THE ESSENTIAL WRITINGS
OF
B. R. AMBEDKAR

The Essential Writings
of
B. R. Ambedkar

THE ESSENTIAL WRITINGS
OF
B. R. AMBEDKAR

edited by
Valerian Rodrigues

OXFORD
UNIVERSITY PRESS

OXFORD
UNIVERSITY PRESS

Oxford University Press is a department of the University of Oxford.
It furthers the University's objective of excellence in research, scholarship, and
education by publishing worldwide. Oxford is a registered trademark ofOxford
University Press in the UK and in certain other countries

Published in India by
Oxford University Press
22 Workspace, 2nd Floor, 1/22 Asaf Ali Road, New Delhi 110002, India

Edition published in 2002
Oxford India Paperbacks 2004
34th impression 2023

ISBN-13: 978-0-19-567055-4
ISBN-10: 0-19-567055-8

Printed in India by Repro India Limited, Haryana

Preface

Dr Bhimrao Ramji Ambedkar is the hero of this book and an attempt has been made here to highlight the best of his writings, reflecting the depth and range of his life's work, his intellectual incisiveness, and his realistic assessment of the social and political issues that he sought to address. But the selection of 'the best' has been difficult as many other articles and excerpts not included here are as representative of his thoughts as those which finally found their place. Till the last moment one toyed with the possibility of including a few other writings, such as those in which he compares untouchability and slavery; uncovers the bare face of colonialism in India; or argues that different nationalities could co-exist within a state and their decision on whether they would secede from each other depended on factors other than the inexorability of national self-determination.

These writings could have been organized in several other ways. One of the most tempting trajectories was to follow the temporal sequence, keeping in step with Ambedkar's growth. The major phases of his life are engrossing—from his birth in an untouchable community till he embraced Buddhism less than two months before his death. But this path has already been trodden by biographers and eulogists and this presentation of his essential writings would have faced the danger of staleness, instead of offering a fresh, new perspective, as attempted here.

Several of my friends have helped me to look closely and discerningly into what Ambedkar wrote and did. While my friendship will suffice as gratitude to them, I cannot help mentioning

Gopal Guru, presently, Mahatma Gandhi Professor, in the Department of Politics and Public Administration, University of Pune and a noted scholar on Dalit politics, whose association I have enjoyed for over two decades now. The still surviving face of untouchability in India which is so starkly visible through the length and breadth of the country goaded me to pursue this work. There is, probably, no greater cause for India to attend to for years to come than this vast constituency as two of India's greatest sons, Mahatma Gandhi and Dr Ambedkar, realized too well.

A few comments about the mode of selecting these writings might be in place. Except for some correspondence, public speeches, and interventions in Parliament, all the writings of Ambedkar and his speeches in the legislatures and other official platforms are now available in sixteen volumes, under the title *Dr Babasaheb Ambedkar: Writings and Speeches* (BAWS), published by the Government of Maharashtra. Ambedkar wrote primarily in English, if we exclude the Marathi journals that he initiated from time to time. Some of these articles in Marathi are available in the *Source Material on Dr Babasaheb Ambedkar and the Movement of the Untouchables* (2 Vols), published by the Government of Maharashtra. All the writings selected here are from *BAWS*.

Ambedkar's writings abound in quotations and citations, but even though his published works contain some standardized references, this is not always the case. The problem is exacerbated in the manuscripts that he left unpublished, where citations hang in limbo, with no references at all or taken from books that are not easily traceable. I have tried to meet these requirements with limited success. I have divided the references into two categories; my references are marked numerically while those of Ambedkar and the editor of BAWS are sequenced separately on each page that they appear. Since Ambedkar did not use diacritical marks in his writings, we have retained his pattern even in the index.

I am grateful to the editors of OUP for suggesting the idea of this work to me. I have not kept to my schedule, but the editorial staff have been patient, save for their gentle but persuasive reminders. Dr Babasaheb Ambedkar Source Material Publication Committee, Government of Maharashtra has kindly granted permission to reproduce the extracts from *BAWS*. I am particularly grateful to its editor and officer on special duty, Sri Vasant Moon.

For a related study I had used the Bodleian Library, Oxford; India Office Library; and the Library of the London School of Economics, London and have freely drawn material required here from them. The Mangalore University Library and the Library of the Indian Institute of Advanced Study, Shimla have been of immense help, particularly in sorting out the literature that have filled this volume. Betilda, Melanie and Shaunna have extended valuable support to me during the course of this endeavour and must forgive me if I have behaved as if they owe me gratitude for acquainting them with Ambedkar!

July 2002   *Valerian Rodrigues*

Contents

Introduction

The role played by Bhimrao Ramji Ambedkar has left its imprint on the social tapestry of the country after Independence, and shaped the political and civic contours of India today. It would have been a different India without him and, in all probability, a much more inequitable and unjust one. He attempted to forge India's moral and social foundations anew and strove for a political order of constitutional democracy that is sensitive to disadvantage, inherited from the past or engendered by prevailing social relations. He became deeply aware of the resources that history and culture offered for an emancipatory project but argued that they can become effective only through the matrix of the present. Undoubtedly, he had the highest academic credentials for an Indian of his time, and his erudition and scholarship have been widely acknowledged.[1] He is the bearer of the modern idiom, the language of the social sciences. He deployed its concepts, cited its authority and negotiated with the world, voicing its theories with intellectual clarity. He rose to become a deeply regarded and most widely acknowledged leader of the 'Untouchables' and, beyond death, his stature has grown larger over the years.

ESSENTIAL WRITINGS

A representative or essential selection from Ambedkar's writings presents a host of problems, some of them characteristic of any such venture and others specific to Ambedkar. There is a huge body of writings to choose from spanning a period of forty years.[2]

There is the variety of subject matter to attend to. He traversed a forbidding range of topics, made possible by an intellectual grooming in liberal education of varied specialized areas such as history, economics, anthropology, politics, and law, which imparted multifaceted resources and orientations to him. In his public life, Ambedkar was observed in several roles: as scholar, teacher, lawyer, parliamentarian, administrator, journalist, publicist, negotiator, agitationist, leader, and devotee. It is difficult to demarcate the areas of his writing given the fact that Ambedkar resorted to various modes of expression—dissertations, research papers, documents, outlines, notes, early drafts, statements, briefs, memoranda, disputations and investigations—as he was often under pressure to play these roles always under the public eye. There is a great deal of unevenness across these modes of expression. Besides, there were too many issues clamouring for attention and in the later days they gathered storm, in spite of his failing health.

Ambedkar privileged the written word.[3] He would make written submissions before committees and commissions to negotiate across the authority of a formulated text. In a culture that was largely oral, the written word gave him a distinctiveness which earlier the upper castes in general and Brahmins in particular had tended to usurp. The written word enabled him to reach out to a larger world, conferring some degree of permanence or immortality and allowing him to usurp some of the Brahmanical authority. The writings, therefore, cannot be separated from their nexus to power, though they are caught in this nexus in variegated ways, some in the immediate sense and others with permanent implications. This nexus can insinuate the significance of a text differently from other writings.

Ambedkar left behind several unpublished drafts, with passages and quotations to be inserted. There are some published texts where adequate references and annotations have not been given, in contrast to his other writings. Sometimes parts of a text are very carefully drafted while the threads of the rest are allowed to hang loose. Several unpublished manuscripts spell out the break-up of the theme under consideration, elaborating certain parts but not according to the given chronological order.[4]

Then there are speeches delivered by Ambedkar for various occasions and different fora, from the Constituent Assembly to mobilizational gatherings. His ideas and reflections may be best represented in these contexts or may not find expression anywhere else. A large body of writings remained unpublished at the time of Ambedkar's death, some of which were still at the initial stage of formulation. They remained scattered, either with his colleagues, the libraries of the institutions set up by him, or in the institutions headed by his associates and relatives. Some of these writings did not see the light of the day as they were caught up in legal wrangles concerning the estate, until they came to be published under government auspices recently.[5] Many of them are still to be subjected to scholarly scrutiny.

At times, there is the problem of determining whether a piece of writing was by Ambedkar or not. Besides there are several drafts of the same text that are occasionally available.[6] Even if one determines their temporal sequences, a later text need not necessarily be more advanced than the earlier one. Compilations of Ambedkar's writings have been brought out by different publications by juxtaposing papers written at wide intervals, addressing different audiences and with varying purposes. The kind of reading such compilations cumulatively offer might be very different from the reading of a discrete text. Several writings of Ambedkar are deeply influenced by the specific context. There are others which have a covert political objective although their subject matter of study might seem far from it.[7] Ambedkar's position on several issues underwent significant changes. He himself was not hesitant to state them openly.[8] These changes were due to a host of reasons, including his own reading and understanding, the context, the audience, the issues and so on.

Ambedkar wanted to revise and publish some of his writings, sometimes succeeding but often not finding adequate time. Occasionally, he expressed the desire to bring out collections of his related writings with appropriate changes and revisions but regretted the lack of time.[9] Some of his works are of a collaborative kind. This is particularly the case with a large body of memoranda, petitions, proposals, and constitutional drafts. Some of them were formulated in the company of comrade-in-arms and sometimes in the committees of which he was a member. Ambedkar's influence on such texts is always palpable but varies very widely. Some of the documents, such as the Constitution of India, were collectively negotiated enterprises. However, Ambedkar left his imprint, even on such documents, organizing the concerned text in a particular way, employing a specific set of concepts, deploying a particular kind of language, and crafting the parts cohesively. Even today there is a section of a reflective audience in India which disregards Ambedkar as a thinker and statesman or actively opposes him, while those who regard him as a leader of worth, vary in their response to the significance of different texts. For thousands of people he is a major cult figure, but they have their own ways of apportioning the order of merit to his writings.

As mentioned earlier, Ambedkar himself gave a great deal of importance to writing compared to several other activities, including speaking, that men of his generation, background and erudition indulged in. He carefully planned the outlines of a text. He ascribed a great deal of authority to his own texts and combated with characteristic vehemence those he considered inimical to his perspective, such as *Manusmriti*. Where Ambedkar took such an antagonistic stance *vis-à-vis* a text or privileged his own formulation, we find extended quotations drawn from relevant texts, including those of the adversary, to buttress his argument.[10] This is particularly the case when the theme is related to the *Shastras*. In combative encounters with *Brahminism*, which he believed tended to monopolize learning and knowledge, he demonstrated not merely his own erudition but through a double reversal argued that true learning and knowledge is different from what Brahminism upheld. Besides, writing does not merely impart meaning but also constitutes space to undermine inimical positions, retrieve support and to position oneself. Sometimes, Ambedkar made a text the battleground where, massing his troops, he launched an attack on the 'enemy territory', the adversary-text, point by point. The way he handled *Manusmiriti*,[11] *Bhagwad Gita*,[12] Jaimini's *Mimamsa*[13] or Gandhi[14] are apt illustrations of this. Ambedkar thought that winning these battles was crucial for reformulating social relations. The expressions of his ideals constituted in the texts had to be reinforced by his acceptance or condemnation of an adversary-text, which makes it even more difficult to pin down his essential writings.

We can, however, identify certain writings of Ambedkar as more significant than others although there is bound to be a shade of subjective preference in such a selection. We have employed the following criteria for the purpose, criteria that need to be considered cumulatively rather than singly:

1. Writings that are distinctive to Ambedkar and those where his contribution to a subject matter is widely acknowledged.

2. There are certain themes and issues that constantly recur in his writings and practices. Writings which highlight these themes and issues could be considered as core writings such as those on caste, untouchability, constitutionalism, Hinduism etc.

3. Writings that focus on favoured themes with a reflective attention rather than merely descriptive or enumerative accounts. In such a reflective focus, the criteria for such reflection are often highlighted, and a great deal of painstaking investigation carried out to buttress the judgements or explanations arrived at. Sometimes, the texts themselves may reflect the significance they had for him through footnotes, or references, or there might be circumstantial evidence in terms of the time that he invested in writing the text.

4. Texts which a knowledgeable community or the savants in the concerned field consider as important. Its modern form is the review. It might be that a text comes to be cited as an authority. For instance, Ambedkar's book on *The Evolution of Provincial Finance in British India*[15] and *The Problem of the Rupee*[16] received very commendatory reviews. Gandhi recommended that *Annihilation of Caste* must be read by every reformer[17] and *Pakistan or Partition of India*, came to be cited as a reference text[18] very widely.

5. Texts that advance knowledge such as Ambedkar's writings on untouchability or present an interpretation that draws attention to issues and concerns hitherto not in focus, such as *The Buddha and His Dhamma*.

6. Writings which express or seem to express the hopes and aspirations of large multitudes and are regarded by them as representative over a period. The Constitution and writings on untouchability fall in this category.[19]

7. Writings which have provoked widespread hostility from large multitudes[20] or combated a prevalent tendency or doctrine, such as *Annihilation of Caste* or *Hindu Code Bill*.

8. Works that led to fashioning institutions and processes on which the life of a number of people depended and which have stood their ground over the period, such as his writings on minorities, the Constitution, and rights.

9. Writings that have changed the lives of people and so acknowledged by them through a set of gestures such as *The Buddha and His Dhamma*.

10. Writings that have a universal import as concepts or theories or that are morally grounded.

11. Writings that constitute legacies and which a tradition made of supporters and opponents consider as significant.

Apart from these criteria there are the constraints of this volume, which required a selection of a wide array of equally linked papers or excerpts of texts. Therefore, what is selected is indicative rather than representative.

LIFE-SKETCH

In the interface between colonialism and nationalism in India, Ambedkar was to intervene in his own distinctive way and attempt shape issues and perceptions particularly from the later half of the 1920s. The platform of the 'Untouchables' in which he invested much of his life's work became his launching pad.

It would not be an exaggeration to say that in the struggle for socio-political space in India, untouchability, as a distinct social entity, came to be recognized only in the twentieth century. Earlier, even the most empathetic of social reformers, such as Jotirao Phule[21] and Narayana Guru Swami[22] in the nineteenth and early twentieth centuries, located it within the framework of the caste system. It was the 1911 Census which for the first time brought home the awesome proportions of what was hitherto described as the Depressed Castes or Classes. The Congress issued the call for the removal of social disabilities suffered by these classes only in 1917. By the early 1920s, the 'Untouchables' had begun to organize themselves as an autonomous political constituency at the all-India level with its base in the provinces. Ambedkar stepped into the public domain at this juncture. He argued that the emancipation of 'Untouchables' had to be fought for by the 'Untouchables' themselves, with any support forthcoming from others and that the movement of the 'Untouchables' was an integral part of the universal movement for freedom, equality and belonging to society as a whole. From this perspective, the national movement itself came to be judged in terms of a two-fold objective, i.e. to what extent it would further the emancipation of the 'Untouchables' and the extent to which it would herald an order embodying freedom, equality of social and economic consideration and the bond of community.

Ambedkar belonged to the Mahar caste, one of the numerous Untouchable castes in Maharashtra. His ancestral village was Ambavade in Mandangad Taluk of Ratnagiri district of the erstwhile Bombay province. This region underwent a momentous social, economic and political upheaval in the wake of the European mercantile and later political expansion. Mahars in this region joined the British army in large numbers.[23] Ambedkar himself was born on 14 April 1891 in Mhow, near Indore, where his father, Ramji Sakpal was the instructor in the local military school. Ramji, like the Mahars of western Maharashtra, was deeply attached to the devotional mystical Varkari sect.[24] He became a follower of the Kabirpanth,[25] and was an admirer of Jotirao Phule, who pioneered major reforms among the lower classes in Maharashtra from the later part of the nineteenth century. There was much devotional singing and recitation of holy texts in Ambedkar's house. His mother, Bhimabai, belonged to a Mahar Kabirpanthi household that boasted of several generations of military service in the British army. She died in 1896 in Satara, where Ramji had found a job after his retirement from the army. Ambedkar was, then, just five years old. Of the fourteen children of Ramji and Bhimabai only five survived, the youngest being Ambedkar.

Although Ambedkar belonged to the highly respected Mahar community, he experienced the pangs of untouchability when he had to interact with people of social layers beyond the confines of the untouchable castes. 'You must remain in your assigned place', seemed to be the constant refrain of the rest of the world.

Ramji dreamt of a different future for his sons. He shifted to Bombay in 1904 and admitted Ambedkar to Elphinstone High School where the boy completed matriculation in 1907. They lived in Parel, then populated by textile labour, where social cleavages, this time in an urban setting, were negotiated, not without conflict, with the demands of industrial employment. Ambedkar married Ramabai, who was just nine years old, in 1908. He completed his B.A. from Elphinstone College in 1912 with English and Persian as his subjects, with some financial assistance from Maharaja Sayaji

Rao of Baroda. A certain facility in Persian and the cultured world it embodied is visible in several of Ambedkar's writings.

Ambedkar joined the armed forces of Baroda as a Lieutenant after his B.A. but had to return to Bombay within a few days when news of the death of his father reached him. However, he secured one of the two scholarships which the Maharaja of Baroda had instituted for backward caste students to study abroad and joined the Columbia University in 1913. It was here that Ambedkar came to shape his learning and perspectives, from great teachers such as John Dewey, Edwin Seligman and A. A. Goldenweiser.

Columbia University itself was in the throes of major institutional refocusing during this period, in an attempt to cultivate leaders and professionals for the great American society of the future. Social scientific knowledge was perceived as a reliable guide for the formulation of appropriate policy measures. Here Ambedkar completed an M.A. with a dissertation on *Administration and Finance of East India Company* and his Ph.D. on *National Dividend: A Historical and Analytical Study*. He also wrote a major paper on 'Castes in India: Their Mechanism, Genesis and Development'.

However, degrees of British universities were the mark of excellence then, particularly in India and ensured privileges for its recipients in their academic and professional careers. Considering Ambedkar's orientation and the inclination of Edwin Seligman, his guide, the London School of Economics (LSE) seemed a better option, given its progressive ambience. Seligman introduced Ambedkar to Sidney Webb, the economist and socialist, one of the founders of the London School of Economics, in glowing terms.[26] Ambedkar joined the college in 1916. He imbibed a great deal of Fabianism from Sidney and Beatrice Webb and came to privilege the role of the state as expounded by J. A. Hobson and L. T. Hobhouse, then members of the faculty and prominent members of the school known as British Idealism. He also joined the Grey's Inn for the Bar-at-Law. However, he had to interrupt his studies and return to India in 1917, as he had executed a bond to serve the Baroda State in return for the scholarship for study abroad. However, the environment at Baroda both at the Accountant General's office, where he was placed as probationer, and outside became humiliating and hostile once people got to know that he was an untouchable.

He returned to Bombay and picked up some odd jobs, but

remained mainly unemployed. He was appointed as Professor of Political Economy at Sydenham College which was then modelled on the pattern of the London School of Economics. He made submissions before the Southborough Committee in January 1919, which was inquiring into the issue of franchise on the eve of the Montagu-Chelmsford reforms of 1919. He pleaded for a separate electorate for the Depressed Classes as had been conceded for Muslims. He also started a fortnightly called *Mooknayak* on 31 January 1920. In its opening issue, he pleaded its necessity as a forum 'to deliberate on the injustices let loose or likely to be imposed on us and other depressed people and to think of their future development and appropriate strategies towards it critically'.[27] In 1920, he collaborated with Shahu Maharaj of Kohlapur in forming the Depressed Classes Forum which organized the First All India Conference of the Depressed Classes in Nagpur, where he argued that the emancipation of the Depressed Classes was possible only through their own initiative.

Ambedkar rejoined the London School of Economics in September 1920. He obtained an M.Sc. degree in 1921, which was essential to proceed on the doctoral studies. He worked on 'The Problem of the Rupee', the dissertation for his D.Sc. under Edwin Cannon, one of the best known professors of economics of the time. This thesis was published by King and Co., London in 1923 under the title *The Problem of the Rupee, Its Origin and Its Solution*. In 1925, Ambedkar's Ph.D. thesis at Columbia University was brought out by the same publishers under the title *The Evolution of Provincial Finance in British India*. In 1922, Ambedkar spent three months at Berlin attempting to pursue further studies there but could not proceed as he had to return to London in connection with his D.Sc. at the London School of Economics. In 1922, he was called to the Bar at Grey's Inn, London. Ambedkar returned to India in 1923 and started legal practice at the Bombay High Court. He taught mercantile law, part-time, at Batliboi's Accountancy Training Institute, Bombay from June 1925 to March 1928. From June 1928 to March 1929 he was professor of law in the Government Law College, Bombay.

In 1924, Ambedkar founded the Bahishkrit Hitkarni Sabha. The organization started a hostel in Sholapur for Depressed Classes. In 1927, he led the famous Mahad satyagraha or non-violent resistance to assert the right of the Untouchables to have access to wells and tanks used by all. This resulted in confrontation with caste Hindus. The *Manusmriti* was publicly burnt by Ambedkar and his followers on 25 December 1927 to show that Untouchables were no longer prepared to abide by the religious and ritual confinement upheld by caste Hindus. On 3 April 1927, Ambedkar had begun publishing a fortnightly journal, *Bahishkrit Bharat*. As its name suggested, it was an attempt to wrest the initiative for the depressed classes in their struggles.

During this period, Ambedkar attempted to radicalize the initiatives taken by Gandhi to bring about a social transformation and weld the nation together. He introduced a Bill in the Bombay Legislature for amending the Bombay Hereditary Offices Act, 1874, which would have benefited inferior hereditary officers, particularly the *Watandar* Mahars by freeing them from traditional social bonds and duties and letting them pursue vocations of their choice. He formed the Samaj Samata Sangh in September 1927 and the Samata Sainik Dal in December 1927, organizations meant to vigorously pursue the agenda of social equality.[28]

Ambedkar who was appointed as a Member of the Legislative Assembly of Bombay Province in 1927 for five years (the appointment was renewed in 1932 for a further five years) attempted to maintain the radical edge in his crusade while carrying out his duties in the Assembly. His speeches on the budget inveighed against the burden imposed on the poor, taking the administration to task for being neither representative nor accountable.[29] As a Member of the Committee of the Bombay Legislature, deputized for the purpose, he submitted a statement before the Indian Statutory Commission, popularly known as the Simon Commission on 29 May 1928, that differed from the rest of the Committee. This statement is a major text on constitutional democracy depicting the perspective of the Depressed Classes and outlining Ambedkar's political stance for years to come. He also submitted a statement on behalf of the Bahishkrit Hitkarni Sabha on the state of education of the Depressed Classes and made a plea for an administration based on universal adult franchise. He also gave oral evidence before the Commission in October 1928.

In June 1928 he took the initiative for the establishment of the Depressed Classes Education Society which established hostels in Panvel, Thane, Nasik, Pune and Dharwad for high school students belonging to these sections. Ambedkar also played a prominent part in the Kalaram Temple movement in 1930, for the entry of the Depressed Classes to this temple, in Nasik. He also became the president of the All India Depressed Classes Congress in Nagpur in August 1930. Ambedkar's experience of a decade of political involvement in the 1920s drove home certain lessons. The British administration was not sympathetic to the pleas of the 'Untouchables'. In fact, one of the choicest indictments of the colonial authority from the perspective of this class was to be written by Ambedkar during this period. Ambedkar also realized that the upper castes were not prepared to bring about, or even concede to social and religious changes that embodied equality. He felt that Gandhi was too soft on orthodoxy and its proponents. As the 1930s advanced, Ambedkar increasingly turned against Gandhi and also against what he called Brahminism.

Ambedkar started a fortnightly, called *Janata*, on 24 November 1930 which became a weekly after a year. It was later published as *Prabudd Bharat* from 4 February 1956. Ambedkar attended the first Round Table Conference (RTC) in London, in 1930 as a representative of the Depressed Classes. The stand adopted by the representatives of various communities and interests, the pressure exerted by several associations of Depressed Classes in India, the near impossibility of the introduction of universal adult franchise and eventually, the attitude of the Congress and Gandhi towards the 'Untouchables' drove Ambedkar to change his stance in favour of a separate electorate for the Depressed Classes. It was at the second RTC that Ambedkar came to a head-on collision with Gandhi. When there was an impasse between contending interests, Ambedkar negotiated with the representatives of the minorities and signed a pact called the Minorities Pact. The Round Table Conference was a major platform from which Ambedkar deployed his learning and his ability to think on his feet to supreme effect. He advanced alternative documents for possible constitutional reforms in India. Several suggestions then voiced and expressed in these documents were to be incorporated in the India Act, 1935.

The bombshell was the Communal Award of 1932 that granted a separate electorate to the 'Untouchables'. Gandhi resorted to a fast unto death against the Award as he had threatened at the Round Table Conference. The Award left space for changes if the communities concerned suggested an alternative scheme, a leeway Ambedkar used to negotiate on behalf of the Depressed Classes, resulting in the Poona Pact.[30] The core of this pact was the promise of a joint electorate with reservations for Depressed Classes, a decision that anticipated the 1950 Constitution of India, but this pact could not satisfy anyone eventually. The orthodox Hindus rallied against Gandhi for conceding too great a share of seats to the Depressed Classes, while Ambedkar felt that the joint electorate was a mechanism for selecting a member of the Depressed Classes who was acceptable to caste Hindus rather than someone who could authentically represent the interests of the 'Untouchables'. He said, 'The communal award was intended to free the Untouchables from the thraldom of the Hindus. The Poona Pact is designed to place them under the domination of the Hindus'.[31]

Ambedkar became a member of the Indian Franchise Committee, popularly known as the Lothian Committee, in December 1931, that looked into the issue of franchise and representation as required by the Round Table Conference. Touring the country, he found that there was an attempt to scale down the existence of the Depressed Classes both quantitatively and qualitatively. Following the Poona Pact, an Anti-Untouchability League, later named the Harijan Sevak Sangh, was set up. Ambedkar accepted membership of its executive committee, following the euphoria of the pact. He, however, found himself totally opposed to Gandhi's understanding and strategy for removing untouchability[32] and resigned from it in 1933.

Ambedkar attended the Third Round Table Conference proceedings from 17 November to 24 December 1932. He accepted a part-time professorship in the Government Law College, Bombay, in June 1934, and after a year, was appointed the Principal of this college for the subsequent three years. However, his wife died on 27 May 1935. She had spent a life of loneliness and privation, saddened also by the loss of three sons and a daughter.

By 1935, Ambedkar had lost all hope that Hinduism could be reformed. On 13 October 1935 at a meeting of the Depressed Classes at Yeola, in Nasik, he suggested that people who belonged to these classes should give up Hinduism. In May 1936, he called a conference of Mahars to discuss this issue with them. Ambedkar's declaration of conversion provoked widespread reaction. Although some dialogue was initiated, particularly with the Sikhs,[33] he was to put off the issue of conversion for the next twenty years.[34] His later writings demonstrate that he did not forget the issue and took to an intense study of Hinduism and comparative religion for the next twenty years. In 1936, Ambedkar wrote a long speech called *Annihilation of Caste* to address the *Jat Pat Todak Mandal*, an organization for social reforms based in Lahore, as it invited him to preside over their annual conference. He cancelled his appointment with the *Mandal* following a disagreement with it regarding certain passages in the text. However, the address, which he published, generated an intense debate between Gandhi and Ambedkar regarding the nature of Hinduism and how to engage with it. In late 1930s, Ambedkar attempted to broad-base some of his concerns. He introduced a Bill for the abolition of the *Khoti* system of land tenure in the Bombay Legislative Assembly in 1936. On 15 August 1936, he founded the Independent Labour Party which contested 17 seats in the elections of 1937 and won 15 of them. In 1938, he joined hands with the Left in Bombay to oppose the Industrial Trade Dispute Bill, introduced by the Congress Government in the Bombay Legislature, a Bill that was perceived as seeking to impose curbs on the labour movement. He also extended his cooperation to the government in its war efforts. However, it was a qualified support.[35]

Ambedkar was probably the first to grapple with the implications of the Lahore resolution of the Muslim League, in 1940, for a separate Pakistan in a full-length study, *Pakistan or the Partition of India*. He felt that the appeal of Pakistan for the Muslim masses was on account of the failure of the Congress to strive for social reforms and democratize society. He repeated these concerns in an important paper presented on the 101th birth anniversary of Ranade at the Gokhale Institute, Poona, in 1943. He argued that once an identity becomes a political force then the consequences of its formation have to be faced. Once Muslims constituted themselves on a separate platform, in a decisive sense, he saw no alternative to forging an identity-based front to demand a share of power. It led to the founding of the Scheduled Caste Federation (SCF) in July 1942 in the wake of the Cripps Mission, in that year. Ambedkar began to project the Scheduled Castes as a third party, other than Hindus and Muslims, in the constitutional developments sought in India.

In December 1942, Ambedkar wrote *Mr Gandhi and the Emancipation of the Untouchables*, for a conference in Quebec organized by the Pacific Relations Committee.

Ambedkar was appointed a member of the Viceroy's Council on 27 July 1942 for a period of five years. It was during this period that Ambedkar, as Labour member of the Council, worked out a fairly comprehensive policy for reservation for Scheduled Castes in the services; several labour legislations were enacted and the tripartite linkages between labour, industry and government were built. It was also during this period that the foundation for a comprehensive welfare legislation for labour was designed. Ambedkar also took a great deal of interest in some of the major multi-purpose developmental projects such as the Damodar Valley Corporation and the Mahanadi River projects. In fact, it was in designing the foundations of the emerging welfare state that Ambedkar played a major role. Apart from his ideological orientation and studies, this experience made him seek the portfolio of Planning, that was denied to him in the Nehru Cabinet in 1951.

Events started moving rapidly following the end of the Second World War. The Scheduled Caste Federation fared badly in the elections held at the end of 1945. Eventually when elections were held to the Constituent Assembly, Ambedkar had to get himself elected from Bengal. However, he advanced the case that the support of the Scheduled Castes has not shifted to the Congress. In the primary elections, wherever the candidates of the organized Scheduled Castes, including those of the Scheduled Castes Federation, had confronted those of the Congress, the success rate of the former was far higher than the latter. However, in the final election those who were at the bottom of the poll came to the top due to caste Hindu votes. The Cabinet Mission arrived in India in March 1946. Ambedkar made several representations to Lord Pethik Lawrence and A. V. Alexander, members of the Cabinet Mission, but they were not prepared to offer much of a quarter to him, citing the electoral debacle of the SCF. At the end of June 1946, the Scheduled Castes started an agitation, under the leadership of Ambedkar, seeking clarification regarding their position in future India. These were trying times for Ambedkar. He was quite desperate and even rushed to London to meet Clement Atlee, the Prime Minister. However, Atlee gave a cold shoulder to Ambedkar's pleas. Ambedkar's attempt to carve out a larger role for the Depressed Classes in independent India remained shattered, at least for the time. He had to work his way through again in terms of

other possibilities, a task that did not deter him, as he often loved
to define politics as the 'art of the possible'.

Ideologically charged interventions continued even at a time
of political upheaval. Perhaps the most significant was *What
the Congress and Gandhi Have Done to the Untouchables?*, a tract
written in 1945. This was an attempt to carve out an autonomous
constituency of Scheduled Castes. It was in the same strain as his
political efforts during this period. In 1946, he published *Who
were the Shudras?*, which while showing the internal cleavages
of Hinduism, held Brahmins to ridicule. In *The Untouchables*,
Ambedkar brought the 'Untouchables' throughout India on a
common platform as being 'broken men' and also Buddhists who
have been reduced to the position of untouchables by the strata-
gems of Brahmins. Apart from their scholarship, these works by
Ambedkar clearly showed his intention to try wresting control
over the Scheduled Castes from Gandhi and Brahminism, and
reach out to the non-Brahminical constituency.

However, Ambedkar swallowed much of his pride at the end
of 1946 and offered not merely his friendly hand to work within
the Constituent Assembly without a prior assurance of any
safeguards but even conceptualized a 'United India'[36] with the
Congress and the Muslim League working together. This marked
a major shift in Ambedkar's attitude to the Congress.[37] For the
Congress it was a great opportunity. After Ambedkar lost his seat
from Bengal, following Partition, he was re-elected to the Constituent Assembly from Bombay with Congress support. On 3 August
1947, he joined the Nehru Cabinet as Law Minister. On 19 August
1947, he was made the chairman of the drafting committee of the
Indian Constitution.[38]

Although Ambedkar later described himself as a hack,[39] a large
part of the Constitution was based on his conceptual framework.
In the previous constitutional developments, he was an active
presence in several of them, including the Government of India
Act, 1935. Apart from formulating the issues, it was remarkable
how Ambedkar piloted the draft constitution in the Constituent
Assembly, winning kudos from all quarters.

As law minister, Ambedkar formulated several important bills
including the Hindu Code Bill. The latter was in a way an attempt
by Ambedkar to effectively transform the hierarchical relations
embodied in the Hindu family and the caste system and bring them

in tune with the values that were embodied in the Constitution. The constitutional provisions, his arguments for state socialism and the transformation of the Hindu order, were attempts to implement single-handedly his project of the 1920s, although others may have evinced interest in these projects for their own reasons. In fact, Ambedkar was riding piggyback to bring about this transformation. The strong opposition to the Hindu Code Bill from orthodox Hindus eventually sabotaged this programme. His attempt to achieve from within[40] what he was striving for from outside did not succeed. Indeed, it was a vain attempt. On the personal front, too, this period saw major changes in his life.

Ambedkar had several health problems by the late 1940s, his personal loneliness exacerbating them further. In 1948, he married Dr Sharada Kabir, a doctor by profession and a Saraswat Brahmin by caste.

The break-up with Nehru was swift, and he resigned from the Cabinet in September 1951. The reasons were, among others, some major disagreements with Nehru on Kashmir and issues of foreign policy. He was disappointed when the Planning portfolio he was keen on did not go to him. But the heart of the matter was the Hindu Code Bill. Ambedkar stood from the Bombay–North constituency for the first Lok Sabha elections of 1952 and was defeated, but was elected to the Rajya Sabha from the Bombay Legislative Assembly. He contested the by-election to the Lok Sabha from the Bandara constituency in 1954 and was defeated again. His deliberations to form an alliance with the socialists remained fragile.

Ambedkar made a concerted intervention for the education of the Scheduled Castes from 1945 as a civic initiative, education for deprived groups being a continuing concern. In pursuit of this, he founded the People's Education Society, Bombay in 8 July 1945 and was the driving force behind the establishment of the Siddharth College of Arts and Science, Bombay in 1946. Soon several institutions were set up under the auspices of this society, such as Siddharth Night School (1947); Milind Mahavidyalaya (1950); Siddharth College of Commerce and Economics (1953); Milind Multipurpose High School (1955) and Siddharth College of Law (1956).

In the 1950s, Ambedkar turned to Buddhism as personal faith and as an ideology that offered an alternative to Hinduism. In 1949, he addressed the World Buddhist Conference in Kathmandu on 'Marxism versus Buddhism'. He wrote a paper in the journal of Mahabodhi Society in 1950 on 'The Buddha and Future of His Religion'. He visited Colombo in 1954, to personally study the practice of Buddhism in Sri Lanka. He also attended the World Buddhist Conference, in Rangoon, in 1955. On 14 October 1956 he formally converted to Buddhism, alongwith lakhs of his followers. That it was not a simple socially neutral, journey was evident when Ambedkar administered a set of oaths to his followers to vow that they would renounce certain practices that tied them to Hinduism. Along with Buddhism the ideology that deeply attracted him in the 1950s was Marxism. In fact in November 1956, he made a trip to Nepal to attend the World Buddhist Conference, where he spoke on Karl Marx and Buddha.

There were honours that came his way in the 1950s, the Doctor of Laws (LL.D.-Honoris Causa) conferred on him by the Columbia University, at its special convention on 5 June 1952 and the D.Litt. degree bestowed by the Osmania University.

Before his death on 6 December 1956, Ambedkar wrote the book *The Buddha and His Dhamma*, which was both a preparation for his conversion to Buddhism as well as the construction of the ideal order for which he struggled throughout his life. Shortly before his death, he also suggested the constitution of a new party, the Republican Party of India. It made a promising start, but soon split into a number of factions. There was also a scramble for Ambedkar's legacy. While Dalits in larger numbers and increasingly across India came to iconize Ambedkar, the Indian state too 'employed' the icon of Ambedkar to guard over its increasingly cleft-ridden socio-economic space.

On 24 April 1942, Governor Lumely of the Bombay Province, wrote to the Viceroy, the Marquees of Linlithgow, conjecturing that Ambedkar probably wanted to withdraw from active involvement in terms of his preoccupations: 'He has given me, for sometime, the impression of a man who is no longer really interested in the work he is doing for his own followers and is anxious to reach a different sphere'.[41] One does not know how accurately Lumley read Ambedkar's mind, but if Ambedkar's subsequent choices give us a glimpse of his life at that time, withdrawal from public life was an option he spent little time on.

THE WORKS OF AMBEDKAR

Ambedkar rightly regarded his educational attainments as valuable and even a cursory reading of his work reveal the depth and range of his erudition. He was a bibliophile and a voracious reader. He also felt that the modern knowledges to which he had assiduously dedicated himself gave him an access to understanding which was superior to traditional forms of knowledge. There are some central assumptions in his approach to knowledge and understanding, particularly his belief that modernity is an advance over previous epochs, in that it opened the possibility of human emancipation.[42] The modern approach may have its faults but had much of value too and its own inbuilt corrective measures.[43] He thought that conceptions such as *Kaliyuga*—the present being unpropitious, degenerate and deplorable—are Brahminical devices, of a self-serving nature.[44] The modern establishes the setting for the triumph of reason, emancipating it from magic and rigid religious world-views. He often suggested a three-stage historiography[45] to correspond to them. The triumph of reason led to the assertion of the human person and his unique value. Reason is the attribute of the human being manifested in understanding, evaluation, discernment and judgement; and concretized in science and technology, the rise of modern institutions and in man's interaction with nature. The modern also frees man from being merely a social role and asserts his autonomy as a human person. However, reason can be vitiated and made prey to prejudices and parochial interests.

While distortions in the understanding of the physical world could be rectified by the methods of reason itself,[46] acting on social reality requires a different anchor, that of morality or ethics. Morality is not a set of fixed canons, but is open to rational inquiry and moral dilemmas are subject to rational scrutiny and evaluation. The foundations of morality lie in justice, and justice in turn involves upholding the liberty and equality of the human person and extending to him the bond of the community. The person is the bearer of a body of rights i.e. claims socially warranted. Claims to culture and community are tenable only to the extent to which they embody these rights. Initially, Ambedkar saw these features as characteristic of the modern world but later attributed them to Buddhism. The teleological march in history referred to in his earlier writings is absent in his later writings where the human condition within the ethical realm is seen in stronger ontological terms.

Ambedkar acknowledged the power of religion and upheld its need, but there is no place in his religion for God and the transcendent. He subscribed to a secular religion, moving away from established religions geared towards the sacred *vis-à-vis* the profane. His writings reveal a deep sensitivity to religion, much before his enchantment with Buddhism. He felt that since human beings are part of this world, the primary role of religion is to safeguard the moral domain. Religion deploys sentiments, feelings and culture to secure the moral domain and make it universal. Although he acknowledged that religion may make other claims, he saw these characteristics as appropriate to any religion.

Ambedkar rarely reflected on the first premises of these assumptions nor did he establish the necessary linkages between them, but these assumptions were constantly at play in his assessments and evaluations.

AUTOBIOGRAPHICAL

The intended autobiography of Ambedkar did not see the light of the day[47] as was the case with several of his other ambitious publishing plans. However, there are many passages in his works where he speaks directly about himself. In fact, if we exclude his two doctoral dissertations and essays associated with their themes, his life and writings are intimately associated. Besides, scattered in his writings are a few autobiographical reminiscences. He talked about his experience of untouchability;[48] his three gurus: Buddha, Kabir, and Phule;[49] his iconoclasm[50] and his devotion and wishes.[51] He had no qualms on stating his religious position in public.[52] He had no hesitation in calling a spade a spade, be it Madan Mohan Malaviya[53] or Rajagopalachari[54] or Gandhi,[55] if he considered his assessment as correct. At the same time, he did not want to engage in any acrimony, even though many experiences in his life, particularly in the Constituent Assembly and the legislatures[56] justifiably deserved stronger retaliation.

EXPLORATION OF CONCEPTS

Ambedkar found the need to reflect upon a wide range of concepts: either to substantially explore them, decipher their different determinations; or to chisel and fine tune them by removing the dross. He adopted different approaches to present them, sometimes in the light of historical developments and at other times, in view of contentions. There are times when he attempted to extrapolate them from a mass of data. Occasionally, he appropriated a concept from a scholar and suggested certain innovations, or drew on his or her authority to reinforce certain dimensions of a concept at hand. There are certain concepts that he radically overhauls such as, for instance, the concept of *Kamma*.[57] Sometimes the determinations of a concept are brought out by contrasting it with kindred concepts[58] such as between religion, *dhamma* and *saddhamma*. Dealing with different types of concepts, he is much more at home with concepts that are less abstruse and closer to experience, lending themselves to actual practice and illustration by example. Y. K. Surveyor, the first lady student of Sydenham College of Commerce and Economics, Bombay where Ambedkar taught from 1918 to 1920, recalls him saying, repeatedly, '...an ounce of illustration is worth more than a pound of theory'.[59]

With his focus on concepts and arguments,[60] Ambedkar contributed to building not merely a framework for social sciences in India but also the basis of healthy public debate.

METHODOLOGY

Ambedkar undertook different types of studies, some involving the collection of sizeable data and its processing such as the election studies of 1937 and 1945, focusing on the constituencies reserved for Scheduled Castes.[61] He undertook several case studies, often to drive home a point better.[62] There are studies where he attempted to locate the major changes in policy or issues over a period by dividing the period into appropriate stages. These projects required resort to documents and archives for necessary data, such as both doctoral studies of Ambedkar, which drew not merely from official documents but also from archival data. In them, there are the standard references to the manuscripts and texts. There are studies such as *Who Were The Shudras?*,[63] exegetical in nature, which delve into texts but propose an alternative thesis because the existing explanations of these texts do not account for certain known details or passages.[63] Studies, such as *The Untouchables*, resort to the method of constructing a distinctive thesis centred on a characteristic feature in a determinate group, existing solely in that group and universally shared by it. Ambedkar also dwelt a great deal on interpretation and on the criteria appropriate for it.[64] He argued with Gandhi that Gandhi's interpretation of Hinduism did not stand up to the criteria of interpretation. Further, he felt that interpretations which do not take popularly held beliefs and strong evaluations into account do not materially affect the situation studied.

For all his major works involving a thesis to be advanced, an issue to be explored, or a position to be combated, Ambedkar spells out his methodological route, particularly for *The Evaluation of Provincial Finance in British India*, *The Problem of the Rupee* and *The Untouchables*.

IDEOLOGICAL

The ideas and ideals of John Dewey, Edwin R. A. Seligman, the Fabians and the British Idealists had a deep impact on Ambedkar. He described himself as a 'progressive radical',[65] and occasionally as a 'progressive conservative,'[66] the qualification, 'progressive', being generally present, distinguishing himself from the liberals and the communists depending on the case. He saw the Directive Principles of State Policy of the Indian Constitution as upholding economic democracy. His notion of liberty was avowedly that of the T. H. Green kind.[67] Although he talked of equality before law and considered it as a major contribution of the British rule in India, he was not satisfied with this notion and advanced stronger notions such as equality of consideration,[68] equality of respect and equality of dignity.[69] He was sensitive to the notion of respect, and the notion of community was central in his consideration. The demand for 'fraternity' in the French Revolution was seen by him as a call for 'community'. The Buddha, he argued, strove for building communities while Brahminism attempted to fragment them.

At the same time, Ambedkar recognized the critical role of the state, the legacies of Columbia University, London School of Economics and the colonial state in India being in consonance with such recognition. He strongly defended a developmental and ameliorative, and consequently an interventionist approach, as against the Gandhians and the Liberals. The state was invested with a pivotal role in the economy.[70] But, wherever such a pivotal role for the state is alluded to, it is based on the premise of a regime of rights that suggested the reasons and limits of intervention. He was deeply suspicious of embedded identities asserting themselves in the name of ethnic, linguistic and cultural claims, relating such assertions to the problem of majorities and minorities. When identity assertions took place, he felt, the minorities are likely to be the victims.[71] He qualified majoritarianism with strong grids of the rule of law, special privileges to minorities,[72] and the existence of a civil society which could nurture democracy as a civic virtue.[73] His opinion that policies and institutions deeply affect the question of representation found expression in his suggestion before the Simon Commission, that if adult franchise was introduced he would favour a joint electorate with reservation for Depressed Classes and if limited franchise was continued he would demand a separate electorate.[74]

One of Ambedkar's most important arguments against Hinduism was that caste and untouchability did not let Hindus act as a community. There is the emphasis on moral order for which he sometimes kept company with Edmund Burke.[75] Further, there is the privileging of human agency along with freedom and education for which he falls upon John Dewey.[76] He rarely gave a reductive picture of religions but went into the sociological moorings that threw up a diversity of beliefs and practices.[77] At the same time, he admitted that commonly held religious beliefs had an impact on socially differentiated constituencies. He found a lot of doctrinal cleavages within Hinduism.[78] He had no great fascination for *bhakti* with which he was nourished in his childhood, castigating the *bhakti* saints for failing to attack the *Shastras*, which provided the normative and sacral grids for sustaining and justifying unjust social institutions.[79]

He was quite contemptuous of the dwindling Labour Party in India[80] although, while in Britain, for a while, he had maintained some contacts with the left-wing of the Liberals such as Edwin Montagu, the Secretary for India during 1917–20. In 1945, when Ambedkar was asked to join the Liberal Party in India he squarely refused. He expected the Labour government in England, which came to power after the war, would extend favourable treatment to him. He explained the disadvantaged position of the constituency that he represented and pleaded for special consideration. However, he was patronizingly asked by the members of the

Cabinet Mission, belonging to the Labour Party, why he did not make common cause with the Left instead of seeking separate consideration[81] for the Scheduled Castes. He often felt that the Conservative Party understood the fact of historically inherited identities and social cleavages better than the Labour Party.

Ambedkar watched Gandhi and Gandhian intervention in the national movement very closely and maintained a meticulous account. His three major works *Mr Gandhi and the Emancipation of the Untouchables*, 'Ranade, Gandhi and Jinnah' and *What Congress and Gandhi have done to the Untouchables*, bear witness to it. Ambedkar initially believed that Gandhian intervention would push forward the social reforms agenda and such social transformation would direct the political reforms to come, seeing his own attempt at reforms in the 1920s as deepening and widening the initiative that Gandhi had taken. Although Ambedkar was emphatic on the emancipation of 'Untouchables' on their own impetus, there were no serious differences on the issues they identified for popular mobilization.

Ambedkar felt a rude shock when, in his assessment, Gandhi succumbed to the pressures of orthodoxy and instead of social transformation became the agent of orthodoxy. Gandhi's strategy for the abolition of untouchability, he felt, placed the 'Untouchables' at the behest of caste Hindus. This suspicion became intensified during the Round Table Conference when Ambedkar felt that Gandhi was attempting to placate the Muslims while isolating the Untouchables. There was a thaw in their relations after the Poona Pact when Ambedkar agreed to become a member of the executive committee of the Anti-Untouchability League, later to be named the Harijan Sevak Sangh, but soon Ambedkar resigned from this body as he did not accept the understanding and strategy of the League nor the kind of activity it prioritized.[82] After 1933, Ambedkar fought a relentless battle against Gandhi, although they continued to share a number of concerns in common.

Ambedkar showed an extraordinary interest in Marxism particularly in the 1950s. All his major writings during this period—'Buddha and the Future of his Religion'; *The Buddha and his Dhamma* and 'Buddha and Karl Marx'—refer to Marx as the central figure. Besides, in the 1950s, Ambedkar started working on a book entitled *India and Communism*, which, however, did not progress much. He identified certain crucial areas on which he agreed with

Karl Marx: The task of philosophy is to transform the world; there is conflict between class and class; private ownership of property begets sorrow and exploitation, and good society requires that private property be collectivized. He found that on all these four issues Buddha is in agreement with Marx. He, however, rejected the inevitability of socialism; the economic interpretation of history; the thesis on the pauperization of the proletariat; dictatorship of the proletariat; withering away of the state, and the strategy of violence as a means to seize power. He felt that Buddhism, which called for self-control and a moral foundation for society, could provide the missing dimensions for a socialist project and for the purpose, called for a dialogue between Marxism and Buddhism.[83] Therefore, while liberal and modernist alliances of Buddhism were taking place elsewhere,[84] Ambedkar wanted to relocate Buddhism in the trajectory of Marxism and vice versa.

RELIGION

A large part of Ambedkar's writings had a direct bearing on Hinduism, most of which remained unpublished and in the initial draft form during his life-time. In these studies, which he undertook mainly from the second half of 1940s, Ambedkar argued that Buddhism, which attempted to found society on the basis of reason and morality, was a major revolution, both social and ideological, against the degeneration of the Aryan society. It condemned the *varna* system and gave hope to the poor, the exploited and to women. It rallied against sacrifices, priestcraft and superstition. The Buddhist Sangha became the platform for the movement towards empowering and ennobling the common man. However, Brahminism struck back against the revolution through the counter-revolution launched by Pushyamitra.[85] Here Ambedkar deployed a specific terminology employed to explain mainstream European transitions of nineteenth and twentieth centuries and he felt that the corresponding explanation was appropriate for India too, although the periods in question were wide apart.

For Ambedkar, literature which legitimized and instituted the counter-revolution was *Smriti* literature in general and *Manusmriti* in particular.[86] It made birth, not worth, the principle of assigning human beings to social roles, reduced the Shudra to servitude and condemned women to ignominy. On the contrary, the governing principle during the Vedic period for assigning social roles was *Varna*, the principle of worth, which allowed wide mobility although it ordered society hierarchically. The trajectory of social transformation that Ambedkar traced was divided into the following phases: the Vedic society and its degeneration into Aryan society; the rise of Buddhism and the social and moral transformation it set into motion; and finally, the counter-revolution and the rise of Brahminism.

He found that the Hindu scriptures do not lend themselves to a unified and coherent understanding. There are strong contentions built into them within and across trends and traditions. There are cleavages within the *Vedas*; the *Upanishadic* thought is in contention with the *Vedic* thought; *Smriti* literature arraigns against *Sruti* literature; sometimes the *Vedas* are considered lower than the *Shastras*; gods are pitted against one another and *tantra* is rallied against *Smriti* literature. The icons of Hinduism such as Rama and Krishna have little to recommend them, in that there is nothing morally elevating about them.[87] Further, Ambedkar generally tended to suggest a later date to the central texts of Hinduism as compared to other Indian scholars.[88]

He did not comment much on the *Upanishads*, and compared to the rest of Hindu literature, is relatively favourably disposed towards them.[89] As late as 1936, Ambedkar felt that Hinduism could be redrafted on the basis of Upanishadic thought.[90] For Ambedkar, the *Gita* is a post-Buddhist text. It is primarily a defence of *Karma-kanda* i.e. religious acts and observances, 'by removing the excrescence which had grown over it.'[91] The *Gita* advances a set of philosophical arguments to save Brahminism in the context of the rise of Buddhism and the inability of the former to defend itself by a mere appeal to the rituals and practices of the Vedas. He finds that the *Gita* defends the position of Jaimini's *Mimamsa*[92] against Badarayan's *Brahmasutras*.[93]

Ambedkar developed a new interpretation of Buddhism which made commentators label it 'Ambedkar's Buddhism'.[94] His magnum opus, *The Buddha and His Dhamma* highlights the central issues that concerned him throughout his life and demarcates his view sharply from that of his adversaries. The work contains the central teachings of the Buddha along with a commentary built into it. The commentary transposes the Buddha's teachings to the present and suggests its contemporary relevance with respect to the problems that confront humanity. He saw Buddhism as an ideology that engages with the world, privileging the poor and exploited. Ambedkar repeatedly asserted that Buddha had a social message. Further, he constructed Buddhism in opposition to Hinduism arguing that if there are some traces of Hinduism in Buddhism, they could be attributed to Brahminical interpolations. Ambedkar also upheld the superiority of Buddhism over other religions, particularly Islam and Christianity.[95]

CASTE

Ambedkar's understanding of caste and the caste system underwent certain significant changes over the period of his writings. Initially he had argued that the characteristic of caste was endogamy superimposed on exogamy in a shared cultural ambience.[96] He suggested that such evils as *sati*, child-marriage and prohibition on widow-remarriage were the outcome of caste. Further, if a caste closed its boundaries other castes were also forced to follow suit. The Brahmins closing themselves socially first gave rise to the system of castes. Ambedkar continued to emphasize the endoga-mous characteristic of caste but roped in other features such as the division of labour, absence of inter-dining and the principle of birth[97] which he had earlier largely absorbed within endogamy. He also found that the caste name is an important feature which keeps the solidarity of caste intact. He increasingly argued that graded inequality is the normative anchor of the caste system. Graded inequality restricts the reach of equality to members of the caste, at the most. Ambedkar thought caste is an essential feature of the Hindu religion. Although a few reformers may have denounced it, for the vast majority of Hindus breaking the codes of caste is a clear violation of deeply held religious beliefs. He found Gandhi subscribing to caste initially and later opposing it but upholding *Varna* instead. Ambedkar, however, felt that the principle under-lying Gandhi's conception of *Varna* is the same as that of caste, that is, assigning social agents on the basis of birth rather than worth. It led to upholding graded inequality and the denial of freedom and equality,[98] social relations that cannot beget commu-nity bonds. The solution that Ambedkar proposed was the annihilation of caste. He suggested inter-caste marriage and inter-dining for the purpose although the latter by itself is too weak to forge any enduring bonds. Further, he felt that hereditary priest-hood should go and it should remain open to all the co-religionists endowed with appropriate qualifications as certified by the state.[99] Ambedkar, however, felt that these suggestions would not be acceptable to Hindus. After the early 1930s he gave up any hope of reforming Hinduism except for a brief while with the Hindu Code Bill which was, in a way, the continuation of the agenda that he had set for himself in the 1920s.

UNTOUCHABILITY

Ambedkar's engagement with Untouchability as a researcher, an intellectual and activist, is much more nuanced, hesitant but intimate as compared to his viewpoint on caste, where he is prepared to offer stronger judgements and proffer solutions. However, with untouchability, there is often a failure of words. Grief is merged with anger. He often exclaims how an institution of this kind has been tolerated and even defended. He evinces deep suspicions about the *bona fides* of others in terms of their engagement with it. He distinguished the institution of untouch-ability from that of caste although the former is reinforced by the latter and Brahminism constituted the enemy of both. He felt that it was difficult for outsiders to understand the phenomena of untouchability and explored modes of presenting the same. Once explained, he thought human sympathy would be forthcoming towards alleviating the plight of the 'Untouchables', but at the same time anticipated hurdles to be crossed, hurdles made of age-old prejudices, interests, religious retribution, the burden of the social pyramid above and the feeble resources that the 'Untouch-ables' could muster. He found that the colonial administration did little to ameliorate the lot of the 'Untouchables'. He argued that the track-record of Islam and Christianity, in this regard, is not praiseworthy either, although they may not subscribe to untouch-ability as integral to their religious beliefs.

He felt that Untouchables have to fight their own battle and if others are concerned about them then such a concern has to be expressed in helping them to fight rather than prescribing solutions to them.[100] He discussed attempts to deny the existence of untouch-ables and to reduce the proportion of their population in order to deny them adequate political presence.[101] He resorted to compari-son with what he called the parallel cases, such as the treatment meted out to slaves and Jews[102] but found the lot of the 'Untouchables' worse than theirs. He argued that inspite of differences and cleavages, all 'Untouchables' share common disadvantages and treatment from caste Hindus: they live in ghettoes; they were universally despised and kept outside the fold. He maintained a graphic account of the course of the movement of the 'Untouchables', although this account was much more specific about the movement in the Bombay Presidency.[103] He threw scorn at the Gandhian attempt to remove Untouchability and termed it as a mere façade aimed at buying over the 'Untouchables' with kindness. He presented voluminous empirical data to defend such a thesis,[104] and suggested his own strategies to confront untouchability, warning Untouchables not to fall into the trap of Gandhism. He exhorted them to fight for political power.[105] Although he did not find the lot of Untouchables better among Christians and Muslims, he felt that they had a better option as they did not subscribe to untouchability as a religious tenet.[106] Ambedkar was also deeply sensitive to insinuations offered by others to co-opt untouchables within their political ambit. He illustrated how Raibahadur P. C. K. Raja fell into the trap and eventually came to regret it.[107]

Ambedkar rarely went into the question of the origin of untouchability in history. He rebutted the suggestion that race had anything to do with it,[108] and did not subscribe to the position that caste has its basis in race[109] either. However, in one instance, he proposed a very imaginative thesis that 'Untouchables' were broken men living on the outskirts of village communities who due to their refusal to give up Buddhism and beef-eating, came to be condemned as untouchables.[110] He did not repeat this thesis in any central way later and did not justify the conversion to Buddhism as going back to the fold either. It has to be noted that the thesis was proposed when Ambedkar was fighting for the recognition that 'Untouchables' were a separate element in India and therefore, should be constitutionally endowed with appropriate safeguards while the colonial administration and Gandhian leadership were prepared to recognize only the Muslims and Sikhs as distinct communities.[111]

IDENTITY

As in the case of the 'Untouchables', Ambedkar attempted to construct a separate identity of Shudras as well and this too during the second half of the 40s. He identified himself with the non-Brahmins[112] and attempted to build a non-Aryan Naga identity, ascribing to it the signal achievements of Indian civilization.[113] He also proposed to write on the clash of the Aryans and the Nagas much more elaborately than he was to do.[114] However, his exploration of the Naga identity remained quite thin.

We find in Ambedkar's works a great deal of detail about primitive tribes and what were called 'criminal' tribes. He saw them basically as outside the pale of civilization and blamed Hinduism for confining them to such sub-human levels.[115] He ridiculed the Hindus for applauding their attitude to such degradation in the name of toleration. Ambedkar, however, did not explore the tribal cultures and did not attempt to build a political bridge-head with them, although in terms of deprivation, he felt, the 'Untouchables' and these communities formed a common constituency.[116] Ambedkar did recognize a myriad of other identities in India such as sub-castes, castes, groupings of castes such as Touchables and Untouchables, twice-born or 'regenerated' castes and the Shudras; religious groups, regional identities and sometimes identities resulting from the mutual reinforcement of all these groups.[117] Ambedkar acknowledged the presence of linguistic and cultural identities but he was deeply suspicious of them. It is not so much their proclivity to cast themselves as a nationality that makes him apprehensive but their tendency to exclude minorities that do not share the dominant identity. He, however, considered the fact of identity seriously, going to the length of suggesting that he was a conservative[118] but arguing that identity should be within the bounds of rule of law, the demands of development, justice and participation. For the same reasons the ideal solution for the problem of linguistic states is not 'one language, one state' but 'one state, one language'.[119]

Social reforms in India were increasingly fragmented into regional ambits by the first decade of the twentieth century, becoming part of the emerging regional identities. Ambedkar refocused the reform question at the all-India level once again and, in a way, made Gandhi accord priority to it in spite of the discomfiture of Jawaharlal Nehru and others. Ambedkar also took an active interest in the working class movement and sometimes occupied formal positions in the trade unions. He understood their concerns as he had lived in a working class locality for over two decades. However, he felt that the Indian working class had not come to address the caste question. On the contrary, the division of labour in industrial establishments was based on caste relations, and he pointed out that as long as the working class was fragmented into castes their common bond would prove too fragile to wage determined struggles.

THE ECONOMY

Unlike in the domain of politics and religion, Ambedkar's intervention in relation to economic thought and issues was intermittent though persistent over a long period. For his M.A. at Columbia University, Ambedkar wrote a lengthy dissertation which he did not eventually submit. It was entitled *Ancient Indian Commerce* and included three fascinating chapters on 'Commercial relations of India with the Middle East', 'Commercial relations of India in the middle ages' and 'India on the eve of the Crown Government'. It projected India as a land which had deep and varied ties with other countries based on the nature of its economy. He portrayed very vividly the exploitative nature of the Company's rule in India.[120] In *The Administration and Finance of East India Company*, Ambedkar provided a lucid account of the organization of the East India Company, its sources of revenue and items of expenditure upto 1857.[121] *The Evolution of Provincial Finance in British India*, builds on Ranade's work on provincial finance,[122] looking at the financial relations between the provinces and the centre in British India from 1833 to 1919. The arguments for centralization and decentralization almost echo our arguments in the present, with Ambedkar himself discretely subscribing to financial decentralization on the principle that power and responsibility should belong to that level which can make optimum use of it. Such an allocation while making the states strong and viable would contribute towards a strong and effective central government as well, by taking away from it power and responsibility which it cannot exercise effectively. In his doctoral thesis at the London School of Economics entitled *The Problem of the Rupee: Its Origin and Its Solution*, Ambedkar favoured the gold standard rather than the silver standard that was introduced in India in 1835 or the gold exchange standard as proposed by scholars such as Professor Keynes. After these major forays into the domain of the economy, Ambedkar made only certain selective interventions in this area. His policy interventions in agriculture were basically four-fold: he demanded the abolition of intermediaries between the direct producer and the state as was manifest for instance in the Khoti system,[123] prevailing in the Konkan. He demanded an end to traditional obligations imposed on inferior public servants belonging to lowly castes and demanded that they be replaced with contractual obligations. He suggested the nationalization of agriculture and distribution of all surplus land to the Scheduled Castes. In 1917, Ambedkar brought out a long article on 'Small Holdings in India and their Remedies', arguing for consolidation of holdings though he did not extend unqualified support to the then prevailing position for the enlargement of holdings. His position was 'To a farmer a holding is too small or too large for the other factors of production at his disposal necessary for carrying on the cultivation of his holding as an economic enterprise'.[124]

Ambedkar advanced some very radical proposals for organizing industry where the state was expected to play the dominant role. He took a keen interest in such projects as the Damodar Valley Corporation[125] and the river valley projects in Orissa.[126] As Labour Member in the Council of the Governor-General, he was in the forefront of a wide variety of legislation affecting conditions of labour and employment and industrial relations, often to the chagrin of his other colleagues in the government. He set up the institution of tripartite conferences between unions, industry and government and strove to bring labour legislation in India in tune with the requirements of International Labour Organization (ILO). In fact, Ambedkar was already laying the basis of the emergent developmental and welfare state in India.

COLONIALISM AND NATIONALISM

Ambedkar's critique of colonialism ranges across a whole spectrum from the economy to the nature of the colonial discourse. In terms of the latter, Ambedkar demanded that the terms of the discourse be altered. He had no defence to offer in favour of colonialism but he did not want power to go to those who would promote partisan ends in the name of the people. Ambedkar's considered judgement was that colonialism benefited the 'Untouchables' the least, except for the rule of law which it inaugurated, allowing some space for them.[127] He insisted on a responsible and accountable government based upon adult franchise, and was one of the first top rung leaders in India to demand universal adult franchise early on in his submission before the Simon Commission,[128] in the strongest possible terms.

However, Ambedkar remained wary of nationalism, particularly given the experience of the Second World War.[129] He was primarily concerned with a regime of rights, based on justice and upholding democracy. In a way, he was forced to engage with nationalism seriously when the Muslim League made the demand for a separate Pakistan in 1940. With respect to nationalism Ambedkar placed a great deal of emphasis on the volitional factor. He felt that once large masses of people begin to believe that they are a nationality then their identity as a separate nation had to be faced. He blamed both the Congress and the Muslim League for precipitating this tendency. He, however, felt, that different nationalities had often remained within a single state and have negotiated terms of associated living. National self-determination is not something inevitable, but the pros and cons of whether nationalities decide to live together in a single state or wish to go their own ways, have to be assessed. He felt that under certain conditions it might be better to be separated than to live in a united state.

Ambedkar did not take an active interest in international relations except in its broader ideological implications. But there were some issues that he felt were significant for the future of India. He located India's place firmly in Asia and in the cultural traditions infused with Buddhism. He saw a threat to India from the Communist bloc, particularly given the age-old strategic interests. He was deeply concerned with the occupation of Tibet by communist China and the response of the Nehru government to this issue. His view regarding Jammu and Kashmir was that it comprised three regions: Kashmir, Jammu and Ladakh. He considered it appropriate to hand over Kashmir to Pakistan and to integrate the other two regions with India.

CONSTITUTIONAL DEMOCRACY

The major area of Ambedkar's work was on constitutional democracy. He was adept at interpreting different Constitutions of the world, particularly those that mattered insofar as they were committed to democracy, along with their constitutional developments. This becomes obvious if we note the references that he adduces to the different Constitution, in the debates of the Constituent Assembly. He was a key player in the constitutional developments of India from the mid-1920s and on certain issues such as a uniform Civil Code he was to anticipate some of the major issues that have been the topics for debate[130] in India. Ambedkar evolved certain basic principles of constitutionalism for a complex polity like India but argued that ultimately their resilience would depend on constitutional ethics.

Ambedkar dwelt on several substantive issues of law.[131] In fact, we can understand the significance that law had in his scheme of things by recourse to his larger social and ideological understanding. He was deeply sensitive to the interface between law on one hand, and customs and popular beliefs on the other. He felt that law was definitely influenced by customs and popular beliefs but stressed that customs may defend parochial interests, but may not uphold fairness, and may be based on their usefulness for the dominant classes. They may not be in tune with the demands of time nor in consonance with morality and reason. Ambedkar also admitted the possibility of customs having the upper hand over law when they begin to defend vested interests, but that with its emphasis on freedom and democracy, law could be placed in the service of the common good. On the other hand, customs, while promoting healthy pluralism, may give rise to a highly inegalitarian order. At the same time, he defers to pluralism, if it can uphold rights.

In all these qualifications, his contention is that the legal domain is an autonomous sphere. Ambedkar also deployed a complex understanding of rights to situate the domain of law. He distinguished the realm of constitutional law from the acts of legislature, but acknowledged that popular aspirations and the democratic mandate was the common ground for both. At the same time, it is law which determines what are popular and democratic aspirations and what constitute the relevant categories, given the existence of the domain of rights. The constructionist role of the state, confronted with long-drawn and irreconcilable disputes, is so prominent in Ambedkar's writing that quite often he avoids substantive definitions and resorts to the legal fiction that 'so and so is that as specified by law'. He did not reconcile the tension between democracy and law and in his exposition, the domain of reason and morals are often in contention with that of law. Ideally, of course, he envisaged a democracy informed by law and a law characterized by sensitivity to democracy. At the same time he looked to a system of law which upheld reason and morality, though he saw reason and morality as far too feeble to ensure social bonds without the authoritative dictates expressed in law. Religion, according to him, could play a major role in lightening the task of law. Ambedkar's views on constitutional democracy were reflected in his relations with Gandhi and Nehru on the issues of untouchability and the Hindu Code Bill respectively.

GOVERNANCE

One of the issues that Ambedkar paid close attention to was that of power and governance. He thought that governance must reflect sociological reality as closely as possible lest those wielding power to their advantage suppress the excluded groups. Ambedkar spent a great deal of his time and energy in advancing proposals for the purpose stressing the need to respect justice and equity. While he was opposed to over representation to Muslims as expressed in the constitutional reforms of 1909, he did not accept that minority representation should be exactly in proportion to its population.

His commitment to democracy as the mode of governance was unwavering but he argued that democracy needed to become a way of life. He developed some interesting arguments on why parliamentary democracy was the most suitable form of government for India and advocated feasible modes of representation and franchise. His writings dwell extensively on such monumental issues as the presidential versus parliamentary form of government, the relationship between the executive and legislature, the role of the judiciary and judicial review, constitutional bodies such as the Election Commission, the federal division of powers, states in a federation, the role of the Governor, the Constitution and the legislature, constitutional amendments, political parties, and public opinion.

One of the domains that Ambedkar was engaged in very closely was civil society in terms of its operative dimension. He basically saw it as the conscience-keeper of the political sphere, determining the course of governance in the long run. Civil society is the domain in which one has to struggle for human values. He viewed religion as an important institution of civil society, which included other institutions such as political parties, the press, educational institutions and unions and associations. It is a contentious terrain of agreement and disputations resulting in relatively stable zones of agreement. Religion can play a major role in deciding the nature and stability of such agreement. Ambedkar's loathing for violence as a mode of constituting governmental authority or to settle issues in civil society was to have far-reaching implications for constitutional democracy in India. However, he emphasized the value of transformative interventions, and it is in his own organization of associations and movements and educational institutions, his writings on the need for social transformation, and eventually his conversion to Buddhism, that Ambedkar's role can be seen.

Ambedkar was deeply alive to the fact that ideologies undergo mutation in their interaction with social cleavages. He felt that Islam in India had not succeeded in eliminating caste cleavages but argued that since Islam does not subscribe to the caste ideology, the convert has access to larger spaces of the community which he would not otherwise have had. He engaged in more rigorous study of Christianity in India than of Islam. He rejected Gandhi's opposition to conversion[132] but felt that, given its resources, Christianity should have attracted more converts but it had not due to its own inadequacies.[133]

Ambedkar was ambivalent towards conversion as a strategy till he opted for Buddhism. This ambivalence was particularly true with respect to conversion to Islam and Christianity, though he dismissed the argument that most of the conversions were done for material gains. Even if it was so, it did not matter in the longer run and he cited many illustrations for the purpose. He did not agree that all religions are different paths to the divine and they are all equal. There are gradations in religions in terms of the basic values they uphold and conversions were attempts to reach out to these values.

DISADVANTAGE AND SUPPORTIVE POLITY

Ambedkar made two major contributions in terms of evolving a polity which would extend special considerations to the disadvantaged. He was the first major theoretician in India who argued that consideration for the disadvantaged should be the constitutive basis of the state. He developed a complex set of criteria to determine disadvantage and attempted to specify its various gradations. Untouchability was only one of the disadvantages, although one of the most degrading and poignant. Further, he concentrated on the socially engendered disadvantage, not because he was unaware of natural and hereditary disadvantages, but because he felt that most disadvantages are engendered by dominant social relations that attempted to convert them into natural disadvantages. He distinguished disadvantage from difference—cultural, religious, ethnic, or linguistic—and approached these issues separately for the adoption of appropriate policy measures. His second contribution was to develop a system of safeguards for the disadvantaged in general and the 'Untouchables' in particular which could be enforceable, quantifiable and accountable, a system he evolved from early on but found its shape at the time of his deputation before the Simon Commission. This system further evolved through the participation of the disadvantaged, particularly the depressed classes themselves. These safeguards were negotiated with the broader polity with the inevitable confrontations, such as Gandhi's fast[134] unto death in 1932. A standardized system of safeguards at the all-India level came to be introduced during Ambedkar's tenure as Labour member in the Viceroy's council. The Indian polity has not contested the necessity or range of these policies, for Scheduled Castes and Scheduled Tribes, and segments of society which consider themselves as disadvantaged have resorted to this model to make their claims negotiable, proving the enduring appeal of the scheme that Ambedkar advanced.

THE RELEVANCE OF AMBEDKAR TODAY

Dr Ambedkar is one of the heroes of modern India whose stature has undoubtedly grown over the years, particularly in the last two decades. This growth has been both social and spatial. Newly mobilized social strata in India have resorted to Ambedkar to suggest a rationale for their practices, to forge their unity, to express their common sense of belonging and to posit an exemplar. The low castes in India may identity themselves with diverse and even opposed politico-ideological persuasions and at the same time ardently avow their belonging to his political lineage and vision of good life. The Dalit masses all over India and irrespective of their social, religious and political cleavages have shown their proclivity to swear by his legacy. The non-resident Dalits in several countries today, as part of the Indian diaspora, have embraced him as their cultural icon. The disadvantaged groups in India have drawn on his legacy to argue for a specific set of preferences for themselves, and communities, attempting to retain or carve out a socio-political space for themselves against the homogenizing drive of the nation-state, have looked to him for support. He is no longer confined to a territorial region in India or to the urban locale but has reached even the most remote hamlets as evidenced by his statues and public places built or dedicated in his honour. At the same time all these groups and strata, in order to take recourse to Ambedkar, must subscribe to a regime of rights and equal worth.

Ambedkar's foray into the socio-political space in India is taking place in the context of a two-fold failure of nationalist India: the failure of the civil society to rally round the socially low and the economically disadvantaged, as Gandhi envisaged[135] and the inability of the Indian state to ensure certain basic primary goods, essential for a sense of worth and dignity, for a vast multitude of its people. While the civil endeavour on the social issue became a damp squib after Gandhi, the initiative of the state has remained confined to a small constituency where state largesse has been dispensed through policies of protective discrimination.

Ambedkar is being appropriated by the lower strata in a society which is deeply divided and increasingly getting fragmented as the old order based on hierarchy, deference and insularity is caving in. The social groups reaching out to Ambedkar wish to bring about changes in the prevailing social relations. They assert a different kind of politics, seeing it not as a stratagem for reproducing existing relations but as a way of bringing about profound changes in them. Given this assertion from these groups, Ambedkar has moved, from being a villain of Indian nationalism,[136] to its centre-stage in the socio-political contestation in India.

This appropriation of Ambedkar is more symbolic than ideological. Given the hermeneutic sites that a symbol affords, there have been systematic and sustained attempts to own him up by several other contenders on the scene in their own ways. One of the most important attempt in this direction has been by the Indian state by orchestrating certain policies, such as preferential treatment for low castes and dalits, erecting statues, celebration of festivals, establishment of institutions and dolling out state largesse. It would be too feeble a rule if it does not reach out to newly assertive constituencies and in ways they can identify themselves with, however minimal and insignificant it might be. There have been attempts by major political forces to incorporate him in their bandwagon too. This is done by attempting to align him with substantive issues of their ideology or subscribing to a framework of politics and invoking Ambedkar as their advocate too. Given the size of Dalits, low castes and the disadvantaged in general, no political party can afford to ignore the electoral dividends that Ambedkar as an ally can bestow. For the state to sustain a modicum of hegemony Ambedkar has become an indispensible necessity today.

This attempt of the political society to woo Ambedkar, however, has not fostered a similar quest in the civil society. Mainstream civil society continues to be ill-disposed, if not hostile, to Ambedkar.[137]

There are, therefore, attempts at domesticating Ambedkar as well as deploying him for an alternative politics. Such contestation has been facilitated in the absence of a major attempt to critically scrutinize ideas and perspectives distinctive to Ambedkar and deploy such a scrutiny to the ideological field of contestations in India. This is irrespective of whether Ambedkar could have outlived such a scrutiny.

What are some of those concepts, issues and explanations in Ambedkar's writings which at this juncture would have facilitated a transition from the symbolic to a more engaged, transparent and reflective response, particularly from the point of view of the deprived classes and strata?

CONCEPT OF EXPLOITATION

For Ambedkar, economic exploitation, was a major issue to contend against. It explains his life-long critical engagement with Marxism. However, he felt that there are other sources of exploitation and marginalization besides economic exploitation which deprive people of those basic goods indispensable for the constitution of a confident self, a life of mutual recognition and participation in collective affairs. They limit people to narrow confines, depriving them of access to resources and solidarities through which people could strive to overcome their subalternity. The role of the superstructures including the way discourses construct and articulate themselves have to be taken into account to understand why specific modes of exploitation reinforce themselves and to devise ways to overcome the same.[138]

REASON, RIGHTS AND IDENTITY

Ambedkar argued that it was in the modern era that human reason came into its own and extricated itself from bonding with myths, customs and religious ideologies. There has been a reversal of the relation between myths and traditions on one hand, and reason on the other. Customs and traditions on one hand, and religion and theology on the other, can be acknowledged as valid to the extent that they are reasonable. It was not that every value, religious tenet or way of life was rejected by him in the process; they were seen as tenable, if they were compatible with human reason.[139]

The world and man, he argued, can be explained by human reason and endeavour. You do not need to invoke the supernatural, for the purpose. The supernatural is the product of weak human capacities or underdeveloped state of affairs. This radical secularity went along with his assertion of the autonomy of man. Besides, knowledge is eminently practical. Speculative knowledge that did not engage with the affairs of human beings, on the contrary, easily leads to priest-craft and superstition. Ambedkar's attitude towards religion remained ambivalent. While he was suspicious of belief in a personal God and revelation, he felt that a religion in a secular society is a prerequisite for any enduring and collective pursuit of a good life. He felt that it elevates baser orientations, providing a better perspective to resolve conflicts and interests. It upholds altruism, making people reach out to others, binding people in solidarity and concern. It nurtures; cares; is oriented towards service; militates against exploitation, injustice and wrongdoing and teaches respect for others.[140] Ambedkar, therefore, did not view religion as in a private affair.

He saw freedom, equality and fraternity as essential conditions for a good life and argued that they should be understood and pursued as one entity. It was only on their foundation that a comprehensive regime of rights could be built. While different moral and religious pursuits might be reasonable, the premises of liberty and equality suggest that they are unavoidable. Once social agents are conceived of as free and equal, a plurality of moral and religious pursuits and identities inevitably beget themselves.

DISADVANTAGE AND PREFERENTIAL TREATMENT

There are diverse types of disadvantages that men and women suffer and a common yardstick cannot be applied for their amelioration. However, there are common principles on the basis of which ameliorative measures to handle disadvantages can be pursued. It is not enough that equal resources and opportunities are assigned to people, for if people suffer from disadvantages such resources and opportunities may not beget equal results in spite of the best efforts of social agents. Therefore, the disadvantaged need to be extended certain preferences that result in giving a fair opportunity to them. He envisaged such support at various levels from collective decision-making to placement in jobs and services. Eventually he thought that such considerations need to become civic virtues rather than the authoritative dispensations of the state. He, however, believed that social roles call for skills and capacities which are acquired through nurture and education, therefore the assignment of social agents must be done in accordance with their capabilities.

PRIVILEGING BUDDHISM

While Ambedkar acknowledged the possibility of diverse religious and moral standpoints that were reasonable he did not see them as equally predisposed towards freedom, equality and fraternity. Religious standpoints may not cherish human autonomy, striving for knowledge and engagement with the world. Buddhism alone cherished such goals comprehensively and intimately and offered a close complimentarity to freedom, equality and fraternity. Buddhism also embodied a just and emancipatory order, akin to Marxism in several respects. It is, therefore, eminently suited to be the moral basis of society.

PLURALISM AND ITS LIMITS

Ambedkar attempted to underplay nationalism as an exclusive or overriding identity and looked to a political order where diverse identities based upon different conceptions of the good are at play. He saw nationalism as an imagined identity which privileges certain elements from collective memory and common belonging but silences others.[141] He describes nationalism as a wild outpouring of energy that needs to be tamed by a regime of rights buttressed by the rule of law. Nationalism has a tendency to promise miracles and needs to be chastened with deference to rights. He, therefore, refused to sacrifice what he felt were the claims of Dalits before the promises of nationalism. He argued that true nationalism is the one which proceeds by acknowledging those claims.

Further, given the diverse conceptions of good, everyone would try to privilege the conception he or she believes in. Those who are powerful would hold the state to ransom for the purpose, and worse still, some may take up arms in the pursuit of ends dear to them, destroying the regime of rights.

Given the exclusive and overriding claims of nationalism, and the different, and conflicting conceptions of the good, civil society and state acquire an added significance. There needs to be a forceful assertion of society in defence and furtherance of rights. Civil society is the terrain where rights form the grids for the pursuit of different ways of life and law becomes a self-ordained injunction rather than the dictate of an external authority. However, if this is not the case, the state must sustain the order of rights, if need be, by the show of force. In a country like India, he saw the social order deeply ill-disposed towards rights making a strong state necessary if people have to pursue the conceptions of the good dear to them.[142]

Ambedkar felt that a liberal democracy has a natural tilt towards the culture and way of life of the majority.[143] It posits itself as the normal and the expected. If the political society is relatively homogenous such a tendency may not provoke deep resentment, but in societies which are culturally plural it may spell doom for the identity of minorities. Therefore, it is necessary that proper safeguards be provided for the expression of these identities.

CONSTITUTIONALISM AND RULE OF LAW

Ambedkar felt that to sustain rights, to let identities thrive as well as make them respect rights, to maintain an order favouring the disadvantaged and to facilitate a vibrant civil society, constitutional order expressed in the rule of law becomes imperative. A healthy constitutional order sustains public reason and popular participation and keeps emotive elements at bay, making it possible for common people to devise ways and means to run their common affairs. If the emotive and the heroic are allowed to have their way they throw up messiahs giving rise to dependency and servitude.

A STRONG AWARENESS OF THE WORLD

Both in his training and in vision of life, Ambedkar was deeply aware of the larger dynamics of the world, its complexity and differential bearing on social groups, localities and nations. Although he took the current ideological alignment of the world seriously into account he was not wholly swayed by it and always qualified ideological postures with historical, strategic and cultural positionings. He felt that the ideological articulation expressed in a specific society cannot offer blueprints for others. For instance, he felt that the Labour Party in England was not sensitive to the specific exploitation and disadvantage that Dalits suffered in India although it claimed to represent the labouring masses. He felt that the liberal Left in India perceived the Dalit situation in the same way. On the other hand, the Conservative Party in England had the sensitivity to perceive differences, group identity and inequalities across groups. He negotiated with them without subscribing to their normative stances on social relations. Ambedkar was also acutely aware that colonialism was on its way out and nation-states were the order of the day. He, however, went a step further. His concern became the kind of nationalism that would imbue these emerging states and the ways in which they would treat their national minorities, particularly if they were the disadvantaged section.

He increasingly saw Asia as the ambience in which India has to negotiate its way through. Although his attachment to Buddhism played a role in forming this opinion, he was deeply aware of the shared cultural sensibilities and socio-political concerns that unified this region as a whole.

APPRECIATION OF THE HERE AND NOW

Ambedkar refused to be swayed by the promises or trends of his day. Gandhi left his powerful impress on men and matters of his times. Ambedkar remained no exception, but he refused to budge from his understanding of what he thought were the ground realities. He deeply resented the pressures brought on him on the eve of the Poona Pact and steered clear from what he felt were its unholy embraces[144] as soon as an occasion presented itself. He refused to accept Atlee's advice that he make his peace with the Congress, given his electoral setback in 1946, and he defended the claims of the Scheduled Castes on independent India's political order when others went along with the mainstream. This dogged determination to pursue the causes dear to him wherever he was and under all circumstances, without donning the cloak of a saint or a renouncer, distinguished Ambedkar from most of his contemporaries. These complex issues which Ambedkar explained and defended, although not always to the satisfaction of many and sometimes not as rigorously as required, have continued to claim intellectual and political attention to this day in many societies and especially in India. He also argued that these issues be approached not through a formal positioning but in their discrete articulations through specific investigations and political programmes. He was pragmatic in his approach although not in his concerns. The backward classes in India, while avowing the political legacy of Ambedkar, are yet to engage with the understanding that marked his political involvement while their dominant counterparts will probably rest content in retaining him merely as a symbol.

I
Reminiscence: On the way to Goregaon[145]

The following is a case-study, the first in a package of six case-studies entitled *Waiting for a Visa*, regarding the treatment meted out to 'Untouchables' by ordinary people in ordinary circumstances. Four of them are autobiographical and were first published by the People's Education Society, Mumbai, in 1990, from the manuscripts in its possession. It is not certain when they were first written but it was surely after 6 March 1938 as the date is mentioned in the sixth episode, and they were probably written between 1946–7. These accounts are notionally addressed to an anonymous foreigner, a character who figures prominently in the other writings of the period, including *What Congress and Gandhi have done to the Untouchables*, who does not have any idea of what it means to be an 'Untouchable' and was all eyes and ears for the version doled out by the Congress. The phrase '*Waiting for a Visa*' is aptly satirical, conveying the situation of exclusion of 'Untouchables' and their being at the mercy of others. Ambedkar felt that case-studies of 'Untouchability' were probably more suited to acquaint a foreigner on this social phenomenon than 'a general description'.

The following case-study, the first of the series, highlights an instance in Ambedkar's childhood, portraying how social relations were often determined by the presence of untouchability.

The above case-studies are not individually titled. The title is supplied by the editor.

1

On the Way to Goregaon

Our family came originally from Dapoli Taluka of the Ratnagiri District of the Bombay Presidency. From the very commencement of the rule of the East India Company my fore-fathers had left their hereditary occupation for service in the Army of the Company. My father also followed the family tradition and sought service in the Army. He rose to the rank of an officer and was a Subhedar when he retired. On his retirement my father took the family to Dapoli with a view to settling down there. But for some reasons my father changed his mind. The family left Dapoli for Satara where we lived till 1904. The first incident which I am recording as well as I can remember, occurred in about 1901 when we were at Satara. My mother was then dead. My father was away on service as a cashier at a place called Goregaon[146] in Khatav Taluka in the Satara District, where the Government of Bombay had started the work of excavating a Tank for giving employment to famine-stricken people who were dying by thousands. When my father went to Goregaon he left me, my brother who was older than myself, and two sons of my eldest sister who was dead, in charge of my aunt and some kind neighbours. My aunt was the kindest soul I know, but she was of no help to us. She was somewhat of a dwarf and had some trouble with her legs which made it very difficult for her to move about without the aid of somebody. Often times she had to be lifted. I had sisters. They were married and were away living with their families. Cooking our food became a problem with us, especially as our aunty could not on account of her helplessness, manage the job. We four children went to school and we also cooked our food. We could not prepare bread. So we lived on *pulav* which we found to be the easiest dish to prepare, requiring nothing more than mixing rice and mutton.

Being a cashier, my father could not leave his station to come to Satara to see us, therefore he wrote to us to come to Goregaon and spend our summer vacation with him. We children were thoroughly excited over the prospect especially as none of us had up to that time seen a railway train.

Great preparations were made. New shirts of English make, bright bejewelled caps, new shoes, new silk-bordered dhoties were ordered for the journey. My father had given us all particulars regarding our journey and had told us to inform him on which day we were starting so that he would send his peon to the Railway Station to meet us and to take us to Goregaon. According to this arrangement myself, my brother and one of my sister's sons left Satara, our aunt remaining in charge of our neighbours who promised to look after her. The Railway Station was 10 miles distant from our place and *tonga* (a one-horse carriage) was engaged to take us to the Station. We were dressed in the new clothing specially made for the occasion and we left our home full of joy but amidst the cries of my aunt who was almost prostrate with grief at our parting.

When we reached the station my brother bought tickets and gave me and my sister's son two annas each as pocket money to be spent at our pleasure. We at once began our career of riotous living and each ordered a bottle of lemonade at the start. After a short while, the train whistled in and we boarded it as quickly as we could, for fear of being left behind. We were told to detrain at Masur, the nearest railway station for Goregaon.

The train arrived at Masur at about 5 in the evening and we got down with our luggage. In a few minutes all the passengers who had got down from the train had gone away to their destinations. We four children remained on the platform looking out for my father or his servant whom he had promised to send. Long did we wait but no one turned up. An hour elapsed and the station-master came to enquire. He asked us for our tickets. We showed them to him. He asked us why we tarried. We told him that we were bound for Goregaon and that we were waiting for father or his servant to come but that neither had turned up and that we did not know how to reach Goregaon. We were well-dressed children.

From our dress or talk no one could make out that we were children of the untouchables. Indeed the station-master was quite sure we were Brahmin children and was extremely touched at the plight in which he found us. As is usual among the Hindus, the station-master asked us who we were. Without a moment's thought I blurted out that we were Mahars. (Mahar is one of the communities which are treated as untouchables in the Bombay Presidency). He was stunned. His face underwent a sudden change. We could see that he was overpowered by a strange feeling of repulsion. As soon as he heard my reply he went away to his room and we stood where we were. Fifteen to twenty minutes elapsed; the sun was almost setting. The father had not turned up nor had he sent his servant, and now the station-master had also left us. We were quite bewildered, and the joy and happiness which we felt at the beginning of the journey gave way to the feeling of extreme sadness.

After half an hour the station-master returned and asked us what we proposed to do. We said that if we could get a bullock-cart on hire we would go to Goregaon and if it was not very far we would like to start straightway. There were many bullock-carts plying for hire. But my reply to the station-master that we were Mahars had gone round among the cartmen and not one of them was prepared to suffer being polluted and to demean himself carrying passengers of the untouchable classes. We were prepared to pay double the fare but we found that money did not work. The station-master who was negotiating on our behalf stood silent, not knowing what to do. Suddenly a thought seemed to have entered his head and he asked us, 'Can you drive the cart?' Feeling that he was finding out a solution of our difficulty we shouted, 'Yes, we can.' With that answer he went and proposed on our behalf that we were to pay the cartman double the fare and drive the cart and that he should walk on foot along with the cart on our journey. One cartman agreed as it gave him an opportunity to earn his fare and also saved him from being polluted.

It was about 6.30 p.m. when we were ready to start. But we were anxious not to leave the station until we were assured that we would reach Goregaon before it was dark. We therefore questioned the cartman as to the distance and the time he would take to reach Goregaon. He assured us that it would be no more than 3 hours. Believing in his word, we put our luggage in the cart, thanked the station-master and got into the cart. One of us took the reins and the cart started with the man walking by our side.

Not very far from the station there flowed a river. It was quite dry except at places where there were small pools of water. The owner of the cart proposed that we should halt there and have our meal as we might not get water on our way. We agreed. He asked us to give a part of his fare to enable him to go to the village and have his meal. My brother gave him some money and he left, promising to return soon. We were very hungry and were glad to have had an opportunity to have a bite. My aunty had pressed our neighbours' women folk into service and had some nice food for us to take on our way. We opened the tiffin basket and started eating. We needed water to wash things down. One of us went to the pool of water in the river basin nearby. But the water really was no water. It was thick with mud and urine and excreta of the cows and buffaloes and other cattle who went to the pool to drink water. In fact, that water was not intended for human use. At any rate the stink of the water was so strong we could not drink it. We had therefore to close our meal before we were satisfied and wait for the arrival of the cartman. He did not come for a long time and all that we could do was to look for him in all directions. Ultimately he came and we started on our journey. For some four or five miles we drove the cart and he walked on foot. Then he suddenly jumped into the cart and took the reins from our hand. We thought this to be rather a strange conduct on the part of a man who had refused to let the cart on hire for fear of pollution, to have set aside all his religious scruples and to have consented to sit with us in the same cart but we dared not ask him any questions on the point. We were anxious to reach Goregaon, our destination, as quickly as possible. And for sometime we were interested in the movement of the cart only. But soon there was darkness all around us. There were no street lights to relieve the darkness. There were no men or women or even cattle passing by to make us feel that we were in their midst. We became fearful of the loneliness which surrounded us. Our anxiety was growing. We mustered all the courage we possessed. We had travelled far from Masur. It was more than three hours. But there was no sign of Goregaon. There arose a strange thought within us. We suspectd that the cartman intended treachery and that he was taking us to some lonely spot to kill us. We had lot of gold ornaments on us and that helped to strengthen our suspicion. We started asking him how far Goregaon was, why we were so late in reaching it. He kept on saying, 'It is not very far, we shall soon reach it'. It was about 10.00 at night when finding that there was no trace of Goregaon we children started crying and abusing the cartman. Our lamentations and wailing continued for long. The cartman made no reply. Suddenly we saw a light burning at some distance. The cartman said, 'Do you see that light? That is a light of the toll-collector. We will rest there for the night.' We felt some relief and stopped crying. The light was distant, but we could never seem to reach it. It took us two hours to reach the toll-collector's hut. The interval increased our anxiety and we kept on asking the cartman all sorts of questions, as to why there was delay in reaching the place, whether we were going on the same road, etc.

Ultimately by midnight the cart reached the toll-collector's hut. It was situated at the foot of a hill but on the other side of the hill. When we arrived we saw a large number of bullock-carts there, all resting for the night. We were extremely hungry and wanted very much to eat. But again there was the question of water. So we asked our driver whether it was possible to get water. He warned us that the toll-collector was a Hindu and that there was no possibility of our getting water if we spoke the truth and said that we were Mahars. He said, 'Say you are Mohammedans and try your luck'. On his advice I went to the toll-collector's hut and asked him if he would give us some water. 'Who are you?', he inquired. I replied that we were Musalmans. I conversed with him in Urdu which I knew very well so as to leave no doubt that I was a real Musalman. But the trick did not work and his reply was very curt. 'Who has kept water for you? There is water on the hill, if you want to go and get it, I have none.' With this he dismissed me. I returned to the cart and conveyed to my brother his reply. I don't know what my brother felt. All that he did was to tell us to lie down

The bullocks had been unyoked and the cart was placed sloping down on the ground. We spread our beds on the bottom plank inside the cart, and laid down our bodies to rest. Now that we had come to a place of safety we did not mind what happened. But our minds could not help turning to the latest event. There was plenty of food with us. There was hunger burning within us; with all this we were to sleep without food; that was because we could get no water and we could get no water because we were untouchables. Such was the last thought that entered our mind. I said, we had come to a place of safety. Evidently my elder brother had his misgivings. He said it was not wise for all four of us to go to sleep. Anything might happen. He suggested that at one time two should sleep and two should keep watch. So we spent the night at the foot of that hill.

Early at 5 in the morning our cartman came and suggested that we should start for Goregaon. We flatly refused. We told him that we would not move until 8 o'clock. We did not want to take any chance. He said nothing. So we left at 8 and reached Goregaon at 11. My father was surprised to see us and said that he had received no intimation of our coming. We protested that we had given intimation. He denied the fact. Subsequently it was discovered that the fault was of my father's servant. He had received our letter but failed to give it to my father.

This incident has a very important place in my life. I was a boy of nine when it happened. But it has left an indelible impression on my mind. Before this incident occurred, I knew that I was an untouchable and that untouchables were subjected to certain indignities and discriminations. For instance, I knew that in the school I could not sit in the midst of my class students according to my rank but that I was to sit in a corner by myself. I knew that in the school I was to have a separate piece of gunny cloth for me to squat on in the class room and the servant employed to clean the school would not touch the gunny cloth used by me. I was required to carry the gunny cloth home in the evening and bring it back the next day. While in the school I knew that children of the touchable classes, when they felt thirsty, could go out to the water tap, open it and quench their thirst. All that was necessary was the permission of the teacher. But my position was separate. I could not touch the tap and unless it was opened for me by a touchable person, it was not possible for me to quench my thirst. In my case the permission of the teacher was not enough. The presence of the school peon was necessary, for he was the only person whom the class teacher could use for such a purpose. If the peon was not available I had to go without water. The situation can be summed up in the statement—no peon, no water. At home I knew that the work of washing clothes was done by my sisters. Not that there were no washermen in Satara. Not that we could not afford to pay the washermen. Washing was done by my sisters because we were untouchables and no washerman would wash the clothes of an untouchable. The work of cutting the hair or shaving the boys including myself was done by our elder sister who had become quite an expert barber by practising the art on us, not that there were no barbers in Satara, not that we could not afford to pay the barber. The work of shaving and hair cutting was done by my sister because we were untouchables and no barber would consent to shave an untouchable. All this I knew. But this incident gave me a shock such as I never received before, and it made me think about untouchability which, before this incident happened, was with me a matter of course as it is with many touchables as well as the untouchables.

II

Concepts

Ambedkar deployed a large body of concepts to explain and engage with the world. In this selection, we have chosen excerpts of seven articles or essays, each expressing his views on these concepts. The first is on religion and *dhamma* where he makes a sharp distinction between the two in *The Buddha and His Dhamma*, first published in 1957. In this excerpt he posits the concepts of religion and *dhamma* and demarcates them from each other.

The concept of democracy[147] (The title is the editor's), is drawn from *What Congress and Gandhi have done to the Untouchables*, published in 1946. In this book, Ambedkar attempted to debunk the initiative of Gandhi and the Congress regarding the removal of untouchability. The excerpt is from the chapter 'A Plea to the Foreigner'. A concept of democracy is extrapolated here by wrestling with the limitations of parliamentary democracy and its class-biases.

In his statement submitted to the Indian Statutory Commission (ISC), popularly known as the Simon Commission, in 1928, Ambedkar dwelt on several concepts of political economy including that of franchise.[148] Here are series of arguments justifying universal adult franchise and the right to franchise is clearly dissociated from levels of literacy.

Ambedkar dwelt on the concept of representation[149] in his statement submitted to the Indian Statutory Commission (ISC) under the title 'electorate'. He rejected certain modes of representation and approved others, fine-tuning his distinctions. (The title is the editor's)

56 • THE ESSENTIAL WRITINGS OF B. R. AMBEDKAR

Eliciting the active involvement of minorities in public life is a major task confronting representative democracies. In this regard, Ambedkar argued that the quantum of representation of minorities[150] should not be merely in accordance with the proportion of their population. The principle of adequacy too should be taken into account. The excerpt is from Ambedkar's statement before the ISC in 1928. (The title is the editor's)

Here Ambedkar identifies a set of criteria to be employed to demarcate *Untouchability*.[151] (The title is the editor's)

This excerpt is taken from Ambedkar's Note to the Indian Franchise Committee (Lothian Committee) submitted in May 1932. The Committee was constituted on the recommendation of the Franchise Sub-committee of the *Round Table Conference* (RTC) in December 1931. Ambedkar was a member of this committee.

This excerpt on caste and class[152] is from Ambedkar's proposed work *Can I be a Hindu?* of which only a chapter 'Symbols of Hinduism' came to be written. It was probably written in the early part of 1950s when Ambedkar displayed a great deal of interest in Buddhism and Marxism. It was first published in 1987. (The editor has titled this excerpt)

2

Religion and Dhamma

WHAT IS RELIGION?

1. The word 'religion' is an indefinite word with no fixed meaning.

2. It is one word with many meanings.

3. This is because religion has passed through many stages. The concept at each stage is called Religion though the concept at one stage has not had the same meaning which it had at the preceding stage or is likely to have at the succeeding stage.

4. The conception of religion was never fixed.

5. It has varied from time to time.

6. Because most of the phenomena such as lightning, rain and floods, the occurrence of which the primitive man could not explain, any weird performance done to control the phenomenon was called magic. Religion therefore came to be identified with magic.

7. Then came the second stage in the evolution of religion. In this stage, religion came to be identified with beliefs, rituals, ceremonies, prayers and sacrifices.

8. But this conception of religion is derivative.

9. The pivotal point in religion starts with the belief that there exists some power which causes these phenomena which primitive man did not know and could not understand. Magic lost its place at this stage.

10. This power was originally malevolent. But later it was felt that it could also be benevolent.

11. Beliefs, rites, ceremonies and sacrifices were necessary both to propitiate a benevolent power and also to conciliate an angry power.

12. Later that power was called God or the Creator.

13. Then came the third stage that it is this God who created this world and also man.

14. This was followed by the belief that man has a soul and the soul is eternal and is answerable to God for man's action in the world.

15. This is, in short, the evolution of the concept of Religion.

16. This is what Religion has come to be and this is what it connotes—belief in God, belief in soul, worship of God, curing of the erring soul, propitiating God by prayers, ceremonies, sacrifices, etc.

HOW DHAMMA DIFFERS FROM RELIGION

1. What the Buddha calls Dhamma differs fundamentally from what is called Religion.

2. What the Buddha calls Dhamma is analogous to what the European theologians call Religion.

3. But there is no greater affinity between the two. On the other hand, the differences between the two are very great.

4. On this account some European theologians refuse to recognize the Buddha's Dhamma as Religion.

5. There need be no regrets over this. The loss is theirs. It does no harm to the Buddha's Dhamma. Rather, it shows what is wanting in Religion.

6. Instead of entering into this controversy it is better to proceed to give an idea of Dhamma and show how it differs from Religion.

7. Religion, it is said, is personal and one must keep it to oneself. One must not let it play its part in public life.

8. Contrary to this, Dhamma is social. It is fundamentally and essentially so.

9. Dhamma is righteousness, which means right relations between man and man in all spheres of life.

10. From this it is evident that one man if he is alone does not need Dhamma.

11. But when there are two men living in relation to each other they must find a place for Dhamma whether they like it or not. Neither can escape it.

12. In other words, Society cannot do without Dhamma.

13. Society has to choose one of the three alternatives.

14. Society may choose not to have any Dhamma, as an instrument of Government. For Dhamma is nothing if it is not an instrument of Government.

15. This means Society chooses the road to anarchy.

16. Secondly, Society may choose the police, i.e., dictatorship as an instrument of Government.

17. Thirdly, Society may choose Dhamma plus the Magistrate wherever people fail to observe the Dhamma.

18. In anarchy and dictatorship, liberty is lost.

19. Only in the third liberty survives.

20. Those who want liberty must therefore have Dhamma.

21. Now what is Dhamma, and why is Dhamma necessary? According to the Buddha, Dhamma consists of Prajna and Karuna.

22. What is Prajna? And why Prajna? Prajna is understanding. The Buddha made Prajna one of the two corner-stones of His Dhamma because he did not wish to leave any room for superstition.

23. What is Karuna? And why Karuna? Karuna is love. Because, without it Society can neither live nor grow, that is why the Buddha made it the second corner-stone of His Dhamma.

24. Such is the definition of the Buddha's Dhamma.

25. How different is this definition of Dhamma from that of Religion.

26. So ancient, yet so modern is the definition of Dhamma given by the Buddha.

27. So aboriginal yet so original.

28. Not borrowed from anyone, yet so true.

29. A unique amalgam of Prajna and Karuna is the Dhamma of the Buddha.

30. Such is the difference between Religion and Dhamma.

3

Democracy

Habits of constitutional morality may be essential for the maintenance of a constitutional form of government. But the maintenance of a constitutional form of government is not the same thing
as a self-government by the people. Similarly, it may be granted
that adult suffrage can produce government of the people in the
logical sense of the phrase, i.e., in contrast to the government of
a king. But it cannot by itself be said to bring about a democratic
government, in the sense of the government by the people and for
the people.

Anyone who knows the tragic fate of Parliamentary Democracy
in Western Europe will not require more and better evidence to
prove the fallacy underlying such notions of democracy.[a] If I may
quote myself from what I have said in another place, the causes
which have led to the failure of democracy in Western Europe may
be summarized in the following words:

The government of human society has undergone some very significant
changes. There was a time when the government of human society had
taken the form of autocracy by Despotic Sovereigns. This was replaced
after a long and bloody struggle by a system of government known as
Parliamentary Democracy. It was felt that this was the last word in the
framework of government. It was believed to bring about the millennium
in which every human being will have the right to liberty, property and
pursuit of happiness. And there were good grounds for such high hopes.

[a] Labour and Parliamentary Democracy—A lecture delivered on 17th
September 1943 to the All-India Trade Union Workers' Study Camp held
in Delhi.

In parliamentary democracy there is the Legislature to express the voice of the people; there is the executive which is subordinate to the Legislature and bound to obey the Legislature. Over and above the Legislature and the Executive there is the Judiciary to control both and keep them both within prescribed bounds. Parliamentary democracy has all the marks of a popular government, a government of the people, by the people and for the people. It is therefore a matter of some surprise that there has been a revolt against parliamentary democracy although not even a century has elapsed since its universal acceptance and inauguration. There is revolt against it in Italy, in Germany, in Russia and in Spain, and there are very few countries in which there has not been discontent against parliamentary democracy. Why should there be this discontent and dissatisfaction against parliamentary democracy? It is question worth considering. There is no country in which the urgency of considering this question is greater than it is in India. India is negotiating to have parliamentary democracy. There is a great need of some one with sufficient courage to tell Indians: 'Beware of parliamentary democracy, it is not the best product as it appears to be.'

Why has parliamentary democracy failed? In the country of the dictators it has failed because it is a machine whose movements are very slow. It delays swift action. In a parliamentary democracy the Executive may be held up by the Legislature which may refuse to pass the laws which the Executive wants and if it is not held up by the Legislature it may be held up by the judiciary which may declare the laws as illegal. Parliamentary democracy gives no free hand to dictatorship and that is why it became a discredited institution in countries like Italy, Spain and Germany which readily welcomed dictatorships. If dictators alone were against parliamentary democracy it would not have mattered at all. Their testimony against parliamentary democracy would be welcomed for the reason that it can be an effective check upon dictatorship. But unfortunately there is a great deal of discontent against parliamentary democracy even in countries where people are opposed to dictatorship. That is the most regrettable fact about Parliamentary democracy. This is all the more regrettable because parliamentary democracy has not been at a standstill. It has progressed in three directions. It began with equality of political rights in the form of equal suffrage. There are very few countries having parliamentary democracy which have not adult suffrage. It has progressed by expanding the notion of equality of political rights to equality of social and economic opportunity. It has recognised that the State cannot be held at bay by corporations which are anti-social in their purpose. With all this, there is immense discontent against parliamentary democracy even in countries pledged to democracy. The reasons for discontent in such countries must obviously be different from those assigned by the dictator countries. There is no time to go into details.

But it can be said in general terms that the discontent against parliamentary democracy is due to the realization that it has failed to assure to the masses the right to liberty, property or the pursuit of happiness. If this is true, it is important to know the causes which have brought about this failure. The causes for this failure may be found either in wrong ideology or wrong organization or in both. I think the causes are to be found in both.

Of the erroneous ideologies which have been responsible for the failure of parliamentary democracy I have no doubt that the idea of freedom of contract is one of them. The idea became sanctified and was upheld in the name of liberty. Parliamentary democracy took no notice of economic inequalities and did not care to examine the result of freedom of contract on the parties to the contract, in spite of the fact that they were unequal in their bargaining power. It did not mind if the freedom of contract gave the strong the opportunity to defraud the weak. The result is that parliamentary democracy in standing out as a protagonist of liberty has continuously added to the economic wrongs of the poor, the downtrodden and the disinherited class.

The second wrong ideology which has vitiated parliamentary democracy is the failure to realize that political democracy cannot succeed where there is no social and economic democracy. Some may question this proposition. To those who are disposed to question it, I will ask a counter-question. Why did parliamentary democracy collapse so easily in Italy, Germany and Russia? Why did it not collapse so easily in England and the USA. To my mind there is only one answer. It is that there was a greater degree of economic and social democracy in the latter countries than existed in the former. Social and economic democracy are the tissues and the fibre of a political democracy. The tougher the tissue and the fibre, the greater the strength of the body. Democracy is another name for equality. Parliamentary democracy developed a passion for liberty. It never made even a nodding acquaintance with equality. It failed to realize the significance of equality and did not even endeavour to strike a balance between liberty and equality, with the result that liberty swallowed equality and has made democracy a name and a farce.

I have referred to the wrong ideologies which in my judgment have been responsible for the failure of parliamentary democracy. But I am equally certain that more than bad ideology it is bad organization which has been responsible for the failure of democracy. All political societies get divided into two classes—the Rulers and the Ruled. This is an evil. If the evil stopped here it would not matter much. But the unfortunate part of it is that the division becomes so stereotyped and stratified that Rulers are always drawn from the ruling class and the class that is ruled never becomes the ruling class. This happens because generally people do not care to see that they govern themselves. They are content to establish a government and leave it to govern them. This explains why parliamentary democracy has never been a government of the people or by the people and why it has been in reality a government of a hereditary subject class by a hereditary ruling class. It is this vicious organization of political life which has made parliamentary democracy such a dismal failure. It is because of this that parliamentary democracy has not fulfilled the hope it held out to the common man of ensuring to him liberty, property and pursuit of happiness.

If this analysis of the causes which have led to the failure of democracy is correct, it must serve as a warning to the protagonists of democracy that there are certain fundamental considerations which go to the root of democracy and which they cannot ignore without peril to democracy. For the sake of clarity these considerations may be set down in serial order.

First is the recognition of the hard fact of history that in every country there exist two classes,—the governing class and the servile class between whom there is a continuous struggle for power. *Second* is that by reason of its power and prestige the governing class finds it easy to maintain its supremacy over the servile class. *Third* is that adult suffrage and frequent elections are no bar against governing class reaching places of powers and authority. *Fourth* is that on account of their inferiority complex the members of the servile classes regard the members of the governing class as their natural leaders and the servile classes themselves volunteer to elect members of the governing classes as their rulers. *Fifth* is that the existence of a governing class is inconsistent with democracy and self-government and that given the fact that where the governing class retains its power to govern, it is wrong to believe that democracy and self-government have become realities of life. *Sixth* is that self-government and democracy become real not when a constitution based on adult suffrage comes into existence but when the governing class loses its power to capture the power to govern. *Seventh* is that while in some countries the servile classes may succeed in ousting the governing class from the seat of authority with nothing more than adult suffrage, in other countries the governing class may be so deeply entrenched that the servile classes will need other safeguards besides adult suffrage to achieve the same end.

That there is great value in having these considerations drawn up and hung up, so to say on the wall, before every lover of democracy, so that he may see them and note them, goes without saying. For they will help, as nothing else can, to make him realize that in devising a Constitution for democracy he must bear in mind: that the principal aim of such a Constitution must be to dislodge the governing class from its position and to prevent it from remaining as a governing class for ever; that the machinery for setting up a democratic government cannot be a matter of dogma; that ousting the governing class from power being the main object the machinery for setting up a democratic government cannot be uniform and that variations in the machinery of democracy must not merely be tolerated but accepted for the reason that the processes by which the governing classes obtain their mastery over the servile classes vary from country to country.

This is what democracy means and involves. But unfortunately Western writers on politics from whom the foreigner draws his notions have failed to take such a realistic view of democracy. Instead, they have taken a very formal and a very superficial view of it by making constitutional morality, adult suffrage and frequent elections as the be-all and end-all of democracy.

Those who propound the view that democracy need involve no more than these three devices are probably unaware of the fact that they are doing nothing more than and nothing different from expressing the point of view of the governing classes. The governing classes know by experience that such mechanisms have not proved fatal to their power and their position. Indeed, they have helped to give to their power and prestige the virtue of legality and made themselves less vulnerable to attack by the servile classes.

4

Franchise

My[153] colleagues have recommended that the franchise in urban areas should remain as it is and that in rural areas the land revenue assessment should be halved. I am unable to agree to this. My colleagues have treated the question of franchise as though it was a question of favour rather than of right. I think that such a view is too dangerous to be accepted as the basis of political society in any country. For if the conception of a right to representation is to be dismissed as irrelevant; if a moral claim to representation is to be deemed as nothing but a metaphysical or sentimental obstruction; if franchise is considered a privilege to be given or withheld by those in political power according to their own estimate of the use likely to be made of it, then it is manifest that the political emancipation of the unenfranchised will be entirely at the mercy of those that are enfranchised. To accept such a conclusion is to accept that slavery is no wrong. For slavery, too, involves the hypothesis that men have no right but what those in power choose to give them. A theory which leads to such a conclusion must be deemed to be fatal to any form of popular Government, and as such I reject it in toto.

My colleagues look upon the question of franchise as though it was nothing but a question of competency to put into a ballot box a piece of paper with a number of names written thereon. Otherwise they would not have insisted upon literacy as a criterion for the extension of the franchise. Such a view of the franchise is undoubtedly superficial and involves a total misunderstanding of what it stands for. If the majority had before its mind the true conception of what franchise means they would have realised that franchise, far from being a transaction concerned with the marking of the ballot paper, 'stands for direct and active participation in the regulation of the terms upon which associated life shall be sustained and the permit of good carried on'. Once this conception of franchise is admitted, it would follow that franchise is due to every adult who is not a lunatic. For, associated life is shared by every individual and as every individual is affected by its consequences, every individual must have the right to settle its terms. From the same premises it would further follow that the poorer the individual the greater the necessity of enfranchising him. For in every society based on private property the terms of associated life as between owners and workers are from the start set against the workers. If the welfare of the worker is to be guaranteed from being menaced by the owners the terms of their associated life must be constantly resettled. But this can hardly be done unless the franchise is dissociated from property and extended to all propertyless adults. It is therefore clear that judged from either point of view the conclusion in favour of adult suffrage is irresistible. I accept that conclusion and recommend that the franchise should be extended to all adults, male and female, above the age of 21.

Political justice is not the only ground for the introduction of adult suffrage. Even political expediency favours its introduction. One of the reasons why minorities like the Mohamedan insist upon communal electorates is the fear that in a system of joint electorates the voters of the majority community would so largely influence the election that seats would go to men who were undesirable from the standpoint of the minority. I have pointed out in a subsequent part of the report that such a contention could be effectively disposed of by the introduction of adult suffrage. The majority has given no thought to the importance of adult suffrage as an alternative to communal electorates. The majority has proceeded as though communal electorates were a good to be preserved and have treated adult suffrage as though it was an evil to be kept within bonds. My view of them is just the reverse. I hold communal electorates to be an evil and adult suffrage to be a good. Those who agree with me will admit that adult suffrage should be introduced not only because of its inherent good but also because it can enable us to get rid of the evil of communal electorates. But even those whose political faith does not include a belief in adult suffrage, will, I am sure, find no difficulty in accepting this view. For it is only commonsense to say that a lesser evil is to be preferred to a greater evil and there is no doubt that adult suffrage, if it is at all an evil, is a lesser evil than communal electorate. Adult suffrage, which is supported by political justice and favoured by political expediency, is also, I find, demanded by a substantial body of public opinion. The Nehru Committee's[154] report, which embodies the views of all the political parties in India except the Non-Brahmins and the Depressed Classes, favours the introduction of adult suffrage. The Depressed Classes have also insisted upon it. The Sindh Mohamedan Association, one Mohamedan member and one Non-Brahmin member of the Government of Bombay, have expressed themselves in favour of it. There is thus a considerable volume of public opinion in support of adult franchise. My colleagues give no reason why they have ignored this volume of public opinion.

Two things appear to have weighed considerably with my colleagues in their decision against the introduction of adult suffrage. One is the extent of illiteracy prevalent in the country. No one can deny the existence of illiteracy among the masses of the country. But that this factor should have any bearing on the question of franchise is a view the correctness of which I am not prepared to admit. First of all, illiteracy of the illiterate is no fault of theirs. The Government of Bombay for a long time refused to take upon itself the most important function of educating the people, and, when it did, it deliberately confined the benefit of education to the classes and refused to extend it to the masses.[a]

It was not until 1854, that the government declared itself in favour of mass education as against class education.[155] But the anxiety of the government for the spread of education among the masses has gone very little beyond the passing of a few resolutions. In the matter of financial support the government always treated education with a most niggardly provision. It is notorious, how the government, which is always in favour of taxation, refused to consent to the proposal of the Honourable Mr Gokhale for

[a] Lest this fact should be regarded as a fiction, I invite attention to the extracts from the Report of the Board of Education of the Bombay Presidency for the year 1850-1.

compulsory primary education, although it was accompanied by a measure of taxation. The introduction of the Reform has hardly improved matters. Beyond the passing of a Compulsory Primary Education Act in the Presidency there has not been any appreciable advance in the direction of mass education. On the contrary there has been a certain amount of deterioration owing to the transfer of education to local authorities which are manned, comparatively speaking, by people who being either indifferent or ignorant, are seldom keen for the advancement of education.

In the case of the Depressed Classes the opportunity for acquiring literacy has in fact been denied to them. Untouchability has been an insuperable bar in their way to education. Even the government has bowed before it and has sacrificed the rights of the Depressed Classes to admission in public schools to the exigencies of the social system in India. In a resolution of the year 1856, the Government of Bombay in rejecting the petition of a Mahar boy to a school in Dharwar observed:[156]

The question discussed in the correspondence is one of very great practical difficulty...

1. There can be no doubt that the Mahar petitioner has abstract justice in his side; and Government trust that the prejudices which at present prevent him from availing himself of existing means of education in Dharwar may be are long removed.

2. But Government are obliged to keep in mind that to interfere with the prejudices of ages in a summary manner, for the sake of one or few individuals, would probably do a great damage to the cause of education. The disadvantage under which the petitioner labours is not one which has originated with this Government, and it is one which Government cannot summarily remove by interfering in his favour, as he begs them to do.

The Hunter Commission[157] which followed after the lapse of 26 years did say that the government should accept the principle that nobody be refused admission to a Government College or School merely on the ground of caste. But it also felt it necessary to say that the principle should 'be applied with due caution' and the result of such caution was that the principle was never enforced. A bold attempt was, no doubt, made in 1921 by Dr Paranjpye, when he was the Minister of Education.[158] But as his action was without any sanction behind it, his circular regarding admission of the Depressed Classes to Schools is being evaded, with the result that illiteracy still continues to be a deplorable feature of the life of the Depressed Classes.

To the question that is often asked is how can such illiterate people be given the franchise, my reply therefore is, who is responsible for their illiteracy? If the responsibility for illiteracy falls upon the government, then to make literacy a condition precedent to franchise is to rule out the large majority of the people who, through no fault of their own, have never had an opportunity of acquiring literacy provided to them. Granting that the extension of franchise must follow the removal of illiteracy, what guarantee is there that efforts will be made to remove illiteracy as early as possible? The question of education like other nation-building questions is ultimately a question of money. So long as money is not forthcoming in sufficient amount, there can be no advance in education. How to find this money is therefore the one question that has to be solved. That a Council elected on the present franchise will never be in a position to solve the problem is beyond dispute. For the simple reason that money for education can only be provided by taxing the rich and the rich are the people who control the present Council. Surely the rich will not consent to tax themselves for the benefit of the poor unless they are compelled to do so. Such a compulsion can only come by a radical change in the composition of the Council which will give the poor and illiterate adequate voice therein. Unless this happens, the question of illiteracy will never be solved. To deny them that right is to create a situation full of injustice. To keep people illiterate and then to make their illiteracy the ground for their non-enfranchisement is to add insult to injury. But the situation indeed involves more than this. In involves an aggravation of the injury. For to keep people illiterate and then to deny them franchise, which is the only means whereby they could effectively provide for the removal of their illiteracy, is to perpetuate their illiteracy and postpone indefinitely the day of their enfranchisement.

It might be said that the question is not who is responsible for illiteracy; the question is whether illiterate persons should be given the right to vote. My answer is that the question cannot be one of literacy or illiteracy; the question can be of intelligence alone. Those who insist on literacy as a test and insist upon making it a condition precedent to enfranchisement, in my opinion, commit two mistakes. Their first mistake consists in their belief that an illiterate person is necessarily an unintelligent person. But everyone knows that, to maintain that an illiterate person can be a very intelligent person, is not to utter a paradox. Indeed an appeal to experience would fortify the conclusion that illiterate people all over the world including India have intelligence enough to understand and manage their own affairs. At any rate the law presumes that above a certain age every one has intelligence enough to be entrusted with the responsibility of managing his own affairs. The illiterate might easily commit mistakes in the exercise of the franchise. But then the Development Department of Bombay has fallen into mistakes of judgment equally great which though they are condemned, are all the same tolerated. And even if they fall into greater errors it may still be well that they should have franchise. For all belief in free and popular government rests ultimately on the conviction that a people gains more by experience than it loses by the errors of liberty and it is difficult to perceive why a truth that holds good of individuals in non-political field should not hold good in the political field. Their second mistake lies in supposing that literacy necessarily imparts a higher level of intelligence or knowledge than what the illiterate possesses. On this point the words of Bryce might be quoted.[159] In his survey of 'Modern Democracies' he raises the question how far ability to read and write goes towards civic competence and answers thus:

Because it is the only test practically available, we assume it to be an adequate test. Is it really so? Some of us remember, among the English rustics of sixty years ago shrewd men, unable to read but with plenty of mother wit, and by their strong sense and solid judgment quite as well qualified to vote as are their grand-children today who read a newspaper and revel in the cinema... The Athenian voters...were better...fitted for civic franchise than most of the voters in modern democracies. These Greek voters learnt politics not from the printed and, few even from any written page, but by listening to accomplished orators and by talking to one another. Talking has this advantage over reading, that in it the mind is less passive. It is thinking that matters, not reading, and by thinking, I mean the power of getting at facts, and arguing consecutively from them. In conversation there is a clash of wits, and to that some mental exertion must go... But in these days of ours reading has become substitute for thinking. The man who reads only the newspaper of his own party, and reads its political intelligence in a medley of other stuff, narratives of crimes and descriptions of football matches, need not know that there is more than one side to a question and seldom asks if there is one, nor what is the evidence for what the paper tells him. The printed page, because it seems to represent some unknown power, is believed more readily than what he hears in talk. He takes from it statements, perhaps groundless, perhaps invented, which he would not take from one of his followers in the workshop or the counting house. Moreover, the Tree of Knowledge is the Tree of the Knowledge of Evil as well as of Good. On the printed page Truth has no better chance than Falsehood, except with those who read widely and have the capacity of discernment. A party organ, suppressing some facts, misrepresenting some others, is the worst of all guides, because it can by incessantly reiterating untruth produce a greater impression than any man or body of men, save only ecclesiastics clothed with a spiritual authority, could produce before printing was invented. A modern voter so guided by his party newspapers is no better off than his grandfather who eighty years ago voted at the bidding of his landlord or his employer or (in Ireland) of his Priest. The grandfather at least knew whom he was following, while the grandson, who only reads what is printed on one side of a controversy may be the victim of selfish interests who own the organs which his simplicity assumes to express public opinion or to have the public good at heart. So a democracy that has been taught only to read and not also to reflect and judge, will not be better for the ability to read.

It seems to me that too much is being made out of the illiteracy of the masses in India. Take the English voter and inquire into his conduct as a voter and what do we find? This is what the Times Literary Supplement of 21 August 1924, says about him:

The mass of the people have no serious interest. Their votes decide all political issues, but they know nothing of politics. It is a disquieting, but too well-founded reflection that the decision about tariff reform or taxation or foreign policy is now said by men and women who have never read a dozen columns of serious politics in their lives. Of the old narrow electorate of eight years ago probably at least two–thirds eagerly studied political speeches on the question of the day. Today not five per cent of the voters read either debates or leading articles. The remnant, however remarkable, is small. Democracy as a whole is as content with gross amusement as Bottles was with vulgar ones, and like him it leases his mind to its newspaper which makes his Sundays much more degrading than those which he spent under his Baptist Minister. This is the atmosphere against whose poisonous gases the schools provide in vain the helmet of their culture.

Surely if British Democracy—say the British Empire is content to be ruled by voters such as above, it is arguable that Indians who are opposed to adult suffrage are not only unjust and visionaries but are protesting too much and are laying themselves open to the charge that they are making illiteracy of the masses an excuse to pocket their political power. For, to insist that a thorough appreciation of the niceties of political creeds and the ability to distinguish between them are necessary tests of political intelligence is, to say the least, hypercritical. On small political questions no voter, no matter in what country he is, will ever be accurately informed. Nor is such minute knowledge necessary. The most that can be expected from the elector is the power of understanding broad issues and of choosing the candidate who in his opinion will serve him best. This, I make bold to say, is not beyond the capacity of an average Indian.

The other thing which apparently weighed with my colleagues in refusing to accept adult suffrage is the analogy of the countries like England. It is argued that the extension of the franchise from forty shilling freehold in 1429 to adult suffrage in 1832 there were less than 500,000 persons who had the right to vote in the election of members of Parliament; that it was not until the Reform Act of that year that the number of voters was increased to nearly 1,000,000; that no further step was taken to lower the franchise till the passing of the Act of 1867 which increased it to 2,500,000; that the next step was taken 17 years after when the Act of 1884 increased it again to 5,500,000; and that adult suffrage did not come till after a lapse of 34 years when People's Representation Act of 1918 was passed. This fact has been used for very different purposes by different set of peoples. A set of politicians who are social tories and political radicals use this in support of their plea that the legislature can be given full powers although it may not be fully representative and in reply to this argument of their opponents that the transference of power to a legislature so little representative will be to transfer it to an oligarchy. By others in support of their plea that in the matter of franchise, we must proceed slowly and go step by step as other nations have done. To the second group of critics my reply is that there is no reason why we should follow in the footsteps of the English nation in this particular matter. Surely the English people had not devised any philosophy of action in the matter of franchise. On the other hand, if the extension was marked by such long intervals it was because of the self-seeking character of the English ruling classes. Besides, there is no reason why every nation should go through the same stages and enact the same scenes as other nations have done. To do so is to refuse to reap the advantage which is always open to those who are born later. To the other section of critics my reply is that their contention as a fact is true, that Parliament did exercise full powers of a sovereign state even when it represented only a small percentage of the population. But the question is, with what results to the nation? Anyone who is familiar with the history of social legislation by the unreformed Parliament as told by Lord Shaftesbury certainly will not wish the experiment to be repeated in this country. This result was the inevitable result of the restricted franchise which obtained in England. The facts relied upon by these critics in my opinion do not go to support a government based upon a restricted franchise. It is a worse form of government in that it gives rise to the rule of oligarchy. Such a result was never contemplated by the authors of the Joint Report.[160] Indeed they were so conscious of the evil that in paragraph 262 of their Report they were particular enough to say that among the matters for consideration the Statutory Commission should consider the working of the franchise and the constitution of electorates, including the important matter of the retention of communal representation. 'Indeed we regard the development of a broad franchise as the arch on which the edifice of self-government must be raised: for we have no intention that our reforms should result merely in the transfer of powers from a bureaucracy to an oligarchy.'

What is however the remedy for preventing oligarchy? The only remedy that I can think of is the grant of adult suffrage. It is pertinent to remark that the members of the Ceylon Commission of 1928[161] who like the authors of the Joint Report were conscious that 'the grant of a responsible government to an electorate of these small dimensions would be tantamount to placing an oligarchy in power without any guarantee that the interests of the remainder of the people would be consulted by those in authority' and who felt it 'necessary to observe that his Majesty's Government is the trustee not merely of the wealthier and more highly educated elements in Ceylon but quite as much of the peasant and the coolie, and of all those poorer classes which form the bulk of the population' and who held that 'to hand over the interests of the latter to the unfettered control of the former would be a betrayal of its trust,' came 'to the conclusion that literacy should not remain as one of the qualifications for voters at election of State Council.'[162]

They said 'the development of responsible government requires, in our opinion, an increasing opportunity to the rank and file of the people to influence the Government and the franchise cannot be fairly or wisely confined to the educated classes.' If adult franchise can be prescribed for Ceylon the question that naturally arises is why should it not be prescribed for India? Similarity in the political, social, economic, and educational conditions of the two countries is so striking that to treat them differently in the matter of franchise is to create a distinction when there is no real difference to justify the same. Analogy apart and considering the case purely on merits it is beyond doubt that of the two if any one of them is more fitted to be trusted with the exercise of adult franchise it is the people of India and more so the people of the Bombay Presidency wherein the system of adult suffrage is already in vogue in the village panchayats.

5

Representation

The existing Legislative Council is composed of 114 Members of whom 26 are nominated and 86 are elected. The nominated Members fall into two groups (a) officials to represent the reserved half of the government and (b) the non-officials to represent (1) the Depressed Classes, (2) Labouring Classes, (3) Anglo-Indians, (4) Indian Christians and (5) the Cotton Trade. Of the elected members (1) some are elected by class-electorates created to represent the interests of the landholders, commerce and industry, (2) some by reserved electorates for Maratha and allied castes and the rest, (3) by communal electorates which are instituted for the Muhammadans and the Europeans. The question is whether this electoral structure should be preserved without alteration. Before any conclusion can be arrived at, it is necessary to evaluate it, in the light of considerations both theoretical as well as practical.

NOMINATED MEMBERS

Against the nominated Members it is urged that their presence in the Council detracts a great deal from its representative character. Just as the essence of responsible self-government is the responsibility of the Executive to the Legislature, so the essence of representative government lies in the responsibility of the legislature to the people. Such a responsibility can be secured only when the legislature is elected by the people. Not only does the system of nominated Members make the House unrepresentative, it also tends to make the Executive irresponsible. For by virtue of the power of nominations, the Executive on whose advice that power is exercised, appoints nearly 25 per cent of the legislature with the result that such a large part of the House is in the position of the servants of the Executive rather than its critics. That the nominated non-officials are not the servants of the government cannot go to subtract anything from this view. For the nominated non-official can always be bought and the Executive has various ways open to it for influencing an elected member with a view to buy up his independence. A direct conferment of titles and honours upon a member, or bestowal of patronage on his friends and relatives, are a few of such methods. But the nominated non-official Members are already in such an abject state of dependence that the Executive has not to buy their independence. They never have any independence to sell. They are the creatures of the Executive and they are given seats on the understanding, if not on the condition, that they shall behave as friends of the Executive. Nor is the Executive helpless against a nominated member who has the audacity to break the understanding. For, by the power of renomination which the Executive possesses, it can inflict the severest penalty by refusing to renominate him and there are instances where it has inflicted that punishment. Like the King's veto, the knowledge that this power to renominate exists, keeps every nominated member at the beck and call of the Executive.

Another evil arising from the system of nomination must also be pointed out. The nominated non-official Members were to represent the interests of certain communities for whose representation the electoral system as devised, was deemed to be inadequate just as the nominated official Members were appointed to support the interests of the government. The regrettable thing is that while the nominated officials served the interests of the government, the nominated non-officials failed to serve the interests of their constituents altogether. Indeed a nominated non-official cannot serve his community. For more often than not the interests of the communities can only be served by influencing governmental action, and this is only possible when the Executive is kept under fire and is made to realize the effects of an adverse vote. But this means is denied to a nominated member by the very nature of his being, with the result that the Executive, being assured of his support, is indifferent to his cause and the nominated member, being denied his independence, is helpless to effect any change in the situation of those whom he is nominated to represent. Representation by nomination is thus no representation. It is only mockery.

Another serious handicap of the system of nomination is that the nominated non-officials are declared to be ineligible for ministership. In theory there ought not to be limitations against the right of a member of the legislature to be chosen as a minister of an administration. Even assuming that such a right is to be limited, the purpose of such limitation must be the interests of good and efficient administration. Not only that is not the purpose of this limitation but that the limitation presses unequally upon different communities owing to the difference in the manner of their representation and affects certain communities which ought to be free from its handicap. Few communities are so greatly in need of direct governmental action as the Depressed Classes for effecting their betterment. It is true that no degree of governmental action can alter the face of the situation completely or quickly. But making all allowance for this, no one can deny the great benefits that wise legislation can spread among the people. All these classes do in fact begin and often complete their lives under a weight of inherited vices and social difficulties, for the existence of which society is responsible, and of the mitigation of which much can be done by legislation. The effect of legislation to alter the conditions under which the lives of individuals are spent has been recognized everywhere in the world. But this duty to social progress will not be recognized unless those like the Depressed Classes find a place in the Cabinet of the country. The system of nomination must therefore be condemned. Its only effect has been to produce a set of people who eventually subordinate the care of the constituents to the desire for place.

ELECTED MEMBERS

CLASS ELECTORATES

These class electorates are a heritage of the Morley–Minto Reforms.[163] The Morley–Minto Scheme was an attempt at make-believe. For under it the bureaucracy without giving up its idea to rule was contriving to create legislatures by arranging the franchise and the electorates in such a manner as to give the scheme the appearance of popular rule without the reality of it. To such a scheme of things, these class electorates were eminently suited. But the Montagu–Chelmsford Scheme[164] was not a make-believe. It contemplated the rule of the people. Consequently it was expected to suggest the abolition of such class electorates. Owing, however, to the powerful influence, which these classes always exercised, the authors of the Report were persuaded to recommend their continuance, which recommendation was given effect to by the Southborough Committee. Whatever the reason that led to the retention of these class electorates, there is no doubt that their existence cannot be reconciled with the underlying spirit of popular government. Their class character is a sufficient ground for their condemnation. In a deliberative assembly like the legislature, where questions of public interest are decided in accordance with public opinion, it is essential that members of the Council who take part in the decision should each represent that opinion. Indeed no other person can be deemed to be qualified to give a decisive vote on the issues debated on the floor of the House. But the representatives of class interests merely reflect the opinions one might say, the prejudices of their class, and should certainly be deemed to be disqualified from taking part in the decision of issues which lie beyond the ambit of the interests of their class. Notwithstanding their class character as Members of the legislature they acquire the competence to vote upon all the issues whether they concern their own class or extend beyond. This, in my opinion, is quite subversive of the principle of popular government. It might be argued that representatives of such class interests are necessary to give expert advice on those sectional issues with which the unsectional house is not familiar. As against this, it is necessary to remember that in a democracy, the ultimate principle is after all self-government and that means that the final decision on all matters must be made by popularly elected persons and not by experts. It is moreover not worthy that the advice of such people is not always serviceable to the house. For their advice invariably tends to become eloquent expositions of class ideology rather than a careful exposition of the formulae in dispute.

Assuming, however, that it is necessary either to safeguard the interests of these classes or to tender advice to the House on their behalf, it is yet to be proved that these interests will not secure sufficient representation through general electorates. Facts, such as we have, show that they can. Taking the case of the Inamdars,[165] though they have been given three seats through special electorates of their own, they have been able to secure 12 seats through the general electorates. Indeed by virtue of the solidarity which they have with other landholding members of the Council, they felt themselves so strong in numbers that only a few months back they demanded a ministerial post for the leader of their class. Besides, it is not true that without class-electorates there will be no representation of the interests of these classes in the Council. Such interests will be amply safeguarded by a Member belonging to that class, even if he is elected by a general constituency. This will be clear if we bear in mind that a Member taking his seat in the legislature, although he represents directly his constituency, yet indirectly he does represent himself and to that extent also his class. Indeed, from the very nature of things this tendency on the part of a Member, indirectly to represent himself, although it might be checked, controlled and over-ruled, so surely manifests itself that it throws, and must necessarily throw, direct representation into the background. No one for instance can believe that a European gentleman representing a Chamber of Commerce will only represent the interests of commerce and will not represent the interests of the European community because he is elected by a Chamber of Commerce and not by the general European community. It is in the nature of things that a man's self should be nearer to him than his constituency. There is a homely saying that a man's skin sits closer to him than his shirt and without imputation on their good faith so it is with the Members of the legislature. It is the realization of this fact which had led the English people who at one time wished that the shipping trade, the woollen trade and the linen trade should each have its spokesman in the House of Commons, to abandon the idea of such class-electorates. It is difficult to understand why a system abandoned elsewhere should be continued in India. It is not necessary in the interests of these classes and it is harmful to the body politic. The only question is whether or not persons belonging to the commercial and individual classes can secure election through the general constituencies. I know of nothing that can be said to handicap these classes in the race of election. That there is no handicap against them is proved by the success of Sardars[166] and Inamdars in general election. Where Inamdars and Sardars have succeeded there is no reason why representatives of commerce and industry should not.

RESERVED ELECTORATES

Three objections can be raised against the system of reserved electorates. One is that it seeks to guarantee an electoral advantage to a majority. It is true that the Marathas and the allied castes form a majority in the Marathi speaking part of the Presidency both in population as well as in voting strength and as such deserve no political protection. But it must be realized that there is all the difference in the world between a power informed and conscious of its strength and power so latent and suppressed that its holders are hardly aware of that they may exercise it. That the Marathas and the allied castes are not conscious of their power, is sufficiently evident if we compare the voting strength of the Marathas and the allied castes in those constituencies wherein, seats are reserved for them, with the rank of their representatives among the different candidates contesting the elections. In every one of such constituencies the Maratha voters, it must be remembered, have a preponderance over the voters of other communities. Yet in the elections of 1923 and 1926, out of the seven seats allotted to them, they could not have been returned in three had it not been for the fact that the seats were reserved for them. It is indeed strange that the candidates of a community which is at the top in the electoral roll, should find themselves at the bottom, almost in a sinking position. This strange fact is only an indication that this large community is quite unconscious of the power it possesses, and is subject to some influence acting upon it from without.

The second ground of objection, urged by the Members of the higher classes who are particularly affected by the system of reserved seats, is that it does an injustice to them in that it does not permit them the benefit of a victory in a straight electoral fight. It is true that the system places a restriction upon the right of the higher classes to represent the lower classes. But is there any reason why 'the right to represent,' as distinguished from 'a right to representation,' should be an unrestricted right? Modern politicians have spent all their ingenuity in trying to find out the reason for restricting the right to vote. In my opinion there is a greater necessity why we should strive to restrict the right of a candidate to represent others. Indeed, there is no reason why the implications of the representative function should not define the condition of assuming it. It would be no invasion of the right to be elected to the Legislature to make it depend, for example, upon a number of years' service on a local authority and to rule out all those who do not fulfil that condition. It would be perfectly legitimate to hold that service in a legislative assembly is so important in its results, that proof of aptitude and experience must be offered before the claim to represent can be admitted. The argument for restricting the rights of the higher classes to represent the lower classes follows the same line. Only it makes a certain social attitude as a condition precedent to the recognition of the right to represent. Nor can it be said that such a requirement is unnecessary. For aptitude and experience are not more important than the social attitude of a candidate towards the mass of men whom he wishes to represent. Indeed, mere aptitude and experience will be the cause of ruination if they are not accompanied and regulated by the right sort of social attitude. There is no doubt that the social attitude of the higher classes towards the lower classes is not of the right sort. It is no doubt always said to the credit of these communities that they are intellectually the most powerful communities in India. But it can with equal truth be said that they have never utilized their intellectual powers to the services of the lower classes. On the other hand, they have always despised, disregarded and disowned the masses in belonging to a different strata, if not to a different race than themselves. No class has a right to rule another class, much less a class like the higher classes in India. By their code of conduct, they have behaved as the most exclusive class steeped in its own prejudices and never sharing the aspirations of the masses, with whom they have nothing to do and whose interests are opposed to theirs. It is not, therefore, unjust to demand that a candidate who is standing to represent others shall be such as shares the aims, purposes and motives of those whom he desires to represent.

The third objection to the system of reserved electorates is that it leads to inefficiency inasmuch as a candidate below the line gets the seat in supersession of a candidate above the line. This criticism is also true. But here, again, there are other considerations which must be taken into account. First of all, as Professor Dicey rightly argues:

It has never been a primary object of constitutional arrangement to get together the best possible Parliament in intellectual capacity. Indeed, it would be inconsistent with the idea of representative government to attempt to form a Parliament far superior in intelligence to the mass of the nation.

Assuming, however, that the displacement of the intellectual classes by the candidates belonging to the non-intellectual classes is a loss, that loss will be more than amply recompensed by the natural idealism of the backward communities. There is no doubt that the representatives of the higher orders are occupied with the pettiest cares and are more frequently concerned with the affairs of their own class than with the affairs of the nation. Their life is too busy or too prosperous and the individual too much self-contained and self-satisfied for the conception of the social progress to be more than a passing thought of a rare moment. But the lower orders are constantly reminded of their adversity, which can be got over only by a social change. The consciousness of mutual dependence resulting from the necessities of a combined action makes for generosity, while the sense of untrained powers and of undeveloped faculties gives them aspirations. It is to the lower classes that we must look for the motive power for progress. The reservation of seats to the backward Hindu communities makes available for the national service such powerful social forces, in the absence of which any Parliamentary government may be deemed to be poorer.

COMMUNAL ELECTORATES

That some assured representation is necessary and inevitable to the communities in whose interests communal electorates have been instituted must be beyond dispute. At any rate, for some time to come the only point that can be open to question is, must such communal representation be through communal electorates? Communal electorates have been held by their opponents to be responsible for the communal disturbances that have of late taken place in the different parts of the country. One cannot readily see what direct connection there can be between communal electorates and communal disturbances. On the contrary it has been argued that by satisfying the demand of the Mohamedans, communal electorates have removed one cause of discontent and ill-feeling. But it is equally true that communal electorates do not help to mitigate communal disturbances and may in fact help to aggrevate them. For communal electorates do tend to the intensification of communal feeling and that they do make the leaders of the two communities feel no responsibility towards each other, with the result that instead of leading their people to peace, they are obliged to follow the momentary passions of the crowd.

The Mohamedans who have been insisting upon the retention of the communal electorates take their stand on three grounds. In the first place they say that the interests of the Mohamedan community are separate from those of the other communities, and that to protect these interests they must have separate electorates. Apart from the question whether separate electorates are necessary to protect separate interests, it is necessary to be certain that there are any interests which can be said to be separate in the sense that they are not the interests of any other community. In the secular, as distinguished from the religious field, every matter is a matter of general concern to all. Whether taxes should be paid or not, if so, what and at what rate; whether national expenditure should be directed in any particular channel more than any other; whether education should be free and compulsory; whether government lands should be disposed of on restricted tenure or occupancy tenure; whether State aid should be granted to industries; whether there should be more police in any particular area; whether the State should provide against poverty of the working classes by a scheme of social insurance against sickness, unemployment or death; whether the administration of justice is best served by the employment of honorary magistrates, and whether the code of medical ethics or legal ethics should be altered so as to produce better results are some of the questions that usually come before the Council. Of this list of questions, is there any which can be pointed out as being the concern of the Mohamedan community only? It is true that the Mohamedan community is particularly interested in the question of education and public service. But there again it must be pointed out that the Mohamedan community is not the only community which attaches particular importance to these questions. That the non–Brahmin and the depressed classes are equally deeply interested in this question becomes evident from the united effort that was put forth by all three in connection with the University Reform Bill[167] in the Bombay Legislative Council. The existence of separate interests of the Mohamedan community is therefore a myth. What exists is not separate interests but special concern in certain matters.

Assuming, however, that separate interests do exist, the question is, are they better promoted by separate electorates than by general electorates and reserved seats? My emphatic answer is that the separate or special interests of any minority are better promoted by the system of general electorates and reserved seats than by separate electorates. It will be granted that injury to any interest is, in the main, caused by the existence of irresponsible extremists. The aim should therefore be to rule out such persons from the councils of the country. If irresponsible persons from both the communities are to be ruled out from the councils of the country, the best system is the one under which the Mohamedan candidates could be elected by the suffrage of the Hindus and the Hindu candidates elected by the suffrage of the Mohamedans. The system of joint electorates is to be preferred to that of communal electorates, because it is better calculated to bring about that result than is the system of separate electorates. At any rate, this must be said with certainty that a minority gets a larger advantage under joint electorates than it does under a system of separate electorates. With separate electorates the minority gets its own quota of representation and no more. The rest of the House owes no allegiance to it and is therefore not influenced by the desire to meet the wishes of the minority. The minority is thus thrown on its own resources and as no system of representation can convert a minority into a majority, it is bound to be overwhelmed. On the other hand, under a system of joint electorates and reserved seats the minority not only gets its quota of representation but something more. For, every Member of the majority who has partly succeeded on the strength of the votes of the minority if not a Member of the minority, will certainly be a Member for the minority. This, in my opinion, is a very great advantage which makes the system of mixed electorates superior to that of the separate electorates as a means of protection to the minority. The Mohamedan minority seems to think that the Council is, like the Cardinals' conclave, convened for the election of the Pope, an ecclesiastical body called for the determination of religious issues. If that was true then their insistence on having few men but strong men would have been a wise course of conduct. But it is time the community realized that Council far from being a religious conclave is a secular organization intended for the determination of secular issues. In such determination of the issues, the finding is always in favour of the many.

If this is so, does not the interest of the minority itself justify a system which compels others besides its own members to support its cause?

The second ground on which the claim to separate electorates is made to rest is that the Mohamedans are a community by themselves; that they are different from other communities not merely in religion but that their history, their traditions, their culture, their personal laws their social customs and usages have given them such a widely different outlook on life quite uninfluenced by any common social ties, sympathies or amenities; that they are in fact a distinct people and that they do so regard themselves even though they have lived in this country for centuries. On this assumption it is argued that if they are compelled to share a common electorate with other communities, the political blending consequent upon it will impair the individuality of their community. How far this assumption presents a true picture, I do not step to consider. Suffice it to say, that in my opinion it is not one which can be said to be true to life. But conceding that it is true and conceding further that the preservation of the individuality of the Mohamedan community is an ideal which is acceptable to that community one does not quite see why communal electorates should be deemed to be necessary for the purpose. India is not the only country in which diverse races are sought to be brought under a common government. Canada and South Africa are two countries within the British Empire where two diverse races are working out a common system of government. Like the Hindus and the Mohamedans in India, the British and the Dutch in South Africa and the British and the French in Canada are two distinct communities with their own distinctive cultures. But none has ever been known to object to common electorates on the ground that such a common cycle of participation for the two communities for electoral purposes is injurious to the preservation of their individualities. Examples of diverse communities sharing common electorates outside the Empire are by no means few. In Poland there are Poles, Ruthenians, Jews, White Russians, Germans and Lithuanians. In Latvia, there are Latvians, Russians, Jews, Germans, Poles, Lithuanians and Esthonians. In Esthonia, there are Germans, Jews, Swedes, Russians, Latvians and Tartars. In Czechoslovakia, there are Czechs, Slovaks, Germans, Magyars, Ruthenians, Jews and Poles. In Austria, there are Germans, Czechs and Slovenes; while in Hungary there are Hungarians. Germans, Slovaks, Roumanians, Ruthenians, Croatians, and Serbians. All these groups are not mere communities. They are nationalities each with a live and surging individuality of their own, living in proximity of each other and under a common government. Yet none of them have objected to common electorates on the ground that a participation in them would destroy their individuality.

But it is not necessary to cite cases of non-Moslem communities to show the futility of the argument. Cases abound in which Mohamedan minorities in other parts of the world have never felt the necessity of communal electorates for the preservation of their individuality against what might be termed the infectious contagion of political contact with other communities. It does not seem to be sufficiently known that India is not the only country where Mohamedans are in a minority. There are other countries, in which they occupy the same position. In Albania, the Mohamedans form a very large community. In Bulgaria, Greece and Roumania they form a minority and in Yugoslavia and Russia they form a very large minority. Have the Mohamedan communities there insisted upon the necessity of separate communal electorates? As all students of political history are aware the Mohamedans in these countries have managed without the benefit of separate electorates; nay, they have managed without any definite ratio of representation assured to them. In India, at any rate, there is a consensus of opinion, that as India has not reached a stage of complete secularization of politics, adequate representation should be guaranteed to the Mohamedan community, lest it should suffer from being completely eclipsed from the political field by the religious antipathy of the majority. The Mohamedan minorities, in other parts of the world are managing their affairs even without the benefit of this assured quota. The Mohamedan case in India, therefore, overshoots the mark and in my opinion, fails to carry conviction.

The third ground on which it is sought to justify the retention of separate communal electorates of the Mohamedans, is that the voting strength of the Mohamedans in a mixed electorate may be diluted by the non-Mohamedan vote to such an extent that the Mohamedan returned by such a mixed electorate, it is alleged, will be a weak and instead of being a true representative of the Mohamedans will be a puppet in the hands of the non-Mohamedan communities. This fear has no doubt the look of being genuine, but a little reasoning will show that it is groundless. If the mass of the non–Muslim voters were engaged in electing a Mohamedan candidate, the result anticipated by the Mohamedans may perhaps come true if the non–Muslims are bent on mischief. But the fact is that at the time of general election there will be many non–Mohamedan candidates standing for election. That being the case, the full force of all the non–Muslim voters will not be directed on the Mohamedan candidates. Nor will the non–Mohamedan candidates allow the non–Mohamedan voters to waste their votes by concentrating themselves on the Mohamedan candidates. On the contrary, they will engage many voters, if not all, for themselves. If this analysis is true, then it follows that very few non–Mohamedan voters will be left to participate in the election of the Mohamedan candidates, and that the fear of the Mohamedans of any mass action against Muslim candidates by non–Muslim voters is nothing but a hallucination. That the Mohamedans themselves do not believe in it is evident from what are known as the 'Delhi' proposals.[168] According to these proposals, which have been referred to in an earlier part of this report, the Mohamedans have shown their willingness to give up communal electorates, in favour of joint electorates, provided the demand for communal Provinces and certain other concessions regarding the representation of the Muslims in the Punjab and Bengal are given to them. Now, assuming that these communal Provinces have no purpose outside their own, and it is an assumption which we must make, it is obvious that the Mohamedan minority in any province must be content with such protection as it can derive from joint electorates. It is therefore a question as to why joint electorates should not suffice without the addition of communal Provinces when they are said to suffice with the addition of communal Provinces. But this consideration apart, if there is any substance in the Muslim view that the watering of votes is an evil which attaches itself to the system of joint electorates, then the remedy in my opinion does not lie in the retention of communal electorates. The remedy lies in augmenting the numbers of the Mohamedan electors to the fullest capacity possible by the introduction of adult suffrage, so that the Mohamedan community may get sufficiently large voting strength to neutralize the effects of a possible dilution by an admixture of the non–Muslim votes.

All this goes to show that the case for communal electorates cannot be sustained on any ground which can be said to be reasonable. What is in its favour is feeling and sentiment only. I do not say that feeling and sentiment have no place in the solution of political problems. I realize fully that loyalty to the government is a matter of faith and faith is a matter of sentiment. This faith should be secured if it can be done without detriment to the body politic. But communal representation is so fundamentally wrong that to give in to sentiment in its case would be to perpetuate an evil. The fundamental wrong of the system, has been missed even by its opponents. But its existence will become apparent to any one who will look to its operation. It is clear that the representatives of the Muslims give law to the non–Muslims. They dispose of revenue collected from the non–Muslims. They determine the education of the non–Muslims, they determine what taxes and how much the non–Muslims shall pay. These are some of the most vital things which Muslims as legislators do, whereby affect the welfare of the non–Muslims. A question may be asked by what right can they do this? The answer, be it noted, is not by right of being elected as representatives of the non–Muslims. The answer is by a right of being elected as the representatives of the Muslims! Now, it is an universally recognized canon of political life that the government must be by the consent of the governed. From what I have said above communal electorates are a violation of that canon. For, it is government without consent. It is contrary to all sense of political justice to approve of a system which permits the members of one community to rule other communities without their having submitted themselves to the suffrage of those communities. And if as the Mohamedans allege that they are a distinct community with an outlook on life widely different from that of the other communities, the danger inherent in the system becomes too terrible to be passed over with indifference.

Such are the defects in the existing structure of the Council. It was framed by the Southborough Committee in 1919. The nature of the framework prepared by that Committee was clearly brought forth by the Government of India in their Despatch No. 4 of 1919 dated 23rd April 1919, addressed to the Secretary of State in which they observed:

Before we deal in detail with the report (of the Southborough Committee) one preliminary question of some importance suggests itself. As you will see, the work of the Committee has not to any great extent been directed towards the establishment of principles. In dealing with the various problems that came before them they have usually sought to arrive at agreement rather than to base their solution upon general reasonings.

My colleagues have not cared to consider the intrinsic value of the framework as it now stands. They have no doubt recommended that the system of nominations should be done away with and in that I agree with them. But excepting that they have kept the whole of the electoral structure intact, as though it was free from any objection. In this connection I differ from them. As I have pointed out, the whole structure is faulty and must be overhauled. I desire to point out that the object of the Reforms as embodied in the pronouncement of August 1917,[169] declares the goal to be the establishment of self-governing institutions. The electoral structure then brought into being was only a half-way house towards it and was justified only because it was agreed that a period of transition from the rule of the bureaucracy to the rule of the people, was a necessity. This existing electoral structure can be continued only on the supposition that the present system of divided government is to go on. The existing system of representation would be quite incompatible with a full government and must therefore be over-ruled.

There is also another reason why the present system of representation should be overhauled. Representative government is everywhere a party government. Indeed a party government is such a universal adjunct of representative government that it might well be said that representative government cannot function except through a party government. The best form of party government is that which obtains under a two-party-system both of ensuring stable as well as responsible government. An executive may be made as responsible as it can be made by law to the legislature. But the responsibility will only be nominal if the legislature is so constituted that it could not effectively impose its will on the executive. A stable government requires absence of uncertainty. An executive must be able to plan its way continuously to an ordered scheme of policy. But that invokes an unwavering support of a majority. This can be obtained only out of a two-party-system. It can never be obtained out of a group system. Under the group system the executive will represent not a general body of opinion, but a patch-work of doctrines held by the leaders of different groups who have agreed to compromise their integrity for the sake of power. Such a system can never assure the continuous support necessary for a stable government since the temptation to reshuffling the groups for private advantage is ever present. The existing Council by reason of the system of representation is, to use the language of Burke, 'a piece of joinery so crossly indented and whimsically dovetailed, a piece of diversified mosaic, a tessellated pavement without cement, patriots and courtiers, friends of government and open enemies. This curious show of a Legislature utterly unsafe to touch and unsure to stand on'[170] can hardly yield to a two-party-system of government, and without a party system there will neither be stable government nor responsible government. The origin of the group system must be sought in the formation of the electorates. For, after all, the electorates are the moulds in which the Council is cast. If the Council is to be remodelled so that it may act with efficiency, then it is obvious that the mould must be recast.

In making my suggestions for the recasting of the electoral system I have allowed myself to be guided by three considerations: (1) Not to be led away by the fatal simplicity of many a politician in India that the electoral system should be purely territorial and should have no relation with the social conditions of the country, (2) Not to recognize any interest, social or economic, for special representation which is able to secure representation through territorial electorates, (3) When any interest is recognized as deserving of special representation, its manner of representation shall be such as will not permit the representatives of such interest the freedom to form a separate group.

Of these three considerations, the second obviously depends upon the pitch of the franchise. In another part of this Report I have recommended the introduction of adult suffrage. I am confident that it will be accepted. I make my recommendations therefore on that basis. But in case it is not, and if the restricted franchise continues, it will call for different recommendations, which I also proposed to make. For the reasons given above and following the last mentioned consideration I suggest that—

I. If adult suffrage is granted there shall be territorial representation except in the case of the Mohamedans, the Depressed Classes, and the Anglo–Indians.

II. If the franchise continues to be restricted, all representation shall be territorial except in the case of the Mohamedans, the Depressed Classes, Anglo-Indians, the Marathas and the allied castes and labour.

III. That such special representation shall be by general electorates and reserved seats and of labour by electorate made up of registered trade unions.

From these suggestions it will be seen that I am for the abolition of all class electorates, such as those for (1) Inamdars and Sardars, (2) Trade and Commerce, whether Indian or European, (3) Indian Christians, and (4) Industry; and merge them in the general electorates. There is nothing to prevent them from having their voice heard in the Councils by the ordinary channel. Secondly, although I am for securing the special representation of certain classes, I am against their representation though separate electorates. Territorial electorates and separate electorates are the two extremes which must be avoided in any scheme of representation that may be devised for the introduction of a democratic form of government in this most undemocratic country. The golden mean is the system of joint electorates with reserved seats. Less than that would be insufficient, more than that would defeat the ends of good government. For obvious reasons I make an exception in the case of the European community. They may be allowed to have their special electorates. But they shall be general electorates and not class electorates.

6

Representation
of Minorities

Equal treatment of all the minorities in the matter of representation is only a part of the problem of the representation of minorities. To determine a satisfactory quantitative measure for the distribution of seats is another and a more important part of the problem. But this is a most controversial question. Of the two opposing theories one is that the representation of a minority should be in a strict proportion to its population. The other theory which is strongly held by the minorities is that such representation must be adequate. I do not think that the arithmetical theory of representation can be agreed to. If the Legislative Council was a zoo or a museum wherein a certain number of each species was to be kept, such a theory of minority representation would have been tolerable. But it must be recognized that the Legislative Council is not a zoo or a museum. It is a battle ground for the acquisition of rights, the destruction of privileges and the prevention of injustice. Viewed in this light a minority may find that its representation is in full measure of its population yet it is so small that in every attempt it makes to safeguard or improve its position against the onslaught of an hostile majority it is badly beaten. Unless the representation of minorities is intended to provide political fun the theory of representation according to population must be discarded and some increase of representation beyond their population ratio must be conceded to them by way of weightage.

To recognize the necessity of weightage is no doubt important. But what is even of greater importance is to recognize that this weightage must be measured out to the minorities on some principle that is both intelligent and reasonable. For it must be recognized that the minorities under the pretext of seeking adequate protection are prone to make demands which must be characterized as preposterous. To avoid this we must define what we mean by adequacy of representation. No doubt adequacy is not capable of exact definition, but its indefiniteness will be considerably narrowed if we keep before our mind certain broad considerations. First of all, a distinction must be made in the matter of minority representation between adequacy on the one hand and supremacy on the other. By supremacy, I mean such a magnitude of representation as would make the minority a dictator. By adequacy of representation I mean such a magnitude of representation as would make it worth the while of any party from the majority to seek an alliance with the minority. Where a party is compelled to seek an alliance with a minority, the minority is undoubtedly in the position of a dictator. On the other hand where a party is only drawn to seek an alliance with the minority, the minority is only adequately represented. The first thing, therefore, that should be kept in mind in the matter of the allotment of seats to minorities is to avoid both the extremes—inadequacy as well as supremacy. These extremes can in my opinion be avoided if we adopt the rule that minority representation shall, in the main, be so regulated that the number of seats to which a minority is entitled will be a figure which will be the ratio of its population to the total seats multiplied by some factor which is greater than one and less than two.

This principle, it is true, merely defines the limits within which the representation of a minority must be fixed. It still leaves unsettled and vague with what this multiplier should vary. My suggestion is that it should vary with the needs of the particular minority concerned. By this method we arrive at a principle for measuring out the weightage to the minorities which is both intelligible and reasonable. For, the needs of a minority are capable of more or less exact ascertainment. There will be general agreement that the needs of a minority for political protection are commensurate with the power it has to protect itself in the social struggle. That power obviously depends upon the educational and economic status of the minorities. The higher the educational and economic status of a minority the lesser is the need for that minority of being politically protected. On the other hand the lower the educational and economic status of a minority, the greater will be the need for its political protection.

7

Untouchability

I have agreed to confine the term depressed classes to untouchables only. In fact, I have myself sought to exclude from the untouchables all those in whom there cannot be the same consciousness of kind as is shared by those who suffer from the social discrimination that is inherent in the system of untouchability[171] and who are therefore likely to exploit the untouchables for their own purposes. I have also raised no objection to the utilization of tests 7 and 8 referred to in the Committee's report for the ascertainment of the untouchable classes. But as I find that different persons seek to apply them in different ways, or put different constructions on them I feel it necessary to explain my point of view in regard to this matter.

In the first place it is urged in some quarters that whatever tests are applied for ascertaining the untouchable classes they must be applied uniformly all over India. In this connection, I desire to point out that in a matter of this sort it would hardly be appropriate to apply the same test or tests all over India. India is not a single homogeneous country. It is a continent. The various Provinces are marked by extreme diversity of conditions and there is no tie of race or language. Owing to absence of communication each Province has evolved along its own lines with its own peculiar manners and modes of social life. In such circumstances, the degree of uniformity with which most of the tests of untouchability are found to apply all over India is indeed remarkable. For instance, bar against temple entry exists everywhere in India. Even the tests of well-water and pollution by touch apply in every Province, although not with the same rigidity everywhere. But to insist on absolute uniformity in a system like that of untouchability which after all is a matter of social behaviour and which must therefore vary with the circumstances of each Province and also of each individual is simply to trifle with the problem. The Statutory Commission[172] was quite alive to this possible line of argument and after careful consideration rejected it by recognizing the principle of diversity in the application of tests of untouchability. On page 67 of Vol. II which contains its recommendations it observed,

It will plainly be necessary, after the main principles of the new system of representation have been settled, to entrust to some specially appointed body (like the former Franchise Committee) the task of drawing up fresh electoral rules to carry these principles into effect, and one of the tasks of such a body will be to frame for each province a definition of 'depressed classes' (which may well vary, sometimes even between parts of the same province), and to determine their numbers as so defined.

Another point which I wish to emphasize is the futility of insisting upon the application of uniform tests of untouchability all over India. It is a fundamental mistake to suppose that differences in tests of untouchability indicate differences in the conditions of the untouchables. On a correct analysis of the mental attitude they indicate, it will be found that whether the test is causing pollution by touch or refusal to use common well, the notion underlying both is one and the same. Both are outward registers of the same inward feeling of defilement, odium, aversion and contempt. Why will not a Hindu touch an untouchable? Why will not a Hindu allow an untouchable to enter the temple or use the village well? Why will not a Hindu admit an untouchable in the inn? The answer to each one of these questions is the same. It is that the untouchable is an unclean person not fit for social intercourse. Again, why will not a Brahmin priest officiate at religious ceremonies performed by a untouchable? Why will not a barber serve an untouchable? In these cases also the answer is the same. It is that it is below dignity to do so. If our aim is to demarcate the class of people who suffer from social odium then it matters very little which test we apply. For as I have pointed out each of these tests is indicative of the same social attitude on the part of the touchables towards the untouchables.

In the second place the view is put forth that in applying the test of 'causing pollution by touch' for ascertaining the untouchable classes effect must be given to it in its literal sense—and not in its notional sense. In the literal sense untouchables are only those persons whose touch not only causes pollution and is therefore avoided, or if not avoided is washed off by purification. In the notional sense an untouchable is a person who is deemed to belong to a class which is commonly held to cause pollution by touch, although contact with such a person may for local circumstances not be avoided or may not necessitate ceremonial purification. According to those who seek to apply the test in its literal sense the conclusion would be the so-called untouchables should cease to be reckoned as untouchables wherever conditions have so changed that people do not avoid the touch of an untouchable, or do not trouble to purify themselves of the pollution caused by their touch. I cannot accept this view which, in my opinion, is based on a misconception. An individual may not be treated as an untouchable in the literal sense of the term on account of various circumstances. None the less outside the scope of such compelling circumstances he does continue to be regarded as an impure person by reason of his belonging to the untouchable class. This distinction is well brought out by the Census Superintendent of Bihar and Orissa in his Census Report of 1921 from which the following is an extract. Speaking of the relaxation of caste rules he says:

Such incidents however which we have only noticed amongst the upper and more educated castes that are aspiring to the upper ranks, are to be regarded not as sign portending the collapse of the caste system, but of its adjustment to modern conditions. The same may be said with regard to modifications of the rules about personal contact or the touching of what is eaten or drunk.... In places like Jamshedpur where work is done under modern conditions men of all castes and races work side by side in the mill without any misgivings regarding the caste of their neighbours. But, because the facts of everyday life make it impossible to follow the same practical rules as were followed a hundred years ago, it is not to be supposed that the distinctions of pure and impure, touchable and untouchable are no longer observed. A high caste Hindu will not allow an 'untouchable' to sit on the same seat, to smoke the same hookah or to touch his person, his seat, his food or the water that he drinks.

If this is a correct statement of the facts of life then the difference between untouchability in its literal and notional sense is a distinction which makes no difference to the ultimate situation; for as the extract shows untouchability in its notional sense persists even where untouchability in its literal sense has ceased to obtain. This is why I insist that the test of untouchability must be applied in its notional sense.

In the third place the idea is broadcast that untouchability is rapidly vanishing. I wish to utter a word of caution against the acceptance of this view, and to point out the necessity of distinguishing facts from propaganda. In my opinion what is important to be borne in mind in drawing inference from instances showing the occasional comingling of Brahmins and non-Brahmins, touchables and untouchables is that the system of caste and the system of untouchability form really the steel frame of Hindu society. This division cannot easily be wiped out for the simple reason that it is not based upon rational, economic or racial grounds. On the other hand, the chances are that untouchability will endure far longer into the future than the optimist reformer is likely to admit on account of the fact that it is based on religious dogma. What makes it so difficult, to break the system of untouchability is the religious sanction which it has behind it. At any rate the ordinary Hindu looks upon it as part of his religion and there is no doubt that in adopting towards untouchables what is deemed to be an inhuman way of behaviour he does so more from the sense of observing his religion than from any motive of deliberate cruelty. Based on religion the ordinary Hindu only relaxes the rules of untouchability where he cannot observe them. He never abandons them. For abandonment of untouchability to him involves a total abandonment of the basic religious tenets of Hinduism as understood by him and the mass of Hindus. Based on religion, untouchability will persist as all religious notions have done. Indian history records the attempts of many a Mahatma to uproot untouchability from the Indian soil. They include such great men as Buddha, Ramanuja and the Vaishnava saints of modern times. It would be hazardous to assume that a system which has withstood all this onslaught will collapse. The Hindu looks upon the observance of untouchability as an act of religious merit, and non-observance of it as sin. My view therefore is that so long as this notion prevails untouchability will prevail.

8

Caste and Class

An old agnostic is said to have summed up his philosophy in the following words:

The only thing I know is that I know nothing; and I am not quite sure that I know that...'

Sir Denzil Ibbetston[173] undertaking to write about caste in Punjab said that the words of this agnostic about his philosophy expressed very exactly his own feelings regarding caste. It is no doubt true that owing to local circumstances there does appear a certain diversity about caste matters and that it is very difficult to make any statement regarding any one of the castes. Absolutely true as it may be, as regards one locality which will not be contradicted with equal truth as regards the same caste in some other area.

Although this may be true yet it cannot be difficult to separate the essential and fundamental features of caste from its non-essential and superficial features. An easy way to ascertain this is to ask what are the matters for which a person is liable to be excluded from caste. Mr. Bhattacharya[174] has stated the following as causes for expulsion from caste. (1) Embracing Christianity or Islam (2) Going to Europe or America (3) Marrying a widow (4) Publicly throwing the sacred thread (5) Publicly eating beef, pork or fowl (6) Publicly eating kachcha food prepared by a Mahomedan, Christian or low-caste Hindu (7) Officiating at the house of a very low-caste Shudra (8) By a female going away from home for immoral purposes (9) By a widow becoming pregnant.

This list is not exhaustive and omits the three most important causes which entail expulsion from caste. They are (10) Intermarrying outside caste (11) Interdining with persons of another caste and (12) Change of occupation. The second defect in the statement of Mr. Bhattacharya is that it does not make any distinction between essentials and non-essentials.

Of course, when a person is expelled from his caste the penalty is uniform. His friends, relatives and fellowmen refuse to partake of his hospitality. He is not invited to entertainments in their houses. He cannot obtain brides or bridegrooms for his children. Even his married daughters cannot visit him without running the risk of being excluded from his caste. His priest, his barber and washerman refuse to serve him. His fellow castemen severe their connection with him so completely that they refuse to assist him even at the funeral of a member of his household. In some cases the man excluded from caste is debarred access to public temples and to the cremation or burial ground.

These reasons for expulsion from caste indirectly show the rules and regulations of the caste. But all regulations are not fundamental. There are many which are unessential. Caste can exist even without them. The essential and unessential can be distinguished by asking another question. When can a Hindu who has lost caste regain his caste? The Hindus have a system of *prayaschitas* which are penances and which a man who has been expelled from caste must perform before he can be admitted to caste fellowship. With regard to these prayaschitas or penances certain points must be remembered. In this first place, there are caste offences for which there is no prayaschita. In the second place, the prayaschitas vary according to the offence. In some cases the prayaschitas involve a very small penalty. In other cases the penalty involved is a very severe one.

The existence of a prayaschita and the absence of it have a significance which must by clearly understood. The absence of prayaschita does not mean that anyone may commit the offence with impunity. On the contrary it means that the offence is of an immeasurable magnitude and the offender once expelled is beyond reclamation. There is no re-entry for him in the caste from which he is expelled. The existence of a prayaschita means that the offence is compoundable. The offender can take the prescribed prayaschita and obtain admission in the caste from which he is expelled.

There are two offences for which there is no penance. These are (1) change from the Hindu religion to another religion (2) Marriage with a person of another caste or another religion. It is obvious if a man loses caste for these offences he loses it permanently.

Of the other offences the prayaschitas prescribed are of the severest kind, are two—(1) interdining with a person of another caste or a non-Hindu and (2) Taking to an occupation which is not the occupation of the caste. In the case of the other offences the penalty is a light one, almost nominal.

The surest clue to find out what are the fundamental rules of caste and what caste consists in is furnished by the rules regarding prayaschitas. Those for the infringement of which there is no prayaschita constitute the very soul of caste and those for the infringement of which the prayaschita is of the severest kind make up the body of caste. It may therefore be said without any hesitation that there are four fundamental rules of caste. A caste may be defined as a social group having (a) belief in the Hindu religion and bound by certain regulations as to (b) marriage (c) food and (d) occupation. To this one more characteristic may be added, namely a social group having a common name by which it is recognized.

In the matter of marriage the regulation lays down that the caste must be endogamous. There can be no intermarriage between members of different castes. This is the first and the most fundamental idea on which the whole fabric of the caste is built up. In the matter of food the rule is that a person cannot take food from and dine with any person who does not belong to his caste. This means that only those who can intermarry can also interdine. Those who cannot intermarry cannot interdine. In other words, caste is an endogamous unit and also a communal unit. In the matter of occupation the regulation is that a person must follow the occupation which is the traditional occupation of his caste and if the caste has no occupation then he should follow the occupation of his father. In the matter of status of a person it is fixed and is hereditary. It is fixed because a person's status is determined by the status of the caste to which he belongs. It is hereditary because a Hindu is stamped with the caste to which his parents belonged, a Hindu cannot change his status because he cannot change his caste. A Hindu is born in a caste and he dies a member of the caste in which he is born. A Hindu may lose his status if he loses caste. But he cannot acquire a new or a better or different status.

What is the significance of a common name for a caste? The significance of this will be clear if we ask two questions which are very relevant and a correct answer to each is necessary for a complete idea of this institution of caste. Social groups are either organized or unorganized. When the membership of the group and the process of joining and leaving the groups, are the subject of definite social regulations and involve certain duties and privileges in relation to other members of the group, then the group is an organized group. A group is a voluntary group in which members enter with a full knowledge of what they are doing and the aims which the association is designed to fulfil. On the other hand, there are groups of which an individual person becomes a member without any act of volition, and becomes subject to social regulation and traditions over which he has no control of any kind.

Now it is hardly necessary to say that caste is a highly organized social grouping. It is not a loose or a floating body. Similarly, it is not necessary to say that caste is an involuntary grouping. A Hindu is born in a caste and he dies as a member of that caste. There is no Hindu without caste, cannot escape caste and being bounded by caste from birth to death he becomes subject to social regulations and traditions of the caste over which he has no control.

The significance of a separate name for a caste lies in this— namely, it makes caste an organized and an involuntary grouping. A separate and a distinctive name for a caste makes caste akin to a corporation with a perpetual existence and a seal of separate entity. The significance of separate names for separate castes has not been sufficiently realized by writers on caste. In doing that they have lost sight of a most distinctive feature of caste. Social groups there are and they are bound to be in every society. Many social groups in many countries can be equated to various castes in India and may be regarded as their equivalent. Potters, washermen, intellectuals as social groups are everywhere. But in other countries they have remained as unorganized and voluntary groups while in India they have become castes because in other countries the social groups were not given a name while in India they did. It is the name which the caste bears which gives it fixity and continuity and individuality. It is the name which defines who are its members and in most cases a person born in a caste carries the name of the caste as a part of his surname. Again it is the name which makes it easy for the caste to enforce its rules and regulations. It makes it easy in two ways. In the first place, the name of the caste forming a surname of the individual prevents the offender in passing off as a person belonging to another caste and thus escape the jurisdiction of the caste. Secondly, it helps to identify the offending individual and the caste to whose jurisdiction he is subject so that he is easily handed up and punished for any breach of the caste rules.

This is what caste means. Now as to the caste system. This involves the study of the mutual relations between different castes. Looked at as a collection of castes, the caste system presents several features which at once strike the observer. In the first place there is no interconnection between the various castes which form a system. Each caste is separate and distinct. It is independent and sovereign in the disposal of its internal affairs and the enforcement of caste regulations. The castes touch but they do not interpenetrate. The second feature relates to the order in which one caste stands in relation to the other castes in the system. That order is vertical and not horizontal.

Such is the caste and such is the caste system. The question is, is this enough to know the Hindu social organization? For a static conception of the Hindu social organization an idea of the caste and the caste system is enough. One need not trouble to remember more than the facts that the Hindus are divided into castes and that the castes form a system in which all hang on a thread which runs through the system in such a way that while encircling and separating one caste from another it holds them all as though it was a string of tennis balls hanging one above the other. But this will not be enough to understand caste as a dynamic phenomenon. To follow the workings of caste in action it is necessary to note one other feature of caste besides the caste system, namely the class-caste system.

The relationship between the ideas of caste and class has been a matter of lively controversy. Some say that caste is analogous to class and that there is no difference between the two. Others hold that the idea of castes is fundamentally opposed to that of class. This is an aspect of the subject of caste about which more will be said hereafter. For the present it is necessary to emphasize one feature of the caste system which has not been referred to hereinbefore. It is this. Although caste is different from and opposed to the notion of class yet the caste-system—as distinguished from caste—recognizes a class system which is somewhat different from the graded status referred to above. Just as the Hindus are divided into so many castes, castes are divided into different classes of castes. The Hindu is caste conscious. He is also class conscious. Whether he is caste conscious or class conscious depends upon the caste with which he comes in conflict. If the caste with which he comes in conflict is a caste within the class to which he belongs he is caste conscious. If the caste is outside the class to which he belongs he is class conscious. Anyone who needs any evidence on this point may study the Non-Brahmin Movement in the Madras and the Bombay Presidency. Such a study will leave no doubt that to a Hindu caste periphery is as real as class periphery and caste consciousness is as real as class consciousness.

Caste, it is said, is an evolution of the *Varna* system. I will show later on that this is nonsense. Caste is a perversion of *Varna*. At any rate it is an evolution in the opposite direction. But while caste has completely perverted the Varna system it has borrowed the class system from the Varna system. Indeed the class-caste system follows closely the class cleavages of the Varna system.

Looking at the caste system from this point of view one comes across several lines of class cleavage which run through this pyramid of castes dividing the pyramid into blocks of castes. The first line of cleavage follows the line of division noticeable in the ancient *Chaturvarna* system. The old system of Chaturvarna made a distinction between the first three *Varnas*, the *Brahmins, Kshatriyas, Vaishyas* and the fourth *Varna*, namely, the *Shudra*. The three former were classed as the regenerate classes. The *Shudra* was held as the unregenerate class. This distinction was based upon the fact that the former were entitled to wear the sacred thread and study the Vedas. The *Shudra* was entitled to neither and that is why he was regarded as the unregenerate class. The line of cleavage is still in existence and forms the basis of the present day class division separating the castes which have grown out of the vast class of *Shudras* from those which have grown out of the three classes of *Brahmins*, the *Kshatriyas* and *Vaishyas*. This line of class cleavage is the one which is expressed by the terms High Castes and Low Castes and which are short forms for the High Class Castes and Low Class Castes.

Next, after this line of cleavage, there runs through the pyramid a second line of class cleavage. It runs just below the Low Class

Castes. It sets above all the castes born out of the four *Varnas* i.e., the high castes as well as the low castes above the remaining castes which I will merely describe as the 'rest'. This line of class cleavage is again a real one and follows the well-defined distinction which was a fundamental principle of the Chaturvarna system. The Chaturvarna system as is pointed out made a distinction between the four Varnas putting the three Varnas above the fourth. But it also made an equally clear distinction between those within the Chaturvarna and those outside the Chaturvarna. It had a terminology to express this distinction. Those within the Chaturvarna— high or low, Brahmin or Shudra were called *Savarna* i.e. those with the stamp of the Varna. Those outside the Chaturvarna were called *Avarna* i.e., those without the stamp of Varna. All the castes which have evolved out of the four Varnas are called Savarna Hindus— which is rendered in English by the term Caste Hindus—the 'rest' are the *Avarnas* who in present parlance are spoken of by Europeans as Non-caste Hindus i.e., those who are outside the four original castes or Varnas.

Much that is written about the caste system has reference mostly to the caste system among the Savarna Hindus. Very little is known about the Avarna Hindus. Who are these Avarna Hindus, what is their position in Hindu Society, how are they related to the Savarna Hindus are questions to which no attention has so far been paid. I am sure that without considering these questions no one can get a true picture of the social structure the Hindus have built. To leave out the class cleavage between the Savarna Hindus and the Avarna Hindus is to relate a Grimm's Fairy Tale[175] which leaves out the witches, the goblins and the ogres.

III

Methodology

For Ambedkar, a study dealt with categories and concepts: their formulation, change, displacement and reformulation. The central thrust of any research agenda is the relationship across concepts or a body of concepts. There are different methods of study depend-ing on the nature of the concepts in question.

On Provincial Finance[176] is the introduction to *The Evolution of Provincial Finance in British India* published in 1925. This study is a revised version of Ambedkar's Ph.D. thesis at Columbia University, submitted in 1917. (The title is the editor's)

On Untouchables is the preface to the book *The Untouchables, Who were They and Why They became Untouchables?* published in 1948. It was a sequel to his book entitled *Who Were the Shudras? How They came to be the Fourth Varna in the Indo-Aryan Society.* However, the methods that he employed for these studies were very different. While the second study employed exegesis, the former set up its hypothesis based on studies engaged with similar phenomena under study and argued that since it succeeds in explaining all the known data, its plausibility could be accepted. (The title is the editor's)

9

On Provincial Finance

A student of Indian Finance has two chief sources of information and guidance open to him. One is the Annual Budget Statement, and the other is the annual volume of Finance and Revenue Accounts. Though separately issued, the two are really companion volumes inasmuch as the Financial Statement forms, so to speak, an exhaustive explanatory memorandum of the annual financial transactions, the details of which are recorded in the volume of Finance and Revenue Accounts.

Helpful as these sources are, they are not without their puzzles. A reference to the latest volume of Finance and Revenue Accounts will show that the accounts therein are classified under four different categories: (1) Imperial, (2) Provincial, (3) Incorporated Local, and (4) Excluded Local. But this is by no means uniformly so. For instance, a volume of the same series before 1870 will not be found to contain the accounts called 'Provincial,' nor will the accounts styled 'Local' be found in any volume prior to 1863. Similarly, any volume of the Financial Statements before 1870 will be found to divide the financial transactions covered therein into— Imperial and Local only. But a volume of the same series after 1908 curiously enough groups the accounts not under Imperial and Local but under (1) Imperial, and (2) Provincial, while the Financial Statements after 1921 cover only the Imperial Transactions. Nothing is more confusing to a beginner than the entrance of the new, and the exit of the old, categories of accounts.[a] The natural question

---

[a] It is surprising that the category of accounts, called 'Excluded Local,' which is to be found in the volume of Finance and Revenue Accounts, never

that he will ask is, how did these different categories evolve, and how are they related to one another?

In the present study, an endeavour is made to explain the rise and growth of one of them, namely, the 'Provincial'. But in order that there may be no difficulty in following the argument it is deemed advisable to preface this study with an outline defining its subject matter and indicating the interrelations of the parts into which it is divided. To facilitate a thorough understanding of the subject the study is divided into four parts, each one dealing with the Origin, Development and Organization of Provincial Finance and the final form in which it was cast by the constitutional changes of 1919. In Part I a somewhat thorny, untrodden and yet necessary ground has been covered in order to give a complete idea of the origin of Provincial Finance. While due homage is paid to the adage which requires students of the present to study the past, nothing more than the past of the present has been dealt with. In Chapter I, Part I, an attempt is made to present a picture of the system of Finance as it existed before the inauguration of the Provincial Finance and to state the causes that called for a change in its organization. In Chapter II a rival system of Finance proposed during the period of reconstruction is brought to light and shown why it failed of general acceptance. Chapter III is devoted to the discussion of a plan which was a compromise between the existing system and its rival, and the circumstances which forced its reception.

---

appears in the Financial Statement. The author has not been able to trace the reason for its exclusion. In the *Madras Manual* (Vol. I, Chapter V, pp. 467–9) it is argued that the ground for the exclusion is technical and consists in the circumstance that the Excluded Funds are not collected by the ordinary revenue collecting agency of the Central Government and are not subject to its interference. Another technical ground may also be found in a ruling given in the third edition of the Civil Account Code (p. 137), according to which Funds were called Excluded, i.e. from the Financial Statement, because they were not required to be lodged in the Government Treasury. But a ruling on the same point given in the seventh and latest edition (p. 122) of the same seems to imply that every public fund must of necessity be lodged in a Government Treasury. The more probable explanation is that given in the *Moral and Material Progress Report* for 1882–3 (Part I, p. 107), where it is said that these funds have no place in General Finance because they 'consist chiefly of special trusts and endowments.'

Having explained the Origin in Part I, the Development of Provincial Finance is made the subject of Part II. How far the arrangement followed in Part I is helpful must in the absence of anything to compare with it be left to the opinion of the reader. In regard to Part II, however, it is to be noted that the arrangement is different from what is adopted in the only fragmentary sketch published on the subject of Provincial Finance in 1887 by the late Justice Ranade. As will be seen from a perusal of Part II, one of the features of Provincial Finance was that the revenues and charges incorporated into the Provincial Budgets were revised every fifth year. Justice Ranade in his pamphlet, which simply covers the ground traversed in Part II of this study, and that too up to 1882 only, has taken this feature as a norm by which to mark off the different stages in the growth of Provincial Finance from one to another. Consequently, each quinquennial period to him becomes a stage, and in his hands the history of Provincial Finance falls into as many stages as the quinquenniums into which it can be divided. It may, however, be submitted that if every revision had changed the fundamentals of Provincial Finance, such an arrangement would not have been illogical. But as a matter of fact, Provincial Finance did not change its hue at every revision. What the revisions did was to temper the wind to the shorn lamb. If the history of the development of Provincial Finance is to be divided into stages according to the changes in the fundamental basis thereof, then emphasis has to be laid on features altogether different in character. Writers on the theory of Public Finance seem to conceive the subject as though it were primarily a matter of equity in taxation and economy in expenditure. But to a Chancellor of the Exchequer finance is eminently practical with a problem to solve, namely, how to bring about an equilibrium in the Budget. If we scan the history of Provincial Finance in British India with a view to discover the method of meeting the problem of equilibrium in Provincial Budgets and the changes introduced in it from time to time, we shall find that Provincial Finance has evolved through three distinct stages, each with its own mode of supply, namely, Assignments, Assigned Revenues and Shared Revenues. Consequently, instead of following the mechanical plan of Justice Ranade, it is believed to be more logical and instructive to divide the stages in the growth of Provincial Finance according to the method of supply to the Provincial Governments adopted by the

Government of India. Consequently, Part II, which deals with the Development of Provincial Finance, is divided into three Chapters: (1) Budget by Assignment, (2) Budget by Assigned Revenues, and (3) Budget by Shared Revenues.

This discussion of the Origin and Development of Provincial Finance is followed in Part III by an examination of its Organization. Chapter VII in Part III is devoted to the analysis of the hitherto neglected rules of limitations on the financial powers of Provincial Governments primarily to bring out the fact that Provincial Finance was not independent in its organization. The analysis of the true position of Provincial Finance is, however, reserved for Chapter VIII, in which the conclusion is fortified by a reference to the character of these limitations, that, notwithstanding the high-sounding appellation of Provincial Finance, there were neither provincial revenues nor provincial services as separate from Imperial revenues and Imperial services, so that instead of being federal in its organization the system remained essentially Imperial. Chapter IX discusses how far it was possible to enlarge the scope of Provincial Finance without jeopardy to the constitutional responsibilities of the Government of India under the old law.

Part IV is a discussion of the changes introduced into the mechanism of Provincial Finance by the Reforms Act of 1919. Chapter X of this Part is devoted to the analysis of the causes which led to these changes. In Chapter XI a full description of the changes effected by the new law is given, while Chapter XII forms a critique of the new regime.

In view of the fact that students of Indian Finance ordinarily content themselves with the phrase 'Decentralization of Finance', to indicate Provincial Finance, a word of explanation in justification of what may rather be called the too cumbersome title of this study. No student of Indian Finance, who is sufficiently acquainted with the branching off of the system in different directions, will fail to mark the inadequacy of the phrase Decentralization of Finance to mean Provincial Finance. If there were in the Indian system only the Provincial Decentralization there would have been no necessity to labour for a new title. As a matter of fact, the starting points of decentralization are by no means the same, and the systems evolved through it are quite different in character. For instance, the centre of decentralization and the systems evolved by the policy of decentralization brought into operation in 1855 were different from the centre and the systems evolved therefrom by the policy of decentralization initiated in 1870. Again, the centre which is gradually being decentralized since 1892, be it noted, is different from those affected by the decentralization of 1855 or 1870. To put it more clearly, the decentralization of 1855 was the decentralization of Indian Finance resulting in—

(I) the separation of Local from Imperial Finance.

The decentralization of 1870 was the decentralization of Imperial Finance resulting in—

(II) the separation of Provincial from Imperial Finance.

And the decentralization commencing from 1882 is the decentralization of Provincial Finance resulting in—

(III) the separation of Local from Provincial Finance.

Obviously then, 'Decentralization of Finance' far from being indicative of Provincial Finance, is a general name for this variegated and multifarious process of decentralization described above, and it cannot but be confusing to use as a title to the study of one line of decentralization a phrase which can be generically applied to all the three lines of decentralization distinguished above. In order, therefore, that this study may not be taken to pertain to a line of decentralization other than the one it purports to investigate, it has been thought proper to designate it 'The Evolution of Provincial Finance in British India' with a sub-title, 'A Study in the Provincial Decentralization of Imperial Finance', where the words Provincial and Imperial must be read with the emphasis due to them. How careless the phraseology often is may be instanced by the fact that Justice Ranade's pamphlet referred to above is styled 'Decentralization of Provincial Finance.' Although it deals with the development of Provincial Finance, it is likely to be passed over by the student, for its title implies that its subject-matter must be the growth of Local Finance. If Justice Ranade had been conscious of the varieties of decentralization, he would have probably realized that the title of his pamphlet was false to its contents.

10

On Untouchables

This book may, therefore, be taken as a pioneer attempt in the exploration of a field so completely neglected by everybody. The book, if I may say so, deals not only with every aspect of the main question set out for inquiry, namely, the origin of Untouchability, but it also deals with almost all questions connected with it. Some of the questions are such that very few people are even aware of them; and those who are aware of them are puzzled by them and do not know how to answer them. To mention only a few, the book deals with such questions as: Why do the Untouchables live outside the village? Why did beef-eating give rise to Untouchability? Did the Hindus never eat beef? Why did non-Brahmins give up beef-eating? What made the Brahmins become vegetarians, etc.? To each one of these, the book suggests an answer. It may be that the answers given in the book to these questions are not all-embracing. Nonetheless it will be found that the book points to a new way of looking at old things.

The thesis on the origin of Untouchability advanced in the book is an altogether novel thesis. It comprises the following propositions:

1. There is no racial difference between the Hindus and the Untouchables;

2. The distinction between the Hindus and Untouchables in its original form before the advent of Untouchability, was the distinction between Tribesmen and Broken Men from alien Tribes. It is the Broken Men who subsequently came to be treated as Untouchables;

3. Just as Untouchability has no racial basis so also it has no occupational basis;

4. There are two roots from which Untouchability has sprung:

(a) contempt and hatred of the Broken Men as of Buddhists by the Brahmins:

(b) Continuation of beef-eating by the Broken Men after it had been given up by others.

5. In searching for the origin of Untouchability care must be taken to distinguish the Untouchables from the Impure. All ortho-dox Hindu writers have identified the Impure with the Untouch-ables. This is an error. Untouchables are distinct from the Impure.

6. While the Impure as a class came into existence at the time of the Dharma Sutras the Untouchables came into being much later AD 400.

These conclusions are the result of such historical research as I have been able to make. The ideal which a historian should place before himself has been well defined by Goethe who said:[a]

The historian's duty is to separate the true from the false, the certain from the uncertain, and the doubtful from that which cannot be accepted... Every investigator must before all things look upon himself as one who is summoned to serve on a jury. He has only to consider how far the statement of the case is complete and clearly set forth by the evidence. Then he draws his conclusion and gives his vote, whether it be that his opinion coincides with that of the foreman or not.

There can be no difficulty in giving effect to Goethe's direction when the relevant and necessary facts are forthcoming. All this advice is of course very valuable and very necessary. But Goethe does not tell what the historian is to do when he comes across a missing link, when no direct evidence of connected relations between important events is available. I mention this because in the course of my investigations into the origin of Untouchability and other interconnected problems I have been confronted with many missing links. It is true that I am not the only one who has been confronted with them. All students of ancient Indian history have had to face them. For as Mountstuart Elphinstone

[a] Maxims and Reflections of Goethe, nos 453, 543.[177]

has observed in Indian history[178] 'no date of a public event can be fixed before the invasion of Alexander: and no connected relation of the natural transactions can be attempted until after the Mohamedan conquest.' This is a sad confession but that again does not help. The question is: 'What is a student of history to do? Is he to cry halt and stop his work until the link is discovered?' I think not. I believe that in such cases it is permissible for him to use his imagination and intuition to bridge the gaps left in the chain of facts by links not yet discovered and to propound a working hypothesis suggesting how facts which cannot be connected by known facts might have been inter-connected. I must admit that rather than hold up the work, I have preferred to resort to this means to get over the difficulty created by the missing links which have come in my way.

Critics may use this weakness to condemn the thesis as violating the canons of historical research. If such be the attitude of the critics I must remind them that if there is a law which governs the evaluation of the results of historical results then refusal to accept a thesis on the ground that it is based on direct evidence is bad law. Instead of concentrating themselves on the issue of direct evidence *versus* inferential evidence and inferential evidence *versus* speculation, what the critics should concern themselves with is to examine (i) whether the thesis is based on pure conjecture, and (ii) whether the thesis is possible and if so, does it fit in with facts better than mine does?

On the first issue I could say that the thesis would not be unsound merely because in some parts it is based on guess. My critics should remember that we are dealing with an institution the origin of which is lost in antiquity. The present attempt to explain the origin of Untouchability is not the same as writing history from texts which speak with certainty. It is a case of reconstructing history where there are no texts, and if there are, they have no direct bearing on the question. In such circumstances what one has to do is to strive to divine what the texts conceal or suggest without being even quite certain of having found the truth. The task is one of gathering survivals of the past, placing them together and making them tell the story of their birth. The task is analogous to that of the archaeologist who constructs a city from broken stones or of the palaeontologist who conceives an extinct animal from scattered bones and teeth or of a painter who reads the lines of the horizon and the smallest vestiges on the slopes of the hill to make up a scene. In this sense the book is a work of art even more than of history. The origin of Untouchability lies buried in a dead past which nobody knows. To make it alive is like an attempt to reclaim to history a city which has been dead since ages past and present it as it was in its original condition. It cannot but be that imagination and hypothesis should play a large part in such a work. But that in itself cannot be a ground for the condemnation of the thesis. For without trained imagination no scientific inquiry can be fruitful and hypothesis is the very soul of science. As Maxim Gorky has said:[179]

Science and literature have much in common; in both, observation, comparison and study are of fundamental importance; the artist like the scientist, needs both imagination and intuition. Imagination and intuition bridge the gaps in the chain of facts by its as yet undiscovered links and permit the scientist to create hypothesis and theories which more or less correctly and successfully direct the searching of the mind in its study of the forms and phenomenon of nature. They are of literary creation; the art of creating characters and types demands imagination, intuition, the ability to make things up in one's own mind.

It is therefore unnecessary for me to apologize for having resorted to constructing links where they were missing. Nor can my thesis be said to be vitiated on that account for nowhere is the construction of links based on pure conjecture. The thesis in great part is based on facts and inferences from facts. And where it is not based on facts or inferences from facts, it is based on circumstantial evidence of presumptive character resting on considerable degree of probability. There is nothing that I have urged in support of my thesis which I have asked my readers to accept on trust. I have at least shown that there exists a preponderance of probability in favour of what I have asserted. It would be nothing but pedantry to say that a preponderance of probability is not a sufficient basis for a valid decision.

On the second point with the examination of which, I said, my critics should concern themselves what I would like to say is that I am not so vain as to claim any finality for my thesis. I do not ask them to accept it as the last word. I do not wish to influence their judgement. They are of course free to come to their own conclusion. All I say to them is to consider whether this thesis is not a workable and therefore, for the time being, a valid hypothesis if the test of a valid hypothesis is that it should fit in with all surrounding facts, explain them and give them a meaning which in its absence they do not appear to have. I do not want anything more from my critics than a fair and unbiased appraisal.

IV

Ideology

Ambedkar's work is replete with ideologically combative stances. He distanced himself from classical liberalism and engaged with Marxism. Brahmanism and Gandhism constituted his *bete noires*. He reformulated Buddhism as an ideology explaining and engaging with the world as Marxism had done for many years.

Ranade, Gandhi and Jinnah[180] is an excerpt from an address entitled *Ranade, Gandhi and Jinnah* delivered on the 101st birth anniversary of Justice Govind Ranade at the Gokhale Memorial Hall, Pune on 18 January 1943. A preface to the published version of the address sums up its thrust:

I am no worshipper of idols. I believe in breaking them. I insist that if I hate Mr Gandhi and Mr Jinnah—I dislike them, I do not hate them—it is because I love India more. That is the true faith of a nationalist. I have hopes that my countrymen, will some day learn that the country is greater than the men, that the worship of Mr Gandhi or Mr Jinnah and service to India are two very different things and may even be contradictory of each other.[181]

Caste, Class and Democracy[182] is taken from *What Congress and Gandhi have done to the Untouchables*, published in 1946. The chapter from which it is excerpted has the title, 'A plea to the foreigner', referring to foreigners in general and the Labour Government, led by Clement Atlee in particular, who, Ambedkar felt, sympathized with the Congress. Ambedkar refuted the belief that the Congress was fighting for the freedom of the country. He advanced a class analysis of India and in the process made a double critique—how an inadequate conception of democracy made the foreigner embrace the Congress because it represented the upper castes and the upper classes in India. (The title is the editor's.)

Gandhism[183] is an excerpt from *What the Congress and Gandhi have done to the Untouchables*, from the chapter with the same title. It is a critique of certain central tenets of the Gandhian ideology, particularly in terms of its bearing on the Untouchables. We have retained certain long quotations from Gandhi found in the text to demonstrate Ambedkar's meticulous pursuit of *Gandhiyana* and the mode of his refutation of the same.

It is said the Buddha or Karl Marx[184] was part of a larger study, but Ambedkar could only complete the paper reproduced here. We have, however, omitted Buddha's sermon regarding King Strongtyre, distinguishing rule by righteousness and the rule of law. In its main aspects this paper contains the address that Ambedkar delivered at Kathmandu, in November 1956 for the Buddhist World Conference. In fact, a comparison between Buddha and Marx and Buddhism and Marxism is a recurrent theme in Ambedkar's writings in the 1950s.[185]

11

Ranade, Gandhi and Jinnah

Ranade's greatest opponents came from the political school of the intelligentsia. These politicals developed a new thesis. According to that thesis political reform was to have precedence over social reform. The thesis was argued from platform to platform and was defended by eminent people like Mr Justice Telang, a Judge of the Bombay High Court, with the consummate skill of an acute lawyer. The thesis caught the imagination of the people. If there was one single cause to which the blocking of the Social Reform movement could be attributed, it was this cry of political reform. The thesis is unsupportable, and I have no doubt that the opponents of Ranade were wrong and in pursuing it did not serve the best interests of the country. The grounds on which Mr Justice Telang defended the politicians' thesis were of course logical. But he totally forgot that logic is not reason, and analogy is not argument. Neither did he have a correct understanding of the inter-relation between the 'social' and the 'political' which Ranade had. Let us examine the reasons for the thesis. Those that were advanced were not very impressive. But I am prepared to meet the most impressive arguments that could be advanced. Even then the thesis will not stand. The following strike me as being the most impressive. In the first place, it could be said that we want political power first because we want to protect the rights of the people. This answer proceeds from a very frugal theory of Government as was propounded by the American statesman Jefferson according to whom politics was only an affair of policing by the State so that the rights of people were maintained without disturbance.

Assume that the theory is a sound one. The question is, what is there for the State to police if there are no rights? Rights must exist before policing becomes a serious matter of substance. The thesis that political reform should precede social reform becomes on the face of it an absurd proposition, unless the idea is that the government is to protect those who have vested rights and to penalize those who have none. The second ground that could be urged in support of the thesis is that they wanted political power because they wanted to confer on each individual certain fundamental rights by law and that such conferring of the political rights could not take place unless there was political power first obtained. This of course sounds very plausible. But is there any substance in it? The idea of fundamental rights has become a familiar one since their enactment in the American Constitution and in the Constitution framed by Revolutionary France. The idea of making a gift of fundamental rights to every individual is no doubt very laudable. The question is how to make them effective? The prevalent view is that once rights are enacted in a law then they are safeguarded. This again is an unwarranted assumption. As experience proves, rights are protected not by law but by the social and moral conscience of society. If social conscience is such that it is prepared to recognize the rights which law chooses to enact, rights will be safe and secure. But if the fundamental rights are opposed by the community, no Law, no Parliament, no Judiciary can guarantee them in the real sense of the word. What is the use of the fundamental rights to the Negroes in America, to the Jews in Germany and to the Untouchables in India? As Burke said, there is no method found for punishing the multitude. Law can punish a single solitary recalcitrant criminal. It can never operate against a whole body of people who are determined to defy it. Social conscience—to use the language of Coleridge—that calm incorruptible legislator of the soul without whom all other powers would 'meet in mere oppugnancy—is the only safeguard of all rights fundamental or non-fundamental.'

The third argument of the politicals could be based on the right to self-government. That self-government is better than good government is a well-known cry. One cannot give it more value than one can give to a slogan, and all would like to be assured that self-government would also be a good government. There is no doubt that the politicals wanted good government and their aim was to establish a democratic form of government. But they never stopped to consider whether a democratic form of government was possible. Their contention was founded on a series of fallacies. A democratic form of government presupposes a democratic form of society. The formal framework of democracy is of no value and would indeed be a misfit if there was no social democracy. The politicals never realized that democracy was not a form of government: it was essentially a form of society. It may not be necessary for a democratic society to be marked by unity, by community of purpose, by loyalty to public ends and by mutuality of sympathy. But it does unmistakably involve two things. The first is an attitude of mind, an attitude of respect and equality towards their fellows. The second is a social organization free from rigid social barriers. Democracy is incompatible and inconsistent with isolation and exclusiveness, resulting in the distinction between the privileged and the unprivileged. Unfortunately, the opponents of Ranade were never able to realize the truth of this fact.

One may judge it by any test and it will be found that the stand that Ranade took in this controversy and his plan of work were correct and fundamental to if they were not the pre-requisites of political reform. Ranade argued that there were no rights in the Hindu society which the moral sense of man could recognize. There were privileges and disabilities, privileges for a few and disabilities for a vast majority. Ranade struggled to create rights. Ranade wanted to vitalize the conscience of the Hindu society which had become moribund as well as morbid. Ranade aimed to create a real social democracy, without which there could be no sure and stable politics. The conflict was between two opposing points of view and it centred round the question which is more important for the survival of a nation, political freedom or strong moral fibre. Ranade took the view that moral stamina was more important than political freedom. This was also the view of Lecky the great historian who after a careful and comparative study of history came to the conclusion that:

The foundation of a Nation's strength and prosperity is laid in pure domestic life, in commercial integrity, in a high standard of moral worth, and of public spirit, in simple habits, in courage, uprightness, and a certain soundness and moderation of judgement which springs quite as much from character as from intellect. If you would form a wise judgment of the future of a nation, observe carefully whether these qualities are increasing or decaying. Observe carefully what qualities count for most in public life. Is character becoming of greater or less importance? Are the men who obtain the highest posts in the nation men of whom, in private life, irrespective of party competent judges speak with genuine respect? Are they of sincere convictions, consistent lives and indisputable integrity? It is by observing this current that you can best cast the horoscope of a nation.[186]

Ranade was not only wise but he was also logical. He told his opponents against playing the part of Political Radicals and Social Tories. In clear and unmistakable terms he warned them saying:

You cannot be liberal by halves. You cannot be liberal in politics and conservative in religion. The heart and the head must go together. You cannot cultivate your intellect, enrich your mind, enlarge the sphere of your political rights and privileges, and at the same time keep your hearts closed and cramped. It is an idle dream to expect men to remain enchained and enshackled in their own superstition and social evils, while they are struggling hard to win rights and privileges from their rulers. Before long these vain dreamers will find their dreams lost.[187]

Experience has shown that these words of Ranade have been true, even prophetic. Let those who deny this consider: Where are we today in politics and why are we where we are? It is now 50 years since the National Congress was born. Its stewardship has passed hands, I won't say from the sane to the insane, or from realists to idealists, but from moderates to radicals. Where does the country stand today at the end of 50 years of political marching? What is the cause of this deadlock? The answer is simple. The cause of deadlock is the absence of communal settlement. Ask why is communal settlement necessary for political settlement and you realize the fundamental importance of the stand that Ranade took. For the answer to this question is to be found in the wrong social system, which is too undemocratic, too over-weighed in favour of the classes and against the masses, too class conscious and too communally minded. Political democracy would become a complete travesty if it were built upon its foundations. That is why nobody except the high caste Hindus will agree to make it the case of a political democracy without serious adjustments. Well some people may argue to their satisfaction that the deadlock is the creation of the British Government. People like to entertain thoughts which soothe them and which throw responsibility on others. This is the psychology of escapism. But it cannot alter the fact that it is the defects of social system which has given rise to the communal problem and which has stood in the way of India getting political power.

Ranade's aim was to cleanse the old order if not to build a new one. He insisted on improving the moral tone of Hindu society. If he had been heard and followed, the system would have at least lost its rigours and its rigidity. If it could not have avoided communal settlement it would have made it easy. For his attempts, limited as they were, would have opened the way to mutual trust. But the politicals had developed a passion for political power which had so completely blinded them that they refused to see virtue in anything else. Ranade has had his revenge. Is not the grant of political safeguard a penalty for denying the necessity of social reform?

How much did Ranade achieve in the field in which he played so dominant a part? In a certain sense the question is not very important. Achievement is never the true measure of greatness. 'Alas,' as Carlyle said, 'we know very well that ideals can never be completely embodied in practice. Ideals must ever lie a very great way off; and we will right thankfully content ourselves with any not intolerable approximation thereto!' 'Let no man', as Schiller says, too querulously 'measure by a scale of perfection the meagre product of reality' in this poor world of ours. We will esteem him no wise man; we will esteem him a sickly discontented foolish man. And yet Ranade's record of achievement was not altogether bare. The problems facing the then social reformers contained in the statement on social reform prepared by Rai Bahadur P. Anandcharly were five: (1) early marriage; (2) remarriages of widows; (3) liberty for our countrymen to travel—or sojourn in foreign lands; (4) women's rights of property and (5) education of women. Of this programme he achieved a great part. If he did not achieve all, there were the odds against him, which should never be forgotten. A clever, determined and an insincere intelligentsia came forward to defend orthodoxy and give battle to Ranade. The scenes were exciting, as exciting as those of a dread grim of battle. And battle it was. One cannot recall the spirit of the time when this controversy over social reform was raging in this country. It is not possible for decency to enter into the abuses that were hurled, the calumnies that were uttered, the strategies that were employed by the orthodox section against the social reformers. It is impossible to read the writing of those who supported orthodoxy in their opposition to the Age of Consent Bill without realizing the depth of the degradation to which the so-called leaders of the peoples had fallen. The Bill aimed to punish a husband who would have sexual intercourse with his wife if she had not attained the age of 12. Could any sane man, could any man with a sense of shame oppose so simple a measure? But it was opposed, and Ranade had to bear the brunt of the mad orthodoxy. Assuming that Ranade's achievements were small; who could take pride or exultation in his failure to achieve more? There was no cause for exultation. The decline of social reform was quite natural. The odium of social reform was too great. The appeal of political power too alluring. The result was that social reform found fewer and fewer adherents. In course of time the platform of the Social Reform Conference was deserted and men flocked to the Indian National Congress. The politicians triumphed over the social reformers. I am sure that nobody will now allow that their triumph was a matter for pride. It is certainly a matter of sorrow. Ranade may not have been altogether on the winning side, but he was not on the wrong side and certainly never on the side of the wrong as some of his opponents were.

How does Ranade compare with others? Comparisons are always odious and unpleasant. At the same time it is true that there is nothing more illuminating than comparisons. Of course in making them one must bear in mind that to be interesting and instructive comparisons must be between those that are alike. Fortunately there is field for comparison. Ranade was a social reformer and as a social reformer he could be usefully compared with other social reformers. Particularly illuminating will be the comparison between Ranade and Jotiba Phule. Phule was born in 1827 and died in 1890. Ranade was born in 1842 and died in 1901. Thus Phule and Ranade were contemporaries and both were foremost social reformers. Some may perhaps demur to the wisdom of comparing Ranade with other politicians. This can only be on the ground that Ranade was not a politician. To say that Ranade was not a politician is to impose a very narrow and very restricted meaning upon the term 'politician'. A politician does not merely trade in politics but he also represents particular faith covering both—the method as well as the metaphysics of politics. Ranade was the founder of a school of politics which was distinctive for its method as well as for metaphysics. Used in this sense Ranade was a politician and could be usefully compared with other politicians. Comparisons of Ranade with social reformers and with politicians cannot but be illuminating and there is enough material for such comparisons. The question really is one of time and taste. Time will not permit any extensive comparison of Ranade being made both with social reformers as well as with politicians. I must really choose between comparing Ranade with social reformers or with politicians. This is a matter of taste. Left to myself I would have preferred to use my available time to compare Ranade with Phule. For I regard social reform more fundamental than political reform. Unfortunately my taste is different from the taste of the audience and I feel that in detaining the audience I must be guided more by its likes and dislikes than my own. The ardour for social reform has cooled down. The craze for politics has held the Indian public in its grip. Politics has become an appetizer—the more one tastes it the more one craves it. The task I am undertaking is a very unpleasant one and if I venture upon it, it is only because it is my duty to expound fully and the desire of the public to know truly the value of Ranade's political philosophy and his place among politicians of today.

Who are the present day politicians with whom Ranade is to be compared? Ranade was a great politician of his day. He must therefore be compared with the greatest of today. We have on the horizon of India two great men, so big that they could be identified without being named—Gandhi and Jinnah. What sort of a history they will make may be a matter for posterity to tell. For us it is enough that they do indisputably make headlines for the Press. They hold leading strings. One leads the Hindus, the other leads the Muslims. They are the idols and heroes of the hour. I propose to compare them with Ranade. How do they compare with Ranade? It is necessary to make some observations upon their temperaments and methods with which they have now familiarized us. I can give only my impressions of them, for what they are worth. The first thing that strikes me is that it would be difficult to find two persons who would rival them for their colossal egotism, to whom personal ascendency is everything and the cause of the country a mere counter on the table. They have made Indian politics a matter of personal feud. Consequences have no terror for them; indeed they do not occur to them until they happen. When they do happen they either forget the cause, or if they remember it, they overlook it with a complacency which saves them from any remorse. They choose to stand on a pedestal of splendid isolation. They wall themselves off from their equals. They prefer to open themselves to their inferiors. They are very unhappy at and impatient of criticism, but are very happy to be fawned upon by flunkeys. Both have developed a wonderful stagecraft and arrange things in such a way that they are always in the limelight wherever they go. Each of course claims to be supreme. If supremacy was their only claim, it would be a small wonder. In addition to supremacy each claims infallibility for himself. Pius IX during whose sacred regime as Pope the issue of infallibility was raging said—'Before I was Pope I believed in Papal infallibility, now I feel it.'[188] This is exactly the attitude of the two leaders whom Providence—may I say in his unguarded moments—has appointed to lead us. This feeling of supremacy and infallibility is strengthened by the Press. One cannot help saying that. The language used by Gardiner to describe the Northcliffe brand of journalism,[189] in my opinion, quite appropriately describes the present state of journalism in India. Journalism in India was once a profession. It has now become a trade. It has no more moral function than the manufacture of soap. It does not regard itself as the responsible adviser of the public. To give the news uncoloured by any motive, to present a certain view of public policy which it believes to be for the good of the community, to correct and chastise without fear all those, no matter how high, who have chosen a wrong or a barren path, is not regarded by journalism in India its first or foremost duty. To accept a hero and worship him has become its principal duty. Under it, news gives place to sensation, reasoned opinion to unreasoning passion, appeal to the minds of responsible people to appeal to the emotions of the irresponsible. Lord Salisbury spoke of the Northcliffe journalism as written by office-boys for office-boys. Indian journalism is all that plus something more. It is written by drum-boys to glorify their heroes. Never has the interest of country been sacrificed so senselessly for the propagation of hero-worship. Never has hero-worship become so blind as we see it in India today. There are, I am glad to say, honourable exceptions. But they are too few and their voice is never heard. Entrenched behind the plaudits of the Press, the spirit of domination exhibited by these two great men has transgressed all limits. By their domination they have demoralized their followers and demoralized politics. By their domination they have made half their followers fools and the other half hypocrites. In establishing their supremacy they have taken the aid of 'big business' and money magnates. For the first time in our country money is taking the field as an organized power. The questions which President Roosevelt propounded for the American public to consider will arise here, if they have not already arisen: Who shall rule—wealth or man? Which shall lead, money or intellect? Who shall fill public stations, educated and patriotic free men or the feudal serfs of corporate capital? For the present, Indian politics, at any rate the Hindu part of it, instead of being spiritualized has become grossly commercialized, so much so that it has become a byword for corruption. Many men of culture are refusing to concern themselves in this cesspool. Politics has become a kind of sewage system intolerably unsavoury and insanitary. To become a politician is like going to work in the drain.

Politics in the hands of these two great men has become a competition in extravaganza. If Mr Gandhi is known as Mahatma, Mr Jinnah must be known as Qaid-i-Azam. If Gandhi has the Congress, Mr Jinnah must have the Muslim League. If the Congress has a Working Committee and the All-India Congress Committee, the Muslim League must have its Working Committee and its Council. The session of the Congress must be followed by a session of the League. If the Congress issues a statement, the League must also follow suit. If the Congress passes a Resolution of 17,000 words, the Muslim League's Resolution must exceed it by at least a thousand words. If the Congress President has a Press Conference, the Muslim League President must have his. If the Congress must address an appeal to the United Nations, the Muslim League must not allow itself to be outbidden. When is all this to end? When is there to be a settlement? There are no near prospects. They will not meet, except on preposterous conditions. Jinnah insists that Gandhi should admit that he is a Hindu. Gandhi insists that Jinnah should admit that he is one of the leaders of the Muslims. Never has there been such a deplorable state of bankruptcy of statesmanship as one sees in these two leaders of India. They are making long and interminable speeches, like lawyers whose trade it is to contest everything, concede nothing and talk by the hour. Suggest anything by way of solution for the deadlock to either of them, and it is met by an everlasting 'Nay' Neither will consider a solution of the problems which is not eternal. Between them Indian politics has become 'frozen' to use a well-known banking phrase and no political action is possible.

How does Ranade strike as compared to these two? I have no personal impression to give. But reading what others have said I think I can say what he must have been like. He had not a tinge of egotism in him. His intellectual attainments could have justified any amount of pride, nay, even insolence. But he was the most modest of men. Serious youths were captivated by his learning and geniality. Many, feeling completely under his sway, responded to his ennobling influence and moulded their whole lives with the passionate reverence for their adored master. He refused to be satisfied with the praises of fools, and was never afraid of moving in the company of equals and of the give and take it involves. He never claimed to be a mystic relying on the inner voice. He was a rationalist prepared to have his views tested in the light of reason and experience. His greatness was natural. He needed no aid of the stage nor the technique of an assumed eccentricity nor the means of a subsidized press. As I said, Ranade was principally a social reformer. He was not a politician in the sense of one who trades in politics. But he has played an important part in the political advancement of India. To some of the politicians he acted as the teacher who secured such signal successes and who dazzled their critics by their brilliance. To some he acted as the guide, but to all he acted as the philosopher.

What was the political philosophy of Ranade? It may be summed up in three propositions:

1. We must not set up as our ideal something which is purely imaginary. An ideal must be such that it must carry the assurance that it is a practicable one.

2. In politics, sentiment and temperament of the people are more important than intellect and theory. This is particularly so in the matter of framing a Constitution. A Constitution is as much a matter of taste as clothes are. Both must fit, both must please.

3. In political negotiations the rule must be what is possible. That does not mean that we should be content with what is offered.

No. It means that you must not refuse what is offered when you know that your sanctions are inadequate to compel your opponent to concede more.

These are the three main doctrines of Ranade's political philosophy. It would be quite easy to illustrate them by appropriate quotations from his writings and his speeches. There is no time for that nor is there any necessity, for they must be clear to every student of Ranade's speeches and writings. Who could quarrel with Ranade on these three propositions and if there be one, on which? On the first only a visionary will quarrel. We need not take any notice of him. The second proposition is so evident that we could only ignore it at our peril. The third proposition is something on which a difference of opinion is possible. Indeed it is this which divided the Liberals from the Congressmen. I am not a liberal, but I am sure the view Ranade held was the right one. There can be no compromise on principle, and there should not be. But once the principle is agreed upon, there can be no objection to realize it by instalments. Graduation in politics is inevitable, and when the principle is accepted it is not harmful and indeed it may in certain circumstances be quite advantageous. On this third proposition there was really no difference between him and Tilak, except this: Tilak would have the possible maximized by the application of sanctions; Ranade would look askance at sanctions. This is all. On the rest they were agreed. The absence of sanctions in Ranade's political philosophy need not detract much from its worth. We all know what sanctions are available to us. We have tried all, old as well as new, with what effect I need not stop to describe.

12

Caste, Class and Democracy

I

In taking the side of the Congress as an organization 'fighting for freedom,' the foreigner does not stop to make a distinction between the freedom of a country and the freedom of the people in the country. In not stopping to make this distinction, the foreigner, it must be said, far from understanding the matter, is allowing himself to be misled, if not deceived. For words such as society, nation and country are just amorphous, if not ambiguous, terms. There is no gainsaying that 'Nation', though one word, means many classes. Philosophically it may be possible to consider a nation as a unit but sociologically it cannot but be regarded as consisting of many classes and the freedom of the nation if it is to be a reality must vouchsafe the freedom of the different classes comprised in it, particularly those who are treated as the servile classes. Consequently, it is foolish to take solace in the fact that because the Congress is fighting for the freedom of India, it is, therefore, fighting for the freedom of the people of India and of the lowest of the low.

The question whether the Congress is fighting for freedom has very little importance as compared to the question for whose freedom is the Congress fighting. This is a pertinent and necessary inquiry and it would be wrong for any lover of freedom to support the Congress without pursuing the matter and finding out what the truth is. But the foreigner who takes the side of the Congress does not care even to raise such a question? Why is the foreigner so indifferent to so important a question? So far as I am able to judge, the reason for such indifference is to be found in the wrong notions of self-government and democracy which are prevalent in the West and which form the stock-in-trade of the foreigner who takes interest in Indian politics.

It is propounded by Western writers on politics that all that is necessary for the realization of self-government is the existence among a people of what Grote called constitutional morality. By constitutional morality is meant[a]

Habits of paramount reverence for the form of the constitution, enforcing obedience to the authorities acting under and within those forms yet combined with the habit of open speech, of action subject only to definite legal control, and unrestrained censure of those very authorities as to all their public acts—combined, too, with a perfect confidence in the bosom of every citizen, admits the bitterness of party contest, that the forms of constitution will be not less sacred in the eyes of his opponents than in his own.

If in a populace these habits are present, then according to Western writers on politics, self-government can be a reality and nothing further need be considered. Similarly, Western writers on democracy believe that what is necessary for the realization of the ideal of democracy, namely, government by the people, of the people and for the people, is the establishment of universal adult suffrage. Other means have been suggested such as recall, plebiscite and short parliaments and in some countries they have been brought into operation. But in a majority of countries nothing more than adult suffrage is deemed to be necessary.

I have no hesitation in saying that both these notions are fallacious and grossly misleading. If democracy and self-government have failed everywhere, it is largely due to these wrong notions. Habits of constitutional morality may be essential for the maintenance of a constitutional *form* of government. But the maintenance of a constitutional form of government is not the same thing as a self-government by the people. Similarly, it may be granted that adult suffrage can produce government of the people in the logical sense of the phrase, i.e. in contrast to the government of a king. But it cannot by itself be said to bring about a democratic government, in the sense of government by the people and for the people.

[a] Grote History of Greece, vol. III, p. 347.

These views of Western writers on politics regarding democracy and self-government are erroneous for very many reasons. In the first place, they omit to take into account the incontrovertible fact that in every country there is a governing class grown up by force of historical circumstances, which is destined to rule, which does rule and to whom adult suffrage and constitutional morality are no bar against reaching places of power and authority and to whom the servile classes, by reason of the fact that they regard the members of the governing classes as their natural leaders, volunteer to elect as rulers. Secondly, they fail to realize that the existence of a governing class is inconsistent with democracy and self-government and that given the fact that where the governing class retains its power to govern, it is wrong to say that democracy and self-government exist unless democracy and self-government are regarded as mere matters of form. Thirdly, they do not seem to be aware that self-government and democracy become real not when a Constitution based on adult suffrage comes into existence but when the governing class loses its power to capture the power to govern. Fourthly, they seem to overlook the fact that while in some countries the servile classes may succeed in ousting the governing class from the seat of authority with nothing more than adult suffrage, in other countries the governing class may be so well entrenched that the servile classes will need other safeguards besides adult suffrage to achieve the same end. Lastly, they seem to pay no heed to the fact that given the existence of the governing class what matters most in the consideration of any scheme of democracy and self-government is the social outlook and social philosophy of the governing class, for so long as the governing class retains its means to capture the power to govern, the freedom and the well-being of the servile classes must depend upon the social outlook, the social conscience of the governing class and its philosophy of life.

The recognition of the existence of a governing class as a fundamental and a crucial fact confronting democracy and self-government is the only safe and realistic approach to those who wish for democracy and self-government to come into their own. It is a fatal blunder to omit to take account of it in coming to a conclusion as to whether in a free country freedom will be the privilege of the governing class only or it will be the possession of all. In my view, therefore, what the foreigner who chooses to side with the Congress should ask is not whether the Congress is fighting for freedom. He should ask: For whose freedom is the Congress fighting? Is it fighting for the freedom of the governing class in India or is it fighting for the freedom of the people of India? If he finds that the Congress is fighting for the freedom of the governing class, he should ask Congressmen: Is the governing class in India fit to govern? This is the least he can do before siding with the Congress.

What are the answers which Congressmen have to give to these questions? I do not know. But I can give what I think are the only true answers to these questions.

II

To start with it is well to know who constitute the governing class in India. The governing class in India consists principally of the Brahmins. It is strange that the present-day Brahmins repudiate the allegation that they belong to the governing class though at one time they described themselves as *Bhudevas* (God on Earth). What can this *volte face* be due to? Is it due to a guilty conscience born out of the realization that they have committed criminal breach of the trust imposed upon the intellectual sections in every community by the sacred law of humanity not to serve the interest of their own class but to safeguard the interest of all and therefore dare not stand before the bar of the world? Or is it due to their sense of modesty? It is unnecessary to stop to speculate as to which is the truth.

That the Brahmins are a governing class is hardly open to question. There are two tests one could apply. First is the sentiment of the people and the second is the control of administration. I am sure there cannot be better and more decisive tests than these two. As to the first, there cannot be any doubt. Taking the attitude of the people, the person of the Brahmin is sacred. In ancient times, he could not be hanged no matter what offence he committed. As a sacred person he had immunities and privileges which were denied to the servile class. He was entitled to first fruits. In Malabar, where the Sambandham marriage[190] prevails, the servile classes such as the Nairs regard it an honour to have their females kept as mistresses by Brahmins. Even kings invited

Brahmins[b] to deflower their queens on *prima noctis*. There was a time when no person of the servile class could take his food without drinking the water in which the toes of the Brahmins were washed. Sir P. C. Ray[193] once described how in his childhood, rows of children belonging to the servile classes used to stand for hours

[b] The traveller Ludovico Di Varthema who came to India in the middle of the 16th Century and visited Malabar says:

. 'It is proper and at the same time a pleasant thing to know who these Brahmins are. You must know that they are the chief persons of the faith, as priests are among us. And when the king takes a wife he selects the most worthy and the most honoured of these Brahmins and makes him sleep the first night with his wife, in order that he may deflower her. Do not imagine that the Brahmin goes willingly to perform this operation. The king is obliged to pay him four hundred to five hundred ducats. The king only and no other person in Calicut adopts this practice'—*Voyages of Varthema* (Hakluyat Society), vol. I, p. 141.

Other travellers tell that the practice was widespread. Hamilton in his *Account of the East Indies* says:

'When the Samorin marries, he must not cohabit with his bride till the Nambourie (Nambudri) or chief priest, has enjoyed her, and if he pleases he may have three nights of her company, because the first fruits of her nuptials must be a holy oblation to the God she worships and some of the nobles are so complacent as to allow the clergy the same tribute; but the common people cannot have that compliment paid to them, but are forced to supply the priests places themselves.'—vol. I, p. 308.

Buchanan in his Narrative refers to the practice in the following terms:

'The ladies of the Tamuri family are generally impregnated by Nambudries; although if they choose they many employ the higher ranks of Nairs; but the sacred character of the Nambudries always procures them a preference.'—*Pinkerton's Voyages*, vol. VIII, p. 734.

'Mr C. A. Innes, ICS., Editor of the *Gazetteer* of Malabar and Anjengo issued under the authority of the Government of Madras says:

Another institution found amongst all the classes following the *marukakh kattayam*[191] system, as well as amongst many of those who observe *makkattayam*,[192] is that known as 'Tali-tying wedding' which has been described as 'the most peculiar, distinctive and unique' among Malayali marriage customs. Its essence is the tying of a *tali* (a small piece of gold or other metal, like a locket, on a string) on a girl's neck before she attains the age of puberty. This is done by a man of the same or

TABLE 12.1

Communities	Approximate population in lakhs	Percentage of population	No. of posts held out of total no. gazetted posts (2200)	Percentage of appointments held	Non-gazetted posts			
					Over Rs 100 Total No. 7000		Over Rs 35 Total No. 20,782	
					No. held by	Percentage of appointments held	No. held by	Percentage of appointments held
Brahmins	15	3	820	37.0	3280	43.73	8812	42.4
Christians	20	4	190	9.0	750	10.0	1655	8.0
Mohamedans	37	7	150	7.0	497	6.63	1624	7.8
Depressed Classes	70	14	25	1.5	39	0.52	144	0.69
Non-Brahmins								
Forward Non-brahmins	113	22	620	27.0	2543	33.9	8440	40.6
Backward Classes	245	50	50	2.0	–	–	–	–
Non-Asiatic and Anglo-Indians	–	–	–	–	372	5.0	83	0.4
Other Communities	–	–	–	–	19	0.5	24	0.11

Distribution of gazetted posts between the Brahmins and other communities in 1948.

together in the morning on the roadside in Calcutta with cups of water in their hands waiting for a Brahmin to pass ready to wash his feet and take it to their parents waiting to sip it before taking their food. Under the British Government and by reason of its equalitarian jurisprudence these rights, immunities and privileges of the Brahmins have ceased to exist. Nonetheless the advantages they gave still remain and the Brahmin is still pre-eminent and sacred in the eyes of the servile classes and is still addressed by them as 'Swami' which means 'Lord.'

The second test gives an equally positive result, to take only the Madras Presidency by way of illustration. Consider Table 12.1 (see page 137). It shows the distribution of gazetted posts between the Brahmins and other communities in the year 1948.

Similar data from other Provinces could also be adduced to support this conclusion. But it is unnecessary to labour the point. Whether the Brahmins claim themselves to be members of the governing class or not, the facts that they control the administration and that their supremacy is accepted by the servile classes, are enough to establish the point.

History shows that the Brahmin has always had other classes as his allies to whom he was ready to accord the status of a governing class provided they were prepared to work with him in subordinate co-operation. In ancient and medieval times he made such an alliance with the Kshatriyas or the warrior class and the two ruled the masses, indeed ground them down, the Brahmin with his pen and the Kshatriya with his sword. At present, the Brahmin has made an alliance with the Vaishya class called Banias. The shifting of this alliance from Kshatriya to Bania is natural. In these days of commerce money is more important than sword. That is one reason for this change in party alignment. The second reason is the need for money to run the political machine. Money can

of a higher caste (the usages of different classes differ), and it is only after it has been done that the girl is at liberty to contract a *sambandham*. It seems to be generally considered that the ceremony was intended to confer on the *tali tier or manavalan* (bridegroom) a right to cohabit with the girl; and by some the origin of the ceremony is found in the claim of the *Bhudevas* or "Earth-Gods," (that is the Brahmins), and on a lower plane of Kshatriyas or ruling classes, to the first-fruits of lower caste womanhood, a right akin to the mediaeval *droit de seigneurie*.'—vol. I, p. 101.

come only from the Bania. It is the Bania who is financing the Congress largely because Mr Gandhi is a Bania and also because he has realized that money invested in politics gives large dividends. Those who have any doubts in the matter might do well to read what Mr Gandhi told Mr Louis Fisher on 6 June 1942. Reports Fisher:[c]

'I said I had several questions to ask him about the Congress Party. Very highly placed Britishers, I recalled, had told me that Congress was in the hands of big business and that Gandhi was supported by the Bombay millowners who gave him as much money as he wanted. 'What truth is there in these assertions,' I asked.
'Unfortunately, they are true,' he declared simply, 'Congress hasn't enough money to conduct its work. We thought in the beginning to collect four annas (about eight cents) from each member per year and operate on that. But it hasn't worked.'
'What proportion of the Congress budget,' I asked, 'is covered by rich Indians?'
'Practically all of it, ' he stated. 'In this ashram, for instance, we could live much more poorly than we do and spend less money. But we do not and the money comes from our rich friends.'

For this reason, it is impossible for the Brahmin to exclude the Bania from the position of a governing class. In fact, he has established not merely a working but a cordial alliance with the Bania. The result is that the governing class in India today is a Brahmin-Bania instead of the Brahmin–Kshatriya combine as it used to be.

The existence of the governing class does not cover the whole story. What is significant is that the members of the governing class in India are quite conscious of the fact that they do belong to the governing class and that they alone are destined to rule. The late Mr Tilak could never forget that he was a Brahmin and belonged to the governing class. The same is reported to be the case about Pandit Jawaharlal Nehru[d] and his sister Mrs Vijaya Laxmi Pandit.

[c] Louis Fisher, *A Week with Gandhi*, Allen & Unwin, 1943, p. 41.
[d] Mr Pattabhi Sitaramaya in his introduction to the Life of Pandit Jawaharlal Nehru by Mr Y. G. Krishnamurti, says Pandit Nehru is very conscious of the fact that he is a Brahmin. This will shock many who are under the impression that Pandit Nehru is a Socialist and does not believe in caste. But Mr Pattabhi Sitaramaya ought to know what he is saying. Not only is Pandit Nahru conscious of the fact that he is a Brahmin but his sister Mrs

Nor is Mr Vallabhbhai Patel free from the feeling that he belongs to the governing class. Mr Tilak is held out as the father of the Swaraj movement. Pandit Nehru and Mr Vallabhbhai Patel are the leading members of the Congress High Command. Not only are they conscious of the fact that they belong to the governing class but some of them hold that the servile classes are a contemptible people, who must remain servile and who must never aspire to rule. Indeed, they have felt no shame and no remorse in giving public expression to such views. In 1918, when the Non-Brahmins and the Backward Classes had started an agitation for separate representation in the Legislature, Mr Tilak in a public meeting held in Sholapur said he did not understand why the oil pressers, tobacco shopkeepers, washermen, etc.—that was his description of the Non-Brahmins and the Backward Classes—should want to go into the Legislature. In his opinion, their business was to obey the laws and not to aspire for power to make laws. In 1942, Lord Linlithgow invited 52 important Indians representing different sections of the people to discuss what steps could be taken to make the Central Government more popular with a view to enlist the sympathy and co-operation of all Indians in war effort. Among those that were invited were members belonging to the Scheduled Castes. Mr Vallabhbhai Patel could not bear the idea that the Viceroy should have invited such a crowd of mean men. Soon after the event, Mr Vallabhbhai Patel made a speech in Ahmedabad and said:[c]

The Viceroy sent for the leaders of the Hindu Mahasabha, he sent for the leaders of the Muslim League and he sent for Ghanchis (oil pressers), Mochis (cobblers) and the rest.

Although Mr Vallabhbhai Patel in his malicious and stinging words referred only to *Ghanchis* and *Mochis*, his speech is indicative

---

Vijaya Laxmi Pandit, also seems to be conscious that she is a Brahmin. It is said that at the All-India Women's Conference held in Delhi in December 1940, the question of not declaring one's caste in the Census Return was discussed. Mrs. Pandit disapproved of the idea and said she did not see any reason why she should not be proud of her Brahmin blood and declare herself as a Brahmin at the Census—See *Sense and Nonsense in Politics* Serial No. XII by Mr J. E. Sanjana in the *Rast Rahabar* (a Bombay Gujarathi Weekly), 14th January' 45.

[c] Quoted by Mr Sanjana in *Sense and Nonsense in Politics.*

of the general contempt in which the governing class and the members of the Congress High Command hold the servile classes of this country. Further illustrations of this attitude of the governing class and the Congress High Command can be found from incidents that have taken place in the election campaigns. They are so relevant and so revealing that a special mention must be made of them.

Ever since 1919 when Mr Gandhi captured the Congress, Congressmen have looked upon the boycott of the Legislature as one of the sanctions for making the British Government concede the demand for Swaraj. Under this policy, every time there was an election in which the Congress decided not to take part, the Congress would not only refuse to put candidates on the Congress ticket but would carry on propaganda against any Hindu proposing to stand for election as an independent candidate. One need not quarrel over the merits of such a policy. But what were the means adopted by the Congress to prevent Hindus standing on an independent ticket? The means adopted were to make the legislatures objects of contempt. Accordingly, the Congress in various Provinces started processions carrying placards saying 'Who will go to the Legislatures? Only barbers, cobblers, potters and sweepers.' In the processions one man would utter the question as part of the slogan and the whole crowd would repeat as answer the second part of the slogan. When Congressmen found that this was not enough to deter persons from standing for the elections, they decided to adopt sterner measures. Believing that respectable people would not be prepared to stand for election if they felt certain that they would have to sit with barbers, potters and sweepers, etc. in the legislatures, the Congress actually went to the extent of putting up candidates from these despised communities on the Congress ticket and got them elected. A few illustrations of this outrageous conduct of the Congress may be mentioned. In the 1920 election, the Congress elected a cobbler[f] to the Central Provinces legislature. In the 1930 election, they elected to the Central Provinces two cobblers,[g] one milkman[h] and one barber[i]

[f] Faguwa Rohidas.
[g] Guru Gosain Agamdas and Balaraj Jaiswar.
[h] Chunnu.
[i] Arjunlal.

and in the Punjab one sweeper.[j] In 1934, the Congress elected a potter[k] to the Central Legislature. It might be said that this is old history. Let me correct such an impression by referring to what happened in 1943, in the Municipal Elections in Andheri—a suburb of Bombay. The Congress put up a barber to bring the Municipality in contempt.

What an enormity! The Sinn Fein in Ireland boycotted the British Parliament. But did they make such hideous use of their own countrymen for effecting their purposes? The campaign of boycott of the Legislature which took place in 1930 is of particular interest. The elections to the Provincial Legislatures in 1930 in which these instances occurred coincided with Mr Gandhi's Salt Satyagraha campaign of 1930! I hope that the future (the official historian Dr Pattabhi Sitamayya has failed to do so) historian of Congress while recording how Mr Gandhi decided to serve notice on the Viceroy, Lord Irwin, presenting him with a list of demands to be conceded before a certain date and on failure by the Viceroy in this behalf, how Mr Gandhi decided to launch a campaign of civil disobedience, how Mr Gandhi elected an Englishman to carry his notice, how Mr Gandhi selected the Salt Act as a target for attack, how he selected Dandi as a scene of battle, how he decided to put himself at the head of the campaign, how he marched out from his Ashram in Ahmedabad with all pomp and ceremony, how the women of Ahmedabad came out with *Arthi* and applied *tilak* (saffron mark) to his forehead wishing him victory, how Mr Gandhi assured them by saying that Gujarat alone will win Swaraj for India, how Mr Gandhi proclaimed his determination by saying that he will not return to Ahmedabad until he has won Swaraj, will not fail to record that while on the one hand Congressmen were engaged in fighting for Swaraj which they said they wanted to win in the name and for the masses, on the other hand and in the very year they were committing the worst outrages upon the very masses by exhibiting them publicly as objects of contempt to be shunned and avoided.

Such is the mentality of the governing classes in India towards the servile classes.

[j] Bansi Lal Chaudhari.
[k] Bhagat Chandi Mal Gola.

III

What is to be the fate of the servile classes of India under this governing class?

The Congress promises to do wonders for the servile classes—the Congress speaks of masses, it ought really to speak of them as the servile classes held in bondage by the governing classes—when Swaraj comes. It says that it would like to make revolutionary changes but it has no power to make them and it must wait for Swaraj. It is this glib talk which goes to deceive the gullible foreigner. Leaving aside the boast and bluster which lie behind the statement, one may ask what really can happen if India does become a sovereign and an independent state? One thing is certain. The governing class will not disappear by the magic wand of Swaraj. It will remain as it is and having been freed from the incubus of British Imperialism will acquire greater strength and vigour. It will capture power as the governing classes in every country do. In short, Swaraj will not be government *by* the people but it will be a government run by the governing class and in the absence of government *by* the people, government *for* the people will be what the governing class will choose to make of it.

What will the governing class do when India becomes a sovereign and independent state? Some hope that they will undertake reform of tenancy laws, enlarge factory legislation, extend primary education, introduce prohibition and train people to ply *charkha*, construct roads and canals, improve currency, regulate weights and measures, open dispensaries and undertake other measures to ameliorate the condition of the servile classes. No one from the servile class can be very enthusiastic about such a programme. In the first place, there is nothing very great in it. In the world of today, no governing class can omit to undertake reforms which are necessary to maintain society in a civilized state. Personally, I have grave doubts about the governing class in India coming forward to carry out even such a modest programme of social amelioration. Most people forget that what leads the Congress today to mouth such a programme is the desire to show that the Congress is better than the British bureaucracy. But once the bureaucracy is liquidated, will there be the same incentive to better the lot of the masses? I entertain very grave doubts on the point. Apart from this, is social amelioration the be-all and end-all of

Swaraj? Speaking for the servile classes, I have no doubt that what they expect to happen in a sovereign and free India is a complete destruction of Brahminism as a philosophy of life and as a social order. If I may say so, the servile classes do not care for social amelioration. The want and poverty which has been their lot is nothing to them as compared to the insult and indignity which they have to bear as a result of the vicious social order. Not bread but honour, is what they want. The question therefore is: Will the governing classes in India having captured the machinery of the State, undertake a programme for the reform of the social order as distinguished from a programme of social amelioration?

The statement by Congressmen that Congress can do wonders if only India was a sovereign and an independent State, supposing that it is an honest aspiration and not mere propaganda, proceeds on the assumption that for a man to do what he wants, nothing more is necessary than power. Such a belief is not only pitiable but is really a dangerous illusion. Those who are inclined to cherish such an illusion forget that there are serious limitations on sovereignty, no matter how absolute it is. None has described these limitations in more telling language than Dicey. In his Law of the Constitution, he says:

The actual exercise of authority by any sovereign whatever, and notably by Parliament, is bounded or controlled by two limitations. Of these the one is an external, the other is an internal limitation.

The external limit to the real power of a sovereign consists in the possibility or certainty that his subjects or a large number of them will disobey or resist his laws.

This limitation exists even under the most despotic monarchies. A Roman Emperor, or a French King during the middle of the eighteenth century, was (as is the Russian Czar at the present day) in strictness a 'sovereign' in the legal sense of that term. He had absolute legislative authority. Any law made by him was binding, and there was no power in the empire or kingdom which could annul such law.... But it would be an error to suppose that the most absolute ruler who ever existed could in reality make or change every law at his pleasure...

The authority, that is to say, even of a despot, depends upon the readiness of his subjects or of some portion of his subjects to obey his behests; and this readiness to obey must always be in reality limited. This is shown by the most notorious facts of history. None of the early Caesars could at their pleasure have subverted the worship of fundamental institutions of the Roman world,...The Sultan could not abolish

Mahommedanism. Louis the Fourteenth at the height of his power could revoke the Edict of Nantes, but he would have found it impossible to establish the supremacy of Protestantism, and for the same reason which prevented James the Second from establishing the supremacy of Roman Catholicism... What is true of the power of a despot or of the authority of a constituent assembly is specially true of the sovereignty of Parliament; it is limited on every side by the possibility of popular resistance. Parliament might legally establish an Episcopal Church in Scotland; Parliament might legally tax the Colonies; Parliament might without any breach of law change the succession to the throne or abolish the monarchy; but everyone knows that in the present state of the world the British Parliament will do none of these things. In each case widespread resistance would result from legislation which, though legally valid, is in fact beyond the stretch of parliamentary power... The internal limit to the exercise of sovereignty arises from the nature of the sovereign power itself. Even a despot exercises his powers in accordance with his character, which is itself moulded by the circumstances under which he lives, including under that head the moral feelings of the time and the society to which he belongs. The Sultan could not if he would, change the religion of the Mahommedan world, but if he could do so it is in the very highest degree improbable that the head of Mahommedanism should wish to overthrow the religion of Mahomet; the internal check on the exercise of the Sultan's power is at least as strong as the external limitation. People sometimes ask the idle question why the Pope does not introduce this or that reform? The true answer is that a revolutionist is not the kind of man who becomes a Pope, and that the man who becomes a Pope has no wish to be a revolutionist...[194]

None can gainsay the truth of what Dicey has said. What the governing class may do depends not so much upon the degree of its sovereignty as upon what Dicey calls the external and internal limitations in sovereignty. Of these two, if the failure to do good arises out of the external limitations, nobody need blame the governing class. The fear of external limitations blocking progress need not cause much apprehension. For it is the internal limitations of the governing class that have a greater determining force than the external limitations. Progress depends more upon internal limitations of the governing class than upon external limitations. What are the factors which determine these internal limitations? The internal limitations are born out of the outlook, traditions, vested interests and the social philosophy of the governing class. The purpose of this discussion is to warn the foreigner that before believing what the Congress proposes to do for the servile classes, he should make it a point to ask: What is the outlook of the governing class? What are its traditions? What is its social philosophy?

To take the Brahmins first. Historically they have been the most inveterate enemy of the servile classes (Shudras and the Untouchables) who together constitute about 80 per cent of the total Hindu population. If the common man belonging to the servile classes in India is today so fallen, so degraded, so devoid of hope and ambition, it is entirely due to the Brahmins and their philosophy. The cardinal principles of this philosophy of Brahmanism are five: (1) graded inequality between the different classes; (2) complete disarmament of the Shudras and the Untouchables; (3) complete prohibition of the education of the Shudras and the Untouchables; (4) ban on the Shudras and the Untouchables occupying places of power and authority; (5) ban on the Shudras and the Untouchables acquiring property. (6) complete subjugation and suppression of women. Inequality is the official doctrine of Brahminism and the suppression of the lower classes aspiring to equality has been looked upon by them and carried out by them without remorse as their bounden duty. There are countries where education did not spread beyond a few. But India is the only country where the intellectual class, namely, the Brahmins not only made education their monopoly but declared acquisition of education by the lower classes, a crime punishable by cutting off of the tongue or by the pouring of molten lead in the ear of the offender. The Congress politicians complain that the British are ruling India by a wholesale disarmament of the people of India. But they forget that disarmament of the Shudras and the Untouchables was the rule of law promulgated by the Brahmins. Indeed, so strongly did the Brahmins believe in the disarmament of the Shudras and the Untouchables that when they revised the law to enable the Brahmins to arm themselves for the protection of their own privileges, they maintained the ban on the Shudras and the Untouchables as it was without lessening its rigour. If the large majority of people of India appear today to be thoroughly emasculated, spiritless, with no manliness, it is the result of the Brahminic policy of wholesale disarmament to which they have been subjected for the untold ages. There is no social evil and no social wrong to which the Brahmin does not give his support. Man's inhumanity to man, such as the feeling of caste, untouchability, unapproachability and unseeability is a religion to him. It would, however, be a mistake to suppose that only the wrongs of man are a religion to him. For the Brahmin has given his support to the worst wrongs that women have suffered from in any part of the world. Widows were burnt alive as sattees. The Brahmin gave his fullest support to *Sattee*, the burning alive of a widow. Widows were not allowed to remarry. The Brahmin upheld the doctrine. Girls were required to be married before 8 and the husband had the right to consummate the marriage at any time thereafter, whether she had reached puberty or not did not matter. The Brahmin gave the doctrine his strongest support. The record of the Brahmins as law-givers for the Shudras, for the Untouchables and for women is the blackest as compared with the record of the intellectual classes in other parts of the world. For no intellectual class has prostituted its intelligence to invent a philosophy to keep his uneducated countrymen in a perpetual state of ignorance and poverty as the Brahmins have done in India. Every Brahmin today believes in this philosophy of Brahminism propounded by his forefathers. He is an alien element in the Hindu Society. The Brahmin *vis-à-vis* Shudras and the Untouchables is as foreign as the German is to the French, as the Jew is to the Gentile or as the White is to the Negro. There is a real gulf between him and the lower classes of Shudras and Untouchables. He is not only alien to them but he is also hostile to them. In relationship with them, there is no room for conscience and there is no call for justice.

The Bania is the worst parasitic class known to history. In him the vice of money-making is unredeemed by culture or conscience. He is like an undertaker who prospers when there is an epidemic. The only difference between the undertaker and the Bania is that the undertaker does not create an epidemic while the Bania does. He does not use his money for production. He uses it to create poverty and more poverty by lending money for unproductive purposes. He lives on interest and as he is told by his religion that money lending is the occupation prescribed to him by Manu, he looks upon it as both right and righteous. With the help and assistance of the Brahmin judge who is ready to decree his suits, he is able to carry on his trade. Interest, interest on interest, he adds on and on and thereby draws families perpetually into his net. Pay him as much as a debtor may, he is always in debt. With no conscience, there is no fraud, and no chicanery that he will not commit. His grip over the nation is complete. The whole of poor, starving, illiterate India is mortgaged to the Bania.

To sum up, the Brahmin enslaves the mind and the Bania enslaves the body. Between them, they divide the spoils which belong to the governing classes. Can anyone who realizes what the outlook, tradition and social philosophy of the governing class in India is, believe that under the Congress regime, a sovereign and independent India will be different from the India we have today?

13

Gandhism

THE DOOM OF THE UNTOUCHABLES

I

Hitherto when Indians have been talking about the reconstruction of Indian social and economic life they have been talking in terms of individualism *versus* collectivism, capitalism *versus* socialism, conservatism *versus* radicalism and so on. But quite recently a new 'ism' has come on the Indian horizon. It is called Gandhism. It is true that very recently Mr Gandhi had denied that there is such a thing as Gandhism. This denial is nothing more than the usual modesty which Mr Gandhi wears so well. It does not disprove the existence of Gandhism. There have been quite a number of books with the title of Gandhism without any protest from Mr Gandhi. It has already caught the imagination of some people both inside and outside India. Some have so much faith in it that they do not hesitate to offer it as an alternative to Marxism.

The followers of Gandhism who may happen to read what is said in the foregoing pages may well ask: Mr Gandhi may not have done what the Untouchables expected him to do; but does not Gandhism offer any hope to the Untouchables? The followers of Gandhism may accuse me of remembering only the short, slow, intermittent steps taken by Mr Gandhi for the sake of the Untouchables and of forgetting the potential length of the principles enunciated by him. I am prepared to admit that it does sometimes happen that a person who enunciates a long principle takes only a short step and that he may be forgiven for the short step in the hope that some day the principle will by its native dynamics force a long step covering all who were once left out. Gandhism is in itself a very interesting subject for study. But to deal with Gandhism after having dealt with Mr Gandhi is bound to be a tedious task and therefore my first reaction was to leave out the consideration of Gandhism and Untouchables. At the same time, I could hardly remain indifferent to the facts that the effect of my omission to consider the subject might be very unfortunate. For Gandhists, notwithstanding my exposure of Mr Gandhi, might take advantage of it and continue to preach that if Mr Gandhi has failed to solve the problem of the Untouchables still the Untouchables will find their salvation in Gandhism. It is because I wish to leave no room for such propaganda that I have overcome my original disinclination and engage upon discussion of Gandhism.

II

What is Gandhism? What does it stand for? What are its teachings about economic problems? What are its teachings about social problems?

At the outset, it is necessary to state that some Gandhists have conjured up a conception of Gandhism which is purely imaginary. According to this conception, Gandhism means return to the village and making the village self-sufficient. It makes Gandhism a mere matter of regionalism. Gandhism, I am sure, is neither so simple nor so innocent as regionalism is. Gandhism has a much bigger content than regionalism. Regionalism is a small insignificant part of it. It has a social philosophy and it has an economic philosophy. To omit to take into account the economic and social philosophy of Gandhism is to present deliberately a false picture of Gandhism. The first and foremost requisite is to present a true picture of Gandhism.

To start with Mr Gandhi's teachings on social problems. Mr Gandhi's views on the caste system—which constitutes the main social problem in India—were fully elaborated by him in 1921-2 in a Gujarathi Journal called *Nava-Jivan*. The article[a] is written in Gujarathi. I give below an English translation of his views as near as possible in his own words. Says Mr Gandhi:

[a] It is reprinted in vol. II of the series called *Gandhi Sikshan* as No. 18.

1. I believe that if Hindu Society has been able to stand it is because it is founded on the caste system.

2. The seeds of Swaraj are to be found in the caste system. Different castes are like different sections of military division. Each division is working for the good of the whole...

3. A community which can create the caste system must be said to possess unique power of organization.

4. Caste has a readymade means for spreading primary education. Every caste can take the responsibility for the education of the children of the caste. Caste has a political basis. It can work as an electorate for a representative body. Caste can perform judicial functions by electing persons to act as judges to decide disputes among members of the same caste. With castes it is easy to raise a defence force by requiring each caste to raise a brigade.

5. I believe that interdining or intermarriage are not necessary for promoting national unity. That dining together creates friendship is contrary to experience. If this was true there would have been no war in Europe... Taking food is as dirty an act as answering the call of nature. The only difference is that after answering call of nature we get peace while after eating food we get discomfort. Just as we perform the act of answering the call of nature in seclusion so also the act of taking food must also be done in seclusion.

6. In India children of brothers do not intermarry. Do they cease to love because they do not intermarry? Among the Vaishnavas many women are so orthodox that they will not eat with the members of the family nor will they drink water from a common water pot. Have they no love? The caste system cannot be said to be bad because it does not allow interdining or intermarriage between different castes.

7. Caste is another name for control. Caste puts a limit on enjoyment. Caste does not allow a person to transgress caste limits in pursuit of his enjoyment. That is the meaning of such caste restrictions as interdining and intermarriage.

8. To destroy the caste system and adopt the Western European social system means that Hindus must give up the principle of hereditary occupation which is the soul of the caste system. Hereditary principle is an eternal principle. To change it is to create disorder. I have no use for a Brahmin if I cannot call him a Brahmin for my life. It will be a chaos if every day a Brahmin is to be changed into a Shudra and a Shudra is to be changed into a Brahmin.

9. The caste system is a natural order of society. In India it has been given a religious coating. Other countries not having understood the utility of the caste system it existed only in a loose condition and

consequently those countries have not derived from caste system the same degree of advantage which India has derived.

These being my views I am opposed to all those who are out to destroy the caste system.

In 1922, Mr Gandhi was a defender of the caste system. Pursuing the inquiry, one comes across a somewhat critical view of the caste system by Mr Gandhi in the year 1925. This is what Mr Gandhi said on 3 February 1925:

I gave support to caste because it stands for restraint. But at present caste does not mean restraint, it means limitations. Restraint is glorious and helps to achieve freedom. But limitation is like a chain. It binds. There is nothing commendable in castes as they exist today. They are contrary to the tenets of the *shastras*. The number of castes is infinite and there is a bar against intermarriage. This is not a condition of elevation. It is a state of fall.

In reply to the question: What is the way out Mr Gandhi said:

The best remedy is that small castes should fuse themselves into one big caste. There should be four such big castes so that we may reproduce the old system of four varnas.

In short, in 1925 Mr Gandhi became an upholder of the *Varna* system.

The old *Varna* system prevalent in ancient India had society divided into four orders: (1) Brahmins, whose occupation was learning; (2) Kshatriyas whose occupation was warfare; (3) Vaishyas, whose occupation was trade and (4) Shudras, whose occupation was service of the other classes. Is Mr Gandhi's *Varna* System the same as this old *Varna* system of the orthodox Hindus? Mr Gandhi explained his *Varna* system in the following terms:[b]

1. I believe that the divisions into *Varna* is based on birth.

2. There is nothing in the *Varna* system which stands in the way of the *Shudra* acquiring learning or studying military art of offence or defence. Contra it is open to a Kshatriya to serve. The *Varna* system is no bar to him. What the *Varna* system enjoins is that a Shudra will not make learning a way of earning a living. Nor will a Kshatriya adopt service

[b] The extracts are taken from an article by Mr Gandhi on the subject and is reproduced in the *Varna Vayavastha*—a book which contains Mr Gandhi's writings in original Gujarathi, translated by Ramnarayan Choudhuri, Ahmedabad, Navjivan, 1959.

as a way of earning a living. (Similarly a Brahmin may learn the art of war or trade. But he must not make them a way of earning his living. In contras a Vaishya may acquire learning or may cultivate the art of war. But he must not make them a way of earning his living.)

3. The *Varna* system is connected with the way of earning a living. There is no harm if a person belonging to one *Varna* acquired the knowledge or science and art specialized in by persons belonging to other *Varnas*. But as far as the way of earning his living is concerned he must follow the occupation of the *Varna* to which he belongs which means he must follow the hereditary profession of his forefathers.

4. The object of the *Varna* system is to prevent competition and class struggle and class war. I believe in the *Varna* system because it fixes the duties and occupations of persons.

5. *Varna* means the determination of a man's occupation before he is born.

6. In the *Varna* system no man has any liberty to choose his occupation. His occupation is determined for him by heredity.

Turning to the field of economic life, Mr Gandhi stands for two ideals:

One of these is the opposition to machinery. As early as 1921, Mr Gandhi gave vent to his dislike for machinery. Writing in the *Young India* of 19 January 1921, Mr Gandhi said:

Do I want to put back the hand of the clock of progress? Do I want to replace the mills by hand-spinning and hand-weaving? Do I want to replace the railway by the countrycart? Do I want to destroy machinery altogether? These questions have been asked by some journalists and public men. My answer is: I would not weep over the disappearance of machinery or consider it a calamity.

His opposition to machinery is well evidenced by his idolization of *charkha* (the spinning wheel) and by insistence upon hand-spinning and hand-weaving. This opposition to machinery and his love for *charkha* is not a matter of accident. It is a matter of philosophy. This philosophy Mr Gandhi took special occasion to propound in his presidential address at the Kathiawad Political Conference held on 8th January 1925. This is what Mr Gandhi said:

Nations are tired of the worship of lifeless machines multiplied *ad infinitum*. We are destroying the matchless living machines viz., our own bodies by leaving them to rust and trying to substitute lifeless machinery for them. It is a law of God that the body must be fully worked and utilized. We dare not ignore it. The spinning wheel is the auspicious symbol of Sharir Yajna—body labour. He who eats his food without offering this sacrifice steals it. By giving up this sacrifice we became traitors to the country and banged the door in the face of the Goddess of Fortune.

Anyone who has read Mr Gandhi's booklet on *Hind Swaraj* (Indian Home Rule) will know that Mr Gandhi is against modern civilization. The book was first published in 1908. But there has been no change in his ideology. Writing in 1921 Mr Gandhi said:[c]

The booklet is a severe condemnation of 'modern civilization.' It was written in 1908. My conviction is deeper today than ever. I feel that, if India would discard 'Modern civilization' she can only gain by doing so.

In Mr Gandhi's views:[d]

'Western civilization is the creation of Satan.'

The second ideal of Mr Gandhi is the elimination of class-war and even class struggle in the relationship between employers and employees and between landlords and tenants. Mr Gandhi's views on the relationship between employers and employees were set forth by him in an article on the subject which appeared in the *Nava-Jivan* of 8 June 1921 from which the following is an extract:

Two paths are open before India, either to introduce the Western principle of 'Might is right' or to uphold the Eastern principle that truth alone conquers, that truth knows no mishap, that the strong and the weak have alike a right to secure justice. The choice is to begin with the labouring class. Should the labourers obtain an increment in their wages by violence? Even if that be possible, they cannot resort to anything like violence, howsoever legitimate may be their claims. To use violence for securing rights may seem an easy path, but it proves to be thorny in the long run. Those who live by sword die also by sword. The swimmer often dies by drowning. Look at Europe. No one seems to be happy there, for not one is contented. The labourer does not trust the capitalist and the capitalist has no faith in the labourer. Both have a sort of vigour and strength but even the bulls have it. They fight to the very bitter end. All motion is not progress. We have got no reason to believe, that the people of Europe are progressing. Their possession of wealth does not argue the possession of any moral or spiritual qualities.

[c] *Young India*, 26 January 1921.
[d] *Dharma Manthan*, p. 65.

What shall we do then? The labourers in Bombay made a fine stand. I was not in a position to know all the facts. But this much I could see that they could fight in a better way. The millowner may be wholly in the wrong. In the struggle between capital and labour, it may be generally said that more often than not the capitalists are in the wrong box. But when labour comes fully to realize its strength, I know it can become more tyrannical than capital. The millowners will have to work on the terms dictated by labour, if the latter could command intelligence of the former. It is clear, however, that labour will never attain to that intelligence. If it does, labour will cease to be labour and become itself the master. The capitalists do not fight on the strength of money alone. They do possess intelligence and tact.

The question before us is this: When the labourers, remaining what they are, develop a certain consciousness, what should be their course? It would be suicidal if the labourers rely upon their numbers or brute-force, i.e., violence. By so doing, they will do harm to industries in the country. If, on the other hand, they take their stand on pure justice and suffer in their person to secure it, not only will they always succeed but they will reform their masters, develop industries and both master and men will be as members of one and the same family.

Referring to the same theme on another occasion Mr Gandhi said:[e]

Nor was it otherwise before. India's history is not one of strained relations between capital and labour.

Particularly noteworthy are the views of Mr Gandhi on strike as a weapon in the hand of the workers to improve their economic condition. Mr Gandhi says:[f]

Speaking, therefore, as one having handled large successful strikes, I repeat the following maxims, already stated in these pages, for guidance of all strike leaders:

(1) There should be *no strike without a real grievance*.

(2) There should be no strike, if the persons concerned are not able to support themselves out of their own savings or by engaging in some temporary occupation, such as carding, spinning and weaving. *Strikers should never depend upon public subscriptions or other charity.*

(3) *Strikers must fix an unalterable minimum demand, and declare it before embarking upon their strike.*

[e] *Young India*, 23 February 1922.
[f] *Young India*, 11 August 1921. Italics not in the original.

A strike may fail in spite of a just grievance and the ability of strikers to hold out indefinitely, if there are workers to replace them. A wise man, therefore, will not strike for increase of wages or other comforts, if he feels that he can be easily replaced. But a philanthropic or patriotic man will strike in spite of supply being greater than the demand, when he feels for and wishes to associate himself with his neighbour's distress. Needless to say, there is no room in a civil strike of the nature described by me for violence in the shape of intimidation, incendiarism or otherwise... Judged by the test suggested by me, it is clear that friends of the strikers could never have advised them to apply for or receive Congress or any other public funds for their support. The value of the strikers' sympathy was diminished to the extent, that they received or accepted financial aid. The merit of a sympathetic strike lies in the inconvenience and the loss suffered by the sympathisers.

Mr Gandhi's view on the relationship between landlords and tenants were expounded by him in the *Young India* of 18 May 1921 in the form of instruction[g] to the tenants of UP who had risen against their landlords. Mr Gandhi said:

Whilst the UP Government is crossing the bounds of propriety, and intimidating people, there is little doubt that the Kisans too are not making wise use of their newly found power. In several Zamindaries, they are said to have overstepped the mark, taken the law into their own hands and to have become impatient of anybody who would not do as they wish. They are abusing social boycott and are turning it into an instrument of violence. They are reported to have stopped the supply of water, barber and other paid services to their Zamindars in some instances and even suspended payment of the rent due to them. The Kisan movement has received an impetus from Non-co-operation but it is anterior to and independent of it. *Whilst we will not hesitate to advise the Kisans when the moment comes, to suspend payment of taxes to Government, it is not contemplated that at any stage of Non-co-operation we would seek to deprive the Zamindars of their rent. The Kisan movement must be confined to the improvement of status of the Kisans and the betterment of the relations between the Zamindars and them.* The Kisans must be advised scrupulously to abide by the terms of their agreement with the Zamindars, whether such is written or inferred from custom. Where a custom or even a written contract is bad, they may not try to uproot it by violence or without previous reference to the Zamindars. In every case there should be a friendly discussion with the Zamindars and an attempt made to arrive at a settlement.

[g] Italics are not in the original. *Kisan* means 'a tenant' and *zamindar* means 'landlord'.

Mr Gandhi does not wish to hurt the propertied class. He is even opposed to a campaign against them. He has no passion for economic equality. Referring to the propertied class Mr Gandhi said quite recently that he does not wish to destroy the hen that lays the golden egg. His solution for the economic conflict between the owners and workers, between the rich and the poor, between landlords and tenants and between the employers and the employees is very simple. The owners need not deprive themselves of their property. All that they need to do is to declare themselves Trustees for the poor. Of course the Trust is to be a voluntary one carrying only a spiritual obligation.

III

Is there anything new in the Gandhian analysis of economic ills? Are the economics of Gandhism sound? What hope does Gandhism hold out to the common man, to the down-and out? Does it promise him a better life, a life of joy, and culture, a life of freedom, not merely freedom from want but freedom to rise, to grow to full stature which his capacities can reach?

There is nothing new in the Gandhian analysis of economic ills in so far as it attributes them to machinery and the civilization that is built upon it. The arguments that machinery and modern civilization help to concentrate management and control into relatively few hands, and with the aid of banking and credit facilitate the transfer into still fewer hands of all materials and factories and mills in which millions are bled white in order to support huge industries thousands of miles away from their cottages, or that machinery and modern civilization cause deaths, maimings and cripplings far in excess of the corresponding injuries by war, and are responsible for disease and physical deterioration caused directly and indirectly by the development of large cities with their smoke, dirt, noise, foul air, lack of sunshine and out-door life, slums, prostitution and unnatural living which they bring about, are all old and worn out arguments. There is nothing new in them. Gandhism is merely repeating the views of Rousseau, Ruskin, Tolstoy and their school.

The ideas which go to make up Gandhism are just primitive. It is a return to nature, to animal life. The only merit is their simplicity. As there is always a large corps of simple people who are attracted by them, such simple ideas do not die, and there is always some simpleton to preach them. There is, however, no doubt that the practical instincts of men—which seldom go wrong—have found them unfruitful and which society in search of progress has thought it best to reject.

The economics of Gandhism are hopelessly fallacious. The fact that machinery and modern civilization have produced many evils may be admitted. But these evils are no argument against them. For the evils are not due to machinery and modern civilization. They are due to wrong social organization which has made private property and pursuit of personal gain matters of absolute sanctity. If machinery and civilization have not benefited everybody the remedy is not to condemn machinery and civilization but to alter the organization of society so that the benefits will not be usurped by the few but will accrue to all.

In Gandhism the common man has no hope. It treats man as an animal and no more. It is true that man shares the constitution and functions of animals, nutritive, reproductive, etc. But these are not distinctively human functions. The distinctively human function is reason, the purpose of which is to enable man to observe, meditate, cogitate, study and discover the beauties of the Universe and enrich his life and control the animal elements in his life. Man thus occupies the highest place in the scheme of animate existence. If this is true what is the conclusion that follows? The conclusion that follows is that while the ultimate goal of a brute's life is reached once his physical appetites are satisfied, the ultimate goal of man's existence is not reached unless and until he has fully cultivated his mind. In short, what divides the brute from man is culture. Culture is not possible for the brute, but it is essential for man. That being so, the aim of human society must be to enable every person to lead a life of culture which means the cultivation of the mind as distinguished from the satisfaction of mere physical wants. How can this happen?

Both for society and as well as for the individual there is always a gulf between merely living and living worthily. In order that one may live worthily one must first live. The time and energy spent upon mere life, upon gaining of subsistence detracts from that available for activities of a distinctively human nature and which go to make up a life of culture. How then can a life of culture be made possible? It is not possible unless there is sufficient leisure.

For it is only when there is leisure that a person is free to devote himself to a life of culture. The problem of all problems which human society has to face is how to provide leisure to every individual. What does leisure mean? Leisure means the lessening of the toil and effort necessary for satisfying the physical wants of life. How can leisure be made possible? Leisure is quite impossible unless some means are found whereby the toil required for producing goods necessary to satisfy human needs is lessened. What can lessen such toil? Only when machine takes the place of man. There is no other means of producing leisure. Machinery and modern civilization are thus indispensable for emancipating man from leading the life of a brute, and for providing him with leisure and making a life of culture possible. The man who condemns machinery and modern civilization simply does not understand their purpose and the ultimate aim which human society must strive to achieve.

Gandhism may be well suited to a society which does not accept democracy as its ideal. A society which does not believe in democracy may be indifferent to machinery and the civilization based upon it. But a democratic society cannot. The former may well content itself with life of leisure and culture for the few and a life of toil and drudgery for the many. But a democratic society must assure a life of leisure and culture to each one of its citizens. If the above analysis is correct then the slogan of a democratic society must be machinery, and more machinery, civilization and more civilization. Under Gandhism the common man must keep on toiling ceaselessly for a pittance and remain a brute. In short, Gandhism with its call of back to nature, means back to nakedness, back to squalor, back to poverty and back to ignorance for the vast mass of the people.

The division of life into separate functions and of society into separate classes may not be altogether obliterated. In spite of many social and economic changes, in spite of the abolition of legal serfdom, legal slavery and the spread of the notion of democracy, with the extension of science, of general education through books, newspapers, travel and general intercourse in schools and factories there remains and perhaps will remain enough cleavage in society into a learned and an ignorant class, a leisure and a labouring class.

But Gandhism is not satisfied with only *notional* class distinctions. Gandhism insists upon class structure. It regards the class structure of society and also the income structure as sacrosanct with the consequent distinctions of rich and poor, high and low, owners and workers as permanent parts of social organization. From the point of view of social consequences nothing can be more pernicious. Psychologically, class structure sets in motion influences which are harmful to both the classes. There is no common plane on which the privileged and the subject classes can meet. There is no endosmosis, no give and take of life's hopes and experiences. The social and moral evils of this separation to the subject class are of course real and obvious. It educates them into slaves and creates all the psychological complex which follows from a slave mentality. But those affecting the privileged class, though less material and less perceptible, are equally real. The isolation and exclusiveness following upon the class structure creates in the privileged classes the anti-social spirit of a gang. It feels it has interests 'of its own' which it makes its prevailing purpose to protect against everybody even against the interests of the State. It makes their culture sterile, their art showy, their wealth luminous and their manners fastidious. Practically speaking in a class structure there is, on the one hand, tyranny, vanity, pride, arrogance, greed, selfishness and on the other, insecurity, poverty, degradation, loss of liberty, self-reliance, independence, dignity and self-respect. Democratic society cannot be indifferent to such consequences. But Gandhism does not mind these consequences in the least. It is not enough to say that Gandhism is not satisfied with mere class distinctions. It is not enough to say that Gandhism believes in a class structure. Gandhism stands for more than that. A class structure which is a faded, jejune, effete thing—a mere sentimentality, a mere skeleton is not what Gandhism wants. It wants class structure to function as a living faith. In this there is nothing to be surprised at. For class structure in Gandhism is not a mere accident. It is its official doctrine.

The idea of trusteeship which Gandhism proposes as a panacea by which the moneyed classes will hold their properties in trust for the poor is the most ridiculous part of it. All that one can say about it is that if anybody else had propounded it the author would have been laughed at as a silly fool who had not known the hard realities of life and was deceiving the servile classes by telling them that a little dose of moral rearmament to the propertied classes— those who by their insatiable cupidity and indomitable arrogance have made and will always make this world a vale of tears for the toiling millions—will recondition them to such an extent that they will be able to withstand the temptation to misuse the tremendous powers which the class structure gives them over servile classes.

The social ideal of Gandhism is either *caste* or *Varna*. Though it may be difficult to say which, there can be no doubt that the social ideal of Gandhism is not democracy. For whether one takes for comparison *caste* or *Varna* both are fundamentally opposed to democracy. It would have been something if the defence of caste system which Gandhism offers was strong and honest. But his defence of the caste system is the most insensible piece of rhetoric one can think of. Examine Mr Gandhi's arguments in support of caste and it will be found that everyone of them is specious if not puerile. To run through the arguments summarized earlier in this chapter.[195]

The first three arguments call for pity. That the Hindu Society has been able to stand while others have died out or disappeared is hardly a matter for congratulation. If it has survived it is not because of caste but because the foreigner who conquered the Hindus did not find it necessary to kill them wholesale. There is no honour in mere survival. What matters is the plane of survival. One can survive by unconditional surrender. One can survive by beating a cowardly retreat and one can survive by fighting. On what plane have the Hindus survived? If they can be said to have survived after fighting and beating their enemies the virtue ascribed to the caste system by Mr Gandhi could be admitted. The history of the Hindus has been one of surrender—abject surrender. It is true others have surrendered to their invaders. But in their case surrender is followed by a revolt against the foreign ruler. The Hindus have not only never withstood the onslaught of the foreign invader, they have never even shown the capacity to organize a rebellion to throw off the foreign yoke. On the other hand the Hindus have tried to make slavery comfortable. On this one may well argue the contrary, namely that this helpless condition of the Hindus is due entirely to the caste system.

Argument in para 4 is plausible. But it cannot be said that caste is the only machinery for discharging such functions as the spread of primary education or the judicial settlement of disputes. Caste is probably the worst instrument for the discharge of such functions. It can be easily influenced and easily corrupted. Such functions have been discharged in other countries much better than they have been in India although they have had no caste system. As to using the caste as a basis for raising military units the idea is simply fantastic. Under the occupational theory underlying the caste system this is unthinkable. Mr Gandhi knows that not a single caste in his own Province of Gujarat has ever raised a military unit. It did not do it in the present World War. But it did not do so even in the last World War, when Mr Gandhi toured through Gujarat as a Recruiting Agent of British Imperialism. In fact under the caste system a general mobilization of the people for defence is impossible since mobilization requires a general liquidation of the occupational theory underlying the caste system.

Arguments contained in para 5 and 6 are as stupid as they are revolting. The argument in para 5 is hardly a good argument. It is quite true the family is an ideal unit in which every member is charged with love and affection for another member although there is no intermarriage among members of a family. It may even be conceded that in a Vaishnava family members of the family do not interdine and yet they are full of love and affection for one another. What does all this prove? It does not prove that interdining and intermarrying are not necessary for establishing fraternity. What it proves is that where there are other means of maintaining fraternity—such as consciousness of family tie—inter-dining and inter-marriage are not necessary. But it cannot be denied that where—as in the caste system—no binding force exists inter-marriage and inter-dining are absolutely essential. There is no analogy between family and caste. Inter-caste dinner and inter-caste marriage are necessary because there are no other means of binding the different castes together while in the case of a family there exists other forces to bind them together. Those who have insisted upon the ban against inter-dining and inter-marriage have treated it as a question of relative values. They have never elevated it to the level of a question of absolute value. Mr Gandhi is the first one to do it. Inter-dining is bad and even if it was capable of producing good it should not be resorted to anyway. Because eating is a filthy act, as filthy as answering the call of nature! The caste system has been defended by others. But this is the first time I have seen such an extraordinary if not a shocking argument used to support it. Even the orthodox may say, 'Save us from Mr Gandhi.' It shows what a deep-dyed Hindu Mr Gandhi is. He has outdone the most orthodox of orthodox Hindus. It is not enough to say that it is an argument of a cave man. It is really an argument of a mad man.

The argument in favour of the caste system outlined in para 7 is not worth much in terms of building up moral strength. The caste system no doubt prohibits a man from satisfying his lust for a woman who is not of his caste. The caste system no doubt prohibits a man from satisfying his craving for food cooked in the house of a man who is not of his caste. If morality consists of observing restraints without regard to the sense or sensibility of restraints then the caste system may be admitted to be a moral system. But Mr Gandhi does not see that these easy restraints are more than balanced by vast liberties permitted by Hinduism. For Hinduism places no restraint upon a man marrying hundred women and keeping hundred prostitutes within the ambit of his caste. Nor does it stop him from indulging in his appetite with his castemen to any degree.

The argument in para 8 begs the whole question. The hereditary system may be good or may not be good. It may be agreeable to some. It may be disagreeable to others. Why elevate it into an official doctrine? Why make it compulsory? In Europe it is not an official doctrine and it is not compulsory. It is left to the choice of individuals most of whom do follow the profession of their ancestors and some don't. Who can say that compulsory system has worked better than the voluntary system? If a comparison of the economic condition of the people in India and the people of Europe is any guide there would be very few rationally-minded people who would be found to support the caste system on this ground. As to the difficulty in changing nomenclature to keep pace with frequent changes in occupation it is only artificial. It arises out of the supposed necessity of having labels for designating persons following a particular profession. The class labels are quite unnecessary and could well be abolished altogether without causing difficulty. Besides what happens today in India? Men's callings and their class labels are not in accord. A Brahmin sells shoes. Nobody is disturbed because he is not called a Chamar. A Chamar becomes an officer of the State. Nobody is disturbed because he is not called a Brahmin. The whole argument is based on a misunderstanding. What matters to society is not the label by which the individual's class is known but the service he offers.

The last argument set out in para 9 is one of the most astounding arguments I have heard in favour of the caste system. It is historically false. No one who knows anything about the Manu Smriti can say that the caste system is a natural system. What does Manu Smriti show? It shows that the caste system is a legal system maintained at the point of a bayonet. If it has survived it is due to (1) prevention of the masses from the possession of arms; (2) denying to the masses the right to education and (3) depriving the masses of the right to property. The caste system far from natural is really an imposition by the ruling classes upon the servile classes.

That Mr Gandhi changed over from the caste system to the varna system does not make the slightest difference to the charge that Gandhism is opposed to democracy. In the first place, the idea of *Varna* is the parent of the idea of *caste*. If the idea of caste is a pernicious idea it is entirely because of the viciousness of the idea of *Varna*. Both are evil ideas and it matters very little whether one believes in *Varna* or in *caste*. The idea of *Varna* was most mercilessly attacked by the Buddhists who did not believe in it. Orthodox or the Sanatan Vedic Hindus had no rational defence to offer. All that they could say was that it was founded on the authority of the *Vedas* and that as the *Vedas* were infallible so was the *Varna* system. This argument was not enough to save the *Varna* system against the rationalism of the Buddhists. If the idea of the *Varna* survived it was because of the *Bhagvad Gita*, which gave a philosophical foundation to the *Varna* system by arguing that the *Varna* was based on the innate qualities of man. The *Bhagvad Gita* made use of the Sankhya philosophy to bolster and buttress the *Varna* idea which would have otherwise petered away by making sense of a thing that is absolute nonsense. *Bhagvad Gita* had done enough mischief by giving a fresh lease of life to the *Varna* system by basing it upon a new and plausible foundation, namely that of innate qualities.

The *Varna* system of the *Bhagvad Gita* has at least two merits. It does not say that it is based on birth. Indeed it makes a special point that each man's *Varna* is fixed according to his innate qualities. It does not say that the occupation of the son shall be that of the father. It says that the profession of a person shall be according to his innate qualities, the profession of the father according to the father's innate quality and that of the son according to the son's innate qualities. But Mr Gandhi has given a new interpretation of the *Varna* system. He has changed it out of recognition. Under the old orthodox interpretation *caste* connoted hereditary occupation but *Varna* did not. Mr Gandhi by his own whim has given a new connotation to the *Varna*. With Mr Gandhi *Varna* is determined by birth and the profession of a *Varna* is determined by the principle of heredity so that *Varna* is merely another name for *caste*. That Mr Gandhi changed from *caste* to *Varna* does not indicate the growth of any new revolutionary ideology. The genius of Mr Gandhi is elvish, always and throughout. He has all the precocity of an elf with no little of its outward guise. Like an elf he can never grow up and grow out of the caste ideology.

Mr Gandhi sometimes speaks on social and economic subjects as though he was a blushing red. Those who will study Gandhism will not be deceived by the occasional aberrations of Mr Gandhi in favour of democracy and against capitalism. For Gandhism is in no sense a revolutionary creed. It is conservatism in excelsis. So far as India is concerned, it is a reactionary creed blazoning on its banner the call of Return to Antiquity. Gandhism aims at the resuscitation and reanimation of India's dread, dying past.

Gandhism is a paradox. It stands for freedom from foreign domination which means the destruction of the existing political structure of the country. At the same time it seeks to maintain intact a social structure which permits the domination of one class by another on a hereditary basis which means a perpetual domination of one class by another. What is the explanation of this paradox? Is it a part of a strategy by Mr Gandhi to win the whole-hearted support of the Hindus, orthodox and unorthodox, to the campaign of Swaraj? If it is the latter, can Gandhism be regarded as honest and sincere? Be that as it may there are two features of Gandhism which are revealing but to which unfortunately no attention has so far been paid. Whether they will make Gandhism more acceptable than Marxism is another matter. But as they do help to distinguish Gandhism from Marxism, it may be well to refer to them.

The first special feature of Gandhism is that its philosophy helps those who have, to keep what they have and to prevent those who have not from getting what they have a right to get. No one who examines the Gandhian attitude to strikes, the Gandhian reverence for caste and the Gandhian doctrine of Trusteeship by the rich for the benefit of the poor can deny that this is upshot of Gandhism. Whether this is the calculated result of a deliberate design or whether it is a matter of accident may be open to argument. But the fact remains that Gandhism is the philosophy of the well-to-do and the leisure class.

The second special feature of Gandhism is to delude people into accepting their misfortunes by presenting them as best of good fortunes. One or two illustrations will suffice to bring out the truth of this statement.

The Hindu sacred law penalized the *Shudras* (Hindus of the fourth class) from acquiring wealth. It is a law of enforced poverty unknown in any other part of the world. What does Gandhism do? It does not lift the ban. It blesses the *Shudra* for his moral courage to give up property! It is well worth quoting Mr Gandhi's own words. Here they are:[h]

The Shudra who only serves (the higher caste) as a matter of religious duty, and who will never own any property, who indeed has not even the ambition to own anything, is deserving of thousand obeisance... The very Gods will shower down flowers on him.

Another illustration in support is the attitude of Gandhism towards the scavenger. The sacred law of the Hindus lays down that a scavenger's progeny shall live by scavenging. Under Hinduism scavenging was not a matter of choice, it was a matter of force. What does Gandhism do? It seeks to perpetuate this system by praising scavenging as the noblest service to society! Let me quote Mr Gandhi: As a President of a Conference of the Untouchables, Mr Gandhi said:[i]

I do not want to attain *Moksha*. I do not want to be reborn. But if I have to be reborn, I should be born an untouchable, so that I may share their sorrows, sufferings and the affronts levelled at them, in order that I may endeavour to free myself and them from that miserable condition. I, therefore prayed that if I should be born again, I should do so not as a Brahmin, Kshatriya, Vaishya, or Shudra, but as an Atishudra...

I love scavenging. In my Ashram, an eighteen years old Brahmin lad is doing the scavenger's work in order to teach the Ashram scavenger cleanliness. The lad is no reformer. He was born and bred in orthodoxy...

[h] Quoted from *Varna Vyavastha*, p. 51.
[i] *Young India*, 27 April 1921.

But he felt that his accomplishments were incomplete until he had become also a perfect sweeper, and that, if he wanted the Ashram sweeper to do his work well, he must do it himself and set an example.

You should realize that you are cleaning Hindu Society.

Can there be a worse example of false propaganda than this attempt of Gandhism to perpetuate evils which have been deliberately imposed by one class over another? If Gandhism preached the rule of poverty for all and not merely for the Shudra the worst that could be said about it is that it is a mistaken idea. But why preach it as good for one class only? Why appeal to the worst of human failings, namely, pride and vanity in order to make him voluntarily accept what on a rational basis he would resent as a cruel discrimination against him? What is the use of telling the scavenger that even a Brahmin is prepared to do scavenging when it is clear that according to Hindu *Shastras* and Hindu notions even if a Brahmin did scavenging he would never be subject to the disabilities of one who is a born scavenger? For in India a man is not a scavenger because of his work. He is a scavenger because of his birth irrespective of the question whether he does scavenging or not. If Gandhism preached that scavenging is a noble profession with the object of inducing those who refuse to engage in it, one could understand it. But why appeal to the scavenger's pride and vanity in order to induce him and him only to keep on scavenging[j] by telling him that scavenging is a noble profession and that he need not be ashamed of it? To preach that poverty is good for the *Shudra* and for none else, to preach that scavenging is good for the Untouchables and for none else and to make them accept these onerous impositions as voluntary purposes of life, by appeal to their failings is an outrage and a cruel joke on the helpless classes which none but Mr Gandhi can perpetuate with equanimity and impunity. In this connection one is reminded of the words of Voltaire who in repudiation of an 'ism' very much like Gandhism said:

Oh! Mockery to say to people that the suffering of some brings joy to others and works good to the whole! What solace is it to a dying man to know that from his decaying body a thousand worms will come into life?[196]

[j] Some of the Provinces of India have laws which make refusal by a scavenger to do scavenging a crime for which he can be tried and punished by a criminal court.

Criticism apart, this is the technique of Gandhism, to make wrongs done appear to the very victim as though they were his privileges. If there is an 'ism' which has made full use of religion as an opium to lull the people into false beliefs and false security, it is Gandhism. Following Shakespeare one can well say: Plausibility! Ingenuity! Thy name is Gandhism.

IV

Such is Gandhism. Having known what is Gandhism the answer to the question, 'Should Gandhism become the law of the land what would be the lot of the Untouchables under it,' cannot require much scratching of the brain. How would it compare with the lot of the lowest Hindu? Enough has been said to show what would be his lot should the Gandhian social order come into being. In so far as the lowest Hindu and the Untouchable belong to the same disinherited class, the Untouchable's lot cannot be better. If anything it might easily be worse. Because in India even the lowest man among the Caste Hindus—why even the aboriginal and Hill Tribe man—though educationally and economically not very much above the Untouchables is still superior to the Untouchables. It is not that he regards himself as superior to the Untouchables. The Hindu society accepts his claim to superiority over the Untouchables. The Untouchable will therefore continue to suffer the worst fate as he does now namely, in prosperity he will be the last to be employed and in depression the first to be fired.

What does Gandhism do to relieve the Untouchables from this fate? Gandhism professes to abolish Untouchability. That is hailed as the greatest virtue of Gandhism. But what does this virtue amount to in actual life? To assess the value of this anti-Untouchability which is regarded as a very big element in Gandhism, it is necessary to understand fully the scope of Mr Gandhi's programme for the removal of Untouchability. Does it mean anything more than that the Hindus will not mind touching the Untouchables? Does it mean the removal of the ban on the right of the Untouchables to education? It would be better to take the two questions separately.

To start with the first question, Mr Gandhi does not say that a Hindu should not take a bath after touching the Untouchables. If Mr Gandhi does not object to it as a purification of pollution then it is difficult to see how Untouchability can be said to vanish by touching the Untouchables. Untouchability centres round the idea of pollution by contact and purification by bath to remove the pollution. Does it mean social assimilation with the Hindus? Mr Gandhi has most categorically stated that removal of Untouchability does not mean inter-dining or inter-marriage between the Hindus and the Untouchables. Mr Gandhi's anti-Untouchability means that the Untouchables will be classed as *Shudras* instead of being classed as Ati-Shudras.[k] There is nothing more in it. Mr Gandhi has not considered the question whether the old Shudras will accept the new Shudras into their fold. If they don't then the removal of Untouchability is a senseless proposition for it will still keep the Untouchables as a separate social category. Mr Gandhi probably knows that the abolition of Untouchability will not bring about the assimilation of the Untouchables by the *Shudras*. That seems to be the reason why Mr Gandhi himself has given a new and a different name to the Untouchables. The new name registers by anticipation what is likely to be the fact. By calling the Untouchables *Harijans* Mr Gandhi has killed two birds with one stone. He has shown that assimilation of the Untouchables by the Shudras is not possible. He has also by his new name counteracted assimilation and made it impossible.

Regarding the second question, it is true that Gandhism is prepared to remove the old ban placed by the Hindu *Shastras* on the right of the Untouchables to education and permit them to acquire knowledge and learning. Under Gandhism the Untouchables may study law, they may study medicine, they may study engineering or anything else they may fancy. So far so good. But will the Untouchables be free to make use of their knowledge and learning? Will they have the right to choose their profession? Can they adopt the career of lawyer, doctor or engineer? To these questions the answer which Gandhism gives is an emphatic 'no.'[l] The Untouchables must follow their hereditary professions. That those occupations they are unclean is no answer: That before the occupation became hereditary it was the result of force and not volition does not matter. The argument of Gandhism is that what is once settled is settled for ever even if it was wrongly settled.

[k] *Young India*, 5 February 1925.
[l] See *supra*, pages 275–7 for Mr Gandhi's views on the subject.

Under Gandhism the Untouchables are to be eternal scavengers. There is no doubt that the Untouchables would much prefer the orthodox system of Untouchability. A compulsory state of ignorance imposed upon the Untouchables by the Hindu Shastras made scavenging bearable. But Gandhism which compels an educated Untouchable to do scavenging is nothing short of cruelty. The grace in Gandhism is a curse in its worst form. The virtue of the anti-Untouchability plank in Gandhism is quite illusory. There is no substance in it.

<h1 style="text-align:center">V</h1>

What else is there in Gandhism which the Untouchables can accept as opening a way for their ultimate salvation? Barring this illusory campaign against Untouchability, Gandhism is simply another form of *Sanatanism* which is the ancient name for militant orthodox Hinduism. What is there in Gandhism which is not to be found in orthodox Hinduism? There is caste in Hinduism, there is caste in Gandhism. Hinduism believes in the law of hereditary profession, so does Gandhism. Hinduism enjoins cow-worship. So does Gandhism. Hinduism upholds the law of *karma*, predestination of man's condition in this world, so does Gandhism. Hinduism accepts the authority of the Shastras. So does Gandhism. Hinduism believes in *avatars* or incarnations of God. So does Gandhism. Hinduism believes in idols, so does Gandhism.[m] All that Gandhism has done is to find a philosophic justification for Hinduism and its dogmas. Hinduism is bald in the sense that it is just a set of rules which bear on their face the appearance of a crude and cruel system. Gandhism supplies the philosophy which smoothens its surface and gives it the appearance of decency and respectability and so alters it and embellishes it as to make it even attractive. What philosophy does Gandhism propound to cover the nudity of Hinduism? This philosophy can be put in a nutshell. It is a philosophy which says that 'All that is in Hinduism is well, all that is in Hinduism is necessary for public good.' Those who are familiar with Voltaire's *Candide* will recognize that it is the philosophy of Master Pangiloss and recall the mockery

[m] Mr Gandhi's articles of faith have been outlined by him in *Young India* of 6 October 1921.

Voltaire made of it. The Hindus are of course pleased with it. No doubt it suits them and accords with their interest. Professor Radhakrishnan—whether out of genuine feeling or out of syco-phancy we need not stop to inquire—has gone to the length of describing Mr Gandhi as 'God on earth.'[197] What do the Untouch-ables understand this to mean? To them it means that: 'This God by name Gandhi came to console an afflicted race: He saw India and changed it not saying all is well and will be, if the Hindus will only fulfil the law of caste. He told the afflicted race, "I have come to fulfil the law of caste." Not a tittle, not a jot shall I allow to abate from it.'

What hope can Gandhism offer to the Untouchables? To the Untouchables Hinduism is a veritable chamber of horrors. The sanctity and infallibility of the Vedas, Smritis and Shastras, the iron law of caste, the heartless law of karma and the senseless law of status by birth are to the Untouchables veritable instruments of torture which Hinduism has forged against the Untouchables. These very instruments which have mutilated, blasted and blighted the life of the Untouchables are to be found intact and untarnished in the bosom of Gandhism. How can the Untouchables say that Gandhism is a heaven and not a chamber of horrors as Hinduism has been? The only reaction and a very natural reaction of the Untouchables would be to run away from Gandhism.

Gandhists may say that what I have stated applies to the old type of Gandhism. There is a new Gandhism, Gandhism without caste. This has reference to the recent statement[n] of Mr Gandhi that caste is an anachronism. Reformers were naturally gladdened by this declaration of Mr Gandhi. And who would not be glad to see that a man like Mr Gandhi having such terrible influence over the Hindus, after having played the most mischievous part of a social reactionary, after having stood out as the protagonist of the caste system, after having beguiled and befooled the unthinking Hindus with arguments which made no distinction between what is fair and foul should have come out with this recantation? But is this really a matter for jubilation? Does it change the nature of Gandhism? Does it make Gandhism a new and a better 'ism' than it was before. Those who are carried away by this recantation of Mr Gandhi, forget two things. In the first place all that Mr Gandhi

[n] *Hindustan Times*, 15 April 1945.

has said is that caste is an anachronism. He does not say it is an evil. He does not say it is anathema. Mr Gandhi may be taken to be not in favour of caste. But Mr Gandhi does not say that he is against the *Varna* system. And what is Mr Gandhi's *Varna* system? It is simply a new name for the caste system and retains all the worst features of the caste system.

The declaration of Mr Gandhi cannot be taken to mean any fundamental change in Gandhism. It cannot make Gandhism acceptable to the Untouchables. The Untouchables will still have ground to say: 'Good God! Is this man Gandhi our Saviour?'

14

Buddha or Karl Marx

A comparison between Karl Marx and Buddha may be regarded as a joke. There need be no surprise in this. Marx and Buddha are divided by 2381 years. Buddha was born in 563 BC and Karl Marx in AD 1818. Karl Marx is supposed to be the architect of a new ideology-policy—a new Economic system. The Buddha on the other hand is believed to be no more than the founder of a religion which has no relation to politics or economics. The heading of this essay 'Buddha or Karl Marx' which suggests either a comparison or a contrast between two such personalities divided by such a lengthy span of time and occupied with different fields of thought is sure to sound odd. The Marxists may easily laugh at it and may ridicule the very idea of treating Marx and Buddha on the same level. Marx so modern and Buddha so ancient! The Marxists may say that the Buddha as compared to their master must be just primitive. What comparison can there be between two such persons? What could a Marxist learn from the Buddha? What can Buddha teach a Marxist? Nonetheless a comparison between the two is attractive and instructive. Having read both and being interested in the ideology of both, a comparison between them just forces itself on me. If the Marxists keep back their prejudices and study the Buddha and understand what he stood for I feel sure that they will change their attitude. It is of course too much to expect that having been determined to scoff at the Buddha they will remain to pray. But this much can be said that they will realize that there is something in the Buddha's teachings which is worth their while to take note of.

THE CREED OF THE BUDDHA

The Buddha is generally associated with the doctrine of Ahimsa. That is taken to be the be-all and end-all of his teachings. Hardly any one knows that what the Buddha taught is something very vast; far beyond Ahimsa. It is therefore necessary to set out in detail his tenets. I enumerate them below as I have understood them from my reading of the *Tripitaka*:

1. Religion is necessary for a free Society.

2. Not every Religion is worth having.

3. Religion must relate to facts of life and not the theories and speculations about God, or Soul or Heaven or Earth.

4. It is wrong to make God the centre of Religion.

5. It is wrong to make salvation of the soul as the centre of Religion.

6. It is wrong to make animal sacrifices to be the centre of religion.

7. Real Religion lives in the heart of man and not in the *Shastras*.

8. Man and morality must be the centre of Religion. If not, religion is a cruel superstition.

9. It is not enough for Morality to be the ideal of life. Since there is no God it must become the law of life.

10. The function of Religion is to reconstruct the world and to make it happy and not to explain its origin or its end.

11. That the unhappiness in the world is due to conflict of interest and the only way to solve it is to follow the *Ashtanga Marga*.

12. That private ownership of property brings power to one class and sorrow to another.

13. That it is necessary for the good of Society that this sorrow be removed by removing its cause.

14. All human beings are equal.

15. Worth and not birth is the measure of man.

16. What is important is high ideals and not noble birth.

17. *Maitri* or fellowship towards all must never be abandoned. One owes it even to one's enemy.

18. Everyone has a right to learn. Learning is as necessary for man to live as food is.

19. Learning without character is dangerous.

20. Nothing is infallible. Nothing is binding forever. Everything is subject to inquiry and examination.

21. Nothing is final.

22. Everything is subject to the law of causation.

23. Nothing is permanent or *sanatan*. Everything is subject to change. Being is always Becoming.

24. War is wrong unless it is for truth and justice.

25. The victor has duties towards the vanquished.

This is the creed of the Buddha in a summary form. How ancient but how fresh! How wide and how deep are his teachings!

THE ORIGINAL CREED OF KARL MARX

Let us now turn to the creed of Karl Marx as originally propounded by him. Karl Marx is no doubt the father of modern socialism or Communism but he was not interested merely in propounding the theory of Socialism. That had been done long before him by others. Marx was more interested in proving that his Socialism was scientific. His crusade was as much against the capitalists as it was against those whom he called the Utopian Socialists. He disliked them both. It is necessary to note this point because Marx attached the greatest importance to the scientific character of his Socialism. All the doctrines which Marx propounded had no other purpose than to establish his contention that his brand of Socialism was scientific and not Utopian.

By scientific socialism what Karl Marx meant was that his brand of socialism was *inevitable* and *inescapable* and that society was moving towards it and that nothing could prevent its march. It is to prove this contention of his that Marx principally laboured.

Marx's contention rested on the following theses. They were:

(i) That the purpose of philosophy is to reconstruct the world and not to explain the origin of the universe.

(ii) That the forces which shape the course of history are primarily economic.

(iii) That society is divided into two classes, owners and workers.

(iv) That there is always a class conflict going on between the two classes.

(v) That the workers are exploited by the owners who misappropriate the surplus value which is the result of the workers' labour.

(vi) That this exploitation can be put to an end by nationalization of the instruments of production, i.e. abolition of private property.

(vii) That this exploitation is leading to greater and greater impoverishment of the workers.

(viii) That this growing impoverishment of the workers is resulting in a revolutionary spirit among the workers and the conversion of the class conflict into a class struggle.

(ix) That as the workers outnumber the owners, the workers are bound to capture the State and establish their rule which he called the dictatorship of the proletariat.

(x) These factors are irresistible and therefore socialism is inevitable.

I hope I have reported correctly the propositions which formed the original basis of Marxian Socialism.

WHAT SURVIVES OF THE MARXIAN CREED

Before making a comparison between the ideologies of the Buddha and Karl Marx it is necessary to note how much of this original corpus of the Marxian creed has survived; how much has been disproved by history and how much has been demolished by his opponents.

The Marxian Creed was propounded sometime in the middle of the nineteenth century. Since then it has been subjected to much criticism. As a result of this criticism much of the ideological structure raised by Karl Marx has broken to pieces. There is hardly any doubt that Marxist claim that his socialism was inevitable has been completely disproved. The dictatorship of the Proletariat was first established in 1917 in one country after a period of something like seventy years after the publication of his *Das Capital* the gospel of socialism. Even when Communism—which is another name for the dictatorship of the Proletariat—came to Russia, it did not come as something inevitable without any kind of human effort. There was a revolution and much deliberate planning had to be done with a lot of violence and bloodshed, before it could step into Russia. The rest of the world is still waiting for coming of the Proletarian Dictatorship. Apart from this general falsification of the Marxian thesis that Socialism is inevitable, many of the other propositions stated in the lists have also been demolished both by logic as well as by experience. Nobody now accepts the economic interpretation of history as the only explanation of history. Nobody accepts that the proletariat has been progressively pauperized. And the same is true about his other premises.

What remains of Karl Marx is a residue of fire, small but still very important. The residue in my view consists of four items:

(i) The function of philosophy is to reconstruct the world and not to waste its time in explaining the origin of the world.

(ii) That there is a conflict of interest between class and class.

(iii) That private ownership of property brings power to one class and sorrow to another through exploitation.

(iv) That it is necessary for the good of society that the sorrow be removed by the abolition of private property.

COMPARISON BETWEEN BUDDHA AND KARL MARX

Taking the points from the Marxian Creed which have survived one may now enter upon a comparison between the Buddha and Karl Marx.

On the first point there is complete agreement between the Buddha and Karl Marx. To show how close is the agreement I quote below a part of the dialogue between Buddha and the Brahmin Potthapada.

Then, in the same terms, Potthapada asked (the Buddha) each of the following questions:

1. Is the world not eternal?
2. Is the world finite?
3. Is the world infinite?

4. Is the soul the same as the body?
5. Is the soul one thing, and the body another?
6. Does one who has gained the truth live again after death?
7. Does he neither live again, nor not live again, after death?

And to each question the exalted one made the same reply: It was this.

That too, Potthapada, is a matter on which I have expressed no opinion.

But why has the Exalted One expressed no opinion on that?

(Because) This question is not calculated to profit, it is not concerned with (the Dhamma) it does not rebound even to the elements of right conduct, nor to detachment nor to purification from lust, nor to quietude, nor to tranquilisation of heart, nor to real knowledge, nor to the insight (of the higher stages of the Path), nor to Nirvana. Therefore it is that I express no opinion upon it.

On the second point I give below a quotation from a dialogue between Buddha and King Pasenadi of Kosala:

Moreover, there is always strife going on between kings, between nobles, between Brahmins, between householders, between mother and son, between son and father, between brother and sister, between sister and brother, between companion and companion...

Although these are the words of Pasenadi, the Buddha did not deny that they formed a true picture of society.

As to the Buddha's own attitude towards class conflict his doctrine of Ashtanga Marga recognizes that class conflict exists and that it is the class conflict which is the cause of misery.

On the third question I quote from the same dialogue of Buddha with Potthapada:

Then what is it that the Exalted One has determined?
I have expounded, Potthapada, that sorrow and misery exist!

I have expounded, what is the origin of misery. I have expounded what is the cessation of misery; I have expounded what is the method by which one may reach the cessation of misery.

'And why has the Exalted One put forth a statement as to that?'

Because that question Potthapada, is calculated to profit, is concerned with the Dhamma, rebounds to the beginnings of right conduct, to detachment, to purification from lusts, to quietude, to tranquilisation of heart, to real knowledge, to the insight of the higher stages of the Path and to Nirwana. Therefore is it, Potthapada that I have put forward a statement as to that.

That language is different but the meaning is the same. If for misery one reads exploitation, Buddha is not away from Marx.

On the question of private property the following extract from a dialogue between Buddha and Ananda is very illuminating. In reply to a question by Ananda the Buddha said:

'I have said that avarice is because of possession. Now in what way that is so, Ananda, is to be understood after this manner. Where there is no possession of any sort or kind whatever by anyone or anything, then there being no possession whatever, would there, owing to this cessation of possession, be any appearance of avarice?'

'There would not, Lord.'

'Wherefore, Ananda, just that is the ground, the basis, the genesis, the cause of avarice, to wit, possession.

'I have said that tenacity is the cause of possession. Now in what way that is so, Ananda, is to be understood after this manner. Where there is no tenacity of any sort or kind whatever shown by any one with respect to any thing, then there being whatever, would there owing to this cessation of tenacity, be any appearance of possession?'

'There would not, Lord.'

'Wherefore, Ananda, just that is the ground, the basis, the genesis, the cause of possession, to wit tenacity.'

On the fourth point no evidence is necessary. The rules of the Bhikshu Sangh will serve as the best testimony on the subject.

According to the rules, a Bhikku can have private property only in the following eight articles and no more. These eight articles are:

1-3. Three robes or pieces of cloth for daily wear.

4. a girdle for the loins.

5. an alms-bowl.

6. a razor.

7. a needle.

8. a water-strainer.

Further a Bhikku was completely forbidden to receive gold or silver for fear that with gold or silver he might buy something beside the eight things he is permitted to have.

These rules are far more rigorous than are to be found in Communism in Russia.

THE MEANS

We must now come to the means. The means of bringing about communism which the Buddha propounded were quite definite. The means can be divided into three parts.

Part I consisted in observing the *Pancha Silas*.

The Enlightenment gave birth to a new gospel which contains the key to the solution of the problem which was haunting him.

The foundation of the New Gospel is the fact that the world was full of misery and unhappiness. It was a fact not merely to be noted but to be regarded as being the first and foremost in any scheme of salvation. The recognition of this fact was the starting point of Buddha's gospel.

To remove this misery and unhappiness was to him the aim and object of the gospel if it is to serve any useful purpose.

Asking what could be the causes of this misery, the Buddha found that there could be only two.

A part of the misery and unhappiness of man was the result of his own misconduct. To remove this cause of misery he preached the practice of *Pancha Sila*.

The *Pancha Sila* comprised the following observations:

(1) To abstain from destroying or causing destruction of any living thing; (2) To abstain from stealing i.e. acquiring or keeping by fraud or violence, the property of another; (3) To abstain from telling untruth; (4) To abstain from lust; (5) To abstain from intoxicating drinks.

A part of the misery and unhappiness in the world was according to the Buddha the result of man's inequity towards man. How was this inequity to be removed? For the removal of man's inequity towards man the Buddha prescribed the Noble Eight-Fold Path. The elements of the Noble Eight-Fold Path are:

(1) Right views i.e. freedom from superstition; (2) Right aims, high and worthy of the intelligent and earnest men; (3) Right speech i.e. kindly, open, truthful; (4) Right conduct i.e. peaceful, honest and pure; (5) Right livelihood i.e. causing hurt or injury to no living being; (6) Right perseverance in all the other seven; (7) Right mindfulness i.e. with a watchful and active mind; and (8) Right contemplation i.e. earnest thought on the deep mysteries of life.

The aim of the Noble Eight-Fold Path is to establish on earth the kingdom of righteousness, and thereby to banish sorrow and unhappiness from the face of the world.

The third part of the Gospel is the doctrine of Nibbana. The doctrine of Nibbana is an integral part of the doctrine of the Noble Eight-Fold Path. Without Nibbana the realization of the Eight-Fold Path cannot be accomplished

The doctrine of Nibbana tells us what the difficulties in the way of the realization of the Eight-Fold Path are.

The chief of these difficulties are ten in number. The Buddha called them the Ten *Asavas*, fetters or hindrances.

The first hindrance is the delusion of self. So long as a man is wholly occupied with himself, chasing after every bauble that he vainly thinks will satisfy the cravings of his heart, there is no noble path for him. Only when his eyes have been opened to the fact that he is but a tiny part of a measureless whole, only when he begins to realize how impermanent a thing is his temporary individuality, can he even enter upon this narrow path.

The second is doubt and indecision. When a man's eyes are opened to the great mystery of existence, the impermanence of every individuality, he is likely to be assailed by doubt and indecision as to his action. To do or not to do, after all my individuality is impermanent, why do anything—are questions, which make him indecisive or inactive. But that will not do in life. He must make up his mind to follow the teacher, to accept the truth and to enter the struggle or he will get no further.

The third is dependence on the efficacy of rites and ceremonies. No good resolutions, however firm will lead to anything unless a man gets rid of ritualism; of the belief that any outward acts, any priestly powers, and holy ceremonies, can afford him assistance of any kind. It is only when he has overcome this hindrance, that men can be said to have fairly entered upon the stream and have a chance sooner or later to win a victory.

The fourth consists of the bodily passions.

The fifth is ill-will towards other individuals.

The sixth is the suppression of the desire for a future life with a material body and the seventh is the desire for a future life in an immaterial world.

The eighth hindrance is pride and nineth is self-righteousness. These are failings which it is most difficult for men to overcome, and to which superior minds are peculiarly liable—a prosaical contempt for those who are less able and less holy than themselves.

The tenth hindrance is ignorance. When all other difficulties are conquered this will even remain, the thorn in the flesh of the wise and good, the last enemy and the bitterest foe of man.

Nibbana consists in overcoming these hindrances to the pursuit of the Noble Eight-Fold Path.

The doctrine of the Noble Eight-Fold Path tells what disposition of the mind which a person should sedulously cultivate. The doctrine of Nibbana tells of the temptation or hindrance which a person should earnestly overcome if he wishes to trade along with the Noble Eight-Fold Path.

The fourth part of the new Gospel is the doctrine of *Paramitas*. The doctrine of Paramitas inculcates the practice of ten virtues in one's daily life.

These are those ten virtues—(1) *Panna* (2) *Sila* (3) *Nekkhama* (4) *Dana* (5) *Virya* (6) *Khanti* (7) *Succa* (8) *Aditthana* (9) *Metta* and (10) *Upekka*.

Panna or wisdom is the light that removes the darkness of *Avijja*, *Moha* or nescience. Panna requires that one must get all his doubts removed by questioning those wiser than himself, associate with the wise and cultivate the different arts and sciences which help to develop the mind.

Sila is moral temperament, the disposition not to do evil and the disposition to do good; to be ashamed of doing wrong. To avoid to do evil for fear of punishment is Sila. Sila means fear of doing wrong.

Nekkhama is renunciation of the pleasures of the world.

Dana means the giving of one's possessions, blood and limbs and even one's life for the good of the others without expecting anything in return.

Virya is right endeavour. It is doing with all your might with no thought of turning back, whatever you have undertaken to do.

Khanti is forbearance. Not to meet hatred by hatred is the essence of it. For hatred is not appeased by hatred. It is appeased only by forbearance.

Succa is truth. An aspirant for Buddha never speaks a lie. His speech is truth and nothing but truth.

Aditthana is resolute determination to reach the goal.

Metta is fellow-feeling extending to all beings, foe and friend, beast and man.

Upekka is detachment as distinguished from indifference. It is a state of mind where there is neither like nor dislike. Remaining unmoved by the result and yet engaged in the pursuit of it.

These virtues one must practice to his utmost capacity. That is why they are called *Paramitas* (States of Perfection).

Such is the gospel the Buddha enunciated as a result of his enlightenment to end the sorrow and misery in the world.

It is clear that the means adopted by the Buddha were to convert a man by changing his moral disposition to follow the path voluntarily.

The means adopted by the Communists are equally clear, short and swift. They are (1) Violence and (2) Dictatorship of the Proletariat.

The Communists say that there are the only two means of establishing Communism. The first is violence. Nothing short of it will suffice to break up the existing system. The other is dictatorship of the proletariat. Nothing short of it will suffice to continue the new system.

It is now clear what the similarities and differences between Buddha and Karl Marx are. The differences are about the means. The end is common to both.

EVALUATION OF MEANS

We must now turn to the evaluation of means. We must ask whose means are superior and lasting in the long run. There are, however, some misunderstandings on both sides. It is necessary to clear them up.

Take violence. As to violence there are many people who seem to shiver at the very thought of it. But this is only a sentiment. Violence cannot be altogether dispensed with. Even in non-Communist countries a murderer is hanged. Does not hanging amount to violence? Non-Communist countries go to war with non-Communist countries. Millions of people are killed. Is this no violence? If a murderer can be killed, because he has killed a citizen if a soldier can be killed in war because he belongs to a hostile nation why cannot a property owner be killed if his ownership leads to misery for the rest of humanity? There is no reason to make an exception in favour of the property owner, why one should regard private property as sacrosanct.

The Buddha was against violence. But he was also in favour of justice and where justice required he permitted the use of force. This is well illustrated in his dialogue with Sinha Senapati, the Commander-in-chief of Vaishali. Sinha having come to know that the Buddha preached Ahimsa went to him and asked:

The Bhagvan preaches Ahimsa. Does the Bhagvan preach an offender to be given freedom from punishment? Does the Bhagvan preach that we should not go to war to save our wives, our children and our wealth? Should we suffer at the hands of criminals in the name of Ahimsa?

Does the Tathagata prohibit all war even when it is in the interest of Truth and Justice?

Buddha replied, 'You have wrongly understood what I have been preaching. An offender must be punished and an innocent man must be freed. It is not a fault of the Magistrate if he punishes an offender. The cause of punishment is the fault of the offender. The Magistrate who inflicts the punishment is only carrying out the law. He does not become stained with Ahimsa. A man who fights for justice and safety cannot be accused of Ahimsa. If all the means of maintaining peace have failed then the responsibility for Himsa falls on him who starts war. One must never surrender to evil powers. War there may be. But it must not be for selfish ends....'

There are of course other grounds against violence such as those urged by Professor John Dewey. In dealing with those who contend that the end justifies the means is morally perverted doctrine, Dewey has rightly asked—what can justify the means if not the end? It is only the end that can justify the means.[198]

Buddha would have probably admitted that it is only the end which would justify the means. What else could? And he would have said that if the end justified violence, violence was a legitimate means for end in view. He certainly would not have exempted property owners from force if force was the only means for that end. As we shall see his means for the end were different. As Professor Dewey has pointed out that violence is only another name for the use of force and although force must be used for creative purposes a distinction between use of force as energy and use of force as violence needs to be made. The achievement of an end involves the destruction of many other ends which are integral with the one that is sought to be destroyed. Use of force must be so regulated that it should save as many ends as possible in destroying the evil one. Buddha's Ahimsa was not as absolute as the Ahimsa preached by Mahavira the founder of Jainism. He would have allowed force only as energy. The Communists preach Ahimsa as an absolute principle. To this the Buddha was deadly opposed.

As to dictatorship, the Buddha would have none of it. He was born a democrat and he died a democart. At the time he lived there were 14 monarchical states and 4 republics. He belonged to the Sakyas and the Sakya's kingdom was a republic. He was extremely in love with Vaishali which was his second home because it was a republic. Before his *Mahaparinirbban* he spent his *Varshavasa* in Vaishali. After the completion of his *Varshavasa* he decided to leave Vaishali and go elsewhere as was his wont. After going some distance he looked back on Vaishali and said to Ananda, 'This is the last look of Vaishali which the Tathagata is having.' So fond was he of this republic.

He was a thorough equalitarian. Originally the Bhikkus, including the Buddha himself, wore robes made of rags. This rule was enunciated to prevent the aristocratic classes from joining the Sangh. Later Jeevaka, the great physician prevailed upon the Buddha to accept a robe which was made of a whole cloth. The Buddha at once altered the rule and extended it to all the monks.

Once the Buddha's mother, Mahaprajapati Gotami who had joined the Bhikkuni Sangh, heard that the Buddha had got a chill. She at once started preparing a scarf for him. After having completed it she took it to the Buddha and asked him to wear it. But he refused to accept it saying that if it is a gift it must be a gift to the whole Sangh and not to an individual member of the Sangh. She pleaded and pleaded but he refused to yield.

The Bhikshu Sangh had the most democratic constitution. The Buddha was only one of the Bhikkus. At the most he was like a Prime Minister among members of the Cabinet. He was never a dictator. Twice before his death he was asked to appoint someone as the head of the Sangh to control it. But each time he refused saying that the Dhamma is the Supreme Commander of the Sangh. He refused to be a dictator and refused to appoint a dictator.

What about the value of the means? Whose means are superior and lasting in the long run?

Can the Communists say that in achieving their valuable end they have not destroyed other valuable ends? They have destroyed private property. Assuming that this is a valuable end, can the Communists say that they have not destroyed other valuable ends in the process of achieving it? How many people have they killed for achieving their end. Has human life no value? Could they not have taken property without taking the life of the owner?

Take dictatorship. The end of dictatorship is to make the revolution a permanent revolution. This is a valuable end. But can the Communists say that in achieving this end they have not destroyed other valuable ends? Dictatorship is often defined as absence of liberty or absence of Parliamentary Government. Both interpretations are not quite clear. There is no liberty even when there is Parliamentary Government. For law means want of liberty. The difference between dictatorship and Parliamentary Government lies in this. In Parliamentary Government every citizen has a right to criticize the restraint on liberty imposed by the government. In Parliamentary Government you have a duty and a right; the duty to obey the law and right to criticize it. In dictatorship you have only duty to obey but no right to criticize it.

Whose Means are More Efficacious

We must not consider whose means are more lasting. One has to choose between government by force and government by moral disposition.

As Burke has said, force cannot be a lasting means. In his speech on conciliation with America he uttered this memorable warning:

First, Sir, permit me to observe, that the use of force alone is but temporary. It may subdue for a moment; but it does not remove the necessity of subduing again; and a nation is not governed which is perpetually to be conquered.

My next objection is its uncertainty. Terror is not always the effect of force, and an armament is not a victory. If you do not succeed, you are without resource, for, conciliation failing, force remains; but force failing, no further hope of reconciliation is left. Power and authority are sometimes bought by kindness; but they can never be begged as alms by an impoverished and defeated violence.

A further objection to force is, that you impair the object by your very endeavours to preserve it. The thing you fought for is the thing which you recover, but depreciated, sunk, wasted and consumed in the contest.[199]

What the Buddha wanted was that each man should be morally so trained that he may himself become a sentinel for the kingdom of righteousness.

WITHERING AWAY OF THE STATE

The Communists themselves admit that their theory of the State as a permanent dictatorship is a weakness in their political philosophy. They take shelter under the plea that the State will ultimately wither away. There are two questions which they have to answer. When will it wither away? What will take the place of the State when it withers away? To the first question they can give no definite time. Dictatorship for a short period may be good and a welcome thing even for making democracy safe. Why should not dictatorship liquidate itself after it has done its work, after it has removed all the obstacles and boulders in the way of democracy and has made the path of democracy safe. Did not Asoka set an example? He practised violence against the Kalingas. But thereafter he renounced violence completely. If our victors today not only disarm their victims but also disarm themselves there would be peace all over the world.

The Communists have given no answer. At any rate no satisfactory answer to the question what would take the place of the State when it withers away, though this question is more important than the question when the State will wither away. Will it be succeeded by anarchy? If so the building up of the Communist State is a useless effort. If it cannot be sustained except by force and if it results in anarchy when the force holding it together is withdrawn what good is the communist State?

The only thing which could sustain it after force is withdrawn is religion. But to the Communists religion is anathema. Their hatred of religion is so deep-seated that they will not even discriminate between religions which are helpful to Communism and religions which are not. The Communists have carried their hatred of Christianity to Buddhism without waiting to examine the difference between the two. The charge against Christianity levelled by the Communists was two-fold. Their first charge against Christianity was that they made people other worldly and made them suffer poverty in this world. As can be seen from quotations from Buddhism in the earlier part of this tract such a charge cannot be levelled against Buddhism.

The second charge levelled by the Communists against Christianity cannot be levelled against Buddhism. This charge is summed up in the statement that religion is the opium of the people. This charge is based upon the Sermon on the Mount which is to be found in the Bible. The Sermon on the Mount sublimates poverty and weakness. It promises heaven to the poor and the weak. There is no Sermon on the Mount to be found in the Buddha's teachings. His teaching is to acquire wealth. I give below his Sermon on the subject to Anathapindika, one of his disciples.

Once Anathapindika came to where the Exalted One was staying. Having come he made obeisance to the Exalted One and took a seat at one side and asked 'Will the Enlightened One tell what things are welcome, pleasant, agreeable, to the householder but which are hard to gain.'

The Enlightened One having heard the question put to him said 'Of such things the first is to acquire wealth lawfully.'

'The second is to see that your relations also get their wealth lawfully.'

'The third is to live long and reach great age.'

'Of a truth, householder, for the attainment of these four things, which in the world are welcome, pleasant, agreeable but hard to gain, there are also four conditions precedent. They are the blessing of faith, the blessing of virtuous conduct, the blessing of liberality and the blessing of wisdom.

The blessing of virtuous conduct which abstains from taking life, thieving, unchastity, lying and partaking of fermented liquor.

The blessing of liberality consists in the householder living with mind free from the taint of avarice, generous, open-handed, delighting in gifts, a good one to be asked and devoted to the distribution of gifts.

Wherein consists the blessing of wisdom? He knows that a householder who dwells with his mind overcome by greed, avarice, ill-will, sloth, drowsiness, distraction and flurry, commits wrongful deeds and neglects that which ought to be done, and by so doing, is deprived of happiness and honour.

Greed, avarice, ill-will, sloth and drowsiness, distraction and flurry and doubt are stains of the mind. A householder who gets rid of such stains of the mind acquires great wisdom, abundant wisdom, clear vision and perfect wisdom.

Thus to acquire wealth legitimately and justly, earned by great industry, amassed by strength of the arm and gained by sweat of the brow is a great blessing. The householder makes himself happy and cheerful and preserves himself full of happiness; also makes his parents, wife, and children, servants, and labourers, friends and companions happy and cheerful, and preserves them full of happiness.

The Russians do not seem to be paying any attention to Buddhism as an ultimate aid to sustain Communism when force is withdrawn. The Russians are proud of their Communism. But they forget that the wonder of all wonders is that the Buddha established Communism so far as the Sangh was concerned without dictatorship. It may be that it was Communism on a very small scale but it was Communism without dictatorship, a miracle which Lenin failed to do.

The Buddha's method was different. His method was to change the mind of man: to alter his disposition: so that whatever man does, he does it voluntarily without the use of force or compulsion. His main means to alter the disposition of men was his Dhamma and the constant preaching of his Dhamma. The Buddha's way was not to force people to do what they did not like to do although it was good for them. His way was to alter the disposition of men so that they would do voluntarily what they would not otherwise do.

It has been claimed that the Communist dictatorship in Russia has wonderful achievements to its credit. There can be no denial of it. That is why I say that a Russian dictatorship would be good for all backward countries. But this is no argument for permanent dictatorship. Humanity does not only want economic values, it also wants spiritual values to be retained. Permanent dictatorship has paid no attention to spiritual values and does not seem to intend to. Carlyle called Political Economy a Pig Philosophy. Carlyle was of course wrong. For man needs material comforts. But the Communist Philosophy seems to be equally wrong for the aim of their philosophy seems to be fatten pigs as though men are no better than pigs. Man must grow materially as well as spiritually. Society has been aiming to lay a new foundation was summarized by the French Revolution in three words, Fraternity, Liberty and Equality. The French Revolution was welcomed because of this slogan. It failed to produce equality. We welcome the Russian Revolution because it aims to produce equality. But it cannot be too much emphasized that in producing equality, society cannot afford to sacrifice fraternity or liberty. Equality will be of no value without fraternity or liberty. It seems that the three can co-exist only if one follows the way of the Buddha. Communism can give one but not all.

V

Religion

Although the ideological and the religious domains overlap, there is a clear distinction between them. Ideologies are contested in a field of conflict while religion is accepted by its adherents as upholding a specific universality. Human reason has greater space to intervene in the sphere of ideologies than religion. This is a tentative distinction, as the meaning of religion and ideology and their conceptual boundaries are very fragile.

Krishna and His Gita.[200] This excerpt is taken from 'Krishna and His Gita', a chapter in the uncompleted work *Revolution and Counter-revolution* that Ambedkar worked on in 1950s.

Ambedkar distinguished Hindu scriptures on the basis of pre-Buddhist and post-Buddhist. He considered the *Vedas*, *Brahmanas* and Upanishads as pre-Buddhist while the *Bhagavad Gita* and *Manudharmashastra* etc. were post-Buddhist. Following Pushyamitra and his regicide, Brahmanism was ascendent and attempted to weed out Buddhism. For Ambedkar, the *Gita* is a text which legitimized this counter-revolution while appearing close to Buddha's teachings. He argued that the *Gita* has to be read not as a general treatise on ethics, as commonly projected, but in relation to the discursive context in which it is situated.[201]

The Buddha and His Predecessors.[202] The *Buddha and His Dhamma* is the last major work of Ambedkar posthumously published in 1957. Ambedkar conceived it as the Gospel of Buddhism as well as its defence against its critics. This excerpt spells out the critique that the Buddha made of the different schools of Hinduism.

Does the Buddha have a social message?[203] Ambedkar engaged himself in a specific hermeneutic with regard to the exposition of Buddhism. He questioned the prevailing interpretations and suspected the quality of scholarship deployed for the purpose. In the short passage excerpted from *The Buddha and His Dhamma*, he asserted the contemporaneous relevance of Buddha's message. (The title is slightly changed from the original.)

Conversion ('Away from Hindus').[204] Ambedkar's conversion to Buddhism has often drawn jeers. Here he offers a justification for conversion, looking at the role that religion has played in social existence. This article, compact and forceful, remained unpublished along with his critical reflections on conversion to Christianity and Islam till 1989. It was written following the Mahar Conference in 1936 where a resolution was passed to renounce Hinduism.

As the ideas expressed in this article are of a wider significance, we felt it appropriate to change its title. The original title is given in brackets.

15

Krishna and His Gita

It cannot but be a matter of great surprise to find such a variety of opinion as to the message which the *Bhagvad Gita* preaches. One is forced to ask why there should be such divergence of opinion among scholars? My answer to this question is that scholars have gone on a false errand. They have gone on a search for the message of the *Bhagvad Gita* on the assumption that it is a gospel as the *Koran*, the *Bible* or the *Dhammapada* is. In my opinion this assumption is quite a false assumption. The *Bhagvad Gita* is not a gospel and it can therefore have no message and it is futile to search for one. The question will no doubt be asked: What is the *Bhagvad Gita* if it is not a gospel? My answer is that the *Bhagvad Gita* is neither a book of religion nor a treatise on philosophy. What the *Bhagvad Gita* does is to defend certain dogmas of religion on philosophic grounds. If on that account anybody wants to call it a book of religion or a book of philosophy he may please himself. But essentially it is neither. It uses philosophy to defend religion. My opponents will not be satisfied with a bare statement of view. They would insist on my proving my thesis by reference to specific instances. It is not at all difficult. Indeed it is the easiest task.

The first instance one comes across in reading the *Bhagvad Gita* is the justification of war. Arjuna had declared himself against the war, against killing people for the sake of property. Krishna offers a philosophic defence of war and killing in war.[a] This philosophic defence of war will be found in Chapter 11, verses 11 to 28. The

---

[a] And see, too, Chapter VII, stanza 17, where the man of knowledge is declared to be 'dear' to Krishna.

philosophic defence of war offered by the *Bhagvad Gita* proceeds along two lines of argument. One line of argument is that anyhow the world is perishable and man is mortal. Things are bound to come to an end. Man is bound to die. Why should it make any difference to the wise whether man dies a natural death or whether he is done to death as a result of violence? Life is unreal, why shed tears because it has ceased to be? Death is inevitable, why bother how it has resulted? The second line of argument in justification of war is that it is a mistake to think that the body and the soul are one. They are separate. Not only are the two quite distinct but they differ inasmuch as the body is perishable while the soul is eternal and imperishable. When death occurs it is the body that dies. The soul never dies. Not only does it never die but air cannot dry it, fire cannot burn it, and a weapon cannot cut it. It is therefore wrong to say that when a man is killed his soul is killed. What happens is that his body dies. His soul discards the dead body as a person discards his old clothes—wears new one and carries on. As the soul is never killed, killing a person can never be a matter of any movement. War and killing need therefore give no ground to remorse or to shame, so argues the *Bhagvad Gita*.

Another dogma to which the *Bhagvad Gita* comes forward to offer a philosophic defence is Chaturvarnya. The *Bhagvad Gita*, no doubt, mentions that the Chaturvarnya is created by God and therefore sacrosanct. But it does not make its validity dependent on it. It offers a philosophic basis to the theory of Chaturvarnya by linking it to the theory of innate, inborn qualities in men. The fixing of the Varna of man is not an arbitrary act says the *Bhagvad Gita*. But it is fixed according to his innate, inborn qualities.[b]

The third dogma for which the *Bhagvad Gita* offers philosophic defence is the *Karma Marga*. By Karma marga the *Bhagvad Gita* means the performance of the observances, such as *Yajnas* as a way to salvation. The *Bhagvad Gita* most stands out for the Karma marga throughout and is a great upholder of it. The line it takes to defend Karma yoga is by removing the excrescences which had grown upon it and which had made it appear quite ugly. The first excrescence was blind faith. The *Gita* tries to remove it by introducing the principle of *Buddhi yoga*[c] as a necessary condition

---

[b] *Bhagvad Gita* IV, p. 13.
[c] *Bhagvad Gita* II, pp. 39–53.

for Karma yoga. To become *Stihtaprajna* i.e., 'befitted with *Buddhi*' there is nothing wrong in the performance of *Karma kanda*. The second excrescence on the Karma kanda was the selfishness which was the motive behind the performance of the Karmas. The *Bhagvad Gita* attempts to remove it by introducing the principle of Anasakti i.e. performance of karma without any attachment for the fruits of the Karma.[d] Founded in Buddhi yoga and dissociated from selfish attachment to the fruits of Karma what is wrong with the dogma of Karma kanda? This is how the *Bhagvad Gita* defends the karma marga.[e] It would be quite possible to continue in this strain, to pick up other dogmas and show how the *Gita* comes forward to offer a philosophic defence in their support where none existed before. But this could be done only if one were to write a treatise on the *Bhagvad Gita*. It is beyond the scope of a chapter, the main purpose of which is to assign to the *Bhagvad Gita* its proper place in ancient Indian literature. I have therefore selected the most important dogmas just to illustrate my thesis.

Two other questions are sure to be asked in relation to my thesis. Which are the dogmas for which the *Bhagvad Gita* offers this philosophical defence? Why did it become necessary for the *Bhagvad Gita* to defend these dogmas?

To begin with the first question, the dogmas which *the Gita* defends are the dogmas of counter-revolution as put forth in the Bible of counter-revolution, namely Jaimini's *Purva Mimansa*.[205] There ought to be no difficulty in accepting this proposition. If there is any it is largely due to wrong meaning attached to the word Karma yoga. Most writers on the *Bhagvad Gita* translate the word Karma yoga as 'action' and the word Jnana yoga, as 'knowledge' and proceed to discuss the *Bhagvad Gita* as though it was engaged in comparing and contrasting knowledge versus action in a generalized form. This is quite wrong. The *Bhagvad Gita* is not concerned with any general, philosophical discussion of action versus knowledge. As a matter of fact, the *Gita* is concerned with the particular and not with the general. By Karma yoga or action, *the Gita* means the dogmas contained in Jaimini's Karma kanda and by Jnana yoga or knowledge it means the dogmas contained in Badarayana's *Brahma Sutras*. That the *Gita* in speaking of Karma

---

[d] *Bhagvad Gita II*, p. 47.

[e] This is well summed up in *Bhagvad Gita II*, p. 48.

is not speaking of activity or inactivity, quieticism or energism, in general terms but religious acts and observances cannot be denied by anyone who has read the *Bhagvad Gita*. It is to lift the *Gita* from the position of a party pamphlet engaged in a controversy on small petty points and make it appear as though it was a general treatise on matters of high philosophy that this attempt is made to inflate the meaning of the words Karma and Jnana and make them words of general import. Mr Tilak is largely to be blamed for this trick of patriotic Indians. The result has been that these false meanings have misled people into believing that the *Bhagvad Gita* is an independent self-contained book and has no relation to the literature that has preceded it. But if one were to keep to the meaning of the word Karma yoga as one finds it in the *Bhagvad Gita* itself one would be convinced that in speaking of Karma yoga the *Bhagvad Gita* is referring to nothing but the dogmas of Karma kanda as propounded by Jaimini which it tries to renovate and strengthen.

To take up the second question: Why did the *Bhagvad Gita* feel it necessary to defend the dogmas of counter-revolution? To my mind the answer is very clear. It was to save them from the attack of Buddhism that the *Bhagvad Gita* came into being. Buddha preached non-violence. He not only preached it but the people at large—except the Brahmins—had accepted it as the way of life. They had acquired a repugnance to violence. Buddha preached against Chaturvarnya. He used some of the most offensive similes in attacking the theory of Chaturvarnya. The framework of Chaturvarnya had been broken. The order of Chaturvarnya had been turned upside down. Shudras and women could become *sannyasis*, a status which counter-revolution had denied them. Buddha had condemned the Karma kanda and the Yajnas on the ground of *Himsa* or violence. He condemned them also on the ground that the motive behind them was a selfish desire to obtain a bonus. What was the reply of the counter-revolutionaries to this attack? Only this. These things were ordained by the *Vedas*, the *Vedas* were infallible, therefore the dogmas were not to be questioned. In the Buddhist age, which was the most enlightened and the most rationalistic age India has known, dogmas resting on such silly, arbitrary, unrationalistic and fragile foundations could hardly stand. People who had come to believe in non-violence as a principle of life and had gone so far as to make it a rule of life—

how could they be expected to accept the dogma that the Kshatriya may kill without sinning because the *Vedas* say that it is his duty to kill? People who had accepted the gospel of social equality and who were remaking society on the basis of each one according to his merits—how could they accept the Chaturvarnya theory of gradation, and separation of man based on birth simply because the *Vedas* say so? People who had accepted the doctrine of Buddha that all misery in society is due to *tanha* or what Tawny calls acquisitive instinct—how could they accept the religion which deliberately invited people to obtain boons by sacrifices merely because there is behind it the authority of the *Vedas?* There is no doubt that under the furious attack of Buddhism, Jaimini's counter-revolutionary dogmas were tottering and would have collapsed had they not received the support which the *Bhagvad Gita* gave them. The philosophic defence of the counter-revolutionary doctrines given by the *Bhagvad Gita* is by no means impregnable. The philosophic defence offered by the *Bhagvad Gita* of the Kshatriya's duty to kill is to say the least puerile. To say that killing is no killing because what is killed is the body and not the soul is an unheard of defence of murder. This is one of the doctrines which make some people say that the doctrines make one's hair stand on their end. If Krishna were to appear as a lawyer acting for a client who is being tried for murder and pleaded the defence set out by him in the *Bhagvad Gita* there is not the slightest doubt that he would be sent to the lunatic asylum. Similarly childish is the defence of the *Bhagvad Gita* of the dogma of Chaturvarnya. Krishna defends it on the basis of the *Guna* theory of the Sankhya. But Krishna does not seem to have realized what a fool he has made of himself. In the Chaturvarnya there are four Varnas. But the gunas according to the Sankhya are only three. How can a system of four varnas be defended on the basis of a philosophy which does not recognize more than three varnas? The whole attempt of the *Bhagvad Gita* to offer a philosophic defence of the dogmas of counter-revolution is childish—and does not deserve a moment's serious thought. Nonetheless there is not the slightest doubt that without the help of the *Bhagvad Gita* the counter-revolution would have died out, out of sheer stupidity of its dogmas. Mischievous as it may seem to the revolutionaries the part played by the *Bhagvad Gita*, there is no doubt that it resuscitated counter-revolution and if the counter-revolution lives even today, it is entirely due to the plausibility of the philosophic defence which it received from the *Bhagvad Gita*—anti-Veda and anti-Yajna. Nothing can be a greater mistake than this. As will appear from other portions of the *Bhagvad Gita* that it is not against the authority of the *Vedas* and *Shastras* (XVI, 23, 24: XVII, 11, 13, 24). Nor is it against the sanctity of the yajnas (III. 9–15). It upholds the virtue of both. There is therefore no difference between Jaimini's *Purva Mimansa* and the *Bhagvad Gita*. If anything, the *Bhagvad Gita* is a more formidable supporter of counter-revolution than Jaimini's *Purva Mimansa* could have ever been. It is formidable because it seeks to give to the doctrines of counter-revolution that philosophic and therefore permanent basis which they never had before and without which they would never have survived. Particularly formidable than Jaimini's *Purva Mimansa* is the philosophic support which the *Bhagvad Gita* gives to the central doctrine of counter-revolution—namely Chaturvarnya. The soul of the *Bhagvad Gita* seems to be the defence of Chaturvarnya and securing its observance in practice, Krishna does not merely rest content with saying that Chaturvarnya is based on *Guna-karma* but he goes further and issues two positive injunctions. The first injunction is contained in Chapter III verse 26. In this Krishna says: that a wise man should not by counter-propaganda create a doubt in the mind of an ignorant person who is a follower of Karma kanda which of course includes the observance of the rules of Chaturvarnya. In other words, you must not agitate or excite people to rise in rebellion against the theory of Karma kand and all that it includes. The second injunction is laid down in Chapter XVIII verses 41–8. In this Krishna tells that every one do the duty prescribed for his Varna and no other and warns those who worship him and are his devotees that they will not obtain salvation by mere devotion but by devotion accompanied by observance of duty laid down for his Varna. In short, a Shudra however great he may be as a devotee will not get salvation if he has transgressed the duty of the Shudra—namely to live and die in the service of the higher classes. The second part of my thesis is that the essential function of the *Bhagvad Gita* being to give new support to Jaimini at least those portions of it which offer philosophic defence of Jaimini's doctrines—have come to be written after Jaimini's *Purva Mimansa* had been promulgated. The third part of my thesis is that this philosophic defence of the

Bhagvad Gita of the doctrines of counter-revolution became necessary because of the attack to which they were subjected by the revolutionary and rationalistic thought of Buddhism.

I must now turn to the objections that are likely to be raised against the validity of my thesis. I see one looming large before me. I shall be told that I am assuming that the *Bhagvad Gita* is posterior in time to Buddhism and to Jaimini's *Purva Mimansa* and that this assumption has no warrant behind it. I am aware of the fact that my thesis runs counter to the most cherished view of Indian scholars all of whom, seem to be more concerned in fixing a very ancient date to the composition of the *Bhagvad Gita* far anterior to Buddhism and to Jaimini than in finding out what is the message of the *Bhagvad Gita* and what value it has as a guide to man's life. This is particularly the case with Mr Telang and Mr Tilak. But as Garbe[f] observes 'To Telang, as to every Hindu—how much so ever enlightened—it is an article of faith to believe in so high an antiquity of the *Bhagvad Gita* and where such necessities are powerful criticism indeed comes to an end.'

Professor Garbe observes:

The task of assigning a date to the Gita has been recognized by every one who has earnestly tried to solve the problem, as being very difficult; and the difficulties grow (all the more) if the problem is presented two fold, viz., to determine as well the age of the original Gita as also of its revision. I am afraid that generally speaking, we shall succeed in arriving, not at any certainties, but only at probabilities in this mater.

What are the probabilities? I have no doubt that the probabilities are in favour of my thesis. Indeed so far as I can see there is nothing against it. In examining this question, I propose first to advance direct evidence from the *Gita* itself showing that it has been composed after Jaimini's *Purva Mimansa* and after Buddhism.

Chapter III, verses 9-13 of the *Bhagvad Gita* have a special significance. In this connection it is true that the *Bhagvad Gita* does not refer to Jaimini by name: nor does it mention *Mimansa* by name. But is there any doubt that in Chapter III, verses 9-18 the *Bhagvad Gita* is dealing with the doctrines formulated by Jaimini in his *Purva Mimansa*? Even Mr Tilak[g] who believes in the antiquity of the *Bhagvad Gita* has to admit that here the *Gita* is

[f] Introduction (Indian Antiquary Supplement) p. 30.

[g] *Gita Rahasya*, vol. II, 916-22.

engaged in the examination of the *Purva Mimansa* doctrines. There is another way of presenting this argument. Jaimini preaches pure and simple Karma yoga. The *Bhagvad Gita* on the other hand preaches *anasakti karma*. Thus the *Gita* preaches a doctrine which is fundamentally modified. Not only the *Bhagvad Gita* modifies the Karma yoga but attacks the upholders of pure and simple Karma yoga in somewhat severe terms.[h] If the *Gita* is prior to Jaimini one would expect Jaimini to take note of this attack of the *Bhagvad Gita* and reply to it. But we do not find any reference in Jaimini to this anasakti karma yoga of the *Bhagvad Gita*. Why? The only answer is that this modification came after Jaimini and not before—which is simply another way of saying that the *Bhagvad Gita* was composed after Jaimini's *Purva Mimansa*.

If the *Bhagvad Gita* does not mention *Purva Mimansa* it does mention by name the *Brahma Sutras*[i] of Badarayana. This reference to *Brahma Sutras* is a matter of great significance for it furnishes direct evidence for the conclusion that the Gita is later than the *Brahma Sutras*.

Mr Tilak[j] admits that the reference to the *Brahma Sutras* is a clear and definite reference to the treatise of that name which we now have. It may be pointed out that Mr Telang[k] discusses the subject in a somewhat cavalier fashion by saying that the treatise '*Brahma Sutras*' referred to in the *Bhagvad Gita* is different from the present treatise which goes by that name. He gives no evidence for so extraordinary a proposition but relies on the conjectural statement of Mr Weber[206]—given in a footnote of his treatise in Indian Literature, again without any evidence—that the mention of *Brahma Sutras* in the *Bhagvad Gita* 'may be taken as an appellative rather than as a proper name.' It would not be fair to attribute any particular motives to Mr Telang for the view he has taken on this point. But there is nothing unfair in saying that Mr Telang[l] shied at admitting the reference to *Brahma Sutras* because he saw that Weber had on the authority of Winternitz assigned AD 500 to the

[h] *Bhagvad Gita* II, 42–6 and XVIII 66.
[i] *Bhagvad Gita* XIII, p. 4.
[j] *Gita Rahasya* II, p. 749.
[k] *Bhagvad Gita* (SBE) Introduction, p. 31.
[l] On the other hand, it may be said that Mr Tilak readily admitted the reference because it was his opinion that *Brahma Sutras* were a very ancient treatise—*see* Gita Rahasya, vol. II.

composition of the *Brahma Sutras*, which would have destroyed his cherished theory regarding the antiquity of the *Bhagvad Gita*. There is thus ample internal evidence to support the conclusion that the *Gita* was composed after Jaimini's *Purva Mimansa* and Badarayana's *Brahma Sutras*.

Is the *Bhagvad Gita* anterior to Buddhism? The question was raised by Mr Telang:

We come now to another point. What is the position of the Gita in regard to the great reform of Sakya Muni? The question is one of much interest, having regard particularly to the remarkable coincidences between Buddhistic doctrines and the doctrines of the Gita to which we have drawn attention in the footnotes to our translation. But the materials for deciding the question are unhappily not forthcoming. Professor Wilson, indeed, thought that there was an allusion to Buddhism in the *Gita*,[m] but his idea was based on a confusion between the Buddhists and the *Charvakas* or materialists.[n] Failing that allusion, we have nothing very tangible but the unsatisfactory 'negative argument' based on mere non-mention of Buddhism in the *Gita*. That argument is not quite satisfactory to my own mind, although, as I have elsewhere pointed out,[o] some of the ground occupied by the *Gita* is common to it with Buddhism, and although various previous thinkers are alluded to directly or indirectly in the *Gita*. There is, however, one view of the facts of this question, which appears to me to corroborate the conclusion deducible by means of the negative argument here referred to. The main points on which Buddha's protest against Brahminism rests, seem to be the true authority of the Vedas and the true view of the differences of caste. On most points of doctrinal speculation, Buddhism is still but one aspect of the older Brahminism.[p] The various coincidences to which we have drawn attention show that, if there is need to show it. Well now, on both these points, the *Gita*, while it does not go the whole length which Buddha goes, itself embodies a protest against the views current about the time of its composition. The *Gita* does not, like Buddhism, absolutely reject the *Vedas*, but it shelves them. The *Gita* does not totally root out caste. It places caste on a less untenable basis. One of two hypothesis therefore presents itself as a rational theory of these facts. Either the *Gita* and Buddhism were alike

[m] Essays on Sanskrit Literature, vol. III, p. 150.

[n] See our remarks on this point in the Introductory Essay to our *Gita* in verse p. 11 seq.

[o] Introduction to Gita in English verse, p. v, seq.

[p] Cr. Max Muller's Hibbert Lectures, p. 137; Weber's Indian Literature, pp. 288, 289; and Rhys Davids' excellent little volume on Buddhism, p. 151; and see also p. 83 of Mr Davids' book.

the outward manifestation of one and the same spiritual upheaval which shook to its centre the current religion, the *Gita* being the earlier and less thorough going form of it; or Buddhism having already begun to tell on Brahminism, the *Gita* was an attempt to bolster it up, so to say, at its least weak points, the weaker ones being altogether abandoned. I do not accept the latter alternative, because I cannot see any indication in the *Gita* of an attempt to compromise with a powerful attack on the old Hindu system while the fact that, though strictly orthodox, the author of the *Gita* still undermines the authority, as unwisely venerated, of the Vedic revelation; and the further fact, that in doing this, he is doing what others also had done before him or about his time; go, in my opinion, a considerable way towards fortifying the results of the negative argument already set forth. To me Buddhism is perfectly intelligible as one outcome of that play of thought on high spiritual topics, which in its other, and as we may say, less thorough going, manifestation we see in the *Upanishads* and the *Gita*.[q]

I have quoted this passage in full because it is typical of all Hindu scholars. Everyone of them is most reluctant to admit that the *Bhagvad Gita* is anyway influenced by Buddhism and is ever ready to deny that the *Gita* has borrowed anything from Buddhism. It is the attitude of Professor Radhakrishnan and also of Tilak. Where there is any similarity in thought between the *Bhagvad Gita* and Buddhism too strong and too close to be denied, the argument is that it is borrowed from the *Upanishads*. It is typical of the mean mentality of the counter-revolutionaries not to allow any credit to Buddhism on any account.

The absurdity of these views must shock all those who have made a comparative study of the *Bhagvad Gita* and the Buddhist *Suttas*. For if it is true to say that Gita is saturated with Sankhya philosophy it is far more true to say that the *Gita* is full of Buddhist ideas.[r] The similarity between the two is not merely in ideas but also in language. A few illustrations will show how true it is.

[q] Cf. Weber's History of Indian Literature, p. 285. In Mr Davids' Buddhism, p. 94 we have a noteworthy extract from a standard Buddhistic work, touching the existence of the soul. Compare that with the corresponding doctrine in the *Gita*. It will be found that the two are at one in rejecting the identity of the soul with the senses. The *Gita* then goes on to admit a soul separate from these. Buddhism rejects that also, and sees nothing but the senses.

[r] On this point compare *Bhagvad Gita* by S. D. Budhiraja MA, LLB. Chief Judge, Kashmere. At every point the author has attempted to draw attention to textual similarities between the *Gita* and Buddhism.

The *Bhagvad Gita* discusses *Brahma-Nirvana*.[s] The steps by which one reaches Brahma-Nirvana are stated by the *Bhagvad Gita* to be (1) *Shraddha* (faith in oneself); (2) *vyavasaya* (firm determination); (3) *Smriti* (rememberance of the goal); (4) *samadhi* (earnest contemplation) and (5) *prajna* (insight or true knowledge). From where has the *Gita* borrowed this *Nirvana* theory? Surely it is not borrowed from the *Upanishads*. For no *Upanishad* even mentions the word Nirvana. The whole idea is peculiarly Buddhist and is borrowed from Buddhism. Anyone who has any doubt on the point may compare this Brahma-Nirvana of the *Bhagvad Gita* with the Buddhist conception of Nirvana as set out in the *Mahaparinibbana Sutta* . It will be found that they are the same which the *Gita* has laid down for Brahma-Nirvana. Is it not a fact that the *Bhagvad Gita* has borrowed the entire conception of Brahma Nirvana instead of Nirvana for no other reason except to conceal the fact of its having stolen it from Buddhism?

Take another illustration. In Chapter VII, verses 13–20, there is a discussion as to who is dear to Krishna; one who has knowledge, or one who performs karma or one who is a devotee. Krishna says that the devotee is dear to him but adds that he must have the true marks of devotee. What is the character of a true devotee? According to Krishna the true devotee is one who practises (1) *maitri*; (loving kindness); (2) *karuna* (compassion); (3) *mudita* (sympathizing joy) and (4) *upeksa* (unconcernedness). From where has the *Bhagvad Gita* borrowed these qualifications of a perfect devotee? Here again, the source is Buddhism. Those who want proof may compare the *Mahapadana Sutta*,[t] and the *Tevijja Sutta*[u] where Buddha has preached what *Bhavanas* (mental attitudes) are necessary for one to cherish the training of the heart. This comparison will show that the whole ideology is borrowed from Buddhism and that too word for word.

Take a third illustration. In chapter XIII the *Bhagvad Gita* discusses the subject of *Kshetra-Kshetrajna*. In verses 7–11 Krishna points out what is knowledge and what is ignorance in the following language:

Pridelessness (Humility), Unpretentiousness, Non-injury or Harmlessness, Forgiveness, Straightforwardness, (uprightness), Devotion to

---

[s] Max Muller *Mahapari-Nibbana Sutta*, p. 63.

[t] See *Mahapadana Sutta*.

[u] *Tevijja Sutta*.

Preceptor, Purity, Steadiness, Self-restraint, Desirelessness towards objects of sense, Absence of Egoism, Reflection on the suffering and evil of birth, death, decrepitude and disease, Non-attachment, Non-identification of oneself with regard to son, wife and home and the rest, Constant even-mindedness of approach to both (what is) agreeable and (what is) disagreeable Unswerving devotion to Me with undivided meditation of Me, Resort to sequestered spots (contemplation, concentration, in solitude), Distaste for the society of worldly men, Incessant application to the knowledge relating to self, Perception or realisation of the true purport of the knowledge of the Tattvas (Samkhya Philosophy), all this is called 'knowledge'; what is Ajnana (Ignorance) is the reverse thereof.

Can anyone who knows anything of the Gospel of Buddha deny that the *Bhagvad Gita* has not in these stanzas reproduced word for word the main doctrines of Buddhism?

In Chapter XIII, verses 5, 6, 18, 19, the *Bhagvad Gita* gives a new metaphorical interpretation of karmas under various heads (1) *Yajnas* (sacrifices); (2) *Dana* (Gifts); (3) *Tapas* (penances); (4) *Food* and (5) *Svadhyaya* (Vedic study). What is the source of this new interpretation of old ideas? Compare with this what Buddha is reported to have said in the *Majjhina Nikaya* I, 286 *Sutta* XVI. Can anyone doubt that what Krishna says in verses 5, 6, 18, 19 of chapter XVII is a verbatim reproduction of the words of Buddha?

These are only a few illustrations I have selected those of major doctrinal importance. Those who are interested in pursuing the subject may take up the reference to similarities between the *Gita* and Buddhism given by Telang in the footnotes to his edition of the *Bhagvad Gita* and satisfy their curiosity. But the illustrations I have given will be enough to show how greatly the *Bhagvad Gita* is permeated by Buddhistic ideology and how much the *Gita* has borrowed from Buddhism. To sum up the *Bhagvad Gita* seems to be deliberately modelled on Buddhist *Suttas*. The Buddhist *Suttas* are dialogues. So is the *Bhagvad Gita*. Buddha's religion offered salvation to women and *Shudras*, Krishna also comes forward to offer salvation to women and *Shudras*. Buddhists say, 'I surrender to Buddha, to Dhamma and to Sangha.' So Krishna says, 'Give up all religions and surrender unto Me.' No parallel can be closer than what exists between Buddhism and the *Bhagvad Gita*.

16

The Buddha and
the Vedic Rishis

1. The *Vedas* are a collection of *Mantras*, i.e., hymns or chants. The reciters of these hymns are called Rishis.

2. The *Mantras* are mere invocations to deities such as *Indra*, *Varuna*, *Agni*, *Soma*, *Isana*, *Prajapati*, *Bramha*, *Mahiddhi*, *Yama* and others.

3. The invocations are mere prayers for help against enemies, for gift of wealth, for accepting the offerings of food, flesh and wine from the devotee.

4. There is not much philosophy in the Vedas. But there were some Vedic sages who had entered into speculations of a philosophical nature.

5. These Vedic sages were: (1) Aghamarsana; (2) Prajapati Parmesthin; (3) Brahmanaspati, otherwise known as Brihaspati; (4) Anila; (5) Dirghatamas; (6) Narayan; (7) Hiranyagarbha; and (8) Visvakarman.

6. The main problem of these Vedic philosophers were: How did the world originate? In what manner were individual things created? Why have they their unity and existence? Who created, and who ordained? From what did the world spring up and to what again will it return?

7. Aghamarsana said that the world was created out *of tapas* (heat). Tapas was the creative principle from which eternal law and truth were born. From these were produced the night (*tamas*).

Tamas produced water and from water originated time. Time gave birth to the sun and the moon, the heaven and the earth, the firmament and light and ordained the days and nights.

8. Brahmanaspati postulated the genesis of being from non-being. By the term non-existence, he denoted apparently the infinite. The existent originally sprang up from the non-existent. The non-existent (*asat, nonens*) was the permanent foundation of all that is existent (*sat, ens*) and of all that is possible and yet non-existent (*asat*).

9. Prajapati Parmesthin started with the problem: 'Did being come out of non-being?' His view was that this was an irrelevant question. For him water was the original substance of that which exists. For him the original matter—water—came neither under the definition of being nor under that of non-being.

10. Paramesthin did not draw any distinction between matter and motive power. According to him water transformed itself into particular things by some inherent principle to which he gave the name Kama, Cosmic Desire.

11. Anila was another Vedic philosopher. To him the principal element was air (vayu). It possesses the inherent capacity for movement. It is endowed with the generating principle.

12. Dirghatamas maintained that all living beings rest and depend ultimately on the sun. The sun held up and propelled by its inherent force went backward and forward.

13. The sun is composed of a grey coloured substance and so are lightning and fire.

14. The sun, lightning and fire formed the germ of water. Water forms the germ of plants. Such were the views of Dirghatamas.

15. According to Narayana, Purusha (God) is the first cause of the universe. It is from Purusha that the sun, the moon, the earth, water, fire, air, mid-air, the sky, the regions, the seasons, the creatures of the air, all animals, all classes of men, and all human institutions, had originated.

16. Hiranyagarbha. From the doctrinal point of view he stood midway between Parmeshthin and Narayan. Hiranyagarbha means the golden germ. It was the great power of the universe, from which all other powers and existences, divine and earthly, were derived.

17. Hiranayagarbha means fire. It is fire that constituted the solar essence, the generating principle of the universe.

18. From the point of view of Vishvakarman it was quite inadequate and unsatisfactory to hold that water was the primitive substance of all that is, and then to derive from it this world as a whole by giving it an inherent power of movement. If water be the primitive substance which is endowed with the inherent principle of change, we have yet to account for that from which water derived its being, and derived the motive power, the generating principle, the elemental forces, the laws and all the rest.

19. Vishvakarman held the view that it was God which was the motive power. God is first and God is last. He is earlier than the visible universe; he had existed before all cosmic forces came into being. He is the sole God who created and ordained this universe. God is one, and the only one. He is the unborn one (aja) in whom all the existing things abide. He is the one who is mighty in mind and supreme in power. He is the maker—the disposer. As father he generated us, and as disposer he knows the fate of all that is.

20. The Buddha did not regard all the Vedic sages as worthy of reverence. He regarded just ten Vedic Rishis as the most ancient and as the real authors of the Mantras.

21. But in the Mantras he saw nothing that was morally elevating.

22. In his view the *Vedas* were as worthless as a desert.

23. The Buddha, therefore, discarded the Mantras as a source from which to learn or to borrow.

24. Similarly, the Buddha did not find anything in the philosophy of the Vedic Rishis. They were groping to reach the truth. But they had not reached it.

25. Their theories were mere speculations not based on logic nor on facts. Their contributions to philosophy created no social values.

26. He therefore rejected the philosophy of the Vedic Rishis as useless.

KAPILA—THE PHILOSOPHER

1. Among the ancient philosophers of India, the most pre-eminent was Kapila.

2. His philosophical approach was unique, and as philosopher he stood in a class by himself. His philosophy was known as the Sankhya philosophy.

3. The tenets of his philosophy were of a startling nature.

4. Truth must be supported by proof. This is the first tenet of the Sankhya system. There is no truth without proof.

5. For purposes of proving the truth Kapila allowed only two means of proof—(1) perception and (2) inference.

6. By perception is meant mental apprehension of a present object.

7. Inference is threefold: (1) from cause to effect, as from the presence of clouds to rain; (2) from effect to cause, as from the swelling of the streams in the valleys to rain in the hills, and (3) by analogy, as when we infer from the fact that a man alters his place when he moves that the stars must also move, since they appear in different places.

8. His next tenet related to causality—creation and its cause.

9. Kapila denied the theory that there was a being who created the universe. In his view a created thing really exists beforehand in its cause just as the clay serves to form a pot, or the threads go to form a piece of cloth.

10. This is the first ground on which Kapila rejected the theory that the universe was created by a being.

11. But there are other grounds which he advanced in support of his point of view.

12. The non-existent cannot be the subject of an activity: There is no new creation. The product is really nothing else than the material of which it is composed: the product exists before its coming into being in the shape of its material of which it is composed. Only a definite product can be produced from such material; and only a specific material can yield a specific result.

13. What then is the source of the empirical universe?

14. Kapila said the empirical universe consists of things evolved (*Vyakta*) and things that are not evolved (*Avyakta*).

15. Individual things (Vyakta Vastu) cannot be the source of unevolved things (Avyakta Vastu).

16. Individual things are all limited in magnitude and this is incompatible with the nature of the source of the universe.

17. All individual things are analogous, one to another and, therefore, no one can be regarded as the final source of the other. Moreover, as they all come into being from a source, they cannot constitute that source.

18. Further, argued Kapila, an effect must differ from its cause, though it must consist of the cause. That being so, the universe cannot itself be the final cause. It must be the product of some ultimate cause.

19. When asked why the unevolved cannot be perceived, why does it not show movement which would make it perceivable, Kapila replied:

20. 'It may be due to various causes. It may be that its fine nature makes it imperceptible, just as other things of whose existence there is no doubt, cannot be perceived; or because of their too great a distance or proximity; or through the intervention of a third object, or through admixture with similar matter; or through the presence of some more powerful sensation, or the blindness or other defect of the senses or the mind of the observer.'

21. When asked: 'What then is the source of the universe? What makes the difference between the evolved and unevolved part of the universe?'

22. Kapila's reply was: 'Things that have evolved have a cause and the things that have not evolved have also a cause. But the source of both is uncaused and independent.'

23. 'The things that have evolved are many in number and limited in space and name. The source is one, eternal and all-pervasive. The things evolved have activities and parts: the source is imminent in all, but has neither activities nor parts.'

24. Kapila argued that the process of development of the unevolved is through the activities of three constituents of which it is made up, *Sattva*, *Rajas* and *Tamas*. These are called three *Gunas*.

25. The first of the constituents, or factors, corresponds to what we call as light in nature, which reveals, which causes pleasure to men; the second is that impels and moves, what produces activity; the third is what is heavy and puts under restraint, what produces the state of indifference or inactivity.

26. The three constituents act essentially in close relation, they overpower and support one another and intermingle with one another. They are like the constituents of a lamp, the flame, the oil and wick.

27. When the three Gunas are in perfect balance, none overpowering the other, the universe appears static (*achetan*) and ceases to evolve.

28. When the three Gunas are not in balance, one overpowers the other, the universe becomes dynamic (*sachetan*) and evolution begins.

29. Asked why the Gunas become unbalanced, the answer which Kapila gave was this disturbance in the balance of the three Gunas was due to the presence of *dukha* (suffering).

30. Such were the tenets of Kapila's philosophy.

31. Of all the philosophers the Buddha was greatly impressed by the doctrines of Kapila.

32. He was the only philosopher whose teachings appeared to the Buddha to be based on logic and facts.

33. But he did not accept everything which Kapila taught. Only three things did the Buddha accept from Kapila.

34. He accepted that reality must rest on proof. Thinking must be based on rationalism.

35. He accepted that there was no logical or factual basis for the presumption that God exists or that he created the universe.

36. He accepted that there was *dukha* (suffering) in the world.

37. The rest of Kapila's teachings he just bypassed as being irrelevant for his purpose.

THE BRAHMANAS

1. Next to the *Vedas* are the religious books known as the Brahmanas. Both were held as sacred books. Indeed the Brahmanas are a part of the *Vedas*. The two went together and were called by a common name *Sruti*.

2. There were four theses on which the Brahmanic Philosophy rested.

3. The first thesis was that the Vedas are not only sacred but that they are infallible and, they are not to be questioned.

4. The second thesis of the Brahmanic Philosophy was that salvation of the soul—that is escape from transmigration—can be had only by the due performance of Vedic sacrifices and observances of religious rites and ceremonies and the offering of gifts to Brahmins.

5. The Brahmins had not only a theory of an ideal religion as contained in the Vedas but they also had a theory for an ideal society.

6. The pattern of this ideal society they named *Chaturvarna*. It is imbedded in the Vedas and as the Vedas are infallible and as their authority cannot be questioned so also Chaturvarna as a pattern of society was binding and unquestionable.

7. This pattern of society was based upon certain rules.

8. The first rule was that society should be divided into four classes: (1) Brahmins; (2) Kshatriyas; (3) Vaishyas; and (4) Shudras.

9. The second rule was that there cannot be social equality among these four classes. They must be bound together by the rule of graded inequality.

10. The Brahmins to be at the top, the Kshatriyas to be kept below the Brahmins but above the Vaishyas, the Vaishyas to be below the Kshatriyas but above the Shudras and the Shudras to be the lowest of all.

11. These four classes were not to be equal to one another in the matter of rights and privileges. The rule of graded inequality governed the question of rights and privileges.

12. The Brahmin had all the rights and privileges which he wished to claim. But a Kshatriya could not claim the rights and privileges which a Brahmin could. He had more rights and privileges than a Vaishya could claim. The Vaishya had more rights and privileges than a Shudra. But he could not claim the rights and privileges which a Kshatriya could. And the Shudra was not entitled to any right, much less any privilege. His privilege was to subsist without offending the three superior classes.

13. The third rule of Chaturvarna related to the division of occupations. The occupation of the Brahmin was learning and teaching and the performance of religious observances. The

occupations of the Kshatriya was fighting. Trade was assigned to the Vaishyas. The occupations of the Shudras was service of the three superior classes. These occupations assigned to different classes were exclusive. One class could not trespass upon the occupation of the other.

14. The fourth rule of Chaturvarna related to the right to education. The pattern of Chaturvarna gave the right to education to the first three classes, the Brahmins, Kshatriyas and Vaishyas. The Shudras were denied the right to education. This rule of Chaturvarna did not deny the right to education to the Shudras only. It denied the right to education to all women including those belonging to the class of Brahmins, Kshatriyas and Vaishyas.

15. There was a fifth rule. According to it, man's life was divided into four stages. The first stage was called *Bramhacharya*; the second stage was called *Grahastashram*; the third stage was called *Vanaprasta* and the fourth stage was called *Sannyasa*.

16. The object of the first stage was study and education. The object of the second stage was to live a married life. The object of the third stage was to familiarize a man with the life of a hermit, i.e., severing family ties, but without deserting his home. The object of the fourth stage was to enable a man to go in search of God and seek union with him.

17. The benefits of these stages were open only to the male members of the three superior classes. The first stage was not open to the Shudras and women. Equally the last stage was not open to the Shudras and women.

18. Such was the divine pattern of an ideal society called Chaturvarna. The Brahmins had idealized the rule and had realized the ideal without leaving any cracks or loopholes.

19. The fourth thesis of Brahmanic Philosophy was the doctrine of Karma. It was part of the thesis of transmigration of the soul. The Karma of the Brahmins was an answer to the question: 'Where did the soul land on transmigration with his new body on new birth?' The answer of the Brahmanic Philosophy was that it depended on a man's deeds in his past life. In other words, it depended on his Karma.

20. The Buddha was strongly opposed to the first tenet of Brahmanism. He repudiated their thesis that the *Vedas* are infallible and their authority could never be questioned.

21. In his opinion, nothing was infallible and nothing could be final. Everything must be open to re-examination and reconsideration whenever grounds for re-examination and reconsideration arise.

22. Man must know the truth and real truth. To him freedom of thought was the most essential thing. And he was sure that freedom of thought was the only way to the discovery of truth.

23. Infallibility of the *Vedas* meant complete denial of freedom of thought.

24. For these reasons this thesis of the Brahmanic Philosophy was most obnoxious to him.

25. He was equally an opponent of the second thesis of the Brahmanic Philosophy. The Buddha did admit that there was any virtue in a sacrifice. But be made a distinction between true sacrifice and false sacrifice.

26. Sacrifice in the sense of self-denial for the good of others he called true sacrifice. Sacrifice in the sense of killing an animal as an offering to God for personal benefit he regarded as a false sacrifice.

27. The Brahmanic sacrifices were mostly sacrifices of animals to please their gods. He condemned them as false sacrifices. He would not allow them even though they be performed with the object of getting salvation for the soul.

28. The opponents of sacrifices used to ridicule the Brahmins by saying: 'If one can go to heaven by sacrificing an animal why should not one sacrifice one's own father. That would be a quicker way of going to heaven.'

29. The Buddha wholeheartedly agreed with this view.

30. The theory of Chaturvarna was as repugnant to the Buddha as the theory of sacrifices was repulsive to him.

31. The organization of society set up by Brahmanism in the name of Chaturvarna did not appear to him a natural organization. Its class composition was compulsory and arbitrary. It was a society made to order. He preferred an open society and a free society.

32. The Chaturvarna of the Brahmins was a fixed order never to be changed. Once a Brahmin always a Brahmin. Once a Kshatriya always a Kshatriya, once a Vaishya always a Vaishya and once a

Shudra always a Shudra. Society was based on status conferred upon an individual by the accident of his birth. Vice, however heinous, was no ground for degrading a man from his status, and virtue, however great, had no value to raise him above it. There was no room for worth nor for growth.

33. Inequality exits in every society. But it was different with Brahmanism. The inequality preached by Brahmins was its official doctrine. It was not a mere growth. Brahmanism did not believe in equality. In fact, it was opposed to equality.

34. Brahmanism was not content with inequality. The soul of Brahmanism lay in graded inequality.

35. Far from producing harmony, graded inequality, the Buddha thought, might produce in society an ascending scale of hatred and a descending scale of contempt, and might be a source of perpetual conflict.

36. The occupations of the four classes were also fixed. There was no freedom of choice. Besides, they were fixed not in accordance with skill but in accordance with birth.

37. On a careful review of the rules of Chaturvarna the Buddha had no difficulty in coming to the conclusion that the philosophic foundations on which the social order was reared by Brahmanism were wrong if not selfish.

38. It was clear to him that it did not serve the interests of all, much less did it advance the welfare of all. Indeed, it was deliberately designed to make many serve the interests of the few. In it man was made to serve a class of self-styled supermen.

39. It was calculated to suppress and exploit the weak and to keep them in a state of complete subjugation.

40. The law of Karma as formulated by the Brahmins, thought the Buddha, was calculated to sap the spirit of revolt completely. No one was responsible for the suffering of man except he himself. Revolt could not alter the state of suffering; for suffering was fixed by his past Karma as his lot in this life.

41. The Shudras and women—the two classes whose humanity was most mutilated by Brahmanism, had no power to rebel against the system.

42. They were denied the right to knowledge with the result that by reason of their enforced ignorance they could not realize what

had made their condition so degraded. They could not know that Brahmanism had robbed them completely of the significance of their life. Instead of rebelling against Brahmanism they had become the devotees and upholders of Brahmanism.

43. The right to bear arms is the ultimate means of achieving freedom which a human being has. But the Shudras were denied the right to bear arms.

44. Under Brahmanism the Shudras were left as helpless victims of a conspiracy of selfish Brahmanism, powerful and deadly Kshatriyas and wealthy Vaishyas.

45. Could it be amended? Knowing that it was a divinely ordained social order, he knew that it could not be. It could only be ended.

46. For these reasons the Buddha rejected Brahmanism as being opposed to the true way of life.

THE UPANISHADS AND THEIR TEACHINGS

1. The *Upanishads* constituted another piece of literature. It is not part of the *Vedas*. It is uncanonical.

2. All the same they did form a part of religious literature.

3. The number of the *Upanishads* is quite large. Some important, some quite unimportant.

4. Some of them were ranged against the Vedic theologians, the Brahmin priests.

5. All of them agreed in viewing Vedic study as a study of nescience or ignorance (*avidya*).

6. They were all agreed in their estimate of the four Vedas and the Vedic science as the lower knowledge.

7. They were all agreed in questioning the divine origin of the Vedas.

8. They were all agreed in denying the efficacy attributed to sacrifices, to the funeral oblations, and the gifts to the priests which are the fundamentals of the Brahmanic philosophy.

9. This, however, was not the main topic with which the Upanishads were concerned. Their discussions centred round Brahman and Atman.

10. *Brahman* was the all-pervading principle which binds the universe and that salvation lay in the *Atman* realizing that it is Brahman.

11. The main thesis of the *Upanishads* was that Brahman was a reality and that Atman was the same as Brahman. The Atman did not realize that it was Brahman because of the *Upadhis* in which it was entangled.

12. The question was: Is Brahmana a reality? The acceptance of the Upanishadic thesis depended upon the answer to this question.

13. The Buddha could find no proof in support of the thesis that Brahman was a reality. He, therefore, rejected the thesis of the *Upanishads.*

14. It is not that questions on this issue were not put to the authors of the *Upanishads.* They were:

15. Such questions were put to no less a person that Yajnavalkya, a great seer who plays so important a part in the *Brahadarnyka Upanishad.*

16. He was asked: 'What is Brahman? What is Atman?' All that Yajnavalkya could say: '*Neti! Neti!* I know not! I know not!'

17. 'How can anything be a reality about which no one knows anything,' asked the Buddha. He had, therefore, no difficulty in rejecting the Upanishadic thesis as being based on pure imagination.

17

Does the Buddha have a Social Message?

1. 'What are the teachings of the Buddha?'

2. This is a question on which no two followers of the Buddha or the students of Buddhism agree.

3. To some Samadhi is his principal teaching.

4. To some it is *Vipassana* (a kind of *Pranayam*).

5. To some Buddhism is esoteric. To others it is exoteric.

6. To some it is a system of barren metaphysics.

7. To some it is sheer mysticism.

8. To some it is a selfish abstraction from the world.

9. To some it is a systematic repression of every impulse and emotion of the heart.

10. Many other views regarding Buddhism could be collected.

11. This divergence of views is astonishing.

12. Some of these views are those of men who have a fancy for certain things. Such are those who regard that the essence of Buddhism lies in Samadhi or Vipassana, or Esoterism.

13. The other views are the results of the fact that the majority of the writers on Buddhism are students of ancient Indian history. Their study of Buddhism is incidental and occasional.

14. Some of them are not students of Buddhism.

15. They are not even students of anthropology, the subject matter which deals with the origin and growth of religion.

16. The question that arises is—'Did the Buddha have no social message?'

17. When pressed for an answer, students of Buddhism refer to the two points. They say—

18. 'The Buddha taught ahimsa.'

19. 'The Buddha taught peace!'

20. Asked—'Did the Buddha give any other social message?'

21. 'Did the Buddha teach justice?'

22. 'Did the Buddha teach love?'

23. 'Did the Buddha teach liberty?'

24. 'Did the Buddha teach equality?'

25. 'Did the Buddha teach fraternity?'

26. 'Could the Buddha answer Karl Marx?'

27. These questions are hardly ever raised in discussing the Buddha's Dhamma.

28. My answer is that the Buddha has a social message. He answers all these questions. But they have been buried by modern authors.

18

Conversion

AWAY FROM THE HINDUS

A large majority of Untouchables who have reached a capacity to think out their problem believe that one way to solve the problem of the Untouchables is for them to abandon Hinduism and be converted to some other religion. At a Conference of the Mahars held in Bombay on 31 May 1936 a resolution to this effect was unanimously passed. Although the Conference was a Conference of the Mahars[a] the resolution had the support of a very large body of Untouchables throughout India. No resolution had created such a stir. The Hindu community was shaken to its foundation and curses, imprecations and threats were uttered against the Untouchables who were behind this move.

Four principal objections have been urged by the opponents against the conversion of the Untouchables:

1. What can the Untouchables gain by conversion? Conversion can make no change in the status of the Untouchables.

2. All religions are true, all religions are good. To change religion is a futility.

3. The conversion of the Untouchables is political in its nature.

4. The conversion of the Untouchables is not genuine as it is not based on faith.

[a] The Conference was confined to Mahars because the intention was to test the intensity of feeling communitywise and to take soundings from each community.

It cannot take much argument to demonstrate that the objections are puerile and inconsequential.

To take the last objection first. History abounds with cases where conversion has taken place without any religious motive. What was the nature of its conversion of Clovis and his subjects to Christianity? How did Ethelbert and his Kentish subjects become Christians? Was there a religious motive which led them to accept the new religion? Speaking on the nature of conversions to Christianity that had taken place during the middle ages Rev. Reichel says:[b]

One after another the nations of Europe are converted to the faith; their conversion is seen always to proceed from above, never from below. Clovis yields to the bishop Remigius and forthwith he is followed by the Baptism of 3,000 Franks. Ethelbert yields to the mission of Augustine and forthwith all Kent follows his example; when his son Eadbald apostatises, the men of Kent apostatise with him. Essex is finally won by the conversion of King Sigebert, who under the influence of another king, Oswy, allows himself to be baptised. Northumberland is temporarily gained by the conversion of its king, Edwin but falls away as soon Edwin is dead. It anew accepts the faith, when another king, Oswald, promotes its diffusion. In the conversion of Germany, a bishop, Boniface, plays a prominent part, in close connection with the princes of the country, Charles Martel and Pepin; the latter, in return for his patronage receiving at Soissons the Church's sanction to a violent act of usurpation. Denmark is gained by the conversion of its kings, Herald Krag, Herald Blastand and Canute, Sweden by that of the two Olofs; and Russia, by the conversion of its sovereign, Vladimir. Everywhere Christianity addresses itself first to kings and princes; everywhere the bishops and abbots appear as its only representatives.

Nor was this all, for where a king had once been gained, no obstacle by the Mediaeval missionaries to the immediate indiscriminate baptism of his subjects. Three thousand warriors of Clovis following the example of their king, were at once admitted to the sacred rite; the subjects of Ethelbert were baptised in numbers after the conversion of their prince, without preparation, and with hardly any instruction. The Germans only were less hasty in following the example of others. In Russia, so great was the number of those who crowded to be baptised after the baptism of Vladimir, that the sacrament had to be administered to hundreds at a time.

History records cases where conversion has taken place as a result of compulsion or deceit.

[b] *The Sea of Rome*, pp. 143–5.

Today religion has become a piece of ancestral property. It passes from father to son, so does inheritance. What genuineness is there in such cases of conversion? The conversion of the Untouchables if it did take place would take place after full deliberation of the value of religion and the virtue of the different religions. How can such a conversion be said to be not a genuine conversion? On the other hand, it would be the first case in history of genuine conversion. It is therefore difficult to understand why the genuineness of the conversion of the Untouchables should be doubted by anybody.

The third objection is an ill-considered objection. What political gain will accrue to the Untouchables from their conversion has been defined by nobody. If there is a political gain, nobody has proved that it is a direct inducement to conversion.

The opponents of conversion do not even seem to know that a distinction has to be made between a gain being a direct inducement to conversion and its being only an incidental advantage. This distinction cannot be said to be a distinction without a difference. Conversion may result in a political gain to the Untouchables. It is only where a gain is a direct inducement that conversion could be condemned as immoral or criminal. Unless therefore the opponents of conversion prove that the conversion desired by the Untouchables is for political gain and for nothing else their accusation is baseless. If political gain is only an incidental gain then there is nothing criminal in conversion. The fact, however, is that conversion can bring no new political gain to the Untouchables. Under the constitutional law of India every religious community has got the right to separate political safeguards. The Untouchables in their present condition enjoy political rights similar to those which are enjoyed by the Muslims and the Christians. If they change their faith the change is not to bring into existence political rights which did not exist before. If they do not change they will retain the political rights which they have. Political gain has no connection with conversion. The charge is a wild charge made without understanding.

The second objection rests on the premise that all religions teach the same thing. It is from the premise that a conclusion is drawn that since all religions teach the same thing there is no reason to prefer one religion to other. It may be conceded that all religions agree in holding that the meaning of life is to be found in the pursuit of 'good'. Up to this point the validity of the premise may be conceded. But when the premise goes beyond and asserts that because of this there is no reason to prefer one religion to another it becomes a false premise.

Religions may be alike in that they all teach that the meaning of life is to be found in the pursuit of 'good'. But religions are not alike in their answers to the question 'What is good?' In this they certainly differ. One religion holds that brotherhood is good, another caste and untouchability is good.

There is another respect in which all religions are not alike. Besides being an authority which defines what is good, religion is a motive force for the promotion and spread of the 'good'. Are all religions agreed in the means and methods they advocate for the promotion and spread of good? As pointed out by Professor Tiele,[c] religion is:

One of the mightiest motors in the history of mankind, which formed as well as tore asunder nations, united as well as divided empires, which sanctioned the most atrocious and barbarous deeds, the most libidinous customs, inspired the most admirable acts of heroism, self-renunciation, and devotion, which occasioned the most sanguinary wars, rebellions and persecutions, as well as brought about the freedom, happiness and peace of nations—at one time a partisan of tyranny, at another breaking its chains, now calling into existence and fostering a new and brilliant civilization, then the deadly foe to progress, science and art.

Apart from these oscillations there are permanent differences in the methods of promoting good as they conceive it. Are there not religions which advocate violence? Are there not religions which advocate non-violence? Given these facts how can it be said that all religions are the same and there is no reason to prefer one to the other.

In raising the second objection the Hindu is merely trying to avoid an examination of Hinduism on its merits. It is an extraordinary thing that in the controversy over conversion not a single Hindu has had the courage to challenge the Untouchables to say what is wrong with Hinduism. The Hindu is merely taking shelter under the attitude generated by the science of comparative religion. The science of comparative religion has broken down the arrogant claims of all revealed religions that they alone are true and all others which are not the results of revelation are false. That revelation

[c] Quoted by Crawley, *Tree of life*, p. 5.

was too arbitrary, too capricious a test to be accepted for distinguishing a true religion from a false and was undoubtedly a great service which the science of comparative religion has rendered to the cause of religion. But it must be said to the discredit of that science that it has created the general impression that all religions are good and there is no use and purpose in discriminating them.

The first objection is the only objection which is worthy of serious consideration. The objection proceeds on the assumption that religion is a purely personal matter between man and God. It is supernatural. It has nothing to do with social. The argument is no doubt sensible. But its foundations are quite false. At any rate, it is a one-sided view of religion and that too based on aspects of religion which are purely historical and not fundamental.

To understand the function and purposes of religion it is necessary to separate religion from theology. The primary things in religion are the usages, practices and observances, rites and rituals. Theology is secondary. Its object is merely to rationalize them. As stated by Professor Robertson Smith:[d]

Ritual and practical usages were, strictly speaking the sum total of ancient religions. Religion in primitive times was not a system of belief with practical applications; it was a body of fixed traditional practices, to which every member of society conformed as a matter of courage, Men would not be men if they agreed to do certain things without having a reason for their action; but in ancient religion the reason was not first formulated as a doctrine and then expressed in practice, but conversely, practice preceded doctrinal theory.

Equally necessary it is not to think of religion as though it was supernatural. To overlook the fact that the primary content of religion is social is to make nonsense of religion. The savage society was concerned with life and the preservation of life and it is these life processes which constitute the substance and source of the religion of the savage society. So great was the concern of the savage society for life and the preservation of life that it made them the basis of its religion. So central were the life processes in the religion of the savage society that everything which affected them became part of its religion. The ceremonies of the savage society were not

[d] *The Religion of the Semites.*

only concerned with the events of birth, attaining of manhood, puberty, marriage, sickness, death and war but they were also concerned with food.

Among the pastoral peoples the flocks and herds are sacred. Among agricultural peoples seedtime and harvest are marked by ceremonies performed with some reference to the growth and the preservation of the crops. Likewise drought, pestilence, and other strange irregular phenomena of nature occasion the performance of ceremonials. As pointed out by Professor Crawley, the religion of the savage begins and ends with the affirmation and consecration of life.

In life and preservation of life therefore consists the religion of the savage. What is true of the religion of the savage is true of all religions wherever they are found for the simple reason that constitutes the essence of religion. It is true that in the present-day society with its theological refinements this essence of religion has become hidden from view and is even forgotten. But that life and the preservation of life constitute the essence of religion even in the present day society is beyond question. This is well illustrated by Professor Crawley, when speaking of the religious life of man in the present day society he says how:

Man's religion does not enter into his professional or social hours, his scientific or artistic moments; practically its chief claims are settled on one day in the week from which ordinary worldly concerns are excluded. In fact, his life is in two parts; but the moiety with which religion is concerned is the elemental. Serious thinking on ultimate questions of life and death is, roughly speaking, the essence of his Sabbath; add to this the habit of prayer, the giving of thanks at meals, and the subconscious feeling that birth and death, continuation and marriage are rightly solemnized by religion, while business and pleasure may possibly be consecrated, but only metaphorically or by an overflow of religious feeling.

Students of the origin and history of religion when they began their study of the savage society became so much absorbed in the magic, the tabu and totem and the rites and ceremonies connected therewith they found in the savage society that they not only overlooked the social processes of the savage as the primary content of religion but they failed even to appreciate the proper function of magic and other supernatural processes. This was a great mistake and has cost all concerned in religion very dearly. For it is responsible for the grave misconception about religion[e] which prevails today among most people. Nothing can be a greater error than to explain religion as having arisen in magic or being concerned only in magic for magic sake. It is true that savage society practises magic, believes in tabu and worships the totem. But it is wrong to suppose that these constitute the religion or form the source of religion. To take such a view is to elevate what is incidental to the position of the principal. The principal thing in the religion of the savage are the elemental facts of human existence such as life, death, birth, marriage, etc. Magic, tabu and totem are not the ends. They are only the means. The end is life and the preservation of life. Magic, tabu, etc. are resorted to by the savage society not for their own sake but to conserve life and to exercise evil influence from doing harm to life. Why should such occasions as harvest and famine be accompanied by religious ceremonies? Why are magic, tabu and totem of such importance to the savage? The only answer is that they all affect the preservation of life. The process of life and its preservation form the main purpose. Life and preservation of life is the core and centre of the religion of the savage society. That today God has taken the place of magic, does not alter the fact that God's place in religion is only as a means for the conservation of life and that the end of religion is the conservation and consecration of social life.

The point to which it is necessary to draw particular attention and to which the foregoing discussion lends full support is that it is an error to look upon religion as a matter which is individual, private and personal. Indeed as will be seen from what follows, religion becomes a source of positive mischief if not danger when it remains individual, private and personal. Equally mistaken is the view that religion is the flowering of special religious instinct inherent in the nature of the individual. The correct view is that religion like language is social for the reason that either is essential for social life and the individual has to have it because without it he cannot participate in the life of the society.

If religion is social in the sense that it primarily concerns society, it would be natural to ask what is the purpose and function of religion.

[e] The word 'religion' inserted here is not in the original MS—Ed.

The best statement regarding the purpose of religion which I have come across is that of Professor Charles A Ellwood.[f] According to him:

...religion projects the essential values of human personality and of human society into the universe as a whole. It inevitably arises as soon as man tries to take valuing attitude towards his universe, no matter how small and mean that universe may appear to him. Like all the distinctive things in human, social and mental life, it of course, rests upon the higher intellectual powers of man. Man is the only religious animal, because through his powers of abstract thought and reasoning, he alone is self-conscious in the full sense of that term. Hence he alone is able to project his values into the universe and finds necessity of so doing. Given, in other words, the intellectual powers of man, the mind at once seeks to universalise its values as well as its ideas. Just as rationalizing processes give man a world of universal ideas, so religious processes give man a world of universal values. The religious processes are, indeed, nothing but the rationalizing processes at work upon man's impulses and emotions rather than upon his precepts. What the reason does for ideas, religion does, then, for the feelings. It universalizes them; and in universalizing them, it brings them into harmony with the whole of reality.

Religion emphasizes, universalizes social values and brings them to the mind of the individual who is required to recognize them in all his acts in order that he may function as an approved member of the society. But the purpose of religion is more than this. It spiritualizes them. As pointed out by Professor Ellwood:[g]

Now these mental and social values, with which religion deals, men call 'spiritual'. It is something which emphasizes as we may say, spiritual values, that is, the values connected especially with the personal and social life. It projects these values, as we have seen, into the universal reality. It gives man a social and moral conception of the universe, rather than a merely mechanical one as a theatre of the play of blind, purposeless forces. While religion is not primarily animistic philosophy, as has often been said, nevertheless it does project mind, spirit, life, into all things. Even the most primitive religion did this; for in 'primitive dynamism' there was a feeling of the psychic, in such concepts as *mana* or *manitou*. They were closely connected with persons and proceeded from person,

[f] Professor Charles A Ellwood, *The Reconstruction of Religion: A Sociological View*, New York, the Macmillan Company, 1925, pp. 39–40.
[g] Ibid., pp. 45–6.

or things which were viewed in an essentially personal way. Religion, therefore, is a belief in the reality of spiritual values, and projects them, as we have said, into the whole universe. All religion—even so-called atheistic religions—emphasizes the spiritual, believes in its dominance, and looks to its ultimate triumph.

The function of religion in society is equally clear. According to Professor Ellwood[h] the function of religion:

Is to act as an agency of social control, that is, of the group controlling the life of the individual, for what is believed to be the good of the larger life of the group. Very early, as we have seen any beliefs and practices which gave expression to personal feelings or values of which the group did not approve were branded as 'black magic' or baleful superstitions; and if this had not been done it is evident that the unity of the life of the group might have become seriously impaired. Thus the almost necessarily social character of religion stands revealed. We cannot have such a thing as purely personal or individual religion which is not at the same time social. For we live a social life and the welfare of the group is, after all, the chief matter of concern.

Dealing with the same question in another place, he says:[i]

...The function of religion is the same as the function of Law and Government. It is a means by which society exercises its control over the conduct of the individual in order to maintain the social order. It may not be used consciously as a method of social control over the individual. Nonetheless the fact is that religion acts as a means of social control. As compared to religion, Government and Law are relatively inadequate means of social control. The control through law and order does not go deep enough to secure the stability of the social order. The religious sanction, on account of its being supernatural has been on the other hand the most effective means of social control, far more effective than law and Government have been or can be. Without the support of religion, law and Government are bound to remain a very inadequate means of social control. Religion is the most powerful force of social gravitation without which it would be impossible to hold the social order in its orbit.

The foregoing discussion, although it was undertaken to show that religion is a social fact, that religion has a specific social purpose and a definite social function it was intended to prove that

[h] *The Religious Reconstruction*, pp. 42-3.

[i] Professor Charles A. Ellwood, *Sociology in its Psychological Aspects*, New York and London, D. Appleton & Co., 1912, pp. 356-7.

it was only proper that a person if he was required to accept a religion should have the right to ask how well it has served the purposes which belong to religion. This is the reason why Lord Balfour was justified in putting some very straight questions to the positivists before he could accept Positivism to be superior to Christianity. He asked in quite trenchent language.

...what has (positivism) to say to the more obscure multitude who are absorbed, and well nigh overwhelmed, in the constant struggle with daily needs and narrow cares; who have but little leisure or inclination to consider the precise role they are called on to play in the great drama of 'humanity' and who might in any case be puzzled to discover its interest or its importance? Can it assure them that there is no human being so insignificant as not to be of infinite worth in the eyes of Him who created the Heavens, or so feeble but that his action may have consequences of infinite moment long after this material system shall have crumbled into nothingness? Does it offer consolation to those who are bereaved, strength to the weak, forgiveness to the sinful, rest to those who are weary and heavy laden?

The Untouchables can very well ask the protagonists of Hinduism the very questions which Lord Balfour asked the Positivists. Nay the Untouchables can ask many more. They can ask: Does Hinduism recognize their worth as human beings? Does it stand for their equality? Does it extend to them the benefit of liberty? Does it at least help to forge the bond of fraternity between them and the Hindus? Does it teach the Hindus that the Untouchables are their kindred? Does it say to the Hindus it is a sin to treat the Untouchables as being neither man nor beast? Does it tell the Hindus to be righteous to the Untouchables? Does it preach to the Hindus to be just and humane to them? Does it inculcate upon the Hindus the virtue of being friendly to them? Does it tell the Hindus to love them, to respect them and to do them no wrong. In fine, does Hinduism universalize the value of life without distinction?

No Hindu can dare to give an affirmative answer to any of these questions? On the contrary the wrongs to which the Untouchables are subjected by the Hindus are acts which are sanctioned by the Hindu religion. They are done in the name of Hinduism and are justified in the name of Hinduism. The spirit and tradition which makes lawful the lawlessness of the Hindus towards the Untouchables is founded and supported by the teachings of Hinduism. How can the Hindus ask the Untouchables to accept

Hinduism and stay in Hinduism? Why should be Untouchables adhere to Hinduism which is solely responsible for their degradation? How can the Untouchables stay in Hinduism? Untouchability is the lowest depth to which the degradation of a human being can be carried. To be poor is bad but not so bad as to be an Untouchable. The poor can be proud. The Untouchable cannot be. To be reckoned low is bad but it is not so bad as to be an Untouchable. The low can rise above his status. An Untouchable cannot. To be suffering is bad but not so bad as to be an Untouchable. They shall some day be comforted. An Untouchable cannot hope for this. To have to be meek is bad but it is not so bad as to be an Untouchable. The meek if they do not inherit the earth may at least be strong. The Untouchables cannot hope for that.

In Hinduism there is no hope for the Untouchables. But this is not the only reason why the Untouchables wish to quit Hinduism. There is another reason which makes it imperative for them to quit Hinduism. Untouchability is a part of Hinduism. Even those who for the sake of posing as enlightened reformers deny that untouchability is part of Hinduism are found to observe untouchability. For a Hindu to believe in Hinduism does not matter. It enhances his sense of superiority by the reason of this consciousness that there are millions of Untouchables below him. But what does it mean for an Untouchable to say that he believes in Hinduism? It means that he accepts that he is an Untouchable and that he is an Untouchable is the result of divine dispensation. For Hinduism is divine dispensation. An Untouchable may not cut the throat of a Hindu. But he cannot be expected to give an admission that he is an Untouchable and rightly so. Which Untouchable is there with soul so dead as to give such an admission by adhering to Hinduism. That Hinduism is inconsistent with the self-respect and honour of the Untouchables is the strongest ground which justifies the conversion of the Untouchables to another and nobler faith.

The opponents of conversion are determined not to be satisfied even if the logic of conversion was irrefutable. They will insist upon asking further questions. There is one question which they are always eager to ask largely because they think it is formidable and unanswerable; what will the Untouchables gain materially by changing their faith? The question is not at all formidable. It is simple to answer. It is not the intention of the Untouchables to make conversion an opportunity for economic gain. The Untouchables it is true will not gain wealth by conversion. This is however no less because while they remain as Hindus they are doomed to be poor. Politically the Untouchables will lose the political rights that are given to the Untouchables. This is, however, no real loss. Because they will be entitled to the benefit of the political rights reserved for the community which they would join through conversion. Politically there is neither gain nor loss. Socially, the Untouchables will gain absolutely and immensely because by conversion the Untouchables will be members of a community whose religion has universalized and equalized all values of life. Such a blessing is unthinkable for them while they are in the Hindu fold.

The answer is complete. But by reason of its brevity it is not likely to give satisfaction to the opponents of conversion. The Untouchables need three things. First thing they need is to end their social isolation. The second thing they need is to end their inferiority complex. Will conversion meet their needs? The opponents of conversion have a feeling that the supporters of conversion have no case. That is why they keep on raising questions. The case in favour of conversion is stronger than the strongest case. Only one does wish to spend long arguments to prove what is so obvious. But since it is necessary to put an end to all doubt, I am prepared to pursue the matter. Let me take each point separately.

How can they end their social isolation? The one and the only way to end their social isolation is for the Untouchables to establish kinship with and get themselves incorporated into another community which is free from the spirit of caste. The answer is quite simple and yet not many will readily accept its validity. The reason is, very few people realize the value and significance of kinship. Nevertheless its value and significance are very great. Kinship and what it implies has been described by Professor Robertson Smith in the following terms:[j]

A kin was a group of persons whose lives were so bound up together, in what must be called a physical unity, that they could be treated as parts of one common life. The/members of one kindred looked on themselves as one living whole, a single animated mass of blood, flesh and bones, of which no member could be touched without all the members suffering.

[j] *Religion of the Semites*, p. 273.

The matter can be looked at from the point of view both of the individual as well as from that of the group. From the point of the group, kinship calls for a feeling that one is first and foremost a member of the group and not merely an individual. From the point of view of the individual, the advantages of his kinship with the group are no less and no different than those which accrue to a member of the family by reason of his membership of the family. Family life is characterized by parental tenderness. As pointed out by Professor McDougall:[k]

From this emotion (parental tenderness) and its impulse to cherish and protect, spring generosity, gratitude, love, pity, true benevolence, and altruistic conduct of every kind; in it they have their main and absolutely essential root, without which they would not be.

Community as distinguished from society is only an enlarged family. As such it is characterized by all the virtues which are found in a family and which have been so well described by Professor McDougall.

Inside the community there is no discrimination among those who are recognized as kindred bound by kinship. The community recognizes that everyone within it is entitled to all the rights equally with others. As Professor Dewey and Tufts have pointed out:

A State may allow a citizen of another country to own land, to sue in its courts, and will usually give him a certain amount of protection, but the first-named rights are apt to be limited, and it is only a few years since Chief Justice Taney's dictum stated the existing legal theory of the United States to be that the Negro 'had no rights which the white man was bound to respect'. Even where legal theory does not recognize race or other distinctions, it is often hard in practice for an alien to get justice. In primitive clan or family groups this principle is in full force. Justice is a privilege which falls to a man as belonging to some group—not otherwise. The member of the clan or the household or the village community has a claim, but the Stranger has nothing standing. He may be treated kindly, as a guest, but he cannot demand 'justice' at the hands of any group but his own. In this conception of rights within the group we have the prototype of modern civil law. The dealing of clan with clan is a matter of war or negotiation, not of law; and the clanless man is an 'outlaw' in fact as well as in name.

[k] William Mcdougall, *Introduction to Social Psychology*, London, Methuen & Co., 1945, p. 61.

Kinship makes the community take responsibility for vindicating the wrong done to a member. Blood-flood which objectively appears to be a savage method of avenging a wrong done to a member is subjectively speaking a manifestation of sympathetic resentment by the members of the community for a wrong done to their fellow. This sympathetic resentment is a compound of tender emotion and anger such as those which issue out of parental tenderness when it comes face to face with a wrong done to a child. It is kinship which generates, this sympathetic resentment, this compound of tender emotion and anger. This is by no means a small value to an individual. In the words of Professor McDougall:

This intimate alliance between tender emotion and anger is of great importance for the social life of man, and the right understanding of it is fundamental for a true theory of the moral sentiments; for the anger evoked in this way is the germ of all moral indignation and on moral indignation justice and the greater part of public law are in the main founded.[207]

It is kinship which generates generosity and invokes its moral indignation which is necessary to redress a wrong. Kinship is the will to enlist the support of the kindred community to meet the tyrannies and oppressions by the Hindus which today the Untouchables have to bear single-handed and alone. Kinship with another community is the best insurance which the Untouchable can effect against Hindu tyranny and Hindu oppression.

Anyone who takes into account the foregoing exposition of what kinship means and does should have no difficulty in accepting the proposition that to end their isolation the Untouchables must join another community which does not recognize caste.

Kinship is the antithesis of isolation. For the Untouchables to establish kinship with another community is merely another name for ending their present state of isolation. Their isolation will never end so long as they remain Hindus. As Hindus, their isolation hits them from front as well as from behind. Notwithstanding their being Hindus, they are isolated from the Muslims and the Christians because as Hindus they are aliens to all—Hindus as well as Non-Hindus. The isolation can end only in one way and in no other way. That way is for the Untouchables to join some non-Hindu community and thereby become its kith and kin.

That this is not a meaningless move will be admitted by all those who know the disadvantages of isolation and the advantages of kinship. What are the consequences of isolation? Isolation means social segregation, social humiliation, social discrimination and social injustice. Isolation means denial of protection, denial of justice, denial of opportunity. Isolation means want of sympathy, want of fellowship and want of consideration. Nay, isolation means positive hatred and antipathy from the Hindus. By having kinship with other community on the other hand, the Untouchables will have within that community equal position, equal protection and equal justice, will be able to draw upon its sympathy, its good-will.

This I venture to say is a complete answer to the question raised by the opponents. It shows what the Untouchables can gain by conversion. It is, however, desirable to carry the matter further and dispose of another question which has not been raised so far by the opponents of conversion but may be raised. The question is: why is conversion necessary to establish kinship?

The answer to this question will reveal itself if it is borne in mind that there is a difference between a community and a society and between kinship and citizenship.

A community in the strict sense of the word is a body of kindred. A society is a collection of many communities or of different bodies of kindreds. To bond which holds a community together is called kinship while the bond which holds a society together is called citizenship.

The means of acquiring citizenship in a society are quite different from the means of acquiring kinship in a community. Citizenship is acquired by what is called naturalization. The condition precedent for citizenship is the acceptance of political allegiance to the State. The conditions precedent for acquiring kinship are quite different. At one stage in evolution of man the condition precedent for adoption into the kindred was unity of blood. For the kindred is a body of persons who conceive themselves as sprung from one ancestor and as having in their veins one blood. It does not matter whether each group has actually and in fact sprung from a single ancestor. As a matter of fact, a group did admit a stranger into the kindred though he did not spring from the same ancestor. It is interesting to note that there was a rule that if a stranger intermarried with a group for seven generations, he became a member of the kindred. The point is that, fiction though it be, admission into the kindred required as a condition precedent unity of blood.

At a later stage of Man's Evolution, common religion in place of unity of blood became a condition precedent to kinship. In this connection it is necessary to bear in mind the important fact pointed out by Prof. Robertson Smith[1] that in a community the social body is made not of men only, but of gods and men and therefore any stranger who wants to enter a community and forge the bond of kinship can do so only by accepting the God or Gods of the community. The Statement in the Old Testament such as those of Naomi to Ruth saying: 'Thy sister is gone back into her people and unto her gods' and Ruth's reply 'Thy people shall be my people, and thy god my God' or the calling of the Mobites the sons and daughters of Chemosh are all evidences which show that the bond of kinship in a community is the consequence of their allegiance to a common religion. Without common religion there can be no kinship.

Where people are waiting to find faults in the argument in favour of conversion it is better to leave no ground for fault-finders to create doubt or misunderstanding. It might therefore be well to explain how and in what manner religion is able to forge the bond of kinship. The answer is simple. It does it through eating and drinking together.[m] The Hindus in defending their caste system ridicule the plea for inter-dining. They ask: What is there in inter-dining? The answer from a sociological point of view is that is everything in it. Kinship is a social covenant of brotherhood. Like all covenants it required to be signed, sealed and delivered before it can become binding. The mode of signing, sealing and delivery is the mode prescribed by religion and that mode is the participation in a sacrificial meal. As said by Prof. Smith:[n]

What is the ultimate nature of the fellowship which is constituted or declared when men eat and drink together? In our complicated society fellowship has many types and many degrees; men may be united by bonds of duty and honour for certain purposes, and stand quite apart in all other things. Even in ancient times—for example, in the old

---

[1] The Religion of the Semites, Lecture II. Prof. Smith makes this distinction as though it was a distinction between ancient society and modern society. It is of wider importance. In reality, it is a distinction which marks off a community from a society.

[m] On this subject see Smith, The Religion of the Semites, pp. 270–1.

[n] Ibid., pp. 271–2.

Testament—we find the sacrament of a common meal introduced to seal engagements of various kinds. But in every case the engagement is absolute and inviolable; it constitutes what in the language of ethics is called a duty of perfect obligation. Now in the most primitive society there is only one kind of fellowship which is absolute and inviolable. To the primitive man all other men fall under two classes, those to whom his life is sacred and those to whom it is not sacred. The former are his fellows: the latter are strangers and potential foemen, with whom it is absurd to think of forming any inviolable tie unless they are first brought into the circle within which each man's life is sacred to all his comrades.

If for the Untouchables mere citizenship is not enough to put an end to their isolation and the troubles which ensure therefrom, if kinship is the only cure then there is no other way except to embrace the religion of the community whose kinship they seek.

The argument so far advanced was directed to show how conversion can end the problem of the isolation of the Untouchables. There remain two other questions to be considered. One is, will conversion remove their inferiority complex? One cannot of course dogmatize. But one can have no hesitation in answering the question in the affirmative. The inferiority complex of the Untouchables is the result of their isolation, discrimination and the unfriendliness of the social environment. It is these which have created a feeling of helplessness which are responsible for the inferiority complex which cost him the power of self-assertion.

Can religion alter this psychology of the Untouchables? The psychologists are of opinion that religion can effect this cure provided it is a religion of the right type; provided that the religion approaches the individual not as a degraded worthless outcastes but as a fellow human being; provided religion gives him an atmosphere in which he will find that there are possibilities for feeling himself the equal of every other human being. There is no reason why conversion to such a religion by the Untouchables should not remove their age-long pessimism which is responsible for their inferiority complex. As pointed out by Professor Ellwood:°

Religion is primarily a valuing attitude, universalizing the will and the emotions, rather than the ideas of man. It thus harmonizes men, on the side of will and emotion, with his world. Hence, it is the fee of pessimism and despair. It encourages hope, and gives confidence in the battle of life,

° Charles A Ellwood, *The Reconstruction of Religion*, op. cit., pp. 40-1.

to the savage as well as to the civilized man. It does so, as we have said, because it braces vital feeling; and psychologists tell us that the reason why it braces vital feeling is because it is an adaptive process in which all of the lower centres of life are brought to reinforce the higher centres. The universalization of values means, in other words, in psycho-physical terms, that the lower nerve centres pour their energies into the higher nerve centres, thus harmonizing and bringing to a maximum of vital efficiency life on its inner side. It is thus that religion taps new levels of energy, for meeting the crisis of life, while at the same time it brings about a deeper harmony between the inner and the outer.

Will conversion raise the general social status of the Untouchables? It is difficult to see how there can be two opinions on this question.

The oft-quoted answer given by Shakespeare to the question what is in a name hardly shows sufficient understanding of the problem of a name. A rose called by another name would smell as sweet would be true if names served no purpose and if people instead of depending upon names took the trouble of examining each case and formed their opinions and attitudes about it on the basis of their examination. Unfortunately, names serve a very important purpose. They play a great part in social economy. Names are symbols. Each name represents association of certain ideas and notions about a certain object. It is a label. From the label people know what it is. It saves them the trouble of examining each case individually and determine for themselves whether the ideas and notions commonly associated with the object are true. People in society have to deal with so many objects that it would be impossible for them to examine each case. They must go by the name that is why all advertisers are keen in finding a good name. If the name is not attractive the article does not go down with the people.

The name 'Untouchable' is a bad name. It repels, forbids, and stinks. The social attitude of the Hindu towards the Untouchable is determined by the very name 'Untouchable'. There is a fixed attitude towards 'Untouchables' which is determined by the stink which is imbedded in the name 'Untouchable'. People have no mind to go into the individual merits of each Untouchable no matter how meritorious he is. All Untouchables realize this. There is a general attempt to call themselves by some name other than the 'Untouchables'. The Chamars call themselves Ravidas or

Jatavas. The Doms call themselves Shilpakars. The Pariahs call themselves Adi-Dravidas, the Madigas call themselves Arundhatyas, the Mahars call themselves Chokhamela or Somavamshi and the Bhangis call themselves Balmikis. All of them if away from their localities would call themselves Christians.

The Untouchables know that if they call themselves Untouchables they will at once draw the Hindu out and expose themselves to his wrath and his prejudice. That is why they give themselves other names which may be likened to the process of undergoing protective discolouration.

It is not seldom that this discolouration completely fails to serve its purpose. For to be a Hindu is for Hindus not an ultimate social category. The ultimate social category is caste, nay sub-caste if there is a sub-caste. When the Hindus meet 'May I know who are you' is a question sure to be asked. To this question 'I am a Hindu' will not be a satisfactory answer. It will certainly not be accepted as a final answer. The inquiry is bound to be further pursued. The answer 'Hindu' is bound to be followed by another; 'What caste?' The answer to that is bound to be followed by question: 'What subcaste?' It is only when the questioner reaches the ultimate social category which is either caste or sub-caste that he will stop his questionings.

The Untouchable who adopts the new name as a protective discolouration finds that the new name does not help and that in the course of relentless questionings he is, so to say, run down to earth and made to disclose that he is an Untouchable. The concealment makes him the victim of greater anger than his original voluntary disclosure would have done.

From this discussion two things are clear. One is that the low status of the Untouchables is bound upon with a stinking name. Unless the name is changed there is no possibility of a rise in their social status. The other is that a change of name within Hinduism will not do. The Hindu will not fail to penetrate through such a name and make the Untouchable confer himself as an Untouchable.

The name matters and matters a great deal. For, the name can make a revolution in the status of the Untouchables. But the name must be the name of a community outside Hinduism and beyond its power of spoilation and degradation. Such name can be the property of the Untouchable only if they undergo religious conversion. A conversion by change of name within Hinduism is a clandestine conversion which can be of no avail.

This discussion on conversion may appear to be somewhat airy. It is bound to be so. It cannot become material unless it is known which religion the Untouchables choose to accept. For what particular advantage would flow from conversion would depend upon the religion selected and the social position of the followers of that religion. One religion may give them all the three benefits, another only two and a third may result in conferring upon them only one of the advantages of conversion. What religion the Untouchables should choose is not the subject matter of this chapter. The subject matter of this chapter is whether conversion can solve the problem of untouchability. The answer to that question is emphatically in the affirmative.

The force of the argument, of course, rests on a view of religion which is somewhat different from the ordinary view according to which religion is concerned with man's relation to God and all that it means. According to this view, religion exists not for the saving of souls but for the preservation of society and the welfare of the individual. It is only those who accept the former view of religion that find it difficult to understand how conversion can solve the problem of untouchability. Those who accept the view of religion adopted in this chapter will have no difficulty in accepting the soundness of the conclusion.

VI

Caste

Ambedkar made a close study of the institution of caste, the changes and resilience it displayed, and its impact on social relations. He ascribed most of the evils of Hinduism to this institution and called for its annihilation.

Castes in India, their Origin, Mechanism and Development[208]— this essay was written for the anthropology seminar of Dr A. A. Goldenweisser, at Columbia University in 1916 and published in the journal of *Indian Antiquity*, in August 1917. In the essay, Ambedkar identified the chief characteristic of caste as endogamy superimposed on exogamy in a culturally homogenous ambience. Here, the Durkheimean functional explanation regarding the reproduction of caste has gone along with its description as 'an enclosed class', *a la* Max Weber. He saw the caste system as the ranking of castes following the example set by the Brahmins.

Annihilation of Caste[209] Ambedkar was invited by a Lahore-based organization, called Jat-Pat-Todak Mandal, a forum for social reforms, to address its annual conference in May 1936. The address that Ambedkar drafted went beyond the limited agenda of the Mandal and demanded the rejection of the *Shastras* that justified the caste system. Ambedkar also repeated the pledge made at the Yeola conference that he might not continue to remain in the Hindu fold. When the Mandal sought to rein in the radical thrust of the address by trying to omit certain passages, Ambedkar cancelled his appointment with the Mandal and published the report independently. Except for the sections dealing with the severity of caste injunctions, the need for social reforms and the futility of the socialist ideal that ignores caste, the rest of the address is reproduced here.

Reply to the Mahatma.[210] Gandhi reviewed *Annihilation of Caste* in the *Harijan*, dated 11 July 1936 and felt that no reformer should ignore the address. In its issue of 18 July 1936, he made an extended comment on Hindu scriptures and how to interpret them. The essay is Ambedkar's response to Gandhi.

19

Castes in India

THEIR MECHANISM, GENESIS AND DEVELOPMENT

Many of us, I dare say, have witnessed local, national or international expositions of material objects that make up the sum total of human civilization. But few can entertain the idea of there being such a thing as an exposition of human institutions. Exhibition of human institutions is a strange idea; some might call it the wildest of ideas. But as students of Ethnology I hope you will not be hard on this innovation, for it is not so, and to you at least it should not be strange.

You all have visited, I believe, some historic place like the ruins of Pompeii, and listened with curiosity to the history of the remains as it flowed from the glib tongue of the guide. In my opinion a student of Ethnology, in one sense at least, is much like the guide. Like his prototype, he holds up (perhaps with more seriousness and desire of self-instruction) the social institutions to view, with all the objectiveness humanly possible, and inquires into their origin and function.

Most of our fellow students in this Seminar, which concerns itself with primitive *versus* modern society, have ably acquitted themselves along these lines by giving lucid expositions of the various institutions, modern or primitive, in which they are interested. It is my turn now, this evening to entertain you, as best I can, with a paper on 'Castes in India: Their mechanism, genesis and development'.

I need hardly remind you of the complexity of the subject I intend to handle. Subtler minds and abler pens than mine have been brought to the task of unravelling the mysteries of caste; but unfortunately it still remains in the domain of the 'unexplained', not to say of the 'un-understood'. I am quite alive to the complex intricacies of a hoary institution like caste, but I am not so pessimistic as to relegate it to the region of the unknowable, for I believe it can be known. The caste problem is a vast one, both theoretically and practically. Practically, it is an institution that portends tremendous consequences. It is a local problem, but one capable of much wider mischief, for 'as long as caste in India does exist, Hindus will hardly intermarry or have any social intercourse with outsiders; and if Hindus migrate to other regions on earth, Indian caste would become a world problem.'[a] Theoretically, it has defied a great many scholars who have taken upon themselves, as a labour of love, to dig into its origin. Such being the case, I cannot treat the problem in its entirety. Time, space and acumen, I am afraid, would all fail me, if I attempted to do otherwise than limit myself to a phase of it, namely, the genesis, mechanism and spread of the caste system, I will strictly observe this rule, and will dwell on extraneous matters only when it is necessary to clarify or support a point in my thesis.

To proceed with the subject. According to well-known ethnologists, the population of India is a mixture of Aryans, Dravidians, Mongolians and Scythians. All these stocks of people came into India from various directions and with various cultures, centuries ago, when they were in a tribal state. They all in turn elbowed their entry into the country by fighting with their predecessors, and after a stomachful of it settled down as peaceful neighbours. Through constant contact and mutual intercourse they evolved a common culture that superseded their distinctive cultures. It may be granted that there has not been a thorough amalgamation of the various stocks that make up the peoples of India, and to a traveller from within the boundaries of India, the East presents a marked contrast in physique and even in colour to the West, as does the South to the North. But amalgamation can never be the sole criterion of homogeneity as predicated of any people. Ethnically,

[a] Shridhar, V. Ketkar, A. M., *The History of Caste in India*, Ithaca, N. Y., Messers Taylor & Carpenter, 1909, p. 4.

all people are heterogeneous. It is the unity of culture that is the basis of homogeneity. Taking this for granted, I venture to say that there is no country that can rival the Indian peninsula with respect to the unity of its culture. It has not only a geographic unity, but it has over and above all, a deeper and a much more fundamental unity—the indubitable cultural unity that covers the land from end to end. But it is because of this homogeneity that caste becomes a problem so difficult to be explained. If Hindu society were a mere federation of mutually exclusive units, the matter would be simple enough. But caste is a parcelling of an already homogeneous unit, and the explanation of the genesis of caste is the explanation of this process of parcelling.

Before launching into our field of enquiry, it is better to advise ourselves regarding the nature of a caste. I will, therefore, draw upon a few of the best students of caste for their definitions of it:

1. Mr Senart, a French authority, defines a caste as 'a close corporation, in theory at any rate rigorously hereditary: equipped with a certain traditional and independent organization, including a chief and a council, meeting on occasion in assemblies of more or less plenary authority and joining together at certain festivals: bound together by common occupations, which relate more particularly to marriage and to food and to questions of ceremonial pollution, and ruling its members by the exercise of jurisdiction, the extent of which varies, but which succeeds in making the authority of the community more felt by the sanction of certain penalties and, above all, by final irrevocable exclusion from the group.'[211]

2. Mr Nesfield defines a caste as 'a class of the community which disowns any connection with any other class and can neither intermarry nor eat nor drink with any but persons of their own community.'[212]

3. According to Sir H. Risley, 'a caste may be defined as a collection of families or groups of families bearing a common name which usually denotes or is associated with specific occupation, claiming common descent from a mythical ancestor, human or divine, professing to follow the same professional callings and are regarded by those who are competent to give an opinion as forming a single homogeneous community.'[213]

4. Dr Ketkar defines caste as 'a social group having two characteristics: (i) membership is confined to those who are born of members and includes all persons so born; (ii) the members are forbidden by an inexorable social law to marry outside the group.'[214]

To review these definitions is of great importance for our purpose. It will be noticed that taken individually the definitions of three of the writers include too much or too little: none is complete or correct by itself and all have missed the central point in the mechanism of the caste system. Their mistake lies in trying to define caste as an isolated unit by itself, and not as a group within, and with definite relations to, the system of caste as a whole. Yet collectively all of them are complementary to one another, each one emphasizing what has been obscured in the other. By way of criticism, therefore, I will take only those points common to all castes in each of the above definitions which are regarded as peculiarities of caste and evaluate them as such.

To start with Mr Senart. He draws attention to the 'idea of pollution' as a characteristic of caste. With regard to this point it may be safely said that it is by no means a peculiarity of caste as such. It usually originates in priestly ceremonialism and is a particular case of the general belief in purity. Consequently its necessary connection with caste may be completely denied without damaging the working of caste. The 'idea of pollution' has been attached to the institution of caste, only because the caste that enjoys the highest rank is the priestly caste: while we know that priest and purity are old associates. We may therefore conclude that the 'idea of pollution' is a characteristic of caste only in so far as caste has a religious flavour. Mr Nesfield in his way dwells on the absence of messing with those outside the caste as one of its characteristics. In spite of the newness of the point we must say that Mr Nesfield has mistaken the effect for the cause. Caste, being a self-enclosed unit naturally limits social intercourse, including messing etc. to members within it. Consequently, this absence of messing with outsiders is not due to positive prohibition, but is a natural result of caste, i.e. exclusiveness. No doubt this absence of messing originally due to exclusiveness, acquired the prohibitory character or a religious injunction, but it may be regarded as a later growth. Sir H. Risley, makes no new point deserving of special attention.

We now pass on to the definition of Dr Ketkar who has done much for the elucidation of the subject. Not only is he a native, but he has also brought a critical acumen and an open mind to bear on his study of caste. His definition merits consideration, for he has defined caste in its relation to a system of castes, and has concentrated his attention only on those characteristics which are absolutely necessary for the existence of a caste within a system, rightly excluding all others as being secondary or derivative in character. With respect to his definition it must, however, be said that in it there is a slight confusion of thought, lucid and clear as otherwise it is. He speaks of *prohibition of intermarriage* and *membership by autogeny* as the two characteristics of caste. I submit that these are but two aspects of one and the same thing, and not two different things as Dr Ketkar supposes them to be. If you prohibit intermarriage the result is that you limit membership to those born within the group. Thus the two are the obverse and the reverse sides of the same medal.

This critical evaluation of the various characteristics of caste leave no doubt that prohibition, or rather the absence of intermarriage—endogamy, to be concise—is the only one that can be called the essence of caste when rightly understood. But some may deny this on abstract anthropological grounds, for there exist endogamous groups without giving rise to the problem of caste. In a general way this may be true, as endogamous societies, culturally different, making their abode in localities more or less removed, and having little to do with each other are a physical reality. The Negroes and the Whites and the various tribal groups that go by name of American Indians in the United States may be cited as more or less appropriate illustrations in support of this view. But we must not confuse matters, for in India the situation is different. As pointed out before, the peoples of India form a homogeneous whole. The various races of India occupying definite territories have more or less fused into one another and do possess cultural unity, which is the only criterion of a homogeneous population. Given this homogeneity as a basis, caste becomes a problem altogether new in character and wholly absent in the situation constituted by the mere propinquity of endogamous social or tribal groups. Caste in India means an artificial chopping off of the population into fixed and definite units, each one prevented from fusing into another through the custom of endogamy. Thus the conclusion is inevitable that *endogamy is the only characteristic that is peculiar to caste*, and if we succeed in showing how endogamy is maintained, we shall practically have proved the genesis and also the mechanism of caste.

It may not be quite easy for you to anticipate why I regard endogamy as a key to the mystery of the caste system. Not to strain your imagination too much, I will proceed to give you my reasons for it.

It may not also be out of place to emphasize at this moment that no civilized society of today presents more survivals of primitive times than does the Indian society. Its religion is essentially primitive and its tribal code, in spite of the advance of time and civilization, operates in all its pristine vigour even today. One of these primitive survivals, to which I wish particularly to draw your attention is the *custom of exogamy*. The prevalence of exogamy in the primitive worlds is a fact too well-known to need any explanation. With the growth of history, however, exogamy has lost its efficacy, and excepting the nearest blood-kins, there is usually no social bar restricting the field of marriage. But regarding the people of India, the law of exogamy is a positive injunction even today. Indian society still savours of the clan system, even though there are no clans; and this can be easily seen from the law of matrimony which centres round the principle of exogamy, for it is not that *sapindas* (blood-kins) cannot marry, but a marriage even between *sagotras* (of the same class) is regarded as a sacrilege.

Nothing is therefore more important for you to remember than the fact that endogamy is foreign to the people of India. The various *gotras* of India are and have been exogamous: so are the other groups with totemic organization. It is no exaggeration to say that with the people of India exogamy is a creed and none dare infringe it, so much so that, in spite of the endogamy of the castes within them, exogamy is strictly observed and that there are more rigorous penalties for violating exogamy than there are for violating endogamy. You will, therefore, readily see that with exogamy as the rule there could be no caste, for exogamy means fusion. But we have castes; consequently in the final analysis creation of castes, so far as India is concerned, means the superposition of endogamy on exogamy. However, in an originally exogamous population an easy working out of endogamy (which is equivalent to the creation of caste) is a grave problem, and it is in the consideration of the means utilized for the preservation of endogamy against exogamy that we may hope to find the solution of our problem.

Thus the superimposition of endogamy on exogamy means the creation of caste. But this is not an easy affair. Let us take an imaginary group that desires to make itself into a caste and analyse what means it will have to adopt to make itself endogamous. If a group desires to make itself endogamous, a formal injunction against intermarriage with outside groups will be of no avail, especially if prior to the introduction of endogamy, exogamy had been the rule in the matrimonial relations. Again, there is a tendency in all groups lying in close contact with one another to assimilate and amalgamate, and thus consolidate into a homogeneous society. If this tendency is to be strongly counteracted in the interest of caste formation, it is absolutely necessary to circumscribe a circle outside which people should not contract marriages.

Nevertheless, this encircling to prevent marriages from without creates problems from within which are not very easy of solution. Roughly speaking, in a normal group the two sexes are more or less evenly distributed, and generally speaking there is an equality between those of the same age. The equality is, however, never quite realized in actual societies. At the same time to the group that is desirous of making itself into a caste, the maintenance of equality between the sexes becomes the ultimate goal, for without it endogamy can no longer subsist. In other words, if endogamy is to be preserved, conjugal rights from within have to be provided for, otherwise members of the group will be driven out of the circle to take care of themselves in any way they can. But in order that the conjugal rights be provided for from within, it is absolutely necessary to maintain a numerical equality between the marriageable units of the two sexes within the group desirous of making itself into a caste. It is only through the maintenance of such an equality that the necessary endogamy of the group can be kept intact, and a very large disparity is sure to break it.

The problem of caste, then ultimately resolves itself into one of repairing the disparity between the marriageable units of the two sexes within it. Left to nature, the much needed parity between the units can be realized only when a couple dies simultaneously. But this is a rare contingency. The husband may die before the wife and create a *surplus woman*, who must be disposed of, else through intermarriage she will violate the endogamy of the group. In like manner the husband may survive his wife and be a *surplus man*, whom the group, while it may sympathize with him for the sad bereavement, has to dispose of, else he will marry outside the caste and will break the endogamy. Thus both the *surplus man* and the *surplus woman* constitute a menace to the caste if not taken care of, for not finding suitable partners inside their prescribed circle (and left to themselves they cannot find any, for if the matter be not regulated there can only be just enough pairs to go round) very likely they will transgress the boundary, marry outside and import offspring that is foreign to the caste.

Let us see what out imaginary group is likely to do with this *surplus man* and *surplus woman*. We will first take up the case of the *surplus woman*. She can be disposed of in two different ways so as to preserve the endogamy of the caste.

First: burn her on the funeral pyre of her deceased husband and get rid of her. This, however, is rather an impracticable way of solving the problem of sex disparity. In some cases it may work, in others it may not. Consequently, every surplus woman cannot thus be disposed of, because it is an easy solution but a hard realization. And so the *surplus woman* (= widow), if not disposed of, remains in the group: but in her very existence lies a double danger. She may marry outside the caste and violate endogamy, or she may marry within the caste and through competition encroach upon the chances of marriage that must be reserved for the potential brides in the caste. She is therefore a menace in any case, and something must be done to her if she cannot be burned along with her deceased husband.

The second remedy is to enforce widowhood on her for the rest of her life. So far as the objective results are concerned, burning is a better solution than enforcing widowhood. Burning the widow eliminates all the three evils that a *surplus woman* is fraught with. Being dead and gone she creates no problem of remarriage either inside or outside the caste. But compulsory widowhood is superior to burning because it is more practicable. Besides being comparatively human it also guards against the evils of remarriage as does burning; but it fails to guard the morals of the group. No doubt under compulsory widowhood the woman remains, and just because she is deprived of her natural right of being a legitimate wife in future, the incentive to immoral conduct is increased. But this is by no means an insuperable difficulty. She can be degraded to a condition in which she is no longer a source of allurement.

The problem of *surplus man* (= widower) is much more important and much more difficult than that of the *surplus woman* in a group that desires to make itself into a caste. From time immemorial man as compared with woman has had the upper hand. He is a dominant figure in every group and of the two sexes has greater prestige. With this traditional superiority of man over woman, his wishes have always been consulted. Woman, on the other hand, has been an easy prey to all kinds of iniquitous injunctions, religious, social or economic. But man as a maker of injunctions is most often above them all. Such being the case, you cannot accord the same kind of treatment to a *surplus man* as you can to a *surplus woman* in a caste.

The project of burning him with his deceased wife is hazardous in two ways: first of all it cannot be done, simply because he is a man. Secondly, if done, a sturdy soul is lost to the caste. There remain then only two solutions which can conveniently dispose of him. I say conveniently, because he is an asset to the group.

Important as he is to the group, endogamy is still more important, and the solution must assure both these ends. Under these circumstances he may be forced or I should say induced, after the manner of the widow, to remain a widower for the rest of his life. This solution is not altogether difficult, for without any compulsion some are so disposed as to enjoy self-imposed celibacy, or even to take a further step of their own accord and renounce the world and its joys. But, given human nature as it is, this solution can hardly be expected to be realized. On the other hand, as is very likely to be the case, if the *surplus man* remains in the group as an active participator in group activities, he is a danger to the morals of the group. Looked at from a different point of view celibacy, though easy in cases where it succeeds, is not so advantageous even then to the material prospects of the caste. If he observes genuine celibacy and renounces the world, he would not be a menace to the preservation of caste endogamy or caste morals as he undoubtedly would be if he remained a secular person. But as an ascetic celibate he is as good as burned, so far as the material well-being of his caste is concerned. A caste, in order that it may be large enough to afford a vigorous communal life, must be maintained at a certain numerical strength. But to hope for this and to proclaim celibacy is the same as trying to cure atrophy by bleeding.

Imposing celibacy on the *surplus man* in the group, therefore, fails both theoretically and practically. It is in the interest of the caste to keep him as a *Grahastha* (one who raises a family), to use a Sanskrit technical term. But the problem is to provide him with a wife from within the Caste. At the outset this is not possible, for the ruling ratio in a caste has to be one man to one woman and none can have two chances of marriage, for in a caste thoroughly self-enclosed there are always just enough marriageable women to go round for the marriageable men. Under these circumstances, the *surplus man* can be provided with a wife only by recruiting a bride from the ranks of those not yet marriageable in order to tie him down to the group. This is certainly the best of the possible solutions in the case of the *surplus man*. By this, he is kept within the caste. By this means, numerical depletion through constant outflow is guarded against, and by this endogamy morals are preserved.

It will now be seen that the four means by which numerical disparity between the two sexes is conveniently maintained are: (1) burning the widow with her deceased husband; (2) compulsory widowhood—a milder form of burning; (3) imposing celibacy on the widower and (4) wedding him to a girl not yet marriageable. Though, as I said above, burning the widow and imposing celibacy on the widower are of doubtful service to the group in its endeavour to preserve its endogamy, all of them operate as *means*. But means, as forces, when liberated or set in motion create an end. What then is the end that these means create? They create and perpetuate endogamy, while caste and endogamy, according to our analysis of the various definitions of caste, are one and the same thing. Thus the existence of these means is identical with caste and caste involves these means.

This, in my opinion, is the general mechanism of a caste in a system of castes. Let us now turn from these high generalities to the castes in Hindu society and inquire into their mechanism. I need hardly premise that there are a great many pitfalls in the path of those who try to unfold the past, and caste in India to be sure is a very ancient institution. This is especially true where there exist no authentic or written records or where the people, like the Hindus, are so constituted that to them writing history is a folly, for the world is an illusion. But institutions do live, though for a long time they may remain unrecorded and as often as not customs and morals are like fossils that tell their own history. If this is true, our task will be amply rewarded if we scrutinize the solution the Hindus arrived at to meet the problems of the *surplus man* and *surplus woman*.

Complex though it be in its general working Hindu society, even to a superficial observer, presents three singular uxorial customs, namely:

(i) *Sati* or the burning of the widow on the funeral pyre of her deceased husband.

(ii) Enforced widowhood by which a widow is not allowed to remarry.

(iii) Girl marriage.

In addition, one also notes a great hankering after *Sannyasa* (renunciation) on the part of the widower, but this may in some cases be due purely to psychic disposition.

So far as I know, no scientific explanation of the origin of these customs is forthcoming even today. We have plenty of philosophy to tell us why these customs were honoured, but nothing to tell us the causes of their origin and existence. *Sati* had been honoured[215] because it is a 'proof of the perfect unity of body and soul' between husband and wife and of 'devotion beyond the grave', because it embodied the ideal of wifehood, which is well expressed by Uma when she said, 'Devotion to her Lord is woman's honour, it is her eternal heaven: and O Maheshvara', she adds with a most touching human cry, 'I desire not paradise itself if thou are not satisfied with me!' Why compulsory widowhood is honoured I know not, nor have I yet met with any one who sang in praise of it, though there are a great many who adhere to it. The eulogy in honour of girl marriage is reported by Dr Ketkar to be as follows: 'A really faithful man or woman ought not to feel affection for a woman or a man other than the one with whom he or she is united. Such purity is compulsory not only after marriage, but even before marriage, for that is the only correct ideal of chastity. No maiden could be considered pure if she feels love for a man other than the one to whom she might be married. As she does not know to whom she is going to be married, she must not feel affection for any man at all before marriage. If she does so, it is a sin. So it is better for a girl to know whom she has to love before any sexual consciousness has been awakened in her.[b] Hence girl marriage.

This high-flown and ingenious sophistry indicates why these institutions were honoured, but does not tell us why they were practised, My own interpretation is that they were honoured because they were practised. Anyone slightly acquainted with the

[b] S. V. Ketkar, op. cit., p. 32.

rise of individualism in the eighteenth century will appreciate my remark. At all times, it is the movement that is most important; and the philosophies grow around it long afterwards to justify it and give it a moral support. In like manner I urge that the very fact that these customs were so highly eulogized proves that they needed eulogy for their prevalence. Regarding the question as to why they arose, I submit that they were needed to create the structure of caste and the philosophies in honour of them were intended to popularize them, or to gild the pill, as we might say, for they must have been so abominable and shocking to the moral sense of the unsophisticated that they needed a great deal of sweetening. These customs are essentially of the nature of *means*, though they are represented as ideals. But this should not blind us from understanding the *results* that flow from them. One might safely say that idealization of means is necessary and in this particular case was perhaps motivated to endow them with greater efficacy. Calling a means an end does no harm, except that it disguises its real character; but it does not deprive it of its real nature, that of a means. You may pass a law that all cats are dogs, just as you can call a means an end. But you can no more change the nature of means thereby than you can turn cats into dogs; consequently I am justified in holding that, whether regarded as ends or as means, *Sati, enforced widowhood* and *girl marriage* are customs that were primarily intended to solve the problem of the *surplus man* and *surplus woman* in a caste and to maintain its endogamy. Strict endogamy could not be preserved without these customs, while caste without endogamy is a fake.

Having explained the mechanism of the creation and preservation of caste in India, the further question as to its genesis naturally arises. The question of origin is always an annoying question and in the study of caste it is sadly neglected; some have connived at it, while others have dodged it. Some are puzzled as to whether there could be such a thing as the origin of caste and suggest that 'if we cannot control our fondness for the word "origin", we should better use the plural form, viz. "origins of caste"'. As for myself I do not feel puzzled by the origin of caste in India for, as I have established before, endogamy is the only characteristic of caste and when I say *origin of caste* I mean *the origin of the mechanism for endogamy*.

The atomistic conception of individuals in a society so greatly popularized—I was about to say vulgarized—in political orations is the greatest humbug. To say that individuals make up society is trivial; society is always composed of classes. It may be an exaggeration to assert the theory of class-conflict, but the existence of definite classes in a society is a fact. Their basis may differ. They may be economic or intellectual or social, but an individual in a society is always a member of a class. This is a universal fact and early Hindu society could not have been an exception to this rule, and, as a matter of fact, we know it was not. If we bear this generalization in mind, our study of the genesis of caste would be very much facilitated, for we have only to determine what was the class that first made itself into a caste, for class and caste, so to say, are next door neighbours, and it is only a span that separates the two. *A caste is an enclosed class.*

The study of the origin of caste must furnish us with an answer to the question—what is the class that raised this 'enclosure' around itself? The question may seem too inquisitorial, but it is pertinent, and an answer to this will serve us to elucidate the mystery of the growth and development of castes all over India. Unfortunately, a direct answer to this question is not within my power. I can answer it only indirectly. I said just above that the customs in question were current in the Hindu society. To be true to facts it is necessary to qualify the statement, as it connotes universality of their prevalence. These customs in all their strictness are obtainable only in one caste, namely the Brahmins, who occupy the highest place in the social hierarchy of the Hindu society; and as their prevalence in non-Brahmin castes is derivative of their observance is neither strict nor complete. This important fact can serve as a basis of an important observation. If the prevalence of these customs in the non-Brahmin caste is derivative, as can be shown very easily, then it needs no argument to prove what class is the father of the institution of caste. Why the Brahmin class should have enclosed itself into a caste is a different question, which may be left as an employment for another occasion. But the strict observance of these customs and the social superiority arrogated by the priestly class in all ancient civilizations are sufficient to prove that they were the originators of this 'unnatural institution' founded and maintained through these unnatural means.

I now come to the third part of my paper regarding the question of the growth and spread of the caste system all over India. The question I have to answer is: How did the institution of caste spread among the rest of the non-Brahmin population of the country? The question of the spread of the caste all over India has suffered a worse fate than the question of genesis. And the main cause, as it seems to me, is that the two questions of spread and of origin are not separated. This is because of the common belief among scholars that the caste system has either been imposed upon the docile population of India by a law-giver as a divine dispensation, or that it has grown according to some law of social growth peculiar to the Indian people.

I first propose to handle the law-giver of India. Every country has its law-giver, who arises as an incarnation (*avatar*) in times of emergency to set right a sinning humanity and give it the laws of justice and morality. Manu, the law-giver of India, if he did exist, was certainly an audacious person. If the story that he gave the law of caste be credited, then Manu must have been a dare-devil fellow and the humanity that accepted his dispensation must be a humanity quite different from the one we are acquainted with. It is unimaginable that the law of caste was *given*. It is hardly an exaggeration to say that Manu could not have outlived his law, for what is that class that can submit to be degraded to the status of brutes by the pen of a man, and suffer him to raise another class to the pinnacle? Unless he was a tyrant who held all the population in subjection it cannot be imagined that he could have been allowed to dispense his patronage in this grossly unjust manner, as may be easily seen by a mere glance at his 'Institutes'. I may seem hard on Manu but I am sure my force is not strong enough to kill his ghost. He lives, like a disembodied spirit and is appealed to, and I am afraid will yet live long. One thing I want to impress upon you is that Manu did not *give the law* of caste and that he could not do so. Caste existed long before Manu. He was an upholder of it and therefore philosophized about it, but certainly he did not and could not ordain the present order of Hindu society. His work ended with the codification of existing caste rules and the preaching of caste *dharma*. The spread and growth of the caste system is too gigantic a task to be achieved by the power or cunning of an individual or of a class. Similar in argument is the theory that the

Brahmins created the caste. After what I have said regarding Manu, I need hardly say anything more, except to point out that it is incorrect in thought and malicious in intent. The Brahmins may have been guilty of many things, and I dare say they were, but the imposing of the caste system on the non-Brahmin population was beyond their mettle. They may have helped the process by their glib philosophy, but they certainly could not have pushed their scheme beyond their own confines. To fashion society after one's own pattern! How glorious! How hard! One can take pleasure and eulogize its furtherance, but cannot further it very far. The vehemence of my attack may seem to be unnecessary; but I can assure you that it is not uncalled for. There is a strong belief in the mind of orthodox Hindus that the Hindu society was somehow moulded into the framework of the caste system and that it is an organization consciously created by the *Shastras*. Not only does this belief exist, but it is being justified on the ground that it cannot but be good, because it is ordained by the *Shastras* and the *Shastras* cannot be wrong. I have urged so much on the adverse side of this attitude, not because the religious sanctity is grounded on scientific basis, nor to help those reformers who are preaching against it. Preaching did not make the caste system neither will it unmake it. My aim is to show the falsity of the attitude that has exalted religious sanction to the position of a scientific explanation.

Thus the great man theory does not help us very far in solving the spread of caste in India. Western scholars, probably not much given to hero-worship have attempted other explanations. The nuclei, round which have 'formed' the various castes in India, are, according to them: (1) occupation; (2) survivals of tribal organizations etc.; (3) the rise of new beliefs; (4) cross-breeding and (5) migration.

The question may be asked whether these nuclei do not exist in other societies and whether they are peculiar to India. If they are not peculiar to India, but are common to the world, why is it that they did not 'form', caste in other parts of this planet? Is it because those parts are holier than the land of the *Vedas*, or that the professors are mistaken? I am afraid that the latter is the truth.

In spite of the high theoretic value claimed by the several authors for their respective theories based on one or other of the above nuclei, one regrets to say that on close examination they are nothing more than filling illustrations—what Matthew Arnold means by 'the grand name without the grand thing in it'. Such are the various theories of caste advanced by Sir Denzil Ibbetson,[216] Mr Nesfield, Mr Senart and Sir H. Risley. To criticize them in a lump would be to say that they are a disguised form of the *Petitio Principii* of formal logic. To illustrate: Mr Nesfield says that 'function and function only... was the foundation upon which the whole system of Castes in India was built up'. But he may rightly be reminded that he does not very much advance our thought by making the above statement, which practically amounts to saying that castes in India are functional or occupational, which is a very poor discovery! We have yet to know from Mr Nesfield why is it that an occupational group turned into an occupational caste? I would very cheerfully have undertaken the task of dwelling on the theories of other ethnologists, had it not been for the fact that Mr Nesfield's is a typical one.

Without stopping to criticize those theories that explain the caste system as a natural phenomenon occurring in obedience to the law of disintegration, as explained by Herbert Spencer in his formula of evolution, or as natural as 'the structural differentiation within an organism'[217]—to employ the phraseology of orthodox apologists—or as an early attempt to test the laws of eugenics—as all belonging to the same class of fallacy which regards the caste system as inevitable, or as being consciously imposed in anticipation of these laws on a helpless and humble population, I will now lay before you my own view on the subject.

We shall be well-advised to recall at the outset that the Hindu society, in common with other societies, was composed of classes and the earliest known are the (1) Brahmins or the priestly class; (2) the Kshatriya, or the military class; (3) the Vaishya, or the merchant class and (4) the Shudra, or the artisan and menial class. Particular attention has to be paid to the fact that this was essentially a class system, in which individuals, when qualified, could change their class, and therefore classes did change their personnel. At some time in the history of the Hindus, the priestly class socially detached itself from the rest of the body of people and through a closed-door policy became a caste by itself. The other classes being subject to the law of social division of labour underwent differentiation, some into large, others into very minute groups. The Vaishya and Shudra classes were the original inchoate plasm, which formed the sources of the numerous castes of today. As the military occupation does not very easily lend itself to very minute sub-division, the Kshatriya class could have differentiated into soldiers and administrators.

This sub-division of a society is quite natural. But the unnatural thing about these sub-divisions is that they have lost the open-door character of the class system and have become self-enclosed units called castes. The question is: were they compelled to close their doors and become endogamous, or did they close on their own accord? I submit that there is a double line of answer: *Some closed the door: Others found it closed against them.* The one is a psychological interpretation and the other is mechanistic, but they are complementary and both are necessary to explain the phenomena of caste-formation in its entirety.

I will first take up the psychological interpretation. The question we have to answer in this connection is: Why did these sub-division or classes, if you please, industrial, religious or otherwise, become self-enclosed or endogamous? My answer is because the Brahmins were so. Endogamy or the closed-door system, was a fashion in the Hindu society, and as it had originated from the Brahmin caste it was whole-heartedly imitated by all the non-Brahmin sub-divisions or classes, who, in their turn, became endogamous castes. It is 'the infection of imitation' that caught all these sub-divisions on their onward march of differentiation and has turned them into castes. The propensity to imitate is a deep-seated one in the human mind and need not be deemed an inadequate explanation for the formation of the various castes in India. It is so deep-seated that Walter Bagehot argues that,

We must not think of...imitation as voluntary, or even conscious. On the contrary it has its seat mainly in very obscure parts of the mind, whose notions, so far from being consciously produced, are hardly felt to exist; so far from being conceived beforehand, are not even felt at the time. The main seat of the imitative part of our nature is our belief, and the causes predisposing us to believe this or disinclining us to believe that are among the obscurest parts of our nature. But as to the imitative nature of credulity there can be no doubt.[c]

[c] Walter Bagehot, *Physics and Politics or Thoughts on the Application of The Principles of Natural Selection and Inheritance to Political Society*, London, Kegan Paul, Trench, Trubner & Co., 1915, p. 60.

This propensity to imitate has been made the subject of a scientific study by Gabriel Tarde, who lays down three laws of imitation. One of his three laws is that imitation flows from the higher to the lower or, to quote his own words, 'Given the opportunity, a nobility will always and everywhere imitate its leaders, its kings or sovereigns, and the people likewise, given the opportunity, its nobility.'[d] Another of Tarde's laws of imitation is: that the extent or intensity of imitation varies inversely in proportion to distance, or in his own words:

The thing that is most imitated is the most superior one of those that are nearest. In fact, the influence of the model's example is efficacious universally to its *distance* as well as directly to its superiority. Distance is understood here in its sociological meaning. However distant in space a stranger may be, he is close by, from this point of view, if we have numerous and daily relations with him and if we have every facility to satisfy our desire to imitate him. This law of the imitation of the nearest, of the least distant, explains the gradual and consecutive character of the spread of an example that has been set by the higher social ranks.[e]

In order to prove my thesis—which really needs no proof—that some castes were formed by imitation, the best way, it seems to me, is to find out whether or not the vital conditions for the formation of castes by imitation exist in Hindu society. The conditions for imitation, according to this standard authority are: (1) that the source of imitation must enjoy prestige in the group and (2) that there must be 'numerous and daily relations' among members of a group. That these conditions were present in India there is little reason to doubt. The Brahmin is a semi-god and very nearly a demi-god. He sets up a mode and moulds the rest. His prestige is unquestionable and is the fountain-head of bliss and good. Can such a being, idolized by scriptures and venerated by the priest-ridden multitude, fail to project his personality on the suppliant humanity? Why, if the story be true, he is believed to be the very end of creation. Such a creature is worthy of more than mere imitation, but at least of imitation; and if he lives in an endogamous enclosure, should not the rest follow his example? Frail humanity! Be it embodied in a grave philosopher or a frivolous housemaid, it succumbs. It cannot be otherwise. Imitation is easy and invention is difficult.

[d] *Laws of Imitation*, tr. by E. C. Parsons, 2nd edition, p. 217.
[e] Ibid., p. 224.

Yet another way of demonstrating the play of imitation in the formation of castes is to understand the attitude of non-Brahmin classes towards those customs which supported the structure of caste in its nascent days until, in the course of history, it became imbedded in the Hindu mind and hangs there to this day without any support—for now it needs no prop but belief—like a weed on the surface of a pond. In a way, but only in a way, the status of a caste in the Hindu Society varies directly with the extent of the observance of the customs of *Sati*, enforced widowhood, and girl marriage. But observance of these customs varies directly with the *distance* (I am using the word in the Tardian sense) that separates the caste. Those castes that are nearest to the Brahmins have imitated all the three customs and insist on the strict observance thereof. Those that are less near have imitated enforced widowhood and girl marriage; others, a little further off, have only girl marriage and those furthest off have imitated only the belief in the caste principle. This imperfect imitation, I dare say, is due partly to what Tarde calls 'distance' and partly to the barbarous character of these customs. This phenomenon is a complete illustration of Tarde's law and leaves no doubt that the whole process of caste-formation in India is a process of imitation of the higher by the lower. At this juncture I will turn back to support a former conclusion of mine, which might have appeared to you as too sudden or unsupported. I said that the Brahmin class first raised the structure of caste by the help of those three customs in question. My reason for that conclusion was that their existence in other classes was derivative. After what I have said regarding the role of imitation in the spread of these customs among the non-Brahmin castes, as means or as ideals, though the imitators have not been aware of it, they exist among them as derivatives; and, if they are derived, there must have been prevalent one original caste that was high enough to have served as a pattern for the rest. But in a theocratic society, who could be the pattern but the servant of God?

This completes the story of those that were weak enough to close their doors. Let us now see how others were closed in as a result of being closed out. This I call the mechanistic process of the formation of caste. It is mechanistic because it is inevitable. That this line of approach, as well as the psychological one, to the explanation of the subject has escaped my predecessors is entirely due to the fact that they have conceived caste as a unit by itself and not as one within a System of Caste. The result of this oversight or lack of sight has been very detrimental to the proper understanding of the subject matter and therefore its correct explanation. I will proceed to offer my own explanation by making one remark which I will urge you to bear constantly in mind. It is this: that *caste in the singular number is an unreality. Castes exist only in the plural number.* There is no such thing as a caste: there are always castes. To illustrate my meaning: while making themselves into a caste, the Brahmins, by virtue of this, created non-Brahmin caste; or, to express it in my own way, while closing themselves in they closed others out. I will clear my point by taking another illustration. Take India as a whole with its various communities designated by the various creeds to which they owe allegiance, to wit, the Hindus, Mohammedans, Jews, Christians and Parsis. Now, barring the Hindus, the rest within themselves are non-caste communities. But with respect to each other they are castes. Again, if the first four enclose themselves, the Parsis are directly closed out, but are indirectly closed in. Symbolically, if Group A wants to be endogamous, Group B has to be so by sheer force of circumstances.

Now apply the same logic to the Hindu society and you have another explanation of the 'fissiparous' character of caste, as a consequence of the virtue of self-duplication that is inherent in it. Any innovation that seriously antagonizes the ethical, religious and social code of the caste is not likely to be tolerated by the caste, and the recalcitrant members of a caste are in danger of being thrown out of the caste, and left to their own fate without having the alternative of being admitted into or absorbed by other castes. Caste rules are inexorable and they do not wait to make nice distinctions between kinds of offence. Innovation may be of any kind, but all kinds will suffer the same penalty. A novel way of thinking will create a new caste for the old ones will not tolerate it. The noxious thinker respectfully called Guru (Prophet) suffers the same fate as the sinners in illegitimate love. The former creates a caste of the nature of a religious sect and the latter a type of mixed caste. Castes have no mercy for a sinner who has the courage to violate the code. The penalty is excommunication and the result is a new caste. It is not peculiar Hindu psychology that induces the excommunicated to form themselves into a caste; far from it.

On the contrary, very often they have been quite willing to be humble members of some caste (higher by preference) if they could be admitted within its fold. But castes are enclosed units and it is their conspiracy with clear conscience that compels the excommunicated to make themselves into a caste. The logic of this obdurate circumstance is merciless, and it is in obedience to its force that some unfortunate groups find themselves enclosed, because others in enclosing, themselves have closed them out, with the result that new groups (formed on any basis obnoxious to the caste rules) by a mechanical law are constantly being converted into castes to a bewildering multiplicity. Thus is told the second tale in the process of caste formation in India.

Now to summarize the main points of my thesis. In my opinion there have been several mistakes committed by the students of caste, which have misled them in their investigations. European students of caste have unduly emphasized the role of colour in the caste system. Themselves impregnated by colour prejudices, they very readily imagined it to be the chief factor in the caste problem. But nothing can be farther from the truth, and Dr Ketkar is correct when he insists that

All the princes whether they belonged to the so-called Aryan race, or the so-called Dravidian race, were Aryas. Whether a tribe or a family was racially Aryan or Dravidian was a question which never troubled the people of India, until foreign scholars came in and began to draw the line. The colour of the skin had long ceased to be a matter of importance.[f]

Again, they have mistaken mere descriptions for explanation and fought over them as though they were theories of origin. There are occupational, religious etc., castes, it is true, but it is by no means an explanation of the origin of caste. We have yet to find out why occupational groups are castes; but this question has never even been raised. Lastly they have taken caste very lightly as though a breath had made it. On the contrary, caste, as I have explained it, is almost impossible to be sustained: for the difficulties that it involves are tremendous. It is true that caste rests on belief, but before belief comes to be the foundation of an institution, the institution itself needs to be perpetuated and fortified. My study of the caste problem involves four main points: (1) that in spite of the composite make-up of the Hindu population, there is a deep

[f] Ketkar, op. cit., p. 82.

cultural unity; (2) that caste is a parcelling into bits of a larger
cultural unit; (3) that there was one caste to start with and (4) that
classes have become castes through imitation and excommunication.

Peculiar interest attaches to the problem of caste in India today;
as persistent attempts are being made to do away with this
unnatural institution. Such attempts at reform, however, have
aroused a great deal of controversy regarding its origin, as to
whether it is due to the conscious command of a Supreme
Authority, or is an unconscious growth in the life of a human
society under peculiar circumstances. Those who hold the latter
view will, I hope, find some food for thought in the standpoint
adopted in this paper. Apart from its practical importance the
subject of caste is an all absorbing problem and the interest aroused
in me regarding its theoretic foundations has moved me to put
before you some of the conclusions, which seem to me well
founded, and the grounds upon which they may be supported. I
am not, however, so presumptuous as to think them in any way
final, or anything more than a contribution to a discussion of the
subject. It seems to me that the car has been shunted on wrong
lines, and the primary object of the paper is to indicate what I
regard to be the right path of investigation, with a view to arrive
at a serviceable truth. We must, however, guard against approaching the subject with a bias. Sentiment must be outlawed from
the domain of science and things should be judged from an
objective standpoint. For myself I shall find as much pleasure
in a positive destruction of my own ideology, as in a rational
disagreement on a topic, which, notwithstanding many learned
disquisitions is likely to remain controversial forever. To conclude,
while I am ambitious to advance a Theory of Caste, if it can be
shown to be untenable I shall be equally willing to give it up.

20

Annihilation of Caste

I

It is a pity that caste even today has its defenders. The defences are many. It is defended on the ground that the caste system is but another name for division of labour and if division of labour is a necessary feature of every civilized society then it is argued that there is nothing wrong in the caste system. Now the first thing to be urged against this view is that caste system is not merely division of labour. *It is also a division of labourers.* Civilized society undoubtedly needs division of labour. But in no civilized society is division of labour accompanied by this unnatural division of labourers into water-tight compartments. The caste system is not merely a division of labourers which is quite different from division of labour—it is an hierarchy in which the division of labourers are graded one above the other. In no other country is the division of labour accompanied by this gradation of labourers. There is also a third point of criticism against this view of the caste system. This division of labour is not spontaneous, it is not based on natural aptitudes. Social and individual efficiency requires us to develop the capacity of an individual to the point of competency to choose and to make his own career. This principle is violated in the caste system in so far as it involves an attempt to appoint tasks to individuals in advance, selected not on the basis of trained original capacities, but on that of the social status of the parents. Looked at from another point of view this stratification of occupations which is the result of the caste system is positively pernicious. Industry is never static. It undergoes rapid and abrupt changes. With such changes an individual must be free to change his occupation. Without such freedom to adjust himself to changing circumstances it would be impossible for him to gain his livelihood. Now the caste system will not allow Hindus to take to occupations where they are wanted if they do not belong to them by heredity. If a Hindu is seen to starve rather than take to new occupations not assigned to his caste, the reason is to be found in the caste system. By not permitting readjustment of occupations, caste becomes a direct cause of much of the unemployment we see in the country. As a form of division of labour the caste system suffers from another serious defect. The division of labour brought about by the caste system is not a division based on choice. Individual sentiment, individual preference has no place in it. It is based on the dogma of predestination. Considerations of social efficiency would compel us to recognize that the greatest evil in the industrial system is not so much poverty and the suffering that it involves as the fact that so many persons have callings which make no appeal to those who are engaged in them. Such callings constantly provoke one to aversion, ill-will and the desire to evade. There are many occupations in India which on account of the fact that they are regarded as degraded by the Hindus provoke those who are engaged in them to aversion. There is a constant desire to evade and escape from such occupations which arises solely because of the blighting effect which they produce upon those who follow them owing to the slight and stigma cast upon them by the Hindu religion. What efficiency can there be in a system under which neither men's hearts nor their minds are in their work? As an economic organization caste is therefore a harmful institution, inasmuch as, it involves the subordination of man's natural powers and inclinations to the exigencies of social rules.

II

Some have dug a biological trench in defence of the caste system. It is said that the object of caste was to preserve purity of race and purity of blood. Now ethnologists are of opinion that men of pure race exist nowhere and that there has been mixture of all races in all parts of the world. Especially is this the case with the people of India. Mr D. R. Bhandarkar in his paper on *Foreign Elements in the Hindu Population* has stated that:

There is hardly a class, or Caste in India which has not a foreign strain in it. There is an admixture of alien blood not only among the warrior classes—the Rajputs and the Marathas—but also among the Brahmins who are under the happy delusion that they are free from all foreign elements.

The caste system cannot be said to have grown as a means of preventing the admixture of races or as a means of maintaining purity of blood. As a matter of fact caste system came into being long after the different races of India had commingled in blood and culture. To hold that distinctions of castes are really distinctions of race and to treat different castes as though they were so many different races is a gross perversion of facts. What racial affinity is there between the Brahmin of the Punjab and the Brahmin of Madras? What racial affinity is there between the untouchable of Bengal and the untouchable of Madras? What racial difference is there between the Brahmin of the Punjab and the Chamar of the Punjab? What racial difference is there between the Brahmin of Madras and the Pariah of Madras? The Brahmin of the Punjab is racially of the same stock as the Chamar of the Punjab and the Brahmin of Madras is of the same race as the Pariah of Madras. The caste system does not demarcate racial division. The caste system is a social division of people of the same race. Assuming it, however, to be a case of racial divisions one may ask: What harm could there be if a mixture of races and of blood was permitted to take place in India by intermarriages between different castes? Men are no doubt divided from animals by so deep a distinction that science recognizes men and animals as two distinct species. But even scientists who believe in purity of races do not assert that the different races constitute different species of men. They are only varieties of one and the same species. As such they can interbreed and produce an offspring which is capable of breeding and which is not sterile. An immense lot of nonsense is talked about heredity and eugenics in defence of the caste system. Few would object to the caste system if it was in accord with the basic principle of eugenics because few can object to the improvement of the race by judicious mating. But one fails to understand how the caste system secures judicious mating. Caste system is a negative thing.

It merely prohibits persons belonging to different castes from intermarrying. It is not a positive method of selecting which two among a given caste should marry. If caste is eugenic in origin then the origin of sub-castes must also be eugenic. But can anyone seriously maintain that the origin of sub-caste is eugenic? I think it would be absurd to contend for such a proposition and for a very obvious reason. If caste means race then differences of sub-castes cannot mean differences of race because sub-castes become *ex hypothesia* sub-divisions of one and the same race. Consequently the bar against intermarrying and interdining between sub-castes cannot be for the purpose of maintaining purity of race or of blood. If sub-castes cannot be eugenic in origin there cannot be any substance in the contention that caste is eugenic in origin. Again if castes is eugenic in origin one can understand the bar against intermarriage. But what is the purpose of the interdict placed on interdining between castes and sub-castes alike? Interdining cannot infect blood and therefore cannot be the cause either of the improvement or of deterioration of the race. This shows that caste had no scientific origin and that those who are attempting to give it an eugenic basis are trying to support by science what is grossly unscientific. Even today eugenics cannot become a practical possibility unless we have definite knowledge regarding the laws of heredity. Professor Bateson in his *Mendel's Principles of Heredity* says,

There is nothing in the descent of the higher mental qualities to suggest that they follow any single system of transmission. It is likely that both they and the more marked developments of physical powers result rather from the coincidence of numerous factors than from the possession of any one genetic element.

To argue that the caste system was eugenic in its conception is to attribute to the forefathers of present-day Hindus a knowledge of heredity which even the modern scientists do not possess. A tree should be judged by the fruits it yields. If caste is eugenic what sort of a race of men it should have produced? Physically speaking the Hindus are a C_3 people. They are a race of Pygmies and dwarfs stunted in stature and wanting in stamina. It is a nation nine-tenths of which is declared to be unfit for military service. This shows that the caste system does not embody the eugenics of modern scientists. It is a social system which embodies the arrogance and selfishness of a perverse section of the Hindus who were superior enough in social status to set it in fashion and who had authority to force it on their inferiors.

III

Caste does not result in economic efficiency. Caste cannot and has not improved the race. Caste has however done one thing. It has completely disorganized and demoralized the Hindus.

The first and foremost thing that must be recognized is that Hindu society is a myth. The name Hindu is itself a foreign name. It was given by the Mohammedans to the natives for the purpose of distinguishing themselves. It does not occur in any Sanskrit work prior to the Mohammedan invasion. They did not feel the necessity of a common name because they had no conception of their having constituted a community. Hindu society as such does not exist. It is only a collection of castes. Each caste is conscious of its existence. Its survival is the be all and end all of its existence. Castes do not even form a federation. A caste has no feeling that it is affiliated to other castes except when there is a Hindu-Muslim riot. On all other occasions each caste endeavours to segregate itself and to distinguish itself from other castes. Each caste not only dines among itself and marries among itself but each caste prescribes its own distinctive dress. What other explanation can there be of the innumerable styles of dress worn by the men and women of India which so amuse the tourists? Indeed the ideal Hindu must be like a rat living in his own hole refusing to have any contact with others. There is an utter lack among the Hindus of what the sociologists call 'consciousness of kind'. There is no Hindu consciousness of kind. In every Hindu the consciousness that exists is the consciousness of his caste. That is the reason why the Hindus cannot be said to form a society or a nation. There are however many Indians whose patriotism does not permit them to admit that Indians are not a nation, that they are only an amorphous mass of people. They have insisted that underlying the apparent diversity there is a fundamental unity which marks the life of the Hindus in as much as there is a similarity of habits and customs, beliefs and thoughts which obtain all over the continent of India. Similarity in habits and customs, beliefs and thoughts there is. But one cannot accept the conclusion that therefore, the Hindus constitute a society. To do so is to misunderstand the essentials which go to make up a society. Men do not become a society by living in physical proximity any more than a man ceases to be a member of his society by living so many miles away from other men. Secondly, similarity in habits and customs, beliefs and thoughts is not enough to constitute men into society. Things may be passed physically from one to another like bricks. In the same way habits and customs, beliefs and thoughts of one group may be taken over by another group and there may thus appear a similarity between the two. Culture spreads by diffusion and that is why one finds similarity between various primitive tribes in the matter of their habits and customs, beliefs and thoughts, although they do not live in proximity. But no one could say that because there was this similarity the primitive tribes constituted one society. This is because similarly in certain things is not enough to constitute a society. Men constitute a society because they have things which they possess in common. To have similar things is totally different from possessing things in common. And the only way by which men can come to possess things in common with one another is by being in communication with one another. This is merely another way of saying that society continues to exist by communication indeed in communication. To make it concrete, it is not enough if men act in a way which agrees with the acts of others. Parallel activity, even if similar, is not sufficient to bind men into a society. This is proved by the fact that the festivals observed by the different castes amongst the Hindus are the same. Yet these parallel performances of similar festivals by the different castes have not bound them into one integral whole. For that purpose what is necessary is for a man to share and participate in a common activity so that the same emotions are aroused in him that animate the others. Making the individual a sharer or partner in the associated activity so that he feels its success as his success, its failure as his failure is the real thing that binds men and makes a society of them. The caste system prevents common activity and by preventing common activity it has prevented the Hindus from becoming a society with a unified life and a consciousness of its own being.

IV

The Hindus often complain of the isolation and exclusiveness of a gang or a clique and blame them for anti-social spirit. But they conveniently forget that this anti-social spirit is the worst feature of their own caste system. One caste enjoys singing a hymn of hate against another caste as much as the Germans did in singing their hymn of hate against the English during the last war. The literature of the Hindus is full of caste genealogies in which an attempt is made to give a noble origin to one caste and an ignoble origin to other castes. The *Sahyadrikhand*[218] is a notorious instance of this class of literature. This anti-social spirit is not confined to caste alone. It has gone deeper and has poisoned the mutual relations of the sub-castes as well. In my province[219] the Golak Brahmins, Deorukha Brahmins, Karada Brahmins, Palshe Brahmins and Chitpavan Brahmins, all claim to be sub-divisions of the Brahmin caste. But the anti-social spirit that prevails between them is quite as marked and quite as virulent as the anti-social spirit that prevails between them and other non-Brahmin castes. There is nothing strange in this. An anti-social spirit is found wherever one group has 'interests of its own' which shut it out from full interaction with other groups, so that its prevailing purpose is protection of what it has got. This anti-social spirit, this spirit of protecting its own interests is as much a marked feature of the different castes in their isolation from one another as it is of nations in their isolation. The Brahmin's primary concern is to protect 'his interest' against those of the non-Brahmins and the Non-Brahmins's primary concern is to protect their interests against those of the Brahmins. The Hindus, therefore, are not merely an assortment of castes but they are so many warring groups each living for itself and for its selfish ideal. There is another feature of caste which is deplorable. The ancestors of the present-day English fought on one side or the other in the wars of the Roses and the Cromwellian War. But the descendents of those who fought on the one side do not bear any animosity—any grudge against the descendents of those who fought on the other side. The feud is forgotten. But the present-day non-Brahmins cannot forgive the present-day Brahmins for the insult their ancestors gave to Shivaji. The present-day Kayasthas will not forgive the present-day Brahmins for the infamy cast upon their forefathers by the forefathers of the latter. To what is this difference due? Obviously to the caste system. The existence of caste and caste consciousness has served to keep the memory of past feuds between castes green and has prevented solidarity.

V

The recent discussion about the excluded and partially included areas[220] has served to draw attention to the position of what are called the aboriginal tribes in India. They number about 13 millions if not more. Apart from the questions whether their exclusion from the new Constitution is proper or improper, the fact still remains that these aborigines have remained in their primitive uncivilized state in a land which boasts of a civilization thousands of years old. Not only are they not civilized but some of them follow pursuits which have led to their being classified as criminals. Thirteen million people living in the midst of civilization are still in a savage state and are leading the life of hereditary criminals! But the Hindus have never felt ashamed of it. This is a phenomenon which in my view is quite unparallelled. What is the cause of this shameful state of affairs? Why has no attempt been made to civilize these aborigines and to lead them to take to a more honourable way of making a living? The Hindus will probably seek to account for this savage state of the aborigines by attributing to them congenital stupidity. They will probably not admit that the aborigines have remained savages because they had made no effort to civilize them, to give them medical aid, to reform them, to make them good citizens. But supposing a Hindu wished to do what the Christian missionary is doing for these aborigines, could he have done it? I submit not. Civilizing the aborigines means adopting them as your own, living in their midst, and cultivating fellow-feeling, in short loving them. How is it possible for a Hindu to do this? His whole life is one anxious effort to preserve his caste. Caste is his precious possession which he must save at any cost. He cannot consent to lose it by establishing contact with the aborigines, the remnants of the hateful Anaryas of the *Vedic* days. Not that a Hindu could not be taught the sense of duty to fallen humanity, but the trouble is that no amount of sense of duty can enable him to overcome his duty to preserve his caste. Caste is, therefore, the real explanation as to why the Hindu has let the savage remain a savage in the midst of his civilization without blushing or without feeling any sense of remorse or repentance. The Hindu has not realized that these aborigines are a source of potential danger. If these savages remain savages they may not do any harm to the Hindu.

But if they are reclaimed by non-Hindus and converted to their faiths they will swell the ranks of the enemies of the Hindus. If this happens the Hindu will have to thank himself and his caste system.

VI

Not only has the Hindu made no effort for the humanitarian cause of civilizing the savages but the higher-caste Hindus have deliberately prevented the lower castes who are within the pale of Hinduism from rising to the cultural level of the higher castes. I will give two instances, one of the Sonars and the other of the Pathare Prabhus. Both are communities quite well-known in Maharashtra. Like the rest of the communities desiring to raise their status these two communities were at one time endeavouring to adopt some of the ways and habits of the Brahmins. The Sonars were styling themselves Daivadnya Brahmins and were wearing their 'dhotis' with folds on and using the word namaskar for salutation. Both, the folded way of wearing the 'dhoti' and the namaskar were special to the Brahmins. The Brahmins did not like this imitation and this attempt by Sonars to pass off as Brahmins. Under the authority of the Peshwas the Brahmins successfully put down this attempt on the part of the Sonars to adopt the ways of the Brahmins. They even got the President of the Councils of the East India Company's settlement in Bombay to issue a prohibitory order against the Sonars residing in Bombay. At one time the Pathare Prabhus had widow-remarriage as a custom of their caste. This custom of widow-remarriage was later on looked upon as a mark of social inferiority by some members of the caste especially because it was contrary to the custom prevalent among the Brahmins. With the object of raising the status of their community some Pathare Prabhus sought to stop this practice of widow-remarriage that was prevalent in their caste. The community was divided into two camps, one for and the other against the innovation. The Peshwas took the side of those in favour of widow-remarriage and thus virtually prohibited the Pathare Prabhus from following the ways of the Brahmins. The Hindus criticize the Mohammedans for having spread their religion by the use of the sword. They also ridicule Christianity on the score of the inquisition. But really speaking who is better and more worthy of our respect—the Mohammedans and Christians who attempted to thrust down the throats of unwilling persons what they regarded as necessary for their salvation or the Hindu who would not spread the light, who would endeavour to keep others in darkness, who would not consent to share his intellectual and social inheritance with those who are ready and willing to make it a part of their own make-up? I have no hesitation in saying that if the Mohammedan has been cruel, the Hindu has been mean and meanness is worse than cruelty.

VII

Whether the Hindu religion was or was not a missionary religion has been a controversial issue. Some hold the view that it was never a missionary religion. Others hold that it was. That the Hindu religion was once a missionary religion must be admitted. It could not have spread over the face of India, if it was not a missionary religion. That today it is not a missionary religion is also a fact which must be accepted. The question therefore is not whether or not the Hindu religion was a missionary religion. The real question is why did the Hindu religion cease to be a missionary religion? My answer is this: Hindu religion ceased to be a missionary religion when the caste system grew up among the Hindus. Caste is inconsistent with conversion. Inculcation of beliefs and dogmas is not the only problem that is involved in conversion. To find a place for the convert in the social life of the community is another and a much more important problem that arises in connection with conversion. That problem is where to place the convert, in what caste? It is a problem which must baffle every Hindu wishing to make aliens converts to his religion. Unlike the club the membership of a caste is not open to all and sundry. The law of caste confines its membership to person born in the caste. Castes are autonomous and there is no authority anywhere to compel a caste to admit a newcomer to its social life. Hindu society being a collection of castes and each caste being a close corporation there is no place for a convert. Thus it is the caste which has prevented the Hindus from expanding and from absorbing other religious communities. So long as caste remains, Hindu religion cannot be made a missionary religion and *Shudhi* will be both a folly and a futility.

VIII

The reason which has made *Shudhi*[221] impossible for Hindus is also responsible for making *Sanghatan* impossible. The idea underlying *Sanghatan*[222] is to remove from the mind of the Hindu that timidity and cowardice which so painfully mark him off from the Mohammedan and the Sikh and which have led him to adopt the low ways of treachery and cunning for protecting himself. The question naturally arises: From where does the Sikh or the Mohammedan derive his strength which makes him brave and fearless? I am sure it is not due to relative superiority of physical strength, diet or drill. It is due to the strength arising out of the feeling that all Sikhs will come to the rescue of a Sikh when he is in danger and that all Mohammedans will rush to save a Muslim if he is attacked. The Hindu can derive no such strength. He cannot feel assured that his fellows will come to his help. Being one and fated to be alone he remains powerless, develops timidity and cowardice and in a fight surrenders or runs away. The Sikh as well as the Muslim stands fearless and gives battle because he knows that though one he will not be alone. The presence of this belief in the one helps him to hold out and the absence of it in the other makes him to give way. If you pursue this matter further and ask what is it that enables the Sikh and the Mohammedan to feel so assured and why is the Hindu filled with such despair in the matter of help and assistance you will find that the reasons for this difference lie in the difference in their associated mode of living. The associated mode of life practised by the Sikhs and the Mohammedans produces fellow-feeling. The associated mode of life of the Hindus does not. Among Sikhs and Muslims there is a social cement which makes them *Bhais*.[223] Among Hindus there is no such cement and one Hindu does not regard another Hindu as his *Bhai*. This explains why a Sikh says and feels that one Sikh, or one Khalsa is equal to *Sava Lakh*[224] men. This explains why one Mohammedan is equal to a crowd of Hindus. This difference is undoubtedly a difference due to caste. So long as caste remains, there will be no *Sanghatan* and so long as there is no *Sanghatan* the Hindu will remain weak and meek. The Hindus claim to be a very tolerant people. In my opinion this is a mistake. On many occasions they can be intolerant and if on some occasions they are tolerant that is because they are too weak to oppose or too indifferent to oppose.

This indifference of the Hindus has become so much a part of their nature that a Hindu will quite meekly tolerate an insult as well as a wrong. You see amongst them, to use the words of Morris:

The great reading down the little, the strong beating down the weak, cruel men fearing not, kind men daring not and wise men caring not.

With the Hindu Gods all forbearing, it is not difficult to imagine the pitiable condition of the wronged and the oppressed among the Hindus. Indifferentism is the worst kind of disease that can infect a people. Why is the Hindu so indifferent? In my opinion this indifferentism is the result of the caste system which has made *Sanghatan* and cooperation even for a good cause impossible.

IX

The assertion by the individual of his own opinions and beliefs, his own independence and interest as over against group standards, group authority and group interests is the beginning of all reform. But whether the reform will continue depends upon what scope the group affords for such individual assertion. If the group is tolerant and fair-minded in dealing with such individuals they will continue to assert and in the end succeed in converting their fellows. On the other hand if the group is intolerant and does not bother about the means it adopts to stifle such individuals they will perish and the reform will die out. Now a caste has an unquestioned right to excommunicate any man who is guilty of breaking the rules of the caste and when it is realized that excommunication involves a complete cesser of social intercourse it will be agreed that as a form of punishment there is really little to choose between excommunication and death. No wonder individual Hindus have not had the courage to assert their independence by breaking the barriers of caste. It is true that man cannot get on with his fellows. But it is also true that he cannot do without them. He would like to have the society of his fellows on his terms. If he cannot get it on his terms then he will be ready to have it on any terms even amounting to complete surrender. This is because he cannot do without society. A caste is ever ready to take advantage of the helplessness of a man and insist upon complete conformity to its code in letter and in spirit. A caste can easily organize itself into a conspiracy to make the life of a reformer a hell and if a conspiracy is a crime I do not understand why such a nefarious act as an attempt to excommunicate a person for daring to act contrary to the rules of caste should not be made an offence punishable in law. But as it is, even law gives each caste an autonomy to regulate its membership and punish dissenters with excommunication. Caste in the hands of the orthodox has been a powerful weapon for persecuting the reformers and for killing all reform.

X

The effect of caste on the ethics of the Hindus is simply deplorable. Caste has killed public spirit. Caste has destroyed the sense of public charity. Caste has made public opinion impossible. A Hindu's public is his caste. His responsibility is only to his caste. His loyalty is restricted only to his caste. Virtue has become caste-ridden and morality has become caste-bound. There is no sympathy to the deserving. There is no appreciation of the meritorious. There is no charity to the needy. Suffering as such calls for no response. There is charity but it begins with the caste and ends with the caste. There is sympathy but not for men of other caste. Would a Hindu acknowledge and follow the leadership of a great and good man? The case of a Mahatma apart, the answer must be that he will follow a leader if he is a man of his caste. A Brahmin will follow a leader only if he is a Brahmin, a Kayastha if he is a Kayastha and so on. The capacity to appreciate merits in a man apart from his caste does not exist in a Hindu. There is appreciation of virtue but only when the man is a fellow caste-man. The whole morality is as bad as tribal morality. My caste-man, right or wrong; my caste-man, good or bad. It is not a case of standing by virtue and not standing by vice. It is a case of standing or not standing by the caste. Have not Hindus committed treason against their country in the interests of their caste?

XI

I would not be surprised if some of you have grown weary listening to this tiresome tale of the sad effects which caste has produced. There is nothing new in it. I will therefore turn to the constructive side of the problem. What is your ideal society if you do not want caste is a question that is bound to be asked of you. If you ask me, my ideal would be a society based on *Liberty, Equality* and *Fraternity*. And why not? What objection can there be to fraternity? I cannot imagine any. An ideal society should be mobile, should be full of channels for conveying a change taking place in one part to other parts. In an ideal society there should be many interests consciously communicated and shared. There should be varied and free points of contact with other modes of association. In other words there must be social endosmosis. This is fraternity, which is only another name for democracy. Democracy is not merely a form of government. It is primarily a mode of associated living, of conjoint communicated experience. It is essentially an attitude of respect and reverence towards fellowmen. Any objection to liberty? Few object to liberty in the sense of a right to free movement, in the sense of a right to life and limb. There is no objection to liberty in the sense of a right to property, tools and materials as being necessary for earning a living to keep the body in due state of health. Why not allow liberty to benefit by an effective and competent use of a person's powers? The supporters of caste who would allow liberty in the sense of a right to life, limb and property, would not readily consent to liberty in this sense, inasmuch as it involves liberty to choose one's profession. But to object to this kind of liberty is to perpetuate slavery. For slavery does not merely mean a legalized form of subjection. It means a state of society in which some men are forced to accept from others the purposes which control their conduct. This condition obtains even where there is no slavery in the legal sense. It is found where, as in the caste system, some persons are compelled to carry on certain prescribed callings which are not of their choice. Any objection to equality? This has obviously been the most contentious part of the slogan of the French Revolution. The objection to equality may be sound and one may have to admit that all men are not equal. But what of that? Equality may be a fiction but nonetheless one must accept it as the governing principle. A man's power is dependent upon (1) physical heredity, (2) social inheritance or endowment in the form of parental care, education, accumulation of scientific knowledge, everything which enables him to be more efficient than the savage, and finally, (3) on his own efforts. In all these three respects men are undoubtedly unequal. But the question is, shall we treat them as unequal because they are unequal? This is a question which the opponents of equality must answer. From the standpoint of the individualist it may be just to treat men unequally so far as their efforts are unequal. It may be desirable to give as much incentive as possible to the full development of everyone's powers. But what would happen if men were treated unequally as they are, in the first two respects? It is obvious that those individuals in whose favour there is also birth, education, family name, business connections and inherited wealth would be selected in the race. But selection under such circumstances would not be a selection of the able. It would be the selection of the privileged. The reason therefore, which forces that in the third respect we should treat men unequally demands that in the first two respects we should treat men as equally as possible. On the other hand it can be urged that if it is good for the social body to get the most out of its members, it can get most out of them only by making them equal as far as possible at the very start of the race. That is one reason why we cannot escape equality. But there is another reason why we must accept equality. A statesman is concerned with vast numbers of people. He has neither the time nor the knowledge to draw fine distinctions and to treat each equitably i.e. according to need or according to capacity. However desirable or reasonable an equitable treatment of men may be, humanity is not capable of assortment and classification. The statesman, therefore, must follow some rough and ready rule and that rough and ready rule is to treat all men alike not because they are alike but because classification and assortment is impossible. The doctrine of equality is glaringly fallacious but taking all in all it is the only way a statesman can proceed in politics which is a severely practical affair and which demands a severely practical test.

XII

But there is a set of reformers who hold out a different ideal. They go by the name of the Arya Samajists and their ideal of social organization is what is called Chaturvarnya or the division of society into four classes instead of the four thousand castes that we have in India. To make it more attractive and disarm opposition the protagonists of Chaturvarnya take great care to point out that their Chaturvarnya is based not on birth but on *guna* (worth).

At the outset, I must confess that notwithstanding the worth-basis of this Chaturvarnya, it is an ideal to which I cannot reconcile myself. In the first place, if under the Chaturvarnya of the Arya Samajists an individual is to take his place in the Hindu society according to his worth I do not understand why the Arya Samajists insist upon labelling men as Brahmin, Kshatriya, Vaishya and Shudra. A learned man would be honoured without his being labelled a Brahmin. A soldier would be respected without his being designated a Kshatriya. If European society honours its soldiers and its servants without giving them permanent labels, why should Hindu society find it difficult to do so is a question, which Arya Samajists have not cared to consider. There is another objection to the continuance of these labels. All reform consists in a change in the notions, sentiment and mental attitudes of the people towards men and things. It is common experience that certain names become associated with certain notions and sentiments, which determine a person's attitude towards men and things. The names, Brahmin, Kshatriya, Vaishya and Shudra, are names which are associated with a definite and fixed notion in the mind of every Hindu. That notion is that of a hierarchy based on birth. So long as these names continue, Hindus will continue to think of the Brahmin, Kshatriya, Vaishya and Shudra as hierarchical divisions of high and low, based on birth, and act accordingly. The Hindu must be made to unlearn all this. But how can this happen if the old labels remain and continue to recall to his mind old notions. If new notions are to be inculcated in the minds of people it is necessary to give them new names. To continue the old name is to make the reform futile. To allow this Chaturvarnya, based on worth to be designated by such stinking labels of Brahmin, Kshatriya, Vaishya, Shudra, indicative of social divisions based on birth, is a snare.

XIII

To me this Chaturvarnya with its old labels is utterly repellent and my whole being rebels against it. But I do not wish to rest my objection to Chaturvarnya on mere grounds of sentiments. There are more solid grounds on which I rely for my opposition to it. A close examination of this ideal has convinced me that as a system of social organization, Chaturvarnya is impracticable, harmful and has turned out to be a miserable failure. From a practical point of view, the system of Chaturvarnya raises several difficulties which its protagonists do not seem to have taken into account. The principle underlying caste is fundamentally different from the principle underlying *Varna*. Not only are they fundamentally different but they are also fundamentally opposed. The former is based on worth. How are you going to compel people who have acquired a higher status based on birth without reference to their worth to vacate that status? How are you going to compel people to recognize the status due to a man in accordance with his worth, who is occupying a lower status based on his birth? For this you must first break up the caste system, in order to be able to establish the *Varna* system. How are you going to reduce the four thousand castes, based on birth, to the four *Varnas*, based on worth? This is the first difficulty which the protagonists of the Chaturvarnya must grapple with. There is a second difficulty which the protagonists of Chaturvarnya must grapple with, if they wish to make the establishment of Chaturvarnya a success.

Chaturvarnya presupposes that you can classify people into four definite classes. Is this possible? In this respect, the ideal of Chaturvarnya has, as you will see, a close affinity to the Platonic ideal.[225] To Plato, men fell by nature into three classes. In some individuals, he believed mere appetites dominated. He assigned them to the labouring and trading classes. Others revealed to him that over and above appetites, they have a courageous disposition. He classed them as defenders in war and guardians of internal peace. Others showed a capacity to grasp the universal reason underlying things. He made them the law-givers of the people. The criticism to which Plato's Republic is subject, is also the criticism which must apply to the system of Chaturvarnya, in so far as it proceeds upon the possibility of an accurate classification of men into four distinct classes. The chief criticism against Plato is that his idea of lumping of individuals into a few sharply marked-off classes is a very superficial view of man and his powers. Plato had no perception of the uniqueness of every individual, of his incommensurability with others, of each individual forming a class of his own. He had no recognition of the infinite diversity of active tendencies and combination of tendencies of which an individual is capable. To him, there were types of faculties or powers in the individual constitution. All this is demonstrably wrong. Modern science has shown that lumping together of individuals into a few sharply marked-off classes is a superficial view of man not worthy of serious consideration. Consequently, the utilization of the qualities of individuals is incompatible with their stratification by classes, since the qualities of individuals are so variable. Chaturvarnya must fail for the very reason for which Plato's Republic must fail, namely that it is not possible to pigeon men into holes, according as he belongs to one class or the other. That it is impossible to accurately classify people into four definite classes is proved by the fact that the original four classes have now become four thousand castes.

There is a third difficulty in the way of the establishment of the system of Chaturvarnya. How are you going to maintain the system of Chaturvarnya, supposing it was established? One important requirement for the successful working of Chaturvarnya is the maintenance of the penal system which could maintain it by its sanction. The system of Chaturvarnya must perpetually face the problem of the transgressor. Unless there is a penalty attached to the act of transgression, men will not keep to their respective classes. The whole system will break down, being contrary to human nature. Chaturvarnya cannot subsist by its own inherent goodness. It must be enforced by law. That, without penal sanction the ideal of Chaturvarnya cannot be realized is proved by the story in the Ramayana of Rama killing Shambuka.[226] Some people seem to blame Rama because he wantonly and without reason killed Shambuka. But to blame Rama for killing Shambuka is to misunderstand the whole situation. Ram Raj was a Raj based on Chaturvarnya. As a king, Rama was bound to maintain Chaturvarnya. It was his duty therefore to kill Shambuka, the Shudra, who had transgressed his class and wanted to be a Brahmin. This is the reason why Rama killed Shambuka. But this also shows that penal sanction is necessary for the maintenance of Chaturvarnya. Not only penal sanction is necessary, but penalty of death is necessary. That is why Rama did not inflict on Shambuka a lesser punishment. That is why Manu-Smriti prescribes such heavy sentences as cutting off the tongue or pouring of molten lead in the ears of the Shudra, who recites or hears the *Veda*. The supporters of Chaturvarnya must give an assurance that they could successfully classify men and they could induce modern society in the twentieth century to reforge the penal sanctions of Manu-Smriti.

The protagonists of Chaturvarnya do not seem to have considered what is to happen to women in their system. Are they also to be divided into four classes, Brahmin, Kshatriya, Vaishya and Shudra? Or are they to be allowed to take the status of their husbands. If the status of the woman is to be the consequence of marriage what becomes of the underlying principle of Chaturvarnya, namely, that the status of a person should be based upon the worth of that person? If they are to be classified according to their worth is their classification to be nominal or real? If it is to be nominal then it is useless and then the protagonists of Chaturvarnya must admit that their system does not apply to women. If it is real, are the protagonists of Chaturvarnya prepared to follow the logical consequences of applying it to women? They must be prepared to have women priests and women soldiers. Hindu society has grown accustomed to women teachers and women barristers. It may grow accustomed to women brewers and women butchers. But he would be a bold person, who would say that it will allow women priests and women soldiers. But that will be the logical outcome of applying Chaturvarnya to women. Given these difficulties, I think no one except a congenital idiot could hope and believe in a successful regeneration of the Chaturvarnya.

XIV

Assuming that Chaturvarnya is practicable, I contend that it is the most vicious system. That the Brahmins should cultivate knowledge, that the Kshatriya should bear arms, that the Vaishya should trade and that the Shudra should serve sounds as though it was a system of division of labour. Whether the theory was intended to state that the Shudra *need not* or that whether it was intended to lay down that he *must not*, is an interesting question. The defenders of Chaturvarnya give it the first meaning. They say, why should the *Shudra* need trouble to acquire wealth, when the three *Varnas* are there to support him? Why need the *Shudra* bother to take to education, when there is the Brahmin to whom he can go when the occasion for reading or writing arises? Why need the *Shudra* worry to arm himself because there is the Kshatriya to protect him? The theory of Chaturvarnya, understood in this sense, may be said to look upon the *Shudra* as the ward and the three *Varnas* as his guardians. Thus interpreted it is a simple, elevating and alluring theory. Assuming this to be the correct view of the underlying conception of Chaturvarnya, it seems to me that the system is neither fool-proof nor knave-proof. What is to happen, if the Brahmins, Vaishyas and Kshatriyas fail to pursue knowledge, to engage in economic enterprise and to be efficient soldiers which are their respective functions? Contrary-wise, suppose that they discharge their functions but flout their duty to the *Shudra* or to one another, what is to happen to the *Shudra* if the three classes refuse to support him on fair terms or combine to keep him down? Who is to safeguard the interests of the *Shudra* or for the matter of that of the Vaishya and Kshatriya when the person, who is trying to take advantage of his ignorance is the Brahmin? Who is to defend the liberty of the *Shudra* and for the matter of that, of the Brahmin and the Vaishya when the person who is robbing him of it is the Kshatriya? Inter-dependence of one class on another class is inevitable. Even dependence of one class upon another may sometimes become allowable. But why make one person depend upon another in the matter of his vital needs? Education everyone must have. Means of defence everyone must have. These are the paramount requirements of every man for his self-preservation. How can the fact that his neighbour is educated and armed help a man who is uneducated and disarmed. The whole theory is absurd. These are the questions, which the defenders of Chaturvarnya do not seem to be troubled about. But they are very pertinent questions. Assuming their conception of Chaturvarnya that the relationship between the different classes is that of ward and guardian is the real conception underlying Chaturvarnya, it must be admitted that it makes no provision to safeguard the interests of the ward from the misdeeds of the guardian. Whether the relationship of guardian and ward was the real underlying conception, on which Chaturvarnya was based, there is no doubt that in practice the relation was that of master and servants. The three classes, Brahmins, Kshatriyas and Vaishyas although not very happy in their mutual relationship managed to work by compromise. The Brahmin flattered the Kshatriya and both let the Vaishya live in order to be able to live upon him. But the three agreed to beat down the Shudra. He was not allowed to acquire wealth lest he should be independent of the three *Varnas*. He was prohibited from acquiring knowledge lest he should keep a steady vigil regarding his interests. He was prohibited from bearing arms lest he should have the means to rebel against their authority. That this is how the *Shudras* were treated by the Tryavarnikas[227] is evidenced by the Laws of Manu. There is no code of laws more infamous regarding social rights than the Laws of Manu. Any instance from anywhere of social injustice must pale before it. Why have the mass of people tolerated the social evils to which they have been subjected? There have been social revolutions in other countries of the world. Why have there not been social revolutions in India is a question which has incessantly troubled me. There is only one answer, which I can give and it is that the lower classes of Hindus have been completely disabled for direct action on account of this wretched system of Chaturvarnya. They could not bear arms and without arms they could not rebel. They were all ploughmen or rather condemned to be ploughmen and they never were allowed to convert their ploughshare into swords. They had no bayonets and therefore everyone who chose could and did sit upon them. On account of the Chaturvarnya, they could receive no education. They could not think out or know the way to their salvation. They were condemned to be lowly and not knowing the way of escape and not having the means of escape, they became reconciled to eternal servitude, which they accepted as their inescapable fate. It is true that even in Europe the strong have not shrunk from exploitation, nay the spoilation of the weak. But in Europe, the strong have never contrived to make the weak helpless against exploitation so shamelessly as was the case in India among the Hindus. Social war has been raging between the strong and the weak far more violently in Europe than it has ever been in India. Yet, the weak in Europe has had in his freedom of military service his *physical weapon*, in suffering his *political weapon* and in education his *moral weapon*. These three weapons for emancipation were never withheld by the strong from the weak in Europe. All these weapons were, however, denied to the masses in India by Chaturvarnya. There cannot be a more degrading system of social organization than the Chaturvarnya. It is the system which deadens, paralyses and cripples the people from helpful activity. This is no exaggeration. History bears ample evidence. There is only one period in Indian history which is a period of freedom, greatness and glory. That is the period of the Maurya Empire. At all other times the country suffered from defeat and darkness. But the Maurya period was a period when Chaturvarnya was completely annihilated, when the Shudras, who constituted the mass of the people, came into their own and became the rulers of the country. The period of defeat and darkness is the period when Chaturvarnya flourished to the damnation of the greater part of the people of the country.

XV

Chaturvarnya is not new. It is as old as the *Vedas*. That is one of the reasons why we are asked by the Arya Samajists to consider its claims. Judging from the past as a system of social organization, it has been tried and it has failed. How many times have the Brahmins annihilated the seed of the Kshatriyas! How many times have the Kshatriyas annihilated the Brahmins! The Mahabharata and the Puranas are full of incidents of the strife between the Brahmins and the Kshatriyas. They even quarreled over such petty questions as to who should salute first, as to who should give way first, the Brahmins or the Kshatriyas, when the two met in the street. Not only was the Brahmin an eyesore to the Kshatriya and the Kshatriya an eyesore to the Brahmin, it seems that the Kshatriyas had become tyrannical and the masses, disarmed as they were under the system of Chaturvarnya, were praying Almighty God for relief from their tyranny. The Bhagwad tells us very definitely that Krishna had taken *Avtar* for one sacred purpose and that was to annihilate the Kshatriyas. With these instances of rivalry and enmity between the different *Varnas* before us, I do not understand how any one can hold out Chaturvarnya as an ideal to be aimed at or as a pattern, on which Hindu society should be remodelled.

XVI

I have dealt with those, who are without you and whose hostility to your ideal is quite open. There appear to be others who are neither without you nor with you. I was hesitating whether I should deal with their point of view. But on further consideration I have come to the conclusion that I must and that for two reasons. Firstly, their attitude to the problem of caste is not merely an attitude of neutrality, but is an attitude of armed neutrality. Secondly, they probably represent a considerable body of people. Of these, there is one set which finds nothing peculiar nor odious in the caste system of the Hindus. Such Hindus cite the case of

Muslims, Sikhs and Christians and find comfort in the fact that they too have castes amongst them. In considering this question you must at the outset bear in mind that nowhere is human society one single whole. It is always plural. In the world of action, the individual is one limit and society the other. Between them lie all sorts of associative arrangements of lesser and larger scope, families, friendship, cooperative associations, business combines, political parties, bands of thieves and robbers. These small groups are usually firmly welded together and are often as exclusive as castes. They have a narrow and intensive code, which is often anti-social. This is true of every society, in Europe as well as in Asia. The question to be asked in determining whether a given society is an ideal society, is not whether there are groups in it, because groups exist in all societies. The questions to be asked in determining what is an ideal society are: How numerous and varied are the interests which are consciously shared by the groups? How full and free is the interplay with other forms of associations? Are the forces that separate groups and classes more numerous than the forces that unite? What social significance is attached to this group life? Is its exclusiveness a matter of custom and convenience or is it a matter of religion? It is in the light of these questions that one must decide whether caste among non-Hindus is the same as caste among Hindus. If we apply these considerations to castes among Mohammedans, Sikhs and Christians on the one hand and to castes among Hindus on the other, you will find that caste among Non-Hindus is fundamentally different from caste among Hindus. First, the ties, which consciously make the Hindus hold together, are non-existent, while among non-Hindus there are many that hold them together. The strength of a society depends upon the presence of points of contact, possibilities of interaction between different groups which exist in it. These are what Carlyle calls 'organic filaments' i.e. the elastic threads which help to bring the disintegrating elements together and to reunite them. There is no integrating force among the Hindus to counteract the disintegration caused by caste while among the non-Hindus there are plenty of these organic filaments which bind them together. Again it must be borne in mind that although there are castes among non-Hindus, as there are among Hindus, caste has not the same social significance for non-Hindus as it has for Hindus. Ask Mohammedan or a Sikh, who he is? He tells you that he is a Mohammedan or a Sikh as the case may be. He does not tell you his caste although he has one and you are satisfied with his answer. When he tells you that he is a Muslim, you do not proceed to ask him whether he is a Shiya or a Sunni; Sheikh or Saiyad; Khatik or Pinjari. When he tells you he is a Sikh, you do not ask him whether he is Jat or Roda; Mazbi or Ramdasi. But you are not satisfied, if a person tells you that he is a Hindu. You feel bound to inquire into his caste. Why? Because so essential is caste in the case of a Hindu that without knowing it you do not feel sure what sort of a being he is. That caste has not the same social significance among non-Hindus as it has among Hindus is clear if you take into consideration the consequences which follow breach of caste. There may be castes among Sikhs and Mohammedans but the Sikhs and the Mohammedans will not outcaste a Sikh or a Mohammedan if he broke his caste. Indeed, the very idea of excommunication is foreign to the Sikhs and the Mohammedans. But with the Hindus the case is entirely different. He is sure to be outcasted if he broke caste. This shows the difference in the social significance of caste of Hindus and non-Hindus. This is the second point of difference. But there is also a third and a more important one. Caste among the non-Hindus has no religious consecration; but among the Hindus most decidedly it has. Among the non-Hindus, caste is only a practice, not a sacred institution. They did not originate it. With them it is only a survival. They do not regard caste as a religious dogma. Religion compels the Hindus to treat isolation and segregation of castes as a virtue. Religion does not compel the non-Hindus to take the same attitude towards caste. If Hindus wish to break caste, their religion will come in their way. But it will not be so in the case of Non-Hindus. It is, therefore, a dangerous delusion to take comfort in the mere existence of caste among Non-Hindus, without caring to know what place caste occupies in their life and whether there are other 'organic filaments', which subordinate the feeling of caste to the feeling of community. The sooner the Hindus are cured of this delusion the better.

The other set denies that caste presents any problem at all for the Hindus to consider. Such Hindus seek comfort in the view that the Hindus have survived and take this as a proof of their fitness to survive. This point of view is well expressed by Professor S. Radhakrishnan in his *Hindu View of Life*. Referring to Hinduism he says,

The civilization itself has not been a short-lived one. Its historic records date back for over four thousand years and even then it had reached a stage of civilization which has continued its unbroken, though at times slow and static, course until the present day. It has stood the stress and strain of more than four or five millenniums of spiritual thought and experience. Though peoples of different races and cultures have been pouring into India from the dawn of History, Hinduism has been able to maintain its supremacy and even the proselytizing creeds backed by political power have not been able to coerce the large majority of Hindus to their views. The Hindu culture possesses some vitality which seems to be denied to some other more forceful currents. It is no more necessary to dissect Hinduism than to open a tree to see whether the sap still runs.[228]

The name of Professor Radhakrishnan is big enough to invest with profundity whatever he says and impress the minds of his readers. But I must not hesitate to speak out my mind. For, I fear that his statement may become the basis of a vicious argument that the fact of survival is proof of fitness to survive. It seems to me that the question is not whether a community lives or dies; the question is on what plane does it live. There are different modes of survival. But all are not equally honourable. For an individual as well as for a society, there is a gulf between merely living and living worthily. To fight in a battle and to live in glory is one mode. To beat a retreat, to surrender and to live the life of a captive is also a mode of survival. It is useless for a Hindu to take comfort in the fact that he and his people have survived. What he must consider is what is the quality of their survival. If he does that, I am sure he will cease to take pride in the mere fact of survival. A Hindu's life has been a life of continuous defeat and what appears to him to be life everlasting is not living everlastingly but is really a life which is perishing everlastingly. It is a mode of survival of which every right-minded Hindu, who is not afraid to own up the truth, will feel ashamed.

XVII

There is no doubt, in my opinion, that unless you change your social order you can achieve little by way of progress. You cannot mobilize the community either for defence or for offence. You cannot build anything on the foundations of caste. You cannot build up a nation, you cannot build up a morality. Anything that you will build on the foundations of caste will crack and will never be a whole.

The only question that remains to be considered is—*How to bring about the reform of the Hindu social order? How to abolish caste?* This is a question of supreme importance. There is a view that in the reform of caste, the first step to take, is to abolish sub-castes. This view is based upon the supposition that there is a greater similarity in manners and status between sub-castes than there is between castes. I think, this is an erroneous supposition. The Brahmins of Northern and Central India are socially of lower grade, as compared with the Brahmins of the Deccan and Southern India. The former are only cooks and water-carriers while the latter occupy a high social position. On the other hand, in Northern India, the Vaishyas and Kayasthas are intellectually and socially on par with the Brahmins of the Deccan and Southern India. Again, in the matter of food there is no similarity between the Brahmins of the Deccan and Southern India, who are vegetarians and the Brahmins of Kashmir and Bengal who are non-vegetarians. On the other hand, the Brahmins of the Deccan and Southern India have more in common so far as food is concerned with such non-Brahmins as the Gujaratis, Marwaris, Banias and Jains. There is no doubt that from the standpoint of making the transit from one caste to another easy, the fusion of the Kayasthas of Northern India and the other non-Brahmins of Southern India with the non-Brahmins of the Deccan and the Dravid country is more practicable than the fusion of the Brahmins of the South with the Brahmins of the North. But assuming that the fusion of sub-castes is possible, what guarantee is there that the abolition of sub-castes will necessarily lead to the abolition of castes? On the contrary, it may happen that the process may stop with the abolition of sub-castes. In that case, the abolition of sub-castes will only help to strengthen the castes and make them more powerful and therefore more mischievous. This remedy is therefore neither practicable nor effective and may easily prove to be a wrong remedy. Another plan of action for the abolition of caste is to begin with inter-caste dinners. This also, in my opinion, is an inadequate remedy. There are many castes which allow inter-dining. But it is a common experience that inter-dining has not succeeded in killing the spirit of caste and the consciousness of caste. I am convinced that the real remedy is inter-marriage. Fusion of blood can alone create the feeling of being kith and kin and unless this feeling of kinship, of being kindred, becomes paramount the separatist feeling—the feeling of being aliens—created by caste will not vanish. Among the Hindus inter-marriage must necessarily be a factor of greater force in social life than it need be in the life of the non-Hindus. Where society is already well-knit by other ties, marriage is an ordinary incident of life. But where society is cut as under, marriage as a binding force becomes a matter of urgent necessity. *The real remedy for breaking caste is inter-marriage. Nothing else will serve as the solvent of caste.* Your Jat-Pat-Todak Mandal has adopted this line of attack. It is a direct and frontal attack, and I congratulate you upon a correct diagnosis and more upon your having shown the courage to tell the Hindus what is really wrong with them. Political tyranny is nothing compared to social tyranny and a reformer, who defies society, is a much more courageous man than a politician, who defies government. You are right in holding that caste will cease to be an operative force only when inter-dining and inter-marriage have become matters of common course. You have located the source of the disease. But is your prescription the right prescription for the disease? Ask yourselves this question; Why is it that a large majority of Hindus do not inter-dine and do not inter-marry? Why is it that your cause is not popular? There can be only one answer to this question and it is that inter-dining and inter-marriage are repugnant to the beliefs and dogmas which the Hindus regard as sacred. Caste is not a physical object like a wall of bricks or a line of barbed wire which prevents the Hindus from co-mingling and which has, therefore, to be pulled down. Caste is a notion, it is a state of the mind. The destruction of caste does not therefore mean the destruction of a physical barrier. It means a *notional* change. Caste may be bad. Caste may lead to conduct so gross as to be called man's inhumanity to man. All the same, it must be recognized that the Hindus observe caste not because they are inhuman or wrong headed. They observe caste because they are deeply religious. People are not wrong in observing caste. In my view, what is wrong is their religion, which has inculcated this notion of caste. If this is correct, then obviously the enemy, you must grapple with is not the people who observe caste, but the *Shastras* which teach them this religion of caste. Criticizing and ridiculing people for not inter-dining or inter-marrying or occasionally holding inter-castes dinners and celebrating inter-caste marriages, is a futile method of achieving the desired end. The real remedy is to destroy the belief in the sanctity of the *Shastras*. How do you expect to succeed, if you allow the *Shastras* to continue to mould the beliefs and opinions of the people? Not to question the authority of the *Shastras* to permit the people to believe in their sanctity and their sanctions and to blame them and to criticize them for their acts as being irrational and inhuman is a incongruous way of carrying on social reform. Reformers working for the removal of untouchability including Mahatma Gandhi, do not seem to realize that the acts of the people are merely the results of their beliefs inculcated upon their minds by the *Shastras* and that people will not change their conduct until they cease to believe in the sanctity of the *Shastras* on which their conduct is founded. No wonder that such efforts have not produced any results. You also seem to be erring in the same way as the reformers working in the cause of removing untouchability. To agitate for and to organize inter-caste dinners and inter-caste marriages is like forced feeding brought about by artificial means. Make every man and woman free from the thraldom of the *Shastras*, cleanse their minds of the pernicious notions founded on the *Shastras*, and he or she will inter-dine and inter-marry, without your telling him or her to do so.

It is no use seeking refuse in quibbles. It is no use telling people that the *Shastras* do not say what they are believed to say, grammatically read or logically interpreted. What matters is how the *Shastras* have been understood by the people. You must take the stand that Buddha took. You must take the stand which Guru Nanak took. You must not only discard the *Shastras*, you must deny their authority, as did Buddha and Nanak. You must have courage to tell the Hindus, that what is wrong with them is their religion—the religion which has produced in them this notion of the sacredness of caste. Will you show that courage?

XVIII

What are your chances of success? Social reforms fall into different species. There is a species of reform, which does not relate to the religious notion of people but is purely secular in character. There is also a species of reform, which relates to the religious notions of people. Of such a species of reform, there are two varieties. In one, the reform accords with the principles of the religion and merely invites people, who have departed from it, to revert to them and to follow them. The second is a reform which not only touches the religious principles but is diametrically opposed to those principles and invites people to depart from and to discard their authority and to act contrary to those principles. Caste is the natural outcome of certain religious beliefs which have the sanction of the *Shastras,* which are believed to contain the command of divinely inspired sages who were endowed with a supernatural wisdom and whose commands, therefore, cannot be disobeyed without committing sin. The destruction of caste is a reform which falls under the third category. To ask people to give up caste is to ask them to go contrary to their fundamental religious notions. It is obvious that the first and second species of reform are easy. But the third is a stupendous task, well-nigh impossible. The Hindus hold to the sacredness of the social order. Caste has a divine basis. You must therefore destroy the sacredness and divinity with which caste has become invested. In the last analysis, this means you must destroy the authority of the *Shastras* and the *Vedas.*

I have emphasized this question of the ways and means of destroying caste, because I think that knowing the proper ways and means is more important than knowing the ideal. If you do not know the real ways and means, all your shots are sure to be misfires. If my analysis is correct then your task is herculean. You alone can say whether you are capable of achieving it.

Speaking for myself, I see the task to be well-nigh impossible. Perhaps you would like to know why I think so. Out of the many reasons, which have led me to take this view, I will mention some, which I regard much important. One of these reasons is the attitude of hostility, which the Brahmins have shown towards this question. The Brahmins form the vanguard of the movement for political reform and in some cases also of economic reform. But they are not to be found even as camp-followers in the army raised to break down the barricades of caste. Is there any hope of the Brahmins ever taking up a lead in the future in this matter? I say no. You may ask why? You may argue that there is no reason why Brahmins should continue to shun social reform. You may argue that the Brahmins know that the bane of Hindu society is caste and as an enlightened class could not be expected to be indifferent to its consequences. You may argue that there are secular Brahmins and priestly Brahmins and if the latter do not take up the cudgels on behalf of those who want to break caste, the former will. All this of course sounds very plausible. But in all this it is forgotten that the break up of the caste system is bound to affect adversely the Brahmin caste. Having regard to this, is it reasonable to expect that the Brahmins will ever consent to lead a movement the ultimate result of which is to destroy the power and prestige of the Brahmin caste? Is it reasonable to expect the secular Brahmins to take part in a movement directed against the priestly Brahmins? In my judgment, it is useless to make a distinction between the secular Brahmins and priestly Brahmins. Both are kith and kin. They are two arms of the same body and are bound to fight for the existence of the other. In this connection, I am reminded of some very pregnant remarks made by Professor Dicey in his *English Constitution*. Speaking of the actual limitation on the legislative supremacy of Parliament, Dicey says:[229]

The actual exercise of authority by any sovereign whatever, and notably by Parliament, is bounded or controlled by two limitations. Of these the one is an external, and the other is an internal limitation. The external limit to the real power of a sovereign consists in the possibility or certainty that his subjects or a large number of them will disobey or resist his laws... The internal limit to the exercise of sovereignty arises from the nature of the sovereign power itself. Even a despot exercises his powers in accordance with his character, which is itself moulded by the circumstance under which he lives, including under that head the moral feelings of the time and the society to which he belongs. The Sultan could not, if he would, change the religion of the Mohammedan world, but even if he could do so, it is in the very highest degree improbable that the head of Mohammedanism should wish to overthrow the religion of Mohammed; the internal check on the exercise of the Sultan's power is at least as strong as the external limitation. People sometimes ask the idle question, why the Pope does not introduce this or that reform? The true answer is that a revolutionist is not the kind of man who becomes a Pope and that a man who becomes a Pope has no wish to be a revolutionist.

I think, these remarks apply equally to the Brahmins of India and one can say with equal truth that if a man who becomes a Pope has no wish to become a revolutionary, a man who is born a Brahmin has much less desire to become a revolutionary. Indeed, to expect a Brahmin to be a revolutionary in matters of social reform is as idle as to expect the British Parliament, as was said by Leslie Stephen, to pass an Act requiring all blue-eyed babies to be murdered.

Some of you will say that it is a matter of small concern whether the Brahmins come forward to lead the movement against caste or whether they do not. To take this view is in my judgment to ignore the part played by the intellectual class in the community. Whether you accept the theory of the great man as the maker of history or whether you do not, this much you will have to concede that in every country the intellectual class is the most influential class, if not the governing class. The intellectual class is the class which can foresee; it is the class which can advise and give lead. In no country does the mass of the people live the life of intelligent thought and action. It is largely imitative and follows the intellectual class. There is no exaggeration in saying that the entire destiny of a country depends upon its intellectual class. If the intellectual class is honest, independent and disinterested it can be trusted to take the initiative and give a proper lead when a crisis arises. It is true that intellect by itself is no virtue. It is only a means and the use of means depends upon the ends which an intellectual person pursues. An intellectual man can be a good man but he can easily be a rogue. Similarly an intellectual class may be a band of high-souled persons, ready to help, ready to emancipate erring humanity or it may easily be a gang of crooks or a body of advocates of a narrow clique from which it draws its support. You may think it a pity that the intellectual class in India is simply another name for the Brahmin caste. You may regret that the two are one; that the existence of the intellectual class should be bound with one single caste, that this intellectual class should share the interest and the aspirations of that Brahmin caste, which has regarded itself the custodian of the interest of that caste, rather than of the interests of the country. All this may be very regrettable. But the fact remains, that the Brahmins form the intellectual class of the Hindus. It is not only an intellectual class but it is a class which is held in great reverence by the rest of the Hindus. The Hindus are taught that the Brahmins are *Bhudevas* (Gods on earth) वर्णानाम् ब्राह्मण गुरू: The Hindus are taught that Brahmins alone can be their teachers. Manu says,[230] 'If it be asked how it should be with respect to points of the Dharma which have not been specially mentioned, the answer is that which Brahmins who are *Shishthas* propound shall doubtless have legal force':

अनाम्नातेषु धर्मेषु कथं स्यादिति चेद्भवेत् ।
यं शिष्टा ब्राह्मणा ब्रुयु: स धर्म: स्यादशङ्कित: ।

When such an intellectual class, which holds the rest of the community in its grip, is opposed to the reform of caste, the chances of success in a movement for the break-up of the caste system appear to me very, very remote.

The second reason, why I say the task is impossible, will be clear if you will bear in mind that the caste system has two aspects. In one of its aspects, it divides men into separate communities. In its second aspect, it places these communities in a graded order one above the other in social status. Each castes takes its pride and its consolation in the fact that in the scale of castes it is above some other caste. As an outward mark of this gradation, there is also a gradation of social and religious rights technically spoken of as *Ashtadhikaras* and *Sanskaras*. The higher the grade of a caste, the greater the number of these rights and the lower the grade, the lesser their number. Now this gradation, this scaling of castes, makes it impossible to organize a common front against the caste system. If a caste claims the right to inter-dine and inter-marry with another caste placed above it, it is frozen, instantly it is told by mischief-mongers, and there are many Brahmins amongst such mischief-mongers, that it will have to concede inter-dining and inter-marriage with castes below it! All are slaves of the caste system. But all the slaves are not equal in status. To excite the proletariat to bring about an economic revolution, Karl Marx told them:[231] 'You have nothing to lose except your chains.' But the artful way in which the social and religious rights are distributed among the different castes whereby some have more and some have less, makes the slogan of Karl Marx quite useless to excite the Hindus against the caste system. Castes form a graded system of sovereignties, high and low, which are jealous of their status and which know that if a general dissolution came, some of them stand to lose more of their prestige and power than others do. You cannot, therefore, have a general mobilization of the Hindus, to use a military expression, for an attack on the caste system.

XIX

Can you appeal to reason and ask the Hindus to discard caste as being contrary to reason? That raises the question: Is a Hindu free to follow his reason? Manu has laid down three sanctions to which every Hindu must conform in the matter of his behaviour. वेदः स्मृतिः सदाचारः स्वस्य च प्रियमात्मनः Here there is no place for reason to play its part. A Hindu must follow either *Veda*, *Smriti* or *Sadachar*. He cannot follow anything else. In the first place how are the texts of the *Vedas* and *Smritis* to be interpreted whenever any doubt arises regarding their meaning? On this important question the view of Manu is quite definite. He says:[232]

योऽवमन्येत ते मूले हेतुशास्त्राश्रयात् द्विजः ।
स साधुभिर्बहिष्कार्यो नास्तिको वेदनिन्दकः ॥

According to this rule, rationalism as a canon of interpreting the *Vedas* and *Smritis*, is absolutely condemned. It is regarded to be as wicked as atheism and the punishment provided for it is ex-communication. Thus, where a matter is covered by the *Vedas* or the *Smritis* a Hindu cannot resort to rational thinking. Even when there is a conflict between *Vedas* and *Smritis* on matters on which they have given a positive injunction, the solution is not left to reason. When there is a conflict between two *Shrutis*, both are to be regarded as of equal authority. Either of them may be followed. No attempt is to be made to find out which of the two accords with reason. This is made clear by Manu:[233]

श्रुतिद्वैधं तु यत्र स्यात्तत्र धर्मावुभौ स्मृतौ ।

'When there is a conflict between *Shruti*, and *Smriti*, the *Shruti* must prevail.' But here too, no attempt must be made to find out which of the two accords with reason. This is laid down by Manu in the following *shloka*:[234]

या वेदबाह्याः स्मृतयो याश्च काश्च कुदृष्टयः ।
सर्वास्ता निष्फलाः प्रेत्य तमोनिष्ठा हि ताः स्मृताः ॥

Again, when there is a conflict between two *Smritis*, the Manu-Smriti must prevail, but no attempt is to be made to find out which of the two accords with reason. This is the ruling given by Brihaspati:

वेदार्थोपनिबंधृत्वात् प्रामाण्यं हि मनोः स्मृतम् ।
मन्वर्थविपरीता तु या स्मृतिः सा न शस्यते ॥

It is, therefore, clear that in any matter on which the *Shrutis* and *Smritis* have given a positive direction, a Hindu is not free to use his reasoning faculty. The same rule is laid down in the Mahabharat:

पुराणं मानवो धर्मः सांगो वेदश्चिकित्सितं ।
आज्ञासिद्धानि चत्वारि न हन्तव्यानि हेतुभिः ॥

He must abide by their directions. The caste and *Varna* are matters, which are dealt with by the *Vedas* and the *Smritis* and consequently, appeal to reason can have no effect on a Hindu. So far as caste and *Varna* are concerned, not only do the *Shastras* do not permit the Hindu to use his reason in the decision of the question, but they have taken care to see that no occasion is left to examine in a rational way the foundations of his belief in caste and *Varna*. It must be a source of silent amusement to many a non-Hindu to find hundreds and thousands of Hindus breaking caste on certain occasions, such as railway journeys and foreign travel and yet endeavouring to maintain caste for the rest of their lives! The explanation of this phenomenon discloses another fetter on the reasoning faculties of the Hindus. Man's life is generally habitual and unreflective. Reflective thought , in the sense of active, persistent and careful consideration of any belief or supposed form or knowledge in the light of the grounds that support it and further conclusions to which it tends, is quite rare and arises only in a situation which presents a dilemma—a crisis. Railway journeys and foreign travels are really occasions of crisis in the life of a Hindu and it is natural to expect a Hindu to ask himself why he should maintain caste at all, if he cannot maintain it at all times. But he does not. He breaks caste at one step and proceeds to observe it at the next without raising any question. The reason for this astonishing conduct is to be found in the rule of the *Shastras*, which directs him to maintain caste as far as possible and to undergo *prayaschitta* when he cannot. By this theory of *prayaschitta*, the *Shastras* by following a spirit of compromise have given caste a perpetual lease of life and have smothered reflective thought which would have otherwise led to the destruction of the notion of caste.

There have been many who have worked in the cause of the abolition of caste and untouchability. Of those, who can be mentioned, Ramanuja, Kabir and others stand out prominently. Can you appeal to the acts of these reformers and exhort the Hindus to follow them? It is true that Manu has included *Sadachar* (सदाचार) as one of the sanctions along with *Shruti* and *Smriti*. Indeed, *Sadachar* has been given a higher place than *Shastras*:

यद्यहाचर्यते येन धर्म्य वाऽधर्म्यमेव वा।
देशस्याचरणं नित्यं चरित्रं तद्धिकीर्तितम्॥

According to this, *Sadachar*, whether, it is धर्म्य or अधर्म्य in accordance with *Shastras* or contrary to *Shastras*, must be followed. But what is the meaning of *Sadachar*? If anyone were to suppose that *Sadachar* means right or good acts *i.e.* acts of good and righteous men he would find himself greatly mistaken. *Sadachar* does not mean good acts or acts of good men. It means ancient custom *good* or *bad*. The following verse makes this clear:

यस्मिन् देशे य आचारः पारंपर्यक्रमागतः।
वर्णानां किल सर्वेषां स सदाचार उच्यते॥

As though to warn people against the view that *Sadachar* means good acts or acts of good men and fearing that people might understand it that way and follow the acts of good men, the *Smritis* have commanded the Hindus in unmistakable terms not to follow even Gods in their good deeds, if they are contrary to *Shruti*, *Smriti* and *Sadachar*. This may sound to be most extraordinary, most perverse, but the fact remains that न देवचरितं चरेत् is an injunction, issued to the Hindus by their *Shastras*. Reason and morality are the two most powerful weapons in the armoury of a reformer. To deprive him of the use of these weapons is to disable him for action. How are you going to break up caste, if people are not free to consider whether it accords with reason? How are you going to break up caste if people are not free to consider whether it accords with morality? The wall built around caste is impregnable and the material, of which it is built, contains none of the combustible stuff of reason and morality. Add to this the fact that inside this wall stands the army of Brahmins, who form the intellectual class, Brahmins who are the natural leaders of the Hindus, Brahmins who are there not as mere mercenary soldiers but as an army fighting for its homeland and you will get an idea why I think that breaking-up of caste amongst the Hindus is well-nigh impossible. At any rate, it would take ages before a breach is made. But whether the doing of the deed takes time or whether it can be done quickly, you must not forget that if you wish to bring about a breach in the system then you have got to apply the dynamite to the *Vedas* and the *Shastras*, which deny any part to reason, to *Vedas* and *Shastras*, which deny any part to morality. You must destroy the religion of the *Shrutis* and the *Smritis*. Nothing else will avail. This is my considered view of the matter.

XX

Some may not understand what I mean by destruction of religion; some may find the idea revolting to them and some may find it revolutionary. Let me therefore explain my position. I do not know whether you draw a distinction between principles and rules. But I do. Not only I make a distinction but I say that this distinction is real and important. Rules are practical; they are habitual ways of doing things according to prescription. But principles are intellectual; they are useful methods of judging things. Rules seek to tell an agent just what course of action to pursue. Principles do not prescribe a specific course of action. Rules, like cooking recipes, do tell just what to do and how to do it. A principle, such as that of justice, supplies a main head by reference to which he is to consider the bearings of his desires and purposes, it guides him in his thinking by suggesting to him the important consideration which he should bear in mind. This difference between rules and principles makes the acts done in pursuit of them different in quality and in content. Doing what is said to be good by virtue of a rule and doing good in the light of a principle are two different things. The principle may be wrong but the act is conscious and responsible. The rule may be right but the act is mechanical. A religious act may not be a correct act but must at least be a responsible act. To permit of this responsibility, religion must mainly be a matter of principles only. It cannot be a matter of rules. The moment it degenerates into rules it ceases to be Religion, as it kills responsibility which is the essence of a truly religious act. What is this Hindu religion? Is it a set of principles or is it a code of rules? Now the Hindu religion, as contained in the *Vedas* and the *Smritis*, is nothing but a mass of sacrificial, social, political and sanitary rules and regulations, all mixed up. What is called religion by the Hindus is nothing but a multitude of commands and prohibitions. Religion, in the sense of spiritual principles, truly universal, applicable to all races, to all countries, to all times, is not to be found in them, and if it is, it does not form the governing part of a Hindu's life. That for a Hindu, Dharma means commands and prohibitions is clear from the way the word Dharma is used in *Vedas* and the *Smritis* and understood by the commentators. The word Dharma as used in the Vedas in most cases means religious ordinances or rites. Even Jaimini in his Purva-Mimansa defines Dharma as 'a desirable goal or result that is indicated by injunctive (*Vedic*) passages'. To put it in plain language, what the Hindus call religion is really Law or at best legalized class-ethics. Frankly, I refuse to call this code of ordinances, as religion. The first evil of such a code of ordinances, misrepresented to the people as religion, is that it tends to deprive moral life of freedom and spontaneity and to reduce it (for the conscientious at any rate) to a more or less anxious and servile conformity to externally imposed rules. Under it, there is no loyalty to ideals, there is only conformity to commands. But the worst evil of this code of ordinances is that the laws it contains must be the same yesterday, today and forever. They are iniquitous in that they are not the same for one class as for another. But this iniquity is made perpetual in that they are prescribed to be the same for all generations. The objectionable part of such a scheme is not that they are made by certain persons called Prophets or Law-givers. The objectionable part is that this code has been invested with the character of finality and fixity. Happiness notoriously varies with the conditions and circumstances of a person, as well as with the conditions of different people and epochs. That being the case, how can humanity endure this code of eternal laws, without being cramped and without being crippled? I have, therefore, no hesitation in saying that such a religion must be destroyed and I say, there is nothing irreligious in working for the destruction of such a religion. Indeed I hold that it is your bounden duty to tear the mask, to remove the misrepresentation that is caused by misnaming this law as religion. This is an essential step for you. Once you clear the minds of the people of this misconception and enable them to realize that what they are told as religion is not religion but that it is really law, you will be in a position to urge for its amendment or abolition. So long as people look upon it as religion they will not be ready for a change, because the idea of religion is generally speaking not associated with the idea of change. But the idea of law is associated with the idea of change and when people come to know that what is called religion is really law, old and archaic, they will be ready for a change, for people know and accept that law can be changed.

XXI

While I condemn a Religion of Rules, I must not be understood to hold the opinion that there is no necessity for a religion. On the contrary, I agree with Burke when he says that[235] 'True religion is the foundation of society, the basis on which all true Civil Government rests, and both their sanction.' Consequently, when I urge that these ancient rules of life be annulled, I am anxious that its place shall be taken by a Religion of Principles, which alone can lay claim to being a true religion. Indeed, I am so convinced of the necessity of religion that I feel I ought to tell you in outline what I regard as necessary items in this religious reform. The following in my opinion should be the cardinal items in this reform: (1) There should be one and only one standard book of Hindu religion, acceptable to all Hindus and recognized by all Hindus. This of course means that all other books of Hindu religion such as *Vedas*, *Shastras* and *Puranas*, which are treated as sacred and authoritative, must by law cease to be so and the preaching of any doctrine, religious or social contained in these books should be penalized. (2) It should be better if priesthood among Hindus was abolished. But as this seems to be impossible, the priesthood must at least cease to be hereditary. Every person who professes to be a Hindu must be eligible for being a priest. It should be provided by law that no Hindu shall be entitled to be a priest unless he has passed an examination prescribed by the state and holds a *sanad* from the state permitting him to practise. (3) No ceremony performed by a priest who does not hold a *sanad* shall be deemed to be valid in law and it should be made penal for a person who has no *sanad* to officiate as a priest. (4) A priest should be the servant of the state and should be subject to the disciplinary action by the state in the matter of his morals, beliefs and worship, in addition to his being subject along with other citizens to the ordinary law of the land. (5) The number of priests should be limited by law according to the requirements of the state as is done in the case of the I.C.S. To some, this may sound radical. But to my mind there is nothing revolutionary in this. Every profession in India is regulated. Engineers must show proficiency, doctors must show proficiency, lawyers must show proficiency, before they are allowed to practise their professions. During the whole of their career, they must not only obey the law of the land,

ANNIHILATION OF CASTE • 301

civil as well as criminal, but they must also obey the special code
of morals prescribed by their respective professions. The priest's
is the only profession where proficiency is not required. The
profession of a Hindu priest is the only profession which is not
subject to any code. Mentally a priest may be an idiot, physically
a priest may be suffering from a foul disease, such as syphilis or
gonorrhea, morally he may be a wreck. But he is fit to officiate
at solemn ceremonies, to enter the *sanctum sanctorum* of a Hindu
temple and worship the Hindu God. All this becomes possible
among the Hindus because for a priest it is enough to be born in
a priestly caste. The whole thing is abominable and is due to the
fact that the priestly class among Hindus is subject neither to law
nor to morality. It recognizes no duties. It knows only of rights
and privileges. It is a pest which divinity seems to have let loose
on the masses for their mental and moral degradation. The priestly
class must be brought under control by some such legislation as
I have outlined above. It will prevent it from doing mischief and
from misguiding people. It will democratize it by throwing it open
to every one. It will certainly help to kill the Brahminism and will
also help to kill caste, which is nothing but Brahminism incarnate.
Brahminism is the poison which has spoiled Hinduism. You will
succeed in saving Hinduism if you will kill Brahminism. There
should be no opposition to this reform from any quarter. It should
be welcomed even by the Arya Samajists, because this is merely
an application of their own doctrine of *guna-karma*.

Whether you do that or you do not, you must give a new
doctrinal basis to your religion—a basis that will be in consonance
with Liberty, Equality and Fraternity, in short, with Democracy.
I am no authority on the subject. But I am told that for such
religious principles as will be in consonance with Liberty, Equality
and Fraternity it may not be necessary for you to borrow from
foreign sources and that you could draw for such principles on
the *Upanishads*. Whether you could do so without a complete
remoulding, a considerable scraping and chipping off the ore they
contain, is more than I can say. This means a complete change in
the fundamental notions of life. It means a complete change in
the values of life. It means a complete change in outlook and in
attitude towards men and things. It means conversion; but if you
do not like the word, I will say, it means new life. But a new life
cannot enter a body that is dead. New life can enter only in a

new body. The old body must die before a new body can come into existence and a new life can enter into it. To put it simply, the old must cease to be operative before the new can begin to enliven and to pulsate. This is what I meant when I said you must discard the authority of the *Shastras* and destroy the religion of the *Shastras*.

XXII

I have kept you too long. It is time I brought this address to a close. This would have been a convenient point for me to have stopped. But this would probably be my last address to a Hindu audience on a subject vitally concerning the Hindus. I would therefore like, before I close, to place before the Hindus, if they will allow me, some questions which I regard as vital and invite them seriously to consider the same.

In the first place, the Hindus must consider whether it is sufficient to take the placid view of the anthropologist that there is nothing to be said about the beliefs, habits, morals and outlooks on life, which obtain among the different peoples of the world except that they often differ; or whether it is not necessary to make an attempt to find out what kind of morality, beliefs, habits and outlook have worked best and have enabled those who possessed them to flourish, to go strong, to people the earth and to have dominion over it. As is observed by Professor Carver,[236]

Morality and religion, as the organized expression of moral approval and disapproval, must be regarded as factors in the struggle for existence as truly as are weapons for offence and defence, teeth and claws, horns and hoofs, furs and feathers. The social group, community, tribe or nation, which develops an unworkable scheme of morality or within which those social acts which weaken it and make it unfit it for survival, habitually create the sentiment of approval, while those which would strengthen and enable it to be expanded habitually create the sentiment of disapproval, will eventually be eliminated. It is its habits of approval or disapproval (these are the results of religion and morality) that handicap it, as really as the possession of two wings on one side with none on the other will handicap the colony of flies. It would be as futile in the one case as in the other to argue, that one system is just as good as another.

Morality and religion, therefore, are not mere matters of likes and dislikes. You may dislike exceedingly a scheme of morality, which, if universally practised within a nation, would make that nation the strongest nation on the face of the earth. Yet in spite of your dislike such a nation will become strong. You may like exceedingly a scheme of morality and an ideal of justice, which if universally practised within a nation, would make it unable to hold its own in the struggle with other nations. Yet in spite of your admiration this nation will eventuality disappear. The Hindus must, therefore, examine their religion and their morality in terms of their survival value.

Secondly, the Hindus must consider whether they should conserve the whole of their social heritage or select what is helpful and transmit to future generations only that much and not more. Professor John Dewey, who was my teacher and to whom I owe so much, has said:[237]

Every society gets encumbered with what is trivial, with dead wood from the past, and with what is positively perverse.... As a society becomes more enlightened, it realizes that it is responsible *not* to conserve and transmit the whole of its existing achievements, but only such as make for a better future society.

Even Burke, in spite of the vehemence with which he opposed the principle of change embodied in the French Revolution, was compelled to admit that

A state without the means of some change is without the means of its conservation. Without such means it might even risk the loss of that part of the constitution which it wished the most religiously to preserve.

What Burke said of a state applies equally to a society.

Thirdly, the Hindus must consider whether they must not cease to worship the past as supplying its ideals. The baneful effect of this worship of the past are best summed up by Professor Dewey when he says:[238]

An individual can live only in the present. The present is not just something which comes after the past; much less something produced by it. It is what life is in leaving the past behind it. The study of past products will not help us to understand the present. A knowledge of the past and its heritage is of great significance when it enters into the present, but not otherwise. And the mistake of making the records and remains of the past the main material of education is that it tends to make the past a rival of the present and the present a more or less futile imitation of the past.

The principle, which makes little of the present act of living and growing, naturally looks upon the present as empty and upon the future as remote. Such a principle is inimical to progress and is an hindrance to a strong and a steady current of life.

Fourthly, the Hindus must consider whether the time has not come for them to recognize that there is nothing fixed, nothing eternal, nothing *sanatan*; that everything is changing, that change is the law of life for individuals as well as for society. In a changing society, there must be a constant revolution of old values and the Hindus must realize that if there must be standards to measure the acts of men there must also be a readiness to revise those standards.

XXIII

I have to confess that this address has become too lengthy. Whether this fault is compensated to any extent by breadth or depth is a matter for you to judge. All I claim is to have told you candidly my views. I have little to recommend them but some study and a deep concern in your destiny. If you will allow me to say, these views are the views of a man, who has been no tool of power, no flatterer of greatness. They come from one, almost the whole of whose public exertion has been one continuous struggle for liberty for the poor and for the oppressed and whose only reward has been a continuous shower of calumny and abuse from national journals and national leaders, for no other reason except that I refuse to join with them in performing the miracle—I will not say trick—of liberating the oppressed with the gold of the tyrant and raising the poor with the cash of the rich. All this may not be enough to commend my views. I think they are not likely to alter yours. But whether they do or do not, the responsibility is entirely yours. You must make your efforts to uproot caste, if not in my way, then in your way. I am sorry, I will not be with you. I have decided to change. This is not the place for giving reasons. But even when I am gone out of your fold, I will watch your movement with active sympathy and you will have my assistance for what it may be worth. Yours is a national cause. Caste is no doubt primarily the breath of the Hindus. But the Hindus have fouled the air all over and everybody is infected, Sikh, Muslim and Christian. You, therefore, deserve the support of all those who are suffering from this infection, Sikh, Muslim and Charistian. Yours is more difficult than the other national cause, namely Swaraj. In the fight for Swaraj you fight with the whole nation on your side. In this, you have to fight against the whole nation and that too, your own. But it is more important than Swaraj. There is no use having Swaraj, if you cannot defend it. More important than the question of defending Swaraj is the question of defending the Hindus under the Swaraj. In my opinion only when the Hindu society becomes a casteless society that it can hope to have strength enough to defend itself. Without such internal strength, Swaraj of Hindus may turn out to be only a step towards slavery. Good-bye and good wishes for your success.

21

Reply to the Mahatma

I

I appreciate greatly the honour done to me by the Mahatma in taking notice in his *Harijan*[239] of the speech on caste which I had prepared for the Jat Pat Todak Mandal. From a perusal of his review of my speech it is clear that the Mahatma completely dissents from the views I have expressed on the subject of caste. I am not in the habit of entering into controversy with my opponents unless there are special reasons which compel me to act otherwise. Had my opponent been some mean and obscure person I would not have pursued him. But my opponent being the Mahatma himself I feel I must attempt to meet the case to the contrary which he has sought to put forth. While I appreciate the honour he has done to me, I must confess to a sense of surprise on finding that of all the persons the Mahatma should accuse me of a desire to seek publicity as he seems to do when he suggests that in publishing the undelivered speech my object was to see that I was not 'forgotten' Whatever the Mahatma may choose to say my object in publishing the speech was to provoke the Hindus to think and take stock of their position. I have never hankered for publicity and if I may say so, I have more of it than I wish or need. But supposing it was out of the motive of gaining publicity that I printed the speech who could cast a stone at me? Surely not those, who like the Mahatma live in glass houses.

II

Motive apart, what has the Mahatma to say on the question raised
by me in the speech? First of all anyone who reads my speech will
realize that the Mahatma has entirely missed the issues raised by
me and that the issues he has raised are not the issues that arise
out of what he is pleased to call my indictment of the Hindus. The
principal points which I have tried to make out in my speech
may be catalogued as follows: (1) That caste has ruined the Hindus;
(2) That the reorganization of the Hindu society on the basis of
Chaturvarnya is impossible because the Varnavyavastha[240] is like
a leaky pot or like a man running at the nose. It is incapable of
sustaining itself by its own virtue and has an inherent tendency to
degenerate into a caste system unless there is a legal sanction behind
it which can be enforced against every one transgressing his Varna;
(3) That the reorganization of the Hindu society on the basis of
Chaturvarnya is harmful because the effect of the Varnavyavastha
is to degrade the masses by denying them opportunity to acquire
knowledge and to emasculate them by denying them the right to
be armed; (4) That the Hindu society must be reorganized on a
religious basis which would recognize the principles of Liberty,
Equality and Fraternity; (5) That in order to achieve this object
the sense of religious sanctity behind caste and Varna must be
destroyed; (6) That the sanctity of caste and Varna can be destroyed
only by discarding the divine authority of the Shastras. It will be
noticed that the questions raised by the Mahatma are absolutely
beside the point and show that the main argument of the speech
was lost upon him.

III

Let me examine the substance of the points made by the Mahatma.
The first point made by the Mahatma is that the texts cited by me
are not authentic. I confess I am no authority on this matter. But
I should like to state that the texts cited by me are all taken from
the writings of the late Mr Tilak who was a recognized authority
on the Sanskrit language and on the Hindu Shastras. His second
point is that these Shastras should be interpreted not by the learned
but the saints and that, as the saints have understood them, the
Shastras do not support caste and untouchability. As regards the

first point what I like to ask the Mahatma is what does it avail to anyone if the texts are interpolations and if they have been differently interpreted by the saints? The masses do not make any distinction between texts which are genuine and texts which are interpolations. The masses do not know what the texts are. They are too illiterate to know the contents of the *Shastras*. They have believed what they have been told and what they have been told is that the *Shastras* do enjoin as a religious duty the observance of caste and untouchability.

With regard to the saints, one must admit that howsoever different and elevating their teachings may have been as compared to those of the merely learned they have been lamentably ineffective. They have been ineffective for two reasons. Firstly, none of the saints ever attacked the caste system. On the contrary, they were staunch believers in the system of castes. Most of them lived and died as members of the castes which they respectively belonged. So passionately attached was Jnyandeo to his status as a Brahmin that when the Brahmins of Paithan would not admit him to their fold he moved heaven and earth to get his status as a Brahmin recognized by the Brahmin fraternity. And even the saint Eknath who now figures in the film 'Dharmatma' as a hero for having shown courage to touch the untouchables and dine with them, did so not because he was opposed to caste and untouchability but because he felt that the pollution caused thereby could be washed away by a bath in the sacred waters of the river Ganges.*
The saints have never according to my study carried on a campaign against caste and untouchability. They were not concerned with the struggle between men. They are concerned with the relation between man and God. They did not preach that all men were equal. They preached that all men were equal in the eyes of God— a very different and a very innocuous proposition which nobody can find difficult to preach or dangerous to believe in. The second reason why the teachings of the saints proved ineffective was because the masses have been taught that a saint might break caste but the common man must not. A saint therefore never became an example to follow. He always remained a pious man to be honoured. That the masses have remained staunch believers in

* अंत्यजाचा विटाळ ज्यासी। गंगास्नाने शुद्धत्व त्यासी॥—एकनाथी भागवत, अ. २८, ओ. १६१.

aste and untouchability shows that the pious lives and noble
ermons of the saints have had no effect on their life and conduct
s against the teachings of the *Shastras*. Thus it can be a matter of
ιo consolation that there were saints or that there is a Mahatma
vho understands the *Shastras* differently from the learned few or
gnorant many. That the masses hold different views of the *Shastras*
s a fact which should and must be reckoned with. How is that
o be dealt with except by denouncing the authority of the *Shastras*,
vhich continue to govern their conduct, is a question which the
Mahatma has not considered. But whatever the plan the Mahatma
ιuts forth as an effective means to free the masses from the
eachings of the *Shastras*, he must accept that the pious life led
ιy one good Samaritan may be very elevating to himself but in
ιndia, with the attitude the common man has to saints and to
Mahatmas—to honour but not to follow—one cannot make much
ιut of it.

IV

The third point made by the Mahatma is that a religion professed
by Chaitanya, Jnyandeo, Tukaram, Tiruvalluvar, Ramkrishna
Paramahansa etc. cannot be devoid of merit as is made out by me
and that a religion has to be judged not by its worst specimens but
by the best it might have produced. I agree with every word of this
statement. But I do not quite understand what the Mahatma wishes
to prove thereby. That religion should be judged not by its worst
specimens but by its best is true enough but does it dispose of the
matter? I say it does not. The question still remains—why the worst
number so many and the best so few? To my mind there are two
conceivable answers to this question: (1) That the worst by reason
of some original perversity of theirs are morally uneducable and
are therefore incapable of making the remotest approach to the
religious ideal. Or (2) That the religious ideal is a wholly wrong
ideal which has given a wrong moral twist to the lives of the many
and that the best have become best in spite of the wrong ideal—
in fact by giving to the wrong twist a turn in the right direction.
Of these two explanations I am not prepared to accept the first and
I am sure that even the Mahatma will not insist upon the contrary.
To my mind the second is the only logical and reasonable explanation unless the Mahatma has a third alternative to explain why

the worst are so many and the best so few. If the second is the only explanation then obviously the argument of the Mahatma that a religion should be judged by its best followers carries us nowhere except to pity the lot of the many who have gone wrong because they have been made to worship wrong ideals.

V

The argument of the Mahatma that Hinduism would be tolerable if only many were to follow the example of the saints is fallacious for another reason.[a] By citing the names of such illustrious persons as Chaitanya etc. what the Mahatma seems to me to suggest in its broadest and simplest form is that Hindu society can be made tolerable and even happy without any fundamental change in its structure if all the high caste Hindus can be persuaded to follow a high standard of morality in their dealings with the low caste Hindus. I am totally opposed to this kind of ideology. I can respect those of the caste Hindus who try to realize a high social ideal in their life. Without such men India would be an uglier and a less happy place to live in than it is. But nonetheless anyone who relies on an attempt to turn the members of the caste Hindus into better men by improving their personal character is in my judgment wasting his energy and hugging an illusion. Can personal character make the maker of armaments a good man, *i.e.* a man who will sell shells that will not burst and gas that will not poison? If it cannot, how can you accept personal character to make a man loaded with the consciousness of caste, a good man, *i.e.* a man who would treat his fellows as his friends and equals? To be true to himself he must deal with his fellows either as a superior or inferior according as the case may be; at any rate, differently from his own caste fellows. He can never be expected to deal with his fellows as his kinsmen and equals. As a matter of fact, a Hindu does treat all those who are not of his caste as though they were aliens, who could be discriminated against with impunity and against whom any fraud or trick may be practised without shame. *This is to say that there can be a better or a worse Hindu. But a good Hindu there cannot be.* This is so not because there is anything wrong with his

[a] In this connection see the illuminating article on Morality and the Social Structure by H. N. Brailsford in the *Aryan Path* for April 1936.

personal character. In fact what is wrong is the entire basis of his relationship to his fellows. The best of men cannot be moral if the basis of relationship between them and their fellows is fundamentally a wrong relationship. To a slave his master may be better or worse. But there cannot be a good master. A good man cannot be a master and a master cannot be a good man. The same applies to the relationship between high caste and low caste. To a low caste man a high caste man can be better or worse as compared to other high caste men. A high caste man cannot be a good man in so far as he must have a low caste man to distinguish him as high caste man. It cannot be good to a low caste man to be conscious that there is a high caste man above him. I have argued in my speech that a society based on *Varna* or caste is a society which is based on a wrong relationship. I had hoped that the Mahatma would attempt to demolish my argument. But instead of doing that he has merely reiterated his belief in Chaturvarnya without disclosing the ground on which it is based.

VI

Does the Mahatma practise what he preaches? One does not like to make personal reference in an argument which is general in its application. But when one preaches a doctrine and holds it as a dogma there is a curiosity to know how far he practises what he preaches. It may be that his failure to practise is due to the ideal being too high to be attainable; it may be that his failure to practise is due to the innate hypocrisy of the man. In any case he exposes his conduct to examination and I must not be blamed if I asked how far has the Mahatma attempted to realize his ideal in his own case. The Mahatma is a Bania by birth. His ancestors had abandoned trading in favour of ministership which is a calling of the Brahmins. In his own life, before he became a Mahatma, when occasion came for him to choose his career he preferred law to scales. On abandoning law he became half saint and half politician. He has never touched trading which is his ancestral calling. His youngest son—I take one who is a faithful follower of his father—born a Vaishya has married a Brahmins's daughter and has chosen to serve a newspaper magnate. The Mahatma is not known to have condemned him for not following his ancestral calling. It may be wrong and uncharitable to judge an ideal by its worst specimens.

But surely the Mahatma as a specimen has no better and if he even fails to realize the ideal then the ideal must be an impossible ideal quite opposed to the practical instincts of man. Students of Carlyle know that he often spoke on a subject before he thought about it. I wonder whether such has not been the case with the Mahatma in regard to the subject matter of caste. Otherwise certain questions which occur to me would not have escaped him. When can a calling be deemed to have become an ancestral calling so as to make it binding on a man? Must man follow his ancestral calling even if it does not suit his capacities, even when it has ceased to be profitable? Must a man live by his ancestral calling even if he finds it not to be immoral? If every one must pursue his ancestral calling then it must follow that a man must continue to be a pimp because his grandfather was a pimp and a woman must continue to be a prostitute because her grandmother was a prostitute. Is the Mahatma prepared to accept the logical conclusion of his doctrine? To me his ideal of following one's ancestral calling is not only an impossible and impractical ideal, but it is also morally an indefensible ideal.

VII

The Mahatma sees great virtue in a Brahmin remaining a Brahmin all his life. Leaving aside the fact there are many Brahmins who do not like to remain Brahmins all their lives what can we say about those Brahmins who have clung to their ancestral calling of priesthood? Do they do so from any faith in the virtue of the principle of ancestral calling or do they do so from motives of filthy lucre? The Mahatma does not seem to concern himself with such queries. He is satisfied that these are 'real Brahmins who are living on alms freely given to them and giving freely what they have of spiritual treasures'.[241] This is how a hereditary Brahmin priest appears to the Mahatma—a carrier of spiritual treasures. But another portrait of the hereditary Brahmin can also be drawn. A Brahmin can be a priest to Vishnu—the God of Love. He can be a priest to Shankar—the God of Destruction. He can be a priest at Buddha Gaya worshipping Buddha—the greatest teacher of mankind who taught the noblest doctrine of Love. He also can be a priest to Kali, the Goddess, who must have a daily sacrifice of an animal to satisfy her thirst for blood; He will be a priest of

REPLY TO THE MAHATMA • 313

the temple of Rama—the Kshatriya God! He will also be a priest of the Temple of Parshuram, the God who took *Avatar* to destroy the Kshatriyas! He can be a priest to Brahma, the Creator of the world. He can be a priest to a Pir whose God Allah will not brook the claim of Brahma to share his spiritual dominion over the world! No one can say that this is a picture which is not true to life. If this is a true picture one does not know what to say of this capacity to bear loyalties to gods and goddesses whose attributes are so antagonistic that no honest man can be a devotee to all of them. The Hindus rely upon this extraordinary phenomenon as evidence of the greatest virtue of their religion—namely its catholicity, its spirit of toleration. As against this facile view, it can be urged that what is toleration and catholicity may be really nothing more creditable than indifference or flaccid latitudinarianism. These two attitudes are hard to distinguish in their outer seeming. But they are so vitally unlike in their real quality that no one who examines them closely can mistake one for the other. That a man is ready to render homage to many gods and goddesses may be cited as evidence of his tolerant spirit. But can it not also be evidence of insincerity born of a desire to serve the times? I am sure that this toleration is merely insincerity. If this view is well founded, one may ask what spiritual treasure can there be with a person who is ready to be a priest and a devotee to any deity which it serves his purpose to worship and to adore? Not only must a person be deemed to be bankrupt of all spiritual treasures but for him to practise so elevating a profession as that of a priest simply because it is ancestral, without faith, without belief, merely as a mechanical process handed down from father to son, is not a conservation of virtue; it is really the prostitution of a noble profession which is no other than the service of religion.

VIII

Why does the Mahatma cling to the theory of every one following his or her ancestral calling? He gives his reasons nowhere. But there must be some reason although he does not care to avow it. Years ago writing on 'Caste *versus* Class' in his *Young India* he argued[242] that caste system was better than the class system on the ground that caste was the best possible adjustment of social stability. If that be the reason why the Mahatma clings to the theory of every one following his or her ancestral calling, then he is clinging to a false view of social life. Everybody wants social stability and some adjustment must be made in the relationship between individuals and classes in order that stability may be had. But two things, I am sure nobody wants. One thing nobody wants is a static relationship, something that is unalterable, something that is fixed for all times. Stability is wanted but not at the cost of change when change is imperative. The second thing nobody wants is mere adjustment. Adjustment is wanted but not at the sacrifice of social justice. Can it be said that the adjustment of social relationship on the basis of caste *i.e.* on the basis of each to his hereditary calling avoids these two evils? I am convinced that it does not. Far from being the best possible adjustment I have no doubt that it is of the worst possible kind inasmuch as it offends against both the canons of social adjustment—namely fluidity and equity.

IX

Some might think that the Mahatma had made much progress inasmuch as he now only believes in *Varna* and does not believe in caste. It is true that there was a time when the Mahatma was a full-blooded and a blue-blooded Sanatani Hindu. He believed in the *Vedas*, the *Upanishads*, the *Puranas* and all that goes by the name of Hindu scriptures and therefore in *avatars* and rebirth. He believed in caste and defended it with the vigour of the orthodox. He condemned the cry for inter-dining, inter-drinking and inter-marrying and argued that restraints about inter-dining to a great extent 'helped the cultivation of will-power and the conservation of certain social virtue'. It is good that he has repudiated this sanctimonious nonsense and admitted that caste 'is harmful both to spiritual and national growth,' and maybe, his son's marriage outside his caste has had something to do with this change of view. But has the Mahatma really progressed? What is the nature of the *Varna* for which the Mahatma stands? Is it the *Vedic* conception as commonly understood and preached by Swami Dayanand Saraswati and his followers, the Arya Samajists? The essence of the *Vedic* conception of *Varna* is the pursuit of a calling which is appropriate to one's natural aptitude. The essence of the Mahatma's conception of *Varna* is the pursuit of ancestral calling irrespective of natural aptitude. What is the difference between caste and *Varna* as understood by the Mahatma? I find none. As defined by the Mahatma, *Varna* becomes merely a different name for caste for the simple reason that it is the same in essence—namely the pursuit of ancestral calling. Far from making progress the Mahatma has suffered retrogression. By putting this interpretation upon the *Vedic* conception of *Varna* he has really made ridiculous what was sublime. While I reject the *Vedic Varnavyavastha* for reasons given in the speech I must admit that the *Vedic* theory of *Varna* as interpreted by Swami Dayanand and some others is a sensible and an inoffensive thing. It did not admit birth as a determining factor in fixing the place of an individual in society. It only recognized worth. The Mahatma's view of *Varna* not only makes nonsense of the *Vedic Varna* but it makes it an abominable thing. *Varna* and caste are two very different concepts. *Varna* is based on the principle of each according to his worthwhile caste is based on the principle of each according to his birth. The two are as distinct as chalk is from cheese. In fact there is an antithesis between the two. If the Mahatma believes as he does in everyone following his or her ancestral calling, then most certainly he is advocating the caste system and that in calling it the *Varna* system he is not only guilty of terminological inexactitude, but he is causing confusion worse confounded. I am sure that all his confusion is due to the fact that the Mahatma has no definite and clear conception as to what is *Varna* and what is caste and as to the necessity of either for the conservation of Hinduism. He has said and one hopes that he will not find some mystic reason to change his view that caste is not the essence of Hinduism. Does he regard *Varna* as the essence of Hinduism? One cannot as yet give any categorical answer. Readers of his article on 'Dr Ambedkar's Indictment'[243] will answer 'No'. In that article he does not say that the dogma of *Varna* is an essential part of the creed of Hinduism. Far from making *Varna* the essence of Hinduism he says 'the essence of Hinduism is contained in its enunciation of one and only God as Truth and its bold acceptance of Ahimsa as the law of the human family'. But the readers of his article in reply to Mr Sant Ram will say 'Yes'. In that article he says 'How can a Muslim remain one if he rejects the Koran, or a Christian remain as Christian if he rejects the Bible? If Caste and *Varna* are convertible terms and if *Varna* is an integral part of the *Shastras* which define Hinduism I do not know how a person who rejects caste, *i.e. Varna* can call himself a Hindu?' Why this prevarication? Why does the Mahatma hedge? Whom does he want to please? Has the saint failed to sense the truth? Or does the politician stand in the way of the saint? The real reason why the Mahatma is suffering from this confusion is probably to be traced to two sources. The first is the temperament of the Mahatma. He has almost in everything the simplicity of the child with the child's capacity for self-deception. Like a child he can believe in anything he wants to believe. We must therefore wait till such time as it pleases the Mahatma to abandon his faith in *Varna* as it has pleased him to abandon his faith in caste. The second source of confusion is the double role which the Mahatma wants to play—of a Mahatma and a politician. As a Mahatma he may be trying to spiritualize politics. Whether he has succeeded in it or not politics has certainly commercialized him. A politician must know that society cannot bear the whole truth and that he must not speak the whole truth; if he is speaking the whole truth it is bad for his politics. The reason why the Mahatma is always supporting caste and *Varna* is because he is afraid that if he opposed them he will lose his place in politics. Whatever may be the source of this confusion the Mahatma must be told that he is deceiving himself and also deceiving the people by preaching caste under the name of *Varna*.

X

The Mahatma says that the standards I have applied to test Hindus and Hinduism are too severe and that judged by those standards every known living faith will probably fail. The complaint that my standards are high may be true. But the question is not whether they are high or whether they are low. The question is whether they are the right standards to apply. A people and their religion must be judged by social standards based on social ethics. No other standard would have any meaning if religion is held to be a necessary good for the well-being of the people. Now I maintain that the standards I have applied to test Hindus and Hinduism are the most appropriate standards and that I know of none that are better. The conclusion that every known religion would fail if tested by my standards may be true. But this fact should not give the Mahatma as the champion of Hindus and Hinduism a ground for comfort any more than the existence of one madman

REPLY TO THE MAHATMA • 317

should give comfort to another madman or the existence of one criminal should give comfort to another criminal. I like to assure the Mahatma that it is not the mere failure of the Hindus and Hinduism which has produced in me the feelings of disgust and contempt with which I am charged. I realize that the world is a very imperfect world and anyone who wants to live in it must bear with its imperfections. But while I am prepared to bear with the imperfections and shortcomings of the society in which I may be destined to labour, I feel I should not consent to live in a society which cherishes wrong ideals or a society which having right ideals will not consent to bring its social life in conformity with those ideals. If I am disgusted with Hindus and Hinduism it is because I am convinced that they cherish wrong ideals and live a wrong social life. My quarrel with Hindus and Hinduism is not over the imperfections of their social conduct. It is much more fundamental. It is over their ideals.

XI

Hindu society seems to me to stand in need of a moral regeneration which it is dangerous to postpone. And the question is who can determine and control this moral regeneration? Obviously only those who have undergone an intellectual regeneration and those who are honest enough to have the courage of their convictions born of intellectual emancipation. Judged by this standard the Hindu leaders who count are in my opinion quite unfit for the task. It is impossible to say that they have undergone the preliminary intellectual regeneration. If they had undergone an intellectual regeneration they would neither delude themselves in the simple way of the untaught multitude nor would they take advantage of the primitive ignorance of others as one sees them doing. Notwithstanding the crumbling state of Hindu society these leaders will nevertheless unblushingly appeal to ideals of the past which have in every way ceased to have any connection with the present; which however suitable they might have been in the days of their origin have now become a warning rather than a guide. They still have a mystic respect for the earlier forms which make them disinclined—nay opposed to any examination of the foundations of their society. The Hindu masses are of course incredibly heedless in the formation of their beliefs. But so are the

Hindu leaders. And what is worse is that these Hindu leaders become filled with an illicit passion for their beliefs when any one proposes to rob them of their companionship. The Mahatma is no exception. The Mahatma appears not to believe in thinking. He prefers to follow the saints. Like a conservative with his reverence for consecrated notions he is afraid that if he once starts thinking, many ideals and institutions to which he clings will be doomed. One must sympathize with him. For every act of independent thinking puts some portion of apparently stable world in peril. But it is equally true that dependence on saints cannot lead us to know the truth. The saints are after all only human beings and as Lord Balfour said, 'the human mind is no more a truth finding apparatus than the snout of a pig'. In so far as he does think, to me he really appears to be prostituting his intelligence to find reasons for supporting this archaic social structure of the Hindus. He is the most influential apologist of it and therefore the worst enemy of the Hindus.

Unlike the Mahatma there are Hindu leaders who are not content merely to believe and follow. They dare to think, and act in accordance with the result of their thinking. But unfortunately they are either a dishonest lot or an indifferent lot when it comes to the question of giving right guidance to the mass of the people. Almost every Brahmin has transgressed the rule of caste. The number of Brahmins who sell shoes is far greater than those who practise priesthood. Not only have the Brahmins given up their ancestral calling of priesthood for trading but they have entered trades which are prohibited to them by the *Shastras*. Yet how many Brahmins who break caste every day will preach against caste and against the *Shastras*? For one honest Brahmin preaching against caste and *Shastras* because his practical instinct and moral conscience cannot support a conviction in them, there are hundreds who break caste and trample upon the *Shastras* everyday but who are the most fanatic upholders of the theory of caste and the sanctity of the *Shastras*. Why this duplicity? Because they feel that if the masses are emancipated from the yoke of caste they would be a menace to the power and prestige of the Brahmins as a class. The dishonesty of this intellectual class who would deny the masses the fruits of their thinking is a most disgraceful phenomenon.

The Hindus in the words of Mathew Arnold are 'wandering between two worlds, one dead, the other powerless to be born'.

What are they to do? The Mahatma to whom they appeal for guidance does not believe in thinking and can therefore give no guidance which can be said to stand the test of experience. The intellectual classes to whom the masses look for guidance are either too dishonest or too indifferent to educate them in the right direction. We are indeed witnesses to a great tragedy. In the face of this tragedy all one can do is to lament and say—such be thy Leaders, O! Hindus.

VII

Untouchability

Some of the most important and involved writings of Ambedkar are concerned with untouchability. He provided empirical accounts of its practices; discussed the attitude of caste Hindus and colonial administration towards Untouchables; gave an account of their struggles; pulled out a lot of skeletons from the cupboards of the so-called votaries of their emancipation; highlighted the objectives and strategies of his movement and discussed his own role in it.

Outside the Fold[244] brings out how far removed the Indian village is from the romantic description of Sir Charles Metcalfe and Gandhi. It was first published posthumously along with a number of other moving accounts of Untouchability in 1989. It was written following the discussion on village panchayats in the Constituent Assembly in 1948.

From Millions to Fractions[245] was written sometime after 1932 and was published posthumously from the unpublished manuscripts in 1989.

Ambedkar was a member of the Indian Franchise Committee or the Lothian Committee. The 1911 and 1921 Census made a separate enumeration of Untouchables, identifying certain definite criteria on what constituted Untouchability. There was not much of a reaction when the Census displayed them as forming a significant proportion of the population. However, when the Lothian Committee visited various provinces on the eve of the constitutional reforms of 1935, the figure of the Untouchables were scaled down and the severity of untouchability was assuaged by a majority of the spokesmen of these provinces. Ambedkar saw it as an attempt to deprive the Untouchables of adequate representation in political power in proportion to their numbers. He found that even Backward Classes and Muslims did not come to the support of the Untouchables.

The Untouchables and The Pax Britannica[246] is a much shortened excerpt of a long account bearing the same title that Ambedkar wrote in preparation to the Round Table Conference. This is an assessment of the Raj from the perspective of the Untouchables.

An Anti-untouchability Agenda[247]. After the Poona Pact an Anti-untouchability League, later named as the Harijan Sevak Sangh (HSS), was constituted, associating leaders of the Depressed Classes and Congressmen. Ambedkar was a member of the Central Board of the League. He laid down an anti-untouchability agenda in a letter written to A. V. Thakkar, the secretary of the League. He, however, felt that the thrust of HSS became 'constructive work' rather than the removal of untouchability and consequently resigned from the organization. (The title is the editor's).

Political Safeguards for the Depressed Classes. This is the scheme of safeguards that Ambedkar submitted, along with Rao Bahadur R. Srinivasan, to the sub-committee on Minorities of the Round Table Conference in 1931. This scheme was to form the basis of the various constitutional and legal provisions against Untouchability and for the protection of Untouchables in the subsequent period.

22

Outside the Fold

What is the position of the Untouchables under the Hindu social
order? To give a true idea of their position is the main purpose of
this chapter. But it is not easy to strike upon the best means of
conveying a realistic and concrete picture of the way the Untouchables live or rather are made to live under the Hindu social order
to one who has no conception of it. One way is to draw a model
plant so to say of the Hindu social order and show the place given
to the Untouchables therein. For this it is necessary to go to a
Hindu village. Nothing can serve our purpose better. The Hindu
village is a working plant of the Hindu social order. One can see
there the Hindu social order in operation in full swing. The average
Hindu is always in ecstasy whenever he speaks of the Indian village.
He regards it as an ideal form of social organization to which he
believes there is no parallel anywhere in the world. It is claimed
to be a special contribution to the theory of social organization for
which India may well be proud of.

How fanatic are the Hindus in their belief in the Indian village
as an ideal piece of social organization may be seen from the angry
speeches made by the Hindu members of the Indian Constituent
Assembly in support of the contention that the Indian Constitution should recognize the Indian village as its base of the constitutional pyramid of autonomous administrative units with its own
legislature, executive and judiciary. From the point of view of the
Untouchables, there could not have been a greater calamity. Thank
God the Constituent Assembly did not adopt it. Nevertheless the
Hindus persist in their belief that the Indian village is an ideal form

of social organization. This belief of the Hindus is not ancestral belief, nor does it come from the ancient past. It is borrowed from Sir Charles Metcalfe—a civil servant of the East India Company. Metcalfe, who was a revenue officer, in one of his Revenue Papers described the Indian village in the following terms:[a]

The village communities are little republics, having nearly everything they want within themselves and almost independent of any foreign relations. They seem to last when nothing else lasts. Dynasty after dynasty tumbles down, revolution succeeds to revolution; Hindu, Pathan, Moghul, Maratha, Sikh, English, all are masters in turn, but the village communities remain the same. In times of trouble they arm and fortify themselves. An hostile army passes through the country, the village communities collect their cattle within their walls and let the enemy pass unprovoked. If plunder and devastation be directed against themselves, and the forces employed be irresistible, they flee to friendly villages at a distance; but when the storm has passed over, they return and resume their occupations. If a country remains for a series of years the scene of continued pillage and massacre so that the villages cannot be inhabited, the scattered villagers nevertheless return whenever the power of peaceable possession revives. A generation may pass away, but the succeeding generation will return. The sons will take the place of their fathers; the same site for the village, the same position for their houses, the same lands will be reoccupied by the descendants of those who were driven out when the village was repopulated; and it is not a trifling matter that will drive them out, for they will often maintain their post through times of disturbances and convulsion, and acquire strength sufficient to resist pillage and oppression with success. This union of the village communities, each one forming a little state in itself, has, I conceive, contributed more than any other cause to the preservation of the people of India, through all the revolutions and changes which they have suffered, and is in a high degree conducive to their happiness and to the enjoyment of a great portion of freedom and independence.

Having read this description of an Indian village given by a high-placed member of the governing class, the Hindus felt flattered and adopted his view as a welcome compliment. In adopting this view of the Indian village, the Hindus have not done any justice to their intelligence or their understanding. They have merely exhibited the weakness common to all subject people. Since many foreigners are led to accept this idealistic view of the Indian village, it would be better to present a realistic picture of society as one finds it in an Indian village.

[a] Quoted by Baden Powell in his 'Land System of British India', vol. 1.

The Indian village is not a single social unit. It consists of castes. But for our purposes, it is enough to say:

I. The population in the village is divided into two sections— (i) Touchables and (ii) Untouchables.

II. The Touchables form the major community and the Untouchables a minor community.

III. The Touchables live inside the village and the Untouchables live outside the village in separate quarters.

IV. Economically, the Touchables form a strong and powerful community, while the Untouchables are a poor and a dependent community.

V. Socially, the Touchables occupy the position of a ruling race, while the Untouchables occupy the position of a subject race of hereditary bondsmen.

What are the terms of associated life on which the Touchables and Untouchables live in an Indian village? In every village the Touchables have a code which the Untouchables are required to follow. This code lays down the acts of omissions and commissions which the Touchables treat as offences. The following is the list of such offences:

1. The Untouchables must live in separate quarters away from the habitation of the Hindus. It is an offence for the Untouchables to break or evade the rule of segregation.

2. The quarters of the Untouchables must be located towards the South, since the South is the most inauspicious of the four directions. A breach of this rule shall be deemed to be an offence.

3. The Untouchables must observe the rule of distance pollution or shadow of pollution as the case may be. It is an offence to break the rule.

4. It is an offence for a member of the Untouchable community to acquire wealth, such as land or cattle.

5. It is an offence for a member of the Untouchable community to build a house with tiled roof.

6. It is an offence for a member of the Untouchable community to put on a clean dress, wear shoes, put on a watch or gold ornaments.

7. It is an offence for a member of the Untouchable community to give high-sounding names to their children. Their names be such as to indicate contempt.

8. It is an offence for a member of the Untouchable community to sit on a chair in the presence of a Hindu.

9. It is an offence for a member of the Untouchable community to ride on a horse or a palanquin through the village.

10. It is an offence for a member of the Untouchable community to take a procession of Untouchables through the village.

11. It is an offence for a member of the Untouchable community not to salute a Hindu.

12. It is an offence for a member of the Untouchable community to speak a cultured language.

13. It is an offence for a member of the Untouchable community, if he happens to come into the village on a sacred day which the Hindus treat as the day of fast and at or about the time of the breaking of fast, to go about speaking, on the ground that their breath is held to foul the air and the food of the Hindus.

14. It is an offence for an Untouchable to wear the outward marks of a Touchable and pass himself as a Touchable.

15. An Untouchable must conform to the status of an inferior and he must wear the marks of his inferiority for the public to know and identify him such as—

(a) having a contemptible name.

(b) not wearing clean clothes.

(c) not having tiled roof.

(d) not wearing silver and gold ornaments.

A contravention of any of these rules is an offence.

Next come the duties which the Code requires members of the Untouchable community to perform for the Touchables. Under this head the following may be mentioned:

1. A member of an Untouchable community must carry a message of any event in the house of a Hindu such as death or marriage to his relatives living in other villages no matter how distant these villages may be.

2. An Untouchable must work at the house of a Hindu when a marriage is taking place, such as breaking fuel, and going on errands.

3. An Untouchable must accompany a Hindu girl when she is going from her parent's house to her husband's village no matter how distant it is.

4. When the whole village community is engaged in celebrating a general festivity such as Holi or Dasara, the Untouchables must perform all menial acts which are preliminary to the main observance.

5. On certain festivities, the Untouchables must submit their women to members of the village community to be made the subject of indecent fun.

These duties have to be performed without remuneration.

To realize the significance of these duties, it is important to note why they have come into being. Every Hindu in the village regards himself as a superior person above the Untouchables. As an overlord, he feels it absolutely essential to maintain his prestige. This prestige he cannot maintain unless he has at his command a retinue to dance attendance on him. It is in the Untouchable that he finds a ready retinue which is at his command and for which he does not have to pay. The Untouchables by reason of their helplessness cannot refuse to perform these duties and the Hindu villager does not hesitate to exact them since they are so essential to the maintenance of his prestige.

These offences are not to be found in the Penal Code, enacted by the British Government. Nonetheless so far as the Untouchables are concerned, they are real. A breach of any of them involves sure punishment for the Untouchables.

Another important thing to note is that the punishment for these offences is always collective. The whole community of Untouchables is liable for punishment though the offence may have been committed by an individual.

How do the Untouchables live? How do they earn their living? Without a knowledge of the ways of earning a livelihood which are open to the Untouchables it would not be possible to have a clear idea of their place in Hindu society.

In an agricultural country, agriculture can be the main source of living. But this source of earning a living is generally not open to the Untouchables. This is so for a variety of reasons. In the first place purchase of land is beyond their means. Secondly, even if an Untouchable has the money to purchase land he has no opportunity to do so. In most parts the Hindus would resent an Untouchable coming forward to purchase land and thereby trying to become the equal of the Touchable class of Hindus. Such an act of daring on the part of an Untouchable would not only be frowned upon but might easily invite punishment. In some parts they are disabled by law from purchasing land. For instance in the Province of Punjab there is a law called the Land Alienation Act. This law specifies the communities which can purchase land and the Untouchables are excluded from the list. The result is that in most part the Untouchables are forced to be landless labourers. As labourers they cannot demand reasonable wages. They have to work for the Hindu farmer for such wages as their masters choose to give. On this issue the Hindu farmers can combine to keep the wages to the lowest level possible for it is in their interests to do so. On the other hand the Untouchables have no holding power. They must earn or starve. Nor have they any bargaining power. They must submit to the rate fixed or suffer violence.

The wages paid to the Untouchables are either paid in cash or in corn. In parts of the Uttar Pradesh the corn given to the Untouchables as their wages is called 'Gobaraha' means privy corn or corn contained in the dung of an animal. In the month of March or April when the crop is fully grown, reaped and dried, it is spread on the threshing floor. Bullocks are made to tread over the corn in order to take the corn out of husk by the pressure of their hooves. While treading over the corn, the bullocks swallow up the corn as well as the straw. As their intake is excessive they find it difficult to digest the corn. Next day, the same corn comes out of their stomach along with their dung. The dung is strained and the corn is separated and given to the Untouchable workmen as their wages which they convert into flour and make into bread.

When the agricultural season is over the Untouchables have no employment and no means of earning a living. In such seasons they subsist by cutting grass and firewood from the jungle and sell it in a nearby town. Even when it is open it depends upon the forest guard. Only if he is bribed he will let them take some grass and firewood from the Government forest. When it is brought to the town they have always to face a buyer's market. The Hindus who are the main body of buyers will always conspire to beat down the wages. Having no power to hold out, the Untouchables have to sell their stuff for whatever is offered to them. Often they have to walk 10 miles each way from the village to the town and back to sell their stuff.

There is no trade in which they are engaged themselves as a means of earning a livelihood. They have not the capital for it and even if they had, no one would buy from them.

All these sources of earning are obviously precarious and fleeting. There is no security. There is only one secure source of livelihood open to the Untouchables in some parts of the country known to me. It is the right to beg food from the Hindu farmers of the village. Every village has its machinery of administration. The Untouchables of the village are hereditary menials employed in the village administration. As part of their remuneration the whole body of Untouchables get a small parcel of land assigned in the ancient past which is fixed and is never increased and which the Untouchables prefer to leave uncultivated because of its excessive fragmentations. Coupled with this is given to them the right to beg for food.

Shocking as it may seem, this has become a customary right of the Untouchables and even the government takes into account the value of the food obtained by the Untouchables by begging in fixing the remuneration of an Untouchable if he were to be employed in a government job.

This right to beg for food from the Touchables is now the principal means of livelihood for 60 millions of Untouchables in India. If anyone were to move in a village after the usual dinner time, he will meet with a swarm of Untouchables moving about the village begging for food and uttering the formula.

This statutory beggary as a means of livelihood for the Untouchables has been reduced to a system. The Untouchable families are attached to different Touchable families in the village as did the serfs and villeins to the Lord of the Manors in Medieval Europe. The Untouchable families attached to the Touchable families are at the command of the latter. This relationship has become so personal that one always hears a Touchable speaking of an Untouchable as 'my man' as though he was his slave. This relationship has helped to systematize this matter of begging food by the Untouchables from the Touchable households.

This is the Village Republic of which the Hindus are so proud. What is the position of the Untouchables in this republic? They are not merely the last but are also the least. He is stamped as an inferior and is held down to that status by all ways and means which a majority can command. This inferiority is the destiny not merely of an individual but of the whole class. All Untouchables are inferior to all Touchables irrespective of age or qualification. A Touchable youth is above an aged Untouchable and an educated Untouchable must rank below an illiterate Touchable.

The established order is the law made by the Touchables. The Untouchables have nothing to do with it except to obey it and respect it.

The Untouchables have no rights against the Touchables. For them there is no equal right, no justice by which that which is due to the Untouchables is allowed to them. Nothing is due to them except what the Touchables are prepared to grant. The Untouchables must not insist on rights. They should pray for mercy and favour and rest content with what is offered.

This established order is a hereditary order both in status as well as in function. Once a Touchable, always a Touchable. Once an Untouchable, always an Untouchable. Once a Brahmin, always a Brahmin. Once a sweeper, always a sweeper. Under it, those who are born high, remain high; those who are born low, remain low. In other words, the established order is based on an inexorable law of karma or destiny which is fixed once for all and can never be changed. This destiny has no relation to the merits of the individuals living under it. An Untouchable however superior he may be mentally and morally, is below a Touchable in rank, no matter how inferior he may be mentally or morally. A Touchable however poor he may be, must always take rank above an Untouchable, however rich he may be.

Such is the picture of the inside life in an Indian village. In this republic, there is no place for democracy. There is no room for equality. There is no room for liberty and there is no room for fraternity. The Indian village is the very negation of a republic. If it is a republic, it is a republic of the Touchables, by the Touchables and for the Touchables. The republic is an Empire of the Hindus over the Untouchables. It is a kind of colonialism of the Hindus designed to exploit the Untouchables. The Untouchables have no rights. They are there only to wait, serve and submit. They are there to do or to die. They have no rights because they are outside the village republic and because they are outside the so-called republic, they are outside the Hindu fold. This is a vicious circle. But this is a fact which cannot be gainsaid.

23

From Millions to Fractions

I

What is the total population of the Untouchables of India? This
is bound to be the first question that a person who cares to know
anything about them is sure to ask. It is now easy to answer this
question. For the Census of India taken in 1931 gives it as 50
millions. While it is possible now to give more or less exact figures
of the Untouchable population in India it was not possible to do
so for a long time.

This was due to various causes. Firstly untouchability is not a
legal term. There is no exact legal definition of untouchability
whereby it could be possible to define who is an Untouchable
and who is not. Untouchability is a social concept which has
become embodied in a custom and as custom varies so does
untouchability. Consequently there is always some difficulty in
the way of ascertaining the population of the Untouchables
with mathematical exactitude. Secondly, there has always been
serious opposition raised by high caste Hindus to the enumeration
by caste in the Census Report. They have insisted on the omission
of the question regarding caste from the schedules and the
suppression of the classification of the population by caste and
tribe. A proposal to this effect was made in connection with the
1901 Census mainly on the ground that the distribution of various
castes and tribes in the population changed at large intervals and
that it was not necessary to obtain figures at each decennial
enumeration.

These grounds of objection did not have any effect on the Census Commissioner. In the opinion of the Census Commissioner enumeration by caste was important and necessary. It was argued by the Census Commissioner that:

Whatever view may be taken of the advantages or disadvantages of caste as a social institution, it is impossible to conceive of any useful discussion of the population questions in India in which caste would not be an important element. Caste is still 'the foundation of the Indian social fabric,' and the record of caste is still 'the best guide to the changes in the various social strata in the Indian Society'. Every Hindu (using the term in its most elastic sense) is born into a caste and his caste determines his religious, social, economic and domestic life from the cradle to the grave. In western countries the major factors which determine the different strata of society, viz, wealth, education and vocation are fluid and catholic and tend to modify the rigidity of birth and hereditary position. In India spiritual and social community and traditional occupation override all other factors. Thus, where in censuses of western countries, an economic or occupational grouping of the population affords a basis for the combination of demographic statistics, the corresponding basis in the case of the Indian population is the distinction of religion and caste. Whatever view may be taken of caste as a national and social institution, it is useless to ignore it, and so long as caste continues to be used as one of the distinguishing features of an individual's official and social identity, it cannot be claimed that a decennial enumeration helps to perpetuate an undesirable institution.

The objections to the enumeration by castes in the Census were urged with greater force on the occasion of the Census of 1911 when the special questionnaire containing ten tests was issued for the purpose of grouping together castes which satisfied those tests. There was no doubt that those tests were such as would mark off the Depressed Classes from the Caste Hindus. It was feared by the Caste Hindus that this circular was the result of the Muslim Memorial to the Secretary of State and its aim was to separate the Depressed Classes from the Hindus and thereby to reduce the strength of the Hindu Community and its importance.

This agitation bore no fruit and the objection of separately enumerating in the Census Report those castes which satisfied those ten tests was carried out. The agitation however did not die out. It again cropped up at the Census of 1920. At this time, effort was made to put forth the objection to the caste return in a formal manner. A resolution was tabled in the Imperial Legislative

Council in 1920 attacking the caste inquiry on the grounds (a) that it was undesirable to recognize and perpetuate, by official action, the system of caste differentiation and (b) that in any case the returns were inaccurate and worthless, since the lower castes took the opportunity of passing themselves as belonging to groups of higher status. If this resolution had been carried, it would not have been possible to know the population of the Untouchables. Fortunately, owing to the absence of the mover, the resolution was not discussed and the Census Commissioner of 1921 remained free to carry out his inquiries in the usual manner.

Thirdly, no attempt was made for a separate enumeration of the Untouchables by any of the Census Commissioners previous to the year 1911. The first general Census of India was taken in the year 1881. Beyond listing the different castes and creeds and adding up their numbers so as to arrive at the total figure of the population of India, the Census of 1881 did nothing. It made no attempt to classify the different Hindu castes either into higher and lower or Touchable and Untouchable. The second general Census of India was taken in the year 1891. It was at this census that an attempt to classify the population on the basis of caste and race and grade was made by the Census Commissioner for the first time.

The third general Census of India was taken in 1901. At this census a new principle of classification was adopted namely 'Classification by social precedence as recognized by native public opinion.' For a society like Hindu society which does not recognize equality and whose social system is a system of gradation of higher and lower, this principle was the most appropriate one. Nothing can present a more intelligible picture of the social life and grouping of that large proportion of the people of India which is organized admittedly or tacitly on the basis of caste as this principle of social precedence.

II

The first attempt of a definite and deliberate kind to ascertain the population of the Untouchables was made by the Census Commissioner in 1911.

The period immediately preceding the Census of 1911 was a period during which the Morley-Minto Reforms were in incubation. It was a period when the Mohammedans of India had started their agitation for adequate representation in the legislatures by separate electorates. As a part of their propaganda, the Mohammedans waited upon Lord Morley, the then Secretary of State for India in Council, in deputation and presented him a Memorial on 27 January 1909.[248]

Whether there was any connection between what the Muslim deputation had urged in their memorial regarding the Untouchables in 1907 and the idea of the Census Commissioner four years after to make a separate enumeration of the Untouchables, is a matter on which nothing definite can be said. It is possible that what the Census Commissioner proposed to do in 1911 was only a culmination of the ways adopted by his predecessors in the matter of the demographic study of the population. Be that as it may, there was a great uproar on the part of the Hindus when the Census Commissioner announced his plan of separate enumeration of the Untouchables. It was said that this attempt of the Census Commissioner was the result of a conspiracy between the Musalmans and the British Government to divide and weaken the Hindu Community. It was alleged that what was behind this move was not a genuine desire to know the population of the Untouchables but the desire to break up the solidarity of the Hindu Community by separating the Untouchables from the Touchables. Many protest meetings were held all over the country by the Hindus and condemned in the strongest terms this plan of the Census Commissioner.

The commissioner of Census however undaunted by this storm of protest decided to carry out his plan. The procedure adopted by him for a separate enumeration of the Untouchables was of course a novel one. The Census Superintendents for different Provinces were instructed by the Census Commissioner to make separate enumeration of castes and tribes classed as Hindus but who did not conform to certain standards or who were subject to certain disabilities.

Under these tests the Census Superintendents made a separate enumeration of castes and tribes who (1) denied the supremacy of the Brahmins, (2) did not receive the Mantra from Brahmana or other recognized Hindu Guru, (3) denied the authority of the *Vedas*, (4) did not worship the great Hindu Gods, (5) were not served by good Brahmanas, (6) have no Brahman priests at all, (7) have no access to the interior of the ordinary Hindu temple,

(8) cause pollution, (9) bury their dead and (10) eat beef and do not revere the cow.

The investigation conducted by the Census Commissioner left no room for guessing. For he found as a fact what the population of the Untouchables was. The table below gives the population of the Untouchables, province by province, as found by the Census Commissioner of 1911.[a]

Province	Total population in million	Population of Depressed Classes in million	Total Seats	Seats for the Depressed Classes
Madras	39.8	6.3	120	2
Bombay	19.5	0.6	113	1
Bengal	45.0	9.9	127	1
United Provinces	47.0	10.1	120	1
Punjab	19.5	1.7	85	–
Bihar and Orissa	32.4	9.3	100	1
Central Provinces	12.0	3.7	72	1
Assam	6.0	0.3	54	–
	221.2	41.9	791	7

An outsider might not realize the significance and the bearing of these tests. They might ask what all this got to do with untouchability. But he will realize the significance and the bearing on the question of ascertaining the population of the Untouchables. As has been said there is no legal definition of untouchability and there cannot be any. Untouchability does not express itself through the hair of the head or the colour of the skin. It is not a matter of blood. Untouchability expresses itself in modes of treatment and observance of certain practices. An Untouchable is a person who is treated in a certain way by the Hindus and who follows certain practices which are different from the Hindus. There are definite ways in which the Hindus treat the Untouchables in social matters. There are definite practices which are observed by the Untouchables. That

[a] This Table is reprinted from Dr Babasaheb Ambedkar, Writings & Speeches, vol. 2: Education Department, Government of Maharashtra, Bombay, p. 364. It is not recorded in the MS—Ed.

being so the only method of ascertaining who are Untouchables is to adopt their ways and practices as the criteria and find out the communities which are subject to them. There is no other way. If the outsider bears this in mind, he will understand that even though the tests prescribed by the Census Commissioner do not show any colour of Untouchability, they are in fact the hallmarks of Untouchability. That being so, there can be no manner of doubt that the procedure was proper and the tests were correct. Consequently it can be truly said, the results of this investigation were valuable and the figures obtained were accurate as far they can be in a matter of this sort.

III

The findings of the Census Commissioner of 1911 regarding the total population of the Untouchables were confirmed by the Census Commissioner of 1921.

The Census Commissioner of 1921 also made an investigation to ascertain the population of the Untouchables. In this Report Part I para 1931 the Census Commissioner observed:

It has been usual in recent years to speak of certain section of the community as 'depressed classes'. So far as I am aware, the term has no final definition nor is it certain exactly whom it covers. In the Quinquennial Review on the Progress of Education from 1912/17 (Chapter XVIII paragraph 505)—the depressed classes are specifically dealt with from the point of view of Educational assistance and progress and in Appendix XIII to that Report a list of the castes and tribes constituting this section of the Community is given. The total population classed according to these lists as depressed amounted to 31 million persons or 19 per cent of the Hindu and Tribal population of British India. There is undoubtedly some danger in giving offence by making in a public report social distinction which may be deemed invidious; but in view of the lists already prepared and the fact that the 'Depressed Classes' have, especially in South India, attained a class consciousness and a class organization, are served by special missions, 'raised' by philanthrophic societies and officially represented in the Legislative Assemblies, it certainly seems advisable to face the facts and to attempt to obtain some statistical estimate of their numbers. I therefore asked Provincial Superintendents to let me have an estimate based on census figures of the approximate strength of the castes who were usually included in the category of 'depressed'.

I received lists of some sort from all provinces and states except the United provinces, where extreme delicacy of official sentiment shrank from facing the task of attempting even a rough estimate. The figures given are not based on exactly uniform criteria, as a different view is taken of the position of the same groups in different parts of India, and I have had in some cases to modify the estimates on the basis of the figures in the educational report and of information from the 1911 reports and tables. They are also subject to the general defect; which has already been explained, that the total strength of any caste is not recorded. The marginal statement gives however a rough estimate of the *minimum* members which may be considered to form the 'depressed classes' of the Hindu community. The total of these provincial figures adds up to about 53 millions. This, however, must be taken as a low and conservative estimate since it does not include (1) the full strength of the castes and tribes concerned and (2) the tribal aborigines more recently absorbed in Hinduism, many of whom are considered impure. We may confidently place the numbers of these depressed classes all of whom are considered impure, at something between 55 and 60 millions in India proper.

At the time when the reforms which subsequently became embodied in the Act of 1919 were being discussed, the authors of the Montague-Chelmsford Report clearly recognized the problem of the Untouchables and the authors pledged themselves to make the best arrangement for their representation in the Legislatures. But the Committee that was appointed under the chairmanship of Lord Southborough to devise the franchise and the electoral system ignored them altogether. The Government of India did not approve of this attitude and made the following comments:

They (Untouchables) are one fifth of the total population and have not been represented at all in the Morley-Minto Councils. The Committees's report mentions them (Untouchables) twice, but only to explain that in the absence of satisfactory electorates they have been provided for by nomination. It does not discuss the position of these people, or their capacity for looking after themselves. Nor does it explain the amount of nomination which it suggests for them... The measure of representation which they propose... suggested that one fifth of the entire population of British India should be allotted seven seats out of practically eight hundred. It is true that in all the Councils there will be roughly speaking a one-sixth proportion of officials who may be expected to bear in mind the interests of the (Untouchables); but that arrangement is not, in our opinion, what the Report on reforms aims at. The authors stated that the (Untouchables) also should learn lessons of self protection. It is surely fanciful to hope that this result can be expected from including a single member of the community in an assembly where there are sixty or seventy caste Hindus. To make good the principles of the Report we must treat the outcastes more generously.

The government recommended that the seats allotted to the Untouchables by the Committee should be doubled. Accordingly in place of seven they were given fourteen seats. It will be seen that the generosity of the Government of India when put into practice did not amount to much. It certainly did not do to the Untouchables the justice that was their due.

Then came the inquiry by the Simon Commission which was appointed by the British Parliament in 1929 to examine the working of the Reforms introduced by the Government of India Act of 1919 and to suggest further reforms.

Among the problems that were not properly settled in 1919, was the problem of the Untouchables, which was bound to loom large before the Simon Commission. Quite unexpectedly the problem received a special emphasis at the hands of the late Lord Birkenhead who was then the Secretary of State for India. In a speech which he made on[b]... just before the appointment of the Simon Commission he said—(*Left blank in the MS*—Ed.).

Naturally the problem became a special task of the Simon Commission. Although the problem as presented was one of providing representation—and in that sense a political problem at the bottom it was a problem, of ascertaining the population of the Untouchables. Because unless the population was ascertained the extent of representation in the legislature could not be settled.

The Simon Commission had therefore to make a searching inquiry into the population of the Untouchables. It called upon the various provincial governments to furnish returns showing the numbers of untouchables residing in their area and it is well known that the provincial governments took special care in preparing these returns. There can therefore be no question regarding the accuracy of the figure of the total population of the untouchables.

IV

It is thus clear that the population of the Untouchables has been estimated to be somewhere about 50 millions. That this is the

[b] Date not cited in the MS—Ed.

population of the Untouchables had been found by the Census Commissioner of 1911 and confirmed by the Census Commissioner of 1921 and by the Simon Commission in 1929. This fact was never challenged by any Hindu during the twenty years it stood on the record. Indeed in so far as the Hindu view could be gauged from the reports of the different Committees appointed by the Provincial and Central Legislatures to cooperate with the Simon Commission, there can be no doubt that they accepted this figure without any demur.

Suddenly however in 1932, when the Lothian Committee came and began its investigation, the Hindus adopted a challenging mood and refused to accept this figure as the correct one. In some provinces the Hindus went to the length of denying that there were any Untouchables there at all. This episode reveals the mentality of the Hindus and as such deserves to be told in some details.

The Lothian Committee was appointed in consequence of the recommendations made by the Franchise Sub-Committee of the Indian Round Table Conference. The Committee toured the whole of India, visited all the Provinces except Central Provinces and Assam. To aid the Committee, there were constituted in each Province by the provincial government, Provincial Committees comprising, so far as possible, spokesmen of the various schools of thought and of the various political interests existing in each province. These Provincial Committees were in the main composed of members of the Provincial Councils with non-officials as Chairmen. With a view to concentrating discussion, the Indian Franchise Committee issued a questionnaire covering the field included in its terms of reference. The procedure laid down by the Franchise Committee was that Provincial Governments should formulate their own views on the points raised in the questionnaire and discuss them with the Committee and that the Provincial Committees who were regarded as the authoritative advisers should independently formulate their views and should at their discretion conduct a preliminary examination of witnesses on the basis of their written statements. The Report of the Indian Franchise Committee was therefore a thorough piece of work based upon detailed investigation.

The letter of instruction sent by the Prime Minister to Lord Lothian as Chairman of the Indian Franchise Committee and which constituted the terms of reference of the Committee contained the following observation:

It is evident from the discussions which have occurred in various connections in the (Indian Round Table) Conference that the new constitution must make adequate provision for the representation of the depressed classes and that the method of representation by nomination is no longer regarded as appropriate. As you are aware, there is a difference of opinion whether the system of separate electorates should be instituted for the depressed classes and your committee's investigation should contribute towards the decision of this question by indicating the extent to which the depressed classes would be likely, through such general extension of the Franchise as you may recommend, to secure the right to vote in ordinary electorates. On the other hand, should it be decided eventually to constitute separate electorates for the depressed classes, either generally or in those Provinces in which they form a distinct and separate element in the population, your Committee's inquiry into the general problem of extending the franchise should place you in possession of facts which would facilitate the devising of a method of separate representation for the depressed classes.

Accordingly in the questionnaire that was issued by the Indian Franchise Committee there was included the following Question:

What communities would you include as belonging to Depressed Classes? Would you include classes other than Untouchables, and if so which?

I was a member of the Indian Franchise Committee. When I became a member of the Committee, I was aware that the principal question on which I should have to give battle with the Caste Hindus was the question of joint versus separate electorates for the Untouchables. I knew, that in the Indian Franchise Committee, the odds would be heavily against them. I was to be the only representative of the Untouchables in the Committee as against half a dozen of the Caste Hindus. Against such an unequal fight I had prepared myself. Before accepting membership of the Indian Franchise Committee, I had stipulated that the decision of the question whether the Untouchables should have joint or separate electorates should not form part of the terms of reference to the Committee. This was accepted and the question was excluded from the purview of the Indian Franchise Committee. I had therefore no fear of being out voted on this issue in the Committee—a strategy for which the Hindu Members of the Committee did not forgive me. But there

arose another problem of which I had not the faintest idea. I mean
the problem of numbers. The problem of numbers having been
examined between 1911 to 1929 by four different authorities, who
found that the population of Untouchables was somewhere about
50 millions, I did not feel that there would be any contest over this
issue before the Indian Franchise Committee.

Strange as it may appear the issue of numbers was fought out
most bitterly and acrimoniously before the Indian Franchise
Committee. Committee after Committee and witness after witness
came forward to deny the existence of the Untouchables. It was
an astounding phenomenon with which I was confronted. It would
be impossible to refer to the statement of individual witnesses who
came forward to deny the existence of such a class as the
Untouchables. It would be enough if I illustrate my point by
referring to the views of the Provincial Franchise Committees and
their members relating to the question of the population of the
Untouchables.

PUNJAB

Opinion of the Punjab Government

The Punjab Government is of opinion that the enfranchisement of the
tenant will give the vote to a considerable number of the Depressed Classes
and to that extent will give them influence in the election of representatives to the Council.[c]

As regards the Depressed Classes, the Punjab Government has no
reason to depart from the view which it has already expressed in para 25
of the Memorandum containing the opinions of the official members of
the Government on the recommendations of the Indian Statutory Commission, that these classes are not a pressing problem in the Punjab and
will get some representation as tenants.[d]

Opinion of the Punjab Provincial Franchise Committee

K. B. Din Mahomed and Mr Hansraj (who represented the Untouchables
on the Committee) held that, while there are no depressed classes among

[c] Memorandum by the Punjab Government to Indian Franchise Committee, IFC, vol. III, p. 29.

[d] Supplementary Memorandum by the Punjab Government, IFC, vol. III,
p. 29.

the Musalmans, there exist depressed classes among the Hindus and Sikhs... Their total number being 1,310,709. Mr Hansraj considers this list incomplete.

They held that provision should be made for separate representation by treating the depressed classes as a separate community. Mr Nazir Husain, Rai Bahadur Chaudhri Chhotu Ram, Mr Own Roberts, K. B. Muhammad Hayat, Mr Qureshi, Mr Chatterji, Sardar Bhuta Singh and Pandit Nanak Chand held that it is impossible to say that there are depressed classes in the Punjab in the sense that any person by reason of his religion suffers any diminution of civic rights... The Chairman, Pandit Nanak Chand and Sardar Bhuta Singh are of opinion that the depressed classes do not exist in the sense in which they exist in Southern India, and that, while there are in the villages certain classes who occupy a very definitely inferior economic and social position, it is not possible to differentiate the Hindu leather worker or Chamar who is claimed as a depressed class from the Musalman leather worker or Mochi who no one alleges belongs to a separate class.[e]

It will thus be seen that the Punjab Provincial Government avoided to answer the question. The Punjab Provincial Committee by a majority denied that there existed a class such as depressed or untouchable.

United Provinces
Opinion of the Provincial Franchise Committee

The United Provinces Franchise Committee is of opinion that only those classes should be called 'depressed' which are untouchable. Judged by this test, the problem of untouchability is non-existent in these provinces except in the case of Bhangis, Doms and Dhanuks, whose total population, including those sections which are touchable is only 582,000.[f]

Babu Ram Sahai, a member of the United Provinces Provincial Franchise Committee representing the Untouchable classes, in his minute of dissent gave the numbers[g] of the Untouchables in UP as 11,435,417. Rai Sahib Babu Ramcharan, another member of the United Provinces Provincial Franchise Committee representing the Depressed Classes in his minute of dissent gave the numbers[h] of the Depressed Classes in UP as 20 millions.

[e] Memorandum by the Punjab Franchise Committee, IFC, vol. III, p. 35.
[f] IFC; vol. III, p. 398.
[g] Ibid., p. 440.
[h] IFC; vol. III, p. 285.

The Government of the United Provinces reported[i] that the maximum estimate amounts to 17 million persons; the minimum something less than one million. In its opinion the least number was 6,773,814.

BENGAL

The Bengal Provincial Franchise Committee in its first Report[j] said

The Committee could come to no decision on this question and resolved to put it back for consideration along with the Central Committee.

In its final Report the same Committee said:

According to the criterion laid down viz, untouchability and unapproach-ability, as these terms are understood in other parts of India, the Committee considers that, except Bhuimalis only, there is no such class in Bengal.[k]

Mr Mullick who was a representative of the Depressed Classes on the Bengal provincial Franchise Committee in his minute of dissent gave a list of 86 castes as belonging to the Untouchable Classes.

BIHAR AND ORISSA

The population of the Depressed Classes in Bihar and Orissa according to the Census of 1911 was 9,300,000[l] and according to the Census of 1921 was 8,000,000.[m]

But the Bihar and Orissa Provincial Franchise Committee in its provincial memorandum[n] observed—

It is difficult to give an exhaustive list of the castes or sects who come under the definition of Depressed Classes. The only classes which can be called depressed are *Mushahars, Dusadhs, Chamars, Doms* and *Mehtars*. Their number is not sufficiently large to justify their being grouped in a separate electoral roll. The problem of Depressed Classes is not so acute in Bihar as in Bombay or South India. The Committee considers that there is no need for special representation of the Depressed Classes.

[i] Ibid., pp. 297–8.
[j] Ibid., p. 189.
[k] Ibid., p. 230.
[l] Quoted from *Dr Babasaheb Ambedkar Writings & Speeches, vol. 2, p. 437*—Ed.
[m] Ibid., p. 431—Ed.
[n] IFC, vol. III, p. 129

The same Committee in its final report° said:

The classes which are commonly regarded as Untouchables are Chamar, Dusadh, Dom, Halalkhor, Hari, Mochi, Mushahar, Pan Pasi.... The majority of the Committee, however consider that there is no need for special representation as the Depressed Classes as their grievances are not so acute here as in Bombay or South India.

Why did the Hindus suddenly turn to reduce the population of the Untouchables from millions to fractions? The figure of 50 millions had stood on the record from 1911. It had not been questioned by anyone. How is it that in 1932 the Hindus made so determined an effort without any regard to the means to challenge the accuracy of this figure?

The answer is simple. Up to 1932 the Untouchables had no political importance. Although they were outside the pale of Hindu society which recognizes only four classes, namely, Brahmins, Kshatriyas, Vaishyas and Shudras, yet for political purposes they were reckoned as part of the Hindu society. So that for political purposes such as representation in the Legislature etc., the question of the population of the Untouchables was of no consequence. Up to 1932 the political question was one of division of seats in the Legislature between Hindus and Musalmans only and as there was no question of the seats that came to the lot of the Hindus being partitioned between the Touchables and the Untouchables and as the whole share went to the Touchables they did not care to inquire what the population of the Untouchables was. By 1932 the situation had completely altered. The question of partition was no longer a question between Hindus and Musalmans. The Untouchables had begun to claim that there should not only be a partition between the Hindus and Musalmans but that the share allotted to the Hindus should be further partitioned and the share of the Untouchables given to them to be enjoyed by them exclusively. This claim to separation was recognized and the Untouchables were allowed to be represented by members of their own class at the Indian Round Table Conference. Not only was the separate existence of the Untouchables thus recognized but the Minorities Sub-Committee of the Indian Round Table Conference had accepted the principle that under the new Constitution the Depressed Classes should be given representation in all Legislatures

° IFC, vol. III, p. 188.

in proportion to their population. It is thus that the population of the Untouchables became a subject of importance. The less the population of the Untouchables the greater the share of the political representation that would go to the Touchable Hindus. This will explain why the Touchables who before 1932 did not care to quarrel over the question of the population of the Untouchables, after 1932 began denying the very existence of such a class as Untouchables.

The ostensible grounds urged by the Hindus before the Lothian Committee for reducing the population of the Untouchables were two. One was that the figures given by the Census Commissioner were for Depressed Classes and not for Untouchables and that Depressed Classes included other classes besides Untouchables. The second ground urged by them was that, the definition of the word should be uniform throughout all India and should be applied in all Provinces in determining the population of the Untouchables. In other words they objected to a local test of untouchability.

The first contention was absolutely untrue. The term Depressed Classes was used as a synonym for Untouchables and the term Depressed Classes was used instead of the term Untouchables because the latter, it was felt, would give offence to the people meant to be included under the term. That, it was used to denote only the Untouchables and it did not include the Aboriginals or the Criminal Tribes was made clear in the debate that took place in the Imperial Legislative Council in 1916 on the Resolution moved by the Honourable Mr Dadabhoy. The second contention of the caste Hindus was that the test of untouchability should be uniform. The object of putting forth this contention was to reduce the number of Untouchables. It is well known that there are variations in the forms which untouchability assumes in different parts of India. In some parts of India, Untouchables are unseeables i.e. they cause pollution if they come within the sight of a Touchable Hindu. In some parts Untouchables are unapproachables i.e. they cause pollution if they come within a certain distance of a Touchable Hindu. Of these unapproachables there are two classes. There is a class of unapproachables who cannot come within a certain fixed distance of a Touchable Hindu. There is another class of unapproachables who cannot come so near a Hindu as to let his shadow fall upon him. In some parts of India an Untouchable is not unseeable or unapproachable. It is only his physical contact which causes pollution. In some parts an Untouchable is one who is not allowed to touch water or food. In some parts an Untouchable is one who is not allowed to enter a temple. With these variations it is clear, that if unseeability was taken as the only test of untouchability, then the unapproachables would have to be excluded form the category of Untouchables. If unapproachability was taken as a test, then those whose touch only caused pollution will have to be excluded from the category of Untouchables. If causing pollution by touch be taken as a test, then those whose disability is that they are not allowed to touch water or food or those whose only disability is that they are not allowed to enter the temple, shall have to be excluded. This is what the Hindus wanted to do. By insisting upon a uniform test they wanted to eliminate certain classes from the category of Untouchables and thereby reduce the population of the Untouchables. Obviously their point of view was fallacious. Untouchability is an outward expression of the inner repulsion which a Hindu feels towards a certain person. The form which this repulsion takes is comparatively a matter of small moment. The form merely indicates the degree of repulsion. Wherever there is repulsion there is untouchability. This simple truth the Hindu knew.

But they kept on insisting upon uniformity of test because they wanted somehow to reduce the population of the Untouchables and to appropriate to themselves a larger share of political representation.

VI

This struggle between the Hindus and the Untouchables constituted undoubtedly the main episode. But within this episode there was another which, though of a smaller character, was yet full of significance. It was the struggle between the Backward Classes and the Untouchables. The representatives of the Backward Classes contended that the category known as Depressed Classes should not only include Untouchables in the strict sense of that term but should also include those classes which are economically and educationally backward. The object of those that wanted, that not only the Untouchables but also those who are educationally and economically backward shall also be given separate representation, was a laudable one. In putting forth this contention they were not asking for anything that was new. Under the reformed constitution that came into operation in 1920, the right of the economically and educationally backward communities was recognized in the two provinces of India, namely, Bombay and Madras. In Bombay the Marathas and allied castes and in Madras the non-Brahmins were given separate representation on the only ground that they were economically and educationally backward. It was feared that if special representation was not given to those communities, they would be politically suppressed by the minority of high caste Hindus such as Brahmins and allied castes. There are many communities in other provinces who are in the same position and who need special political representation to prevent their being suppressed by the higher castes. It was therefore perfectly proper for the representatives of the Backward Classes from the Hindus to have claimed special representation for themselves.[P] If their point of view had been accepted the total number of Depressed classes would have swelled to enormous proportions. But they received no support either from the Untouchables or from the high caste Hindus. The Hindus were opposed to the move which was calculated to increase the population of the Depressed classes. The Untouchables did not want to be included in their category any class of people who were not really Untouchables. The proper course for these backward communities was to have asked to make a division of Touchable Hindus into advanced and backward and to have claimed separate representation for the Backward. In that effort the Untouchables would have supported them. But they did not agree to this and persisted in being included among the Depressed Classes largely because they thought that this was easier

[P] The necessity for making such provisions for the Backward Classes in UP from which this demand mainly came was amply demonstrated by what the government of UP said in its Memorandum to the Simon Commission. Regarding the composition of the UP Legislature it said—'In the Province as a whole the four leading Hindu Castes, Brahman, Thakur, Vaishya and Kayastha form 21.5 per cent of the total Hindu population, but these four castes have supplied no less than 93 per cent of the Hindu Members of Council. The Jats, with 1.8 per cent of the population, have contributed another 5 per cent to the Hindu membership; and all the millions included in the multitude of other Hindu Castes, including the real agricultural castes, though they amount to over 76 per cent of the Hindu population have only succeeded in supplying 2 per cent of the representation', p. 560.

way of securing their object. But as the Untouchables opposed this, the backward communities turned and joined the Hindus in denying the existence of Untouchables, more vehemently than the Hindus.

In this struggle between the Touchables and Untouchables the latter did not get any support from the Mohammedans. It will be noticed that in the Punjab Provincial Franchise Committee, only one Mahomedan supported the representative of the Untouchables in his assertion that there are in the Punjab communities which are treated as Untouchables. The rest of the Mohammedans members of the Committee did not join. In Bengal the Hindu and the Mohammedans members of the Bengal Provincial Franchise Committee agreed not to express any view on the matter. It is rather strange that the Mohammedans should have kept mum. It was in their interest that the Untouchables should be recognized as a separate political community. This separation between the Touchables and the Untouchables was to their benefit. Why did they not help the Untouchables in this struggle for numbers? There were two reasons why the Mohammedans took this attitude. In the first place the Mohammedans were asking for more than their population ratio of representation. They were asking for what in Indian political parlance is known as weightage. They knew that their weightage must involve a loss to the Hindus and the only question was which section of the Hindus should bear the loss. The Touchable Hindus would not mind the weightage if it could be granted without reducing their share. How to do this was the problem and the only way out of it was to reduce the share of the Untouchables. To reduce the share meant to reduce the population. This is one reason why the Mahomedans did not help the Untouchables in this struggle for numbers. The second reason why the Mohammedans did not help the Untouchables was the fear of exposure by the Hindus. Although Islam is the one religion which can transcend race and colour and unite diverse people into a compact brotherhood, yet Islam in India has not succeeded in uprooting caste from among the Indian Musalmans. Caste feeling among the Musalmans is not so virulent as it is among the Hindus. But the fact is that it exists. That this caste feeling among the Musalmans leads to social gradation, a feature of the Muslim community in India, has been noticed by all those who have had an occasion to study the subject.

These facts are quite well known to the Hindus and they were quite prepared to cite them against the Muslims if the Muslims went too far in helping the Untouchables in this struggle for numbers and thereby bringing about a dimunition of the seats for Caste Hindus in the Legislature. The Mahomedans knew their own weak points. They did not wish to give an excuse to the Hindus to rake up the social divisions among the Musalmans and thought that their interest would be best served by their taking a non-partisan attitude.

The Untouchables were thus left to themselves to fight for their numbers. But even they could not be depended upon to muster for the cause. When the Hindus found that they could not succeed in reducing the number of the Untouchables, they tried to mislead the Untouchables. They began telling the Untouchables that the government was making a list of the Untouchable communities and it was wrong to have a community's name entered in such list because it would perpetuate untouchability. Acting on this advice, many communities which were actually an Untouchable community would send a petition stating that it was not classed as Untouchable and should not be listed. Much effort had to be made to induce such communities to withdraw such petitions by informing them that the real purpose was to estimate their numbers in order to fix their seats in the Legislature.

Fortunately for all, this struggle is now over and the controversy is closed and the population of the Untouchables can never be open to dispute. The Untouchables are now statutorily defined. Who are Untouchables is laid down by a schedule to the Government of India Act 1935 which describes them as Scheduled Castes. But the struggle reveals a trait of Hindu character. If the Untouchables make no noise, the Hindu feels no shame for their condition and is quite indifferent as to their numbers. Whether they are thousands or millions of them, he does not care to bother. But if the Untouchables rise and ask for recognition, he is prepared to deny their existence, repudiate his responsibility and refuse to share his power without feeling any compunction or remorse.

24

The Untouchables and
the Pax Britannica

Caste and Untouchability are the two great social evils in India.
Caste has disabled the whole Hindu society. Untouchability has
suppressed a large class of people. And yet the British Government
has completely ignored the two evils. One may search in vain the
Indian Code to find any law dealing with caste or with untouchability. It is true that caste and untouchability are social matters.
They will vanish when people will begin to inter-dine and inter-
marry. Law cannot compel a person to dine with another. It is true,
law cannot compel a person to marry with another. But it is also
true that law can prohibit a caste from preventing a person from
marrying a person outside his caste. Caste continues because a caste
can conspire to punish its members if they break the rules of caste
by declaring a social boycott against him. It would have been
perfectly possible to have enacted a law declaring such social
boycott to be a crime. Again in the matter of Untouchability the
disabilities are not merely social. They are fundamentally civic.
Inability to get admission to school, to be able to take water from
a public well, to be able to get into a public conveyance, to be able
to get into public service, are all civic disabilities. It was the duty
of the British Government to legislate at least to the extent
necessary to protect their civic rights. It was possible to do so. A
short Enactment on the lines of Caste Disabilities Removal Act
would have been sufficient. Yet the British Government has gone
on as though these two evils did not exist at all. Indeed it is most
extraordinary thing to note that although Legislative Bodies were

established in India in 1861 and have been passing laws on every
social questions and discussing public questions, yet except on two
occasions the Untouchables were not even mentioned. The first
occasion on which they were mentioned was in 1916, when one
Parsi gentleman Sir Maneckji Dadabhoy moved the following
Resolution in the Central Legislature:[249]

That this Council recommends to the Governor General in Council that
measures be devised with the help, if necessary, of a small representative
committee of officials and non-officials for an amelioration in the moral,
material and educational condition of what are known as the Depressed
Classes, and that, as a preliminary step the Local Government and
Administrations be invited to formulate schemes with due regard to local
conditions.

There was no sympathy to this resolution. The Hindu members
of the Legislature were angry with the mover for his having
brought such a subject before the Legislature.
Pandit Madan Mohan Malviya said:

Sir, it seems rather ungracious to say so, but a sense of the dignity of
the proceedings of this Council compels me to utter a protest against
the manner in which sometimes subjects are brought before it for
consideration...
    In moving the Resolution the object of which I may at once say, has
my whole-hearted support, my friend, the Hon'ble Mr Dadabhoy, went
out of his way to make remarks against the Hindu community which,
I think, he ought to have avoided.... I am not here to defend everything
Hindu that exists. I am not here to apologize for the many prejudices or
superstitions, which I am sadly conscious are to be found among one
portion or another of our community. But it is not the Hindu community
alone which finds it difficult to get rid of prejudices.... Without meaning
the smallest disrespect, I would instance the case of the marriage with a
Deceased Wife's Sister Bill... We Hindus have got some much worse
prejudices to fight against... But I do not think it is within the province
of a member of this Council either to lecture to the Hindus present here
or to those outside as to the socio-religious disabilities among themselves
which they might fight against and remove. I think the province of
Members of this Council is limited to dealing with matters of legislation
or other administrative matters which may properly be taken up by the
Government. As has been already pointed out, the Government have, in
pursuance of a wise and liberal policy, laid it down that they shall not
interfere in matters of a religious or socio-religious character, and
accusations of the character in question ought, therefore, to be avoided

there... I do not wish to descent into a disputation as to the merits of the imputations or the justification for the general observations that have been made.... And yet, if I do not, I am left in the position that I have heard without protest remarks showing that the Hindu Community from one end of the country to the other was guilty of all that my friend, the Hon'ble Mover of the Resolution, has suggested... I am conscious that we Hindus have many prejudices to fight against and conquer; but I submit that this is not the place to tell us of them.

Even a social reformer like Sir Surendranath Bannerjee was not happy. He said:

...I regret very much that my Hon'ble friend the Mover of this Resolution went somewhat out of his way to level (I do not think he did it intentionally) an attack against the Hindu Community. He must bear in mind that we are the inheritors of past traditions, of a civilization as ancient as the world. That civilization undoubtedly had its defects, but that civilization in the morning of the world was the guarantee for law and order and social stability. In the past it afforded consolation to millions. We are trying to evolve a national system in conformity with our present environments, but we cannot push aside all those things which have come down to us from the past. We reverence the venerable fabric which has been built up by our ancestors. We notice their defects, and we are anxious to get rid of them gradually and steadily, not by any revolutionary movement, but the slow, steady process of evolution. My friend must have a little sympathy with us; he must extend to us the hand of generosity in our efforts to deal with the problems. My Hon'ble friend suggests that Government should take measures... We welcome the action of Government in a matter of this kind, but after all, if you analyse the situation, it is a social problem, and the British Government, very properly, as I think, in conformity with its ancient traditions, holds aloof from all interference with social questions.

Government can do a great by way of education, a great deal by helping forward the industrial movement among the Depressed classes. But the vital problem, the problem of problems, is one of social uplifting, and there the Government can only afford to be a benevolent spectator. It may sympathize with our efforts, but it cannot actively participate in them...

The Hon'ble Mr Dadabhoy had to defend himself. In his reply he said:

Sir, I find myself in a very peculiar and unfortunate position. There are two parties in this Council, and they are both on the defensive on this occasion. My justification for bringing in this Resolution, if any justification were needed, is to be found in the unenthusiastic and half hearted support which I have received from my non-official colleagues. It was no pleasure, I assure you, Sir, to me to bring in this Resolution. If I could possibly have avoided it, I would have very cheerfully and very willingly done so. This is the sixth year of the life of this Reformed Council, as Hon'ble Members are aware, and the second term is now approaching expiration. During the major portion of that time—the five years that I have been on this Council—I anticipated that the champions of public liberty, public spirit and public enterprise and culture—men like my friends the Hon'ble Surendra Nath Bannerjee or the Honourable Pandit Madan Mohan Malaviya—would take the trouble of moving a Resolution to this effect. I waited all this time to see if one of these enthusiastic members would bring in a Resolution for the amelioration of the Depressed Classes, but when I found that none of them had taken up the matter—though at times this matter is discussed even in the Congress Pandal in a certain manner; when I found that it was not taken up in this Council.... I, as a Parsee, representing a Hindu constituency thought it my duty to bring this matter for public discussion in this Council.

The government naturally felt relieved by this quarrel. Resting behind the moral support of the Hindu members of the Legislature for covering up their delinquency, Sir Reginald Craddock speaking on behalf of the government disposed of the Resolution.

Why did the British Government leave the Untouchables in the cold without any care or attention?

The explanation for so criminal a neglect was furnished by Sir Reginald Craddock. In replying on behalf of the Government of India on the Resolution moved by Sir Maneckji Dadabhoy in the Imperial legislative Council in 1916, he stated what the position of the British Government took with regard to the Untouchables in the following terms:

With regard to them (i.e. the Untouchables) the difficulty is not that Government does not recognize them, but that until the habits and prejudices of centuries are removed, the hands of their neighbours must necessarily press upon them...you must remember that these people live mostly in villages and very often in the back lane of towns, and that their neighbours have not yet come under these broad and liberal minded influences. Therefore, as many speakers have indicated, the problem in dealing with this question is more social and religious than purely administrative.

I know myself of many difficulties in the matter of schools. There are many places where the Mahar boys will not be allowed into the school; they may be allowed in the Verandah and get only a small part of the master's attention there, or they may be entirely excluded. But it is only gradually that the difficulty can be met. I have constantly dealt with this very problem on the spot. I have reasoned with people; I have said to them: There are tax payers like yourselves, either let them come into the school, or if you wish to indulge in your own prejudices—they may be reasonable prejudices, as you consider them—but if you wish to indulge them, should you not contribute something in order that these boys may have a school of their own? In that what some of the better people have come forward to help in the matter of wells, and schools for the low castes; they have assisted, and the difficulties have been got over. But of course it is a matter which must take time, and Government itself cannot use compulsion. They go rather near to it sometimes for example, in travelling by railway: and when petitions are presented in Court. But they cannot ensure that these people shall always be well-treated in their offices. Very often, I think, some of these classes refrain from seeking service they might otherwise wish to secure, because their neighbours are not likely to treat them warmly. Although the Hon'ble mover described the statement made by the Government of Bombay as a 'magnificent *non-possumus*', I think that it very accurately describes what the real difficulties of the situation are. Even though Government is willing to help in every way these unfortunate people, yet it remains true that 'the position of these castes and tribes in the future depends partly on their own selves, and partly those more favoured Indian Communities, which by extending the hand of human comradeship or hardening their hearts and averting their faces, have it in their power to elevate or to degrade them.'

That Sir, I think, represents very truly and accurately the position of affairs as regards these Depressed Classes.

The same attitude was reiterated in 1928 when the resolution of Mr Jayakar was discussed in the Central Legislative Assembly. Mr Bajpai speaking on behalf of the Government said:

...it is not by increasing the number of special schools or by providing special facilities that you are going to solve this problem (of the Untouchables)... You will solve this problem only by a quickening and broadening the spirit of all sections of the community towards the so-called depressed classes.

Leaving the problem to be solved by the quickening of the consciences of the Hindus, the British Government just neglected the Untouchables and believed that as a Government they were not called upon to do anything to help to improve the lot of the Untouchables. How did the British justify this neglect of so helpless and so downtrodden a class of their subjects as the Untouchables?

The answer is very clear. They did it by taking the view that the evil of Untouchability was not of their making. They argued that if they did not deal with the evil of Untouchability, they are not to be blamed for it because the system did not originate with them. This was clearly enunciated by the Government of Bombay in 1856. In June 1856 a petition was submitted on behalf of a Mahar boy to the Government of Bombay complaining that though willing to pay the usual schooling fee he had been denied admission to the Dharwar Government School. In disposing of the application, the Government of Bombay thought the matter so important that it issued a Resolution dated 21 July 1856 of which the following is the full text:

1. The question discussed in the correspondence is one of very great practical difficulty.

2. There can be no doubt that the Mahar petitioner has abstract justice on his side; and Government trust that the prejudices which at present prevent him from availing himself of existing means of education in Dharwar may be ere long removed.

3. But Government are obliged to keep in mind that to interfere with the prejudices of ages in a summary manner, for the sake of one or few individuals, would probably do a great damage to the cause of education. *The disadvantage under which the petitioner is not one which has originated with the Government*, and it is one which Government cannot summarily remove by interfering in his favour, as he begs them to do.

This is of course an easy view of the duties of a governement. It is not a responsible view. It is certainly not a view which a civilized government would take. A government which is afraid to govern is not a government. It is only a corporation formed to collect taxes. The British Government undoubtedly meant to be more than a mere tax gathering machinery. It claimed to be a civilized government. Then why did it not act to prevent wrong and injustice? Was it because it had no power or was it because it was afraid to use them or was it because it felt that there was nothing wrong in the social and religious system of India?

The answer is that it had the power, the amplest power. It did not use it because for a part of the period it did not think that there was anything wrong in the social system of the Hindus and during the period when it became convinced that things were wrong it was overpowered by sense of fear.

People wanted freedom political, economic and social. This the British Government declined to create:

As a result of this, so far as the moral and social life of the people was concerned, the change of Government by the Moghuls to a Government by the British was only a change of rulers rather than a change of system. Owing to the adoption of the principle of non-interference partly by preference and partly by necessity by the British 'the natives of India found themselves under a Government distinguished in no vital respect from those under which they had toiled and worshipped, lived and died through all their weary and forgotten history. From a political standpoint, the change was but the replacement of one despotism by another. It accepted the arrangements as it found them[a] and preserved them faithfully in the manner of the Chinese tailor who, when given an old coat as a pattern, produced with pride an exact replica, rents, patches and all.'[b]

This policy of non-intervention though understandable, was so far as the Untouchables were concerned, mistaken in its conception and disastrous in its consequences. It may be granted that Untouchables can only be lifted up by the Hindus recognizing his human rights and him as a human being as correct. But that does not dispose of the matter. Question remains how is this recognition of his rights as a human being to be secured. There are only two ways of helping to realize this object. One way is to make him worthy of respect and the other is to punish those who disrespect him and deny him his rights. The first way involves the duty to educate him and to place him in positions of authority. The other way involves social reform by making recognition of Untouchability a penal offence. Neither of this the British Government was prepared to do. It would not give the Untouchables any preferential treatment in public service. It would not undertake to reform Hindu society. The result was that Untouchable has remained what he was before the British, namely an Untouchable. He was a citizen but he was not given the rights of a citizen. He paid taxes out of which schools were maintained but his children could not be admitted into those schools. He paid taxes out of which wells were built but he had no right to take water from

[a] The poll tax has been continued in Burma simply because it was found to exist there on the day of conquest.
[b] Bernard Houghton, *Bureaucratic Government, A Study in Indian Polity*, Madras, G. A. Natesan, 1921.

them. He paid taxes out of which roads were built. But he has no right to use them. He paid taxes for the upkeep of the state. But he himself was not entitled to hold offices in the state. He was a subject but not a citizen. The Untouchable stood most in need of education and supply of water. He stood mostly in need of office to protect himself. Owing to his poverty he should have been exempted from all taxes. All this was reversed. The Untouchable was taxed to pay for the education of the touchable. The Untouchable was taxed to pay for the water supply of the touchable. The Untouchable was taxed to pay for the salary of the touchables in office.

What good has British conquest done to the Untouchables? In education, nothing; in service, nothing; in status, nothing. There is one thing in which they have gained and that is equality in the eye of the law. There is of course nothing special in it because equality before law is common to all. There is of course nothing tangible in it because those who hold office often prostitute their position and deny to the Untouchables the benefit of this rule. With all this, the principle of equality before law has been of special benefit to the Untouchables for the simple reason that they never had it before the days of the British. The Law of Manu did not recognize the principle of equality. Inequality was the soul of the Law of Manu. It pervaded all walks of life, all social relationships and all departments of state. It had fouled the air and the Untouchables were simply smothered. The principle of equality before law has served as a great disinfectant. It has cleansed the air and the Untouchable is permitted to breath the air of freedom. This is a real gain to the Untouchables and having regard to the ancient past it is no small gain.

25

An Anti-Untouchability Agenda

The writer in the *Indian Social Reformer* pleads that Untouchables should be associated with the management of the Sangh.[250] His statement might lead people to believe that Untouchables were never represented on the Central Board of the Sangh. That would be a mistake. The correct position is that when the Sangh was started, prominent Untouchables in substantial numbers were on the Central Board of the Sangh. The statement issued by Mr Birla and Mr Thakkar on 3 November 1932 gives the names of those who were constituting the Central Board. It was announced that:

The Central Board has been constituted with the following organizing members:

Sjt. G. D. Birla, Delhi and Calcutta; Sir Purshotamdas Thakurdas, Bombay; Sir Lallubhai Samaldas, Bombay; Dr B. R. Ambedkar, Bombay; Sheth Ambalal Sarabhai, Ahmedabad; Dr B. C. Roy, Calcutta; Lala Shri Ram, Delhi; Rao Bahadur M. C. Raja, Madras; Dr T. S. S. Rajan, Trichinopoly; Rao Bahadur Srinivasan, Madras; Mr A. V. Thakkar, General Secretary, Delhi.

It will be seen that out of 8 members 3 were drawn from the Untouchables. After my retirement from the Board, the other two, namely, Rao Bahadur M. C. Raja and Rao Bahadur Srinivasan also retired. I do not know the reasons why they dissociated themselves from the Sangh.

It is right and proper that I should state the reasons why I severed my connection with the Sangh. After the Poona Pact I proceeded in a spirit of forget and forgive. I accepted the *bona fides* of Mr Gandhi as I was asked to do by many of his friends. It was in that spirit that I accepted a place on the Central Board of the

Sangh and was looking forward to play my part in its activities. In fact, I wanted to discuss with Mr Gandhi the programme of work which I felt the Sangh should undertake. Before I could do that, I was called to go to London to attend the third Round Table Conference. The next best thing I could do was to communicate my views to Mr A. V. Thakkar, the Secretary of the Sangh. Accordingly I wrote the following letter from the steamer:

M/N 'Victoria,'
Port Said,
14 November 1932.

Dear Mr Thakkar,

I received your wire previous to my departure to London, informing me of the acceptance of my suggestion regarding the nomination of Rao Bahadur Shrinivasan to the Central Board and Mr D. V. Naik to the Bombay Provincial Board. I am glad that this question has been amicably settled and that we can now conjointly work out the programme of the Anti-Untouchability League.[a] I wish I had an opportunity to meet the members of the Central Board to discuss with them the principles which the League should follow in framing its programme of work, but unfortunately owing to my having to leave for London at a very short notice, I have had to forego that opportunity. I am however doing the second best namely to convey to you my views in writing for placing them before the Board for their consideration.

In my opinion there can be two distinct methods of approaching the task of uplifting the Depressed Classes. There is a school, which proceeds on the assumption that the fact of the individual belonging to the Depressed Classes is bound up with his personal conduct. If he is suffering from want and misery it is because he must be vicious and sinful. Starting from this hypothesis this School of social workers concentrates all its efforts and its resources on fostering personal virtue by adopting a programme which includes items such as temperance, gymnasium, co-operation, libraries, schools, etc., which are calculated to make the individual a better and virtuous individual. In my opinion, there is also another method of approach to this problem. It starts with the hypothesis that the fate of the individual is governed by his environment and the circumstances he is obliged to live under, and if an individual is suffering from want and misery it is because his environment is not propitious. I have no doubt that of the two views the latter is the more correct, the former may raise a few stray individuals above the level of

---

[a] Harijan Sevak Sangh was the name given to the League at a later stage.

the class to which they belong. It cannot lift the class as a whole. My view of the aim of the Anti-Untouchability League is that it has come into existence not for helping a few individuals at random or a few selected boys belonging to the Depressed Classes but for raising the whole class to a higher level. Consequently, I would not like the League to dissipate its energies on a programme calculated to foster private virtue. I would like the Board to concentrate all its energies on a programme that will effect a change in the social environment of the Depressed Classes. Having stated in general terms my views, I venture to place some concrete proposals for work to be undertaken by the League.

A CAMPAIGN TO SECURE CIVIL RIGHTS

I think the first thing that the League should undertake is a campaign all over India to secure to the Depressed Classes the enjoyment of their civic rights such as taking water from the village wells, entry in village schools, admission to village chawdi, use of public conveyance, etc. Such a programme if carried into villages will bring about the necessary social revolution in the Hindu Society, without which it will never be possible for the Depressed Classes to get equal social status. The Board must, however, know what difficulties it will have to face if this campaign of civic rights is to be carried through. Here I can speak from experience, because I, as President, know what happened when the Depressed. Classes Institute and the Social Equality League launched such a plan in the Kolaba and the Nasik Districts of the Bombay Presidency. First of all, there will be riots between the Depressed Classes and the caste Hindus which will result in breaking heads and in criminal prosecutions of one side or the other. In this struggle, the Depressed classes will suffer badly because the Police and the Magistracy will always be against them. There has not been a single case in the course of the social struggle carried on in these two districts, in which the Police and the Magistracy have come to the rescue of the Depressed Classes even when justice was on their side. The Police and the Magistracy are as corrupt as they could be, but what is worse is that they are definitely political in the sense that they are out not to see that justice is done but to see that the dignity and interests of the caste Hindus as against the Depressed Classes are upheld. Secondly, the villages will proclaim a complete boycott of the Depressed Classes, the moment they see the latter are trying to reach a status of equality along with them. You know what harrowing tales of harassment, unemployment and starvation, which the Depressed Classes repeated before the Starte Committee of which you were a member. I therefore do not think it necessary to say anything more about the severity of this weapon and of its dreadful power to bring all efforts of the Depressed classes to rise above their degraded station to a standstill.

I have mentioned only two of the many obstacles which the League will have to overcome, if this campaign of civic rights is to be successful and the League will have to have an army of workers in the rural parts, who will encourage the Depressed Classes to fight for their rights and who will help them in any legal proceedings arising therefrom to a successful issue. I am so much convinced by the efficiency of this programme that I have not the slightest hesitation in saying that the League ought to look upon this as primary in comparison to everything else. It is true that this programme involves social disturbance and even bloodshed. But I do not think that it can be avoided. I know the alternative policy of adopting the line of least resistance. I am convinced that it will be ineffective in the matter of uprooting Untouchability. The silent infiltration of rational ideas among the ignorant mass of caste Hindus cannot, I am sure, work for the elevation of the Depressed Classes. First of all, the caste Hindu like all human beings follows his customary conduct in observing Untouchability towards the Depressed Classes. Ordinarily people do not give up their customary mode of behaviour because somebody is preaching against it. But when that customary mode of behaviour has or is believed to have behind it the sanction of religion mere preaching, if it is not resented and resisted, will be allowed to waft along the wind without creating any effect on the mind. The salvation of the Depressed Classes will come only when the Caste Hindu is made to think and is forced to feel that he must alter his ways. For that you must create a crisis by direct action against his customary code of conduct. The crisis will compel him to think and once he begins to think he will be more ready to change than he is otherwise likely to be. The great defect in the policy of least resistance and silent infiltration of rational ideas lies in this that they do not *compel* thought, for they do not produce crisis. The direct action in respect of Chawdar Tank in Mahad, the Kalaram Temple in Nasik and the Gurwayur Temple in Malabar have done in a few days what million days of preaching by reformers would never have done. I therefore strongly recommend this campaign of direct action for securing civic rights of the Depressed Classes for adoption by the Anti-Untouchability League. I know the difficulties of this campaign, and from such experience as I have of it I am convinced that the forces in charge of Law and Order must be on our side, if it is to end in success. It is because of this that I have deliberately excluded temples from its scope and confined it only to public rights of a civic nature, the exercise of which I feel Government is bound to protect.

EQUALITY OF OPPORTUNITY

The second thing I would like the Anti-Untouchability League to work for, is to bring about equality of opportunity for the Depressed Classes. Much of the misery and poverty of the Depressed Classes is due to the absence of equality of opportunity which in its turn is due to Untouchability. I am sure you are aware that the Depressed Classes in villages and even in towns cannot sell vegetables, milk or butter—ways of earning a living which are open to all and sundry. A caste Hindu will buy these things from a non-Hindu, but he will not buy them from the Depressed Classes. In the matter of employment, his condition is the worst. In Government Departments the bar-sinister operates and he is denied the place of a constable or even a messenger. In industries he fares no better. Like the Negro in America he is the last to be employed in days of prosperity and the first to be fired in days of adversity. And even when he gets a foothold, what are his prospects? In the Cotton Mills in Bombay and Ahmedabad he is confined to the lowest paid department where he can earn only Rs 25 per month. More paying departments like the weaving department are permanently closed to him. Even in the low paid departments he cannot rise to the highest rung of the ladder. The place of the boss is reserved for the caste Hindu while the Depressed Class worker must slave as his underdog, no matter how senior or how efficient. In departments where the earning depends on piece work, he has failed to earn as well as Caste Hindu employees because of social discrimination. Depressed Classes women working in the Winding and Reeling Departments have come to me in hundreds complaining that the Naikins instead of distributing the raw material to all employees equally or in fair proportion, give all of it to the caste Hindu women and leave them in the cold. I have given only a few of the instances of the gross inequality of opportunity from which the Depressed Classes are suffering mainly at the hands of the Hindus. I think it would be fit and proper, if the Anti-Untouchability League were to take up this question by creating public opinion in condemnation of it and establishing bureaus to deal with urgent cases of inequality. I would particularly desire the League to tackle the problem of opening the Weaving department of the cotton mills to the Depressed Classes as it is likely to make a very large opening for prosperous employment to members of the Depressed Classes. Much can be done by private firms and companies managed by Hindus by extending their patronage to the Depressed Classes and by employing them in their offices in various grades and occupations suited to the capacities of the applicants.

SOCIAL INTERCOURSE

Lastly, I think the League should attempt to dissolve that nausea, which the touchables feel towards the Untouchables and which is the reason why the two sections have remained so much apart as to constitute separate and distinct entities. In my opinion the best way of achieving it is to establish closer contact between the two. Only a common cycle of participation can help people to overcome the strangeness of feeling which one has, when brought into contact with the other. Nothing can do this more effectively in my opinion than the admission of the Depressed Classes to the houses of the caste Hindus as guests or servants. The live contact thus established will familiarize both to a common and associated life and will pave the way for that unity which we are all striving after. I am sorry that many caste Hindus who have shown themselves responsive are not prepared for this. During those ten days of the Mahatma's fast that shook the Indian world, there were cases in Vile Parle and in Mahad where the caste Hindu servants had struck work because their masters had abrogated the rules of untouchability by fraternising with the Untouchables. I expected that they would end the strike and teach a lesson to the erring masses by filling the vacancies by employing Depressed Classes in their place. Instead of doing that they capitulated with the forces of orthodoxy and strengthened them. I do not know how far such fair-weather friends of the Depressed Classes would be of help to them. People in distress can have very little consolation from the fact that they have sympathisers, if those sympathisers will do nothing more than sympathise, and I may as well tell the League that the Depressed Classes will never be satisfied of the *bona fides* of these caste Hindu sympathisers until it is proved that they are prepared to go to the length of fighting against their own kith and kin actual warfare if it came to that for the sake of the Depressed Classes as the Whites of the North did against their own kith and kin namely, the Whites of the South for the sake of the emancipation of the Negro. But this thing apart, I think it is necessary that the League should endeavour to inculcate upon the mind of the Hindu public the necessity of establishing contact and social intercourse between the touchables and the Untouchables in the way I have mentioned.

AGENCY TO BE EMPLOYED

The League will have to employ a very large army of workers to carry out its programme. The appointment of social workers might perhaps be looked upon as a minor question. Speaking for myself, I attach very great importance to the selection of a proper agency to be employed in this behalf. There can always be found workers to do a particular piece of work or any other for the matter of that if they are paid for it. I am sure such mercenary workers will not serve the purpose of the League. As Tolstoy said: 'Only those who love can serve.' In my opinion that test is more likely to be fulfilled by workers drawn from the Depressed Classes. I should therefore like the League to bear this aspect of the question in mind in deciding upon whóm to appoint and when not to appoint. I do not suggest that there are not scoundrels among the Depressed Classes who have not made social service their last refuge. But largely speaking you can be more sure that a worker drawn from the Depressed Classes will regard the work as love's labour—a thing which is so essential to the success of the League. Secondly, there are agencies which are already engaged in same sort of social service without any confines as to class or purpose—and may be prepared to supplement their activity by taking up the work of Anti-Untouchability League in consideration of a grant-in-aid. I am sure this hire-purchase system of work—if I may use that expression—can produce no lasting good. What is wanted in an agency is a singleminded devotion to one task and one task only. We want bodies and organizations which have deliberately chosen to be narrow-minded in order to be enthusiastic about their cause. The work if it is to be assigned must be assigned to those who would undertake to devote themselves exclusively to the work of the Depressed Classes.

I am afraid I have already trespassed the limits of a letter and I do not think I can err further in that direction without being tediously long. I had many other things to say but I now propose to reserve them for another occasion. Before closing this I wish to say just this. It was Balfour I think who said that what could hold the British Empire together was love and not law. I think that observation applies equally to the Hindu Society. The touchables and the untouchables cannot be held together by law—certainly not by any electoral law substituting joint electorates for separate electorates. The only thing that can hold them together is love. Outside the family justice alone in my opinion can open the possibility of love, and it should be the duty of the Anti-Untouchability League to see that the touchable does, or failing that is made to do, justice to the Untouchable. Nothing else in my opinion can justify the project or the existence of the League.

With best wishes and kind regards.

I am,
Yours sincerely,
(sd/-) B. R. Ambedkar

P. S.

I am releasing this to the Press so that the general public may know my views and have an opportunity to consider them.

To

A. V. Thakkar, Esq.,
General Secretary,
Anti-Untouchability League,
Birla House,
New Delhi.

To my great surprise, I found that no attention was paid to my proposals. Indeed, my letter was not even acknowledged! I felt that there was no use in my remaining in the Sangh. I dissociated myself from it. I found that in my absence the aims and objectives had undergone a complete change. At the meeting held in Cowasjee Jehangir Hall in Bombay on the 30 September 1932 the aims of the organization were stated to be:

Carrying propaganda against Untouchability and taking immediate steps 'to secure as early as practicable that all public wells, dharamshalas, roads, schools, crematoriums, burning ghats and all public temples be declared open to the Depressed Classes, provided that no compulsion or force shall be used and that only peaceful persuasion shall be adopted towards this end.'

But in the statement issued by Mr G. D. Birla and Mr A. V. Thakkar on 3 November two months after its inauguration it was stated:

The League believes that reasonable persons among the Sanatanists are not much against the removal of Untouchability as such, as they are against inter-caste dinners and marriages. Since it is not the ambition of the League to undertake reforms beyond its own scope, it is desirable to make it clear that while the League will work by persuasion among the caste Hindus to remove every vestige of Untouchability, the main line of work will be constructive, such as the uplift of Depressed Classes educationally, economically and socially, which itself will go a great way to remove Untouchability. With such a work even a staunch Sanatanist can have nothing but sympathy. And it is for such work mainly that the League has been established. Social reforms like the abolition of the caste system and inter-dining are kept outside the scope of the League.

Here there was a complete departure from the original aims of the organization. Removal of Untouchability had only a nominal place in the programme. Constructive work became the main part of the work of the Sangh. It is pertinent to ask why this change in the aims and objects was made. This change in the aims and objects could not have been brought about without the knowledge and consent of Mr Gandhi. The only reason one can see is that the original programme was most inconvenient to Mr Gandhi. Removal of Untouchability as a platform was very good, but as a programme of action it was bound to have made Mr Gandhi very unpopular with the Hindus. He was not prepared to court such unpopularity. He therefore preferred the programme of constructive work which had all advantages and no disadvantages. The

Hindus did not mind it. Mr Gandhi could pursue it without incurring the displeasure of the Hindus. The programme of constructive work had no such disadvantage. On the other hand, it had a positive advantage to recommend it. It had the possibility of destroying the independent movement which the Untouchables had built up and which had forced Mr Gandhi in 1932 to yield to its demands by agreeing to the Poona Pact by dangling well before them the benefits of the constructive work, a consummation which all Congressmen so devoutly wish. It could make Untouchables Congressmen and most gracefully too. The programme of constructive work had the possibility of being converted into a plan to kill Untouchables by kindness. This as a matter of fact has happened. The Harijan Sevak Sangh is intolerent of any movement on the part of the Untouchables which is independent and opposed to the Hindus and the Congress and is out to destroy it. Anticipating that such would be the consequences of the change in the aims and objects, I retired from the Sangh.

Since the first batch of the Untouchables left the Sangh no attempt was made by Mr Gandhi to appoint other Untouchables in their places. Instead, the management of the Sangh has been allowed to pass entirely into the hands of the Hindus of the Congress persuasion. Indeed, it is now the policy of the Sangh to exclude Untouchables from the management and higher direction of the Sangh. As will be seen from the refusal of Mr Gandhi to agree to the suggestion made by deputation of Untouchables requesting him to appoint Untouchables to managing body. Mr Gandhi has propounded a new doctrine to console the deputations. He says:

the Welfare work for the Untouchables is a penance which the Hindus have to do for the sin of Untouchability. The money that has been collected has been contributed by the Hindus. From both points of view the Hindus alone must run the Sangh. Neither ethics nor right would justify Untouchables in claiming a seat on the Board of the Sangh.[251]

Mr Gandhi does not realize how greatly he has insulted the Untouchables by his doctrine, the ingenuity of which has not succeeded in concealing its gross and coarse character. If Mr Gandhi's point is that the money is collected by the Hindus and the Untouchables have therefore no right to say how it shall be spent, no self-respecting Untouchable will bother him and fortunately those Untouchables who have gone to him for such favour are just unemployed loafers who are seeking to make politics a source of their livelihood. But Mr Gandhi must realize that what he says is only a justification for the change. It does not explain what has been the cause of this profound change in the original conception of the Sangh. It is pertinent to ask: why at one time he was anxious to have Untouchables on the Governing Body of the Sangh and why he is determined now to exclude them?

26

Political Safeguards for Depressed Classes

The following are the terms and conditions on which the Depressed Classes will consent to place themselves under a majority rule in a self-governing India.

CONDITION NO. I

EQUAL CITIZENSHIP

The Depressed Classes cannot consent to subject themselves to majority rule in their present state of hereditary bondsmen. Before majority rule is established their emancipation from the system of untouchability must be an accomplished fact. It must not be left to the will of the majority. The Depressed Classes must be made free citizens entitled to all the rights of citizenship in common with other citizens of the State.

(A) To secure the abolition of untouchability and to create the equality of citizenship, it is proposed that the following fundamental right shall be made part of the constitution of India.

Fundamental Right

'All subjects of the State in India are equal before the law and possess equal civic rights. Any existing enactment, regulation, order, custom or interpretation of law by which any penalty, disadvantage, disability is imposed upon or any discrimination is made against any subject of the State on account of Untouchability shall, as from the day on which this Constitution comes into operation, cease to have any effect in India.'[a]

(B) To abolish the immunities and exemptions now enjoyed by executive officers by virtue of sections 110 and 111 of the Government of India Act, 1919 and their liability for executive action be made co-extensive with what it is in the case of a European British Subject.[b]

CONDITION NO. II

FREE ENJOYMENT OF EQUAL RIGHTS

It is no use for the Depressed Classes to have a declaration of equal rights. There can be no doubt that the Depressed Classes will have to face the whole force of orthodox society, if they try to exercise the equal rights of citizenship. The Depressed Classes therefore feel that if these declarations of rights are not to be mere pious pronouncements but are to be realities of everyday life then they should be protected by adequate pains and penalties from interference in the enjoyment of these declared rights.

(A) The Depressed Classes therefore propose that the following section should be added to Part XI of the Government of India Act, 1919, dealing with Offences, Procedure and Penalties.

Offence of Infringement of Citizenship

'Whoever denies to any person except for reasons by law applicable to persons of all classes and regardless of any previous condition of Untouchability the full enjoyment of any of the accommodations, advantages, facilities, privileges of inns, educational institutions, roads, paths, streets, tanks, wells and other watering places, public conveyances on land, air or water, theatres or other places of public amusement, resort or convenience whether they are dedicated to or maintained or licensed for the use of the public shall be punished with imprisonment of either description for a

[a] USA Constitution Amendment XIV and Government of Ireland Act, 1920, 10 & 11, Geo. V, Ch. 67, sec. 5 (2).

[b] This is so in all Constitutions, see Prof Keith's remarks in Cmd. 207, p. 56.

term which may extend to five years and shall also be liable to fine.'[c]

(B) Obstruction by orthodox individuals is not the only menace to the Depressed Classes in the way of peaceful enjoyment of their rights. The commonest form of obstruction is the social boycott. It is the most formidable weapon in the hands of the orthodox classes with which they beat down any attempt on the part of the Depressed Classes to undertake any activity if it happens to be unpalatable to them. The way it works and the occasions on which it is brought into operation are well described in the Report of the Committee appointed by the Government of Bombay in 1928 'to enquire into the educational, economic and social condition of the Depressed Classes (Untouchables) and of the Aboriginal Tribes in the Presidency and to recommend measures for their uplift'. The following is an extract from the same.

Depressed Classes and Social Boycott

'102. Although we have recommended various remedies to secure to the Depressed Classes their rights to all public utilities we fear that there will be difficulties in the way of their exercising them for a long time to come. The first difficulty is the fear of open violence against them by the orthodox classes. It must be noted that the Depressed Classes form a small minority in every village, opposed to which is a great majority of the orthodox who are bent on protecting their interests and dignity from any supposed invasion by the Depressed Classes at any cost. The danger of prosecution by the Police has put a limitation upon the use of violence by the orthodox classes and consequently such cases are rare.

'The second difficulty arises from the economic position in which the Depressed Classes are found today. The Depressed Classes have no economic independence in most parts of the Presidency. Some cultivate the lands of the orthodox classes as their tenants at will. Others live on their earnings as farm labourers employed by the orthodox classes and the rest subsist on the food or grain given to them by the orthodox classes in lieu of service

[c] US Statutes at large. Civil Rights Protection Acts of 9 April 1886 and of 1 March 1875 passed in the interest of the Negroes after their emancipation.

rendered to them as village servants. We have heard of numerous instances where the orthodox classes have used their economic power as a weapon against those Depressed Classes in their villages, when the latter have dared to exercise their rights, and have evicted them from their land, and stopped their employment and discontinued their remuneration as village servants. This boycott is often planned on such an extensive scale as to include the prevention of the Depressed Classes from using the commonly used paths and the stoppage of sale of the necessities of life by the village Bania. According to the evidence sometimes small causes suffice for the proclamation of a social boycott against the Depressed Classes. Frequently it follows on the exercise by the Depressed Classes of their right to the use of the common well, but cases have been by no means rare where a stringent boycott has been proclaimed simply because a Depressed Class man has put on the sacred thread, has bought a piece of land, has put on good clothes or ornaments, or has carried a marriage procession with the bridegroom on the horse through the public street.

'We do not know of any weapon more effective than this social boycott which could have been invented for the suppression of the Depressed Classes. The method of open violence pales away before it, for it has the most far-reaching and deadening effects. It is the most dangerous because it passes as a lawful method consistent with the theory of freedom of contact. We agree that this tyranny of the majority must be put down with a firm hand if we are to guarantee the Depressed Classes the freedom of speech and action necessary for their uplift.'

In the opinion of the Depressed Classes the only way to overcome this kind of menace to their rights and liberties is to make social boycott an offence punishable by law. They are therefore bound to insist that the following sections should be added to those included in Part XI of the Government of India Act, 1919, dealing with Offences, Procedure and Penalties:

OFFENCE OF BOYCOTT DEFINED

A person shall be deemed to boycott another who:

(a) refuses to let or use or occupy any house or land, or to deal with, work for hire, or do business with another person, or to render to him or receive for him any service, or refuses to do any of the said things on the terms on which such things should commonly be done in the ordinary course of business, or

(b) abstains from such social, professional or business relations as he would, having regard to such existing customs in the Community which are not inconsistent with any fundamental right or other rights of citizenship declared in the Constitution, ordinarily maintain with such person, or

(c) in any way injures, annoys or interferes with such other person in the exercise of his lawful rights.[d]

PUNISHMENT FOR BOYCOTTING

Whoever, in consequence of any person having done an act which he was legally entitled to do or of his having omitted to do any act which he was legally entitled to omit to do or with intent to cause any person to do any act which he is not legally bound to do or to omit to do any act which he is legally entitled to do, or with intent to cause harm to such person in body, mind, reputation or property, or in his business or means of living, boycotts such person or any person in whom such person is interested, shall be punished with imprisonment of either description for a term which may extend to seven years or with fine or with both.

Provided that no offence shall be deemed to have been committed under this section if the Court is satisfied that the accused person has not acted at the instigation of or in collusion with any other person or in pursuance of or in collusion with any other person or in pursuance of any conspiracy or of any agreement or combination to boycott.

PUNISHMENT FOR INSTIGATING OR PROMOTING A BOYCOTT

Whoever:

(a) publicly makes or publishes or circulates a proposal for, or

(b) makes, publishes or circulates any statement, rumour or

[d] This and the following legal provisions are bodily taken from Burma Anti-Boycott Act, 1922, with a few changes to suit the necessities of the case.

report with intent to, or which he has reason to believe to be likely to, cause, or

(c) in any other way instigates or promotes the boycotting of any person or class of persons, shall be punished with imprisonment which may extend to five years or with fine or with both.

Explanation—An offence under this section shall be deemed to have been committed although the person affected or likely to be affected by any action of the nature referred to herein is not designated by name or class but only by his acting or abstaining from acting in some specified manner.

PUNISHMENT FOR THREATENING A BOYCOTT

Whoever, in consequence of any person having done any act which he was legally entitled to do or of his having omitted to do an act which he was legally entitled to omit to do, or with intent to cause any person to do any act which he is not legally bound to do, or to omit to do any act which he is legally entitled to do, threatens to cause such person or any person in whom such person is interested, to be boycotted shall be punished with imprisonment of either description for a term which may extend to five years or with fine or with both.

Exception—It is not boycott:

(i) to do any act in furtherance of a *bona fide* labour dispute,

(ii) to do any act in the ordinary course of business competition.

N.B.—All these offences shall be deemed to be cognizable offences.

CONDITION NO. III

PROTECTION AGAINST DISCRIMINATION

The Depressed Classes entertain grave fears of discrimination either by legislation or by executive order being made in the future. They cannot therefore consent to subject themselves to majority rule unless it is rendered impossible in law for the legislature or the executive to make any invidious discrimination against the Depressed Classes.

It is therefore proposed that the following Statutory provision be made in the constitutional law of India:

'It shall not be competent for any Legislature or Executive in India to pass a law or issue an order, rule or regulation so as to violate the rights of the subjects of the State, regardless of any previous condition of untouchability, in all territories subject to the jurisdiction of the dominion of India—

(1) to make and enforce contracts, to sue, be parties, and give evidence, to inherit, purchase, lease, sell, hold and convey real and personal property,

(2) to be eligible for entry into the civil and military employ and to all educational institutions except for such conditions and limitations as may be necessary to provide for the due and adequate representation of all classes of the subjects of the State,

(3) to be entitled to the full and equal enjoyment of the accommodations, advantages, facilities, educational institutions, privileges of inns, rivers, streams, wells, tanks, roads, paths, streets, public conveyances on land, air and water, theatres, and other places of public resort or amusement except for such conditions and limitations applicable alike to all subjects of every race, class, caste, colour or creed,

(4) to be deemed fit for and capable of sharing without distinction the benefits of any religious or charitable trust dedicated to or created, maintained or licensed for the general public or for persons of the same faith and religion,

(5) to claim full and equal benefit of all laws and proceedings for the security of person and property as is enjoyed by other subjects regardless of any previous condition of untouchability and be subject to like punishment, pains and penalties and to none other.'

CONDITION NO. IV

ADEQUATE REPRESENTATION IN THE LEGISLATURES

The Depressed Classes must be given sufficient political power to influence legislative and executive action for the purpose of securing their welfare. In view of this they demand that the following provisions shall be made in the electoral law so as to give them:

(1) Right to adequate representation in the Legislatures of the Country, Provincial and Central.

(2) Right to elect their own men as their representatives, (a) by adult suffrage, and (b) by separate electorates for the first ten years and thereafter by joint electorates and reserved seats, it being understood that joint electorates shall not be forced upon the Depressed Classes against their will unless such joint electorates are accompanied by adult suffrage.

N.B.—Adequate Representation for the Depressed Classes cannot be defined in quantitative terms until the extent of representation allowed to other communities is known. But it must be understood that the Depressed Classes will not consent to the representation of any other community being settled on better terms than those allowed to them. They will not agree to being placed at a disadvantage in this matter. In any case the Depressed Classes of Bombay and Madras must have weightage over their population ratio of representation irrespective of the extent of representation allowed to other minorities in the Provinces.

CONDITION NO. V

ADEQUATE REPRESENTATION IN THE SERVICES

The Depressed Classes have suffered enormously at the hands of the high caste officers who have monopolized the Public Services by abusing the Law or by misusing the discretion vested in them in administering it to the prejudice of the Depressed Classes and to the advantage of the caste Hindus without any regard to justice, equity or good conscience. This mischief can only be avoided by destroying the monopoly of caste Hindus in the Public Services and by regulating the recruitment to them in such a manner that all communities including the Depressed Classes will have an adequate share in them. For this purpose the Depressed Classes have to make the following proposals for statutory enactment as part of the constitutional law:

(1) There shall be established in India and in each Province in India a Public Service Commission to undertake the recruitment and control of the Public Services.

(2) No member of the Public Service Commission shall be removed except by a resolution passed by the Legislature nor shall he be appointed to any office under the Crown after his retirement.

(3) It shall be the duty of the Public Service Commission subject to the tests of efficiency as may be prescribed—(a) to recruit the Services in such a manner as will secure due and adequate representation of all communities, and (b) to regulate from time to time priority in employment in accordance with the existing extent of the representation of the various communities in any particular service concerned.

CONDITION No. VI

REDRESS AGAINST PREJUDICIAL ACTION OR NEGLECT OF INTERESTS

In view of the fact that the Majority Rule of the future will be the rule of the orthodox, the Depressed Classes fear that such a Majority Rule will not be sympathetic to them and that the probability of prejudice to their interests and neglect of their vital needs cannot be over-looked. It must be provided against, particularly because, however adequately represented, the Depressed Classes will be in a minority in all legislatures. The Depressed Classes think it very necessary that they should have the means of redress given to them in the constitution. It is therefore proposed that the following provision should be made in the constitution of India:

'(1) In and for each Province and in and for India it shall be the duty and obligation of the Legislature and the Executive or any other Authority established by law to make adequate provision for the education, sanitation, recruitment in Public Services and other matters of social and political advancement of the Depressed Classes and to do nothing that will prejudicially affect them.'

'(2) Where in any Province or in India the provisions of this section are violated an appeal shall lie to the Governor-General in

Council from any act or decision of any Provincial Authority and to the Secretary of State from any act or decision of a Central Authority affecting the matter.'

'(3) In every such case where it appears to the Governor-General in Council or to the Secretary of State the Provincial Authority or Central Authority does not take steps requisite for the due execution of the provisions of this section then and in every such case, and as far only as the circumstances of each case require, the Governor-General in Council or the Secretary of State acting as an appellate authority may prescribe, for such period as they may deem fit, remedial measures for the due execution of the provisions of this section and of any of its decisions under this section and which shall be binding upon the authority appealed against.'ᵉ

CONDITION NO. VII

SPECIAL DEPARTMENTAL CARE

The helpless, hapless and sapless condition of the Depressed Classes must be entirely attributed to the dogged and determined opposition of the whole mass of the orthodox population which will not allow the Depressed Classes to have equality of status or equality of treatment. It is not enough to say of their economic condition that they are poverty-stricken or that they are a class of landless labourers, although both these statements are statements of fact. It has to be noted that the poverty of the Depressed Classes is due largely to the social prejudices in consequence of which many an occupation for earning a living is closed to them. This is a fact which differentiates the position of the Depressed Classes from that of the ordinary caste labourer and is often a source of trouble between the two. It has also to be borne in mind that the forms of tyranny and oppression practised against the Depressed Classes are very various and the capacity of the Depressed Classes to protect themselves is extremely limited. The facts which obtain in this connection and which are of common occurrence throughout India are well described in the Abstracts of Proceedings of the Board of Revenue of the Government of Madras

ᵉ British North America Act, 1867, sec. 93.

dated 5th November 1882, No. 723, from which the following is an extract:

'134. There are forms of oppression only hitherto hinted at which must be at least cursorily mentioned. To punish disobedience of Pariahs, their masters:

(a) Bring false cases in the village court or in the criminal courts.

(b) Obtain, on application, from Government, waste lands lying all round the paracheri, so as to impound the Pariahs' cattle or obstruct the way to their temple.

(c) Have mirasi names fraudulently entered in the Government account against the paracheri.

(d) Pull down the huts and destroy the growth in the backyards.

(e) Deny occupancy right in immemorial sub-tenancies.

(f) Forcibly cut the Pariahs' crops, and on being resisted charge them with theft and rioting.

(g) Under misrepresentations, get them to execute documents by which they are afterwards ruined.

(h) Cut off the flow of water from their fields.

(i) Without legal notice, have the property of sub-tenants attached for the landlords' arrears of revenue.

'135. It will be said there are civil and criminal courts for the redress of any of these injuries. There are the courts indeed; but India does not breed village Hampdens. One must have courage to go to the courts; money to employ legal knowledge, and meet legal expenses; and means to live during the case and the appeals. Further most cases depend upon the decision of the first court; and these courts are presided over by officials who are sometimes corrupt and who generally, for other reasons, sympathize with the wealthy and landed classes to which they belong.'

'136. The influence of these classes with the official world can hardly be exaggerated. It is extreme with natives and great even with Europeans. Every office, from the highest to the lowest, is stocked with their representatives, and there is no proposal affecting their interests but they can bring a score of influence to bear upon it in its course from inception to execution.'

There can be no doubt that in view of these circumstances the uplift of the Depressed Classes will remain a pious hope unless the task is placed in the forefront of all governmental activities and unless equalization of opportunities is realized in practice by a definite policy and determined effort on the part of the Government. To secure this end the proposal of the Depressed Classes is that the Constitutional Law should impose upon the Government of India a statutory obligation to maintain at all times a department to deal with their problems by the addition of a section in the Government of India Act to the following effect:

'1. Simultaneously with the introduction of this Constitution and as part thereof there shall be created in the Government of India a Department to be in-charge of a Minister for the purpose of watching the interests of the Depressed Classes and promoting their welfare.'

'2. The Minister shall hold office so long as he retains the confidence of the Central Legislature.'

'3. It shall be the duty of the Minister in the exercise of any powers and duties conferred upon him or transferred to him by law, to take all such steps as may be desirable to secure the preparation, effectively carrying out and co-ordination of measures preventative of acts of social injustice, tyranny or oppression against the Depressed Classes and conducive to their welfare throughout India.'

'4. It shall be lawful for the Governor-General—

(a) to transfer to the Minister all or any powers or duties in respect of the welfare of the Depressed Classes arising from any enactment relating to education, sanitation, etc.,

(b) to appoint Depressed Classes welfare bureaux in each province to work under the authority of and in co-operation with the Minister.'

CONDITION NO. VIII

DEPRESSED CLASSES AND THE CABINET

Just as it is necessary that the Depressed Classes should have the power to influence governmental action by seats in the Legislature so also it is desirable that the Depressed Classes should have the opportunity to frame the general policy of the Government. This they can do only if they can find a seat in the Cabinet. The Depressed Classes therefore claim that in common with other minorities, their moral rights to be represented in the Cabinet should be recognized. With this purpose in view the Depressed Classes propose:

That in the Instrument of Instructions an obligation shall be placed upon the Governor and the Governor-General to endeavour to secure the representation of the Depressed Classes in his Cabinet.

VIII

Identity[252]

Ambedkar attempted to construct certain identities such as that of the *Shudras* and the Untouchables at the all-India level. Till then these identities were primarily construed at the provincial levels. He draws on his considerable scholarship to link these identities with widespread popular perceptions about them.

Who were the Shudras?[253] The following excerpt is the preface to an important work of Ambedkar entitled *Who were the Shudras? How they came to be the Fourth Varna in the Indo-Aryan Society*, published in 1946. In this work Ambedkar took an exegetical detour supported by certain historical data to argue that the *Shudras* were a Kshatriya community. Having displeased the Brahmins it came to be the fourth *Varna*, being denied the *Upanayana*, the ceremony that enabled one to join the ranks of the twice-born. Along with the *Shudras*, a multitude of other communities came to be condemned to the exclusions and debasement imposed on this community, as the appellation came to be applied to them.

Origin of Untouchability.[254] This is an excerpt from the book *The Untouchables, Who were They and Why They became Untouchables?*, published in 1948. Here Ambedkar developed the argument that the Untouchables were originally broken men, made to live at the outskirts of villages. However, as they continued to be Buddhists and carried on with beef-eating, they came to be treated as Untouchables. Such a construction opened up a space to claim the Buddhist and tribal inheritance for the Scheduled Castes. (The title is the editor's.)

27

Who were the Shudras?

In the present stage of the literature on the subject, a book on the *Shudras* cannot be regarded as a superfluity. Nor can it be said to deal with a trivial problem. The general proposition that the social organization of the Indo-Aryans was based on the theory of Chaturvarnya and that Chaturvarnya means the division of society into four classes—*Brahmins* (priests), *Kshatriyas* (soldiers), *Vaishyas* (traders) and *Shudras* (menials) does not convey any idea of the real nature of the problem of the *Shudras* nor of its magnitude. Chaturvarnya would have been a very innocent principle if it meant no more than mere division of society into four classes. Unfortunately, more than this is involved in the theory of Chaturvarnya. Besides dividing society into four orders, the theory goes further and makes the principle of graded inequality the basis for determining the terms of associated life as between the four *Varnas*. Again, the system of graded inequality is not merely notional. It is legal and penal. Under the system of Chaturvarnya, the *Shudra* is not only placed at the bottom of the gradation but he is subjected to innumerable ignominies and disabilities so as to prevent him from rising above the condition fixed for him by law. Indeed until the fifth *Varna* of the Untouchables came into being, the *Shudras* were in the eyes of the Hindus the lowest of the low. This shows the nature of what might be called the problem of the *Shudras*. If people have no idea of the magnitude of the problem it is because they have not cared to know what the population of the *Shudras* is. Unfortunately, the Census does not show their population separately. But there is no doubt that, excluding the Untouchables, the *Shudras* form about 75 to 80 per cent of the population of Hindus. A treatise which deals with so vast a population cannot be considered to be dealing with a trivial problem.

The book deals with the *Shudras* in the Indo-Aryan Society. There is a view that an inquiry into these questions is of no present-day moment. It is said by no less a person than Mr Sherring[255] in his *Hindu Tribes and Castes*[a] that:

Whether the Shudras were Aryans, or aboriginal inhabitants of India, or tribes produced by the union of the one with the other, is of little practical moment. They were at an early period placed in a class by themselves, and received the fourth or last degree of rank, yet at a considerable distance from the three superior castes. Even though it be admitted that at the outset they were not Aryans, still, from their extensive intermarriages with the three Aryan Castes, they have become so far Aryanized that, in some instances as already shown, they have gained more than they have lost, and certain tribes now designated as Shudras are in reality more Brahmins and Kshatriyas than anything else. In short, they have become as much absorbed in other races as the Celtic tribes of England have become absorbed in the Anglo-Saxon race; and their own separate individuality, if they ever had any, has completely vanished.

This view is based on two errors. Firstly, the present-day *Shudras* are a collection of castes drawn from heterogeneous stocks and are racially different from the original *Shudras* of the Indo-Aryan society. Secondly, in the case of *Shudras* the centre of interest is not the *Shudras* as a people but the legal system of pains and penalties to which they are subjected. The system of pains and penalties was no doubt originally devised by the Brahmins to deal with the *Shudras* of the Indo-Aryan society, who have ceased to exist as a distinct, separate, identifiable community. But strange as it may seem, the Code intended to deal with them has remained in operation and is now applied to all low-class Hindus, who have no lock stock with the original *Shudras*. How this happened must be a matter of curiosity to all. My explanation is that the *Shudras* of the Indo-Aryan Society in course of time became so degraded as a consequence of the severity of the Brahmanical laws that they really came to occupy a very low state in public life. Two consequences followed from this. One consequence was a change in the

[a] Vol. I, Introduction, p. xxi.

connotation of the word *Shudra*. The word *Shudra* lost its original meaning of being the name of a particular community and became a general name for a low-class people without civilization, without culture, without respect and without position. The second consequence was that the widening of the meaning of the word *Shudra* brought in its train the widening of the application of the Code. It is in this way that the so-called *Shudras* of the present-day have become subject to the Code, though they are not *Shudras* in the original sense of the word. Be that as it may, the fact remains that the Code intended for the original culprits has come to be applied to the innocents. If the Hindu law-givers had enough historical sense to realize that the original *Shudras* were different from the present-day low-class people, this tragedy—this massacre of the innocents—would have been avoided. The fact, however unfortunate it may be, is that the Code is applied to the present-day *Shudras* in the same rigorous manner in which it was applied to the original *Shudras*. How such a Code came into being cannot therefore be regarded as of mere antiquarian interest to the *Shudras* of today.

While it may be admitted that a study of the origin of the *Shudras* is welcome, some may question my competence to handle the theme. I have already been warned that while I may have a right to speak on Indian politics, religion and religious history of India are not my field and that I must not enter it. I do not know why critics have thought it necessary to give me this warning. If it is an antidote to any extravagant claim made by me as a thinker or a writer, then it is unnecessary. For, I am ready to admit that I am not competent to speak even on Indian politics. If the warning is for the reason that I cannot claim mastery over the Sanskrit language, I admit this deficiency. But I do not see why it should disqualify me altogether from operating in this field. There is very little of literature in the Sanskrit language which is not available in English. The want of knowledge of Sanskrit need not therefore be a bar to my handling a theme such as the present. For I venture to say that a study of the relevant literature, albeit in English translations, for fifteen years ought to be enough to invest even a person endowed with such moderate intelligence like myself, with sufficient degree of competence for the task. As to the exact measure of my competence to speak on the subject, this book will furnish the best testimony. It may well turn out that this attempt of mine is only an illustration of the proverbial fool rushing in where the angels fear to tread. But I take refuge in the belief that even the fool has a duty to perform, namely, to do his bit if the angel has gone to sleep or is unwilling to proclaim the truth. This is my justification for entering the prohibited field.

What is it that is noteworthy about this book? Undoubtedly the conclusions which I have reached as a result of my investigations. Two questions are raised in this book: (1) Who were the *Shudras*? and (2) How they came to be the fourth *Varna* of the Indo-Aryan society? My answers to them are summarized below:

1. The *Shudras* were one of the Aryan communities of the Solar race.

2. There was a time when the Aryan society recognized only three *Varnas*, namely, *Brahmins*, *Kshatriyas* and *Vaishyas*.

3. The *Shudras* did not form a separate *Varna*. They ranked as part of the *Kshatriya Varna* in the Indo-Aryan society.

4. There was a continuous feud between the *Shudra* kings and the *Brahmins* in which the *Brahmins* were subjected to many tyrannies and indignities.

5. As a result of the hatred towards the *Shudras* generated by their tyrannies and oppressions, the *Brahmins* refused to perform the *Upanayana* of the *Shudras*.

6. Owing to the denial of *Upanayana*, the *Shudras* who were *Kshatriyas* became socially degraded, fell below the rank of the *Vaishyas* and thus came to form the fourth *Varna*.

I must of course await the verdict of scholars on these conclusions. That these conclusions are not merely original but they are violently opposed to those that are current is of course evident. Whether these conclusions will be accepted or not will depend upon the mentality of a person claiming to have a right to sit in judgement over the issue. Of course, if he is attached to a particular thesis he will reject mine. I would not however bother about his judgement for he would be an adversary from whom nothing can be expected except opposition. But if a person is an honest critic, howsoever cautious; however conservative he may be, provided that he has an open mind and a readiness to accept facts, I do not despair of converting him to my view. This expectation may fail to materialize, but about one thing I am quite certain. My critics will have to admit that the book is rich in fresh insights and new visions.

Apart from scholars, how the Hindu public will react may be an interesting speculation. The Hindus of today fall into five definite classes. There is a class of Hindus, who are known as orthodox and who will not admit that there is anything wrong with the Hindu social system. To talk of reforming it is to them rank blasphemy. There is a class of Hindus who are known as Arya Samajists. They believe in the *Vedas* and only in the *Vedas*. They differ from the orthodox inasmuch as they discard everything which is not in the *Vedas*. Their gospel is that of return to the *Vedas*. There is a class of Hindus who will admit that the Hindu social system is all wrong, but who hold that there is no necessity to attack it. Their argument is that since law does not recognize it, it is a dying, if not a dead system. There is a class of Hindus, who are politically minded. They are indifferent to such questions. To them *Swaraj* is more important than social reform. The fifth class of Hindus are those who are rationalists and who regard social reforms as of primary importance, even more important than *Swaraj*.

With the Hindus, who fall into the second category, those who are likely to regard the book as unnecessary, I cannot agree. In a way they are right when they say that the existing law in British India does not recognize the caste system prevalent in the Hindu society. It is true that, having regard to Section 11 of the Civil Procedure Code, it would not be possible for a Hindu to obtain a declaration from a civil court that he belongs to a particular *Varna*. If courts in British India have to consider the question whether a person belongs to a particular *Varna*, it is only in cases of marriage, inheritance and adoption, the rules of which vary according to the *Varna* to which the party belongs. While it is true that the law in British India does not recognize the four *Varnas* of the Hindus, one must be careful not to misunderstand what this means. To put it precisely: (1) it does not mean that the observance of the *Varna* system is crime; (2) it does not mean that the *Varna* system has disappeared; (3) it does not mean that the *Varna* system is not given effect to in cases where the observance of its rules are necessary to acquiring civil rights; (4) it only means that the general legal sanction behind the *Varna* system has been withdrawn. Now, law is not the only sanction which goes to sustain social institutions. Institutions are sustained by other sanctions also. Of these, religious sanction and social sanction are the most important. The *Varna* system has a religious sanction. Because it has a religious sanction, the *Varna* system has the fullest social sanction from the Hindu society. With no legal prohibition, this religious sanction has been more than enough to keep the *Varna* system in full bloom. The best evidence to show that the *Varna* system is alive notwithstanding there is no law to enforce it, is to be found in the fact that the status of the *Shudras* and the Untouchables in the Hindu society has remained just what it has been. It cannot therefore be said that a study such as this is unnecessary.

As to the politically-minded Hindu, he need not be taken seriously. His line of approach is generally governed by a short-term view more than by long-range considerations. He is willing to follow the line of least resistance and postpone a matter, however urgent, if it is likely to make him unpopular. It is therefore quite natural if the politically-minded Hindu regards this book as a nuisance.

The book treads heavily on the toes of the Arya Samajists. My conclusions have come in sharp conflict with their ideology at two most important points. The Arya Samajists believe that the four *Varnas* of the Indo-Aryan society have been in existence from the very beginning. The book shows that there was a time when there were only three *Varnas* in the Indo-Aryan society. The Arya Samajists believe that the *Vedas* are eternal and sacrosanct. The book shows that portions of the *Vedas* at any rate, particularly the *Purusha Sukta*, which is the mainstay of the Arya Samajists, are fabrications by *Brahmins* intended to serve their own purposes. Both these conclusions are bound to act like atomic bombs on the dogmas of the Arya Samajists.

I am not sorry for this clash with Arya Samajists. The Arya Samajists have done great mischief in making the Hindu society a stationary society by preaching that the *Vedas* are eternal, without beginning, without end, and infallible, and that the social institutions of the Hindus being based on the *Vedas* are also eternal, without beginning, without end, infallible and therefore requiring no change. To be permeated with such a belief is the worst thing that can happen to a community. I am convinced that the Hindu society will not accept the necessity of reforming itself unless and until this Arya Samajists' ideology is completely destroyed. The book does render this service, if no other.

What the Orthodox Hindu will say about this book I can well imagine for I have been battling with him all these years. The only thing I did not know was how the meek and non-violent looking Hindu can be violent when anybody attacks his Sacred Books. I became aware of it as never before when last year I received a shower of letters from angry Hindus, who became quite unbalanced by my speech on the subject delivered in Madras. The letters were full of filthy abuse, unmentionable and unprintable, and full of dire threats to my life. Last time they treated me as a first offender and let me off with mere threats. I don't know what they will do this time. For on reading the book they are sure to find more cause for anger at what in their eyes is a repetition of the offence in an aggravated form for having brought forth chapter and verse to show that what goes by the name of Sacred Books contains fabrications which are political in their motive, partisan in their composition and fraudulent in their purpose. I do not propose to take any notice of their vilifications or their threats. For I know very well that they are a base crew who, professing to defend their religion, have made religion a matter of trade. They are more selfish than any other set of beings in the world, and are prostituting their intelligence to support the vested interests of their class. It is a matter of no small surprise that when the mad dogs of orthodoxy are let loose against a person who has the courage to raise his voice against the so-called Sacred Books of the Hindus, eminent Hindus occupying lofty places, claiming themselves to be highly educated and who could be expected to have no interest and to have a free and open mind become partisans and join the outcry. Even Hindu Judges of High Courts and Hindu Prime Ministers of Indian States do not hesitate to join their kind. They go further. They not only lead the howl against him but even join in the hunt. What is outrageous is that they do so because they believe that their high stations in life would invest their words with an amount of terror which would be sufficient enough to cow down any and every opponent of orthodoxy. What I would like to tell these amiable gentlemen is that they will not be able to stop me by their imprecations. They do not seem to be aware of the profound and telling words of Dr Johnson who when confronted with analogous situation said, 'I am not going to be deterred from catching a cheat by the menaces of a ruffian.' I do not wish to be rude to these high-placed critics, much less do I want to say that they are playing their part of a ruffian interested in the escape of a cheat. But I do want to tell them two things: firstly that I propose, no matter what happens, to follow the determination of Dr Johnson in the pursuit of historical truth by the exposure of the Sacred Books so that the Hindus may know that it is the doctrines contained in their Sacred Books which are responsible for the decline and fall of their country and their society; secondly, if the Hindus of this generation do not take notice of what I have to say I am sure the future generation will. I do not despair of success. For I take consolation in the words of the poet Bhavabhuti who said, 'Time is infinite and earth is vast, some day there will be born a man who will appreciate what I have said.' Whatever that be the book is a challenge to orthodoxy.

The only class of Hindus, who are likely to welcome the book are those who believe in the necessity and urgency of social reform. The fact that it is a problem which will certainly take a long time to solve and will call the efforts of many generations to come, is in their opinion, no justification for postponing the study of that problem. Even an ardent Hindu politician, if he is honest, will admit that the problems arising out of the malignant form of communalism, which is inherent in the Hindu social organization and which the politically minded Hindus desire to ignore or postpone, invariably will return to plague those very politicians at every turn. These problems are not the difficulties of the moment. They are our permanent difficulties, that is to say, difficulties of every moment. I am glad to know that such a class of Hindus exists. Small though they be, they are my mainstay and it is to them I have addressed my argument.

It will be said that I have shown no respect for the sacred literature of the Hindus which every sacred literature deserves. If the charge be true, I can plead two circumstances in justification of myself. Firstly, I claim that in my research I have been guided by the best tradition of the historian who treats all literature as vulgar—I am using the word in its original sense of belonging to the people—to be examined and tested by accepted rules of evidence without recognizing any distinction between the sacred and the profane and with the sole object of finding the truth. If in following this tradition I am found wanting in respect and reverence for the sacred literature of the Hindus my duty as a scholar must serve as my excuse. Secondly, respect and reverence for the sacred literature cannot be made to order. They are the results of social factors which make such sentiments natural in one case and quite unnatural in another. Respect and reverence for the sacred literature of the Hindus is natural to a Brahmin scholar. But it is quite unnatural in a non-Brahmin scholar. The explanation of this difference is quite simple. That a Brahmin scholar should treat this sacred literature with uncritical reverence and forbear laying on it the heavy hands which the detachment of an intellectual as distinguished from the merely educated is what is to be expected. For what is this sacred literature? It is a literature which is almost entirely the creation of the Brahmins. Secondly, its whole object is to sustain the superiority and privileges of the Brahmins as against the non-Brahmins. Why should not the Brahmins uphold the sanctity of such a literature? The very reason that leads the Brahmin to uphold it makes the non-Brahmin hate it. Knowing that what is called the sacred literature contains an abominable social philosophy which is responsible for their social degradation, the non-Brahmin reacts to it in a manner quite opposite to that of the Brahmin. That I should be wanting in respect and reverence for the sacred literature of the Hindus should not surprise any one if it is borne in mind that I am a non-Brahmin, not even a non-Brahmin but an Untouchable. My antipathy to the sacred literature could not naturally be less than that of the non-Brahmin. As Professor Thorndyke says:[256] that a man thinks is a biological fact, what he thinks is a sociological fact.

I am aware that this difference in the attitude of a Brahmin scholar and a non-Brahmin scholar towards this sacred literature—literature which is the main source of the material for the study of the problems of the social history of the Hindus—the former with his attitude of uncritical commendation and the latter with his attitude of unsparing condemnation is most harmful to historical research.

The mischief done by the Brahmin scholars to historical research is obvious. The Brahmin scholar has a two-fold interest in the maintenance of the sanctity of this literature. In the first place being the production of his forefathers his filial duty leads him to defend it even at the cost of truth. In the second place as it supports the privileges of the Brahmins, he is careful not to do anything which would undermine its authority. The necessity of upholding the system by which he knows he stands to profit, as well as of upholding the prestige of his forefathers as the founders of the system, acts as a silent immaculate premise which is ever present in the mind of the Brahmin scholar and prevents him from reaching or preaching the truth. That is why one finds so little that is original in the field of historical research by Brahmin scholars unless it be a matter of fixing dates or tracing genealogies. The non-Brahmin scholar has none of these limitations and is therefore free to engage himself in a relentless pursuit of truth. That such a difference exists between the two classes of students is not a mere matter of speculation. This very book is an illustration in print. It contains an exposure of the real character of the conspiracy against the *Shudras*, which no Brahmin scholar could have had the courage to present.

While it is true that a non-Brahmin scholar is free from the inhibitions of the Brahmin scholar he is likely to go to the other extreme and treat the whole literature as a collection of fables and fictions fit to be thrown on the dung heap not worthy of serious study. This is not the spirit of an historian. As has been well said, an historian ought to be exact, sincere, and impartial; free from passion, unbiased by interest, fear, resentment or affection; and faithful to the truth, which is the mother of history, the preserver of great actions, the enemy of oblivion, the witness of the past, the director of the future. In short he must have an open mind, though it may not be an empty mind, and readiness to examine all evidence even though it be spurious. The non-Brahmin scholar may find it difficult to remain true to this spirit of the historian. He is likely to import the spirit of non-Brahmin politics in the examination of the truth or falsity of the ancient literature which is not justifiable. I feel certain that in my research I have kept myself free from such prejudice. In writing about the *Shudras* I have had present in my mind no other consideration except that of pure history. It is well-known that there is a non-Brahmin movement in this country which is a political movement of the *Shudras*. It is also well known that I have been connected with it. But I am sure that the reader will find that I have not made this book a preface to non-Brahmin politics.

I am sensible of the many faults in the presentation of the matter. The book is loaded with quotations, too long and too many. The book is not a work of art and it is possible that readers will find it tedious to go through it. But this fault is not altogether mine. Left to myself, I would have very willingly applied the pruning knife. But the book is written for the ignorant and the uninformed *Shudras*, who do not know how they came to be what they are. They do not care how artistically the theme is handled. All they desire is a full harvest of material—the bigger the better. Those of them to whom I have shown the manuscript have insisted upon retaining the quotations. Indeed, their avidity for such material was so great that some of them went to the length of insisting that besides giving translations in English in the body of the book I should also add the original Sanskrit texts in an Appendix. While I had to deny their request for the reproduction of the original Sanskrit texts, I could not deny their request for retaining the translations on the ground that the material is not readily available to them. When one remembers that it is the *Shudras*, who have largely been instrumental in sustaining the infamous system of Chaturvarnya, though it has been the primary cause of their degradation and that only the *Shudras* can destroy the Chaturvarnya, it would be easy to realize why I allowed the necessity of educating and thereby preparing the *Shudras* fully for such a sacred task to outweigh all other considerations which favoured the deletion or if not deletion the abridgement of the quotations.

28

Origin of Untouchability

CONTEMPT FOR BUDDHISTS AS THE ROOT OF UNTOUCHABILITY

I

The Census Reports for India published by the Census Commissioner at the interval of every ten years from 1870 onwards contain a wealth of information nowhere else to be found regarding the social and religious life of the people of India. Before the Census of 1910 the Census Commissioner had a column called 'Population by Religion'. Under this heading the population was shown (1) Muslims, (2) Hindus, (3) Christians, etc. The Census Report for the year 1910 marked a new departure from the prevailing practice. For the first time it divided the Hindus under three separate categories, (i) Hindus, (ii) Animists and Tribal, and (iii) the Depressed Classes or Untouchables. This new classification has been continued ever since.

II

This departure from the practice of the previous Census Commissioners raises three questions. First is what led the Commissioner for the Census of 1910 to introduce this new classification. The second is what were the criteria adopted as a basis for this classification. The third is what are the reasons for the growth of certain practices which justify the division of Hindus into three separate categories mentioned above.

The answer to the first question will be found in the address presented in 1909 by the Muslim Community under the leadership of H.H. The Aga Khan to the then Viceroy, Lord Minto, in which they asked for a separate and adequate representation for the Muslim community in the legislature, executive and the public services. In the address[a] there occurs the following passage:

The Mohamedans of India number, according to the census taken in the year 1901 over sixty-two millions or between one-fifth and one-fourth of the total population of His Majesty's Indian dominions, and *if a reduction be made for the uncivilised portions of the community enumerated under the heads of animist and other minor religions, as well as for those classes who are ordinarily classified as Hindus but properly speaking are not Hindus at all, the proportion of Mohamedans to the Hindu Majority becomes much larger.*[b] We therefore desire to submit that under any system of representation extended or limited a community in itself more numerous than the entire population of any first class European power except Russia may justly lay claim to adequate recognition as an important factor in the State.

We venture, indeed, with Your Excellency's permission to go a step further, and urge that the position accorded to the Mohamedan community in any kind of representation direct or indirect, and in all other ways effecting their status and influence should be commensurate, not merely with their numerical strength but also with their political importance and the value of the contribution which they make to the defence of the empire, and we also hope that Your Excellency will in this connection be pleased to give due consideration to the position which they occupied in India a little more than hundred years ago and of which the traditions have naturally not faded from their minds.

The portion in italics has a special significance. It was introduced in the address to suggest that in comprising the numerical strength of the Muslims with that of the Hindus the population of the animists, tribals and the Untouchables should be excluded. The reason for this new classification of 'Hindus' adopted by the Census Commissioner in 1910 lies in this demand of the Muslim community for separate representation on augmented scale. At any rate this is how the Hindus understood this demand.[c]

[a] For the text of the address see BAWS, vol. 8, pp. 430–45.
[b] Italics not in the original.
[c] This operation came soon after the address given by Muslim community to Lord Minto in 1909 in which they asked for a separate and adequate representation for the Muslim community. The Hindu smelt a rat in it. As the Census Commissioner observed:

Interesting as it is, the first question as to why the Census Commissioner made this departure in the system of classification is of less importance than the second question. What is important is to know the basis adopted by the Census Commissioner for separating the different classes of Hindus into (1) those who were hundred per cent Hindus and (2) those who were not.

The basis adopted by the Census Commissioner for separation is to be found in the circular issued by the Census Commissioner in which he laid down certain tests for the purpose[d] of distinguishing these two classes. Among those who were not hundred per cent Hindus were included castes and tribes which:

(1) Deny the supremacy of the Brahmins.

(2) Do not receive the Mantra from a Brahmin or other recognized Hindu Guru.

(3) Deny the authority of the *Vedas*.

(4) Do not worship the Hindu gods.

(5) Are not served by good Brahmins as family priests.

(6) Have no Brahmin priests at all.

(7) Are denied access to the interior of the Hindu temples.

(8) Cause pollution (a) by touch, or (b) within a certain distance,.

(9) Bury their dead.

(10) Eat beef and do no reverence to the cow.

Out of these ten tests some divide the Hindus from the Animists and the Tribal. The rest divide the Hindus from the Untouchables. Those that divide the Untouchables from the Hindus are (2), (5), (6), (7), and (10). It is with them that we are chiefly concerned.

For the sake of clarity it is better to divide these tests into parts and consider them separately. This Chapter will be devoted only to the consideration of (2), (5), and (6).

'Incidentally, the enquiry generated a certain amount of heat, because unfortunately it happened to be made at a time when the rival claims of Hindus and Mohammedans to representation on the Legislative Councils were being debated and some of the former feared that it would lead to the exclusion of certain classes from the category of Hindus and would thus react unfavourably on their political importance, Part I, p. 116.

[d] See Census of India (1911), Part I, p. 117.

The replies received by the Census Commissioner to questions embodied in tests (2), (5), and (6) reveal (1) that the Untouchables do not receive the Mantra from a Brahmin; (2) that the Untouchables are not served by good Brahmin priests at all; and (3) that Untouchables have their own priests reared from themselves. On these facts the Census Commissioners of all Provinces are unanimous.[e]

Of the three questions the third is the most important. Unfortunately the Census Commissioner did not realize this. For in making his inquiries he failed to go to the root of the matter to find out: Why were the Untouchables not receiving the Mantra from the Brahmin? Why Brahmins did not serve the Untouchables as their family priests? Why do the Untouchables prefer to have their own priests? It is the 'why' of these facts which is more important than the existence of these facts. It is the 'why' of these facts which must be investigated. For the clue to the origin of Untouchability lies hidden behind it.

Before entering upon this investigation, it must be pointed out that the inquiries by the Census Commissioner were in a sense one-sided. They showed that the Brahmins shunned the Untouchables. They did not bring to light the fact that the Untouchables also shunned the Brahmins. Nonetheless, it is a fact. People are so much accustomed to thinking that the Brahmin is the superior of the Untouchables and the Untouchable accepts himself as his inferior; that this statement that the Untouchables look upon the Brahmin as an impure person is sure to come to them as a matter of great surprise. The fact has however been noted by many writers who have observed and examined the social customs of the Untouchables. To remove any doubt on the point, attention is drawn to the following extracts from their writings.

The fact was noticed by Abbe Dubois who says:[f]

Even to this day a Pariah is not allowed to pass a Brahmin Street in a village, though nobody can prevent, or prevents, his approaching or passing by a Brahmin's house in towns. The Pariahs, on their part will under no circumstances, allow a Brahmin to pass through their *paracherries* (collection of Pariah huts) as they firmly believe it will lead to their ruin.

[e] See Census of 1911 for Assam p. 40; for Bengal, Bihar and Orissa p. 282; for C. P. p. 73; for Madras p. 51; for Punjab p. 109; for U.P. p. 121; for Baroda p. 55; for Mysore p. 53; for Rajputana pp. 94–105; for Travancore p. 198.

[f] Abbe Dubois, *Hindu Manners and Customs*, Oxford, Clarendon Press, 1928 (3rd edition), p. 61, fn.

Mr Hemingsway, the Editor of the Gazetteer of the Tanjore District says:

These castes (Parayan and Pallan or Chakkiliyan castes of Tanjore District) strongly object to the entrance of a Brahmin into their quarters believing that harm will result to them therefrom.[g]

Speaking of the Holeyas of the Hasan District of Mysore, Captain J. S. F. Mackenzie says:

Every village has its Holigiri as the quarters inhabited by the Holiars, formerly agrestic serfs, is called outside the village boundary hedge. This, I thought was because they were considered as impure race, whose touch carries defilement with it.[h]

Such is the reason generally given by the Brahmins who refuse to receive anything directly from the hands of a Holiar, and yet the Brahmins consider great luck will wait upon them if they can manage to pass through the Holigiri without being molested. To this Holiars have a strong objection, and, should a Brahmin attempt to enter their quarters, they turn out in a body and slipper him, in former times, it is said, to death. Members of the other castes may come as far as the door, but they must not enter the house, for that would bring the Holiar bad luck. If, by chance, a person happens to get in, the owner takes care to tear the intruder's cloth, tie up some salt in one corner of it, and turn him out. This is supposed to neutralize all the good luck which might have accrued to the tresspasser, and avert any evil which ought to have befallen the owner of the house.

What is the explanation of this strange phenomenon? The explanation must of course fit in with the situation as it stood at the start, i.e. when the Untouchables were not Untouchables but were only Broken Men. We must ask why the Brahmins refused to officiate at the religious ceremonies of the Broken Men? Is it the case that the Brahmins refused to officiate? Or is it that the Broken Men refused to invite them? Why did the Brahmin regard Broken Men as impure? Why did the Broken Men regard the Brahmins as impure? What is the basis of this antipathy?

[g] Gazetteer of Tanjore District, Madras, Government of Madras (1906), p. 80.
[h] Indian Antiquary, 1873, 11.65.

This antipathy can be explained on one hypothesis. It is that the Broken Men were Buddhists. As such they did not revere the Brahmins, did not employ them as their priests and regarded them as impure. The Brahmin on the other hand disliked the Broken Men because they were Buddhists and preached against them with contempt and hatred with the result that the Broken Men came to be regarded as Untouchables.

We have no direct evidence that the Broken Men were Buddhists. No evidence is as a matter of fact necessary when the majority of Hindus were Buddhists. We may take it that they were.

That there existed hatred and abhorrence against the Buddhists in the mind of the Hindus and that this feeling was created by the Brahmins is not without support.

Nilkant in his *Prayaschit Mayukha*[i] quotes a verse from Manu which says:

If a person touches a Buddhist or a flower of Pachupat, Lokayata, Nastika and Mahapataki, he shall purify himself by a bath.

The same doctrine is preached by Apararka in his Smriti.[j] Vradha Harit goes further and declares entry into the Buddhist Temple as sin requiring a purificatory bath for removing the impurity.

How widespread had become this spirit of hatred and contempt against the followers of Buddha can be observed from the scenes depicted in Sanskrit dramas. The most striking illustration of this attitude towards the Buddhists is to be found in the Mricchakatika. In Act VII of that drama, the hero Charudatta and his friend Maitreya are shown waiting for Vasantasena in the park outside the city. She fails to turn up and Charudatta decides to leave the park. As they are leaving, they see the Buddhist monk by name Samvahaka. On seeing him, Charudatta says:

'Friend Maitreya, I am anxious to meet Vasantsena...
Come, let us go. (After walking a little) Ah! Here's an inauspicious sight, a Buddhist monk coming towards us. (After a little reflection) Well, let him come this way, we shall follow this other path.'(Exit.)

In Act VIII, the monk is in the Park of Sakara, the King's brother-in-law, washing his clothes in a pool. Sakara accompanied

[i] Edited by Gharpure, p. 95.
[j] Smriti Sammuchaya I, p. 118.

by Vita, turns up and threatens to kill the monk. The following conversation between them is revealing:

Sakara: Stay, you wicked monk.

 Monk: Ah! Here's the king's brother-in-law! Because some monk has offended him, he now beats up any monk he happens to meet.

Sakara: Stay, I will now break your head as one breaks a radish in a tavern. (*Beats him*).

Vita: Friend, it is not proper to beat a monk who has put on the saffron-robes, being disgusted with the world.

Monk: (*Welcomes*) Be pleased, lay brother.

Sakara: Friend, see. He is abusing me.

Vita: What does he say?

Sakara: He calls me lay brother (*upasaka*). Am I a barber?

Vita: Oh! He is really praising you as a devotee of the Buddha.

Sakara: Why has he come here?

Monk: To wash these clothes.

Sakara: Ah! You wicked monk. Even I myself do not bathe in this pool; I shall kill you with one stroke.

After a lot of beating, the monk is allowed to go. Here is a Buddhist Monk in the midst of the Hindu crowd. He is shunned and avoided. The feeling of disgust against him is so great that the people even shun the road the monk is travelling. The feeling of repulsion is so intense that the entry of the Buddhist was enough to cause the exit of the Hindus. The Buddhist monk is on a par with the Brahmin. A Brahmin is immune from death-penalty. He is even free from corporal punishment. But the Buddhist monk is beaten and assaulted without remorse, without compunction as though there was nothing wrong in it.

If we accept that the Broken Men were the followers of Buddhism and did not care to return to Brahminism when it became triumphant over Buddhism as easily as others did, we have an explanation for both the questions. It explains why the Untouchables regard the Brahmins as inauspicious, do not employ them as their priest and do not even allow them to enter into their quarters. It also explains why the Broken Men came to be regarded as Untouchables. The Broken Men hated the Brahmins because the Brahmins were the enemies of Buddhism and the Brahmins imposed untouchability upon the Broken Men because they would not leave Buddhism. On this reasoning it is possible to conclude that one of the roots of untouchability lies in the hatred and contempt which the Brahmins created against those who were Buddhist.

Can the hatred between Buddhism and Brahminism be taken to be the sole cause why Broken Men became Untouchables? Obviously, it cannot be. The hatred and contempt preached by the Brahmins was directed against Buddhists in general and not against the Broken Men in particular. Since untouchability stuck to Broken Men only, it is obvious that there was some additional circumstance which has played its part in fastening untouchability upon the Broken Men. What that circumstance could have been? We must next direct our effort in the direction of ascertaining it.

BEEF-EATING AS THE ROOT OF UNTOUCHABILITY

We now take up test No. 10 referred to in the circular issued by the Census Commissioner and to which reference has already been made in the previous chapter. The test refers to beef-eating.

The Census Returns show that the meat of the dead cow forms the chief item of food consumed by communities which are generally classified as Untouchable communities. No Hindu community, however low, will touch cow's flesh. On the other hand, there is no community which is really an Untouchable community which has not something to do with the dead cow. Some eat her flesh, some remove the skin, some manufacture articles out of her skin and bones.

From the survey of the Census Commissioner, it is well established that Untouchables eat beef. The question however is: Has beef-eating any relation to the origin of Untouchability? Or is it merely an incident in the economic life of the Untouchables? Can we say that the Broken Men came to be treated as Untouchables because they ate beef? There need be no hesitation in returning an affirmative answer to this question. No other answer is consistent with facts as we know them.

In the first place, we have the fact that the Untouchables or the main communities which compose them eat the dead cow and those who eat the dead cow are tainted with Untouchability and no others. The co-relation between Untouchability and the use of the dead cow is so great and so close that the thesis that it is the root of untouchability seems to be incontrovertible. In the second place if there is anything that separates the Untouchables from the Hindus, it is beef-eating. Even a superficial view of the food taboos of the Hindus will show that there are two taboos regarding food which serve as dividing lines. There is one taboo against meat-eating. It divides Hindus into vegetarians and flesh-eaters. There is another taboo which is against beef-eating. It divides Hindus into those who eat cow's flesh and those who do not. From the point of view of Untouchability the first dividing line is of no importance. But the second, is. For it completely marks off the Touchables from the Untouchables. The Touchables whether they are vegetarians or flesh-eaters are united in their objection to eat cow's flesh. As against them stand the Untouchables who eat cow's flesh without compunction and as a matter of course and habit.[k]

In this context it is not far-fetched to suggest that those who have a nausea against beef-eating should treat those who eat beef as Untouchables.

There is really no necessity to enter upon any speculation as to whether beef-eating was or was not the principal reason for the rise of Untouchability. This new theory receives support from the Hindu *Shastras*. The *Veda Vyas Smriti* contains the following verse which specifies the communities which are included in the category of Antyajas and the reasons why they were so included.[l]

L. 12–13 The *Charmakars* (Cobbler), the *Bhatta* (Soldier), the *Bhilla*, the *Rajaka* (washerman), the *Puskara*, the *Nata* (actor), the *Vrata*, the *Meda*, the *Chandala*, the *Dasa*, the *Svapaka*, and the *Kolika*—these are known as Antyajas as well as others who eat cow's flesh.

Generally speaking, the Smritikars never care to explain the why and the how of their dogmas. But this case is an exception. For in this case, Veda Vyas does explain the cause of untouchability. The clause 'as well as others who eat cow's flesh' is very

[k] The Untouchables have felt the force of the accusation levelled against them by the Hindus for eating beef. Instead of giving up the habit the Untouchables have invented a philosophy which justifies eating the beef of the dead cow. The gist of the philosophy is that eating the flesh of the dead cow is a better way of showing respect to the cow than throwing her carcass to the wind.

[l] Quoted in Kane's *History of Dharma Shastra*, vol. II, Part I, p. 71.

important. It shows that the Smritikars knew that the origin of untouchability is to be found in the eating of beef. The dictum of Veda Vyas must close the argument. It comes, so to say, straight from the horse's mouth and what is important is that it is also rational for it accords with facts as we know them.

The new approach in the search for the origin of Untouchability has brought to the surface two sources of the origin of Untouchability. One is the general atmosphere of scorn and contempt spread by the Brahmins against those who were Buddhists and the second is the habit of beef-eating kept on by the Broken Men. As has been said the first circumstance could not be sufficient to account for stigma of Untouchability attaching itself to the Broken Men. For the scorn and contempt for Buddhists spread by the Brahmins was too general and affected all Buddhists and not merely the Broken Men. The reason why Broken Men only became Untouchables was because in addition to being Buddhists they retained their habit of beef-eating which gave additional ground for offence to the Brahmins to carry their new-found love and reverence to the cow to its logical conclusion. We may therefore conclude that the Broken Men were exposed to scorn and contempt on the ground that they were Buddhists and the main cause of their Untouchability was beef-eating.

IX

Economics

Ambedkar's early work was on political economy and currency. Over the years he made forays in several areas of economic studies, including agricultural holdings, land reforms, planning, budgeting, industrial disputes and labour relations.

The Enlargement of the Scope of Provincial Finance.[257] This chapter is taken from *The Evolution of Provincial Finance in British India*, published in 1925. It was a modified version of his Ph.D. thesis submitted to Columbia University in 1917. The book explored the varying stances that the colonial regime adopted towards the financial autonomy of the provinces. By the end of the nineteenth century, arguments in favour of provincial finance had become stronger and the scale came to be titled towards the provinces with the rise of the popular element in politics and in public life.

The Silver Standard and the Evils of its Instability[258] is a chapter from *The Problem of the Rupee*, Ambedkar's D.Phil. thesis at the London School of Economics. Here Ambedkar explored the consequences that the Indian economy suffered as a silver standard country linked to Britain as a gold standard country, with the dislocation of fixed parity after 1873. Incidentally, it also provides an understanding about the resources that Ambedkar tapped for his research.

29

The Enlargement of the Scope of Provincial Finance

It used to be made a matter of complaint that the system of Provincial Finance was unjust in that under it the Government of India conscripted, at every revision of the financial settlement, the increases in the revenues given over to the management of the Provinces, either for its own benefit on the pretext of meeting the requirements of the Central Exchequer or for the benefit of such of the Provinces as had by inertia not cared to improve their resources on the pretext of tempering the wind to the shorn lamb. There was a good deal of truth in this complaint in the early period of Provincial Finance. Being the custodian of the funds, the Government of India did often put the consideration of Imperial Services above that for the Provincialized Services. In the early period of Provincial Finance the prevailing idea[a] in the distribution of funds was not how much of the revenues assigned under the expiring settlement could be continued to be usefully spent on heads of expenditure controlled by Provincial Governments, but how much of the general revenues consistently with its obligations, and having regard to the growth of demands upon its resources during the currency of the settlement, could the Government of India surrender for a further period to the Provincial Governments in order to enable them to meet whatever expenditure was essential to the conduct of their administration. This attitude of the

[a] Finance Department Resolution, No. 458 of 28 January 1881.

Government of India, justifiable as it was by the financial stringency of the period, changed as the financial condition became easy, so that in the latter period.

The distribution of revenues between the Provincial and Central Governments was made, except on occasions of grave emergency, with direct reference not to the needs of the Central Government, but to the outlay which each Province might reasonably claim to incur upon the services which it administered. The first step taken in concluding a settlement was to ascertain the needs of the Province and assign revenue to meet them; the residue only of the income of the Province coming into the Imperial Exchequer.[b]

With the shifting of emphasis on the competing needs of the Central and Provincial Governments the complaints on the score of unfair distribution of funds ceased, and no fear of an adverse revision remained when the settlements were declared permanent. There, however, remained the other main objection to the system of Provincial Finance, namely, that the limitations imposed upon it tended to reduce the Provincial Government to a nonentity by restricting the scope of their activity within the field allotted to it.

It was said that if the system of Provincial Finance was inaugurated on the understanding by which the Government of India said to the Provinces

Take what we are able to give you, and for the residue take certain powers of taxation and raise it yourself... for there are subjects which can be dealt with far better by local than by imperial taxation.

There was no reason why the Provinces should not have been allowed the freedom to tax. Again, if certain resources had been made over to the Provinces, what justification was there in not allowing them to raise loans for promoting purposes of local utility? This restriction was particularly resented; for, it was pointed out that even the humblest Local Authority in India enjoyed the power to raise loans to effect improvements in its respective jurisdiction, while such an important polity as a Provincial Government was deemed unworthy of shouldering such a responsibility. Indeed it was felt as a most galling restriction, for under it it happened that a Provincial Government which was

---

[b] Finance Department Resolution, No. 27, 18 May 1912.

deemed to have enough credit to be accepted as security by the Government of India against loans to other local bodies subordinate to it, was ruled to have no credit to pledge in its own behalf!

What, again, was the justification for limitations on the spending powers of the Provincial Governments in the matter of staff and establishments? If the administration of certain services had been entrusted to the Provincial Governments, why should they have been circumscribed in the matter of creating new or abolishing old appointments or revising the establishments of their departments? If under the system of Provincial Finance the Provinces were responsible for the services they managed, why should they not have been trusted with powers to make needful changes in the agencies which carried out those services?

Further, it was asked, what justification was there for the limitations on the preparation and execution of the Provincial Budgets? If separate Budgets had been carved for each of the Provinces out of what once formed an Imperial Budget for the whole of India, why should the Provinces have been required to submit their Budgets to the Government of India? Merely as a matter of conveying information the requirement was comparatively of a trifling character. But why should the Government of India have claimed to alter their estimates and compel them to abide by the grants as fixed by it? Was such a scrutiny of Provincial Budgets a cover for dictating a policy to the Provincial Governments? If this was so, what was the scope for initiative and freedom left to the Provinces which it was the primary object of Provincial Finance to promote and of the permanent settlements to ensure? Again, why should a Provincial Government have been required to come to the Government of India for a supplementary grant as it had to do where the excess over estimates could not be met by reappropriations, even when it had balances to its credit so sufficient as not to be reduced below the required minimum by a draft to meet the excess?

For each of these limitations which fettered the Provincial Governments and contracted the scope of Provincial Finance, the Government of India was of course ready with abundant excuses.[c] In the matter of revenue restrictions it urged that the revenues of

[c] In this connection, cf. Evidence of Mr J. S. Meston before the Royal Commission on Decentralization. Mit. of Evid., vol. X, Q. 44807-45336,

India were its constitutional possession for the proper disposal of which it was responsible to the Secretary of State and Parliament. That being the case it was fair that the Government of India should require that the sources assigned to the Provinces should not be alienated nor spent on unauthorized grants or unapproved services. Again, being responsible for all services it followed that the Government of India could not have afforded to weaken its position as to managing the resources of the country by partitioning the taxing or borrowing powers. The field for taxation in India being considerably limited, an indiscriminate levy of taxes by a competing authority, it was feared, would have led either to discontent by additions[d] to the Imperial imposts or to a retrenchment of the field for Imperial taxation. The concentration of borrowing powers in its hands, the Government of India urged, was a natural corollary of the statutory hypothecation of all India revenues to all-India needs. The Government of India could not allow its revenues to be mortgaged by a Provincial Government for its own needs. Besides it was afraid[e] that if this freedom to borrow were granted

the temptation to hypothecate revenues in advance might become inconveniently strong, and the future administration of a Province might be starved because a former Government had been in a hurry to proceed with some costly ambitions and non-productive project.

Moreover, the loan market in India, it was said, was as limited as the taxable capacity of the country. Therefore

if many buckets are dipping into one well and drought cuts short the supply of water, obviously the chief proprietor of the well must take it upon himself to regulate the drawings.[f]

In the matter of specific restrictions on spending powers with respect to staff and establishments, the defence of the Government of India was that such restrictions were necessary in the interest of uniformity and economy. It was urged that if each province was allowed the freedom to regulate the remuneration of the Public

[d] between 1870 and 1879, when the Provinces had a freer hand in the matter of local taxation, all of them selected the already overburdened basis of taxation, viz. land for their levy.

[e] *R.C.D.* Mit. of Evid., vol. X, Q. 45310.

[f] Report on Indian Constitutional Reforms, Cd. 9109 of 1918, p. 94, hereafter called Joint Report.

Service which carried on the actual work of administration the result would probably have been unequal pay for equal work. Such a consequence would have engendered discontent in the servants of the State which it was desirable to prevent in the interest of good administration. Again, if the Provinces had been given full freedom to revise establishments it might have resulted in considerable additions to the recurring expenditure of the Provinces, thereby jeopardizing the stability of the Provincial as well as of the Imperial finance, for in the last resort the Government of India was responsible for maintaining the Provincial Governments.

In the matter of control over the preparation and execution of Provincial Budgets the Government of India urged that the scrutiny was not motivated by a desire to control an unwelcome policy,[g] but was inevitable because of the three important ties by which the Provincial Budgets were bound up with the Budget of the Government of India. These were (1) the incorporation of the income and expenditure of the Provincial Governments into the Budget and the Annual Accounts of the Government of India as an integral part thereof; (2) the system of divided heads of revenue and expenditure, and (3) a common treasury involving a combined 'ways and means' for the transaction of the Central and Provincial Governments. The first two points of inter-relation required that the Government of India should examine the Budget Estimates of the Provincial Governments. It was urged[h] that the power to make such alterations was rendered specially necessary by the inveterate tendency of Local Governments to over-estimate their expenditure and under-estimate their revenue. Estimates which departed widely from actuals meant bad finance and also a provision of larger ways and means for the working of the Treasury. But even if this tendency was absent it was incumbent on the Government of India to scrutinize the Provincial Estimates in order to preserve accuracy in the combined accounts. Besides the interests of accuracy, the Government of India had to ascertain by a scrutiny of their estimates that a Province did not impair the stability of its finances by (1) including in its budget expenditure on schemes which had not received due administrative sanction, or was not likely to receive such sanction in time to be

[g] R.C.D., Mit. of Evid., vol. X, Q. 44981.
[h] R.C.D., Mit. of Evid., vol. X, Q. 44863.

incurred during the year; or (2) by entering on an enhanced scale of expenditure a Province was not unduly depleting its balances. But by far the strongest reason why the Government of India needed to scrutinize the Provincial Estimates consisted in the fact that in so far as some of the Heads of Accounts were shared, the ultimate result of the Central Budget whether there was to be surplus or deficit, depended upon the accuracy of the estimates. The Government of India, it was urged, was thus directly interested in the Provincial Budgets, and could not have abandoned its right to scrutinize them without exposing its budgetary system to serious derangement. The third point of inter-relationship necessitated that the Provincial Governments should work within the grants as fixed finally by the Government of India. To have allowed the Provincial Governments the liberty to exceed the grants because they had ample balances to their credit would have been incompatible[i] with the responsibility of the Imperial Government to provide the ways and means for the whole administration of the country. A provincial balance, it was pointed out, was not a separate balance locked up in a separate provincial chest. It was a part of the general balances on which the Government of India operated daily. If a sudden demand uncontemplated in the Budget were to be made upon these balances, as would have been the case if the Provincial Governments had exceeded their budget grants, it would have disturbed the ways and means transaction and would have involved the Government into insolvency by causing insufficiency of cash.

All these defences of the restrictions on Provincial Governments were plausible defences and could have been decisive if the centralized system of administration in favour of which they were urged could be deemed to have satisfied the ends of good government. But it was not unreasonable to argue as was done by the Provincial Governments[j] that modern tendencies were all moving in the direction of forms of government which placed fullest powers as low down in the administrative scale (i.e. as near the section of population immediately affected) as could be safely arranged. It is reasonable to centralize such powers as could not

[i] *RCD*, Mit. of Evid., vol. X, Q. 44865.
[j] In this connection see the very trenchant memorandum by the Government of Bombay on Decentralization, *RCD*, Mit. of Evid., vol. VIII, Appendix II.

be efficiently exercised otherwise. But it is equally unreasonable to centralize powers where central control or uniformity is not clearly essential or is impracticable. By centralization all progress tends to be retarded, all initiative liable to be checked and the sense of responsibility of Local Authorities greatly impaired. Besides, centralization involves and must involve a serious sacrifice of elasticity, for it is naturally disagreeable to a central department to have to deal with half a dozen different ways of managing the same branch of administration, and which therefore aims at reducing all types to one. Further centralization conflicts with what may be regarded as a cardinal principle of good government, namely, that when administrative business reached an authority fully competent to deal with it, that authority should deal with it finally. Even when there is a higher authority equally competent, to pass the business on to it would at best help to transfer power to the hands of the lower ranks of the official hierachy, by causing congestion of business in the Central Department. Thus centralization, unless greatly circumscribed, must lead to inefficiency. This was sure to occur even in homogeneous states, and above all in a country like India where there are to be found more diversities of race, language, religion, customs and economic conditions than in the whole continent of Europe. In such circumstances there must come a point at which the higher authority must be less competent than the lower, because it cannot by any possibility possess the requisite knowledge of all local conditions. It was therefore obvious that a Central Government for the whole of India could not be said to possess knowledge and experience of all various conditions prevailing in the different Provinces under it. It, therefore, necessarily became an authority less competent[k] to deal with matters of provincial administration than the Provincial

[k] In this connection it may be of interest to draw attention to the semi-serious suggestion made by Mr A. C. Logan, in which he argued that if decentralization 'cannot be effected then there is an alternative method of so remodelling the constitution of the Government of India as to replace the present departments by departments of various local areas each with its own Secretary and Member; thus there should be a department of Bombay with Secretary and Member appointed from that Province dealing with all Bombay questions and the like for other (six) provinces. Thus each Province could govern itself from Calcutta under the supervision of the Governor General'—Vide RCD, Mit. of Evid., vol. VIII, Q. 35531.

Governments, the members of which could not be said to be markedly inferior, and must generally be equal in ability to those of the Central Government, while necessarily superior as a body in point of knowledge.

To these arguments the only reply the Government of India could make was that it concentrated all power in its hands, not from principle but from necessity that necessarily arose out of its constitutional obligations. The law had invested it with the superintendence, direction, and control of the civil and military government and the ordering and management of the revenues of the country. It could not therefore relax its control over the powers it had delegated to the Provincial Governments. It was, of course, impossible to deny the force of this argument. So long as the Government of India remained the authority solely responsible to Parliament it was reasonable to hold that it should be the controlling authority in all matters pertaining to the administration of the country. But it was equally reasonable to ask whether it would not have been possible in the interests of cordiality between the Central and Provincial Governments to have relaxed such of the restrictions on the financial powers of the Provinces as would not have been incompatible with the due discharge by the former of its own responsibilities. That it was possible so to enlarge the scope of Provincial Finance by a relaxation of the limitations without injury to the position of the Government of India must be said to be evident from the following analysis of the suggestions made by the Provincial Governments. These suggestions were

(i) Power of taxation and borrowing on the security of Provincial Revenues.

(ii) Power of sanctioning expenditure on Staff and Establishments up to a limit higher than that allowed by the Government of India.

(iii) Separation of Provincial Estimates from the Imperial Budget and Accounts.

(iv) Abolition of the system of divided heads of revenue and expenditure and the replacement of it by a system of separation of sources and contributions from the yield.

(v) Power to spend part of their balances up to a defined amount without the previous sanction of the Government of India in meeting an excess of expenditure over Budget Estimates.

What objections were there, from the standpoint of the constitutional responsibilities of the Government of India, to the grant of these demands? Clearly it was possible for the Government of India to have marked off certain sources of taxation best suited for provincial levy and unconnected with the imperial imposts. Similarly it was possible to have permitted the Provincial Governments to borrow to a limited extent on the security of the revenues assigned to them. To suggest as did the Government of India, that the Provincial Governments would abuse these powers to the extent of causing discontent or jeopardizing the stability of their financial system, was to believe that such legally recognized polities and the Provincial Governments were run by incompetent administrators unmindful of their obligations. The second demand could have been granted with greater ease. It is to be noted that the Civil Service of the country which deals with revenue and general administration has been divided into

(1) The 'Indian Civil Service' recruited in England by competitive examination, at which natives of India, like other subjects of His Majesty, can compete; and

(2) The 'Provincial' and 'Subordinate' Civil Services, recruited in India, and, as a rule, only open to persons who are natives of the country or domiciled therein.

Each Province has had its own separate 'Provincial' and 'Subordinate' Services, but while it has a free hand in recruiting for the latter, appointments to the former have been regulated by rules laid down by the Government of India. That being the case it would have been only logical that the Government which had the power of recruiting for an appointment should also have the power of regulating the salary. There can be no reason why the salaries of posts of similar grades should be equal in all Provinces; nor can they be equal having regard to the differences in the economic conditions of the Provinces. A Local Government knows better the economic value of a local man, and should therefore have been trusted with powers up to a limit covered by the Provincial and Subordinate Services. The suggestion of the Government of India that the grant of such powers would have resulted in heavy additions to the recurring expenditure of a Province must be said to be too ungracious to be taken seriously.

The acceptance of the third recommendation could not have in any conceivable way affected the responsibility of the Government of India. The only objection which the Government of India urged was that such a separation would have been unwise. To have published accounts or estimates of the Imperial Government which excluded the accounts of the Provincial Governments, when the items excluded covered such a large magnitude, would have misled the public and rendered a wholly incomplete idea of the financial position of the Government of India.[1] Now it must be granted that if such a separation of accounts could have avoided the scrutiny and the consequent restraint on budget-making by the Provinces, not to have done so was to have put the supposed convenience of the student of Accounts above the administrative convenience of the Provincial Governments. Besides, it is to be pointed out that the suggestion was not a novel one. It was only a revival of the old practice which obtained between 1871 and 1877. During that period of financial decentralization Provincial figures did not appear in the Imperial Budget. The Provincial Budget as framed by the Accountant General was passed by the Provincial Government and no more reference was required to the Government of India except to inform it that the estimate was a probable one and that it was within the limits of the revenues assigned to the Province. It is therefore obvious that there could not have been any constitutional objection to the granting of the demand for a separation of accounts.

The fourth recommendation was of the same class as the third, in that it too could not be said to have involved any infringement of the constitutional responsibilities of the Government of India. The abolition of the divided heads of revenue would have clearly eliminated the interference of the Government of India in the preparation of the Budget Estimates by the Provinces. Similarly the abolition of the divided heads of expenditure would have given the Provinces greater[m] freedom in the matter of spending the revenues assigned to them. Under that system a Provincial Government could not spend more on a particular service if it was a divided head unless the Government of India consented to increase its figure for expenditure under that service. If the Government

[1] RCD, Mit. of Evid., vol. X, Q. 44866, 45179-80.
[m] RCD, Mit. of Evid., vol. VIII, Q. 35225-8.

of India reduced its figure the Provincial Government was perforce obliged to reduce its own. The substitution of a system of separation of sources and contributions from the yield for the system of divided heads would have clearly resulted in a greater freedom to the Provincial Governments, without any evil consequence to the Government of India. The objections which the Government of India was able to oppose to this demand was far from convincing. It was urged[n] that the Provincial Governments under complete separation may cease to take such interest as it took in respect of revenues which were divided. But it is evidently a mistaken view that a Provincial government could not have been trusted to administer a tax efficiently unless it had a financial interest in the result. The view supposed that the people engaged in the collection of revenue really knew whether it went to the Imperial or the Provincial credit. As a matter of fact the ultimate credit could in no way have affected the collection of the revenue. And even if that view were true the difficulty could easily have been met by each government having its own staff to collect its own revenues. The employing by one Government to execute its functions the agencies of another, as has been the case in India, is obviously a complicated and awkward system. If separation of agencies had resulted from the separation of sources it would have been a reform all to the good. Besides it was overlooked that the fact that the divided heads gave a personal interest to the Provincial Governments was indeed a point against the system rather than in favour of it. A system which created a vested interest in a revenue apart from the interest of the public was a bad system, for such an interest was sure to lead to harshness and rigidity in collection.[o] As an instance of this may be cited the notorious unwillingness of Provincial Governments in the matters of remitting taxation.[p] If humanizing the Provincial Governments was a desirable end, then the abolition of divided heads was a good means. The other objection which the Government of India was able to oppose was that such a change would have given the share of the Government of India from the revenues raised in the provinces the character of a tribute, and the Government of India

[n] Ibid., vol. IV. Q. 16791.
[o] Cf. in this connection by Professor Urdhal.
[p] RCD, Mt. of Evid., vol X, Q. 44866.

would have appeared to be the pensioner of the Provincial Governments, depending upon them rather than controlling them. This objection must be ruled out as being sentimental.

The fifth and the last suggestion for the enlargement of the scope of Provincial Finance was least obnoxious to the responsibility of the Government of India. There is no reason why there should have been a single-treasury system for both the Governments, Provincial and Central. It is true that a common treasury permits a high state of economy in the cash balances of the country, which it is the duty of every Government to effect, just as any business firm looks upon it as its duty to economize its till money or floating cash. But if a common treasury hindered the use of the balances the gain in freedom would have more than compensated the loss involved by the increase in the cash balances that would have followed the institution of separate treasuries and separate ways and means. But the demand of the Provincial Governments did not ask for a complete separation of Provincial balances from the balances of the Central Government involving separate treasury system and separate ways and means, probably because they anticipated that as such a proposal meant separate possession of provincial revenues the Government of India would raise a constitutional objection to such a demand. All they asked for was a power to spend part of their balances up to a defined amount without reference to the Government of India. The suggestion was accepted[q] as 'reasonable' for its consequences, provided it was not a big amount, would have been not a deprivation of the Government of India's power of control over nor a disturbance in the ways and means, but only a slight increase in the cash balances of the country.

Thus it is clear that the scope of Provincial Finance was unduly restricted by a too narrow and too legalistic an interpretation of the constitutional obligations of the Government of India. From the above analysis of the suggestions made by the Provincial Governments it is clear that without making any breach in the constitutional position of the Government of India it would have been possible, with a more charitable view of their sense of responsibility, to effect the changes they desired. Such concessions would have made Provincial Finance as self-sufficient and as

q *RCD*, Mit. of Evid., vol. X, Q. 44000

autonomous as it was capable of being made. The system would no doubt have rested on pure convention: nonetheless its benefits would have been as real as though it was based on law.

But the time had arrived when the financial arrangements could no longer be looked upon as a matter which concerned the Central and Provincial Governments. There arose a third party whose counsels were rejected in 1870 but which now insisted on having a voice in the disposition of the financial resources of the country. It was the Indian taxpayer, and his clamour had grown so strong that it compelled the powers that be to alter the system so as to permit him to take the part he claimed to play.

30

The Silver Standard and
the Evils of its Instability

The economic consequences of this rupture of the par of exchange
were of the most far-reaching character. It divided the commercial
world into two sharply defined groups, one using gold and the
other using silver as their standard money. When so much gold
was always equal to so much silver, as was the case previous to
1873, it mattered very little, for the purposes of international
transactions, whether a country was on a gold or on a silver
standard; nor did it make any difference in which of the two
currencies its obligations were stipulated and realized. But when,
owing to the dislocation of the fixed par, it was not possible to
define how much silver was equal to how much gold from year
to year or even from month to month, this precision of value, the
very soul of pecuniary exchange, gave place to the uncertainties
of gambling. Of course, all countries were not drawn into this
vortex of perplexities in the same degree and to the same extent,
yet it was impossible for any country which participated in
international commerce to escape from being dragged into it.
This was true of India as it was of no other country. She was a
silver-standard country intimately bound to a gold-standard country, so that her economic and financial life was at the mercy of
blind forces operating upon the relative values of gold and silver
which governed the rupee-sterling exchange.

The fall increased the burden of those who were under an obligation to make gold payments. Amongst such, the most heavily

charged was the Government of India. Owing to the exigencies of its political constitution, that Government has been under the necessity of making certain payments in England to meet: (1) interest on debt and on the stock of the guaranteed railway companies; (2) expenses on account of the European troops maintained in India; (3) pensions and non-effective allowances payable in England; (4) cost of the home administration;[a] and (5) stores purchased in England for use or consumption in India. England being a gold-standard country, these payments were necessarily gold payments. But the revenues of the Government of India out of which these payments were met were received in silver, which was the sole legal-tender money of the country. It is evident that even if the gold payments were a fixed quality their burden must increase *pari passu* with the fall in the gold value of silver. But the gold payments were not a fixed quantity. They have ever been on the increase, so that the rupee cost of the gold payments grew both by reason of the growth in their magnitude, and also by reason of the contraction of the medium, i.e. the appreciation of gold, in which they were payable. How greatly this double levy diminished the revenues of India, the figures in Table 30.1 give a convincing testimony.

The effect of such a growing burden on the finance of the Government may well be imagined; the condition of the government, embarrassing at first, later became quite desperate under this continuously increasing burden. It enforced a policy of high taxation and rigid economy in the finances of the Government Analysing the resource side of the Indian Budgets from the year 1872-3, we find that there was hardly any year which did not expire without making an addition to the existing imports of the country. In 1872-3, there commenced the levy of what were called Provincial Rates. The fiscal year 1875-6 witnessed the addition of Re 1 per gallon in the exise duty on spirits. In 1877-8 the Pass Duty on Malwa opium was raised from Rs 600 to Rs 650 per chest. An addition of a Licence Tax and Local Rates was made in the year 1978-9, and an increase of Rs 50 per chest took place in the Malwa Opium Duty in the following year. With the help of these imposts the Government expected to place its finances on an adequate basis.

[a] Since the Reform Act of 1920 that part of this cost which was 'political' has been placed upon the British Estimates.

TABLE 30.1: Increase in the Rupee Cost of Gold Payments[b]

Financial Year	Average Rate of Exchange for the Year		Total Excess of Rupees needed to provide for the net Sterling Payments of the Year over those required to meet the Sterling Payments of 1874–5	Amount of this Excee due to	
				(1) Fall in the Rate of Exchange over that of 1874–5	(2) Increase in gold payments over those of 1874–5
	s.	d.	R	R	R
1875–6	1	9.626	86,97,980	41,13,723	45,84,257
1876–7	1	8.508	3,15,06,824	1,44,68,234	1,70,38,590
1877–8	1	8.791	1,30,05,481	1,14,58,670	1,15,46,811
1878–9	1	7.794	1,85,23,170	1,04,16,718	81,06,452
1879–80	1	7.961	39,23,570	1,65,37,394	–1,26,13,824
1880–1	1	7.956	3,12,11,981	1,92,82,582	1,19,29,399
1881–2	1	7.895	3,18,19,685	1,98,76,786	–1,19,42,899
1882–3	1	7.525	62,50,518	1,86,35,246	2,48,85,764
1883–4	1	7.536	3,44,16,685	2,33,46,040	1,10,70,645
1884–5	1	7.308	1,96,25,981	2,48,03,423	51,77,442
1885–6	1	6.254	1,82,11,346	2,54,95,337	–4,37,06,683
1886–7	1	5.441	4,69,16,788	4,46,68,299	22,48,489
1887–8	1	4.898	4,63,13,161	4,96,60,537	–33,47,376
1888–9	1	4.379	9,00,38,166	6,59,71,998	2,40,66,168
1889–90	1	4.566	7,75,96,889	6,06,98,370	1,68,98,519
1890–1	1	6.090	9,06,11,857	4,65,48,302	4,40,63,555
1891–2	1	4.733	10,44,44,529	6,54,52,999	3,89,91,530

By the end of 1882, it felt quite secure and even went so far as to remit some of the taxes, which it did by lowering the customs duties and the Patwari Cess in the North-Western Provinces. But the rapid pace in the fall of the exchange soon showed that a resort to further taxation was necessary to make up for the increased cost of the sterling payments. To the existing burdens, therefore, was added in 1886 an Income Tax, a duty of 5 per cent on imported

[b] Compiled from figures in Appendix II, p. 270, of the Indian Currency Committee of 1843.

and also on non-illuminating petroleum. The Salt Duty was raised in 1888 in India from Rs 2 to Rs 2½ and in Burma from 3 annas to Re 1 per maund. The Patwari Cess of the North–Western Provinces, repealed in 1882, was re-imposed in 1888. The rates of duty on imported spirit and the excise duties on spirits were not only raised in 1890, but were afterwards added to in every province. An excise duty on malt liquor was levied in 1893, and another on salted fish at the rate of 6 annas per maund. The yield of the taxes and duties levied from 1882-3 was[c] as follows:

Sources	1882–3	1892–3
	Rs	Rs
Salt	5,67,50,000	8,14,90,000
Excise	3,47,50,000	4,97,90,000
Customs	1,08,90,000	1,41,80,000
Assessed taxes	48,40,000	1,63,60,000

All this additional burden was due to the enhanced cost of meeting the gold payments, and 'would not have been necessary but for the fall in the exchange'.[d]

Along with this increase of resources the Government of India also exercised the virtue of economy in the cost of administration. For the first time in its history, the Government turned to the alternative of employing the comparatively cheaper agency of the natives of the country in place of the imported Englishmen. Prior to 1870, the scope of effecting economy along this line was very limited. By the Civil Service Reforms of 1853[e] the way was cleared for the appointment of Indians to the posts reserved by the Statute of 1793[f] for the members of the covenanted Civil Service. But this reform did not conduce to any economy in the cost of the administration, because the Indian members carried the same high scale of salaries as did the English members of the Civil Service. It was when the Statute of 1870 (33 Vic. c. 3) was passed permitting the appointment by nomination of non-covenanted Indians to

[c] *Report of the Indian Currency Committee*, 1893, App. II, p. 263.

[d] J. E. O'Conor, *Report of the Indian Currency Committee*, 1898, App. II, p. 182.

[e] Cf. *Report of the Public Service Commission*, C. 5327 of 1887.

[f] This provision of the Act has been re-enacted by the Act of 1861.

places reserved for the covenanted Civil Service on a lower scale of salary, that a real scope for economy presented itself to the Government of India. Hard pressed, the Government of India availed itself of the possibilities for economy held out by this Statute. So great was the need for economy and so powerful was the interest of the Government in reducing its expenditure that it proceeded, notwithstanding increased demands for efficient administration, to substitute the less expensive agency of non-covenanted civilians in place of the more expensive agency of the covenanted civilians. The scale on which this substitution was effected was by no means small, for we find that between 1874 and 1889 the strength of the covenanted service recruited in England was reduced by more than 22 per cent, and was further expected to be reduced by about 12 per cent, by the employment of uncovenanted Indians to the posts usually reserved for covenanted civilians.[g] Besides substituting a cheap for a dear agency in the administration, the Government also sought to obtain relief by applying the pruning knife to the rank growth in departmental extravagances.[h] Even with such heroic efforts to increase the revenue and reduce the expenditure the finances of the Government throughout the period of the falling exchange were never in a flourishing state, as is shown in Table 30.2.

Much more regrettable was the inability of the Government, owing to its financial difficulties, to find money for useful public works. The welfare of the Indian people depends upon turning to best account the resources which the country possesses. But the people have had very little of the necessary spirit of enterprise in them. The task, therefore, has fallen upon the Government of India to provide the country with the two prime requisites of a sustained economic life, namely a system of transport and a network of irrigation. With this object in view the Government had inaugurated a policy of developing what were called 'Extraordinary Public Works,' financed by capital borrowings. For such borrowings India, as was to be expected, hardly offered any market, the people being too poor and their savings too scanty to furnish a

[g] Cf. evidence of Mr Jenkins, Q. 12. Mit. of Evid. of the Select Committee on East India (Civil Servants), H. of C. 327 of 1890.

[h] Cf. *Calcutta Civil Finance Committee's Report*, 1886; also *The Report of the Civil Finance* Commissioner (1887), who completed the work of the Committee after it was dissolved.

TABLE 30.2: Revenue and Expenditure of the Government of India

Year	Average rate of exchange	In India			In England		Final result surplus (+) or deficit (−)
		Net revenue	Net expenditure excluding exchange	Surplus	Net sterling revenue	Exchange	
	d.	R.	R.	R.	£	R.	R.
1874-5	22.156	39,564,216	25,897,098	13,667,118	12,562,101	1,045,239	59,778
1875-6	21.626	40,053,419	24,541,923	15,511,496	12,544,813	1,377,428	1,589,255
1876-7	20.508	38,253,366	25,355,285	12,898,081	13,229,646	2,252,611	-2,584,176
1877-8	20.791	39,275,489	27,658,021	11,617,468	13,756,478	2,123,030	-4,262,040
1878-9	19.794	44,415,139	25,778,928	18,636,211	13,610,211	2,891,902	2,134,098
1879-80	19.961	45,258,197	29,384,030	15,874,167	14,223,891	2,878,169	-1,227,893
1880-1	19.956	44,691,119	34,880,434	9,810,085	11,177,231	2,264,848	-3,031,394
1881-2	19.895	45,471,887	27,717,249	17,754,638	11,737,688	2,421,499	3,595,451
1882-3	19.525	42,526,173	25,500,437	17,025,736	13,299,976	3,050,923	674,837
1883-4	19.536	43,591,273	23,566,381	20,024,892	14,770,257	3,375,158	1,879,477
1884-5	19.308	41,585,347	24,763,779	16,821,568	13,844,028	3,363,986	-386,446
1885-6	18.254	42,635,953	27,352,132	15,283,821	13,755,659	4,329,888	-2,801,726
1886-7	17.441	44,804,774	25,124,335	19,680,439	14,172,298	5,329,714	178,427
1887-8	16.898	45,424,150	25,968,025	19,456,125	15,128,018	6,356,939	-2,028,832
1888-9	16.379	46,558,354	25,051,147	21,507,207	14,652,590	6,817,599	37,018
1889-90	16.566	50,005,810	26,367,855	23,637,955	14,513,155	6,512,767	2,612,033
1890-1	18.090	49,403,819	25,579,727	23,824,092	15,176,866	4,959,055	3,688,171
1891-2	16.733	50,023,142	27,013,618	23,009,524	15,716,780	6,825,909	467,535

428 • THE ESSENTIAL WRITINGS OF B. R. AMBEDKAR

modicum of the required capital outlay. Like all governments of poor peoples, the Government of India had therefore to turn to wealthier countries that had surplus capital to lend. All these countries unfortunately happened to be on the gold standard. As long as it was possible to say that so much gold was equal to so much silver, the English investor was indifferent whether the securities of the Government of India were rupee securities or sterling securities. But the fall in the gold value of silver was also a fall in the gold value of the rupee securities, and what was once a secure investment ceased to be so any more. This placed the Government in a difficult position in the matter of financing its extraordinary public works. Figures in Table 30.3 are worth study.

The English investor would not invest in the rupee securities. An important customer for the Indian rupee securities was thus lost. The response of the Indian money market was inadequate. To issue sterling securities was the only alternative to enable the Government to tap a bigger and a more constant reservoir for the drawing of capital to India; but as it was bound to increase the burden of the gold payments, which it was the strongest interest of the Government to reduce, the resort to the London money market, unavoidable as it became, was somewhat restrained,[i] with the result that the expansion of extraordinary public works did not proceed at a pace demanded by the needs of the country. The effects of this financial derangement, consequent on the fall of the exchange, were not confined to the Government of India. They were immediately felt by the municipalities and other local bodies who were dependent upon the Government for financial aid. So long as the cash balances were overflowing in the treasury of the Government, 'one of the most useful ways' to employ them was found in lending a portion of them to these local institutions. As they had just then been inaugurated under the local self-government policy of Lord Ripon's regime, and were looked upon only as an experiment, their taxing and borrowing powers were rigidly limited. Consequently, this financial aid from the Central

---

[i] During the period of falling exchange the distribution of the debt of India was as follows:

	Sterling debt	Rupee debt
End of 1873–4	41,117,617	66,41,72,900
End of 1898–9	124,268,605	1,12,65,04,340

TABLE 30.3: Price Movements of Rupee and Sterling Securities of the Government of India*

Year	Rates of Exchange		Price of 4 per cent Rupee Paper				Price of Sterling India Stock					
			In Calcutta		In London		4 per cent		3 per cent		3 per cent	
	Highest	Lowest	Highest	Lowest	Highest	Low est	Highest	Lowest	Highest	Lowest	Highest	Lowest
1	2	-3	4	5	6	7	8	9	10	11	12	13
	d.	d.										
1873	22⅞	21⅝	105	101⅞	97	94½	106½	101¼				
1874	23⅛	21¾	104½	99½	98	94½	103¾	101				
1875	22 3/16	21¼	102⅞	101¾	94	91	106¼	103¼				
1876	22⅜	18½	101⅞	98¾	89¾	78	105⅞	101⅞				
1877	22¼	20 9/16	98⅞	93¼	88½	81	104⅝	102¼				
1878	21	18¾	96⅞	93½	82½	75⅜	104⅝	99				
1879	20⅝	18⅝	94⅞	91¼	80	77¼	105⅜	100⅞				
1880	20⅜	19¾	100	92 15/16	81⅜	77¾	105⅝	102⅛				
1881	20 1/16	19½	104⅝	100	86	81½	106⅜	103⅞	103⅞	100¾		
1882	20 3/16	19 1/16	102 1/16	95⅝	85	81	105⅛	102⅞	101⅞	99¾		
1883	19 9/16	19 3/16	101⅛	97 9/16	82	79¾	104⅝	102 7/16	103⅛	101⅜		
1884	19¾	18 15/16	100⅝	95 5/16	81¾	78¼	104⅜	101⅝	107⅛	101¾	96¼	91¾

(Contd.)

(TABLE 30.3 contd.)

1	2	3	4	5	6	7	8	9	10	11	12	13
1885	$19\frac{3}{16}$	$17\frac{31}{32}$	$98\frac{7}{16}$	$92\frac{1}{4}$	$77\frac{1}{2}$	$73\frac{1}{4}$	$103\frac{1}{16}$	$98\frac{3}{4}$	$102\frac{3}{4}$	$97\frac{1}{2}$	$91\frac{1}{2}$	$85\frac{3}{4}$
1886	18	$16\frac{1}{8}$	$97\frac{3}{4}$	$97\frac{3}{16}$	73	$66\frac{1}{4}$	$103\frac{1}{2}$	$101\frac{1}{4}$	$102\frac{1}{4}$	$99\frac{3}{4}$	$90\frac{1}{8}$	$86\frac{5}{8}$
1887	$18\frac{3}{16}$	$15\frac{5}{8}$	$99\frac{3}{16}$	$95\frac{5}{16}$	$71\frac{11}{16}$	$67\frac{7}{8}$	$102\frac{3}{4}$	$100\frac{1}{2}$	$103\frac{1}{4}$	$100\frac{1}{4}$	$92\frac{3}{4}$	$95\frac{3}{8}$
1888	$17\frac{7}{8}$	16	$100\frac{3}{16}$	$97\frac{3}{4}$	$69\frac{3}{8}$	$66\frac{1}{4}$	$102\frac{7}{8}$	$100\frac{1}{2}$	$107\frac{1}{4}$	$104\frac{5}{8}$	98	95
1889	$16\frac{15}{16}$	16	$100\frac{3}{8}$	$97\frac{1}{16}$	$69\frac{1}{8}$	$66\frac{3}{8}$			$109\frac{1}{2}$	$106\frac{7}{8}$	$101\frac{1}{8}$	99
1890	$20\frac{29}{32}$	$16\frac{7}{8}$	$103\frac{7}{8}$	$96\frac{13}{16}$	$87\frac{1}{4}$	$68\frac{3}{4}$			$108\frac{1}{2}$	$105\frac{1}{4}$	$100\frac{3}{4}$	$95\frac{1}{4}$
1891	$18\frac{1}{4}$	$16\frac{5}{8}$	$107\frac{13}{16}$	$104\frac{1}{16}$	$80\frac{3}{4}$	$74\frac{1}{4}$			$109\frac{1}{2}$	105	99	$94\frac{1}{2}$
1892	$16\frac{11}{16}$	$14\frac{5}{8}$	$108\frac{15}{16}$	$103\frac{11}{16}$	$74\frac{1}{2}$	62			$109\frac{1}{2}$	$106\frac{1}{8}$	$98\frac{1}{2}$	$94\frac{7}{8}$

* Appendix II to the *Report of the Indian Currency Committee* of 1893, p. 272. These prices differ slightly from those given in Appendix IV to the First Report of the Gold and Silver Commission, 1886, and also from those in the statistics of British India (First Issue) for 1906–07, Part IV, (a) Finance Tables 7 and 8 of the division called Prices.

Government by way of temporary advances was a resource of inestimable value to them. When, however, the cash balances of the Central Government began to diminish owing to the continued losses by exchange, these facilities were severely curtailed,[j] so that the very vitality of these institutions was threatened just at the moment when they needed all help to foster their growth and strengthen their foundations.

Addressing the Secretary of State, the Government of India, in a despatch of 2 February 1886, observed:[k]

10. We do not hesitate to repeat that the facts set forth in the preceding paragraphs are, from the point of Indian interests, intolerable; and the evils which we have enumerated do not exhaust the catalogue. Uncertainty regarding the future of silver discourages the investment of capital in India, and we find it impossible to borrow in silver except at an excessive cost.

On the other hand, the Frontier and Famine Railways which we propose to construct, and the Coast and Frontier defences which we have planned, are imperatively required and cannot be postponed indefinitely.

We are forced, therefore, either to increase our sterling liabilities, to which course there are so many objections, or to do without the railway required for the commercial development of the country, and its protection against invasion and the effects of famine.

11. Nor can the difficulties which local bodies experience in borrowing in India be overlooked. The Municipalities of Bombay and Calcutta require large sums for sanitary improvements, but the high rate of interest which they must pay for silver loans operates to deter them from undertaking expensive works, and we need hardly remind your Lordship that it has quite recently been found necessary for Government to undertake to lend the money required for the construction of docks at Calcutta and Bombay, and that when the Port Commissioners of Calcutta attempted to raise a loan of 75 lakhs of rupees in September, 1885, guaranteed by the Government of India, the total amount of tenders was only Rs 40,200, and no portion of this insignificant amount was offered at par...'

The importation of capital on private account was hampered for similar reasons, to the great detriment of the country. It was urged on all hands, and was even recommended by a Royal Commission,[l] that one avenue of escape from the ravages of recurring famines,

[j] Cf. *Financial Statement*, 1876–7, p. 94.

[k] Sec C. 4868 of 1886, p. 8.

[l] Cf. *The Report of the Famine Commission of* 1880, Part II, C. 2735 of 1880, pp. 175–6.

to which India so pitifully succumbed at such frequent intervals, was the diversification of her industries. To be of any permanent benefit, such diversified industrial life could be based on a capitalistic basis alone. But that depended upon the flow of capital into the country as freely as the needs of the country required. As matters then stood, the English investor, the largest purveyor of capital, looked upon the investment of capital in India as a risky proposition. It was feared that once the capital was spread out in a silver country every fall in the price of silver would not only make the return uncertain when drawn in gold, but would also reduce the capital value of his investment in terms of gold, which was naturally the unit in which he measured all his returns and his outlays. The check to the free inflow of capital was undoubtedly the most serious evil arising out of the rupture of the par of exchange.

Another group of people, who suffered from the fall of exchange because of their obligation to make gold payments, was composed of the European members of the Civil Service in India. Like the Government to which they belonged, they received their salaries in silver, but had to make gold remittances in support of their families, who were often left behind in England. Before 1873, when the price of silver in terms of gold was fixed, this circumstance was of no moment to them. But as the rupee began to fall the face of the situation was completely altered. With every fall in the value of silver they had to pay more rupees out of their fixed salaries to obtain the same amount of gold. Some relief was no doubt given to them in the matter of their remittances. The Civil Servants were permitted, at a sacrifice to the Government, to make their remittances at what was called the Official Rate of Exchange.[m] It is true

[m] As was explained by Mr Waterfield before the Select Committee on East India (Civil Servants). H.C. Return 327 of 1890, Q. 1905-17, it was first instituted in 1824 and was arrived at as follows: In December of each year a calculation was made at the India Office of the cost of sending a rupee to India, based on the market price of silver in London, and of the cost of bringing a rupee from India, based on the price of bills on London in Calcutta. A mean between the two was struck and taken as the adjusting rate for the coming official year between the India Office and the British Treasury in regard to such transactions or payments undertaken by one Government as the agent of the other. It was fixed anew for each and formed a fair average rate, although it was sometimes above and sometimes below the market rate of exchange.

the difference between the market rate and the official rate was not very considerable. Nonetheless, it was appreciable enough for the Civil Servants to have gained by 2½ per cent on the average of the years 1862–90[n] at the cost of the Government. The Military Servants obtained a similar relief to a greater degree, but in a different way. Their salary was fixed in sterling, though payable in rupees. It is true the Royal Warrant which fixed their salary also fixed the rate of exchange between the sterling and the rupee for that purpose. But as it invariably happened that the rate of exchange fixed by the Warrant was higher than the market rate, the Military Servants were compensated to the extent of the difference at the cost of the Indian Exchequer.[o] This relief was, comparatively speaking, no relief to them. The official or the warrant rates of exchange, though better than the market rates of exchange, were much lower than the rate at which they were used to make their remittances before 1873. Their burden, like that of the Government, grew with the fall of siver, and as their burden increased their attitude became alarmist. Many were the memorialists who demanded from the Government adequate compensation for their losses on exchange.[p] The Government was warned[q] that

'the ignorant folk who think India would be benefited by lowering present salaries are seemingly unable to comprehend that such a step would render existence on this reduced pay simply impossible, and that recourse would of necessity be had to other methods of raising money.'

Such, no doubt, was the case in the earlier days of the East India Company, when the Civil Servants fattened on pickings because their pay was small,[r] and it was to put a stop to their extortions

[n] Ibid., Q. 1925–6.

[o] Cf. FS 1887–8, pp. 39–40. This cost was as follows:

| 1847–75 | Rs 6,40,000 | 1885–6 | Rs 4,00,000 |
| 1884–5 | Rs 18,43,000 | 1886–7 | Rs 5,15,000 |

[p] Cf. *Report of the Indian Currency Committee*, 1893, App. I, pp. 185–90 and p. 202, for memorials of the European Civil Servants.

[q] Cf. Col. Hughes-Hallett, M. P., *The Depreciation of the Rupee: its Effect on the Anglo-Indian Official—the Wrong and the Remedy*, London, 1887, p. 14.

[r] The connection between the rapacious conduct of the early European Civil Servants and the smallness of their salaries was well brought out by Clive in his speech dated 30 March 1772, during the course of the debate in the House of Commons on the East India Judicature Bill, *Hansard*, Vol. XVII, pp. 334–9.

that their salaries were raised to what appears an extraordinary level. That such former instances of extortions should have been held out as monitions showed too well how discontented the Civil Service was owing to its losses through exchange.

Quite a different effect the fall had on the trade and industry of the country. It was in a flourishing state as compared with the affairs of the Government or with the trade and industry of a gold-standard country like England. Throughout the period of falling silver there was said to be a progressive decline relatively to population in the employment afforded by various trades and industries in England. The textile manufactures and the iron and coal trade were depressed as well as the other important trades, including the hardware manufactures of Birmingham and Sheffield, the sugar-refining of Greenock, Liverpool, and London, the manufactures of earthenware, glass, leather, paper, and a multitude of minor industries.[s] The depression in English agriculture was so widespread that the Commissioners of 1892 were 'unable to point to any part of the country in which [the effects of the depression] can be said to be entirely absent,' and this notwithstanding the fact that the seasons since 1882 'were on the whole satisfactory from an agricultural point of view.'[t] Just the reverse was the case with Indian trade and industry. The foreign trade of the country, which had bounced up during the American Civil War, showed greater buoyancy after 1870, and continued to grow throughout the period of the falling exchange at a rapid pace. During the short space of twenty years the total imports and exports of the country more than doubled in their magnitude, as is shown by Table 30.4

Not only had the trade of India been increasing, but the nature of her industries was also at the same time undergoing a profound change. Prior to 1870, India and England were, so to say, non-competing groups. Owing to the protectionist policy of the Navigation Laws, and owing also to the substitution of man by machinery in the field of production, India had become exclusively an agricultural and a raw-material-producing country,

[s] Report by Dunraven, Farrer, Muntz, and Lubbock in the *Final Report of the Royal Commission on Depression of Trade and Industry, par.*, 54, C. 4893.

[t] *Final Report of the Royal Commission on Agricultural Depression in England*, C. 8540 of 1897, par. 28.

TABLE 30.4: Imports and Exports (Both Merchandize and Treasure)

Year	Exports R.	Imports	Year	Exports R.	Imports
1870–1	57,556,951	39,913,942	1881–2	83,068,198	60,436,155
1871–2	64,685,376	43,665,663	1882–3	84,527,182	65,548,868
1872–3	56,548,842	36,431,210	1883–4	89,186,397	68,157,311
1873–4	56,910,081	39,612,362	1884–5	85,225,922	69,591,269
1874–5	57,984,549	44,363,160	1885–6	84,989,502	71,133,666
1875–6	60,291,731	44,192,378	1886–7	90,190,633	72,830,670
1876–7	65,043,789	48,876,751	1887–8	92,148,279	78,830,468
1877–8	67,433,324	58,819,644	1888–9	98,833,879	83,285,427
1878–9	64,919,741	44,857,343	1889–90	105,366,720	86,656,990
1879–80	69,247,511	52,821,398	1890–1	102,350,526	93,909,856
1880–1	76,021,043	62,104,984	1891–2	111,460,278	84,155,045

From Appendix II (nos 1 and 2) to the *Report of the Indian Currency Committee of 1898.*

while England had transformed herself into a country which devoted all her energy and her resources to the manufacturing of raw materials imported from abroad into finished goods. How marked was the contrast in the industrial pursuits in the two countries is well revealed by the analysis of their respective exports in Table 30.5.

After 1870, the distribution of their industrial pursuits was greatly altered, and India once again began to assume the role of a manufacturing country. Analysing the figures for Indian imports and exports for the twenty years succeeding 1870, (see Table 30.6) we find that the progress in the direction of manufactures formed one of the most significant features of the period.

This change in the industrial evolution was marked by the growth of two principal manufactures. One of them was the manufacture of cotton. The cotton industry was one of the oldest industries of India, but during 100 years between 1750 and 1850 it had fallen into a complete state of decrepitude. Attempts were made to resuscitate the industry on a capitalistic basis in the sixties of the ninetenth century and soon showed signs of rapid advance. The story of its progress is graphically illustrated in the following summary in Table 30.7

TABLE 30.5: Nature of Industrial Pursuits in England and India*

	Distribution of Indian exports exclusive of treasure					Distribution of English exports exclusive of treasure				
	Manufactured articles	Raw materials	Food articles	Unclassified articles	Total	Manufactured articles	Raw materials	Food articles	Unclassified articles	Total
1	2	3	4	5	6	7	8	9	10	
1857	11	34	22	23	100	90.9	4	4.9	.2	100
1858	6	35	26	33	100	91.4	3.4	5.1	.1	100
1859	6.5	40	15.5	38	100	91.5	3.8	4.6	.1	100
1860	5.7	43.6	17.7	33	100	91.9	3.6	4.4	.3	100
1861	5.8	46.5	15.3	32.4	100	90.4	4.8	4.8	–	100
1862	5	52	16	27	100	90.3	4	4.8	.9	100
1863	3.7	58.7	10.6	27	100	91.0	4	4	1.0	100
1864	4	69.2	9.3	17.5	100	92.5	3.7	3.7	.1	100
1865	3.5	68	12	16.6	100	92.1	3.6	3.6	.7	100
1866	4.2	67.2	10.3	18.3	100	92	3.7	3.7	.4	100
1867	4	58	11	27	100	92.2	3.8	3.7	.3	100
1868	4	58.5	11.5	26	100	92	4.4	3.4	.2	100
1869	4.8	60.5	14	20.7	100	92	4.2	3.1	.7	100

(Contd.)

(TABLE 30.5 contd.)

1	2	3	4	5	6	7	8	9	10	
1870	4.4	63.6	9	23	100	91	4	4	1.0	100
1871	3.7	65.3	11	20	100	90	4.4	4.9	.7	100
1872	3.3	61.4	13.5	21.8	100	91.2	5.4	3.5	.9	100

* The figures for India are calculated from the *Statistical Abstract for British India*, Second Number (1857–66), Table No. 34, and the Eighth Number (1864–73), Table No. 24. Figures for England are taken from Appendix C (Statement 6) to the *First Report of the Royal Commission of the Depression of Trade and Industry*, 1885, with this alteration—that the separate figures in the original under 'Manufactured' and 'Partially Manufactured' are here grouped under 'Manufactured.' The 'Unclassified Articles' under Indian Exports are for the most part 'Jewellery.'

TABLE 30.6: Changes in Industrial Pursuits of India

Year	Imports		Exports	
	Manufactured	Raw	Manufactured	Raw
	Rs	Rs	Rs	Rs
1879	25,98,65,827	13,75,55,837	5,27,80,340	59,67,27,991
1892	36,22,31,872	26,38,18,431	16,42,47,566	85,52,09,499
Percentage of increase	39	91	211	43
Total Annual	2.8	6.5	15	3

*From Ranade's Essays on Indian Economics, p. 104.

TABLE 30.7: The Development of Indian Cotton Trade and Industry

	Growth of trade (average annual quantities in each quinquennium)				
	1870–1 to 1874–5	1875–6 to 1879–80	1880–1 to 1884–5	1885–6 to 1889–90	1890–1 to 1894–5
Imports of raw cotton— thousands or cwts.	23	52	51	74	89
Exports of raw cotton— thousands cwts.	5236	3988	5477	5330	4660
Imports of twist and yarn	33.55	33.55	44.34	49.09	44.79
	Growth of industry (at end of each fifth year)				
Number of mills	48	58	81	114	143
Number of spindles— 000—omitted	1000	1471	2037	2935	3712
Number of looms— 000—omitted	10	13	16	22	34
Number of persons employed	–	39,537	61,836	99,224	–

Another industry which figured largely in this expansion of
Indian manufactures was jute. Unlike the cotton industry of India,
the jute industry was of a comparatively recent origin. Its growth,
different from that of the cotton industry was fostered by the
application of European capital, European management, and

European skill, and it soon took as deep roots as the cotton industry and flourished as well as the latter did, if not better. Its history was one of continued progress as will be seen from Table 30.8

TABLE 30.8: Development of Jute Industry and Trade

Growth	Average Annual of each Quinquennium				
	1870–1 to 1874–5	1875–6 to 1879–80	1880–1 to 1884–5	1885–6 to 1889–90	1890–1 to 1894–5
Exports					
Raw, million cwt.	5.72	5.58	7.81	9.31	10.54
Gunny bags, millions	6.44	35.96	60.32	79.98	120.74
Cloth, million yds.	–	4.71	6.44	19.79	54.20
Growth of industry					
Number of					
Mills	–	21	21	24	26
Looms, 000 omitted	–	5.5	5.5	7	8.3
Spindls, 000 omitted	–	88	88	138.4	172.4
Persons employed in thousand	–	38.8	38.8	52.7	64.3

This increasing trend towards manufactures was not without its indirect effects on the course of Indian agriculture. Prior to 1870 the Indian farmer, it may be said, had no commercial outlook. He cultivated not so much for profit as for individual self-sufficiency. After 1870 farming tended to become a business and crops came more and more to be determined by the course of market prices than by the household needs of the farmer. This is well illustrated by figures in Table 30.9

Table 30.9: Growth of Agricultural Exports of India

	1868–9	1873–4	1877–8	1882–3	1887–8	1891–2
Wheat	100	637.41	2,313.47	5,152.36	4,914.37	11,001.44
Opium	100	118.38	123.83	122.47	120.20	116.82
Seeds	100	111.26	305.87	239.97	403.60	480.99
Rice	100	131.66	119.84	203.28	185.55	220.36
Indigo	100	116.91	121.57	142.17	140.76	126.33
Tea	100	169.35	293.17	507.25	775.09	1,075.75
Coffee	100	86.04	69.98	85.31	64.59	74.11

Such was the contrast in the economic conditions prevalent in the two countries. This peculiar phenomenon of a silver standard country steadily progressing, and a gold-standard country tending to a standstill, exercised the minds of many of its observers. The chief cause was said to be the inability of the English manufacturers to hold out in international competition. This inability to compete with the European rivals was attributed to the prevalence of protective tariffs and subsidies which formed an essential part of the industrial and commercial code of the European countries. Nothing of the kind then existed in India, where trade was as free and industry as unprotected as any could have been, and yet the Lancashire cotton-spinner, the Dundee jute manufacturer and the English wheat-grower complained that they could not compete with their rivals in India. The cause, in this case, was supposed to be the falling exchange.[u] So much were some people impressed by this view that even the extension of the Indian trade to the Far East was attributed to this cause. Already, it was alleged, the dislocation of the par of exchange between gold and silver had produced a kind of segregation of gold-using countries and silver-using countries to the exclusion of each other. In a transaction between two countries using the same metal as standard it was said the element of uncertainty arising from the use of two metals varying in terms of each other was eliminated. Trade between two such countries could be carried on with less risk and less inconvenience than between two countries using different standards, as in the latter case the uncertainty entered into every transaction and added to the expense of the machinery by which trade was carried on. That the Indian trade should have been deflected to other quarters[v] where, owing to the existence of a common standard the situation trade had to deal with was immune from uncertainties, was readily admitted. But it was contended that there was no reason why, as a part of the segregation of commerce, it should have been possible for the Indian manufacturer to oust his English rival from the Eastern markets to the extent he was able to do (see Table 30.10, p. 441).

[u] Cf. *The Final Report of the Royal Commission on Gold and Silver* Part I, pars. 99–101, for a summary of the argument.

[v] The distribution of Indian trade during this period was as shown on page 441.

TABLE 30.10: Exports of Cotton Goods to Eastern Markets

Year	Yarn, lbs., '000 omitted		Piece-goods, yds., '000 omitted	
	from India	from UK	from India	from UK
1877	7927	33,086	15,544	394,489
1878	15,600	36,467	17,545	382,330
1879	21,332	38,951	22,517	523,921
1880	25,862	46,426	25,800	509,099
1881	26,901	47,479	30,424	587,177
1882	30,786	34,370	29,911	454,948
1883	45,378	33,499	41,534	415,956
1884	49,877	38,856	55,565	439,937
1885	65,897	33,061	47,909	562,339
1886	78,242	26,924	51,578	490,451
1887	91,804	35,354	53,406	618,146
1888	113,451	44,643	69,486	652,404
1889	128,907	35,720	70,265	557,004
1890	141,950	37,869	59,496	633,606
1891	169,253	27,971	67,666	595,258

Distribution of Indian Trade
Annual Average for each Quinquennium in Millions of Rupees

Countries	1875–6 to 1879–80			1880–1 to 1884–5		
	Imports	Exports	Total	Imports	Exports	Total
United Kingdom	323.68	278.15	601.83	434.45	344.22	778.67
China	14.05	132.27	146.32	19.23	134.94	154.17
Japan	.02	.33	.35	.19	2.09	2.28
Ceylon	5.74	22.97	28.71	5.35	16.37	21.72
Straits Settlement	10.83	26.11	36.94	15.88	33.65	49.53

Annual Average for each Quinquennium in Millions of Rupees

Countries	1885–6 to 1889–90			1890–1 to 1894–5		
	Imports	Exports	Total	Imports	Exports	Total
United Kingdom	510.47	360.59	871.06	526.24	338.40	864.64
China	21.64	134.54	156.18	28.69	133.30	161.90
Japan	.25	7.27	7.52	1.51	14.44	15.95
Ceylon	5.86	20.56	26.42	6.42	31.18	37.60
Straits Settlement	20.09	42.54	62.63	23.32	52.56	75.88

The causes which effected such trade disturbances formed the subject of a heated controversy.[w] The point in dispute was whether the changes in international trade, such as they were, were attributable to the monetary disturbances of the time. Those who held to the affirmative explained their position by arguing that the falling exchange gave a bounty to the Indian producer and imposed a penalty on the English producer. The existence of this bounty, which was said to be responsible for the shifting of the position of established competitors in the field of international commerce, was based on a simple calculation. It was said that if the gold value of silver fell the Indian exporter got more rupees for his produce and was therefore better off, while by reason of the same fact the English producer got fewer sovereigns and was therefore worse off. Put in this naive form, the argument that the falling exchange gave a bounty to the Indian exporters and imposed a penalty on the English exporters had all the finality of a rule of arithmetic. Indeed, so axiomatic was the formula regarded by its authors that some important inferences as to its bearing on the trade and industrial situation of the time were drawn from it. One such inference was that it stimulated exports from and hindered imports into the silver-using countries. The second inference was that the fall of exchange exposed some English producers more than others to competition from their rivals in silver-using countries. Now, can such results be said to follow from the fall of exchange? If we go behind the bald statement of a fall of exchange and inquire as to what determined the gold price of silver the above inferences appear quite untenable. That the ratio between gold and silver was simply the inverse of the ratio between gold prices and silver prices must be taken to be an unquestionable proposition. If therefore the gold price of silver was falling.it was a counterpart of the more general phenomenon of the fall of the English prices which were measured in gold, and the rise of the Indian prices which were measured in silver. Given such an interpretation of the event of the falling exchange, it is difficult to understand how it can help to increase exports and diminish imports. International trade is governed by the relative advantages

[w] See the evidence and memoranda by Professors Marshall and Nicholson before the Royal Commission on Gold and Silver (1886); also Professor Lexis, 'The Agio on Gold and International Trade' in the *Economic Journal*, Vol. V, 1895.

which one country has over another, and the terms on which it is carried on are regulated by the comparative cost of articles that enter into it. It is, therefore, obvious that there cannot be a change in the real terms of trade between countries except as a result of changes in the comparative cost of these goods. Given a fall in gold prices *all round*, accompanied by a rise in silver prices *all round*, there was hardly anything in the monetary disturbance that could be said to have enabled India to increase her exportation of anything except by diminishing her exportation or increasing her importation of something else. From the same view of the question of the falling exchange it follows that such a monetary disturbance could not depress one trade more than another. If the falling or rising exchange was simply an expression of the level of *general* prices, then the producers of all articles were equally affected. There was no reason why the cotton trade or the wheat trade should have been more affected by the fall of exchange than the cutlery trade.

Not only was there nothing in the exchange disturbance to disestablish existing trade relations in general or in respect of particular commodities, but there was nothing in it to cause benefit to the Indian producer and injury to the English producer. Given the fact that the exchange was a ratio of the two price-levels, it is difficult to see in what sense the English producer, who got fewer sovereigns but of high purchasing power, was worse off than the Indian producer, who got more rupees but of low purchasing power. The analogy of Professor Marshall was very apt. To suppose that a fall of exchange resulted in a loss to the former and a gain to the latter was to suppose that, if a man was in the cabin of a ship only ten feet high, his head would be broken if the ship sank down twelve feet into a trough. The fallacy consisted in isolating the man from the ship when, as a matter of fact, the same force, acting upon the ship and the passenger at one and the same time, produced like movements in both. In like manner, the same force acted upon the Indian producer and the English producer together, for the change in the exchange was itself a part of the more sweeping change in the general price-levels of the two countries. Thus stated, the position of the English and Indian producer was equally good or equally bad, and the only difference was that the former used fewer counters and the latter a larger number in their respective dealings.

444 • THE ESSENTIAL WRITINGS OF B. R. AMBEDKAR

A bounty to the Indian producer and a penalty to the English producer, it is obvious, could have arisen only if the fall of silver in England in terms of gold was greater than the fall of silver in terms of commodities in India. In that case the Indian producer would have obtained a clear benefit by exchanging his wares for silver in England and thus securing a medium which had a greater command over goods and services in India. But *a priori* there could be no justification for such an assumption. There was no reason why gold price of silver should have fallen at a different rate from the gold price of commodities in general, or that there should have been a great difference between the silver prices in England and in India. Statistics show that such *a priori* assumptions were not groundless. (See Table 30.11).

It is obvious that if silver was falling faster than commodities, and if silver prices in India were lower than silver prices in England, we should have found it evidenced by an inflow of silver from England to India. What were the facts? Not only was there no extraordinary flow of silver to India, but the imports of silver during 1871–93 were much smaller than in the twenty years previous to that period.[x] This is as complete a demonstration as could be had of the fact that the silver prices in India were the same as they were outside, and consequently the Indian producer had very little chance of bounty on his trade.

Although such must be said to be the *a priori* view of the question, the Indian producer was convinced that his prosperity was due to the bounty he received. Holding such a position he was naturally opposed to any reform of the Indian currency, for the falling exchange which the Government regarded a curse he considered a boon. But however plausible was the view of the Indian producer, much sympathy would not have been felt for it had it not been coupled with a notion, most commonly held, that the bounty arose from the *export trade*, so that it became an article of popular faith that the fall of exchange was a source of gain to the *nation as a whole*. Now was it true that the bounty arose from the export trade? If it were so, then every fall of exchange ought to give a bounty. But supposing that the depreciation of

[x] It will, however, be noted how closely the flow of silver into India between 1872 and 1893 followed the fall in gold price of silver. See, BAWS, Vol. 6, pp. 335–77.

TABLE 30.11: Movements of Prices, Wages and Silver between India and England*

Net imports of silver into India		Index no. for gold price of silver	Years	Index no. for silver prices of commodities in India	Index no. for wages in India	Index no. for gold prices of commodities in England	Index no. for wages in England
Years	Amount Rs						
(1)	(2)	(3)	(4)	(5)	(6)	(7)	(8)
1871–2	6,587,296	99.7	1871	100	–	100	100
1872–3	739,244	99.2	1872	105	–	109	105.8
1873–4	2,530,824	97.4	1873	107	100	111	112
1874–5	4,674,791	95.8	1874	116	101	102	113
1875–6	1,640,445	93.3	1875	103	97	96	111.6
1876–7	7,286,188	86.4	1876	107	98	95	110
1877–8	14,732,194	90.2	1877	138	97	94	109.8
1878–9	4,057,377	86.4	1878	148	99	87	107
1879–80	7,976,063	84.2	1879	135	100	83	105.8
1880–1	3,923,612	85.9	1880	117	99	88	106.5
1881–2	5,381,410	85.0	1881	106	99	85	106.5
1882–3	7,541,427	84.9	1882	105	100	84	106.5
1883–4	6,433,886	83.1	1883	106	102	82	108

(Contd.)

(TABLE 30.11 contd.)

(1)	(2)	(3)	(4)	(5)	(6)	(7)	(8)
1884–5	7,319,581	83.3	1884	114	101	76	109
1885–6	11,627,028	79.9	1885	113	106	72	108
1886–7	7,191,743	74.6	1886	110	105	69	107
1887–8	9,319,421	73.3	1887	111	114	68	108
1888–9	9,327,529	70.4	1888	119	112	70	109.8
1889–90	11,002,078	70.2	1889	125	112	72	113
1890–1	14,211,408	78.4	1890	125	113	72	118
1891–2	9,165,684	74.3	1891	128	118	72	118
1892–3	12,893,499	65.5	1892	141	110	68	117.4
1893–4	13,759,273.	58.5	1893	138	119	68	117.4

* Col. (2) is from Appendix II, Table No. 2 of the I.C.C. of 1898. Cols (3), (5), (6), and (7) are from Atkinson's 'Silver Prices in India', in the *Journal of the Statistical Society*, March, 1897. Col. (8) is based on the figures given by W. T. Layton in his *Introduction to the Study of Prices* (1912), Table I, Col. 1, p. 150, re-scaled to 1871 as 100.

silver had taken place in India *before* it had taken place in Europe could the fall of exchange thus brought about have given a bounty to the Indian exporter? As was explained above, the Indian exporter stood a chance of getting a bounty only if with the silver he obtained for his produce he was able to buy more goods and services in India. To put the same in simpler language, his bounty was the difference between the price of his product and the price of his outlay. Bearing this in mind, we can confidently assert that in the supposed case of depreciation of silver having taken place in India first, such a fall in the Indian exchange would have been accompanied by a penalty instead of a bounty on his trade. In that case, the exporter from India would have found that though the Indian exchange, i.e. the gold price of silver, had fallen, yet the ratio which gold prices in England bore to silver prices in India had fallen more, i.e. the price he received for his product was smaller than the outlay he had incurred. It is not quite established whether silver had fallen in Europe before it had fallen in India.[y] But even if that were so the possibility of a penalty through the fall of exchange proves that the bounty, it there was any, was not a bounty on the export trade as such, but was an outcome of the disharmony between the general level of prices and the prices of particular goods and services within the country, and *would have existed* even if the country had no export *trade*.

Thus the bounty was but an incident of the general depreciation of the currency. Its existence was felt because prices of *all* goods and services in India did not move in the same uniform manner. It is well known that at any one time prices of certain commodities will be rising, while the general price level is falling. On the other hand, certain goods will decline in price at the same time that the general price-level is rising. But such opposite movements are rare. What most often happens is that prices of some goods and services, though they move in the same direction, do not move at the same pace as the general price level. It is notorious that when general prices fall wages and other fixed incomes, which form the largest item in the total outlay of every employer, do not fall in the same proportion; and when general prices rise they do not rise as fast as general prices, but generally lag behind. And this was just what was happening in a silver-standard country like India and a gold-standard country like England during the period of 1873–93 (see Chart 30.1). Prices had fallen in England, but wages had not fallen to the same extent. Prices had risen in India, but wages had not risen to the same extent. The English manufacturer was penalized, if at all, not by any act on the part of his Indian rival, but by reason of the wages of the former's employees having remained the same, although the price of his products had fallen. The Indian producer got a bounty, if any, not because he had an English rival to feed upon, but because he did not have to pay higher wages, although the price of his product had risen.

The conclusion, therefore, is that the falling exchange could not have disturbed established trade relations or displaced the commodities that entered into international trade. The utmost that could be attributed to it is its incidence in economic incentive. But insofar as it supplied a motive force or took away the incentive, it did so by bringing about changes in the social distribution of wealth. In the case of England, where prices were falling, it was the employer who suffered; in the case of India, where prices were rising, it was the wage-earner who suffered. In both cases there was an injustice done to a part of the community and an easy case for the reform of currency was made out. The need for a currency reform was recognized in England; but in India many people seemed averse to it. To some the stability of the silver standard had made a powerful appeal, for they failed to find any evidence of Indian prices having risen above the level of 1873. To others the bounty of the falling exchange was too great a boon to be easily given away by stabilizing the exchange. The falsity of both the views is patent. Prices in India did rise and that, too, considerably. Bounty perhaps there was, but it was a penalty on the wage-earner. Thus viewed, the need for the reform of Indian currency was far more urgent than could have been said of the English currency. From a purely psychological point of view there is probably much to choose between rising prices and falling prices. But from the point of view of their incidence on the distribution of wealth, very little can be said in favour of a standard which changes in its value and which becomes the *via media* of transferring wealth from the relatively poor to the relatively rich. Scrope said: 'Without stability of value money is a fraud.' Surely, having regard to the magnitude of the interests affected, depreciated money must be regarded as a greater fraud. That being

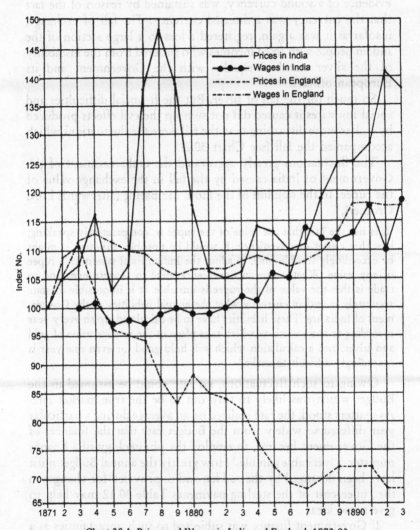

Chart 30.1: Prices and Wages in India and England, 1873-93

so, the prosperity of Indian trade and industry, far from being evidence of a sound currency, was sustained by reason of the fact that the currency was a diseased currency. The fall of exchange, insofar as it was a gain, registered a loss to a large section of the Indian people with fixed incomes who suffered from the instability of the silver standard equally with the Government and its European officers.

So much for the fall of silver. But the financial difficulties and social injustices it caused did not sum up the evil effects produced by it. Far more disturbing than the fall were the fluctuations which accompanied the fall (see Chart 30.2).

The fluctuations greatly aggravated the embarrassment of the Government of India caused by the fall in the exchange value of the rupee. In the opinion of the Hon. Mr Baring (afterwards Lord Cromer),[z]

'It is not the fact that the value of the rupee is, comparatively speaking, low that causes inconvenience. It would be possible, although it might be exceedingly troublesome, to adjust the Indian fiscal system to a rupee of any value. What causes inconvenience alike to Government and to trade is that the value of the rupee is unstable. It is impossible to state accurately in Indian currency what the annual liabilities of the Government of India are. These liabilities have to be calculated afresh every year according to the variations which take place in the relative value of gold and silver, and a calculation which will hold good for even one year is exceedingly difficult to make.'

Owing to such fluctuations, no rate could be assumed in the Budget which was likely to turn out to be the true market rate. As matters stood, the rate realized on an average during a particular year differed so widely from the Budget rate that the finances of the Government became, to employ the phraseology of a finance minister, a 'veritable gamble.' How greatly the annual Budget must have been deranged by the sudden and unprovided for changes in the rupee cost of the sterling payments Table 30.12 may help to give some idea.

If Government finance was subjected to such uncertainties as a result of exchange fluctuations, private trade also became more or less a matter of speculation. Fluctuations in exchange are, of course, a common incident of international trade. But if they are not to produce discontinuity in trade and industry there must be definite

[z] *Financial Statement*, 1883–4, p. 26.

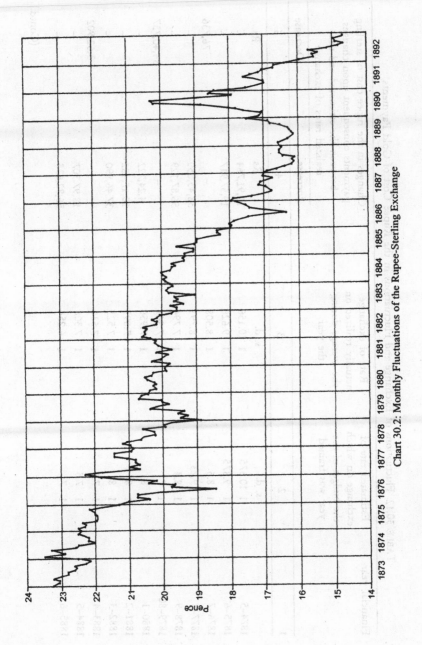

Chart 30.2: Monthly Fluctuations of the Rupee-Sterling Exchange

TABLE 30.12: Fluctuations of Exchange and Fluctuations in the Rupee Cost of Gold Payments*

Financial year	Estimated rate of exchange on which the budget of the year was framed	Rate of exchange actually realized on the average during the year	Changes in the rupee cost of sterling payments consequent upon changes between the estimated and the realized rates of exchange	
			Increase	Decrease
1	2	3	4	5
	s. d.	s. d.	Rs	Rs
1874-5	1 10.375	1 10.156	15,91,764	–
1875-6	1 9.875	1 9.626	19,57,917	–
1876-7	1 8.5	1 8.508	–	76,736
1877-8	1 9.23	1 8.791	38,43,050	–
1878-9	1 8.4	1 7.794	56,87,129	–
1879-80	1 7	1 7.961	–	84,40,737
1880-1	1 8	1 7.956	4,24,722	–
1881-2	1 8	1 7.895	10,17,482	–
1882-3	1 8	1 7.525	37,46,890	–
1883-4	1 7.5	1 7.536	–	3,62,902
1884-5	1 7.5	1 7.308	18,97,307	–
1885-6	1 7	1 6.254	56,82,638	–

(Contd.)

(TABLE 30.12 contd.)

1	2	3	4	5
1886-7	1 6	1 5.441	65,17,721	–
1887-8	1 5.5	1 4.898	71,90,097	–
1888-9	1 4.9	1 4.379	77,98,400	–
1889-90	1 4.38	1 4.566	–	27,31,892
1890-1	1 4.552	1 6.09	–	2,35,51,744
1891-2	1 5.25	1 4.733	80,09,366	–

* Compiled from figures given in the *Final Report of the Gold and Silver Commission*, p. 40, and in App. II, p. 270, to the *Report of the Indian Currency Committee, 1893*.

454 • THE ESSENTIAL WRITINGS OF B. R. AMBEDKAR

limits to such fluctuations. If the limits are ascertainable, trade would be reasonably certain in its calculation, and speculation in exchange would be limited within the known limits of deviations from an established par. Where, on the other hand, the limits are unknown, all calculations of trade are frustrated and speculation in exchange takes the place of legitimate trading. Now, it is obvious that fluctuations in the exchange between two countries will be limited in extent if the two countries have the same standard of value. Where there is no such common standard of value the limits, though they exist, are too indefinite to be of much practical use. The rupture of the fixed par of exchange, having destroyed a common standard of value between gold and silver countries, removed the limits on the exchange fluctuations between such countries. As a result of such variations in the value of the standard measure, trade advanced by 'rushes and pauses' and speculation became feverishly active.[aa]

. That progress of trade depends on stability is a truism which seldom comes home until it is denied in fact. It is difficult to appreciate its importance to healthy enterprise when government is stable, credit is secure, and conditions are uniform. And yet so great is the handicap of instability that everywhere businessmen have been led by a variety of devices to produce stability in domains enveloped by uncertainty. Everywhere there have grown up business barometers forewarning businessmen of impending changes and so enabling them to forearm against them by timely changes in their operations. The whole of insurance business is aimed at giving stability to economic life. The necessity which compelled all regularly established Governments to maintain standard measures by which the true proportion between things as to their quantities might be ascertained and dealings in them regulated with certainty was motivated by the same purpose. The meticulous precision with which every civilized country defines its standard measures, and the large machinery it maintains to preserve them from deviation, are only evidences of the great importance that an economic society must continue to attach to the matter of providing precision of expression and assurance of fulfillment with regard to the contracts entered into by its members in their individual or corporate capacities.

[aa] Evid. Indian Currency Committee, 1898, Q. 6290, 9808-10.

Important as are the standard measures of a community, its measures of a community, its measure of value is by far the most important of them all.[ab] The measures of weight, extension, or volume enter only into particular transactions. If the pound, the bushel, or the yard were altered the evils would be comparatively restricted in scope. But the measure of value is all pervading.

There is no contract,' Peel declared,[ac] 'public or private, no engagement national or individual, which is unaffected by it. The enterprises of commerce, the profits of trade, the arrangements made in all domestic relations of society, the wages, of labour, pecuniary transactions of the highest amount and of the lowest, the payment of national debt, the provision for national expenditure, the command which the coin of the smallest denomination has over the necessaries of life, are all affected...

by changes in the measure of value. This is because every contract, though ultimately a contract in goods, is primarily a contract in value. It is, therefore, not enough to maintain constancy in the measures of weight, capacity, or volume. A contract as one of goods may remain exact to the measure stipulated, but may nevertheless be vitiated as a contract in values by reason of changes in the measure of values. The necessity of preserving stability in its measure of value falls on the shoulders of every Government of an orderly society. But its importance grows beyond disputes as society advances from status to contract. The conservation of the contractual basis of society then becomes tantamount to the conservation of an invariable measure of value.

The work of reconstituting a common measure of value in some form or other, which those misguided legislators of the seventies helped to destroy, it was found, could not be long delayed with impunity. The consequences that followed in the wake of that legislation, as recounted before, were too severe to allow the situation to remain unrectified. That efforts for reconstruction should have been launched before much mischief was done only shows that a world linked by ties of trade will insist, if it can, that its currency systems must be laid on a common gauge.

[ab] Cf. Harris, *An Essay upon Money and Coins* (reprinted by J. R. McCulloch in his volume of *Scarce Tracts on Money*, Part I, Chap. II, para. 21; Part II, Chap. II, paras 11, 13, and 20).

[ac] Cf. his speech dated 6 May 1844, delivered during the Commons debates on the Bank Charter Act., *Hansard*, vol. XXXIV, p. 720.

X

Nationalism

Till 1940, Ambedkar wrote little on nationalism. The Lahore Resolution of the Muslim League, calling for a separate Pakistan, provided an occasion for an intervention. His book, *Thoughts on Pakistan*, published in 1940, which was subsequently published under the title *Pakistan or Partition of India*, became an instant bestseller. There is a strong volitional thrust in Ambedkar's understanding of nationalism and he remained deeply suspicious of it, particularly with the experience of the inter-war period.

Is There a Case for Pakistan? ('A Nation Calling For A Home')[259] Here Ambedkar develops the argument, which is not uncommon in the literature of nationalism, that the feeling of oneness, together with the existence of common territory, constitute the basis of nationalism. However, he emphasized that ascriptive and unreflected social bonds, however widespread they might be, may not succeed in preventing the tide of nationalism.

The title is supplied by the editor. The original title of the chapter is in brackets.

31

Is There a Case for Pakistan?

A NATION CALLING FOR A HOME

That there are factors, administrative, linguistic or cultural, which are the predisposing causes behind these demands for separation, is a fact which is admitted and understood by all. Nobody minds these demands and many are prepared to concede them. But, the Hindus say that the Muslims are going beyond the idea of separation and questions, such as what has led them to take this course, why are they asking for partition, for the annulment of the common tie by a legal divorce between Pakistan and Hindustan, are being raised.

The answer is to be found in the declaration made by the Muslim League in its Resolution that the Muslims of India are a separate nation. It is this declaration by the Muslim League, which is both resented and ridiculed by the Hindus.

The Hindu resentment is quite natural. Whether India is a nation or not, has been the subject-matter of controversy between the Anglo-Indians and the Hindu politicians ever since the Indian National Congress was founded. The Anglo-Indians were never tired of proclaiming that India was not a nation, that 'Indians' was only another name for the people of India. In the words of one Anglo-Indian 'to know India was to forget that there is such a thing as India.' The Hindu politicians and patriots have been, on the other hand, equally persistent in their assertion that India is a nation. That the Anglo-Indians were right in their repudiation cannot be gainsaid. Even Tagore, the national poet of Bengal, agrees with them. But, the Hindus have never yielded on the point even to Dr Tagore.

This was because of two reasons. Firstly, the Hindu felt ashamed to admit that India was not a nation. In a world where nationality and nationalism were deemed to be special virtues in a people, it was quite natural for the Hindus to feel, to use the language of Mr H. G. Wells, that it would be as improper for India to be without a nationality as it would be for a man to be without his clothes in a crowded assembly. Secondly, he had realized that nationality had a most intimate connection with the claim for self-government. He knew that by the end of the nineteenth century, it had become an accepted principle that the people, who constituted a nation were entitled on that account to self-government and that any patriot, who asked for self-government for his people, had to prove that they were a nation. The Hindu for these reasons never stopped to examine whether India was or was not a nation in fact. He never cared to reason whether nationality was merely a question *of calling* a people a nation or was a question of the people *being* a nation. He knew one thing, namely, that if he was to succeed in his demand for self-government for India, he must maintain, even if he could not prove it, that India was a nation.

In this assertion, he was never contradicted by any Indian. The thesis was so agreeable that even serious Indian students of history came forward to write propagandist literature in support of it, no doubt out of patriotic motives. The Hindu social reformers, who knew that this was a dangerous delusion, could not openly contradict this thesis. For, anyone who questioned it was at once called a tool of the British bureaucracy and enemy of the country. The Hindu politician was able to propagate his view for a long time. His opponent, the Anglo-Indian, had ceased to reply to him. His propaganda had almost succeeded. When it was about to succeed comes this declaration of the Muslim League—this rift in the lute. Just because it does not come from the Anglo-Indian, it is a deadlier blow. It destroys the work which the Hindu politician has done for years. If the Muslims in India are a separate nation, then, of course, India is not a nation. This assertion cuts the whole ground from under the feet of the Hindu politicians. It is natural that they should feel annoyed at it and call it a stab in the back.

But, stab or no stab, the point is, can the Musalmans be said to constitute a nation? Everything else is beside the point. This raises the question: What is a nation? Tomes have been written on the subject. Those who are curious may go through them and study the different basic conceptions as well as the different aspects of it. It is, however, enough to know the core of the subject and that can be set down in a few words. Nationality is a social feeling. It is a feeling of a corporate sentiment of oneness which makes those who are charged with it feel that they are kith and kin. This national feeling is a double edged feeling. It is at once a feeling of fellowship for one's own kith and kin and an anti-fellowship feeling for those who are not one's own kith and kin. It is a feeling of 'consciousness of kind' which on the one hand binds together those who have it, so strongly that it overrides all differences arising out of economic conflicts or social gradations and, on the other, severs them from those who are not of their kind. It is a longing not to belong to any other group. This is the essence of what is called a nationality and national feeling.

Now apply this test to the Muslim claim. Is it or is it not a fact that the Muslims of India are an exclusive group? Is it or is it not a fact that they have a consciousness of kind? Is it or is not a fact that every Muslim is possessed by a longing to belong to his own group and not to any non-Muslim group?

If the answer to these questions is in the affirmative, then the controversy must end and the Muslim claim that they are a nation must be accepted without cavil.

What the Hindus must show is that notwithstanding some differences, there are enough affinities between Hindus and Musalmans to constitute them into one nation, or, to use plain language, which make Muslims and Hindus long to belong together.

Hindus, who disagree with the Muslim view that the Muslims are a separate nation by themselves, rely upon certain features of Indian social life which seem to form the bonds of integration between Muslim society and Hindu society.

In the first place, it is said that there is no difference of race between the Hindus, and the Muslims. That the Punjabi Musalman and the Punjabi Hindu, the UP Musalman and the UP Hindu, the Bihar Musalman and the Bihar Hindu, the Bengal Musalman and the Bengal Hindu, the Madras Musalman and the Madras Hindu, and the Bombay Musalman and the Bombay Hindu are racially of one stock. Indeed there is more racial affinity between the Madras Musalman and the Madras Brahmin than there is between the Madras Brahmin and the Punjab Brahmin. In the second place, reliance is placed upon linguistic unity between Hindus and Muslims. It is said that the Musalmans have no common language of their own which can mark them off as a linguistic group separate from the Hindus. On the contrary, there is a complete linguistic unity between the two. In the Punjab, both Hindu and Muslims speak Punjabi. In Sind, both speak Sindhi. In Bengal, both speak Bengali. In Gujarat, both speak Gujarati. In Maharashtra, both speak Marathi. So in every province. It is only in towns that the Musalmans speak Urdu and the Hindus the language of the province. But outside, in the mofussil, there is complete linguistic unity between Hindus and Musalmans. Thirdly, it is pointed out that India is the land which the Hindus and Musalmans have now inhabited together for centuries. It is not exclusively the land of the Hindus, nor is it exclusively the land of the Mahomedans.

Reliance is placed not only upon racial unity but also upon certain common features in the social and cultural life of the two communities. It is pointed out that the social life of many Muslim groups is honeycombed with Hindu customs. For instance, the *Avans* of the Punjab, though they are nearly all Muslims, retain Hindu names and keep their genealogies in the Brahmanic fashion. Hindu surnames are found among Muslims. For instance, the surname Chaudhari is a Hindu surname but is common among the Musalmans of UP and Northern India. In the matter of marriage, certain groups of Muslims are Muslims in name only. They either follow the Hindu form of the ceremony alone, or perform the ceremony first by the Hindu rites and then call the Kazi and have it performed in the Muslim form. In some sections of Muslims, the law applied is the Hindu Law in the matter of marriage, guardianship and inheritance. Before the Shariat Act was passed, this was true even in the Punjab and the NWFP. In the social sphere the caste system is alleged to be as much a part of Muslim society as it is of Hindu society. In the religious sphere, it is pointed out that many Muslim *pirs* had Hindu disciples; and similarly some Hindu *yogis* have had Muslim *chelas*. Reliance is placed on instances of friendship between saints of the rival creeds. At Girot, in the Punjab, the tombs of two ascetics, Jamali

Sultan and Diyal Bhawan, who lived in close amity during the early part of the nineteenth century, stand close to one another, and are reverenced by Hindus and Musalmans alike. Bawa Fathu, a Muslim saint, who lived about AD 1700 and whose tomb is at Ranital in the Kangra District, received the title of prophet by the blessing of a Hindu saint, Sodhi Guru Gulab Singh. On the other hand, Baba Shahana, a Hindu saint whose cult is observed in the Jang District, is said to have been the *chela* of a Muslim *pir* who changed the original name (Mihra), of his Hindu follower, into Mir Shah.

All this, no doubt, is true. That a large majority of the Muslims belong to the same race as the Hindus is beyond question. That all Mahomedans do not speak a common tongue, that many speak the same language as the Hindus cannot be denied. That there are certain social customs which are common to both cannot be gainsaid. That certain religious rites and practices are common to both is also a matter of fact. But the question is: can all this support the conclusion that the Hindus and the Mahomedans on account of them constitute one nation or these things have fostered in them a feeling that they long to belong to each other?

There are many flaws in the Hindu argument. In the first place, what are pointed out as common features are not the result of a conscious attempt to adopt and adapt to each other's ways and manners to bring about social fusion. On the other hand, this uniformity is the result of certain purely mechanical causes. They are partly due to incomplete conversions. In a land like India, where the majority of the Muslim population has been recruited from caste and out-caste Hindus, the Muslimization of the convert was neither complete nor effectual, either from fear of revolt or because of the method of persuasion or insufficiency of preaching due to insufficiency of priests. There is, therefore, little wonder if great sections of the Muslim community here and there reveal their Hindu origin in their religious and social life. Partly it is to be explained as the effect of common environment to which both Hindus and Muslims have been subjected for centuries. A common environment is bound to produce common reactions, and reacting constantly in the same way to the same environment is bound to produce a common type. Partly are these common features to be explained as the remnants of a period of religious amalgamation between the Hindus and the Muslims inaugurated by the

Emperor Akbar, the result of a dead past which has no present and no future.

As to the argument based on unity of race, unity of language and inhabiting a common country, the matter stands on a different footing. If these considerations were decisive in making or unmaking a nation, the Hindus would be right in saying that by reason of race, community of language and habitat the Hindus and Musalmans form one nation. As a matter of historical experience, neither race, nor language, nor country has sufficed to mould a people into a nation. The argument is so well put by Renan that it is impossible to improve upon his language. Long ago in his famous essay on Nationality, Renan observed:

that race must not be confounded with nation. The truth is that there is no pure race; and that making politics depend upon ethnographical analysis, is allowing it to be borne upon a chimera... Racial facts, important as they are in the beginning, have a constant tendency to lose their importance. Human history is essentially different from zoology. Race is not everything, as it is in the sense of rodents and felines.[260]

Speaking about language, Renan points out that:

Language invites re-union; it does not force it. The United States and England, Spanish America and Spain speak the same languages and do not form single nations. On the contrary, Switzerland which owes her stability to the fact that she was founded by the assent of her several parts counts three or four languages. In man there is something superior to language,—will. The will of Switzerland to be united, in spite of the variety of her languages, is a much more important fact than a similarity of language, often obtained by persecution.[261]

As to common country, Renan argued that:

It is no more the land than the race that makes a nation. The land provides a *substratum*, the field of battle and work; man provides the soul; man is everything in the formation of that sacred thing which is called a people. Nothing of material nature suffices for it.[262]

Having shown that race, language, and country do not suffice to create a nation, Renan raises in a pointed manner the question, what more, then is necessary to constitute a nation? His answer may be given in his own words:

A nation is a living soul, a spiritual principle. Two things, which in truth are but one, constitute this soul, this spiritual principle. One is in the past, the other in the present. One is the common possession of a rich heritage of memories; the other is the actual consent, the desire to live together, the will to preserve worthily the undivided inheritance which has been handed down. Man does not improvise. The nation, like the individual, is the outcome of a long past of efforts, and sacrifices, and devotion. Ancestor-worship is therefore, all the more legitimate; for our ancestors have made us what we are. A heroic past, great men, glory,—I mean glory of the genuine kind,—these form the social capital, upon which a national idea may be founded. To have common glories in the past, a common will in the present; to have done great things together, to will to do the like again,—such are the essential conditions for the making of a people. We love in proportion to the sacrifices we have consented to make, to the sufferings we have endured. We love the house that we have built, and will hand down to our descendant. The Spartan hymn, 'We are what you were; we shall be what you are,' is in its simplicity the national anthem of every land.

In the past an inheritance of glory and regrets to be shared, in the future a like ideal to be realised; to have suffered, and rejoiced, and hoped together; all these things are worth more than custom houses in common, and frontiers in accordance with strategical ideas; all these can be understood in spite of diversities of race and language. I said just now 'to have suffered together' for indeed, suffering in common is a greater bond of union than joy. As regards national memories, mournings are worth more than triumphs; for they impose duties, they demand common effort.[263]

Are there any common historical antecedents which the Hindus and Muslims can be said to share together as matters of pride or as matters of sorrow? That is the crux of the question. That is the question which the Hindus must answer, if they wish to maintain that Hindus and Musalmans together form a nation. So far as this aspect of their relationship is concerned, they have been just two armed battalions warring against each other. There was no common cycle of participation for a common achievement. Their past is a past of mutual destruction—a past of mutual animosities, both in the political as well as in the religious fields. As Bhai Parmanand points out in his pamphlet called 'The Hindu National Movement':

In history the Hindus revere the memory of Prithvi Raj, Partap, Shivaji and, Beragi Bir, who fought for the honour and freedom of this land (against the Muslims), while the Mahomedans look upon the invaders of India, like Muhammad Bin Qasim and rulers like Aurangzeb as their national heroes.

In the religious field, the Hindus draw their inspiration from the *Ramayan*, the *Mahabharat*, and the *Gita*. The Musalmans, on the other hand, derive their inspiration from the *Quran* and the *Hadis*. Thus, the things that divide are far more vital than the things which unite. In depending upon certain common features of Hindu and Mahomedan social life, in relying upon common language, common race and common country, the Hindu is mistaking what is accidental and superficial for what is essential and fundamental. The political and religious antagonisms divide the Hindus and the Musalmans far more deeply than the so-called common things are able to bind them together. The prospects might perhaps be different if the past of the two communities can be forgotten by both, Renan points out the importance of forgetfulness as a factor in building up a nation:

Forgetfulness, and I shall even say historical error, form an essential factor in the creation of a nation; and thus it is that the progress of historical studies may often be dangerous to the nationality. Historical research, in fact, brings back to light the deeds of violence that have taken place at the commencement of all political formations, even of those the consequences of which have been most beneficial. Unity is ever achieved by brutality. The union of Northern and Southern France was the results of an extermination, and of a reign of terror that lasted for nearly a hundred years. The king of France who was, if I may say so, the ideal type of a secular crystalliser, the king of France who made the most perfect national unity in existence, lost his prestige when seen at too close a distance. The nation that he had formed cursed him; and today the knowledge of what he was worth, and what he did, belongs only to the cultured.

It is by contrast that these great laws of the history of Western Europe become apparent. In the undertaking which the king of France, in part by his justice, achieved so admirably, many countries came to disaster. Under the crown of St. Stephen, Magyars and Slavs have remained as distinct as they were eight hundred years ago. Far from combining the different elements in its dominions, the house of Hapsburg has held them apart and often opposed to one another. In Bohemia, the Czech element and the German element are superimposed like oil and water in a glass. The Turkish policy of separation of nationalities according to religion has had much graver results. It has brought about the ruin of the East. Take a town like Smyrna or Salonica; you will find there five or six communities each with its own memories, and possessing among them scarcely anything in common. But the essence of the nation is, that all its individual members should have things in common; and also, that all of them should hold many things in oblivion. No French citizen knows whether he is a Burgundian, an Alan, or a Visigoth; every French citizen ought to have forgotten St Bartholomew, and the massacres of the South in the thirteenth century. There are not ten families in France able to furnish proof of a French origin; and yet, even if such a proof were given it would be essentially defective, in consequence of a thousand unknown crosses, capable of deranging all genealogical systems.[264]

The pity of it is that the two communities can never forget or obliterate their past. Their past is embedded in their religion, and for each to give up its past is to give up its religion. To hope for this is to hope in vain.

In the absence of common historical antecedents, the Hindu view that Hindus and Musalmans form one nation falls to the ground. To maintain it is to keep up a hallucinatioin. There is no such longing between the Hindus and Musalmans to belong together as there is among the Musalmans of India.

It is no use saying that this claim of the Musalmans being a nation is an after-thought of their leaders. As an accusation it is true. The Muslims were hitherto quite content to call themselves a community. It is only recently that they have begun to style themselves a nation. But an accusation, attacking the motives of a person, does not amount to a refutation of his thesis. To say that because the Muslims once called themselves a community, they are, therefore, now debarred from calling themselves a nation is to misunderstand the mysterious working of the psychology of national feeling. Such an argument presupposes that wherever there exist a people, who possess the elements that go to the making up of a nation, there *must* be manifested that sentiment of nationality which is their natural consequence and that if they fail to manifest it for sometime, then that failure is to be used as evidence showing the unreality of the claim of being a nation, if made afterwards. There is no historical support for such a contention. As Professor Toynbee points out:

It is impossible to argue a form *priory* the presence one or even several of these factors to the existence of a nationality; they may have been there for ages and kindled no response and it is impossible to argue from one case to another; precisely the same group of factors may produce nationality here, and there have no effect.

This is probably due to the fact, as pointed out by Professor Barker, that it is possible for nations to exist and even for centuries, in unreflective silence, although there exists that spiritual essence of a national life of which many of its members are not aware. Some such thing has no doubt happened in the case of the Musalmans. They were not aware of the fact that there existed for them the spiritual essence of a national life. This explains why their claim to separate nationality was made by them so late. But, it does not mean that the spiritual essence of a national life had no existence at all.

It is no use contending that there are cases where a sense of nationality exists but there is no desire for a separate national existence. Cases of the French in Canada and of the English in South Africa, may be cited as cases in point. It must be admitted that there do exist cases, where people are aware of their nationality, but this awareness does not produce in them that passion which is called nationalism. In other words, there may be nations conscious of themselves without being charged with nationalism. On the basis of this reasoning, it may be argued that the Musalmans may hold that they are a nation but they need not on that account demand a separate national existence; why can they not be content with the position which the French occupy in Canada and the English occupy in South Africa? Such a position is quite a sound position. It must, however, be remembered that such a position can only be taken by way of pleading with the Muslims not to insist on partition. It is no argument against their claim for partition, if they insist upon it.

Lest pleading should be mistaken for refutation, it is necessary to draw attention to two things. First, there is a difference between nationality and nationalism. They are two different psychological states of the human mind. Nationality means 'consciousness of kind, awareness of the existence of that tie of kinship.' Nationalism means 'the desire for a separate national existence for those who are bound by this tie of kinship.' Secondly, it is true that there cannot be nationalism without the feeling of nationality being in existence. But, it is important to bear in mind that the converse is not always true. The feeling of nationality may be present and yet the feeling of nationalism may be quite absent. That is to say, nationality does not in all cases produce nationalism. For nationality to flame into nationalism two conditions must exist. First, there must arise the 'will to live as a nation.' Nationalism is the dynamic expression of that desire. Secondly, there must be a territory which nationalism could occupy and make it a state, as well as a cultural home of the nation. Without such a territory, nationalism, to use Lord Acton's phrase, would be a 'soul as it were wandering in search of a body in which to begin life over again and dies out finding none.' The Muslims have developed a 'will to live as a nation.' For them nature has found a territory which they can occupy and make it a state as well as a cultural home for the new-born Muslim nation. Given these favourable conditions, there should be no wonder, if the Muslims say that they are not content to occupy the position which the French choose to occupy in Canada or the English choose to occupy in South Africa, and that they shall have a national home which they can call their own.

XI

Constitutionalism and Law

Ambedkar drafted several documents which were to shape the constitutional developments in India. He remained a votary of constitutional democracy throughout. He also felt that certain core principles needed to inform not merely the institutional complex of governance but society at large.

Basic Features of the Indian Constitution[265] is taken from Ambedkar's introduction to the draft Constitution in the Constituent Assembly on 4 November 1948.

The title is the editor's.

The Hindu Code Bill was the most vehemently resisted Bill in the Parliament and eventually led Ambedkar to resign from the Nehru Cabinet. Ambedkar's emphasis in his argument on the Bill is to reform Hinduism and to create a large enough public space regulated by rule of law applicable to one and all. He is open to diversity but only under the rule of law. The orthodoxy clearly perceived a threat from the Bill, but even those who supported Ambedkar did not do it for the reasons he stressed. Some of them saw it as a way of consolidating Hinduism freeing it from its fissiparous tendencies, buttressing their viewpoint by the analogy of Sardar Patel consolidating the Indian State. Further, while Ambedkar sought integral and holistic changes in the Hindu Code, his opponents insisted on 'piece-meal' changes.

In the first excerpt here Ambedkar highlights the major provisions of the Bill.[266] However, given the kind of challenges the Bill faced, he made his defence of the Bill by underplaying its radical edge and linking it with the *Shastras*, usages, customs and simple reasonableness.

32

Basic Features of the Indian Constitution

Mr President: I think we shall now proceed with the discussion. I call upon the Honourbale Dr Ambedkar to move his motion.

The Honourable Dr B. R. Ambedkar (Bombay, General): Mr President, Sir, I introduce the Draft Constitution as settled by the Drafting Committee and move that it be taken into consideration.

The Drafting Committee was appointed by a Resolution passed by the Constituent Assembly on 29 August 1947.

The Drafting Committee was in effect charged with the duty of preparing a Constitution in accordance with the decisions of the Constituent Assembly on the reports made by the various Committees appointed by it such as the Union Powers Committee, the Union Constitution Committee, the Provincial Constitution Committee and the Advisory Committee on Fundamental Rights, Minorities, Tribal Areas, etc. The Constituent Assembly had also directed that in certain matters the provisions contained in the Government of India Act, 1935, should be followed. Except on points which are referred to in my letter of the 21 February 1948 in which I have referred to the departures made and alternatives suggested by the Drafting Committee, I hope the Drafting Committee will be found to have faithfully carried out the directions given to it.

The Draft Constitution as it has emerged from the Drafting Committee is a formidable document. It contains 315 Articles and 8 Schedules. It must be admitted that the Constitution of no country could be found to be so bulky as the Draft Constitution. It would be difficult for those who have not been through it to realize its salient and special features.

The Draft Constitution has been before the public for eight months. During this long time friends, critics and adversaries have had more than sufficient time to express their reactions to the provisions contained in it. I dare say that some of them are based on misunderstanding and inadequate understanding of the Articles. But there the criticisms are and they have to be answered.

For both these reasons it is necessary that on a motion for consideration I should draw your attention to the special features of the Constitution and also meet the criticism that has been levelled against it.

Before I proceed to do so I would like to place on the table of the House Reports of three Committees appointed by the Constituent Assembly (1) Report of the Committee on Chief Commissioners Provinces (2) Report of the Expert Committee on Financial Relations between the Union and the States, and (3) Report of the Advisory Committee on Tribal Areas, which came too late to be considered by that Assembly though copies of them have been circulated to Members of the Assembly. As these reports and the recommendations made therein have been considered by the Drafting Committee it is only proper that the House should formally be placed in possession of them.

Turning to the main question. A student of Constitutional Law, if a copy of a Constitution is placed in his hands, is sure to ask two questions. Firstly, what is the form of Government that is envisaged in the Constitution; and secondly, what is the form of Constitution? For these are the two crucial matters which every Constitution has to deal with. I will begin with the first of the two questions.

In the Draft Constitution there is placed at the head of the Indian Union a functionary who is called the President of the Union. The title of this functionary reminds one of the President of the United States. But beyond identity of names there is nothing in common between the forms of Government prevalent in America and the form of Government proposed under the Draft Constitution. The American form of Government is called the Presidential system of Government. What the Draft Constitution proposes is the Parliamentary system. The two are fundamentally different.

Under the Presidential system of America, the President is the Chief head of the Executive. The administration is vested in him. Under the Draft Constitution the President occupies the same position as the King under the English Constitution. He is the head of the State but not of the Executive. He represents the Nation but does not rule the Nation. He is the symbol of the nation. His place in the administration is that of a ceremonial device on a seal by which the nation's decisions are made known. Under the American Constitution the President has under him Secretaries in charge of different Departments. In like manner the President of the Indian Union will have under him Ministers in charge of different Departments of administration. Here again there is a fundamental difference between the two. The President of the United States is not bound to accept any advice tendered to him by any of his Secretaries. The President of the Indian Union will be generally bound by the advice of his Ministers. He can do nothing contrary to their advice nor can he do anything without their advice. The President of the United States can dismiss any Secretary at any time. The President of the Indian Union has no power to do so, so long as his Ministers command a majority in Parliament.

The Presidential system of America is based upon the separation of the Executive and the Legislature. So that the President and his Secretaries cannot be members of the Congress. The Draft Constitution does not recognise this doctrine. The Ministers under the Indian Union are members of Parliament. Only members of Parliament can become Ministers. Ministers have the same rights as other members of Parliament, namely, that they can sit in Parliament, take part in debates and vote in its proceedings. Both systems of Government are of course democratic and the choice between the two is not very easy. A democratic executive must satisfy two conditions—(1) It must be a stable executive and (2) it must be a responsible executive. Unfortunately it has not been possible so far to devise a system which can ensure both in equal degree. You can have a system which can give you more stability but less responsibility or you can have a system which gives you more responsibility but less stability. The American and the Swiss systems give more stability but less responsibility. The British system on the other hand gives you more responsibility but less stability. The reason for this is obvious. The American Executive is a non-Parliamentary Executive which means that it is not dependent for its existence upon a majority in the Congress, while the British system is a Parliamentary Executive which means that it is dependent upon a majority in Parliament. Being a non-Parliamentary Executive, the Congress of the United States cannot dismiss the Executive. A Parliamentary Government must resign the moment it loses the confidence of a majority of members of Parliament. Looking at it from the point of view of responsibility, a non-Parliamentary Executive being independent of Parliament tends to be less responsible to the Legislature, while a Parliamentary Executive being more dependent upon a majority in Parliament becomes more responsible. The Parliamentary system differs from a non-Parliamentary system inasmuch as the former is more responsible than the latter but they also differ as to the time and agency for assessment of their responsibility. Under the non-Parliamentary system, such as the one that exists in the USA, the assessment of the responsibility of the Executive is periodic. It takes place once in two years. It is done by the Electorate. In England, where the Parliamentary system prevails, the assessment of responsibility of the executive is both daily and periodic. The daily assessment is done by members of Parliament, through Questions, Resolutions, No confidence motions, Adjournment motions and Debates on Addresses. Periodic assessment is done by the Electorate at the time of the election which may take place every five years or earlier. The daily assessment of responsibility which is not available under the American system is, it is felt, far more effective than the periodic assessment and far more necessary in a country like India. The Draft Constitution in recommending the Parliamentary system of Executive has preferred more responsibility to more stability.

So far I have explained the form of Government under the Draft Constitution. I will now turn to the other question, namely, the form of the Constitution.

Two principal forms of the Constitution are known to history— one is called Unitary and other Federal. The two essential characteristics of a Unitary Constitution are: (1) the supremacy of the Central Polity and (2) the absence of subsidiary Sovereign polities. Contrarywise, a Federal Constitution is marked: (1) by the existence of a Central polity and subsidiary polities side by side, and (2) by each being sovereign in the field assigned to it. In other words, Federation means the establishment of a Dual Polity. The Draft

Constitution is Federal Constitution inasmuch as it establishes what may be called a Dual Polity. This Dual Polity under the proposed Constitution will consist of the Union at the Centre and the States at the periphery each endowed with sovereign powers to be exercised in the field assigned to them respectively by the Constitution. The dual polity resembles the American Constitution. The American polity is also a dual polity, one of it is known as the Federal Government and the other States which correspond respectively to the Union Government and the States Government of the Draft Constitution. Under the American Constitution the Federal Government is not a mere league of the States nor are the States administrative units or agencies of the Federal Government. In the same way the Indian Constitution proposed in the Draft Constitution is not a league of States nor are the States administrative units or agencies of the Union Government. Here, however, the similarities between the Indian and the American Constitution come to an end. The differences that distinguish them are more fundamental and glaring than the similarities between the two.

The points of differences between the American Federation and the Indian Federation are mainly two. In the USA this dual polity is followed by a dual citizenship. In the USA there is a citizenship of the USA. But there is also a citizenship of the State. No doubt the rigours of this double citizenship are much assuaged by the fourteenth amendment to the Constitution of the United States which prohibits the States from taking away the rights, privileges and immunities of the citizen of the United States. At the same time, as pointed out by Mr William Anderson, in certain political matters, including the right to vote and to hold public office, States may and do discriminate in favour of their own citizens. This favouritism goes even farther in many cases. Thus to obtain employment in the service of a State or local Government one is in most places required to be a local resident or citizen. Similarly in the licensing of persons for the practice of such public professions as law and medicine, residence or citizenship in the State is frequently required; and in business where public regulation must necessarily be strict, as in the sale of liquor, and of stocks and bonds, similar requirements have been upheld.

Each State has also certain rights in its own domain that it holds for the special advantage of its own citizens. Thus wild game and fish in a sense belong to the State. It is customary for the States to

charge higher hunting and fishing license fees to non-residents than
to its own citizens. The States also charge non-residents higher
tuition in State Colleges and Universities, and permit only residents
to be admitted to their hospitals and asylums except in emergencies.

In short, there are a number of rights that a State can grant to
its own citizens or residents that it may and does legally deny to
non-residents, or grant to non-residents only on more difficult
terms than those imposed on residents. These advantages, given to
the citizen in his own State, constitute the special rights of State
citizenship. Taken all together, they amount to a considerable
difference in rights between citizens and non-citizens of the States.
The transient and the temporary sojourner is everywhere under
some special handicaps.

The proposed Indian Constitution is a dual polity with a single
citizenship. There is only one citizenship for the whole of India.
It is Indian citizenship. There is no State citizenship. Every Indian
has the same rights of citizenship, no matter in what State he
resides.

The dual polity of the proposed Indian Constitution differs
from the dual polity of the USA in another respect. In the USA
the Constitutions of the Federal and State Governments are loosely
connected. In describing the relationship between the Federal and
State Governments in the USA, Bryce has said:

The Central or National Government and the State Governments may
be compared to a large building and a set of smaller buildings standing
on the same ground, yet distinct from each other.[267]

Distinct they are, but how distinct are the State Governments
in the USA from the Federal Government? Some idea of this
distinctness may be obtained from the following facts:

1. Subject to the maintenance of the republican form of Government, each State in America is free to make its own Constitution.

2. The people of a State retain for ever in their hands, altogether
independent of the National Government, the power of altering
their Constitution.[268]

To put it again in the words of Bryce:

A State (in America) exists as a commonwealth by virtue of its own
Constitution, and all State Authorities, legislative, executive and judicial
are the creatures of, and subject to the Constitution.[269]

This is not true of the proposed Indian Constitution. No States (at any rate those in Part I) has a right to frame its own Constitution. The Constitution of the Union and of the States is a single frame from which neither can get out and within which they must work.

So far I have drawn attention to the differences between the American Federation and the proposed Indian Federation. But there are some other special features of the proposed Indian Federation which mark it off not only from the American Federation but from all other Federations. All federal systems including the American are placed in a tight mould of federalism. No matter what the circumstances, it cannot change its form and shape. It can never be unitary. On the other hand the Draft Constitution can be both unitary as well as federal according to the requirements of time and circumstances. In normal times, it is framed to work as a federal system. But in times of war it is so designed as to make it work as though it was a unitary system. Once the President issues a Proclamation which he is authorized to do under the Provisions of Article 275, the whole scene can become transformed and the State becomes a unitary State. The Union under the Proclamation can claim if it wants (1) the power to legislate upon any subject even though it may be in the State list, (2) the power to give directions to the States as to how they should exercise their executive authority in matters which are within their charge, (3) the power to vest authority for any purpose in any officer, and (4) the power to suspend the financial provisions of the Constitution. Such a power of converting itself into a unitary State no federation possesses. This is one point of difference between the Federation proposed in the Draft Constitution, and all other Federations we know of.

This is not the only difference between the proposed Indian Federation and other Federations. Federalism is described as a weak if not an effective form of Government. There are two weaknesses from which Federation is alleged to suffer. One is rigidity and the other is legalism. That these faults are inherent in Federalism, there can be no dispute. A Federal Constitution cannot but be a written Constitution and a written Constitution must necessarily be a rigid Constitution. A Federal Constitution means division of Sovereignty by no less a sanction than that of the law of the Constitution between the Federal Government and the States, with.

two necessary consequences (1) that any invasion by the Federal Government in the field assigned to the States and *vice versa* is a breach of the Constitution and (2) such breach is a justiciable matter to be determined by the Judiciary only. This being the nature of federalism, a Federal Constitution cannot escape the charge of legalism. These faults of a Federal Constitution have been found in a pronounced form in the Constitution of the United States of America.

Countries which have adopted Federalism at a later date have attempted to reduce the disadvantages following from the rigidity and legalism which are inherent therein. The example of Australia may well be referred to in this matter. The Australian Constitution has adopted the following means to make its federation less rigid:

(1) By conferring upon the Parliament of the Commonwealth large powers of concurrent Legislation and few powers of exclusive Legislation.

(2) By making some of the Articles of the Constitution of a temporary duration to remain in force only 'until Parliament otherwise provides.'

It is obvious that under the Australian Constitution, the Australian Parliament can do many things, which are not within the competence of the American Congress and for doing which the American Government will have to resort to the Supreme Court and depend upon its ability, ingenuity and willingness to invent a doctrine to justify in the exercise of authority.

In assuaging the rigour of rigidity and legalism the Draft Constitution follows the Australian plan on a far more extensive scale than has been done in Australia. Like the Australian Constitution, it has a long list of subjects for concurrent powers of legislation. Under the Australian Constitution concurrent subjects are 39. Under the Draft Constitution they are 37. Following the Australian Constitution there are as many as six Articles in the Draft Constitution, where the provisions are of a temporary duration and which could be replaced by Parliament at any time by provisions suitable for the occasion. The biggest advance made by the Draft Constitution over the Australian Constitution is in the matter of exclusive powers of legislation vested in Parliament. While the exclusive authority of the Australian Parliament to legislate extends only to about 3 matters, the authority of the

Indian Parliament as proposed in the Draft Constitution will extend to 91 matters. In this way the Draft Constitution has secured the greatest possible elasticity in its federalism which is supposed to be rigid by nature.

It is not enough to say that the Draft Constitution follows the Australian Constitution or follows it on a more extensive scale. What is to be noted is that it has added new ways of overcoming the rigidity and legalism inherent in federalism which are special to it and which are not to be found elsewhere.

First is the power given to Parliament to legislate on exclusively provincial subjects in normal times. I refer to Articles 226, 227 and 229. Under Article 226 Parliament can legislate when a subject becomes a matter of national concern as distinguished from purely Provincial concern, though the subject is in the State list, provided a resolution is passed by the Upper Chamber by two-thirds majority in favour of such exercise of the power by the Centre. Article 227 gives the similar power to Parliament in a national emergency. Under Article 229 Parliament can exercise the same power if Provinces consent to such exercise. Though the last provision also exists in the Australian Constitution the first two are a special feature of the Draft Constitution.

The second means adopted to avoid rigidity and legalism is the provision for facility with which the Constitution could be amended. The provisions of the Constitution relating to the amendment of the Constitution divide the Articles of the Constitution into two groups. In the one group are placed Articles relating to (a) the distribution of legislative powers between the Centre and the States, (b) the representation of the States in Parliament, and (c) the powers of the Courts. All other Articles are placed in another group. Articles placed in the second group cover a very large part of the Constitution and can be amended by Parliament by a double majority, namely, a majority of not less than two-thirds of the members of each House present and voting and by a majority of the total membership of each House. The amendment of these Articles does not require ratification by the States. It is only in those Articles which are placed in group one that an additional safeguard of ratification by the States is introduced.

One can therefore safely say that the Indian Federation will not suffer from the faults of rigidity or legalism. Its distinguishing feature is that it is a flexible federation.

There is another special feature of the proposed Indian Federation which distinguishes it from federations. A Federation being a dual polity based on divided authority with separate legislative, executive and judicial powers for each of the two polities is bound to produce diversity in laws, in administration and in judicial protection. Upto a certain point this diversity does not matter. It may be welcomed as being an attempt to accommodate the powers of Government to local needs and local circumstances. But this very diversity when it goes beyond a certain point is capable of producing chaos and has produced chaos in many Federal States. One has only to imagine twenty different laws— if we have twenty States in the Union—of marriage, of divorce, of inheritance of property, family relations, contracts, torts, crimes, weights and measures, of bills and cheques, banking and commerce, of procedures for obtaining justice and in the standards and methods of administration. Such a state of affairs not only weakens the State but becomes intolerant to the citizen who moves from State to State only to find that what is lawful in one State is not lawful in another. The Draft Constitution has sought to forge means and methods whereby India will have Federation and at the same time will have uniformity in all the basic matters which are essential to maintain the unity of the country. The means adopted by the Draft Constitution are three

(1) a single judiciary,

(2) uniformity in fundamental laws, civil and criminal, and

(3) a common All-India Civil Service to man important posts.

A dual judiciary, a duality of legal codes and a duality of civil services, as I said, are the logical consequences of a dual polity which is inherent in a federation. In the USA the Federal Judiciary and the State Judiciary are separate and independent of each other. The Indian Federation though a Dual Polity has no Dual Judiciary at all. The High Courts and the Supreme Court form one single integrated Judiciary having jurisdiction and providing remedies in all cases arising under the constitutional law, the civil law or the criminal law. This is done to eliminate all diversity in all remedial procedure. Canada is the only country which furnishes a close parallel. The Australian system is only an approximation.

Care is taken to eliminate all diversity from laws which are at the basis of civic and corporate life. The great Codes of Civil & Criminal Laws, such as the Civil Procedure Code, Penal Code, the Criminal Procedure Code, the Evidence Act, Transfer of Property Act, Laws of Marriage, Divorce, and Inheritance, are either placed in the Concurrent List so that the necessary uniformity can always be preserved without impairing the federal system.

The dual polity which is inherent in a Federal system as I said is followed in all Federations by a dual service. In all Federations there is a Federal Civil Service and a State Civil Service. The Indian Federation though a Dual Polity will have a Dual Service but with one exception. It is recognized that in every country there are certain posts in its administrative set-up which might be called strategic from the point of view of maintaining the standard of administration. It may not be easy to spot such posts in a large and complicated machinery of administration. But there can be no doubt that the standard of administration depends upon the calibre of the Civil Servants who are appointed to these strategic posts. Fortunately for us we have inherited from the past system of administration which is common to the whole of the country and we know what are these strategic posts. The Constitution provides that without depriving the States of their right to form their own Civil Services there shall be an All India Service recruited on an All-India basis with common qualifications, with uniform scale of pay and the members of which alone could be appointed to these strategic posts throughout the Union.

Such are the special features of proposed Federation. I will now turn to what the critics have had to say about it.

It is said that there is nothing new in the Draft Constitution, that about half of it has been copied from the Government of India Act of 1935 and that the rest of it has been borrowed from the Constitutions of other countries. Very little of it can claim originality.

One likes to ask whether there can be anything new in a Constitution framed at this hour in the history of the world. More than hundred years have rolled over when the first written Constitution was drafted. It has been followed by many countries reducing their Constitutions to writing. What the scope of Constitution should be has long been settled. Similarly what are the fundamentals of a Constitution are recognized all over the world.

Given these facts all Constitutions in their main provisions must look similar. The only new things, if there can be any, in a Constitution framed so late in the day are the variations made to remove the faults and to accommodate it to the needs of the country. The charge of producing a blind copy of the Constitutions of other countries is based, I am sure, on an inadequate study of the Constitution. I have shown what is new in the Draft Constitution and I am sure that those who have studied other Constitutions and who are prepared to consider the matter dispassionately will agree that the Drafting Committee in performing its duty has not been guilty of such blind and slavish imitation as it is represented to be.

As to the accusation that the Draft Constitution has produced a good part of the provisions of the Government of India Act, 1935, I make no apologies. There is nothing to be ashamed of in borrowing. It involves no plagiarism. Nobody holds any patent rights in the fundamental ideas of a Constitution. What I am sorry about is that the provisions taken from the Government of India Act, 1935, relate mostly to the details of administration. I agree that administrative details should have no place in the Constitution. I wish very much that the Drafting Committee could see its way to avoid their inclusion in the Constitution. But this is to be said on the necessity which justifies their inclusion. Grote, the historian of Greece, has said that:

The diffusion of constitutional morality, not merely among the majority of any community but throughout the whole, is the indispensable condition of government at once free and peaceable; since even any powerful and obstinate minority may render the working of a free institution impracticable, without being strong enough to conquer ascendancy for themselves.

By constitutional morality Grote means

A paramount reverence for the forms of the Constitution, enforcing obedience to authority acting under and within these forms yet combined with the habit of open speech, of action subject only to definite legal control, and unrestrained censure of those very authorities as to all their public acts combined too with a perfect confidence in the bosom of every citizen amidst the bitterness of party contest that the forms of the Constitution will not be less sacred in the eyes of his opponents than in his own. (*Hear, hear*).

While everybody recognizes the necessity of the diffusion of the Constitutional morality for the peaceful working of a democratic Constitution, there are two things interconnected with it which are not, unfortunately, generally recognized. One is that the form of administration has a close connection with the form of the Constitution. The form of the administration must be appropriate to and in the same sense as the form of the Constitution. The other is that it is perfectly possible to prevent the Constitution, without changing its form by merely changing the form of the administration and to make it inconsistent and opposed to the spirit of the Constitution. It follows that it is only where people are saturated with Constitutional morality such as the one described by Grote, the historian that one can take the risk of omitting from the Constitution details of administration and leaving it for the Legislature to prescribe them. The question is, can we presume such a diffusion of Constitutional morality? Constitutional morality is not a natural sentiment. It has to be cultivated. We must realize that our people have yet to learn it. Democracy in India is only a top-dressing on an Indian soil, which is essentially undemocratic.

In these circumstances it is wiser not to trust the Legislature to prescribe forms of administration. This is the justification for incorporating them in the Constitution.

Another criticism against the Draft Constitution is that no part of it represents the ancient polity of India. It is said that the new Constitution should have been drafted on the ancient Hindu model of a State and that instead of incorporating Western theories the new Constitution should have been raised and built upon village Panchayats and District Panchayats. There are others who have taken a more extreme view. They do not want any Central or Provincial Governments. They just want India to contain so many village Governments. The love of the intellectual Indians for the village community is of course infinite if not pathetic (*laughter*). It is largely due to the fulsome praise bestowed upon it by Metcalfe who described them as little republics having nearly everything that they want within themselves, and almost independent of any foreign relations. The existence of these village communities each one forming a separate little State in itself has according to Metcalfe contributed more than any other cause to the preservation of the people of India, through all the revolutions and changes which they have suffered, and is in a high degree conducive to their happiness and to the enjoyment of a great portion of the freedom and independence. No doubt the village communities have lasted where nothing else lasts. But those who take pride in the village communities do not care to consider what little part they have played in the affairs and the destiny of the country; and why? Their part in the destiny of the country has been well described by Metcalfe himself who says:

Dynasty after dynasty tumbles down. Revolution succeeds to revolution. Hindoo, Pathan, Mogul, Maharatha, Sikh, English, are all masters in turn but the village communities remain the same. In times of trouble they arm and fortify themselves. A hostile army passes through the country. The village communities collect their little cattle within their walls and let the enemy pass unprovoked.

Such is the part the village communities have played in the history of their county. Knowing this, what pride can one feel in them? That they have survived through all vicissitudes may be a fact. But mere survival has no value. The question is on what plane they have survived. Surely on a low, on a selfish level. I hold that these villages republics have been the ruination of India. I am therefore surprised that those who condemn Provincialism and communalism should come forward as champions of the village. What is the village but a sink of localism, a den of ignorance, narrow-mindedness and communalism? I am glad that the Draft Constitution has discarded the village and adopted the individual as its unit.

The Draft Constitution is also criticized because of the safeguards it provides for minorities. In this, the Drafting Committee has no responsibility. It follows the decisions of the Constituent Assembly. Speaking for myself, I have no doubt that the Constituent Assembly has done wisely in providing such safeguards for minorities as it has done. In this country both the minorities and majorities have followed a wrong path. It is wrong for the majority to deny the existence of minorities. It is equally wrong for the minorities to perpetuate themselves. A solution must be found which will serve a double purpose. It must recognize the existence of the minorities to start with. It must also be such that it will enable majorities and minorities to merge some day into one. The solution proposed by the Constituent Assembly is to be welcomed because it is a solution which serves this two-fold purpose. To diehards who have developed a kind of fanaticism against minority protection I would like to say two things. One is that minorities are an explosive force which, if it erupts, can blow up the whole fabric of the State. The history of Europe bears ample and appalling testimony to this fact. The other is that the minorities in India have agreed to place their existence in the hands of the majority. In the history of negotiations for preventing the partition of Ireland, Redmond said to Carson 'ask for any safeguard you like for the Protestant minority but let us have a United Ireland.' Carson's reply was 'Damn your safeguards, we don't want to be ruled by you.' No minority in India has taken this stand. They have loyally accepted the rule of the majority which is basically a communal majority and not a political majority. It is for the majority to realize its duty not to discriminate against minorities. Whether the minorities will continue or will vanish must depend upon this habit of the majority. The moment the majority loses the habit of discriminating against the minority, the minorities can have no ground to exist. They will vanish.

The most criticized part of the Draft Constitution is that which relates to Fundamental Rights. It is said that Article 13 which defines fundamental rights is riddled with so many exceptions that the exceptions have eaten up the rights altogether. It is condemned as a kind of deception. In the opinion of the critics Fundamental Rights are not Fundamental Rights unless they are also absolute rights. The critics rely on the Constitution of the United States and the Bill of Rights embodied in the first ten Amendments to that Constitution in support of their contention. It is said that the Fundamental Rights in the American Bill of Rights are real because they are not subjected to limitations or exceptions.

I am sorry to say that the whole of the criticism about fundamental rights is based upon a misconception. In the first place, the criticism in so far as it seeks to distinguish fundamental rights from non-fundamental rights is not sound. It is incorrect to say that fundamental rights are absolute while non-fundamental rights are not absolute. The real distinction between the two is that non-fundamental rights are created by agreement between parties while fundamental rights are the gift of the law. Because fundamental rights are the gift of the State it does not follow that the State cannot qualify them.

In the second place, it is wrong to say that fundamental rights in America are absolute. The difference between the position under the American Constitution and the Draft Constitution is one of form and not of substance. That the fundamental rights in America are not absolute rights is beyond dispute. In support of every exception to the fundamental rights set out in the Draft Constitution one can refer to at least one judgement of the United States Supreme Court. It would be sufficient to quote one such judgement of the Supreme Court in justification of the limitation on the right of free speech contained in Article 13 of the Draft Constitution. In *Gitlow Vs. New York* in which the issue was the constitutionality of a New York 'criminal anarchy' law which purported to punish utterances calculated to bring about violent change, the Supreme Court said:

It is a fundamental principle, long established, that the freedom of speech and of the press, which is secured by the Constitution, does not confer an absolute right to speak or publish, without responsibility, whatever one may choose, or an unrestricted and unbridled license that gives immunity for every possible use of language and prevents the punishment of those who abuse this freedom.

It is therefore wrong to say that the fundamental rights in America are absolute, while those in the Draft Constitution are not.

It is agreed that if any fundamental rights require qualification, it is for the Constitution itself to qualify them as is done in the Constitution of the United States and where it does not do so, it should be left to be determined by the Judiciary upon a consideration of all the relevant considerations. All this, I am sorry to say, is a complete misrepresentation, if not a misunderstanding of the American Constitution. The American Constitution does nothing of the kind. Except in one matter namely the right of assembly, the American Constitution does not itself impose any limitations upon the fundamental rights guaranteed to the American citizens. Nor is it correct to say that the American Constitution leaves it to the Judiciary to impose limitations on fundamental rights. The right to impose limitations belongs to the Congress. The real position is different from what is assumed by the critics. In America, the fundamental rights as enacted by the Constitution were no doubt absolute. Congress, however, soon found that it was absolutely essential to qualify these fundamental rights by limitations. When the question arose as to the constitutionality of these limitations before the Supreme Courts, it was contended that the Constitution gave no power to the United States Congress to impose such limitation, the Supreme Court invented the doctrine of police power and refuted the advocates of absolute fundamental rights by the argument that every State has inherent in police power which is not required to be conferred on it expressly by the Constitution. To use the language of the Supreme Court in the case I have already referred to, it said:

That a State in the exercise of its police power may punish those who abuse this freedom by utterances inimical to the public welfare, tending to corrupt public morals, incite to crime or disturb the public peace, is not open to question...

What the Draft Constitution has done is that instead of formulating fundamental rights in absolute terms and depending upon our Supreme Court to come to the rescue of Parliament by inventing the doctrine of police power, it permits the State directly to impose limitations upon the fundamental rights. There is really no difference in the result. What one does directly the other does indirectly. In both cases, the fundamental rights are not absolute.

In the Draft Constitution the Fundamental Rights are followed by what are called 'Directive Principles'. It is a novel feature in a Constitution framed for Parliamentary Democracy. The only other constitution framed for Parliamentary Democracy which embodies such principles is that of the Irish Free State. These Directive Principles have also come up for criticism. It is said that they are only pious declarations. They have no binding force. This criticism is of course superfluous. The Constitution itself says so in so many words.

If it is said that the Directive Principles have no legal force behind them, I am prepared to admit it. But I am not prepared to admit that they have no sort of binding force at all. Nor am I prepared to concede that they are useless because they have no binding force in law.

The Directive Principles are like the Instrument of Instructions which were issued to the Governor-General and to Governors of the Colonies and to those of India by the British Government under the 1935 Act. Under the Draft Constitution it is proposed to issue such instruments to the President and to the Governors. The texts of these Instruments of Instructions will be found in

Schedule IV of the Constitution. What are called Directive Principles is merely another name for Instrument of Instructions. The only difference is that they are instructions to the Legislature and the Executive. Such a thing is to my mind to be welcomed. Wherever there is a grant of power in general terms for peace, order and good government, it is necessary that it should be accompanied by instructions regulating its exercise.

The inclusion of such instructions in a Constitution such as is proposed in the Draft becomes justifiable for another reason. The Draft Constitution as framed only provides a machinery for the government of the country. It is not a contrivance to install any particular party in power as has been done in some countries. Who should be in power is left to be determined by the people as it must be, if the system is to satisfy the tests of democracy. But whoever captures power will not be free to do what he likes with it. In the exercise of it, he will have to respect these instruments of instructions which are called Directive Principles. He cannot ignore them. He may not have to answer for their breach in a Court of Law. But he will certainly have to answer for them before the electorate at election time. What great value these directive principles possess will be realized better when the forces of right contrive to capture power.

That it has no binding force is no argument against their inclusion in the Constitution. There may be a difference of opinion as to the exact place they should be given in the Constitution. I agree that it is somewhat odd that provisions which do not carry positive obligations should be placed in the midst of provisions which do carry positive obligations. In my judgment their proper place is in Schedules III A & IV which contain Instrument of Instructions to the President and the Governors. For, as I have said they are really Instruments of Instructions to the Executive and the Legislatures as to how they should exercise their powers. But that is only a matter of arrangement.

Some critics have said that the Centre is too strong. Others have said that it must be made stronger. The Draft Constitution has struck a balance. However much you may deny powers to the Centre, it is difficult to prevent the Centre from becoming strong. Conditions in the modern world are such that centralization of powers is inevitable. One has only to consider the growth of the Federal Government in the USA which, notwithstanding the very limited powers given to it by the Constitution, has out-grown its former self and has overshadowed and eclipsed the State Governments. This is due to modern conditions. The same conditions are sure to operate on the Government of India and nothing that one can do will help to prevent it from being strong. On the other hand, we must resist the tendency to make it stronger. It cannot chew more than it can digest. Its strength must be commensurate with its weight. It would be a folly to make it so strong that it may fall by its own weight.

The Draft Constitution is criticized for having one sort of constitutional relations between the Centre and the Provinces and another sort of constitutional relations between the Centre and the Indian States. The Indian States are not bound to accept the whole list of subjects included in the Union List but only those which come under Defence, Foreign Affairs and Communications. They are not bound to accept subjects included in the Concurrent List. They are not bound to accept the State List contained in the Draft Constitution. They are free to create their own Constituent Assemblies and to frame their own constitutions. All this, of course, is very unfortunate and, I submit quite indefensible. This disparity may even prove dangerous to the efficiency of the State. So long as the disparity exists, the Centre's authority over all-India matters may lose its efficacy. For, power is no power if it cannot be exercised in all cases and in all places. In a situation such as may be created by war, such limitations on the exercise of vital powers in some areas may bring the whole life of the State in complete jeopardy. What is worse is that the Indian States under the Draft Constitution are permitted to maintain their own armies. I regard this as a most retrograde and harmful provision which may lead to the break-up of the unity of India and the overthrow of the Central Government. The Drafting Committee, if I am not misrepresenting its mind, was not at all happy over this matter. They wished very much that there was uniformity between the Provinces and the Indian States in their constitutional relationship with the Centre. Unfortunately, they could do nothing to improve matters. They were bound by the decisions of the Constituent Assembly, and the Constituent Assembly in its turn was bound by the agreement arrived at between the two negotiating Committees.

But we may take courage from what happened in Germany. The German Empire as founded by Bismarck in 1870 was a composite

State, consisting of 25 units. Of these 25 units, 22 were monarchical States and 3 were republican city States. This distinction, as we all know, disappeared in the course of time and Germany became one land with one people living under one Constitution. The process of the amalgamation of the Indian States is going to be much quicker than it has been in Germany. On 15 August 1947 we had 600 Indian States in existence. Today by the integration of the Indian States with Indian Provinces or merger among themselves or by the Centre having taken them as Centrally administered Areas there have remained some 20/30 States as viable States. This is a very rapid process and progress. I appeal to those States that remain to fall in line with the Indian Provinces and to become full units of the Indian Union on the same terms as the Indian Provinces. They will thereby give the Indian Union the strength it needs. They will save themselves the bother of starting their own Constituent Assemblies and drafting their own separate Constitution and they will lose nothing that is of value to them. I feel hopeful that my appeal will not go in vain and that before the Constitution is passed, we will be able to wipe off the differences between the Provinces and the Indian States.

Some critics have taken objection to the description of India in Article 1 of the Draft Constitution as a Union of States. It is said that the correct phraseology should be a Federation of States. It is true that South Africa which is a unitary State is described as a Union. But Canada which is a Federation is also called a Union. Thus the description of India as a Union, though its constitution is Federal, does no violence to usage. But what is important is that the use of the word Union is deliberate. I do not know why the word 'Union' was used in the Canadian Constitution. But I can tell you why the Drafting Committee has used it. The Drafting Committee wanted to make it clear that though India was to be a Federation, the Federation was not the result of an agreement by the States to join in a Federation and that the Federation not being the result of an agreement no State has the right to secede from it. The Federation is a Union because it is indestructible. Though the country and the people may be divided into different States for convenience of administration the country is one integral whole, its people a single people living under a single *imperium* derived from a single source. The Americans had to wage a civil war to establish that the States have no right of secession and that their Federation was indestructible. The Drafting Committee thought that it was better to make it clear at the outset rather than to leave it to speculation or to dispute.

The provisions relating to amendment of the Constitution have come in for a virulent attack at the hands of the critics of the Draft Constitution. It is said that provisions contained in the Draft make amendment difficult. It is proposed that the Constitution should be amendable by a simple majority at least for some years. The argument is subtle and ingenious. It is said that this Constituent Assembly is not elected on adult suffrage while the future Parliament will be elected on adult suffrage and yet the former has been given the right to pass the Constitution by a simple majority while the latter has been denied the same right. It is paraded as one of the absurdities of the Draft Constitution. I must repudiate the charge because it is without foundation. To know how simple are the provisions of the Draft Constitution in respect of amending the Constitution one has only to study the provisions for amendment contained in the American and Australian Constitutions. Compared to them, those contained in the Draft Constitution will be found to be the simplest. The Draft Constitution has eliminated the elaborate and difficult procedures such as a decision by a convention or a referendum. The Powers of amendment are left with the Legislatures, Central and Provincial. It is only for amendments of specific matters—and they are only few—that the ratification of the State legislatures is required. All other Articles of the Constitution are left to be amended by Parliament. The only limitation is that it shall be done by a majority of not less than two-thirds of the members of each House present and voting and a majority of the total membership of each House. It is difficult to conceive a simple method of amending the Constitution.

What is said to be the absurdity of the amending provisions is founded upon a misconception of the position of the Constituent Assembly and of the future Parliament elected under the Constitution. The Constituent Assembly in making a Constitution has no partisan motive. Beyond securing a good and workable Constitution it has no axe to grind. In considering the Articles of the Constitution it has no eye on getting through a particular measure. The future Parliament, if it met as a Constituent Assembly, its members, will be acting as partisans seeking to carry amendments to the Constitution to facilitate the passing of party measures which they have failed to get through Parliament by reason of some Article of the Constitution which has acted as an obstacle in their way. Parliament will have an axe to grind while the Constituent Assembly has none. That is the difference between the Constituent Assembly and the future Parliament. That explains why the Constituent Assembly though elected on limited franchise can be trusted to pass the Constitution by simple majority and why the Parliament though elected on adult suffrage cannot be trusted with the same power to amend it.

I believe I have dealt with all the adverse criticisms that have been levelled against the Draft Constitution as settled by the Drafting Committee. I don't think that I have left out any important comment or criticism that has been made during the last eight months during which the Constitution has been before the public. It is for the Constituent Assembly to decide whether they will accept the Constitution as settled by the Drafting Committee or whether they shall alter it before passing it.

But this I would like to say. The Constitution has been discussed in some of the Provincial Assemblies of India. It was discussed in Bombay, CP, West Bengal, Bihar, Madras and East Punjab. It is true that in some Provincial Assemblies serious objections were taken to the financial provisions of the Constitution and in Madras to Article 226. But excepting this, in no Provincial Assembly was any serious objection taken to the Articles of the Constitution. No Constitution is perfect and the Drafting Committee itself is suggesting certain amendments to improve the Draft Constitution. But the debates in the Provincial Assemblies give me courage to say that the Constitution as settled by the Drafting Committee is good enough to make in this country a start with. I feel that it is workable, it is flexible and it is strong enough to hold the country together both in peace time and in war time. Indeed, if I may say so, if things go wrong under the new Constitution, the reason will not be that we had a bad Constitution. What we will have to say is, that Man was vile. Sir, I move.

33

The Hindu Code Bill

MAJOR PROVISIONS OF THE BILL

Sir, this Bill, the aim of which is to codify the rules of Hindu Law which are scattered in innumerable decisions of the High Courts and of the Privy Council, which form a bewildering motley to the common man and give rise to constant litigation, seeks to codify the law relating to seven different matters. Firstly, it seeks to codify the law relating to the rights of property of a deceased Hindu who had died intestate without making a will, both female and male. Secondly, it prescribes a somewhat altered form of the order of succession among the different heirs to the property of a deceased dying intestate. The next topic it deals with is the law of maintenance, marriage, divorce, adoption, minority and guardianship. The House will see what is the ambit and the periphery of this Bill. To begin with the question of inheritance. Under this head the Bill enacts a new principle, at least for certain parts of British India. As many members who are lawyers in this House will know, so far as inheritance is concerned, the Hindus are governed by two different systems of law. One system is known as *Mitakshara* and the other is known as *Dayabhag*. The two systems have a fundamental difference. According to *Mitakshara*, the property of a Hindu is not his individual property. It is property which belongs to what is called a coparcenary, which consists of father, son, grandson and great grandson. All these people have a birth-right in that property and the property on the death of anyone member of this coparcenary passes by what is

496 THE ESSENTIAL WRITINGS OF B. R. AMBEDKAR

called survivorship to the members who remain behind, and does not pass to the heirs of the deceased. The Hindu Code contained in this Bill adopts the *Dayabhag* rule, under which the property is held by the heir as his personal property with an absolute right to dispose it of either by gift or by will or any other manner that he chooses.

That is one, fundamental change which the Bill seeks to make. In other words, it universalizes the law of inheritance by extending the *Dayabhag* rule to the territory in which the rule of the *Mitakshara* now operates.

Coming to the question of the order of succession among the heirs, there is also fundamental difference of a general character between the rule of the *Mitakshara* and the rule of the *Dayabhag*. Under the *Mitakshara* rule the agnates of a deceased are preferred to his cognates; under the *Dayabhag* rule the basis of heirship is blood relationship to the deceased and not the relationship based on cognatic or agnatic relationship. That is one change that the Bill makes; in other words, here also it adopts the rule of the *Dayabhag* in preference to the rule of the *Mitakshara*.

In addition to this general change in the order of succession to a deceased Hindu, the Bill also seeks to make four changes. One change is that the widow, the daughter, the widow of a pre-deceased son, all are given the same rank as the son in the matter of inheritance. In addition to that, the daughter also is given a share in her father's property; her share is prescribed as half of that of the son. Here again, I should like to point out that the only new change which this Bill seeks to make, so far as the female heirs are concerned is confined to daughters; the other female heirs have already been recognized by the Hindu Women's Right to Property Act of 1937. Therefore, so far as that part of the Bill is concerned, there is really no change in the Bill at all; the Bill merely carries the provisions contained in the Act to which I have made reference.

The second change which the Bill makes so far as the female heirs are concerned is that the number of female heirs recognized now is much larger than under either the *Mitakshara* or the *Dayabhag*.

The third change made by the Bill is this that under the law, whether the *Mitakshara* or the *Dayabhag*, a discrimination was made among female heirs, as to whether a particular female was rich or poor in circumstances at the death of the testator, whether she was married or unmarried, or whether she was with issue or without issue. All these consideration which led to discrimination in the female heirs are now abolished by this Bill. A woman who also has a right to inherit gets it by reason of the fact that she is declared to be an heir irrespective of any other considerations.

The last change that is made relates to the rule of inheritance in the *Dayabhag*. Under the *Dayabhag* the father succeeds before in preference to the mother; under the present Bill the position is altered so that the mother comes before the father.

So much for the order of succession of heirs to a deceased male Hindu. I now come to the provisions in the Bill which relates to intestate succession to females. As Members of the House who are familiar with Hindu Law will know, under the existing law the property held by a Hindu female falls into two categories; one is called her *stridhan*, and the other is called 'woman's property'. Taking first the question of *stridhan*, under the existing law *stridhan* falls into several categories; it is now one single category, and the order of succession to the *stridhan* of a female under the existing law varies according to the category of the *stridhan*; one category of *stridhan* has a different law of succession than another category and these rules are alike both as to *Mitakshara* as they are to the *Dayabhag*. So far as *stridhan* is concerned the present Bill makes two changes. The one change it makes is that it consolidates the different categories of *stridhan* into one single category of property and lays down a uniform rule of succession; there is no variety of heirs to the *stridhan* in accordance with the different categories of the *stridhan*—all *stridhan* is one and there is one rule of succession.

The second change which the Bill seeks to make with regard to the heirs is that the son also is now given a right to inherit the *stridhan* and he is given half the share which the daughter takes. Members will realize that in formulating this Bill and making changes in rules of succession, it is provided that while the daughter is getting half the share in the father's property, the son is also getting half the share in the mother's property so that in a certain sense the Bill seeks to maintain an equality of position between the son and the daughter.

Coming to the question of the 'woman's estate', as members of the House will know under the Hindu Law where a woman inherits property she gets only what is called a 'life estate'. She can enjoy the income of the property, but she cannot deal with the corpus of the property except for legal necessity; the property must pass after the death of the woman to the reversioners of her husband. The Bill, here again, introduces two changes. It converts this limited estate into an absolute estate just as the male when he inherits gets an absolute estate in the property that he inherits and secondly, it abolishes the right of the reversioners to claim the property after the widow.

An important provision which is ancillary to the rights of women to inherit property contained in this Bill is a provision which relates to *dowry*. All members of the House know what a scandalous affair this *dowry* is; how, for instance, girls who bring enormous lot of property from their parents either by way of *dowry* or *stridhan* or gift are treated, nonetheless, with utter contempt, tyranny and oppression. The Bill provides in my judgment one of the most salutary provisions, namely that this property which is given as *dowry* to a girl on the occasion of her marriage shall be treated as a trust property, the use of which will inure to the woman and she is entitled to claim that property when she comes to the age of 18, so that neither her husband nor the relations of her husband will have any interest in that property; nor will they have any opportunity to waste that property and make her helpless for the rest of her life.

Coming to the provisions relating to maintenance, there is mostly nothing new in this part of the Bill. The Bill prescribes that the dependents of a deceased shall be entitled to claim maintenance from those who inherit his property either under the rules of intestate succession or who inherit the property under his will. There are 11 different kinds of dependants enumerated in this Bill. I believe, at least speaking for myself, it is an unfortunate thing that even a concubine is included in the category of dependants, but there it is; it is a matter for consideration. The liability to maintenance is cast upon those who take the estate of the deceased. As I said, there is nothing very new in this part of the Bill.

There is another part of the Bill which is important and it relates to the rights of a wife to claim separate maintenance when she lives separate from her husband. Generally, under the provisions of the Hindu law, a wife is not entitled to claim maintenance from her husband if she does not live with him in his house. The Bill, however, recognizes that there are undoubtedly circumstances where if the wife has lived away from the husband, it must be for causes beyond her control and it would be wrong not to recognize the causes and not to give her separate maintenance. Consequently the Bill provides that a wife shall be entitled to claim separate maintenance from her husband if he is (1) suffering from a loathsome disease, (2) if he keeps a concubine, (3) if he is guilty of cruelty, (4) if he has abandoned her for two years, (5) if he has converted to another religion and (6) any other cause justifying her living separately.

The next topic to which I wish to make a reference concerns the question of marriage. The Code recognizes two forms of marriages. One is called 'sacramental' marriage and the other is called 'civil' marriage. As members will know, this is a departure from the existing law. The existing Hindu law recognizes only what is called 'sacramental' marriage, but it does not recognize what we call a 'civil' marriage. When one considers the conditions for a valid sacramental marriage and a valid registered marriage, under the Code there is really very little difference between the two. There are five conditions for a sacramental marriage. Firstly, the bridegroom must be 18 years old, and the bride must be 14 years old. Secondly, neither party must have a spouse living at the time of marriage. Thirdly, parties must not be within prohibited degree of relationship.[270] Fourthly, parties must not be *sapindas*[271] of each other. Fifthly, neither must be an idiot or a lunatic. Except for the fact that similarity of *sapindaship* is not a bar to a registered marriage, so far as other conditions are concerned, there is no difference between the sacramental marriage and the civil marriage. The only other difference is that the registered marriage must be registered in accordance with provisions in the Bill while a sacramental marriage may be registered if parties desire to do so. Comparing the rules of marriage contained in the Bill and the existing law, it may be noticed that there are three differences which the Bill makes. One is this, that while the existing law requires identity of caste and sub-caste for a valid sacramental marriage, the Bill dispenses with this condition. Marriage under the Bill will be valid irrespective of the caste or sub-caste of the parties entering into the marriage.

The second provision in this Bill is that identity of *gotrapravara* is not a bar to a marriage while it is under the existing law. The third distinctive feature is this, that under the old law, polygamy was permissible. Under the new law it is monogamy which is prescribed. The sacramental marriage was a marriage which was indissoluble. There could be no divorce. The present Bill makes a new departure by introducing into the law provisions for the dissolution of marriage. Any party which marries under the new code has three remedies to get out of the contract of marriage. One is to have the marriage declared null and void; secondly, to have the marriage declared invalid; and thirdly, to have it dissolved. Now, the grounds for invalidation of marriage are two: One, if one party to the marriage had a spouse living at the time of marriage, then such a marriage will be null and void. Secondly, if the relationship of the parties fell within what is called the ambit of prohibited-degrees, the marriage could be declared null and void. The grounds for invalidation of the marriage are four. First, impotency. Second, parties being *sapinda*. Third, parties being either idiotic or lunatic. Fourth, the guardian's consent obtained by force or fraud. In order not to keep the sword of dissolution hanging on the head, the Bill, in my judgment very wisely, has provided a limit to an action for invalidation. It provides that a suit for the invalidation of marriage must be filed within three years from the date of the marriage; otherwise the suit will be barred and the marriage will continue as though there was no ground for invalidity. The Bill also provides that even though the marriage may be invalidated and may be declared invalid by a court of Law, the invalidation of marriage will not affect the legitimacy of the children born and they would continue to be legitimate just the same.

Then coming to the question of divorce, there are seven grounds on which divorce could be obtained. (1) desertion, (2) conversion to another religion, (3) keeping a concubine or becoming a concubine, (4) incurably unsound mind, (5) virulent and incurable form of leprosy, (6) venereal diseases in communicable form and (7) cruelty.

Coming to the question of adoption, there again, most of the rules embodied in the Bill are in no way different from the rules obtaining under the present law. There are two new provisions in this part dealing with adoption. Firstly, under the Code, it will be necessary for the husband if he wants to make an adoption to obtain the consent of his wife and if there are more than one, at least the consent of one of them. Secondly, it also lays down that if the widow wants to adopt, she can only adopt if there are positive instructions left by the husband authorizing her to adopt and in order to prevent litigation as to whether the husband has, as a matter of fact, left instructions to his wife, the Code provides that the evidence of such instructions shall be either by registered deed or by a provision in the will. No oral evidence would be admissible, so that chances of litigation are considerably mitigated. The Code also provides that the adoption may also be evidenced by registration. One of the most fruitful sources of litigation in this country is the question of adoption. All sorts of oral evidence is manufactured, concocted; witnesses are suborned; widows are fooled; they one day declare that they have made one adoption and subsequently they make an avowal that they have not adopted and in order that all this litigation may be put a stop to, the Code makes a salutary provision that there may be registration of adoption by a Hindu.

Then there is the question of minority and guardianship, the last subject which the Bill seeks to codify. There is nothing new in this part of the Code and, therefore, I do not propose to say anything so far as that part in the Bill is concerned.

As members will realize, the points which arise out of this Bill for consideration and which are new are these: First, the abolition of birth-right and to take property by survivorship. The second point that arises for consideration is the giving of half-share to the daughter. Thirdly, the conversion of the women's limited estate into an absolute estate. Fourthly, the abolition of caste in the matter of marriage and adoption. Fifthly, the principle of monogamy and sixthly, the principle of divorce. I have sought to enumerate these points separately and categorically because I felt that in view of the limited time we have at our disposal, it would be of help to the Members of this House if I could point out what are the points of debate on which attention may be concentrated. These departures which are made in this Bill undoubtedly requires justification, but I think it would be a waste of time if I at this stage undertook any defence of the departures enacted by this Bill. I propose to hear Honourable Members as to what they have to say on the points which I have enumerated and if I find that it is necessary for me to enter upon a justification, I propose to do so in the course of my reply. Sir, I move.

IN DEFFNCE OF THE HINDU CODE BILL

The Honourable Dr B. R. Ambedkar: Sir, in the ordinary course a speech of the sort which I have made is generally regarded not only appropriate but sufficient for the occasion. But it would be futile on my part to disguise the fact that there is a section—if not a large section, a section in the house—which feels a certain amount of compunction over certain parts of the Bill. Neither can I disguise from myself the fact that outside the House there are many people who are not only interested in the Bill but, if I may say so, very deeply concerned about it. I therefore think that it is only right, if you will permit me, to add a few general observations with regard to the points of controversy which I have noticed in several newspapers which I have been perusing ever since the Bill has been on the anvil. I will take this matter also part by part and section by section. I will deal only with what I regard have been considered as points of controversy. Let me take marriage and divorce. Here I find that there are three points of controversy—The first point of controversy is abolition of castes as a necessary requirement for a valid marriage; the second point of controversy is the prescription of monogamy; and the third part of controversy is permission for divorce.

I will take the first point of controversy, namely—abolition of caste restrictions. So far as this Bill is concerned, what it does is to arrive at a sort of compromise between the new and the old. The Bill says that if a member of the Hindu community wants to follow the orthodox system which requires that a marriage shall not be valid unless the bride and bridegroom belong to the same *varna*, the same caste or the same sub-caste, there is nothing in this Code which can prevent him from giving effect to his wishes or giving effect to what he regards as his *dharma*. In the same way if one Hindu who is a reformist and who does not believe in *varna*, caste or sub-caste, chooses to marry a girl outside his *varna*, outside his caste, outside his sub-caste, the law regards his marriage also as valid. So far as the marriage law is concerned there is therefore no kind of imposition at all. The *vydhikas*, the orthodox, are left free to do what they think is right according to their *dharma*. The reformers who do not follow *dharma* but who follow reason, who follow conscience, have also been left to follow their reason and their conscience.

THE HINDU CODE BILL • 503

Consequently, what will happen in Hindu society so far as marriage law is concerned is there will be a competition between the old and the new. And we hope that those who are following the new path will win subsequently. But, as I say, if they do not, we are quite content to allow two parallel systems of marriage to be operative in this country and anyone may make his choice. There is no violation of a *shastra*, no violation of a *smriti* at all.

With regard to monogamy it may be that it is a new innovation. But I must point out that I do think that any Member in this house will be able to point out having regard to customary law or having regard to our *Shastras* that a Hindu husband had at all times an unfettered, unqualified right to polygamy. That was never the case. Even today, in certain parts of South India there are people who follow this, a section of the Nattukottai Chettiyars—the case has been reported in the Reports of the Privy Council itself, I am not depending on mere heresay evidence—but among the Nattukottai Chettiyars there is a custom that a husband cannot marry a second wife unless he obtains the consent of his wife. Secondly, when a consent is obtained, he must allot to her certain property which I think in the Tamil language is called *moppu*. That property becomes her absolute property so that if after her consent the husband marries and ill-treats her, she has a certain amount of economic competence in her own hands to lead an independent life. I cite that as an illustration to show that there has not been an unqualified right for polygamy.

A second illustration which I would like to give would be from the *Arthashastra* of Kautilya. I do not know how many Members of the House have perused that book, I suppose many of them have. If they have, they will realize that the right to marry a second wife has been considerably limited by Kautilya. In the first place, no man can marry for the first ten or twelve years because he must be satisfied that the woman is not capable of producing children. That was one limitation. The second limitation imposed by Kautilya on the right of second marriage was that the husband was to return to the woman all the *stridhan* that she had acquired at the time of marriage. It is only under these two conditions that Kautilya's *Arthashastra* permitted a Hindu husband to marry a second time.

Thirdly, in our own country, in the legislation that has been passed in various Provinces, monogamy has been prescribed. For instance in the *marumakkathayam*[272] and the *aliyasanthanam*[273] law both of them prescribe monogamy as a rule of marital life. Similarly, with regard to the recent legislation that has been passed in Bombay or in Madras, similarly in Baroda, the law is the law of monogamy.

I hope the House will see from the instances I have given that we are not making any very radical or revolutionary change. We have precedent for what we are doing, both in the laws that have been passed by various States in India, also in the ancient *Shastras* such as Kautilya's *Arthashastra*. If I may go further, we have got the precedent of the whole world which recognizes monogamy as the most salutary principle so far as marital relations are concerned.

Coming to the question of divorce, there again I should like to submit to the House that this is no way an innovation. Everybody in this House knows that communities which are called *Shudra* have customary divorce and what is the total of what we call *Shudra*? Nobody has ever probably made any calculation as to the total number of *Shudras* who go to compose the Hindu society, but I have not the slightest doubt in my mind that the *Shudras* form practically 90 per cent of the total population of the Hindus. What are called the 'regenerated' classes probably do not fill more than ten per cent of the total population of this country, and the question that I want to ask of honourable Members is this: are you going to have the law of the 90 per cent of the people as the general law of this country, or are you going to have the law of the 10 per cent of the people being imposed upon the 90 per cent? That is a simple question which every Member must answer and can answer.

So far as the 'regenerated' classes are concerned there was a time, if one refers for instance to the time when the Narada *smriti* or the Parashara *smriti* were written, when the *smritis* recognized that a woman can divorce her husband when he has abandoned her, when he died, when he has taken *parivrija*,[274] and she was entitled to have a second husband. Consequently, it may be that at a later stage I shall read to you some extracts from your *Shastras* to show (*An honourable member*: 'Your *shastras*'). Yes, because I belong to the other caste.

I shall read the extracts to show that what has happened in this country is that somehow, unfortunately, unnoticed, unconsciously, custom has been allowed to trample upon the text of the *Shastras* which were all in favour of the right sort of marital relations. My submission, therefore, to the house is that so far as any new principles have been introduced in the law of marriage or divorce, whatever has been done is both just and reasonable and supported by precedent not only of our *Shastras* but the experience of the world as a whole.

With regard to adoption, there are again three points of controversy. One point of controversy with regard to adoption is this, that like the old Hindu law we do not make similarity or identity of caste a requisite for a valid adoption. We follow the same rule that we have followed with regard to marriage. Here again, I may say that if a *Brahmin* wants to adopt a *Brahmin* boy, he is free to do so. If a *Kayasth* wants to adopt a *Kayasth* boy, he is free to do so. If a *Shudra* wants to adopt a boy of his own community he is free to do so. If a Brahmin is so enlightened as not to adopt a boy belonging to his own community but adopts a *Shudra*, he is also permitted to do so. There is therefore no kind of imposition.

Seth Govind Das (C. P. and Berar: General): Why do you consider such a Brahmin enlightened?

The Honourable Dr B. R. Ambedkar: Well, I do not know. From my point of view certainly he is enlightened; from your point of view he may be a very dark man, but that is a difference of opinion.

With regard to the question of the limitation on the right of an adopted son to challenge all alienations made by the widow before adoption, I do not think that there can be any controversy at all. There is no reason why we should continue the notion that a boy when adopted becomes the son of the adopted father right from the time when the adopted father died. This is a pure fiction. It has no value at all. It is not merely a fiction; it is fiction which gives rise to tremendous litigation and tremendous difficulties. It is therefore right that the adoption should be simultaneous with the vesting of the property. I do not think any member of the House will think that this is a proposition which we ought not to accept at this stage. (*Shri B. Das*: 'We all accept')

Similarly, as I have stated, the limitation upon the right of a boy who is adopted to divest the mother completely and to make her nothing more than a dependant waiting for such maintenance as the adopted boy may give, I do not think that there is any member of the House who will think that such a situation can be justified on any ground whatsoever. I think it is right that we preserve the right of adoption which the orthodox community cherishes so much, but, Sir, I do not understand why there should be adoption. Most of us who make adoptions have no name to be recorded in history. Personally, I myself certainly would not like my name to go down in history, because my record is probably very poor. I am an unusual member of the Hindu community. But there are many who have no records to go down and I do not understand why they should indulge in adopting a son—a stupid boy, uneducated, without any character—not knowing his possibilities and fastening him and fathering him upon a poor woman, whom he can deprive of every property that she possessed. Therefore, my submission is this, that if you do want to cherish your old notions with regard to adoption at any rate make this provision that the adopted boy does not altogether deprive the mother of the property which is her mainstay. I do not think that that limitation can be at all a point of controversy.

With regard to the question of the abolition of customary adoption, I would like to say two things. There is a general argument which the House will be able to appreciate. It is this. A Code is inconsistent with customary law. That is a fundamental proposition. If you allow a Code to remain and at the same time permit custom to grow and custom to plead against the Code, there is no purpose in having a Code at all, because a custom can always eat into the Code and make the Code *null and void*. With regard to this particular matter of customary adoption such as *Krithrim*[275] adoption, *Godha*[276] adoption and *Dwaimushayan*[277] adoption, my submission is this, that these are really not adoption at all. As the Privy Council in one of its rulings has definitely stated, adoption is purely a religious affair. The getting of property by the adopted son is a secondary matter. He may get property, he may not get property, and even though he may not get property his adoption from a religious point of view may be valid. Therefore, my submission is this, that all these customary adoptions are nothing else but devices to keep property within the two families which enter into this bargain, and in my judgment, since we have passed the Constitution and included in the Directive Principles one article saying that the State should take steps not to allow property being concentrated in the hands of one or a few, such devices like the *Dwaimushayan* where two parties merely agree to share the property and keep it with them ought not to be tolerated. Besides, there is no reason why parties who want to make a genuine adoption should not conform to the rules and regulation regarding the *Dattaka*[278] adoption which is permitted by the law.

I want not to take up the points of controversy relating to the topic of co-parcenary law. The question is raised: Why does the Bill wish to seek to abolish the co-parcenary which is prescribed by what is called the *Mitakshara* law? Now, Sir, having applied my mind in the best way I can for the proper exposition of this subject, I think this is a question which required to be considered from three different points of view. One is how large a volume of property is included within the ambit of what is called co-parcenary property. If the volume that is comprised within what is called co-parcenary property is a very large part of the property which a man in these days holds, then no doubt some serious attention will have to be paid to this question. Therefore, that is the first aspect of the question that one has to examine.

The second aspect that we have to consider with regard to the retention of what is called co-parcenary property is whether any co-parcenary had individually the right to alienate property. Thirdly, whether any co-parcener has a right in himself to break up the co-parcenary. Obviously, if the property included within the class of property called co-parcenary property is a small part of the property, different questions will arise. Similarly, if any co-parcener, under the present existing Hindu law, has already got the right to alienate his share in the property, then obviously, the question whether this law or this Bill is abrogating co-parcenary property would stand on a different footing. Similarly, if under the existing Hindu law a co-parcener has an inherent right to break up a co-parcenary, then my submission is that the question that this Bill breaks up the co-parcenary becomes very much less momentous than is thought of by most members of the House as well as people outside.

Let me therefore take the first question: What is the extent of the non-co-parcenary property which a co-parcener may hold, notwithstanding the fact that he is a member of the co-parcenary? Now, my friends, who have paid attention to this subject and know what the position is under the Hindu law, will know that there is no disqualification upon a co-parcener to hold separate property while he continues to be a co-parcener. A co-parcener may have capacity to hold two different sorts of property—property which belongs to the co-parcenary and property which does not belong to the co-parcenary, but belongs to himself and does not go, by what is called survivorship.

Let me give the House some idea of the extent and nature of the property which a co-parcener can hold, although he is a co-parcener. I have taken from the existing text books on the Hindu law, the following categories of property which a co-parcener can hold, notwithstanding the fact that he is a co-parcener. First, property inherited by a Hindu from a person other than his father, grandfather and great grandfather. If a Hindu gets property from a person who is not his father, grandfather or great grand father, that property is in his hand and is separate property and does not belong to the co-parcenary. Secondly, property inherited by him from his maternal grandfather, thirdly, gift of ancestral movables made to him by his father and fourthly, property granted by government to an individual who is a member of the co-parcenary becomes his personal property and not the property of the co-parcenary. Then fifthly, we have ancestral property lost to the family and recovered without the aid of the family property. That also, although originally co-parcenary property, becomes his private property. Then sixthly, there is the income from separate property and purchases made from the income of such property. They are also private property, seventhly, share of a co-parcener by partition if he has not male issue, eighthly, property held by sole surviving co-parcener when there is no widow with the power to adopt, ninthly, separate earning of a member of a joint family co-parcenary and tenthly, gains of learning . Such vast amount of property included in these 10 categories is today under the Mithakshara law the private property of a co-parcener. It does not become the property of the co-parcenary.

Let me illustrate this by one plain illustration. There are hundreds and hundreds of clerks in our Secretariat, some drawing small salaries, some drawing huge salaries more than the salaries of the Members of the Cabinet—Rs 4000 (Honourable Members: 'Clerks? Are they clerks?'), I mean officers. In a certain sense they are glorified clerks.

The point I want to put to the House is this: that such large income as gains of learning, which come up in individual cases to Rs 4000, if there was a joint family in the true sense of the word,

THE HINDU CODE BILL • 509

ought to go to the joint family for the joint maintenance of that family. What happens? Under the Gains of Learning Act passed only a few years ago, this very Assembly, not I mean the members, passed a law that such gains of learning, which form, as I say, the principal part of the income of a joint family and which a member is enabled to earn by reason of the education that was given to him out of the family income, have now been made his personal and private income. My submission to the House is this: when so large a property, as I have mentioned, included in these ten different categories have already been made in modification of the original laws of *Mitakshara* private property, what is the balance of property that is left which can be said to comprise the co-parcenary property? My submission is that really very, very small volume of property is left to comprise within what is called the co-parcenary. Let me take the other question. It is said that the co-parcenary—I hope Members understand that co-parcenary is something very narrow and very limited and it is not the same thing as a joint family, which is quite a different matter— system enables the Hindus to preserve the property, to retain it, that there can be no break-up, there can be no squandering of money so to say on the part of any member of the family. A question that I want to put to the House is this: Is it true under the existing law of the *Mitakshara* that this property cannot be alienated, cannot be squandered? The answer is completely in the negative. Let me give you one or two illustrations. I am taking the case of the father. The father can alienate joint property for antecedent debt. All that the father has to do is to first of all create a debt, say one thousand or two thousand rupees on a personal promissory note. Subsequently, after six months he becomes entitled to sell the whole of the co-parcenary property, if that becomes necessary for the purpose of meeting that antecedent debt. Now, a submission that I want to make to the House is this: Does the lodgment of such enormous power in the hands of a father to sell the property for purely antecedent and personal debts in order? I want the house to bear in mind that the *Mitakshara* law makes a distinction between the father and the manager so far as the alienation of property is concerned. True a manager cannot alienate a property belonging to the co-parcenary unless and until it is proved that there is a family necessity for which alienation is necessary. But with regard to the father, there is no such obligation at all. A father can create a debt personally for himself and he becomes entitled to alienate that property for a purely personal debt which has not been incurred for the purposes of the family. The only limitation that is imposed upon the right of the alienation of the father under the *Mitakshara* law is that the debt must not be impious, must not be for an immoral purpose and if it is not immoral, then the father can alienate the whole of the property of the co-parcenary. There is no limit at all.

Similarly, take the case of the son. It is also under the *Mitakshara* law within the competence of a son to demand the partition of the family property at any time he likes. I could have well understood the argument for the conservation of the co-parcenary property if the rule of Hindu Law was that no co-parcener was entitled to alienate the property, that the property must remain the property of the co-parcenary, but that is not the case. The root of dissolution, the root of destruction of the co-parcenary property is in the co-parcenary itself, because it is the co-parcenary law that gives a vested right, a right from the very birth to demand partition of the property and disrupt the whole of the society.

Thirdly, even if a son does not alienate his property, he can create a debt on the property for his own personal purposes and the creditor who has advanced that money under *Mitakshara* law has a perfect right to sue for the partition of the co-parcenary in order to recover his debt. A stranger, therefore, under the *Mitakshara* law has a right to break-up the co-parcener. I would like to ask my honourable friends, who are worried about this matter, where a large part of the estate, of the assets lies outside the co-parcenary property and so far as the co-parcenary property is concerned, the father has a right to alienate without any kind of limitation except the immorality of the debt, the son has a right to break up the property at any time he likes and the son has a right to create a charge on the property enabling the creditor to sue for partition, is it something which might be called a solid system, which is fool-proof and knave-proof? My submission is this, that the co-parcenary property law as it stands, contains within itself the elements of disruption. Therefore, the Bill is doing nothing very radical in saying that the share shall be held separately. As we all know to-day the condition is such that everybody wants to live separately. The moment a father dies, the sons claim that there shall be a legal recognition to facts, as they exist to-day. There is nothing that is radical at all in this part of the Bill.

Of course, I should say one thing which I think is generally not realized. I started by saying that a distinction has to be made between co-parcenary and joint family. This Bill while it does away with co-parcenary, maintains the joint family. It does not come in the way of the joint family being maintained. The only thing is that the joint family in the *Mitakshara* law will be on the same footing and of the same character as the joint family under the *Dayabhaga* law. It must not be supposed that because the *Mitakshara* law does not prevail in Bengal that there is no joint family. There is a joint family. The only distinction will be that the members of the joint family instead of holding their rights as joint tenants, will hold them as tenants in common. That will be the only distinction that will be between the existing law in the *Mitakshara* and the future law in the *Mitakshara*.

Now, I come to woman's property. I do not know how many members of this House are familiar with the intricacies of this subject. So far as I have been able to study this subject, I do not think that there is any subject in the Hindu Law which is so complicated, so intricate as the women's property (An honourable Member: 'As the woman herself'): As the woman herself. If you ask the question, what is *stridhan*, before answering that question, you have to ask another question and find an answer for it. You must first of all ask, 'is she a maiden' or 'is she a married woman'. Because what property is *stridhan* and what property is not *stridhan* depends upon the status of the woman. Certain property is *stridhanam* if she has obtained it while she is a maiden; certain property is not *stridhan* if she has obtained it after marriage. Consequently, if you ask the question what is the line of inheritance to the *stridhan*, you have again to ask the question whether the *stridhan* belongs to a maiden or the *stridhan* belongs to a married woman. Because, the line of succession to the *stridhan* of a maiden is quite different from the line of succession to the *stridhan* belonging to a married woman. When you come to the question of succession to married woman's property, you have again to ask the question, does she belong to the Bengal School or does she belongs to the *Mitakshara* School. If you ask the question whether she belongs to the *Mitakshara* school, you will never be able to find a definite answer unless you probe further and ask whether she belongs to the Mithila School or the Benares School or some other School. This is a most complicated subject. At the same time, I should like honourable members to bear two things in mind. One is this: so far as women's property is concerned, generally speaking, it falls into two categories. One category is called her *stridhan* and the other is called widow's property. The latter property is property which she inherits from a male member of her family, and according to the existing law property which she owns only during her lifetime and subsequently that property passes to the reversioners of the male heir. That is the position.

Therefore, so far as women's property is concerned, we have two different sorts of inheritance and two different sets of property, *stridhan* property and widow's property. The heirs to the *stridhan* property are quite different and distinct from the heirs to the property she inherits from a male member. The question, therefore, we have to consider in codifying this particular branch of the Hindu Law is this. Are you going to maintain the two principal divisions which exist at present, namely, *stridhan* property and widow's property? Secondly, are you going to maintain the double line of succession; one line of succession for the *stridhan* property and another line of succession for widow's property? These are the two principal questions which arise when one begin to codify this law. The Committee came to the conclusion that so far as codification was concerned, its purpose would be defeated if we allow the present chaos to continue. We must either decide that a woman will not be entitled to have absolute property or we must decide that a woman should have absolute property. We must also decide what should be the line of heirs for a woman: whether they should be uniform or they should be different. The Committee came to the conclusion that so far as right to property is concerned, there should be uniformity and uniformity should recognize that the woman has absolute property.

I know a great deal of the argument that is always urged against women getting absolute property. It is said that women are imbecile; it is said that they are always subject to the influence of all sorts of people and consequently, it would be very dangerous to leave women in the world subject to the influences of all sorts of wily men who may influence them in one way or another to dispose of property both to the detriment of themselves as well as to the detriment of the family from which they have inherited the family property. The view that the Committee has taken is a very simple one. In certain matters or certain kinds of property which is called *stridhan* property the *Smritis* are prepared to invest woman with absolute right. There can be no question at all that a woman has an absolute right over her *stridhan* property. She can dispose it of in any way she likes. My submission to the House is this. If the woman can be trusted to dispose of her *stridhanam* property in the best way she likes, and nobody has ever raised an argument for the obliteration of that rule of *Mitakshara*, the burden of proof lies upon the opponents who say that the other part of the property, namely, widow's estate, which the woman has inherited, should not become her absolute property. It is they who must prove that while the women are competent to dispose of a certain part of the property which they possess, they are not competent to dispose of a certain other part. The Committee, on a very careful examination, failed to find a satisfactory solution of this dilemma. The Committee, in my judgment, very rightly, came to the conclusion that if in certain cases women were competent and intelligent to sell and dispose of their property, they must be held to be competent in respect of the disposal of the other property also. That is the reason why the Committee have made this rule that women should now possess absolute property.

The other question that arises on this issue, namely women's property is the share of the daughter. I know it would be a very great understatement to say that this is a ticklish question; it is a very anxious question. There are many people in this world, in India today, both orthodox and unorthodox who cannot help producing daughters; they do. I do not know what would happen to this world if daughters were not born. At the same time, they do not want to extend to the daughter the same love and affection which a parent is bound to extend both to the male and female issue. But, I am not going to use any such high level of argument in favour of the proposition which has been enunciated by the Select Committee; I am going to speak on a much lower tone. The first thing that I would like to address myself to this house is this. The inclusion of the daughter among the heirs is not an innovation which is made by this Committee. Honourable members who are familiar with the law of inheritance as it prevails both under the *Mitakshara* and *Dayabhaga*, I am sure, will admit that the daughter is included by both of them under what is called the compact series. As members will know, Hindu heirs are divided into several categories. The first category, is called, compact series. After that, there is a series of heirs spoken of as *sapindas*, then comes *samanodaks*. After that comes the *bandhus*. *Bandhus* are divided into three categories: *Atma bandhus*, *Pitru bandhus* and *Matru bandhus*. The compact series is really a special class of heirs which does not conform strictly to the basic principles of heirship surrounded round *gotraja*, *samanodaka* and *bandhus*, because it is a mixed category. It is a category which is based on double foundation. It is based on propinquity; it is also based on religious efficacy. They do not conform to any of the criteria which have been laid down for determining the categories of *sapindas*, *samanodakas* and *bandhus*.

If you take both the laws, the Mitakshara as well as the *Dayabhaga* you will see that the daughter is included within the category known as compact series. The only distinction between the *Mitakshara* and the *Dayabhaga* is this. According to the *Dayabhaga* the necessary element in heirship is the capacity to offer oblation. Consequently the *Dayabhaga* makes a rule between a daughter who is unmarried, a daughter who is married, a daughter who is married but has a son, and a daughter who is a widow. They give preference to a daughter who is married and has a son. Next to that they give preference to a daughter who is married. The unmarried daughter comes third. But it is within that category, the reason being that a daughter who is married and has a son, is ready there to offer oblation, because her son can offer oblation. A daughter who is unmarried, has no son, and therefore his possibility of offering an oblation does not exist. That is why she has been kept down. But the point I want to emphasize, and which I want the House to bear in mind is that there is no innovation as such in the inclusion of the daughter in the category of compact series. She has always been there both according to the *Mitakshara* and according to the *Dayabhaga*. The only innovation which the Bill seeks to make is to raise the status of the daughter. Under the Bill she becomes simultaneous heir, along with the son, the widow, the widow of the predeceased son, son of a predeceased son of a predeceased son, widow of a predeceased son of a predeceased son.

The point is this that originally, and particularly according to the *Mitakshara* Law, no female was entitled to any kind of share at all. This law was changed in the year 1937 whereby the widow of the deceased, the widow of the predeceased son and of his grandson and great-grandson—they were all made simultaneous heirs along with the son. The only omission that was made was in respect of the daughter. The government at that time was not prepared to lend its support to put the daughter on the same level as the widow and the widows of the predeceased son and the predeceased son's son. This is therefore the only innovation that the Bill makes. It merely raises it up in the order of heirs. It is not that for the first time she has been made an heir.

Now, I come to the question of her share. As the Rau Committee has pointed out, and as many of the witnesses who know the Shastras have pointed out, that it is impossible to deny the fact that the daughter according to the Smritis was a simultaneous heir along with the son and that she was entitled to one-fourth share of her father's property. That has been accepted as a text from the Yagnavalkya and also from Manu. I once counted 137 Smritis and I do not know why our ancient Brahmins were so occupied in writing Smritis and why they did not spend their time doing something else it is impossible to say, assuming that that occupation was a paramount occupation of the day. There is no doubt that the two Smritikars whom I have mentioned—Yagnavalkya and Manu, rank the highest among the 137 who had tried their hands in framing Smritis. Both of them have stated that the daughter is entitled to one-fourth share. It is a pity that somehow for some reason custom has destroyed the efficacy of that text: otherwise, the daughter would have been, on the basis of our own Smritis, entitled to get one-fourth share. I am very sorry for the ruling which the Privy Council gave. It blocked the way for the improvement of our law. The Privy Council in an earlier case said that custom will override law, with the result that it became quite impossible to our Judiciary to examine our ancient codes and to find out what laws were laid down by our Rishis and by our Smritikars. I have not the least doubt about it that if the Privy Council had not given that decision, that custom will override text, some lawyer, some Judge would have found it quite possible to unearth this text of Yagnavalkya and Manusmriti, and women today would have been enjoying, if not more, at least one-fourth of the share of their property.

The original Bill had raised the share of the daughter to one-half. My Select Committee went a step further and made her share full and equal to that of the son. The only innovation that we are making is that her share is increased and that we bring her in the line with the son or the widow. That also, as I say, would not be an innovation if you accept my view that in doing this we are merely going back to the text of the *Smritis* which you all respect.

I might also say that in discussing this question about the share of the daughter, myself, and the members of the Law Department examined every system of inheritance. We examined the Muslim system of inheritance: We examined the Parsi system of inheritance: We examined also the Indian Succession Act and the line of succession that had been laid down and we also examined the British system of inheritance, and nowhere could we find any case where a daughter was excluded from a share. There is no system anywhere in the world where a daughter has been excluded.

Now, Sir, one question has been brought forth constantly— that the giving of the share to the daughter means disruption of the family. I must frankly confess that I cannot appreciate the force of that argument. If a man has twelve sons and one daughter, and if the twelve sons on the day of the death of the father immediately decide on partition and obtain a twelfth of the total property of the father, is the partition going to be much more worse, if there was a daughter, the thirteenth, who also demanded a share?

Twelve share or 12 fragments is not a better situation than 13 fragments. If you want to prevent fragmentation we shall have to do something else, not by the law of inheritance but by some other law, whereby property shall not be fragmented so as to become less useful from a national point of view for purposes of national production.

I think I have, so far as I know, exhausted what I have to say on the various points of controversy which I had seen raised both by members of this House as well as by the members of the public. I hope that the clarification which I have given on the various points will allay the fears of members who are not well disposed towards this measure. They will realize that this is in no sense a revolutionary measure. I say that this is not even a radical measure.

Notes

1. See selected excerpts of the speeches of the members of the Constituent Assembly, *Dr Babasaheb Ambedkar: Writings and Speeches*, BAWS, vol. 13, Bombay, Government of Maharashtra, Department of Education, 1994, pp. 1163-94.

2. Ambedkar wrote several full-length studies during his life-time. He published a number of papers, addresses, and representations independently. Besides, he drafted umpteen memoranda and documents that shaped the constitutional developments in India. He also brought out the journals: *Mooknayak, Bahishkrit Bharat* and *Janata* (subsequently *Prabudd Bharat*) in Marathi. From 1927 till his death in 1956, he often participated in legislative debates, either at the provincial or central level, in different capacities. He also brought out a grammar and dictionary of the Pali language. The Government of Maharashtra has already published *Writings and Speeches*, vols 1-16, beginning from 1979 till 1998. Further, it has published two volumes on *Source Material on Dr Babasaheb Ambedkar and the Movement of Untouchables*. Further volumes on Ambedkar in Parliament, his photographs, letters, and his main writings in Marathi are proposed to be published.

3. The written word still is a major challenge for Dalits in India.

4. For instance, see *India and Communism*, BAWS, vol. 3, pp. 93-148 and *Revolution and Counter-Revolution in Ancient India*, BAWS, vol. 3, pp. 149-437.

5. See the editorial comments to BAWS, 3, 4, 5 and 12.

6. See BAWS, vol. 3, p. 439 (ed. note).

7. For instance, *The Untouchables, Who Were They and Why They Became Untouchables* was published in the beginning of 1948. Ambedkar had worked on it in 1946 and 1947 when community and identity had become very important to advance claims to power. Therefore, the book is not merely an account of the rise of untouchability but establishes the Untouchables as a community, distinct from Hindus, spread across India and at the same time, deeply disadvantaged.

8. See B. R. Ambedkar, 'The Buddha and the Future of His Religion', *Mahabodi, 58, 1950*; his comments on the Constitution, *Manusmriti*, separate electorates etc.

9. This is the case for instance, when he wanted to bring out the third edition of *Annihilation of Caste* in 1944. He wanted to recast the essay by incorporating the essay that he wrote in 1916 entitled 'Castes in India, their Origin and their Mechanism'. See BAWS, vol. 1, p. 26. Also see Preface to 'Ranade, Gandhi and Jinnah', BAWS, vol. 1, pp. 207–8.

10. See BAWS, vol. 3, pp. 271–331, vol. 3, pp. 222–356.

11. BAWS, vol. 3, pp. 357–80.

12. See BAWS, vol. 3, pp. 257–61, 257–9, 362–7, 378–80.

13. See BAWS, vol. 3, pp. 257–9, 362–7, and 378–80.

14. See BAWS, vol. 9; vol. 1, pp. 86–96.

15. See *The Journal of the Royal Economic Society*, vol. XXXVI, p. 111, Rep. in *BAWS*, vol. 6, pp. 313–14.

16. See W. N. Kuber, *B. R. Ambedkar*, New Delhi, Govt. of India, Publication Division, 1981, p. 81.

17. See 'Dr Ambedkar's Indictment', *Harijan*, 11 July 1936 (Rep. BAWS, vol. 1, pp. 81–3). Sant Ramji, the secretary of the Jat-Pat Todak Sangh who sent the aborted invitation to Ambedkar for which he drafted the address *Annihilation of Caste* says, 'as far as I know, it is the most learned thesis on the subject', *Harijan*, 15 August 1936 (Reproduced in BAWS, vol. 1, p. 84).

18. See Preface to the Second edition, BAWS, vol. 8, pp. 1–3.

19. Ambedkar himself mentions his work on *Who were the Shudras? How they came to be the Fourth Varna in the Indo–Aryan Society* as of this kind. See the Preface to the book, BAWS, vol. 7, p. 18.

20. The publication of vol. 4 of *Writings and Speeches* entitled *Riddles in Hinduism*, in 1987 provoked widespread protest from the Shiv Sena and a counter-reaction by the Dalits in Maharashtra, eventually making the editorial committee state that the views

expressed in the book were not the official position of the Government of Maharashtra.

21. For Phule's engagement with the Untouchables, see Gail Omvedt, *Cultural Revolt in a Colonial Society: The Non-Brahmin Movement in Western India—1873-1930*, Mumbai, Scientific Socialist Education Trust, 1976; Rosalind O'Hanlon, *Caste, Conflict and Ideology: Mahatma Jotirao Phule and the Low Caste Protest in Ninteenth Century Western India*, Hyderabad, Cambridge University Press, 1985.

22. For Narayan Guru Swami see, M. S. A. Rao, *Social Movements and Social Transformation: A Study of Two Backward Classes' Movements*, Manohar, Delhi, 1979.

23. When other communities claimed consideration due to their historic importance, Ambedkar drew attention to the contribution made by Mahars, Dusadhs, and Pariahs, to build the British Raj in India. See, 'The Untouchables and the Pax Britannica', BAWS, vol. 12, pp. 84–7.

24. See R. D. Ranade, *Mysticism in Maharashtra*, Pune, 1933; Jayant Lele, *Tradition and Modernity in Bhakti Movements*, Leiden, E. J. Brill, 1981.

25. For an introduction to Kabir and the Kabir tradition, see Daniel Gold, *The Lord as Guru*, Oxford, Oxford University Press, 1987; Ch Vandevelle, *Kabir*, Oxford, Clarendon Press, 1974; Keay, *The Religious Life of India: Kabir and His Followers* and Muhammad Hedayetullah, *Kabir: The Apostle of Hindu-Muslim Unity*, Delhi, Motilal Banarasidas, 1977.

26. The letter is reproduced in C. B. Khairmode, *Dr Bhimrao Ramji Ambedkar* (in Marathi), vol. 1, Bombay, Bharat Bhushan Publishing Press, 1959, p. 779.

27. *Mooknayak*, 31 January 1920.

28. These organizations were patterned on similar organizations of the Indian National Congress, such as the Hindustan Seva Dal. While the Congress adopted nationalist nameplates for its organizations, Ambedkar stressed on democracy, equality, and labouring masses, encompassing all communities.

29. For a glimpse of Ambedkar's budgetary intervention, see vol. 2, pp. 1–34.

30. For details of the Poona Pact, see *What Congress and Gandhi have done to the Untouchables*, Appendix III, BAWS, vol. 9, pp. 307–11 and for explanation, ibid., pp. 67–9.

31. BAWS, vol. 5, p. 355.

32. See BAWS, vol. 9, pp. 133–42.

33. See S. R. Kharat, *Dr Babasaheb Ambedkaranchi Patran* (in Marathi) Poona, Laxmi Rasta, Lekhan Vachan Bhandar, 1961.

34. When he became a member of the Viceroy's Council, The *Indian Information*, 1 March 1943, wrote the following about his intended conversion from Hinduism:

    'But while he is determined not to remain a Hindu and has studied the teachings of several other religions, including Buddhism, Sikhism and Christianity, Dr Ambedkar will not announce his entry into another faith. The untouchables, he feels, still need him. His conversion now would have far-reaching repercussions. His faith and the faith of every follower of his is a matter which each man should settle for himself; and he does not wish to influence his followers in this matter. When he has handed over the leadership of the untouchables to others and retired from public life, he will tell the world of his decision. For the present his crusade must go on.' (BAWS, vol. 10, p. 9)

35. See Dhananjay Keer, *Dr Ambedkar: Life and Mission*, Bombay, Popular Prakashan, 1971.

36. See BAWS, vol. 13, pp. 7–14.

37. This change is clearly visible in Ambedkar's reply to the 'Objectives Resolution' and advancing a radical socialist agenda, See BAWS, vol. 13, pp. 7–14.

38. The entire process of Ambedkar's co-option into the Interim Cabinet and his eventually becoming the chairman of the drafting committee is still to be effectively traced. There is the letter of Rajendra Prasad to B. G. Kher, the Prime Minister of Bombay that Ambedkar be elected to the central legislature from Bombay. See G. Austin, *The Indian Constitution: Cornerstone of a Nation*, Oxford, Clarendon, 1968, p. 13, fn. 44. Also see, D. C. Ahir, *Dr Ambedkar and the Indian Constitution*, Lucknow, Buddha Vihara, 1973, p. ii. The suggested intervention of Gandhi in this regard has not been adequately supported.

39. See BAWS, vol. 15, p. 860.

40. See Chandra Bharill, *Social and Political Ideas of B. R. Ambedkar*, Jaipur, Aalekh Publishers, 1977, p. 83.

41. BAWS, vol. 10, p. 451.

42. See 'Philosophy of Hinduism' BAWS, vol. 3, pp. 3–92 and vol. 9, pp. 274–97.

43. For Ambedkar's approach to Modern Technology, see *What Congress and Gandhi have done to the Untouchables*, Chapter XI, BAWS, vol. 9, pp. 274–97.

44. See BAWS, vol. 4, pp. 288–322.

45. See 'Philosophy of Hinduism', BAWS, vol. 3, pp. 3–92.

46. See *What Congress and Gandhi have Done to the Untouchables*, op. cit., Chapter XI.

47. See BAWS, vol. 5, p. XI.

48. BAWS, vol. 12, pp. 665–85.

49. See M. F. Ganjare (ed.), *Dr Babasaheb Ambedkaranchi Bhashane* (in Marathi), vol. VI, Nagpur, Ashok Prakashan, 1976, p. 100.

50. BAWS, vol. 1, p. 90.

51. BAWS, vol. 11, pp. 595–9.

52. BAWS, vol. 1, p. 90.

53. BAWS, vol. 12, pp. 133–5.

54. BAWS, vol. 15, p. 289.

55. See BAWS, vol. 9.

56. For an illustration see BAWS, vol. 15, pp. 968–73.

57. BAWS, vol. 11, p. 243 and pp. 329–44. Kamma is Pali for Karma, meaning action, is a central concept in Buddhism. Ambedkar argued that the Brahminical doctrine of Karma suggests that birth and rebirth are the consequences of one's action. It upholds the caste system, undermines or limits human freedom and subscribes to permanence and eternity of soul. On the contrary, Buddha's conception of Kamma upholds dissolution of existent beings and their reconstitution into new forms of life. The latter inherit the consequences of action of previous life. (See B. R. Ambedkar, *The Buddha and his Dhamma*, Bombay, Siddharth, 1974, 2nd ed., pp. 245–7).

58. See BAWS, vol. 11, pp. 227–325.

59. Sydenham College of Commerce and Economics, Golden Jubilee 1913-63, *Souvenir*, Bombay, October, 1963, p. 75.

60. For illustration see Ambedkar's debate with Gandhi, BAWS, vol. 1, pp. 81-96.

61. See BAWS, vol. 9: Appendix XIV and XV, 'A critique of the proposals: Analysis of the Cabinet Mission for Indian Constitutional changes in so far as they affect the Scheduled Castes (Untouchables)' pp. 357–75 and 'Results of primary elections held in December', 1945, BAWS, vol. 10, pp. 523–36.

62. See BAWS, vol. 12, pp. 665–91.

63. See Preface to *Who Were The Shudras?*' BAWS, vol. 7, pp. 9–19.
64. See 'Introduction', *The Buddha and His Dhamma*, BAWS, vol. 11, pp. 225–6; and vol. 1, pp. 86–96.
65. 'Constitution First Amendment Bill', BAWS, vol. 15, p. 356.
66. BAWS, vol. 14, p. 283.
67. See T. H. Green, *Lectures on the Principles of Political Obligation and Other Writings*, P. Harris and J. Morrow (eds), Cambridge, Cambridge University Press, 1986.
68. See BAWS, vol. 13, pp. 390–4.
69. See BAWS, vol. 5, pp. 403–21.
70. 'States and Minorities', BAWS, vol. 1, pp. 396–7.
71. See BAWS, vol. 2, pp. 362–3.
72. BAWS, vol. 1, pp. 131–3 and pp. 167–70.
73. See BAWS, vol. 2, pp. 190–6.
74. For the entire range of argument see BAWS, vol. 2, pp. 337–69.
75. For a lucid presentation, see I. Krammick, *The Rage of Edmund Burke*, New York, Basic Books, 1977.
76. Ambedkar's favourite among Dewey's works was *Democracy and Education*, New York, Macmillan, 1916.
77. See for instance, BAWS, vol. 5, pp. 422–44.
78. See *Riddles of Hinduism*, BAWS, vol. 4.
79. BAWS, vol. 1, pp. 87–8.
80. See 'Ranade, Gandhi and Jinnah', BAWS, vol. 1, pp. 235–40.
81. See 'Note of meeting between Cabinet delegation, Field Marshal Viscount Wavell and B. R. Ambedkar, BAWS, vol. 10, p. 485.
82. See Ambedkar's letter to A. V. Thakkar, the Secretary of the League, BAWS, vol. 9, pp. 133–142.
83. See 'Buddha or Karl Marx', BAWS, vol. 3, pp. 441–64.
84. See Richard Gombrich, *Theravada Buddhism*, London, Routledge & Kegan Paul, 1988.
85. See BAWS, vol. 3, pp. 266–9. This refers to the murder of the Buddhist Emperor Brihadratha of the Maurya dynasty by his commander-in-chief Pushymitra Sunga that perhaps took place in 185 BC. For Ambedkar's consideration of the theme, see BAWS, vol. 7, pp. 372–4, BAWS, vol. 3, pp. 240–1, 268–9, and 276–7.
86. See BAWS, vol. 3, pp. 269–331.
87. See the Riddle of 'Rama and Krishna', BAWS, vol. 4, pp. 323–43.

88. See 'Literature of Brahmanishm', BAWS, vol. 3, pp. 239–65.
89. Later, however, the Buddha is shown rejecting the teachings of the Upanishads, See BAWS, vol. 1, p. 226.
90. See BAWS, vol. 1, p. 75.
91. BAWS, vol. 3, p. 362.
92. Jaimini's *Mimamsa*, the principal version of *Purva Mimansa*, upholds the teachings contained in the earlier portions of the Veda, particularly the *Brahmanas*, stresses on performances and action prescribed by them and is deferential to their authority. Badarayana's *Brahmasutras*, also known as *Uttara Mimansa*, which present the teachings of the Upanishads in a summary form, while acknowledging the authority of the Vedas, is little concerned with rituals and performances and emphasizes on the nature of *Brahman* and the realization of self.
93. BAWS, vol. 3, pp. 362–7.
94. See Jeevaka, Review of The Buddha and His Dhamma, *Mahabodi*, 68, December 1959.
95. See Valerian Rodrigues, 'Making a Tradition Critical: Ambedkar's Reading of Buddhism', Peter Robb (ed.), *Dalit Movements and the Meanings of Labour in India*, Delhi, Oxford University Press, 1993, pp. 299–338.
96. BAWS, vol. 1, pp. 3–22.
97. See BAWS, vol. 5, pp. 157–60.
98. See BAWS, vol. 9, pp. 274–97.
99. See BAWS, vol. 1, pp. 66–9 and 76–8.
100. See Letter to V. S. Thakkar BAWS, vol. 9, pp. 134–40.
101. See BAWS, vol. 5, ch. 20.
102. See BAWS, vol. 12, pp. 741–59.
103. See BAWS, vol. 5, ch. 21.
104. See BAWS, vol. 5, pp. 306–28, vol. 5, ch. 25 etc.
105. BAWS, vol. 2, pp. 503–9, pp. 546–54.
106. BAWS, vol. 5, pp. 403–21.
107. BAWS, vol. 5, pp. 358–62.
108. BAWS, vol. 3, pp. 289–304.
109. See BAWS, vol. 7, Ch. VII.
110. See B. R. Ambedkar, *The Untouchables: Who were They and why They became Untouchables?* BAWS, vol. 7, pp. 239–379.
111. See 'A critique of the proposals of the Cabinet Mission for Indian Constitutional Changes in so far as they affect the Scheduled Castes (Untouchables)' BAWS, vol. 10, p. 523.

112. See BAWS, vol. 7, p. 18.
113. On the Nagas, see BAWS, vol. 5, pp. 267–8; vol. 7, pp. 292–8.
114. See the Scheme of Books, BAWS, vol. 3, p. 465.
115. See 'Civilisation or Felony', BAWS, vol. 5, pp. 127–44.
116. Ibid.
117. See BAWS, vol. 5, pp. 145–226. For an enumeration of the Brahmin castes, see BAWS, vol. 5, pp. 210–26.
118. BAWS, vol. 14, p. 283.
119. See 'Thoughts on Linguistic States', BAWS, vol. 1, pp. 131–201.
120. See Ancient Indian Commerce, BAWS, vol. 12, p. 72.
121. See BAWS, vol. 6, pp. 7–48.
122. See BAWS, vol. 6, p. 60.
123. The Khoti system was a minor land tenure system in the former Bombay presidency found mostly in Ratnagiri district and in some parts of Kolaba and Thane districts. Under the Khoti tenure the government employed the services of the Khot for the purpose of collecting revenue.
124. BAWS, vol. 1, p. 468.
125. BAWS, vol. 10, pp. 220–1, 284–90.
126. BAWS, vol. 10, pp. 302–11.
127. For Ambedkar's considered judgement on the issue, see 'The Untouchables and the Pax Britannica', BAWS, vol. 12, pp. 75–146.
128. See BAWS, vol. 2, pp. 344–57.
129. See BAWS, vol. 8, p. 352.
130. For a relevant debate in the Constituent Assembly, see BAWS, vol. 13, particularly p. 363.
131. See BAWS, vol. 12, p. 209.
132. See 'The Condition of the Convert', BAWS, vol. 5, pp. 445–50.
133. See 'Christianising the Untouchable' and 'The Condition of the Convert', BAWS, vol. 5, pp. 426–76.
134. Gandhi went on fast unto death against the award of separate electorate to the Depressed Classes by the British Government. He gave a set of interrelated arguments for taking such an extreme step. Separate electorate, he felt, would 'vivisect' and 'disrupt' Hinduism. The Depressed Classes were dependent on caste Hindus and distributed among them. Separate electorate would sever these age-old bonds and beget extensive violence. The approach to the problems of the Depressed Classes should be primarily 'moral and religious' and not 'political'. Separate

electorate cannot be the solution to the 'crushing degradation' of Depressed Classes. Through his fast Gandhi appealed to the caste Hindus to change their attitude to the Depressed Classes and embrace them into their fold.

Ambedkar, a broad spectrum of non-Congress Dalit leadership and Dalit groups organized outside the Indian National Congress were in favour of separate electorate in 1932. Given Gandhi's opposition to separate electorate which represented the stand of large sections of Congressmen, it led to confrontation within the nationalist forum.

135. Probably no other issue seized the attention of Gandhi as much as the campaign against untouchability. He saw it as a social endeavour rather than a state practice. While the state assumed this task following Independence there has been little social mobilization to go hand in hand. In the absence of a social conscience and public opinion pursuing this issue, the response to it has been officialese and legal. For a version of Gandhi's approach to untouchability, see Pyarelal, *The Epic Fast*, Ahmedabad, Navjivan, 1932 and Bhikhu Parekh, *Colonialism, Tradition and Reform. An Analysis of Gandhi's Political Discourse*, New Delhi/London/Newbury Park, Sage, 1989, pp. 207–46.

136. See C. Rajagopalachari, *Ambedkar Refuted*, Bombay, Hind Kitabs, 1941 and Santhanam K., *Ambedkar's Attack*, New Delhi, Hindustan Times Press, 1946.

137. For distinction between civil society and political society, see Partha Chatterjee (ed.), *Wages of Freedom*, New Delhi, Oxford University Press, 1998, Introduction.

138. See B. R. Ambedkar, 'Annhilation of Caste', BAWS, vol. 1, pp. 23–96, 'Buddha or Karl Marx', BAWS, vol. 3, pp. 441–64.

139. See B. R. Ambedkar, 'Philosophy of Hinduism', BAWS, vol. 3, pp. 3–92; 'The Hindu Social Order: Its Essential Principles', Ibid., pp. 95–115.

140. See B. R. Ambedkar, 'Philosophy of Hinduism', *op. cit.*

141. See B. R. Ambedkar, *Pakistan Or Partition of India*, BAWS, vol. 8.

142. See Ambedkar's reasoning in the Constituent Assembly debates, BAWS, vol. 13.

143. See B. R. Ambedkar, 'States and Minorities', BAWS, vol. 1.

144. See B. R. Ambedkar, Letter to A. V. Thakkar, 14 November 1932, vol. 9, pp. 134–40.

145. From BAWS, vol. 12, pp. 665-71.
146. The BAWS text sometimes terms it as Koregaon and at other times Goregaon. C. B. Khairmode, however, terms it as Goregaon. (See C. B. Khairmode, *Dr Bhimrao Ramji Ambedkar*, vol. 1, p. 44).
147. From BAWS, vol. 9, pp. 444-9.
148. From BAWS, vol. 2, pp. 337-44.
149. Ibid., pp. 344-56.
150. Ibid., pp. 362-3.
151. From BAWS, vol. 2, pp. 491-4.
152. From BAWS, vol. 3, pp. 142-8.
153. Members of the Bombay Legislative Committee associated with the Simon Commission, 1928-9.
154. The All Parties Conference in 1928 appointed a committee to suggest constitutional reforms for India. It was headed by Motilal Nehru. It submitted its report on 10 August 1928. This report is known as the Nehru Report.
155. On this issue see the statement concerning the state of education of the depressed classes in the Bombay Presidency submitted by Dr Ambedkar to the Simon Commission on behalf of the Bahiskrit Hitkarni Sabha on 29 May 1928, BAWS, vol. 2, pp. 407-28.
156. For details see BAWS, vol. 2, pp. 418-20 and vol. 12, pp. 77-147.
157. The Hunter Commission on education was appointed in 1882. For its recommendations, see BAWS, vol. 2, pp. 422-5; also see vol. 12, pp. 107-14.
158. In the Bombay Province.
159. James Bryce, *Modern Democracies*, London, Macmillan and Co. Ltd., 1921, Reprint 1929, pp. 80-92.
160. Montagu-Chelmsford report of constitutional reforms in India, 1919.
161. This commission recommended that the communal electorate be abolished and territorial constituencies be established in the then British colony of Ceylon. For the report of the Commission, see Government of Ceylon, *Report of the Special Commission on the Ceylon Constitution*, Colombo, 1928.
162. Ibid.
163. Political reforms introduced in India in 1909.
164. Political reforms introduced in India in 1919.

165. Landholders on whom title of land was initially conferred by way of a gift.

166. Vassals under the Marathas. The title was used in a wider sense to denote such feudatories in the rest of India as well.

167. For Ambedkar's stance on the Bill see BAWS, vol. 2, pp. 43–63.

168. They were the proposals that were advanced by prominent members of the Muslim community in India for a political settlement on 20 March 1927 in the context of the opposition to a separate electorate. Among others, they included: 1. That Sind should be made a separate province; 2. That NWF province should be treated on the same footing as other provinces; 3. That in Punjab and Bengal the proportion of Muslim representation be in accordance with their population. If these demands were met they showed their willingness to give up the communal electorate in favour of a joint electorate.

169. This was the announcement made by the Secretary of State for India in the House of Commons on 20 August 1917, that expressed the desire that progressive realization of responsible government was the goal of the future British Policy in India.

170. Edmund Burke, 'American Taxation', *Speeches and Letters on American Affairs*, V. Rev. Canon Peter Mckevitt, introduction, London, J. M. Dent & Sons, 1908, p. 49.

171. They were a ban on access to the interior of the ordinary temple and causing pollution, respectively. These tests were initially applied in the Census of 1911 to demarcate the Depressed Classes from the rest of the Hindus.

172. The Simon Commission of 1928.

173. Sir Denzil Ibbetson, *Punjab Castes*, Lahore, Government of Punjab, 1916.

174. Jogendranath Bhattacharya, *Hindu Castes and Sects*, Calcutta, Editions India, 1968, p. 13 (First publication: Calcutta, Thacker Spink & Co., 1896).

175. *Grimm's Fairy Tales*, Bridlington, Priory Books.

176. From BAWS, vol. 6, pp. 59–63.

177. See Johan Woygang Von Goethe, Goethes Werke, Hamburger Ansgabe, Eric Trunz (ed.), Hamburg, Christian Wegner, 1948–60.

178. Mountstuart Elphinstone, *The History of India*, London, John Murray, 1866, p. 19.

179. Maxim Gorky, 'How I learnt to write', *On Literature, Selected Articles*, V. Dober, trans, Moscow, Foreign Languages Publishing House, 1961, pp. 28-9
180. From BAWS, vol. 1, pp. 221-9.
181. From BAWS, vol. 1, p. 209
182. From BAWS, vol. 9, pp. 201-17.
183. From BAWS, vol. 9, pp. 274-97
184. From BAWS, vol. 3, pp. 441-53 & 459-62.
185. See Introduction pp. 23-4.
186. William Edward Hartpole Leeky, *The Map of Life, Conduct and Character*, Longman Green & Co., New York & Bombay, 1899, p. 316.
187. This oft repeated quotation from Justice M. G. Ranade is available in several forms. One of its first versions can be found in his speech as President of the first Bombay Provincial Social Conference held at Satara in May, 1900:

    'You cannot have a good social system when you find yourself low in the scale of political rights, nor can you be fit to exercise political rights and privileges unless your social system is based on reason and justice... If your religious ideals are low and grovelling, you cannot succeed in social, economical or political spheres. This interdependence is not an accident but is the law of nature. Like the members of our body, you cannot have strength in the hands and feet if your internal organs are in disorder. What applies to the human body holds good of the collective humanity, we call society or state', Mrs Ramadevi Ranade, *Miscellaneous Writings of the Hon'ble Mr Justice M. G. Ranade*, Bombay, The Manoranjan Press, 1915, pp. 231-2.
188. Pope Pius IX (1792-1878) during his papacy (1846-78), convened the First Vatican Council (1869-70) during which the doctrine of papal infallibility was authoritatively defined. It decreed that the Pope, when pronouncing on faith and morals, *ex cathedra*, is infallible.

    Pius IX, however, had entertained no doubt, even prior to the resolution of the Council, regarding the elevated status of his office. For a contemporaneous commentory to which this quotation is traceable, see Lord Acton, 'History of the Vatican Council', *North British Review*, LIII, October 1870—January 1871.
189. Alfred Charles William Harmsworth Northcliffe is reputed to be the most successful newspaper publisher in the history of the British Press. He founded popular modern journalism with several weeklies and dailies, starting from *Tit-Bits, Answers, Comic*

Cuts and Forget-Me-Not to *London Evening News* (1894); *Glassgow Daily Record* and *Daily Mail* (1896), *Daily Mirror* (1903); *Observer* (1905) and in 1906 secured control over *The Times*. He introduced a column for women in his papers, kept the price of his publications low and emphasized on their entertainment value.

190. A Nair woman's connubial relations with a Namboodri Brahmin is known as Sambandham (see A. K. Sur, *Sex and Marriage in India*, New Delhi, Allied, 1973).

191. A system of succession and inheritance that was mainly found in Kerala in which descent was traced through the female line. Its legal specification was provided by the Madras Marumakkattayam Act 1932, the Travancore Act (II of 1100), the Travancore Ezhava Act (III of 1100), the Travancore Nanjinad Vellala Act (VI of 1101), the Travancore Krishnanvakh Marummakkattayam Act (XXXIII of 1113) or the Cochin Nayar Act (XXIX of 1113).

192. A system of succession and inheritance that was mainly prevalent among the Thiyas in Kerala.

193. Sir P. C. Roy, who was the scion of a major landowning family in East Bengal, joined as Lecturer in chemistry at Presidency College, Calcutta after obtaining the B.Sc. and D.Sc. degrees from Edinburgh University. He published extensively on Ayurveda. He founded the Bengal Chemical and Pharmaceutical Works in 1892 and was instrumental in laying the foundation of the Indian Chemical Industry. In 1916 he joined the College of Science of Calcutta University as Palit Professor of Chemistry. He was knighted in 1919 and was elected as the President of the Indian Science Congress in 1920. Although he did not participate actively in politics he was deeply involved in social and philanthropic activities, particularly in the campaign against untouchability. (See M. Gupta, *Profulla Chandra Ray: A Biography*, Bharatiya Vidya Bhavan, 1966).

194. A. V. Dicey, *Introduction to the Study of the Law of the Constitution*, London, Macmillan & Co. Limited, 1915, pp. 74-8.

195. See BAWS, vol. 9, pp. 82-4.

196. See Voltaire, *Candide, Zadig and Selected Stories*, Donald M. Frame, Trans., London, Gassell, 1961, pp. 15-101.

197. See, S. Radhakrishnan, 'Gandhi, Religion and Politics', S. Radhakrishnan, ed., *Mahatma Gandhi: Essays and Reflections on his Life and Work*, London, George, Allen and Unwin, pp. 13-40.

530 ● NOTES

198. See John Dewey, *Democracy and Education*, New York, Macmillan, 1916, p. 124.
199. Edmund Burke, 'On Conciliation with Colonies', *Speeches and Letters on American Affairs*, V. Rev. Canon Peter Mckevitt, intro, London, J. M. Dent & Sons, 1908, p. 89.
200. From BAWS, vol. 3, pp. 360–71.
201. From BAWS, vol. 3, pp. 360–71
202. From BAWS, vol. 11, pp. 81–93.
203. Ibid, pp. 225–6
204. From BAWS, vol. 5, pp. 403–21.
205. Ambedkar argued it out in BAWS, vol. 3, pp. 246–9, pp. 257–61.
206. Albrecht Weber, *History of Indian Literature*, John Mann and Theodore Zacharael trans., London, Kegan Paul, Trubner & Co. Ltd., 1872 & 1892.
207. William McDougall, Introduction to Social Psychology, London, Methuen & Co., 1945, p. 61.
208. From BAWS, vol. 1, pp. 5–22.
209. From BAWS, vol. 1, pp. 47–80.
210. Ibid., pp. 86–96.
211. Ambedkar quotes the definition as reproduced by S. V. Ketkar, op. cit., pp. 13–14. Senart, however, was to work out his ideas on caste more in detail, subsequently. He restated its definition as follows: 'Let us picture a corporate group exclusive, in theory at least, rigorously hereditary. It possesses certain traditional and independent organization, a chief and a council, as occasion demands it meets in assemblies endowed with more or less full authority. Often united in the celebration of certain festivals, it is further bounded together by a common profession and by the practice of common customs which bear more especially upon marriage, food and various cases of impurity. Finally it is armed, in order to assure its authority, with a jurisdiction of fairly wide extent, capable of the infliction of certain penalties, especially of banishment, either absolute or revocable, enforcing the power of the community. Such briefly is the caste system, as it appears to us. Emile Senart, *Caste in India, The Facts and the System*, Sir E. Denison Ross, C.I.E. (trans.), London, Methuen & Co. 1930, p. 20.
212. Ambedkar quotes S. V. Ketkar verbatim, op. cit., p. 14.
213. Ambedkar quotes Ketkar, again, verbatim, op. cit., p. 14; also see, H. Risley, *The People of India*, Delhi, Oriental Books, 1969.

214. S. V. Ketkar, op. cit., p. 15.

215. A. K. Coomaraswamy, 'Sati: A Defence of the Eastern Woman', *British Sociological Review*, vol. VI, 1913.

216. Denzil Ibbetson, *Punjab Castes*, Lahore, Government of Punjab, 1916.

217. Herbert Spencer, *First Principles*, New York, D. Appleton & Co., 1885; Spencer's more formal definition of evolution was '...an integration of matter and concomitant dissipation of motion during which the matter passes from an indefinite, incoherent homogeneity to a definite, coherent heterogeneity; and during which the retained motion undergoes a parallel transformation' (Ibid., p. 396).

218. It is a *Purana* devoted to the construction of lineages.

219. Bombay Province.

220. These were areas of British India, generally inhabited by indigenous people such as the North-East, which were kept directly under the control of the Governor-General under the India Act, 1935.

221. It is the practice of purification initiated, on a large scale, by the Arya Samaj towards the lower castes, particularly the untouchables to accommodate them in the Hindus caste hierarchy in the early part of the twentieth century (see Nandini Gooptu, 'Caste and Labour: Untouchable Social Movements in Urban Uttar Pradesh in the early Twentieth Century' Peter Robb (ed.), *Dalit Movements and the Meanings of Labour in India*, New Delhi, Oxford University Press, 1993.

222. Meaning, organization, emphasized by the Arya Samaj and particularly by the Rashtriya Swayam Sevak Sangh, formed in October 1925.

223. Meaning, brothers in the sense of strong kinship or community bond.

224. Literally 1¼ of a lakh, meaning the incomparably superior quality of the person, under consideration, compared to others.

225. See Plato, *Republic*.

226. Shambuka who belonged to a lowly caste is supposed to have been killed by Rama for pursuing an avocation not permitted to his caste.

227. Those belonging to the upper three Varnas: Brahmin, Kshatriya and Vaishya.

228. S. Radhakrishnan, *Hindu View of Life*, London, Unwin, 1963 (impression), p. 11.

229. A. V. Dicey, op. cit., pp. 74–8.

230. Acharya Jagdeeshlal Shastri (ed.), *Manusmriti*, Delhi, Motilal Benarasidas, 1983, Ch. 12, Verse 108.

231. This slogan appears in several forms. The concluding sentence of the *Communist Manifesto* is, 'the proletarians have nothing to lose but their chains. They have a world to win. Working men of all countries unite' (Marx and Engels, *Collected Works*, 1845–48, New York, International Publishers, 1976, p. 519.

232. Acharya Jagdeeshlal Shastri (ed.), *Manusmriti*, op cit., Ch. 2, Verse 11.

233. Ibid., Ch. 2, Verse 14.

234. Ibid., Ch. 12, Verse 95.

235. Edmund Burke, *Reflections on the Revolution in France*, London, Dent, 1910, p. 87.

236. Another version of this position is as follows: 'Not only social institutions, but moral codes, religious, educational systems, fashions, and everything else connected with social life must be considered as having a place, potentially at least, in the process of human adaptation...' Thomas Nixon Carver, *The Essential Factors of Social Evolution*, Cambridge, Harvard University Press, 1935, p. 11.

237. John Dewey, *Democracy and Education: An Introduction to the Philosophy of Education*, New York, The Macmillan Co., 1916, p. 24.

238. Ibid., p. 88.

239. Gandhi's review of Annihilation of caste in *Harijan*, 11 July 1936; 18 July 1936 and 15 August 1936.

240. Social order based on *Varna*.

241. M. K. Gandhi, *Harijan*, 18 July 1936.

242. See *What the Congress and Gandhi have done to the Untouchables*, BAWS, vol. 9, pp. 275–6.

243. M. K. Gandhi, *Harijan*, 11 July 1936.

244. From BAWS, vol. 5, pp. 19–26.

245. Ibid., pp. 229–76.

246. From BAWS, vol. 12, pp. 132–3; 138–40, 145–7.

247. From BAWS, vol. 9, pp. 133–42.

248. It was preceeded by an address presented to Lord Minto, Governor, General, by a deputation of the Muslim Community. The full version of the address and Lord Minto's reply can be seen in *Pakistan or Partition of India*, BAWS, vol. 8, pp. 430–45.

249. For the resolution and the discussion that ensued see BAWS, vol. 12, pp. 132–7.
250. Harijan Seva Sangh.
251. See Gandhi's Statement dated 5 November 1932 in Pyarelal, *The Epic Fast*, Ahmedabad, Navjivan, 1932, pp. 318–22.
252. From BAWS vol. 2, pp. 546–54.
253. From BAWS vol. 7, pp. 9–18.
254. From BAWS vol. 7, pp. 311–20.
255. M. A. Sherring, *Hindu Tribes and Castes*, vol. 1, London 1909, p. xxi.
256. Edward L Thorndike, *The original Nature of the Man*, New York, Teachers College, Columbia University, 1913.
257. From BAWS, vol. 6, pp. 213–24.
258. From BAWS, vol. 6, pp. 415–44.
259. From BAWS, vol. 8 pp. 29–39.
260. E. Renan, 'What is a nation', in Alfred Zimmerin (ed.), *Modern Political Doctrines*, London, Oxford University Press, 1939, p. 197. The essay was initially published in 1882. The translation used by Zimmerin differes slightly from the one used by Ambedkar.
261. Ibid., p. 198.
262. Ibid., p. 202.
263. Ibid., pp. 202–3.
264. Ibid., pp. 190–1.
265. From, BAWS, vol. 13, pp. 49–70.
266. From BAWS, vol. 14, Part 1, pp. 5–12.
267. James Bryce, *The American Commonwealth*.
268. Ibid.
269. Ibid.
270. For prohibited degree of relationships see BAWS, vol. 14, Part I, p. 212.
271. For *sapinda* relationships see BAWS, vol. 14, Part I, pp. 204–10.
272. See note 192.
273. A system of inheritance in the line of the progemy of sisters, mainly prevalent among some communities in Kerala and coastal Karnataka and specified by the Madras Aliyasantha Act, 1949 (Madras Act IV of 1949).
274. Renouncer.
275. Form of adoption traditionally prevalent in and around Mithila, under which even a wife or a widow could adopt a son, although

from the same caste. It was recognized as valid though no ceremonies or documents were required for it. (See D. F. Mulla, *Principles of Hindu Law*, Bombay, N. M. Tripathi Private Limited, 1959, 12th edition, p. 676.)

276. A form of adoption that prevailed in the Mithila Darbhanga region (See D. F. Mulla, op. cit.), p. 676.

277. It was a made of adoption where a person gives his son to another under an agreement that he should be considered to be the son of both the natural and adoptive fathers. The son so given in adoption is called *dvyamushyayana* (See D. F. Mulla, op. cit.), p. 653.

278. It is the ceremony of handing over of the child by the natural parents or guardians and his acceptance by his adoptive parents. Legally, it has the effect of transferring the adopted boy from his family into the family that adopts him.

Bibliography

In terms of modes of presentation we can re-group Ambedkar's writings as follows:

BOOKS AND MONOGRAPHS PUBLISHED BY PROFESSIONAL PUBLISHERS

The Problem of the Rupee (1923) and *The Evolution of Provincial Finance in British India* (1925): King & Co., London. *Thoughts on Pakistan* (1940); *Mr Gandhi and the Emancipation of Untouchables* (1943); *What Congress and Gandhi have done to the Untouchables* (1945); *Who were the Shudras? How they came to be the Fourth Varna in Indo-Aryan Society* (1946); *States and Minorities: What are their Rights and how to Secure them in the Constitution of Free India* (1947) and *Maharashtra as a Linguistic Province* (1948): Thacker & Co., Bombay. *The Untouchables: Who were They and Why they became Untouchables?* (1948): Amrit Book Co., New Delhi. *Case for the Hindu Code* (1949): Beacon Information and Publications, New Delhi. *Thoughts on Linguistic States* (1955): Ram Krishna Printing Press, Bombay. *The Buddha and His Dhamma* (1957): Siddhartha College Publications, Bombay.

Most of these works went through several editions and reprints. Sometimes, the title of the work got changed. For instance, *Thoughts on Pakistan* saw three editions by 1946 with its title changed to *Pakistan or Partition of India* in 1946. Occasionally, publishers changed hands with a new edition. *The Problem of the Rupee*, initially published by King & Co., was brought out as *History of Indian Currency and Banking* by Thacker & Co., in 1946.

BOOKS AND PAPERS PUBLISHED BY AMBEDKAR

Annihilation of Caste (1936); *Ranade, Gandhi and Jinnah* (1943) and *Communal Deadlock and a Way to Solve it—Address to the All India Scheduled Castes Federation* (1945).

ADDRESSES AND LECTURES
PUBLISHED BY SPONSORS

Federation vs Freedom (1939), the Kale Memorial Lecture, by Gokhale Institute of Economics and Political Science. *Conditions Precedent to the Success of Parliamentary Democracy in India* (1953), by V. B. Gogate, Hon. Secretary, Poona District Law Library, Poona.

ARTICLES, PAPERS AND RADIO TALKS

'Castes in India: Their Mechanism, Genesis and Development' in *Indian Antiquity*, 1917; 'Small Holdings in India and their Remedies' and 'Mr Russell and the Reconstruction of Society, a review of Bertrand Russell's *Principles of Social Reconstruction* in *Journal of Indian Economic Society*, vol. 1, 1918; 'The Present Problem in Indian Currency' in *The Servant of India*, 11 & 16 April 1925; Review of H. L. Chablani's *Indian Currency and Exchange* in *The Servant of India*, 25 June 1925; Review of the *Report of the Taxation Enquiry Committee*, 1926 in *The Servant of India*, 29 April 1926; 'What ails the World Today' in *The Indian Readers Digest*, July 1943; 'The Buddha and the Future of His Religion' in *Mahabodhi*, April–May 1950; 'The Rise and Fall of Hindu Women; Who is Responsible for it?' in *Mahabodhi*, May–June, 1951 and 'The Original Home of the Hindus' in *The Organiser*, 23 July 1952.

Ambedkar wrote regularly in his Marathi journals *Mooknayak*; *Bahishkrit Bharat*; *Janata* and *Prabudd Bharat*.

He delivered a talk on 'Prospects of Parliamentary Democracy', BBC, London, 20 May 1956.

INTRODUCTIONS BY AMBEDKAR
ON WRITINGS OF OTHERS

Preface to P. L. Narasu's, *Essence of Buddhism*, Delhi, Bharatiya Publishing House, 1948. Foreword to V. G. Salvi's, *Commodity*

Exchange, 1947. Foreword to M. R. Idgunji's *Social Insurance in India*, 1948.

DOCUMENTS AND REPRESENTATIONS

Ambedkar drew up numerous representations, memoranda and documents. He issued statements on behalf of the interests and constituencies he represented. He also drafted the Constitution and bye-laws of the political parties and organizations set up by him. They included: Evidence before the Southborough Committee (1917); Statement and Deputation before the Simon Commission (1928); Statements on Behalf of the Bahishkrit Hitkarni Sabha before the Simon Commission (1928); Round Table Conference Documents (1930-2) with associated memoranda and Statements including *The Untouchables and the Pax Britannica*; Statement before the Lothian Committee (1932); the Constitution of the Independent Labour Party (1936); The Constitution of the Scheduled Caste Federation (1942); The Confidential report containing the Grievances of the Scheduled Castes presented to the Governor-General (1942); Statement on Cripps Proposals (1942); A critique of the Proposals of the Cabinet Mission (1946) and Memorandum on behalf of the Scheduled Caste Federation submitted to the Cabinet Mission (1946).

He drafted the bills that he initiated before the Bombay Legislature such as the Hereditary Offices (Amendment) Bill (1927) and the Khoti System Abolition Bill (1937). He was the Chairman of the Drafting Committee (1947-9) of the Constitution and was the Chairman of the select Committee on the Hindu Code Bill (1948-51) as Law Minister. He also played a major role in initiating several bills as Labour member of the Viceroy's Council (1942-6) and as Law Minister in the Nehru Cabinet (1947-51).

He prepared supportive evidence to these documents and backed them up through appendices.

UNPUBLISHED WRITINGS

Ambedkar left behind a large number of his writings at various stages of completion. We can divide them mainly into five types:

Early Writings: *Ancient Indian Commerce*, the dissertation that he initially worked on for an MA, at Columbia University (1916); *Administration and Finance of the East India Company* (1916); Responsibilities of Provincial Governments in India, a paper read at the Economic Association of Columbia University (1916).

Notes for his teaching and the conferences that he attended (1924–42).

Writings related to Hinduism: In the context of his decision to give up Hinduism he undertook an extensive study of comparative religions with special reference to Hindu scriptures (1936–56). The debates on the Hindu Code Bill made him to undertake specialized studies on Hindu law and traditions (1948–51).

Writings related to Buddhism and the interface between Hinduism and Buddhism (1940's–56).

Marxism and the relation between Marxism and Buddhism (1940's–56). Ambedkar planned a major work on *India and the Pre-requisites of Communism* but could complete only a part of it. He presented a major address at the World Buddhist Conference in November, 1956 on *Buddha or Karl Marx*.

INTERVENTIONS IN LEGISLATURES, OFFICIAL COMMITTEES AND CONFERENCES

Ambedkar was a nominated member of the Bombay Legislative Assembly (1926–37); an elected member of the Bombay Legislature (1937–42); Labour Member in the Executive Council of the Viceroy (1942–6); A Member of the Constituent Assembly and Central Legislature (1946–52) and Member of the Rajya Sabha (1952–6). He was also a member of several commissions, conferences and the sub-committees appointed by them. Ambedkar made meticulous preparations for the meetings and participated in them very forcefully. The minutes of the proceedings of most of these bodies are available.

LETTERS: PERSONAL AND OFFICIAL

During his long public career Ambedkar was in contact with several public figures. He also was away from his house for very long intervals. He associated with a number of people in different capacities. Letters were the major mode of communication with them.

PUBLIC ADDRESSES

Ambedkar addressed a large audience all over India. Some of his most important arguments and stances came to be announced there. Several of these addresses were carefully drawn up such as the one at the Yeola conference on the reasons for conversion and the speech before the *Baudha* gathering in 1951.

EXCERPTS OF SPEECHES IN NEWSPAPERS, MAGAZINES OR JOURNALS

Ambedkar was reported very extensively in the media, with a mix of kudos and brickbats. He also strongly reacted to the media reports. Lengthy excerpts of his speeches and pronouncements were published in the papers particularly on such occasions as the Poona Pact, the visit of the Cabinet Mission, the debate on the Hindu Code Bill and his conversion to Buddhism.

Compilations of Ambedkar's writings was undertaken from early on, particularly of those writings and speeches found in Marathi. S. R. Kharat brought out *Dr Ambedkaranchi Patran*, Poona, Lekhan Vachan Bhandar, Laxmi Rasta, 1961, the collection of Ambedkar's letters; M. F. Ganjare edited the speeches of Ambedkar in six volumes, *Dr Ambedkaranchi Bhashane*, vols I-VI, Nagpur, Ashok Prakashan, 1974; Bhagwan Das compiled Ambedkar's speeches in English in *Thus Spoke Ambedkar* (Selected Speeches). While vols 1 & 2 of it were brought out by Bheem Patrika Publications, Jullundur, 1963 & 1969, vols 3 & 4 were published by Ambedkar Sahitya Prakashan, Bangalore, 1979. He also compiled a volume on *Rare Prefaces Written by Dr Ambedkar*, Jullundur, Bheem Patrika, 1980. *The Rise and Fall of the Hindu Woman*, was brought out by Hyderabad, Dr Ambedkar Publications, 1965; Compilations from the journals that Ambedkar edited were soon to come: Ratnakar Ganaveer, ed., *Dr Ambedkaranche Bahishkrit Bharatateel Agralekh*, Nagpur, Ratnamitra Prakashan, 1976. He also brought out *Dr Ambedkaranche Bahishkrit Bharatateel Sphut Lekh*, Bhusaval, Ratnamitra Prakashan, 1981. Ratnakar Ganveer also collected Ambedkar's letters written from abroad, under the title, *Vilayatehun Dr Babasahebanchi Patre*, Nagpur, Ratnamitra Prakashan, 1984. S. R. Kharat edited a collection of Ambedkar's letters in *Dr Babasaheb-Ambedkaranchi Patre*, Pune, Indrayani Sahitya, 1990.

In 1976, the Government of Maharashtra set up an advisory committee with the State's Education Minister as Chairman and comprising political followers of Dr Ambedkar, scholars and noted writers to compile the writings and speeches of Ambedkar and have them published. The committee set up an Editorial Board for the purpose with Shri Vasant Moon as officer-on-special duty. Under the overall

supervision of this committee Shri Vasant Moon has compiled and
edited two volumes on *Source Material on Dr Babasaheb Ambedkar and
the Movement of the Untouchables* (Bombay, Department of Education,
Government of Maharashtra, 1982 & 1990) and 16 volumes of
Babasaheb Ambedkar Writings and Speeches (Bombay, Department of
Education, Government of Maharashtra, 1979-98). A few more
volumes on Dr Ambedkar in Parliament—1947 to 1956; Dr Ambedkar's
Correspondence; Dr Ambedkar in photographs and on his writings
in Marathi, his Speeches and Interviews are yet to be published.

A BRIEF GUIDE TO AMBEDKAR'S WRITINGS

The *Babasaheb Ambedkar Writings and Speeches* brought out by the
Government of Maharashtra are not organized thematically except for
the volumes published later where an attempt has been made to
preserve some thematic unity.

There are numerous reasons for it. Even if they are attended to,
a theoretical hurdle would still remain: Given the essential contestability
of the boundaries of a discipline, it is difficult to suggest exclusion and
inclusion of issues in a strong sense, except in certain core areas of
general agreement. However, conventions, feasibility and disciplinary
rootedness make recourse to themes unavoidable. We have employed
the criterion of the significant and the less significant to include or
exclude a piece of writing in slots enumerated below.

ON ECONOMICS

Ambedkar's first writings in this area, 'Small holdings in India and
their remedies', and 'Mr Russell and the Reconstruction of Society,
a review of Bertrand Russell's *Principles of Social Reconstruction*,
appeared in the *Journal of the Indian Economic Society* and have been
reproduced in *BAWS*, vol. 1. *Administration and Finance of the East
India Company and The Evolution of Provincial Finance in British India*,
his MA and Ph.D. dissertations, respectively, at Columbia University
and *The Problem of the Rupee*, the D.Sc. thesis at London School of
Economics are now available in *BAWS*, vol. 6. This volume also
contains Ambedkar's statement before the Royal Commission on
Indian Currency and Finance, 1924-5; his oral evidence before it on
15 December 1925; a summary statement of his position explored in
The Problem of the Rupee, and published in *The Servant of India* as 'The
Present Problem in the Indian Currency' on 1 April 1925; a sequel

BIBLIOGRAPHY ● 541

to it in the same journal on 16 April 1925; his review of H. L. Chablani's book *Indian Currency and Exchange*, published in *The Servant of India* and his forwards to two books dealing on *Commodity Exchange* and *Social Insurance in India* by P. G. Salvi and M. R. Idgunji, respectively. *Ancient Indian Commerce*, the dissertation that he initially intended to submit for the MA requirements of Columbia University, is included in *BAWS*, vol. 12. Ambedkar's initiative in evolving a welfare regime and his large scale forays in labour legislation and planning can be found in *BAWS*, vol. 10. His interventions on the budget in the Bombay legislature, the Hereditary Offices Amendment Bill (1928), a Bill to abolish the Khoti System of land tenure (1937) and his response to the Industrial Disputes Bill (1938) are included in BAWS, vol. 2. While writings critiquing Gandhism and Marxism are placed in BAWS, vol. 13 and vol. 3 respectively writings dealing with affirmative action are scattered across, particularly, in BAWS, vols 2, 10, 13, 15 and 16. His writings and speeches in defence of state socialism are included in BAWS, vols 1, 13 and 15.

SOCIAL INSTITUTIONS

Ambedkar paid a great deal of attention in understanding varna, caste and untouchability. His 'Castes in India, their Mechanism, Genesis and Development', published in 1917, and 'Annihilation of Caste', published in 1936 are found in BAWS, vol. 1. Writings dealing on the caste-system and its implications are included in BAWS, vol. 3, BAWS, vol. 5 contains writings dealing with the social structures and the movement of the Untouchables. The approach of the Congress and Gandhi towards the Untouchables is found in the articles included in BAWS, vol. 9. The confinement of the *Shudras* to the fourth *Varna* and origin of untouchability is discussed in BAWS, vol. 7. The approach of the British towards the Untouchables is discussed in several writings, particularly in the representations of the Bahishkrit Hitkarni Sabha, contained in BAWS, vol. 2 and in the *The Untouchables and the Pax Britannica* in BAWS, vol. 12. Comparison of untouchability with cases akin to it such as slavery and the treatment meted out to Jews is undertaken in writings included in BAWS, vol. 12.

HINDUISM

Since Ambedkar thought that the caste system and untouchability were integral to Hinduism, an understanding of the latter calls for a

study of the former. *Riddles on Hinduism* (BAWS, vol. 4); the three
sections of BAWS, vol. 3—'Philosophy of Hinduism', 'Revolution and
Counter-revolution' and 'India and the Pre-requisites of Communism'—and BAWS, vol. 14 that discusses the Hindu Code contain his
main ideas on Hinduism. The relation between high caste and low
caste Hindus, on one hand, and the Untouchables, on the other, is
discussed in several works, particularly in BAWS, vol. 5 and vol. 9.
The Buddha and His Dhamma included in BAWS, vol. 11 compares
Buddhism with Hinduism. '*Ranade, Gandhi and Jinnah*' and '*Annihilation of Caste*' included in BAWS, vol. 1 stress on the continued
relevance of the agenda of social reforms. Ambedkar's attempt to
highlight the distinct identity of the *Shudras* and Untouchables can be
seen in *Who are the Shudras?* and *The Untouchables* (BAWS, vol. 7).

BUDDHISM

Ambedkar's two major works on Buddhism, i.e. *The Buddha and His
Dhamma and Pali Dictionary and the Buddha Pooja Path* are reproduced
in BAWS, vol. 11 and vol. 16, respectively. Some of the most important speeches of Ambedkar on Buddhism, including the 1951 speech
to the Boudha gathering, are not found in the hitherto published
works of BAWS. One has to take recourse to K. F. Ganjare or Bhagwan
Das for the same. For Ambedkar's construction of Buddhism in
opposition to Hinduism, *Revolution and Counterrevolution in Ancient
India* (BAWS, vol. 3) and *The Untouchables* (BAWS, vol. 7) are important. For the interface between Buddhism and Marxism, apart from
The Buddha and His Dhamma (BAWS, vol. 11) *India and Pre-requisites
of Communism* 'Buddha or Karl Marx' (BAWS, vol. 3), and 'Buddha
and the Future of His Religion' (*Mahabodi*, April–May 1950) are
significant. For the relation between Buddhism and other religions
and Buddhism and the domain of morality and rights, *The Buddha and
His Dhamma* (BAWS, vol. 11) and 'Buddha and the Future of His
Religion' (*Mahabodi*, April–May 1950) and 'Buddha and Karl Marx'
(BAWS, vol. 3) could be consulted.

HISTORY

Ambedkar located issues on a historical trajectory. Therefore, the
historical axis remains the basis of all his writings. Substantially he
addresses a number of issues which historians generally do: *Ancient*

Indian Commerce (BAWS, vol. 12) has three fascinating chapters dealing on ancient Indian commerce, commercial relations of India in the Middle Ages and the devastation wrought by the East India Company in India, respectively. *The Evolution of Provincial Finance in India and History of Indian Currency and Banking* (BAWS, vol. 6) highlight the formation of public policies over a period. *The Administration and Finance of East India Company* (BAWS, vol. 6), brings out the larger involvement of British Society in shaping early colonialism in India. Ambedkar's perspective on nationalism is spelled out in *What Congress and Gandhi have done to the Untouchables* (BAWS, vol. 9); *Pakistan or the Partition of India* (BAWS, vol. 8) and 'Ranade, Gandhi and Jinnah' (BAWS, vol. 1) and in his memoranda, statements and representations (BAWS, vols 2 & 10). The impact of the Raj on the Untouchables is brought out in articles contained in BAWS, vol. 2, 5 and 12. A critical exposition of the history of Christianity in India is undertaken in the articles included in BAWS, vol. 5. The contention between Buddhism and Hinduism is explored in *Revolution and Counter-revolution in India* (BAWS, vol. 3). His conception of History and a critique of the conception of History of Hindu Scriptures can be seen in 'Philosophy of Hinduism' (BAWS, vol. 3) and *Riddles of Hinduism* (BAWS, vol. 4). *Who were the Shudras?* and *The Untouchables* (BAWS, vol. 7), highlight the process of the emergence of two major social constituencies in India over the period. The Buddha in *The Buddha and His Dhamma* (BAWS, vol. 11) is located at a clear historical conjuncture. The Hindu Code Bill (BAWS, vol. 14) explores the changes that customs and traditions have undergone.

POLITICS AND PRAXIS

There is definitely a primacy to politics in Ambedkar's writings as he constructed constituencies and proposed agendas. The key writings in this regard are:

'Evidence before the Southborough Committee' (BAWS, vol. 1); interventions in the Bombay Provincial Legislature (BAWS, vol. 2); on the Mahad Satyagraha and the temple entry movements (Government of Maharashtra, *Source Material On Dr Ambedkar and the Movement of the Untouchables*, vols 1 & 2); Statements before the Simon Commission (BAWS, vol. 2); The deliberations at the RTC and the connected documents (BAWS, vol. 2); the Poona Pact and contest with Gandhi and Gandhism (BAWS, vol. 9); the Constitutions of the Independent Labour Party and the Scheduled Castes Federation (Government of Maharashtra, *Source Material on Dr Ambedkar and the Movement of the Untouchables*, vols 1 & 2); 'Federalism versus Freedom' (BAWS, vol. 1); *Thoughts on Pakistan* (BAWS, vol. 8); interventions as the Labour Member in the Viceroy's Council (BAWS, vol. 10); submissions before the Cripps Mission and the Cabinet Mission (BAWS, vol. 10); 'Communal Deadlock and a Way to Solve it' and 'States and Minorities' (BAWS, vol. 1); the proposals before the Constituent Assembly (BAWS, vol. 13); the Hindu Code Bill (BAWS, vol. 14) and *The Buddha and His Dhamma* (BAWS, vol. 11). In his interventions in the Parliament (BAWS, vol. 15), Ambedkar advances specific and fairly coherent political agendas although there might be changes in emphasis over a period. The periodicals that he published highlighted these political agendas (Government of Maharashtra, *Source Material on Dr Babasaheb Ambedkar and the Movement of the Untouchables*, vol. 2).

LAW

The domain of law has a pivotal importance in Ambedkar's scheme of things. He elaborated it in 'States and Minorities' (BAWS, vol. 1); the draft constitution and the Constituent Assembly debates (BAWS, vol. 13); the Hindu Code Bill and his clash with Nehru in this regard (BAWS, vol. 14, Part I & II); his interventions in Bombay Provincial Legislature (BAWS, vol. 2) and as Law Minister and Member of the Opposition (BAWS, vol. 15). He discussed the relation between law and morality in *The Buddha and His Dhamma* (BAWS, vol. 11) and in 'Buddha and Karl Marx' (BAWS, vol. 3). His critical comments on the traditional Hindu code in general and on *Manudharmashastra*, in particular, are found in several of his writings (BAWS, vols 3 and 4). Besides he reflected upon specific aspects of law in 'Lectures on the English Constitution'. 'The Notes on Acts and Laws', 'Paramountcy and the Claim of the Indian States to be Independent', 'Notes on Parliamentary Procedure' etc. (BAWS, vol. 12).

MINORITIES

Ambedkar singled out the minorities for special consideration in a number of his writings. The most important among them is the

'Evidence before the Southborough Committee' (BAWS, vol. 1); Statement before the Simon Commission and particularly the statements on behalf of the Bahishkrit Hitkarini Sabha before the same commission (BAWS, vol. 2); the deliberations at the RTC (BAWS, vol. 2); 'Federation Versus Freedom' and 'Communal Deadlock and a Way to Solve it' (BAWS, vol. 1); *Pakistan or Partition of India* (BAWS, vol. 8); *What Congress and Gandhi have Done to the Untouchables* and *Mr Gandhi and the Emancipation of the Untouchables* (BAWS, vol. 9); Essays on Untouchables and Untouchability and writings included under Book IV in BAWS, vol. 5; 'States and Minorities' (BAWS, vol. 1); the draft constitution and deliberations in the Constituent Assembly (BAWS, vol. 13) and the Hindu Code Bill (BAWS, vol. 14, Part I & II).

AFFIRMATIVE ACTION

Ambedkar advanced a set of justification and a comprehensive scheme of affirmative action in the 'Evidence before the Southborough Committee (BAWS, vol. 1); his representations before the Simon Commission, Note before the Lothian Committee and deliberations at the RTC (BAWS, vol. 2); certain specific bills and policy measures that he recommended (BAWS, vols 2 and 10); his contentions against the Congress and Gandhi (BAWS, vol. 9); 'The Untouchables and the Pax Britannica' (BAWS, vol. 12); the 'Grievances of the Scheduled Castes', submitted to the Governor General (BAWS, vol. 10); his response to the Cripps Proposals and the proposals of the Cabinet Mission (BAWS, vol. 10), 'States and Minorities' (BAWS, vol. 1); the Constituent Assembly debates and the draft constitution (BAWS, vol. 13); his interventions as Law Minister and Member of the opposition in the Parliament (BAWS, vols 15 & 17) and in 'Thoughts on Linguistic States' (BAWS, vol. 11).

IDENTITIES

Ambedkar is in constant struggle to negotiate the relation between the domain of law, rights, identities and communities. He did not subscribe to the arrangement of these relations expressed in Hinduism (See Hinduism above); He accords a qualified approval to linguistic states (BAWS, vol. 1); is cautious on nationalism (BAWS, vol. 8); subscribes to a specific understanding of religion while at the same time acknowledging its necessity (BAWS, vols 3 and 11) and suggests a specific relation between rights and identity, in 'Annihilation of Caste' (BAWS, vol. 1) and the Hindu Code (BAWS, vol. 14, Part I & II). He approves or disapproves identities on the basis of certain general principles as expressed in 'Federalism versus Freedom' and 'States and Minorities' (BAWS, vol. 1) and *What Congress and Gandhi Have Done to the Untouchables* and *Mr Gandhi and the Emancipation of the Untouchables* (BAWS, vol. 9). Further he established a specific relation between group rights and individual rights (BAWS, vols 2 & 13) and adopted a critical stance towards the practices of conversion while upholding the right to freedom of religion (BAWS, vol. 5).

BIOGRAPHIES

C. B. Khairmode's ambitious project in 14 volumes, *Dr Bhimrao Ramji Ambedkar*, in Marathi, still remains the most authoritative biography of Ambedkar. It's first volume was published in 1952 and Khairmode could see the publication of only six of the volumes before he died on 18 November 1971. The subsequent volumes were published by the Maharashtra Sahitya Sanskriti Mandal, Bombay. The Sugava Publication Pune, has brought out a second edition of this biography. In similar fashion, B. C. Kamble has authored a multi-volume biography, *Samagra Ambedkar Charitra*, Parts 1–11 (Bombay, Author, 1984–7). S. R. Kharat's *Dr Babasaheb Ambedkaranchya Sahavasant* (Pune, Inamdar Bandhu Prakashan, 1982) and *Dr Babasaheb Ambedkarkaranchi Atmakatha* (Pune, Thokal Prakashan, 1977) provide some of the intimate glimpses of Ambedkar.

Dhanajay Keer's, *Dr Ambedkar: Life and Mission* (Bombay, Popular Prakashan, 1962, Second edition), initially published in 1954, still remains the most popular biography in English. He has also brought out *Dr Ambedkar, a Memorial Album* (Bombay, Popular Prakashan, 1982). D. N. Shikare's *Dr Ambedkar* (Jayant & Co. Poona, 1963), was a welcome addition in the beginning but has been supplanted by the new arrivals. In the 'Builders of India' Series, W. N. Kuber provided a biographical account of *Ambedkar* (New Delhi, Ministry of Information and Broadcasting, 1978) following a longer evaluative study from a leftist standpoint entitled, *Dr Ambedkar, A Critical Study* (New Delhi, PPH, 1973). D. C. Ahir, after several other studies on Ambedkar and Buddhism has published *The Legacy of Dr Ambedkar*, (Delhi, B. R., 1990). A detailed chronological account of the main events in Ambedkar's life can be found in K. N. Kadam (ed.), *B. R. Ambedkar and the Significance of His Movement; A chronology*, Bombay, Popular Prakashan, 1991.

Much more numerous are biographies of Ambedkar in the vernacular languages. They have proliferated with the growth of the Dalit movement and emergence of an articulate section of Dalit intellectuals. One of the earliest works in Hindi which focussed on Ambedkar was that of C. P. Jigyasu, *Dr Babasaheb Ambedkar Ka Jivan Sangharsh* (Lucknow, Hindu Samaj Sudhar Karyalaya, 1961). A large number of these biographies in the vernaculars are, however, abridged versions of their better-known counterparts in English or Marathi and have rarely woven local memories of Ambedkar and the movement in their presentation.

SECONDARY WRITINGS

We can identify two kinds of writings in this category. The first, provide a general account of the ideas of Ambedkar and, sometimes, the movement that he led. They often go into several biographical details. The other writings concentrate on specific aspects or look at issues from the vantage point of a set of ideas. This distinction, however, is quite tentative and only holds good within limits.

Among generalist accounts, mention could be made of the following: Joachim Alva, *Man and Superman of Hindusthan*, Bombay, Thacker & Co. 1943; Robbin Jeanette, *Dr Ambedkar and His Movement*, Hyderabad, Dr Ambedkar Publication Society, 1964; V. Chandra Mowli, *B. R. Ambedkar: Man and His Mission*, New Delhi, Sterling, Madhu Limaye, 'B. R. Ambedkar: A Social Revolutionary', in *Prime Movers: Role of Individual in History*, New Delhi, Radiant, 1985, pp. 181–292; D. R. Jatava, *The Social Philosophy of B. R. Ambedkar*, Agra, Phoenix Publication, 1965; Nim Hotilal (ed.), *Thoughts on Dr Ambedkar*, Agra, Siddharth Educational and Cultural society, 1969; Chandra Bharill, *Social and Political ideas of B. R. Ambedkar*, Jaipur, Aalek Pub., 1977; K. L. Chanchreek, *Dr B. R. Ambedkar*, New Delhi, Gyan Pub., 1990; Government of India, *Ambedkar and Social Justice*, New Delhi, Ministry of Information & Broadcasting, 1992; Eleanor Zelliot, *From Untouchable to Dalit*, *Essays on the Ambedkar Movement*, New Delhi, Manohar, 1992 and Arun Shourie, *Worshipping False Gods: Ambedkar and the Facts which have been Erased*, New Delhi, ASA Pub. 1997.

Those which concentrate on specific aspects and provide specialised accounts can be organised around the following themes.

BUDDHISM

Eleanor Zelliot, 'Background of the Mahar Buddhist Conversion', in Robert Sakai (ed.), *Studies on Asia*, Lincoln, University of Nebraska, 1966; 'Buddhism and Politics in Maharashtra', in D. E. Smith (ed.), *South Asian Politics and Religion*, Princeton, Princeton University Press, 1966 and 'Learning the Use of Political Means, the Mahars of Maharashtra', in Rajni Kothari (ed.), *Caste in Modern India*, Poona, Orient and Longman, 1970; Ven, Anand Kausalyayan, ed., *The Buddha and His Dhamma* (in Hindi), Bombay, People's Education Society, Siddharth College, 1971 (This translation was first brought out in 1960. It added extensive footnotes to the text, tracing the sources of the Buddha's teachings. It suggested that the passages of *The Buddha and His Dhamma* are primarily drawn from the Pali Tripitakas, thereby, legitimizing the status of the work for orthodox rendering); Eleanor Zelliot, 'The Psychological Dimension of the Buddhist Movement in India', in G. A. Oddie (ed.), *Religion in South Asia*, Delhi, Manohar, 1977; 'Religion and Legitimation in Mahar Movement', in B. L. Smith (ed.), *Religion and Legitimation of Power in South Asia*, Leiden, Bill, 1978; and 'The Indian Rediscovery of Buddhism', in A. K. Narain (ed.), *Studies in Pali and Buddhism*, New Delhi, D. K., 1979; D. C. Ahir (ed.), *Dr Ambedkar and Buddhism*, Bombay, People's Education Society, 1982; Sanghrakshita, *Ambedkar and Buddhism*, Glasgow, Windrose, 1986; A. K. Narian and D. C. Ahir (eds), *Dr Ambedkar, Buddhism and Social Change*, Delhi, B. R., 1994 and Timothy Fitzgerald, 'Ambedkar, Buddhism and the Concept of Religion', in S. M. Michael (ed.), *Dalits in Modern India*, New Delhi, Vistaar, 1999.

THE CONSTITUTION

D. C. Ahir, *Dr Ambedkar and the Indian Constitution*, Lucknow, Buddha Vihara, 1973; Sharad Prasad Singh and Anil Kumar Singh, *Ambedkar's Vision of the Indian Constitution*, Patna, Swarna Pub., 1987.

CONVERSION

Shanti Deva and C. M. Wagh, *Dr Ambedkar and Conversion*, Dr Ambedkar Pub. Society, 1965; D. R. Jatava, *The Critics of Ambedkar*,

New Delhi, Bharatiya Shoshit Jan Utthan Parishad, 1975 and Rajshekar Shetty, *Ambedkar and His Conversion*, A Critique, Bangalore, Dalit Action Committee, 1980.

ECONOMIC THOUGHT

Narendra Jadhav, *Dr Ambedkar: Economic Thought and Philosophy*, Pune, Sugava Prakashan, 1993.

EDUCATION

M. B. Chitnis, 'Dr Babasaheb Ambedkar as an Educationist', *Souvenir*, All India Buddhist College and University Teachers' Conference, Aurangabad, 8–9 October 1981.

EMANCIPATION

A. M. Rajasekariah, *The Politics of Emancipation*, Bombay, Sindhu, 1971; K. N. Kadam (ed.), *Dr Ambedkar, the Emancipator of the Oppressed*, Bombay, Popular Prakashan, 1993 (Centenary Volume).

HUMAN RIGHTS

R. D. Suman, *Dr Ambedkar: Pioneer of Human Rights*, New Delhi, Bodisattva Pub., 1977; B. K. Ahluwalia and Shashi Ahluwalia (ed.), *Dr Ambedkar and Human Rights*, Delhi, 1981.

JOURNALISM

Gangadhar Pantwane, *Patrakar Dr Babasaheb Ambedkar*, Nagpur, Abhijit Prakashan, 1987; Harishchandra Nirmal, *Dalitanchi Niyatkalike*, Pune, Sugava Prakashan, 1987.

LABOUR

D. K. Baisantry, 'Dr Ambedkar, India's War-time Labour Minister', in Bhagwan Das, ed., *Thoughts on Ambedkar*, Part I, Bheem Patrika, Jalandhar, 1972; Y. D. Phadke, 'The Independent Labour Party and the One-day General Strike of 7 November, 1938', Seminar on the *Dalit Movement in Maharashtra*, Shivaji University, Kolhapur, 9–11 January 1988.

IMPACT ON LITERATURE

Waman Kardak, *Watcal*, Aurangabad, Prabodhan Prakashan, 1972; Eleanor Zelliot and Gail Omvedt, 'Introduction to Dalit Poems', *Bulletin of Concerned Asian Scholars*, 10: 3, 1978; Jayshree B. Gokhale-Turner, 'Bhakti or Vidroha: Continuity and Change in Dalit Sahitya', in Jayant Lele (ed.), Tradition and Modernity in Bhakti Movements, Leiden, E. J. Brill, 1981; Barbara Joshi, ed., *Untouchable! Voices of the Dalit Liberation Movement*, London, Zed Books, 1986; B. D. Phadke, *Dr Ambedkar and Dalit Sahitya*, Kolhapur, Mrs Nandini T. Gaval, 1989 (in Marathi); Arjun Dangle (ed.), *Poisoned Bread: Translations from Marathi Dalit Literature*, New Delhi, Orient Longman, 1992; Krishna Kirwale, *Ambedkari Shahire*, Pune, Nalanda Pub., 1992; Eleanor Zelliot, 'New Voices of the Buddhists of India', in A. K. Narain and D. C. Ahir (eds), *Dr Ambedkar, Buddhism and Social Change*, Delhi, B. R., 1994; Gopal Guru, *Dalit Cultural Movement & Dialectics of Dalit Politics in Maharashtra*, Mumbai, Vikas Adhyayan Kendra, 1997 and Gauri Viswanathan, *Outside*, New Delhi, Oxford University Press, 1998.

MAHAD SATYAGRAHA

Ratnakar Ganvir, *Mahad Samata Sangar*, Jalgaon, Ratnamitra Prakashan, 1981 (in Marathi).

ON THE MOVEMENT

C. Rajagopalachari, *Ambedkar Refuted*, Bombay, Hind Kitabs, 1941; D. Belayudab, *Gandhi or Ambedkar?*, Madras, Gandhi Era Pub., 1945; K. Santhanam, Ambedakar's attack, New Delhi, Hindustan Times Press 1946; Eleanor Zelliot, *Dr Ambedkar and the Mahar Movement*, University of Pennsylvania, Ph.D. Dissertation, 1969; T. S. Wilkinson and M. M. Thomas (ed.), *Ambedkar and the Neo-Buddhist Movement*, Bangalore, CISRS, 1972; Gail Omvedt, *Cultural Revolt in a Colonial Society: The non-Brahmin Movement in Western Maharashtra, 1850–1935*, Poona, Scientific Socialist Education Trust, 1976; Bharat Patankar and Gail Omvedt, 'The Dalit Liberation Movement in Colonial Period, *Economic and Political Weekly*, XIV, pp. 409–504; D. R. Jatav, *Dr Ambedkar's Role in National Movement*, New Delhi, Boudha Sahitya Sammelan, 1979; Y. D. Phadke, *Ambedkar Chalwal*, Pune, Shrividya Prakashan, 1990 (in Marathi); Peter Robb, *Dalit Movements and the Meanings of Labour in India*, Delhi, OUP, 1993; D. R. Nagaraj, *The Flaming Feet, A Study of Dalit Movement*, Bangalore, South Forum Press, 1993; Sandeep Pendse, ed., *Dalit Movement Today*, Bombay, Vikas Adhyayan Kendra, 1994 and Gail Omvedt, *Dalits and the Democratic Revolution, Dr Ambedkar and the Dalit Movement in Colonial India*, New Delhi, Sage, 1994.

POLITICAL THOUGHT

D. R. Jatav, *The Political Philosophy of B. R. Ambedkar*, Agra, Phoenix, Pub. House, 1965; W. N. Kuber, *Dr Ambedkar—A Critical Study*, New Delhi, PPH, 1973; G. S. Lokhande, *Bhimrao Ramji Ambedkar, A Study in Social Democracy*, New Delhi, Intellectual Publishing House, 1977; C. G. J. Lobo, *Ambedkar, the Champion of Social Democracy in India*, Bangalore, Hilerina, 1984; Rao Saheb Kasbe, *Ambedkar and Marx*, Poona, Sugava Prakashan, 1985; K. K. Kavlekar, and A. S. Chousalkar (eds), *Political Ideas and Leadership of Dr B. R. Ambedkar*, Pune, Viswanil, 1989; Thomas Mathew, *Ambedkar: Reform or Revolution*, New Delhi, Segment Books, 1991; Upendra Baxi, 'Collective Conspiracy to Hush up Babasaheb's Burning Thoughts', *Dalit Voice*, 1–15 April, pp. 15–21; Kshirsagar Ramachandra Kamaji, *Political Thought of Dr Babasaheb Ambedkar*, New Delhi, Intellectual Publishing House, 1992; K. Raghavendra Rao, *Babasaheb Ambedkar*, New Delhi, Sahitya Akademi, 1993; M. S. Gore, *The Social Context of an Ideology, Ambedkar's Social and Political Thought*, New Delhi, Sage, 1993 and Gail Omvedt, *Dalit Visions: The Anti-Caste Movement and the Construction of an Indian Identity*, New Delhi, Orient Longman, 1996.

POONA PACT

Pyarelal, *The Epic Fast*, Ahmedabad, Navjivan, 1958; Eleanor Zelliot, 'Gandhi and Ambedkar—A Study in Leadership', in Michael Mahar, ed., *The Untouchables in Contemporary India*, Tucson, University of Arizona Press, 1972 and Ravindra Kumar, 'Gandhi, Ambedkar and the Poona Pact, 1932', in Jim Masselos (ed.), *Struggling and Ruling*, South Asia, Pub. New Delhi, Sterling, 1987.

RECOLLECTIONS

B. H. Varale, *Dr Ambedkarancha Sangati*, Shrividya Prakashan, Pune, 1988 (in Marathi) and Shankaranand Shastri, *My Memories and*

Experiences of Babasaheb Dr B. R. Ambedkar, Ghaziabad, Bheem Sadan, 1989.

SECULARISM

A. M. Dharmalingam, *B. R. Ambedkar and Secularism*, Bangalore, Dalit Sahitya Academy, 1985.

UNTOUCHABILITY

Clark Blake, 'The Victory of an Untouchable', *Reader's Digest*, 56: 107-11, 1950; Owen M. Lynch, *The Politics of Untouchability*, New York and London, Columbia University Press, 1969; J. Michael Mahar (ed.), The Untouchables in Contemporary India, Arizona, Tucson, The University of Arizona Press, 1972.

WOMEN

Urmila Pawar and Meenakshi Moon, *Aamhihi Itihas Ghadwala*, Bombay, Granthali Pub. 1978 (in Marathi); Pillai—Vetschera, T., *The Mahars*, New Delhi, Intercultural Pub. 1994 and 'Ambedkar's Daughters: A Study of Mahar Women in Ahmednagar District of Maharashtra', in S. M. Michael (ed.), *Dalits in Modern India*, New Delhi, Vistaar, 1999; Gopal Guru, 'Dalit Women Talk Differently', *Economic and Political Weekly*, XXX (41/42), Oct: 2548-50; 1995.

Sources of Selection

All the references here below are to volumes and pages of the *Dr Babasaheb Ambedkar Writings and Speeches*, published by Education Department, Government of Maharastra, Mumbai. Corrections to these texts, if any, is indicated in the endnotes.

REMINISCENCE

On the way to Goregaon, 12: 665–71.

CONCEPTS

Religion and Dharmma, 11: 315–17; Democracy, 9: 444–9; Franchise, 2: 337–44; Representation, 2: 344–56; Representation of Minorities, 2: 362–3; Untouchability, 2: 491–4; Caste and Class, 3: 142–8.

METHODOLOGY

On Provincial Finance, 6: 59–63; On Untouchables, 7: 240–5.

IDEOLOGY

Ranade, Gandhi and Jinnah, 1: 221–9; Caste, Class and Democracy, 9: 201–17; Gandhism, 9: 274–97; Buddha or Karl Marx, 3: 441–53 & 459–62.

RELIGION

Krishna and His Gita, 3: 360-71; The Buddha and His Predecessors, 11: 81-93; Does the Buddha have a Social Message?, 11: 225-6; Conversion ('Away from the Hindus'), 5: 403-21.

CASTE

Caste in India: Their Origin, Mechanism and Development, 1: 5-22; Annihilation of Caste, 1: 47-80; Reply to the Mahatma, 1: 86-96.

UNTOUCHABILITY

Outside the Fold, 5: 19-26; From Millions to Fractions, 5: 229-46; The Untouchables and the Pax Britannica, 12: 132-3, 135, 138-40 & 145-7; An anti-untouchability agenda, 9: 133-42; Political Safeguards for Depressed Classes, 2: 546-54.

IDENTITIES

Who were the Shudras?, 7: 9-18; Origin of Untouchability, 7: 311-20.

ECONOMICS

The Enlargement of the Scope of Provincial Finance, 6: 213-24; the Silver Standard and the Evils of its Instability, 6: 415-44.

NATIONALISM

Is there a case for Pakistan ('A National calling for a Home'), 8: 29-39.

CONSTITUTIONALISM

Basic Features of the Indian Constitution, 13: 49-70; The Hindu Code Bill, 14: 4-12 & 267-81.

Chronology

DR B. R. AMBEDKAR (1891–1956)

14 April 1891   Bhimrao Ramji was born at Mhow; the four-teenth child of Ramji, a Subedar Major in the British Army, and Bhimabai. Only three sons, Balaram, Anandrao, and Bhimrao and two daughters, Manjula and Tulasa survived. The family belonged to the Mahar caste, one of the numerous untouchable castes of the then Bombay Province. His ancestral village was Ambavade in Ratnagiri District of Maharashtra. Ramji retired soon after the birth of Bhimrao and went to Dapoli Taluk in Ratnagiri District.

1896   Shift of the family to Satara. Death of Ambedkar's mother. Early studies.

1904   Shifts to Bombay with the family. Lives in Parel, a residential area for textile labourers, in Bombay. Studies in Elphinstone High School.

1907   Completes SSLC examination.

1908   Marries Ramabhai, who was just 9 years old.

1912   Passes BA examination, studying in Elphinstone College.

1913   Joins the armed forces of the Baroda State in the rank of Lieutenant for a while. Death of Ramji.

July 1913   Joins the Faculty of Political Science, Columbia University, USA assisted by a scholarship from Maharaja Sayaji Rao of Baroda.

1915	Completes MA dissertation on *Administration and Finance of the East India Company*.
9 May 1916	Paper on 'Castes in India: Their Mechanism, Genesis and Development', at the Anthropology Seminar of Dr A. A. Goldenweizer, that was eventually published in *Indian Antiquity*, May 1917, Vol. XLI.
June 1916	Submits Ph.D. dissertation on 'National Dividend of India—a Historical and Analytical Study' to Columbia University.
12 October 1916	Joins the London School of Economics as well as the Grey's Inn.
1917	Awarded the Ph.D. degree by Columbia University. Dissertation published by King & Co., London in 1925, after suitable revision, under the title *The Evolution of Provincial Finance in British India*.
July 1917	Returns to India. Joining the services of the Maharaja of Baroda according to the contract. Subjected to indignity as an Untouchable. Leaves the job.
11 November 1918	Appointed Professor of Political Economy at the Sydenham College of Commerce and Economics, Bombay.
January 1919	Representation before the Southborough Committee on Franchise. Plea for separate electorate for the depressed classes.
January 1920	Starts *Mooknayak*, a fortnightly, in Marathi.
30 May 1920 to 1 June	The first All-India Conference of Depressed Classes, presided over by Shahu Maharaj of Kolhapur. Ambedkar's argument for self-help.
September 1920	Returns to LSE for continuation of studies.
June 1921	M.Sc. dissertation on '*Provincial Decentralisation of Imperial Finance in British India*'.
1922	Invited to the Bar-at-law from Grey's Inn.
1922	Submits the D.Sc. dissertation on *The Problem of the Rupee—Its Origin and its Solution* to LSE.
1922	Departs to Berlin University for Studies.
1923	Awarded of D.Sc. degree by LSE. Thesis published by King & Co., London in the same year.

June 1923	Starts law practice in Bombay High Court.
20 July 1924	Formation of the 'Bahishkrit Hitakarini Sabha' (Depressed Classes Welfare Association).
June 1925 to March 1928	Works as part-time teacher in Mercantile law in Batliboi's Accountancy Training Institute, Bombay.
18 February 1927	Nomination to Bombay Legislative Council for five years. Renewed in 1932 for further five years.
20 March 1927	Satyagraha at Chowdar Tank in Mahad begins.
3 April 1927	Starts the fortnightly journal, *Bahiskrit Bharat*, in Marathi (published till 15 November 1929).
4 September 1927	Formation of Samaj Samata Sangh.
December 1927	Formation of Samata Sainik Dal.
25 December 1927	Burning of *Manusmriti* at Mahad.
19 March 1928	Introduction of the Bill to amend the Bombay Hereditary Offices Act, 1874
29 March 1928	Statement before the Simon Commission.
June 1928– March 1929	Becomes Professor of Law in Government Law College, Bombay.
14 June 1928	Founding of Depressed Classes Education Society, Bombay.
29 June 1928	Starting of the fortnightly, *Samata* (closure in 1929).
23 October 1928	Evidence before the Simon Commission.
2 March 1930	Satyagraha at Kalaram Temple, Nasik, begins. Continues for 5 years intermittently.
24 April 1930	Starts the Marathi fortnightly, *Janata*.
8–9 August 1930	Becomes President, First All India Depressed Classes Congress, held in Nagpur.
12 November 1930– 19 January 1931	Participates in the First Round Table Conference.
7 September 1931– 1 December 1931	Appointed as Member, the Second Round Table Conference.
1 May 1932	Note to the Indian Franchise Committee.
24 September 1932	Poona Pact.
17 November 1932– 24 December	Participates in the Third Round Table Conference.
27 May 1935	Death of Ramabai.

June 1935–	Appointed as Principal, Government Law
June 1938	College, Bombay.
October 1935	Yeola Conference announcing conversion to Buddhism.
1936	*Annihilation of Caste.*
15 August 1936	Formation of Independent Labour Party.
7 November 1938	Protest against Industrial Dispute Bill.
1939	*Federation vs Freedom.*
1940	*Thoughts on Pakistan.*
18–20 July 1942	Formation of the Scheduled Castes Federation.
27 July 1942	Labour Member in Viceroy's Council (till July 1946).
1943	*Ranade, Gandhi and Jinnah.*
1943	*Mr Gandhi and the Emancipation of the Untouchables.*
1945	*Communal Deadlock and the Way to Solve it.*
1945	*What Congress and Gandhi have done to the Untouchables.*
8 July 1945	Foundation of People's Education Society, Bombay.
1946	*Who were the Shudras? How they came to be the Fourth Varna in Indo-Aryan Society.*
1946	Establishment of Siddharth College of Arts and Science.
19 July 1946	Elected to the Constituent Assembly from Bengal.
1947	*States and Minorities.*
23 July 1947	Elected to the Constituent Assembly, from Bombay.
3 August 1947	Appointed as Law Minister of Independent India.
19 August 1947	Appointed as Chairman, Drafting Committee of the Indian Constitution.
1948	*The Untouchables: Who were They and Why They became Untouchables?*
26 November 1950	Acceptance of the Indian Constitution.
25 May 1950	Visit to Colombo for an experience of Buddhism.
8 September 1951	Resigns from Nehru's Cabinet.

January 1952	Stands for the Lok Sabha elections from Bombay North Parliamentary Constituency, but is defeated.
March 1952	Elected to Rajya Sabha from Bombay Legislature.
5 June 1952	Doctor of Laws Degree from Columbia University.
December 1954	Participates in the World Buddhist Conference at Rangoon.
1955	*Thoughts on Linguistic States.*
May 1955	*Formation of the Boudha Maha Sabha.*
4 February 1956	Starts *Prabudd Bharat.*
14 October 1956	Embraces Buddhism in Nagpur.
15–16 November 1956	Participates at the World Buddhist Conference in Kathmandu.
6 December 1956	Dies in Delhi.
1957	*Buddha and His Dhamma* (Posthumous).

Index

INDEX • 567

jute trade, 439
movements of prices, wages and
  silver, 444–50
payments in England in gold-
  standard and, 422–55
problem of, 422–55
revenue and expenditure, 426–27
rupee and sterling securities, 428–
  31
rupee cost of gold payments, 423–
  24
rupee-sterling exchange fluctuations, 450–54
trade disturbances, 440–43, 454
Indian Franchise Committee, 12, 56,
  321, 340–42
Indian Social Reformer, 359
Indian Statutory Commission (ISC),
  see, Simon Commission
Indian Succession Act, 516
Indian village, life of untouchables in,
  324–31
Indo-Aryan Society, 386, 388, 390
Industrial Trade Dispute Bill, 13
Innes, C.A., 136*n*
Intellectual class, 293–94
International Labour Organization
  (ILO), 31
Irwin, Lord, 142
Islam, 26–27, 35

Jaimini, 4, 25, 195–202
Jainism, 185
Jamali Sultan tomb, 462–63
Janata, 11
Jat-Pat-Todak Mandal, 13, 239, 289,
  306
Jayakar, 355
Jeevaka, 185
Jefferson, 121
Jinnah, 119
  and Ranade, 127–30
Jnana yoga, 195–96

Jnyandeo, 308–09
Johnson, 391–92
Joint electorate system, 84
Joint Report, 73

Kabir, 19, 296
Kabir, Sharada, 16
Kabirpanth/Kabirpanthi, 7
Kalaram Temple movement, 11
Kamma, 20
Kapila, 207–10
Karada Brahmins, 269
Karma, doctrine of, 212
Karma yoga, 194–96, 200
Karuna, 59
Kautilya, 503–04
Ketkar, Shridhar V., 242, 244–45,
  251, 261
Keynes, 30
Khan, Aga, 397
Khoti system of land tenure, 13, 31
Kinship, 230–35, 289
Koran, 193
Krishnamurti, Y.G., 139*n*,
Kshatriyas, 104, 138–39, 152, 197,
  211–15, 256–57, 269, 278,
  281–82, 284, 288, 313,
  345, 383, 385, 388

Labour Party, 22–23, 42
Labourer, division of, 263–64
Lahore Resolution, of Muslim League,
  13, 457
Land Alienation Act, 328
Lawrene, Pethik, 14
Leeky, William Edward Hartpole,
  123
Legislative Council,
  class electorates, 77–79
  communal electorates, 82–89
  elected members, 77–91
  nominated members, 74–77
  representation in, 74–91
  reserved electorates, 80–82